What Readers Are Saying About *XML and ASP.NET*

"*XML and ASP.NET* is a useful, code-packed tutorial/reference for ASP.NET developers eager to add XML technology to their toolkits."

—Dr. Joseph Feller, *Editor,* Inside XML Solutions, Element K Journals *and Lecturer, Business Information Systems, University College Cork, Ireland*

"Complete guide to XML in ASP.NET from the Ground UP."

—Kunal Cheda, www.DotNeteXtreme.com

"*XML and ASP.NET* provides a comprehensive and invaluable introduction to building XML applications with ASP.NET. The coverage, ranging from building XML documents from database data and XSL Transformations to XML serialization and Web Services, is authoritative, complete, and exceptionally illuminating. The two concluding case studies are especially valuable, demonstrating real world applications of the skills taught in the book."

—Steve Heckler, *President, WestLake Internet Training,* www.westlake.com

XML and ASP.NET

Contents At a Glance

XML and ASP.NET

Kirk Allen Evans
Ashwin Kamanna
Joel Mueller

New Riders

www.newriders.com
201 West 103rd Street, Indianapolis, Indiana 46290
An Imprint of Pearson Education
Boston • Indianapolis • London • Munich • New York • San Francisco

XML and ASP.NET

International Standard Book Number: 0-7357-1200-X

Library of Congress Catalog Card Number: *200194558*

06 05 04 03 02   7 6 5 4 3 2 1

Interpretation of the printing code: The rightmost double-digit number is the year of the book's printing; the right-most single-digit number is the number of the book's printing. For example, the printing code 02-1 shows that the first printing of the book occurred in 2002.

Printed in the United States of America

Trademarks

Warning and Disclaimer

Publisher
David Dwyer

Associate Publisher
Stephanie Wall

Production Manager
Gina Kanouse

Managing Editor
Kristina Knoop

Acquisitions Editor
Deborah Hittel-Shoaf

Development Editor
Anne Marie Walker

Project Editor
Todd Zellers

Product Marketing Manager
Kathy Malmloff

Publicity Manager
Susan Nixon

Copy Editor
Sheri Cain

Indexer
Larry Sweazy

Manufacturing Coordinator
Jim Conway

Book Designer
Louisa Klucznik

Cover Designer
Brainstorm Design, Inc.

Cover Production
Aren Howell

Proofreader
Sossity Smith

Composition
Amy Parker

❖

*We would like to respectfully dedicate this book to the victims
and their families of the September 11, 2001, tragedies.*

May the road rise to meet you,
May the wind blow at your back,
May the sun shine softly on your face.
May the rains fall softly in your fields,
And until we meet again,
May God hold you in the palm of His hand.

❖

Table of Contents

About the Authors

Lead Author

Kirk Allen Evans has been developing applications for over 10 years. His focus remains developing complex, distributed systems using Microsoft technologies. He has written several articles for *Visual Basic Programmer's Journal* and speaks at user groups and conferences. Kirk also developed and maintains vbdna.net, a website devoted to demonstrating techniques for developing distributed systems using Visual Basic. He lives in Cumming, Georgia, and works as a contract developer in the Atlanta area. You can reach him at kaevans@vbdna.net.

Authors

Ashwin Kamanna works as a software engineer at AINS India Pvt. Ltd., in Hyderabad, India. He spends most of his time designing and developing web applications with ASP, Java, XML, and COM. He has written for some ASP and C# online magazines including *ASPToday.com* and *CSharpToday.com*. His special fields of interest are XML and object-oriented design, and he enjoys delving deeper into them. He has a BE (Hons.) in Electrical and Electronics Engineering from Birla Institute of Technology and Science (BITS), Pilani, India. In his leisure time, if Ashwin is not programming or reading, he can be found doing a painting or a sketch to add to his gallery.

Joel Mueller is a senior software engineer at DeLani Technologies (www.delani.com), a leading web development software company, where he has been spearheading the company's Microsoft .NET development effort since July, 2000. Prior to the advent of ASP.NET, Joel did extensive work with Microsoft Active Server Pages and Macromedia ColdFusion. Joel has written several books and articles on the topics of Macromedia ColdFusion and XML.

Contributing Author

Scott Worley is a freelance IT consultant specializing in Microsoft-based technologies and SDLC project management. For the past 10 years, he has worked on many leading-edge development projects, utilizing the latest technologies. Scott is currently focusing all his attention on the .NET Framework and associated technologies, paying specific attention to ASP.NET and distributed web development.

About the Technical Reviewers

These reviewers contributed their considerable hands-on expertise to the entire development process for *XML and ASP.NET*. As the book was being written, these dedicated professionals reviewed all the material for technical content, organization, and flow. Their feedback was critical to ensuring that *XML and ASP.NET* fit our readers' need for the highest-quality technical information.

Ken Cox is a technical writer and web applications programmer in Toronto. After receiving his bachelor's degree in Radio and Television Arts from Ryerson University, he started a career in radio. He was a journalist for 20 years for top-rated stations and news networks in Toronto and Montreal. During that time, he spent seven years as a correspondent in Quebec City. Computers were only his hobby when Microsoft invited Ken into the beta test for a new product code named Denali—later known as Active Server Pages (ASP). To pursue his passion for all things high-tech, Ken earned a college certificate in Technical Communications and began a second career as a t echnical writer for many companies, including Nortel Networks. Thanks to his grounding in Internet technologies, Ken found himself in demand as a writer and technical reviewer of computer books and magazine articles on Microsoft technologies, such as Internet Information Server, ASP.NET, Visual Basic, XML, and HTML. Microsoft has recognized Ken's expertise and volunteer contribution to online newsgroups by making him a Microsoft Most Valuable Professional (MVP). When not at the keyboard, Ken can be found riding his moped around Toronto or listening to 60's rock 'n roll.

Steve Platt has been around computers for the last 17 years. After a start in chemistry/chemical enginering, Steve decided that his hobby was far more interesting and in 1984 turned to computer programming full-time. After a succession of jobs writing mainframe code for blue-chip companies, Steve turned his attention to the Internet. He has worked on many sites mainly for the financial/insurance sector. Steve currently works for a Microsoft Solution Provider in Brighton, UK, and is actively following his dream to emigrate to Australia.

Acknowledgments

Kirk Allen Evans:

I would like to thank my wife, Deanna, for her enduring love throughout the writing of this book. I love you more than I could ever express, and I cherish the life that we have together. You are truly amazing: running our entire household, raising a one-year old, and carrying our unborn child through morning sickness and exhaustion, all while your husband secludes himself in the office for nights on end.

I also thank my child, Carson (a.k.a "Little Bit"), for showing me that God blesses us everyday with the smallest smile and your playful laugh. Thank you for giving up so much time with your daddy while this book was being written. I also thank our unborn child, "Teeny Bit," for showing me that God truly blesses us all.

I thank the people whose hard work and dedication have made this book an enjoyable experience. The folks at New Riders are exemplary, and I am fortunate to have worked with such professionals. Deborah Hittel-Shoaf, thank you for helping me get over difficult hurdles to get the chapters submitted. Anne Marie Walker, thank you for helping make this book more readable.

Thanks to Joel for helping me so much with examples, and thank you Ashwin for your hard work organizing this project from the beginning. Scott, thanks for jumping in so late in the game; you are a life saver.

Special thanks to Ken Cox and Steve Platt for your honest criticisms and great suggestions in your reviews. I learned so much about writing from both of you. Thank you for making this a better book. Thank you for keeping this book honest and the examples true.

Ashwin Kamanna:

Thanks to my dear parents, my sister Preeti, Uncle Prabhu, and Aunt Ranjana for all your love, support, and inspiration. Thanks to my friends Savitha R. and Kumar Alok for being a consistent source of support during the writing of my chapters. Special thanks to my boss and friend, Suresh Basheerbad, for extending the help and flexibility at work, and the CEO of AINS, Mr. Mohinder Goswami, for his encouragement.

Thanks to Kirk for his guidance, the technical reviewers for their immense help in making my work better, the editors, Deb, Anne Marie, and to all the people at New Riders for their help and flexibility.

Tell Us What You Think

As the reader of this book, you are the most important critic and commentator. We value your opinion and want to know what we're doing right, what we could do better, what areas you'd like to see us publish in, and any other words of wisdom you're willing to pass our way.

As the Associate Publisher for New Riders Publishing, I welcome your comments. You can fax, email, or write me directly to let me know what you did or didn't like about this book—as well as what we can do to make our books stronger.

Please note that I cannot help you with technical problems related to the topic of this book, and that due to the high volume of mail I receive, I might not be able to reply to every message.

When you write, please be sure to include this book's title and author as well as your name and phone or fax number. I will carefully review your comments and share them with the author and editors who worked on the book.

Fax: 317-581-4663
Email: stephanie.wall@newriders.com
Mail: Stephanie Wall
        Associate Publisher
        New Riders Publishing
        201 West 103rd Street
        Indianapolis, IN 46290 USA

Introduction

Welcome to *XML and ASP.NET*. This book gives you a complete introduction to XML and its implementation in .NET, focusing on implementations with ASP.NET. XML is a vast subject with many pages devoted to it, covering everything from theory to implementation. The authors strived to give you more complete coverage of XML in the .NET Framework than you can find in any other book. This book provides you with not only a solid understanding of the implementation of XML in the .NET Framework, but also gives you a thorough explanation of the formal XML recommendations and its associated technologies.

XML is either left out of most books on .NET or is covered only in passing. This is unfortunate because XML is the underpinning of much of the .NET strategy. *XML and ASP.NET* strives to convey the concepts of XML processing without stating what you likely already know. It goes deeper into some concepts that you are familiar with, and explains Microsoft's implementation of those concepts in the .NET Framework.

Most books covering XML are formatted in a similar way to the MSDN documentation: give a class, list the properties and methods associated with it, and provide a brief description. Instead of serving as a reference guide, the authors chose real-world examples to teach concepts and how to apply different solutions using XML. Rather than tell you what each object is and does, the authors teach you *why* a particular approach is taken and how you can leverage it.

The authors included many working samples throughout this book to show you not only the *whys*, but the *hows* as well. This is the best way to learn what is really going on with technologies such as XML Schema and XSLT. The examples were developed using Microsoft Visual Studio .NET, and we focused on giving examples rather than explanations. We also included a chapter on MSXML, because it is still an important part of Microsoft's XML strategy.

This book is broken into two parts: XML on the client and XML on the server. This separation helps make the structure of this book more readable than simply discussing various XML-related technologies.

The writing of this book has been a labor of love. We hope that you find the same excitement and passion for XML as we have tried to convey in the following pages.

What's Inside?

This book gives as complete a picture of XML and ASP.NET as possible without trading a book's bulk for its content. We discuss XML from a basic level and quickly move to an advanced discussion on its implementation and the formal recommendations.

Many topics are covered throughout this book, including the following:

- The XML 1.0 Recommendation
- The XML Schema 1.0 Recommendation
- The XPath 1.0 Recommendation
- The XSLT 1.0 Recommendation
- Changes to ASP.NET
- Using XML with ADO.NET
- Creating and manipulating XML documents using the .NET Framework classes
- Whitespace handling in XML
- Validating XML documents
- Using Visual Studio .NET to work with XML
- Other available tools and utilities to work with XML
- Using and controlling XML serialization
- Creating and consuming XML Web Services
- WAP and WML programming

Microsoft has done a great job of including volumes of information on XML in MSDN, and there is plenty of information to sort through on the web as well. We make specific references to documentation, sites, and other books and magazines throughout this book. Rather than list different websites in this section, we suggest you visit www.newriders.com and www.xmlandasp.net for updated articles, code listings, and links to more information.

Who This Book Is For

This book is written for ASP developers who want to learn about XML in the .NET Framework and its application to ASP solutions. We make the assumption that you have created HTML pages and are familiar with server-side and client-side programming. We assume that you have at least a passing familiarity with XML as well. Although it's not required, a previous understanding of XML is helpful to understand the concepts presented in this book. An excellent book on XML is New Riders Publishing's *Inside XML* (2001), written by Steve Holzner.

Who This Book Is Not For

While covering so many areas of XML, this book can not serve all audiences. If you are not familiar with ASP development, we suggest that you first read New Riders Publishing's *Inside ASP.NET* (2002). You might also find that your appetite for XSLT and XML has been whet: For a further discussion on XML and XSLT that introduces implementations outside Microsoft's, we suggest both *Inside XML* and its companion, *Inside XSLT* (2001), both written by Steve Holzner.

The Level of This Book

This book is written at several different levels, from beginning to advanced. This is largely due to the nature of XML itself: Some topics can seem self-explanatory but warrant discussion, while others seem complex and obscure. The examples are written with both Visual Basic and C# developers in mind. Examples usually appear in one language or the other unless certain concepts warrant listing the code in both languages. Some sections, such as XSLT and XSD, are targeted for more advanced developers. Other sections assume little or no previous experience with XML, such as Chapters 1 and 2.

Because this book focuses on using XML with .NET, it assumes familiarity with the .NET Framework to at least a small degree. For example, language constructs can be used in various examples, but this book does not formally teach Visual Basic or C# syntax. Beginning readers should be able to read through this book and gain mastery of the presented concepts.

Conventions Used in This Book

When concepts are introduced in a sample section of code, we highlight the section to draw attention to the pertinent lines. Here's an example:

```
<?xml version="1.0" encoding="UTF-8" ?>
<xsl:stylesheet version="1.1"
xmlns:xsl="http://www.w3.org/1999/XSL/Transform">
    <xsl:template match="/">
        <table>
            <xsl:for-each select="links/link">
                <tr>
                    <td>
                        <xsl:if test="position() mod 2 = 0">
                            <xsl:attribute
name="bgcolor">silver</xsl:attribute>
                        </xsl:if>
                        <xsl:value-of select="@name" />
                    </td>
                </tr>
```

```
        </xsl:for-each>
      </table>
    </xsl:template>
</xsl:stylesheet>
```

Much of the code in this book is also available for download from the web site. When the code is available, it is explicitly referenced in the text.

Sometimes, a bit of information is noteworthy, but might not fit directly within the text being discussed. In those cases, we use a sidebar.

Message Handlers and the xsl:message Element

For the .NET base classes, the `xsl:message` element does not cause a trappable error. Instead, the message is output to the default message handler. For a Windows application project, the default handler is the output window. For a Console application, the default handler is the console window. For Web Forms applications, the message is suppressed.

Generally, code is displayed using a monotype font. For example, the `xsl:template` element is discussed throughout the text, as is the `XmlTextReader` object.

If you have any comments on this book, I would love to hear from you. I am always looking for ways to improve this book and help make it one of the premier books on XML development with .NET.

I

XML on the Client

XML and ASP.NET: The Basics

Welcome to *XML and ASP.NET*. Hopefully, you noticed in the title just what this book is about: XML is covered in respect to how it applies to ASP.NET. Before jumping in, this chapter looks at some basic concepts.

Extensible Markup Language (XML) is just data. That's it. Think of it as data in a file, or data in a string, or data in a stream. XML is just data. XML is not a messaging protocol; it is not a wire transfer specification. XML is just data and how data is represented. Much hype and confusion surrounds XML's definition and what it does for your applications. This chapter makes it clear that XML is just a unified way to represent data.

XML is a rapidly evolving technology, but note that markup languages have existed since computers existed. Various markup formats existed to try to separate content from presentation, and developers often created their own formats for custom needs. This created a need for proprietary parsers, which were applications developed to recognize a certain set of symbols, or *markup*, to read the data contained in a file.

Consider some of the markup formats that you might still regularly use in applications. Rich Text Formatting (RTF) is used in programs such as Microsoft Word. Microsoft Word also supports a native format, which changes slightly from version to version. WordPerfect documents use a slightly different markup to represent the data contained in them. The result is that you need a special add-in to read a WordPerfect document from Microsoft Word.

XML changes the need for different markup formats and parsers by standardizing certain aspects of what an XML document looks like, while allowing custom dialects to represent data. This chapter looks at the components of an XML document, discusses the formal XML 1.0 Specification, and talks about standards bodies such as the World Wide Web Consortium (W3C) and its role in XML and its related technologies. This chapter provides an overview and focuses on the terms that are important to understand XML within the context of .NET. It is not, however, a complete reference to the entire set of XML recommendations.

Why XML?

XML is many things, but it is not a panacea. Simply adding an XML document or two to your application is not going to make anything magically better. There are reasons for XML, and there are certainly cases where XML is not appropriate. Admittedly, much hype surrounds XML. Before jumping into a discussion on what XML is, it is important to ask why you're learning about XML in the first place.

Standardized Generalized Markup Language (SGML) has been around since the late 1960s. But SGML is a broad and complex technology, and did not gain wide acceptance. Then Hypertext Markup Language (HTML) came along, and the world of markup languages changed.

Tim Berners-Lee created HTML in 1989. HTML is a descendant of SGML that displays data by using a fixed set of tags to signify different display elements. HTML is a greatly simplified version of SGML, and quickly gained widespread acceptance because of its ease of use. Although great for presentation, the actual data for an HTML page is intermingled with the display elements. Soon, many people realized that HTML was too simple for complex data requirements.

The designers of XML recognized this and sought to develop a markup language that would truly separate data from its presentation. Thus, XML 1.0 was presented to the W3C as a working draft on November 14, 1996. The W3C working group had the following design goals in mind for XML:

- It must be easily usable over the Internet.
- It needs to support a wide variety of applications.
- It must be compatible with SGML.

- It must be easy to write programs that process XML documents.
- The number of optional features in XML is to be kept to the absolute minimum, ideally zero.
- XML documents should be human-legible and reasonably clear.
- The design needs to be prepared quickly.
- The design needs to be formal and concise.
- XML documents must be easy to create.
- Terseness is of minimal importance.[1]

As you can see, ease of use and understandability were the main goals of XML from its beginning. More importantly, XML is a widely adopted standard markup format that actually achieves the preceding goals. Open a Microsoft Word file in Notepad and look at the markup involved in making a .doc file or a .rtf file: It is not trivial. XML makes the overall structure of a document trivial, leaving the implementation and dialect up to you.

In short, you use XML to describe data in a universal fashion: It's common across the boundaries of language and operating system (OS). You can use XML to create views of data that express relationships through hierarchies. You can use XML because it is clearer and less restrictive than many alternative languages.

Self-Describing Data

The most associated term with XML has to be *self-describing data*. How can something be self-describing? Look at this example.

```
<?xml version="1.0"?>
<Customer>
      <Name>Deanna Evans</Name>
      <Age>29</Age>
      <MaritalStatus>Married</MaritalStatus>
</Customer>
```

You can tell a lot of information by looking at the preceding document. Because the XML is human-readable, you can discern that this data describes a single customer whose first name is Deanna and whose last name is Evans, respectively. You can infer that this customer's age is 29, and can read that the customer's marital status is Married. It's easier to work with the document because of the fact that it's self-describing. Suppose, instead, the information was represented differently, as shown here:

```
$Deanna$1$Evans#1D$Married
```

Try to decipher this odd dialect. Any string value whole word must be pre-fixed with a dollar-sign ($). If a dollar sign is followed by a numerical value, this indicates the number of empty spaces. All actual numbers are prefixed with a pound or hash symbol (#) and must be represented in hexadecimal for-mat. This dialect cannot be easily read, and you certainly cannot intimate that this data belongs to a customer.

Looking at the XML example, you can see the data in a structured manner. XML imposes structure on the data, which makes it usable and understand-able. By using readable tag names, you can designate a type with each element.

The term self-describing is overused and somewhat arbitrary. Consider the-following example:

```
<b/>
```

This document is well-formed because it contains a single root element, the element name is a valid NCName, and the element tag is properly closed.

From this example, we can infer that the root element has no content. Instead of saying "self-describing," it is more important to make a distinction between "human-readable" and "machine-readable." While the previous example does not seem very human-readable, it is certainly machine-readable.

Toolset Support

One of the benefits of XML is that there's no fixed API to work with XML. It is flexible and easy to understand without requiring a single rigid set of meth-ods. Instead, XML enjoys support from a variety of tools, ranging from different parsing APIs targeted for different languages to different text editors to help create XML documents easily. Examples of these tools include the following:

- Xselerator by MarrowSoft is a great XSLT development tool that enables you to debug XSLT stylesheets.
- XmlSpy by Tibco Extensibility is a great IDE for XML development and for working with XML Schemas.

While there is no fixed and rigid API for working with XML, there does exist a recommendation for representing XML as a programmable object model. This recommendation is known as the Document Object Model (DOM), specified in the W3C DOM Level 1 and 2 Core recommendations.

Implementors are urged to adhere to the recommendation within their implementations. Because different vendors adhere to the same recommenda-tion, consistent behavior is expected between different versions (for instance, a Java implementation should work exactly like a Visual Basic implementation). The DOM is explored in Chapter 5, "MSXML Parser," and in Chapter 6, "Exploring the System.Xml Namespace."

Separation of Content and Presentation

Now that you can see how ugly markup can get, look at what is meant by "separation of content and presentation." I assume that you are familiar with HTML at this point, and likely are familiar with XML, at least in passing. What you might not have realized is what XML is achieving: An XML document can contain the data that's being displayed, and a number of different presentation methods can be applied for displaying the data.

For example, a paragraph can actually be spread out over different table rows and table cells to make it more visually appealing. Because the presentation is intermixed with the content, it's difficult to extract the data from an HTML page in a common manner. Screen scraper programs that extract data from other websites typically run into problems when a website's content changes. The parser functions in the screen scraper application might look for something like this:

```
<div id="stockquote">
    <table>
        <tr>
            <td>MSFT</td><td>50.27</td>
            <td>YHOO</td><td>8.11</td>
        </tr>
    </table>
</div>
```

The web page's authors, however, decide to change the look and feel of their page. They change the data to the following:

```
<p>Stock Quote for <i>MSFT</i>: <b>50.27</b></p>
<p>Stock Quote for <i>YHOO</i>: <b>8.11</b></p>
```

The screen scraper program navigates to the remote site, looks for the text in the previous example, but can't grab stock quotes because the data changed and you could not reliably know where in the HTML the stock quote really resided unless you recode your parser.

XML data, however, separates the presentation of data from the actual data itself. If you were interested in the raw data, you might access an XML file that did not contain display logic, such as the following:

```
<?xml version="1.0"?>
<quotes>
<quote symbol="MSFT" price="50.27"/>
<quote symbol="YHOO" price="8.11"/>
</quotes>
```

The XML data is then displayed using HTML, XHTML, PDF, or a variety of other formats, but the raw data remains the same. If the display format changes, the raw data is unaffected.

Interoperability and Data Transfer

One of the design goals of XML was, "XML shall be straightforwardly usable over the Internet." This challenge is more difficult than it first appears. The Internet is composed of many different binary formats, messaging protocols, and operating systems. To complicate matters, users of data might be from different parts of the world and might speak different languages or even use different characters in their text. By standardizing encoding, or the character set used in a document, XML allows a generic template for creating documents without compromising the design goals of making a document readable by humans. Again, the content is separate from the presentation.

XML relies on the International Organization for Standardization's Specification ISO 10646 to represent what a character is and what encoding is allowed. Relying on this standard makes XML accessible through different operating systems and networks. Imagine if no standard existed to represent a character: One operating system might consider a character four bytes of information, while another operating system might consider it two bytes.

Why ASP.NET?

The question, "Why XML?" was answered with a brief history lesson, so I'll do the same with ASP.NET.

The first web pages were HTML documents that displayed HTML. There was nothing else to web pages; they simply displayed formatted text and images while allowing you to link to other HTML documents. Capabilities were soon added to handle user input by using forms. These forms were submitted to an external CGI program for processing data.

As simple CGI programs advanced, users quickly saw HTML's potential and began coding their own web applications. The limitations of CGI were apparent in how it managed memory.

Developers at Microsoft saw the potential in the web and began developing a solution. The result of this effort was *Internet Information Services* (IIS). IIS really hit the mainstream when IIS 3.0 was released as part of the NT Option Pack for Windows NT 4.0. Part of the IIS installation was Active Server Pages, an environment that facilitated web development using VBScript and ADO.

Almost overnight, data-driven web pages became the rage and developers quickly became familiar with bugs, workarounds, and limitations. For example, in IIS 3.0, it was suggested that procedures (subs and functions) not be used to reduce stack space usage. IIS 3.0 also suffered significant performance loss at high volumes, but its popularity continued to rise. It didn't take long for the next release: the NT 4.0 Option Pack included IIS 4.0.

IIS 4.0 greatly stabilized the web server, making web development more reliable and, as a direct result, more popular. Suddenly, complex systems were being developed that needed to take advantage of Microsoft Transaction Server (MTS) and its transactional integration with MSMQ and ADO. As systems became more complex, IIS became even more popular. With the advent of Windows 2000 and COM+ Component Services, IIS was now a stable environment that could host extremely complex systems with significantly high user loads.

The environment was stable, but only if it was used "just right." Countless articles appeared that discussed thread affinity and stored apartment-threaded objects in session state. It is simple to create a COM component and call it from an ASP page, but it can be difficult to do this effectively. Server crashes continued and security exploits popped up on the web, making IIS servers one of the most frequent targets for hacker attacks.

ASP.NET was developed with both security and performance in mind. ASP.NET is built on the Common Language Runtime (CLR). CLR manages memory for the developer and eliminates security vulnerabilities, such as buffer underruns that can lead to most common IIS vulnerabilities. ASP.NET code is compiled and managed by CLR, which means that it is secure and fast.

Why XML and ASP.NET?

The combination of XML and ASP.NET yields an amazingly broad range of possibilities. .NET heavily utilizes XML, as you will see throughout this book (especially in Chapter 7, "ASP.NET Extensibility with XML"). Complex web pages can be designed to present a rich user experience with minimal amounts of code by using XML data from various sources. XSLT transformations can be applied to XML data to provide HTML, WML, or a host of other formats. XML Schemas can validate XML data that is shared between organizations, and XML Web Services provide an XML-based messaging system between organizations.

XML is about data, and ASP.NET is about the manipulation and presentation of data.

The XML Document Structure

You will see the term *document* throughout this book. A document refers to a set of XML tags that follow the XML document syntax. Because the XML can be contained within a file, a stream, or a string, the term document is used to separate the implementation of how the bytes are stored from the logical grouping of those bytes into an informational item.

A document contains three sections: a prologue, a body, and an epilogue. In terms of understanding XML in .NET, you are only going to focus on the body section of an XML document and what an XML document is. Look at the components of XML and how to create your XML documents.

XML Document Syntax

The XML document syntax is the backbone of XML. The document syntax describes what an XML document is.

An XML document:

- Is composed of one or more nodes
- Has one and only one root node
- Has elements whose tags are properly nested
- Has elements that contain both start and end tags

Take a look at some of these concepts in a more familiar manner. (We assume here that you have written at least simple HTML documents.) Consider the following HTML code for creating an anchor tag or hyperlink:

```
<a href="http://www.microsoft.com">Microsoft.com</a>
```

The syntax of XML is recognizable if you have experience with HTML. XML also uses the angle brackets (< and >) for delimiting tags, and HTML uses the same beginning tag and ending tag sequence. The XML document syntax actually refers to an XML element that contains a beginning tag with matching case. Figure 1.1 shows the begin tag, end tag, and content of an XML element.

Figure 1.1 The begin tag, end tag, and content of an XML element.

Many browsers are accepting of poorly formed HTML documents. For example, Internet Explorer gladly renders the following:

```
<H1>This is a heading where the tags don't match</h1>
```

Notice that the tags use a different case: This might be acceptable for HTML browsers, but it is not acceptable for XML. XML is case-sensitive, and begin and end tags must match. Similarly, HTML elements do not always require an ending tag. One such HTML tag is the <br> tag. In XML, all elements require both a start tag and an end tag.

If a document conforms to the preceding syntax rules, the document is said to be well formed. For example, the following can be considered well formed:

```
<parent/>
```

or

```
<parent></parent>
```

or

```
<parent>data</parent>
```

or

```
<parent><teacher>text</teacher><student>name</student></parent>
```

The following is not well formed because it contains multiple root nodes:

```
<parent></parent><teacher></teacher>
```

This example is not well formed because does not have an end tag:

```
<root>
```

Here, you see a document that is not well formed because its children are not properly nested:

```
<parent><teacher>text</student><student>name</teacher></parent>
```

The XML document syntax addresses what a document is and what its structure is. By conforming to these rules, you impose a common structure on your data that's flexible enough to meet different applications. The next step in understanding XML is to understand its building blocks.

Elements

Elements were mentioned in the previous section. An *element* is a type name for an XML entity. The equivalent concept in HTML is a tag. An element is marked by a start tag and an end tag. An element is similar to a tag in HTML. For example, the following HTML creates a table:

```
<table>
    <tr>
        <td>Hello</td><td>World</td>
    </tr>
</table>
```

In XML, you can think of each of the HTML tags as XML elements. But the presence of a tag does not make an XML document. An XML document must conform to the XML document syntax, and the data contained in an element or attribute must not contain certain types of characters. Elements can contain other elements, character data, or both.

The text appearing between the start tag and end tag is called the element's *content*. If no data appears between the start and end tag, the element is said to be empty. An empty tag can be represented either as

```
<customer></customer>
```

or

```
<customer/>
```

An element has a name and is associated with a namespace. See the sections, "Names" and "Namespaces" for more information.

Elements are rather simplistic. This simplicity makes XML a successful technology. The ability to create new elements with little restriction is an integral part of XML.

Attributes

An *attribute* is a simple name and value pairing that describes a facet of an element. An attribute must have an associated name that is unique to the element, and each attribute has a value that does not contain angled brackets (< or >).

```
<?xml version='1.0'?>
<children>
<child nickname="Little Bit">Carson Allen Evans</child>
<child nickname="Teeny Bit"/>
</children>
```

In the preceding example, the `nickname` attribute describes a single facet of the `child` element. The name of the attribute is `nickname`, and the value of the attribute for Carson Allen Evans is `Little Bit`. An attribute name follows the qualified naming syntax (see the section, "Names" for more information).

Because you can structure a document by using elements and/or attributes, the natural question arises, "When should I choose one over the other?" This is a long-standing debate. Some developers argue that attributes are no longer necessary because you can represent any attribute as a child element. Others argue that attributes make a document infinitely more readable. Attributes and child elements are used throughout this book. The only hard and fast rule is that each attribute name must be unique within an element. If you find that an attribute must appear more than once for an element, you need to switch to using nested elements instead of attributes.

Two attributes are predefined in the XML 1.0 Recommendation: `xml:space` and `xml:lang`.

xml:space

The xml:space attribute enables the document's author to explicitly state how white space is to be handled within the document. XML parsers, such as those used in the .NET Framework classes, can strip white space from a document unless otherwise instructed. The xml:space attribute signifies that the current node and its children should be treated accordingly. The valid values for xml:space are preserve and default. Specifying a value of preserve signifies to the processor that the current node and its children should have whitepsace preserved. This behavior can then be overridden in a child node by using a value of default to signify that the default white space handling should again be used.

```
<data xml:space="preserve">
    <a>      </a>
    <b xml:space="default">
       <c>      </c>
    </b>
</data>
```

Using this example, space is preserved for the data and a nodes. The b node overrides the behavior of its parent and uses default white space handling. Node c then uses default white space handling because its parent, b, overrode the handling locally.

Table 1.1 lists the definitions of white space.

Table 1.1 **White Space Characters in XML**

ASCII Character Code	Description
9	Horizontal tab (vbTab)
10	Line feed
13	Carriage return
32	Space character

The .NET Framework classes dealing with XML provide properties to specify white space handling. It is more typical to handle white space formatting in the object model and parser or XSLT stylesheet than it is to explicitly declare the white space formatting within the XML document itself because the document should specify data and not its presentation or behavior.

xml:lang

The xml:lang attribute is used for internationalization. The valid values are defined in ISO 639, RFC 1766, or a user-defined language code. Table 1.2 shows you some examples of valid values for the xml:lang attribute.

Table 1.2   **Examples of ISO 639 Country Codes and Subcodes**

Country Code (and Subcode)	Description
en–US	English (U.S.)
en–GB	English (Great Britain)
Fr	French
sp–MX	Spanish

Here, you see three different languages being used within the same document: U.S. English, French, and Spanish:

```
<?xml version="1.0" encoding="UTF-8"?>
<phrases>
    <phrase xml:lang="en-US">One beer, please</phrase>
    <phrase xml:lang="sp-MX">Uno cerveza, por favor</phrase>
    <phrase xml:lang="fr">Une bière, s'il vous plaît</phrase>
</phrases>
```

xmlns

Actually, one more attribute is valid for elements, <xmlns>, which was not a part of the XML 1.0 Recommendation. This attribute associated a node with a given namespace. Namespaces are discussed in more detail in the section, "Namespaces."

Comments

XML documents can also contain comments. The syntax for creating a comment in XML is the same as it is in HTML:

```
<customer>
   <!--The following nodes are commented out and unreachable
     <foo>Testing</foo>
     <bar>Another test</bar>
   -->
</customer>
```

Comments can contain any type of data, but cannot be nested. XML parsers can ignore comments in their implementation and might not be reachable as a node. The .NET Framework classes that deal with XML recognize comments as a processable node.

CDATA

CDATA sections contain data that would otherwise be recognized as markup. For example, elements cannot contain angled brackets in their content; neither can attributes. They can, however, contain a character entity reference (< or

>), but cannot contain the literal angled bracket. CDATA sections provide a means for containing this type of data.

```
<script language="JavaScript">
var i;
function getIncrement()
{
   return(++i);
}
</script>
```

To represent the preceding JavaScript function block in an XML document, you need to use character entity references to denote the literal values that would otherwise break up the document's organization, as shown here:

```
<?xml version="1.0"?>
<function>
&lt;script&gt; language=&quot;JavaScript&quot;&gt;
var i;
function getIncrement()
{
    return(++i);
}
&lt;/script&gt;
</function>
```

Instead of using character entity references, you can use a CDATA section to contain the data, as follows:

```
<?xml version="1.0"?>
<function>
<![CDATA[
<script language="JavaScript">
var i;
function getIncrement()
{
   return(++i);
}
</script>
]]>
</function>
```

Because the angled brackets and double quotes are contained within the CDATA section, the document is now well formed.

Processing Instructions

Processing instructions (PIs) give the XML processor hints on how the document needs to be handled.

Another processing instruction is commonly used to link an XSL stylesheet to an XML document:

```
<?xml-stylesheet type="text/xsl" href="mystylesheet.xsl"?>
```

This common processing instruction links an XML document to a particular XSL stylesheet.

You can also declare your own processing instructions by using the processing instruction syntax. PIs must use a valid `NCName` and cannot begin with "xml" because the use of that prefix is reserved. Here's an example:

```
<?my-instruction this is my custom PI?>
```

As you can see in the preceding code line, a processing instruction does not need to contain a formal attribute. It can contain any content except for the end tag delimiter, which is `?>`.

A common misconception is that the following is also a PI:

```
<?xml version="1.0" encoding="UTF-8"?>
```

This looks like a PI, but it is actually the optional XML declaration that specifies the XML version and the encoding scheme. The reason this misconception is prevalent is because the only way to create this by using MSXML is to create a PI that looks like the XML declaration. This difference might seem trivial, but it makes a huge difference in the .NET Framework because a distinction is made between processing instructions and the XML declaration. For example, the `XmlDocument` class contains the `CreateProcessingInstruction` method and a separate `CreateXmlDeclaration` method. In addition, a separate class, `XmlDeclaration`, is separate from the `XmlProcessingInstruction` class.

Names

Both elements and attributes have an associated local name and a namespace. A local name, or `NCName`, begins with an underscore or an alphabetic character followed by zero or more alphanumeric characters, periods, hyphens, underscores, or full-stops (periods)[2]. A name cannot have spaces in it. The following element names are valid:

```
<Customers></Customers>
```

and

```
<products></products>
```

and

```
<_orders></_orders>
```

The following element name is not valid because it contains a space:

```
<car type></car type>
```

Namespaces

As mentioned previously, all elements and attributes also have an associated namespace that, combined with the local name, forms the name. A *namespace* is a Uniform Resource Identifier (URI), which is either a Uniform Resource Locator (URL) or Uniform Resource Name (URN). If not expressly declared, an element or attribute falls in to the default namespace, which might be the null namespace.

When using the Visual Studio .NET Schema Designer, it uses a default namespace of www.tempuri.org. This implies that the document must be found at that location; however, this is not the case.

All domain names on the web are unique. For example, I cannot register the domain name Microsoft.com because that domain name is already taken. Because domain names are unique across the Internet, you can easily see the rationale behind using a URL as a unique qualifier for a namespace. Because domain names are unique, it is easy to control the uniqueness of a namespace by using your domain name as its basis. URLs are commonly used and understood, in theory, by most Internet users. URNs, however, are not familiar to many developers, so they simply choose what is convenient or better known. No real advantage exists to one over the other, except a URN can more clearly show that a unique identifier does not imply the resource's location. I could have easily used example.com, tempuri.org, foo.bar, anything.anywhere, or any other valid URL even though I might not have access to that URL and the URL might not even exist. There's no guarantee that the namespace used has anything to do with the location of the document; it only implies the uniqueness.

After you understand that the namespace name does not imply its location, you're ready to move on to the concept of namespaces and their use. Namespaces prevent naming collisions.

The following XML document expresses siblings in the Evans family:

```
<siblings>
    <name>Bob Evans</name>
    <name>Keith Evans</name>
    <name>Michelle Schultz</name>
</siblings>
```

Use the <name> element to designate a sibling's name. But what if you want to distinguish between brothers and sisters? In that case, you need to use namespaces, as follows:

```
<siblings xmlns:brother="urn:sibling:brother"
        xmlns:sister="urn:sibling:sister">
    <brother:name>Bob Evans</brother:name>
    <brother:name>Keith Evans</brother:name>
    <sister:name>Michelle Schultz</sister:name>
</siblings>
```

Now you can differentiate between brother and sister elements while using the same local name, name, for each element. A namespace is composed of a namespace prefix and the URL or URI that's associated with the namespace. Together, the namespace prefix and the identifier form a qualified name, which is also referred to as a QName.

Suppose that you are developing an XSLT stylesheet. You want to output a node, message, and the XSLT namespace also includes a node called message. How do you differentiate between the two nodes and what their meanings are? The answer is to bind a prefix to the namespace and qualify the element names, as shown here:

```
<xsl:stylesheet
        xmlns:xsl="http://www.w3.org/1999/XSL/Transform" version="1.0"
        xmlns="urn:schemas-vbdna:sample">
        <xsl:template match="/">
                <hello>This is a sample, bound to the default
                ➥namespace</hello>
                <message>This element is also bound to the default
                ➥namespace</message>
                <xsl:message>However, this is a message from
                ➥XSLT</xsl:message>
        </xsl:template>
</xsl:stylesheet>
```

Two different namespaces are used in this example. One namespace was declared with a prefix, xsl, and the other used no prefix. By using the namespace prefix xsl, you actually change the name of the element. The XML parser and XPath functions now recognize the element name as <xsl:message>.

The element declared with no prefix at the root level of the document defines the default namespace. The <message> element is bound to the default namespace, as is the <hello> element.

Namespaces do not need to be declared at the root or document level—they can be declared at the element level as well. Here's an example:

```
<?xml version="1.0"?>
<doc>
    <test>This is a test</test>
    <data xmlns="example">
        <child>Bound to the example namespace</child>
        <sibling xmlns="">No longer bound</sibling>
      </data>
</doc>
```

In this example, the doc element is bound to the null namespace. As previously mentioned, every element and attribute name consists of a local name and an associated namespace. The <doc> element is not explicitly bound to any namespace. It belongs to the null namespace. This is also true for the <test> element. The <data> element, however, is explicitly bound to the namespace example. By binding an element to a namespace, all its children are also bound to that namespace unless it's overridden. Therefore, the <child> element is bound to the example namespace.

To override a namespace, simply set the xmlns attribute to a new value. The sibling element, for example, overrode the namespace inherited from its parent. All child elements of the <sibling> element then belong to the null namespace.

> **Note**
> Namespaces are also covered in depth in Chapter 2, "XML Schemas in .NET."

Entities

Documents might need to contain angled brackets or quotation signs in element content. Containing all such data in CDATA sections to handle one or two occurrences of reserved characters would be tedious. In order to handle this, XML provides entity references that represent delimiter characters. Table 1.3 shows the five entity references provided by the XML 1.0 Recommendation.

Table 1.3   **Entity References Provided by XML**

Entity Reference	ASCII Code	Escape Character
&amp;	38	Ampersand (&)
&quot;	34	Double quote (")
&apos;	39	Apostrophe (')
&lt;	60	Less than (<)
&gt;	62	Greater than (>)

Besides entity references, you can also use character references. Character references use either decimal or hexadecimal to represent the character. When using decimal, the value must be preceded by &# and followed by a trailing semicolon, as shown here:

```
     <!-- outputs a non-breaking space-->
```

If using hexadecimal, the value must be preceded by &#x and followed by a trailing semicolon, as shown here:

```
     <!-- outputs a non-breaking space -->
```

Some entity references or character references are only available within a given namespace. For example, the non-breaking space entity reference is defined for HTML, but not for XML or XSLT. If you're using an XSLT stylesheet to generate XHTML, you might want to output a non-breaking space. To do this, you need to use either the decimal or hexadecimal format for a non-breaking space character reference. Chapter 3, "XML Presentation," looks deeper into this issue.

Creating Valid Documents

A schema or Document Type Definition (DTD) contains the rules by which an XML document must abide. Schemas and DTDs are discussed in detail in a moment, but first, think of them as a set of rules. If the XML document conforms to the rules, it is said to be a valid document.

More precisely, XML documents are said to be valid if their content can be validated against either an XML Schema (XSD or XDR) or a DTD. This section discusses both schemas and DTDs, their benefits, shortcomings, and their prospective roles in .NET.

Why Validate Documents?

As with the other sections in this chapter, let's begin by answering some basic questions. Before jumping into how to validate documents, you must understand why you would want to validate a document.

Providing the rules and vocabulary for a document helps to communicate the grammar associated with the document. By describing what is valid content for the document, you develop a vocabulary that can be extended and understood by other developers.

Without explicitly stating the rules to which a document must conform, you put the burden of data validation on the program that generated the data, the program that consumes the data, or both to know the implicit rules associated with the XML document. Instead of relying on implicit validation, the DTD or schema can require explicit conformity to the referenced set of rules that makes the document valid.

Consider a system where you receive a data feed from a customer. How would your customer know what is valid data and what is a valid structure of the document? You could give extensive wording and diagrams, but you risk losing something in the interpretation of a verbose document.

As a benefit, XML tools can also use DTDs or schemas to assist the developer in creating the document. For example, the XML editor included in Visual Studio .NET uses schemas to provide code completion and on-the-fly validation so that you know whether a document is valid during its creation.

Now you're ready to look at DTDs and schemas in more detail.

DTDs

A DTD is simply a syntax for declaring the grammar and vocabulary of an XML document. The DTD enables the developer to convey the structure of XML documents, as well as the content of XML documents.

This section covers DTDs only enough to convey their use and existence. DTDs are quickly losing ground to XML Schemas as the preferred validation mechanism for XML documents. This book focuses on the use of XML Schemas for validation over the use of DTDs.

What Is a DTD?

A DTD declares the structure and content of an XML file. It defines the content model of a document. Consider the following XML document:

```
<?xml version="1.0" encoding="utf-8" standalone="yes" ?>
<SITES>
    <LINKS>
        <LINK>http://www.Microsoft.com</LINK>
        <LINK>http://www.xmlandasp.net</LINK>
    </LINKS>
</SITES>
```

Suppose that business rules are associated with the structure of this document, and that these rules are not immediately obvious. For example, suppose that you only accept one LINKS node as a child of the SITES node. Furthermore, there can be zero or more LINK elements as a child of the LINKS element. Finally, each LINK element contains text content. Here is the sample DTD that validates this data:

```
<?xml version="1.0" encoding="utf-8" standalone="yes" ?>
<!DOCTYPE SITES [
<!ELEMENT SITES (LINKS)?>
<!ELEMENT LINKS (LINK)*>
<!ELEMENT LINK (#PCDATA)>
]>
```

To explain this a little further, begin by declaring the XML processing instruction, version, and the standalone attribute. The next line declares the root element, SITES, using the DOCTYPE keyword. The DOCTYPE is part of the document's prolog, so it appears before the XML body content. Remember that an XML document can have one, and only one, root node so that the root node is associated with the DOCTYPE definition.

The following line declares an element as a child of the SITES node. The child node is named LINKS, and the question mark (?) declares that the element appears only zero or one time(s). Using this definition, the following XML is valid:

```
<?xml version="1.0" encoding="utf-8" standalone="yes" ?>
<SITES/>
```

This is because the LINKS element can occur zero times or one time, but cannot occur more than once.

The following line declares that a child element can occur either zero or many times.

```
<!ELEMENT LINKS (LINK)*>
```

If you want to declare that at least one LINK element must be a child of the LINKS element, use the + notation to signify a cardinality of greater than one:

```
<!ELEMENT LINKS (LINK)+>
```

The following line in the sample DTD declares that the LINK elements content is made up of PCDATA, or character data:

```
<!ELEMENT LINK (#PCDATA)>
```

You can also declare a sequence of child elements. Suppose that you want to add an ARTICLES element as a child of the SITES root node. Furthermore, the LINKS element must always precede the ARTICLES node. To add this, you must change the sample DTD to the following:

```
<?xml version="1.0" encoding="utf-8" standalone="yes" ?>
<!DOCTYPE SITES [
<!ELEMENT SITES (LINKS,ARTICLES)?>
<!ELEMENT LINKS (LINK)*>
<!ELEMENT LINK (#PCDATA)>
<!ELEMENT ARTICLES (ARTICLE*)>
<!ELEMENT ARTICLE (#PCDATA)>
]>
```

The following XML document is now valid using this DTD definition:

```
<?xml version="1.0" encoding="utf-8" standalone="yes" ?>
<!DOCTYPE SITES [
<!ELEMENT SITES (LINKS,ARTICLES)?>
<!ELEMENT LINKS (LINK)*>
<!ELEMENT LINK (#PCDATA)>
<!ELEMENT ARTICLES (ARTICLE*)>
<!ELEMENT ARTICLE (#PCDATA)>
]>
<SITES>
    <LINKS>
        <LINK>http://www.Microsoft.com</LINK>
        <LINK>http://www.xmlandasp.net</LINK>
    </LINKS>
      <ARTICLES>
            <ARTICLE>This is where an article may go</ARTICLE>
        </ARTICLES>
</SITES>
```

The following XML, however, is not valid because the sequence was defined so that LINKS must precede ARTICLES:

```
<?xml version="1.0" encoding="utf-8" standalone="yes" ?>
<!DOCTYPE SITES [
<!ELEMENT SITES (LINKS,ARTICLES)?>
<!ELEMENT LINKS (LINK)*>
<!ELEMENT LINK (#PCDATA)>
<!ELEMENT ARTICLES (ARTICLE*)>
<!ELEMENT ARTICLE (#PCDATA)>
]>
<SITES>
        <ARTICLES>
                <ARTICLE>This is where an article may go</ARTICLE>
        </ARTICLES>
        <LINKS>
            <LINK>http://www.Microsoft.com</LINK>
            <LINK>http://www.xmlandasp.net</LINK>
        </LINKS>
</SITES>
```

Suppose that you want to have a choice between two different element types. Instead of requiring both elements and articles as a child of the root node, suppose that you want one or the other. To represent this, use the OR notation |.

```
<?xml version="1.0" encoding="utf-8" standalone="yes" ?>
<!DOCTYPE SITES [
<!ELEMENT SITES (LINKS | ARTICLES)?>
    <!ELEMENT LINKS (LINK)*>
                <!ELEMENT LINK (#PCDATA)>
    <!ELEMENT ARTICLES (ARTICLE*)>
                <!ELEMENT ARTICLE (#PCDATA)>
]>
<SITES>
        <ARTICLES>
                <ARTICLE>This is where an article may go</ARTICLE>
        </ARTICLES>
</SITES>
```

This document is considered valid. The following document, however, is not valid because both elements are used when the OR condition was specified in the DTD:

```
<?xml version="1.0" encoding="utf-8" standalone="yes" ?>
<!DOCTYPE SITES [
<!ELEMENT SITES (LINKS | ARTICLES)?>
    <!ELEMENT LINKS (LINK)*>
                <!ELEMENT LINK (#PCDATA)>
    <!ELEMENT ARTICLES (ARTICLE*)>
                <!ELEMENT ARTICLE (#PCDATA)>
]>
<SITES>
        <ARTICLES>
```

```
                <ARTICLE>This is where an article may go</ARTICLE>
            </ARTICLES>
        <LINKS>
                <LINK>http://www.xmlandasp.net</LINK>
                <LINK>http://www.microsoft.com</LINK>
        </LINKS>
    </SITES>
```

So far, only elements have been a focus. What if you want to specify an attribute? For example, what if you want to associate a name attribute with each link element? To use attributes, simply specify them in an ATTLIST section in the DTD, as shown here:

```
<?xml version="1.0" encoding="utf-8" standalone="yes"?>
<!DOCTYPE SITES [
    <!ELEMENT SITES (LINKS | ARTICLES)+>
    <!ELEMENT LINKS (LINK*)*>
    <!ELEMENT LINK (#PCDATA)>
    <!ELEMENT ARTICLES (ARTICLE*)*>
    <!ELEMENT ARTICLE (#PCDATA)>
    <!ATTLIST LINK
    name CDATA #REQUIRED
>
]>
<SITES>
    <ARTICLES>
        <ARTICLE>This is where an article may go</ARTICLE>
    </ARTICLES>
    <LINKS>
        <LINK name="xmlandasp.net">http://www.xmlandasp.net</LINK>
        <LINK name="Microsoft">http://www.microsoft.com</LINK>
    </LINKS>
</SITES>
```

The #REQUIRED modifier for the attribute specifies that the attribute is required.

As you can see, DTDs can be useful for defining the structure and content model of an XML document.

Drawbacks of Using DTDs

The first drawback to using DTDs is that an XML parser cannot parse them. DTDs use a syntax that's difficult for parsers to represent. Two types of DTDs exist: *internal* and *external*. In this section, only internal DTDs are used, just to keep things simple. External DTDs are DTDs that are external to the XML document and are referenced from with the XML document. The XML parser cannot represent external DTDs, so working with DTDs becomes problematic because a different toolset must be used outside the XML parser.

As you might have seen throughout the DTD examples, the content of attributes and elements were specified as #PCDATA. This is because DTDs do not support typing of data. You cannot restrict that the content of an element will be a number or a string because everything in an XML document is a string, according to DTDs. You cannot specify the acceptable length of a string, nor can you specify restrictions on the string's contents.

Another drawback to using DTDs is that names in a DTD must be unique. You can reference other elements, but you cannot define a new one by using the same name. For example, suppose that you want to change the DTD so that each ARTICLE element contains a child LINKS node, as follows:

```
<?xml version="1.0" encoding="utf-8" standalone="yes" ?>
<!DOCTYPE ROOT [
<!ELEMENT ROOT (LINKS,ARTICLES)?>
<!ELEMENT LINKS (LINK)*>
<!ELEMENT ARTICLES (ARTICLE)*>
<!ELEMENT LINK (#PCDATA)>
<!ELEMENT ARTICLE (LINKS)>
]>
<ROOT>
    <LINKS>
        <LINK>NewRiders.com</LINK>
    </LINKS>
    <ARTICLES>
        <ARTICLE>
            <LINKS>
                <LINK>Microsoft.com</LINK>
                <LINK>Xmlandasp.net</LINK>
            </LINKS>
        </ARTICLE>
    </ARTICLES>
</ROOT>
```

Notice that both the ROOT and ARTICLE elements declare a child element of type LINKS.

You can reuse definitions, but you cannot redefine names. Suppose that, instead of reusing the LINKS definition, you want to redefine it. You might try something like the following, but this code is invalid because the name is already declared:

```
<?xml version="1.0" encoding="utf-8" standalone="yes" ?>
<!DOCTYPE ROOT [
<!ELEMENT ROOT (LINKS,ARTICLES)?>
<!ELEMENT LINKS (LINK)*>
<!ELEMENT ARTICLES (ARTICLE)*>
<!ELEMENT LINK (#PCDATA)>
<!ELEMENT ARTICLE (LINKS)>
<!ELEMENT LINKS (#PCDATA)>
]>
```

Finally, using namespaces with DTDs is difficult. It is not impossible because using namespaces involves using a qualified name (QName) that consists of a namespace prefix and an associated local name. To the DTD, there is no concept of a namespace; it just treats the name with a colon as any other XML name. But defining a namespace in a DTD is difficult because you must use attribute lists for elements that use the namespace prefix.

XML Schemas are gaining ground on DTDs because schemas can easily represent different names, extend existing definitions, and easily use namespaces.

Validating XML Documents

The easiest way to validate an XML document against a DTD or schema is to load the XML document and its DTD in the XML editor in Visual Studio .NET. Select XML | Validate XML Data from the menu, and Visual Studio .NET reports any errors found in the DTD or in the XML document that violates the DTD.

> **Validation Using Internet Explorer**
>
> Internet Explorer doesn't validate documents with either DTDs or schemas by default. iexmltls.exe, however, is a free add-on to IE that performs validation. See http://msdn.microsoft.com/downloads/default.asp?url=/downloads/sample.asp?url=/ MSDN-FILES/027/000/543/msdncompositedoc.xml to download this add-on.

To validate against a DTD using the ValidatingReader class in .NET, set the ValidationType property of the ValidatingReader object to ValidationType.DTD, as shown here:

```
Sub Validate()
    Dim xmlReader As System.Xml.XmlTextReader = New
System.Xml.XmlTextReader("c:\temp\xmlfile.xml")
    Dim vReader As System.Xml.XmlValidatingReader = New
System.Xml.XmlValidatingReader(xmlReader)

    vReader.ValidationType = ValidationType.DTD
    AddHandler vReader.ValidationEventHandler, AddressOf ValidateCallback
    While vReader.Read()
    End While
End Sub
Public Sub ValidateCallback(ByVal sender As Object, ByVal args As
System.Xml.Schema.ValidationEventArgs)
    Debug.WriteLine(args.Message)
End Sub
```

You can also use the .NET base classes or MSXML to programmatically validate against an XML document. Chapter 2 discusses the ValidatingReader class for validating XML documents, and the ValidatingReader class is discussed in greater detail in Chapter 6, "Exploring the System.Xml Namespace." Chapter 5, "MSXML Parser," discusses how to validate documents by using MSXML.

The W3C

Throughout this chapter, references to the W3C and various recommendations have been mentioned. This is a great time to briefly discuss the W3C and its role in XML development.

Tim Berners-Lee started the W3C to focus the growth of the Internet and help standardize the technologies that were quickly evolving. The mission of the W3C is to lead the World Wide Web to its full potential by developing common protocols that promote its evolution and ensure its interoperability.

You can easily imagine how a company might adopt a particular strategy and integrate it into its products, forcing use of a technology simply through convenience. Many XML developers accuse Microsoft of this approach through their use of XML Data Reduced (XDR) Schemas, although others believe that Microsoft furthered the adoption of schemas by providing a working draft in many of their products, such as BizTalk and Commerce Server. Despite the finger-pointing surrounding standards evolution and adherence, the W3C has been integral in forming working groups from various companies and technology backgrounds to develop vendor-neutral standards and implementations of XML technology.

The W3C is a standards body, but only governments can make official standards by international agreement. For this reason, the W3C issues recommendations that carry the same weight as a standard in the development world.

A technology is first proposed to the W3C who considers the proposal on its merit and decides if it's worth standardization. The next step is to route the proposal through the recommendation track.

The Recommendation Track

As you work with XML, you will see references to outdated recommendations or hear that a particular technology is still a *working draft* or a *release candidate*. What do these terms this mean?

A working draft is essentially the beginnings of a recommendation. When a proposal becomes a working draft, a working group is formed through the W3C who devises a charter. Simply accepting a proposal does not mean that everyone agrees on the proposal: It only means that the working group has committed to pursue the work.

The next step of a proposal is the *last call working draft*. A last call means that the working group is asking for comments or suggestions on the working draft. Comments are solicited from the W3C, other W3C working groups, and the public. At this stage, the working group believes to have fulfilled its charter.

After a proposal becomes a last call working draft and it passes the commenting period, the proposal becomes a *candidate recommendation*. A candidate recommendation is believed by consensus to have met the working group's charter and is published to gain implementation experience and feedback. At this stage, tool vendors usually announce support for an XML-related technology.

After a candidate recommendation passes, it becomes a *proposed recommendation*. A proposed recommendation is a formal notice to the W3C, requesting review. This stage represents sufficient implementation experience to warrant the W3C's consideration to become a W3C recommendation.

When a proposal becomes a W3C recommendation, the technology becomes a standard in the Internet community. Any future revisions to the recommendation result in a new proposal and a new version number is assigned to the recommendation.

Chapter Summary

This chapter covered the groundwork of XML. The basics of XML, from elements and attributes to entities and DTDs, were discussed. A handful of information was left out of this chapter purposefully, however: The W3C recommendation for XML is large, and new recommendations are frequently added to it. For more information on XML, including the document syntax, the XML 1.0 Recommendation, and other W3C proposals, see `www.w3.org` for a listing of the W3C's areas of involvement.

References

[1] `www.w3.org/TR/WD-xml-961114.html#sec1.1`

[2] Box, Don, Aaron Skonnard, and John Lam. *Essential XML, Beyond Markup*. DevelopMentor.

2

XML Schemas in .NET

Similar to Data Type Definitions (DTDs), *XML Schemas* provide for specification of the structure of an XML document. This chapter looks at XML Schemas and how you can use them to validate XML documents.

XML Schemas are well-formed XML documents. This means that, unlike DTD documents, they can be created and manipulated with XML parsers, such as the .NET objects in the System.Xml namespace or the MSXML DOM. XML Schemas have many advantages over DTDs, including support for data types and namespaces. They are readable and provide tremendous flexibility for describing an XML document.

World Wide Web Consortium Recommendation

XML Schemas are a World Wide Web Consortium (W3C) Recommendation, which means that they have passed all other stages of the W3C approval process. This also means that tool support is more widespread now that the working draft is not a moving target.

Understanding Schemas

Before you jump into the code for working with schemas, you must understand what schemas are. The word *Extensible* in Extensible Markup Language refers to the ability to define new elements, therefore creating documents that are self-describing. Schemas take the notion of extensibility and extend it to encompass defining new vocabularies for XML documents. Schemas help you define the structure of a document so that the structure can be easily conveyed within and outside your organization.

What Are Schemas?

The word *schema* is often used in the context of databases to describe the layout of a database. A *database schema* defines the tables, columns, and datatypes for a database. XML Schemas are similar in that you can define not only the layout of the document in terms of relation and datatypes, but also in terms of hierarchy and order of precedence. At their basic definition, XML Schemas are XML files that use predefined elements to define the structure of an XML document. A parser that supports the XML Schema recommendation knows how to react to the predefined elements when validataing your XML document. Usually, a schema is defined in a file with an XSD extension that is separate from the XML document. An XML document can reference the schema to declare the structure to which it should conform, although it's not required.

Some Acronyms to Understand

Two main acronyms are associated with XML schemas. *XML Data Reduced (XDR)* was based on a proposal submitted by Microsoft. XDR Schemas are used and supported in many Microsoft tools, such as SQL Server 2000, BizTalk, and Microsoft Office 2000. XDR has been supported in the MSXML parser since version 2.0; it is supported both in the version 4.0 parser and in .NET. The W3C Working Group evolved XDR into *XML Schema Definition (XSD)* language. XSD is the current implementation of XML Schemas and is currently a W3C Recommendation, which means that the proposal has passed all other stages of the W3C approval process. XSD has superseded XDR, so this book will focus primarily on XSD. However, XDR schemas are used in Chapter 9, "SQL Server 2000 and XML," in conjunction with SQL Server 2000 and are explained within the context. For more information on XDR Schemas, see the XDR Schema Developer's Guide on MSDN Online at `http://msdn. microsoft.com/library/en-us/xmlsdk30/htm/xmconxmlschemadevelopersguide.asp`.

Why Use Schemas?

Schemas allow for validation of the data contained in an XML document. Suppose that your application accepts XML data from a third party. How would you convey what the structure of the XML should be? You could email the structure, "The customer's ID field is 20 characters and is required." This would be troublesome, however, when you need to update the XML format. It would also be inconvenient for validating format because you would still be required to write validation routines to confirm the data is properly formatted according to your email. You would eventually have to recode the same implementation for another document, creating document-specific validation code that is not easily reusable.

Instead of guessing that the XML document conforms to an agreed-upon protocol and risking breaking your application due to malformed XML or missing required elements, you can explicitly convey your document standard by providing an XML Schema. You can make the schema available to developers from other departments or organizations so that they will know how to format their XML documents to effectively share data. When they send you a document, you can validate it using a parser that supports schema validation, such as MSXML4 or the System.Xml objects in .NET. If the XML document conforms to the contract specified in the schema, the XML document is said to be *valid*. If it does not conform, the XML parser notifies you that the document is not valid.

Another reason to consider schemas is their integration throughout .NET. As explained throughout this book, XML is integrated heavily into .NET. For example, Chapter 8, "Database Access with ADO.NET and XML," shows how XML Schemas play an important role in ADO.NET and are used heavily within ADO.NET DataSets to describe the content of the underlying data. Another new concept in .NET is the notion of *typed DataSets*. By using XML Schemas, you have the ability to generate class structures from an XML Schema, or to generate schemas from an existing class structure. This is a powerful concept: You can define your class hierarchies by using an XML Schema document and then use a utility to generate class files so that most of the coding is done for you. This technique is demonstrated in Chapter 4, "XML Tool Support in Visual Studio .NET." Conversely, you can develop your class files and serialize them by using a schema document to validate the serialization. Serialization is covered in Chapter 10, "XML Serialization." Finally, XML Schemas are being integrated into many other Microsoft products, such as SQL Server. SQL Server's extensive use of XML Schemas is covered in Chapter 9, "SQL Server 2000 and XML."

Instance and Schema Documents

A *schema document* is the document that describes the rules and layout for an XML document. An instance document is an XML document that's validated against the schema document.

Referencing a Schema Document Directly

An instance document does not necessarily have to include a reference to the schema document, although it is common to do so. An XML parser that supports XSD should provide a means to specify the schema document's location and/or text without requiring the instance document to include an embedded reference to the schema document.

For most of this chapter, you'll use instance documents with an embedded reference to a schema document. In the cases where an instance document is used without a schema document, it is explicitly stated.

The two things I wanted to know when I first started using schemas were how to represent a class object and how to represent a collection of those objects. Consider the XML document in Listing 2.1.

Listing 2.1 **A Sample Purchase Order XML Document**

```xml
<?xml version="1.0" encoding="utf-8" ?>
<PURCHASEORDER>
    <CUSTOMER>
        <NAME>Carson Allen Evans</NAME>
        <PHONE>(800)555-1212</PHONE>
        <EMAIL>carson.evans@xmlandasp.net</EMAIL>
    </CUSTOMER>
    <ORDER>
        <ITEM>
            <ITEMNAME>Easton BZ70-Z Z-Core Titanium Baseball
            ➥Bat</ITEMNAME>
            <DESCRIPTION>The BZ70-Z Z-Core titanium baseball bat from
            ➥Easton with Sc777 Triple Seven alloy
            ➥construction.</DESCRIPTION>
            <SIZE>33/30</SIZE>
            <PRICE>229.99</PRICE>
        </ITEM>
        <ITEM>
            <ITEMNAME>Mizuno MZP11 Pro Limited</ITEMNAME>
            <DESCRIPTION>Mizuno MZP11 Pro Limited 12 Inch Baseball Glove,
            ➥Pro Sized Pitcher&apos;s Glove.</DESCRIPTION>
            <SIZE>Left hand throw</SIZE>
            <PRICE>175.99</PRICE>
        </ITEM>
    </ORDER>
</PURCHASEORDER>
```

Here, you can see an order for some baseball equipment. This document is the instance document because it contains a data instance of the structure that's defined throughout this chapter. The root node is PURCHASEORDER, which describes the content. You have a CUSTOMER object representation with the properties NAME, PHONE, and EMAIL, respectively. Then you have an ORDER collection that contains multiple ITEMs. You can use an XML Schema to validate the structure of the XML instance document. You can also use that structure as a template and any data contained in an instance of that template can also be validated.

XML Naming Conventions

Listing 2.1 uses all uppercase for element names. Although different conventions exist for naming XML elements, such as Pascal-style casing and camel-casing, the use of all uppercase naming was chosen for this example to yield an important point later regarding typed DataSets and Visual Basic .NET.

Begin by looking at how to associate the instance document with a schema document. Listing 2.1 is an example of an instance document without an embedded schema reference. To embed a reference to the external schema document, you must specify a namespace Uniform Resource Identifier (URI) that points to the schema document, as shown here:

```
<PURCHASEORDER xmlns="http://www.xmlandasp.net/sales/">
...
</PURCHASEORDER>
```

This code uses namespaces to convey the location of the XML schema. *Namespaces* are simply unique identifiers to a document. A URL is used because it is unique across the Internet, but you could have just as easily used a Globally Unique Identifier (GUID) or any other string. For example, the following code is also valid:

```
<PURCHASEORDER xmlns="DeannaEvans">
...
</PURCHASEORDER>
```

Another convention is to use a Uniform Resource Name (URN) to identify your schema. For more information on URNs, search for RFC 1737 on the web by using your favorite search site. Here's an example of using a URN:

```
<PURCHASEORDER xmlns="urn:deanna-evans:wife">
...
</PURCHASEORDER>
```

Because a namespace doesn't have to be a URL, how would the processor locate the schema document referenced in your XML instance document? To answer this question, another namespace declaration is available for use in your instance document, which is described in "XML Schema Part 0: Primer" at www.w3.org/TR/xmlschema-0. This namespace contains the schemaLocation element to provide hints to the physical location of the schema. It accepts pairs of URI references where the first pair references the namespace and the second pair refers to the physical location of the document.

In this code snippet, you can see the use of the xsi namespace to associate a physical document with the associated URN:

```
<PURCHASEORDER xmlns="urn:schemas-xmlandasp-net:po"
xmlns:xsi="http://www.w3.org/2001/XMLSchema-instance"
xsi:schemaLocation="urn:schemas-xmlandaspnet:po
                    http://www.xmlandasp.net/schema/po.xsd">

...
</PURCHASEORDER>
```

Creating a Schema

When creating a schema, you need to decide on what namespace you want to use to reference the document. As you saw before, namespaces are not necessarily URLs to documents on the web, although they can be. Web URLs are typically used because they are unique across the Internet, but you can use a URN or any other unique identifier. In fact, the only requirements for namespaces are that the value for the namespace attribute matches the namespace for the XSD document and they follow the recommendation for naming elements and attributes. URLs are used in this example for clarity.

XML Schemas contain a top-level element named schema and use the namespace www.w3.org/2001/XMLSchema (hereafter referred to as xsd namespace or the XML Schema namespace) so that processors will know how to process XSD schemas. A schema element contains type declarations using simple and complex types as well as element and attribute declarations as its children. Begin by creating the top-level schema element and declaring the namespaces that are used in the document. The convention for working with XML Schemas is to use the prefix xsd when referring to the XML Schema elements.

Should I Use the Default Namespace or a Namespace Prefix?

You can use the XML Schema namespace as the default namespace so that the xsd prefix is not required for all elements and attributes, requiring less typing. I use the xsd prefix on all elements and attributes because this is consistent with most available documentation and tools.

Listing 2.2 shows a sample schema for the XML document in Listing 2.1. Notice that a default namespace is used for this document by declaring the namespace http://www.xmlandasp.net with no namespace prefix.

Listing 2.2   **A Sample Purchase Order Schema**

```
<xsd:schema id="PURCHASEORDER"
xmlns="http://www.xmlandasp.net"
targetNamespace="http://www.xmlandasp.net/schema/Sales.xsd"
xmlns:xsd="http://www.w3.org/2001/XMLSchema"
attributeFormDefault="unqualified"
elementFormDefault="qualified">
<xsd:simpleType name="emailType">
    <xsd:restriction base="xsd:string">
        <xsd:pattern value=""/>
    </xsd:restriction>
</xsd:simpleType>
<xsd:complexType name="customerType">
    <xsd:sequence>
        <xsd:element name="NAME" type="xsd:string" />
        <xsd:element name="PHONE" type="xsd:string" />
        <xsd:element name="EMAIL" type="emailType" />
    </xsd:sequence>
</xsd:complexType>
<xsd:element name="PURCHASEORDER">
    <xsd:complexType>
        <xsd:choice maxOccurs="unbounded">
            <xsd:element name="CUSTOMER" type="customerType"/>
            <xsd:element name="ORDER">
                <xsd:complexType>
                    <xsd:sequence>
                        <xsd:element name="ITEM" minOccurs="1"
                        ↦maxOccurs="unbounded">
                            <xsd:complexType>
                                <xsd:sequence>
                                    <xsd:element name="ITEMNAME"
                                    ↦type="xsd:string" />
                                    <xsd:element name="DESCRIPTION"
                                    ↦type="xsd:string" />
                                    <xsd:element name="SIZE"
                                    ↦type="xsd:integer" />
                                    <xsd:element name="PRICE"
                                    ↦type="xsd:string" />
                                </xsd:sequence>
                            </xsd:complexType>
                        </xsd:element>
                    </xsd:sequence>
                </xsd:complexType>
            </xsd:element>
        </xsd:choice>
    </xsd:complexType>
</xsd:element>
</xsd:schema>
```

The highlighted section in Listing 2.2 shows the various namespaces in use. The default namespace used in this XML document is `http://www.xmlandasp.net`. You can also see the XML Schema namespace declared and aliased with the `xsd` prefix. The `attributeFormDefault` and `elementFormDefault` attributes signify whether the elements and attributes must be qualified using the namespace prefix. (This is discussed in more detail in the section, "Creating Attributes.") The `targetNamespace` attribute signifies to the processor the namespace that is used when referencing this schema.

After declaring the namespaces that are used in the document, the elements that are valid for this schema are declared, the order they must be used in, and the data types for the values contained in the elements.

Creating Elements

Creating an element in an XML Schema document is fairly straightforward. You can use the `xsd:element` tag to declare an element. Suppose that you want to create a document with a single root node, REPORTS, that contains character data, such as the following:

```
<xsd:schema id="REPORTSCHEMA"
xmlns="http://www.xmlandasp.net"
targetNamespace="http://www.xmlandasp.net/schema/sales.xsd"
xmlns:xsd="http://www.w3.org/2001/XMLSchema">
<xsd:element name="REPORTS" type="xsd:string"/>
</xsd:schema>
```

Elements can be declared with a type attribute to signify the character data that they contain. The PURCHASEORDER element in Listing 2.2 is not defined with a type attribute because it does not hold character data; it is simply the top-level element of the document that contains other elements. You can also define elements within hierarchies or define complex types of your own that are element hierarchies, as discussed in the section, "Complex Types."

Creating Attributes

Creating attributes are just as simple as creating elements. An attribute cannot exist on its own; it must be contained within an element. In XML Schemas, you can use the `xsd:attribute` tag to signify the presence of an attribute. However, the `xsd:attribute` tag cannot be a direct descendant of the `xsd:element` tag; it must be a child of a complex type tag (for more information on complex types, see the section, "Complex Types"). Therefore, you need to use the `xsd:attribute` tag as a child of an `xsd:complexType` tag to create an attribute. Add a LOCATION attribute to your REPORTSCHEMA example:

```
<xsd:schema id="REPORTSCHEMA"
xmlns="http://www.xmlandasp.net"
targetNamespace="http://www.xmlandasp.net/schema/sales.xsd"
xmlns:xsd="http://www.w3.org/2001/XMLSchema">
<xsd:element name="REPORTS" type="xsd:string">
    <xsd:complexType>
                    <xsd:attribute name="LOCATION" type="xsd:string"/>
                </xsd:complexType>
</xsd:element>
</xsd:schema>
```

In the PURCHASEORDER schema, you specified attributeFormDefault="qualified", but left it out in this example. If the attribute is left out, its default value is *unqualified*. This means that you do not have to explicitly use the namespace prefix when referencing an attribute. If this had been specified as qualified, the following instance document would be schema-valid:

```
<xmlandasp:REPORTS xmlns:xmlandasp="http://www.xmlandasp.net"
xmlandasp:LOCATION="blah"/>
```

Notice that the REPORTS node is prefixed with the namespace prefix xmlandasp, and the namespace prefix is associated with the proper namespace definition using the xmlns attribute.

Because the elementFormDefault element specified the value qualified, you must use a namespace prefix when referencing the element name. The following would be schema-invalid because no namespace prefix is used to distinguish the element's namespace:

```
<REPORTS xmlns="http://www.xmlandasp.net" LOCATION="blah">
```

Each element and attribute declaration supports the xsd:form attribute to override at the item level that the element's qualification should be:

```
<xsd:attribute name="LOCATION" type="xsd:string" form="qualified"/>
```

To avoid confusion with namespaces and qualified locals, the unqualified form of attributes are going to be used.

Elements and attributes are the easiest part of schemas. The more challenging and artistic aspect of schemas is the ability to define your own types and structures for reuse throughout your document.

Declaring Types

One of the most important aspects of XML Schemas is the ability to define and validate types within an XML document. In the PURCHASEORDER example, you specified that the PHONE element is of type xsd:string. More specifically, it declares that an element named PHONE conforms to the definition of string contained in the xsd namespace. The xsd namespace contains a set of predefined simple types that you can use to define your own types. Types need not be constrained to data types, however. A type can be defined as a set of elements and attributes, as well as other complex types.

Using the Built-In Types

As previously mentioned, the xsd namespace contains data types that are already built into it. Included in this namespace are definitions for string, integer, date, double, and many other data types. An example of using the built-in data types in the following example is the EMAIL element:

```
<xsd:element name="EMAIL" type="xsd:string" />
```

You can easily see that the type is string. A host of data types are built into the XML Schema namespace. Figure 2.1 shows the data types and their hierarchy.

Creating Simple Types

Schemas provide developers with a mechanism to not only use the built-in types, but also to declare your own types. A *simple* type is exactly what it sounds like: It is the simplest form of a type, describing a single value that is not compound. The easiest way to think of a simple type is as a data type in a programming language. C++, C#, Visual Basic, Java, Pascal, and most other languages support the concept of an integer or a string. Simple types can be thought of in the same manner: They describe a single value. A good representation of a simple type might be a type declaration for a numeric zip code or a U.S. Social Security number stored as a string with special formatting. An example of using a simple type in the following example is the EMAIL element:

```
<xsd:element name="EMAIL" type="emailType" />
```

We declared the type as emailType, which was declared elsewhere in the schema document. Creating your own types in schemas is similar to declaring a type in a programming language: You define the new type based on other types and give it a name. With XML Schemas, you can also specify different *content* for the type, including a restriction, list, or union.

A content type of union provides a union between two or more simple types. A content type of list provides a way to give a list of space-separated values. A content type of restriction allows you to provide constraints on a simple type. I focus on using the content type of restriction to provide constraints for a simple type.

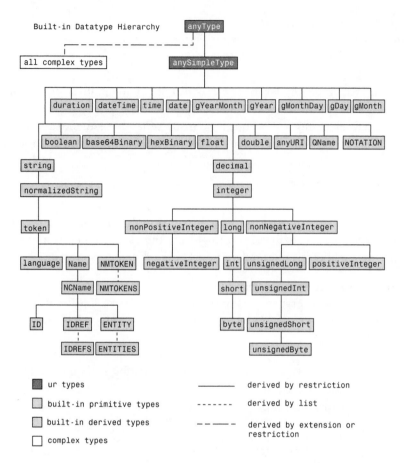

Figure 2.1   The type hierarchy for built-in types.

Note that **anyType** is at the root of this type hierarchy. All built-in types are simple types based (directly or indirectly) on anySimpleType. © May, 2, 2001, World Wide Web Consortium (Massachusetts Institute of Technology, Institut National de Recherche en Informatique et en Automatique, Keio University). All Rights Reserved. www.w3.org/Consortium/Legal/.

You can have multiple constraints for a type, defined by the use of facets. The xsd:pattern facet is specified in the following code, which allows you to specify a regular expression to validate the email address:

```
<xsd:simpleType name="emailType">
    <xsd:restriction base="xsd:string">
        <xsd:pattern value=" \w+([-+.]\w+)*@\w+([-.]\w+)*\.\w+([-.]\w+)*"/>
    </xsd:restriction>
</xsd:simpleType>
```

> **What Are Regular Expressions?**
>
> *Regular expressions* (also called regex or regexp) are sets of symbols and elements used to match patterns in text. They are a powerful method of defining valid XML text element and attribute values.

Besides the data type and facets, you can also use element attributes to further explain an element or attribute. For example, you can specify the `maxOccurs` and `minOccurs` elements to find out how many times an element can occur within a sequence of elements. The following declaration shows that the EMAIL element is optional, but can appear more than once:

```
<xsd:element name="EMAIL" type="xsd:string" minOccurs="0"
maxOccurs="unbounded"/>
```

You can use the `default` attribute to specify a default value for an attribute. If you were defining an attribute, you might use the `use` attribute to specify whether the attribute is required, optional, or prohibited.

> **Attributes and Occurrence Constraints**
>
> By definition, an attribute can only occur once within a single element. Therefore, the `minOccurs` and `maxOccurs` attributes are not valid when declaring a type that will be used within an attribute node.

Furthering the example, you can specify the formatting rules more explicitly by adding validation rules, or *facets,* to the type definition. The following shows how a regular expression is used to validate the email address:

```
<xsd:simpleType name="emailType">
    <xsd:restriction base="xsd:string">
        <xsd:pattern value="\w+([-+.]\w+)*@\w+([-.]\w+)*\.\w+([-.]\w+)*"/>
    </xsd:restriction>
</xsd:simpleType>
```

After the type is properly defined in the schema, you can declare an element or attribute to use the simple type:

```
<xsd:element name="EMAIL" type="emailType" minOccurs="0"
maxOccurs="unbounded"/>
```

By breaking the definition of the simple type apart from the rest of the document, you can reuse the definition of an email address throughout your document.

Simple Type Facets

In the previous email example, a regular expression was used to validate what an email address should look like. To do this, a *facet* was declared to describe an aspect or characteristic of the data type. A facet is a validation rule to express the validation of a given type in more detail than the built-in simple types allows. There are two types of facets: *fundamental* and *constraining*. Constraining facets are the focus of this section. A constraining facet validates a value against the given set of rules. For example, suppose that you define a Quantity property and determine that the minimum quantity value allowed is 1:

```
1 <= Quantity
```

To express this in XML Schema, use the minInclusive facet. You can now write the expression as an XML Schema element:

```
<xsd:simpleType name="creditScoreType">
<xsd:restriction base="xsd:integer">
<xsd:minInclusive value="1">
</xsd:restriction>
</xsd:simpleType>
```

Similarly, the minExclusive facet denotes that an attribute or element of this type must be greater than the specified value. The minInclusive and maxExclusive elements work in the same manner. We want to express that the maximum value for the Quantity element is up to, but not including, 10. Here's an example:

```
1 <= Quantity < 10
```

To express this in XML Schemas, you can combine several facets to form the expression, as follows:

```
<xsd:simpleType name="creditScoreType">
<xsd:restriction base="xsd:integer">
<xsd:minInclusive value="1">
<xsd:maxExclusive value="10">
</xsd:restriction>
</xsd:simpleType>
```

Not all facets are applicable to all types, however. For example, the minLength facet does not apply to a numeric type, and the minInclusive facet does not apply to a string. Figure 2.2 shows the different facets and how they apply.

So far, the focus has been on some basics, such as declaring types, creating types, and performing validation. You have been using elements and attributes all along, but they have not been explained. Refer to Chapter 3, "XML Presentation," for more information on elements and attributes. The following sections show you how to define elements and attributes within an XML Schema.

Complex Types

Suppose that you want to describe an address element that contains child elements describing each part of an address, such as street, city, state, and zip code. You can simply use the following code line:

```
<xsd:element name="Address" type="xsd:string"/>
```

Derivation	Base Type Definition	Applicable Constraining Facets											
		length	minLength	maxLength	pattern	enumeration	whiteSpace	maxInclusive	maxExclusive	minInclusive	minExclusive	totalDigits	fractionDigits
list	(all datatypes)	X	X	X	X	X	X						
union	(all datatypes)				X	X							
atomic	string	X	X	X	X	X	X						
	boolean				X		X						
	float				X	X	X	X	X	X	X		
	double				X	X	X	X	X	X	X		
	decimal				X	X	X	X	X	X	X	X	X
	duration				X	X	X	X	X	X	X		
	dateTime				X	X	X	X	X	X	X		
	time				X	X	X	X	X	X	X		
	date				X	X	X	X	X	X	X		
	gYearMonth				X	X	X	X	X	X	X		
	gYear				X	X	X	X	X	X	X		
	gMonthDay				X	X	X	X	X	X	X		
	gDay				X	X	X	X	X	X	X		
	gMonth				X	X	X	X	X	X	X		
	hexBinary	X	X	X	X	X	X						
	base64Binary	X	X	X	X	X	X						
	anyURI	X	X	X	X	X	X						
	QName	X	X	X	X	X	X						
	NOTATION	X	X	X	X	X	X						

Figure 2.2   Constraining facets and applicable data types.

Steven Holzner. *Inside XML*. New Riders Publishing, 2001 (Indianapolis, IN). ISBN 0-7357-1020-1.

For some uses where the presence and format of an address is not at all critical, this can be an acceptable representation of an address. For other applications that need to differentiate between different components of an address, this would not be acceptable. Using the hypothetical purchase order XML instance document, you might want to require not only a full address, but also that the zip code and state fields within the address conform to a certain format. You can approach this by breaking out the different components of an address into different elements or attributes:

```
<xsd:element name="Name" type="xsd:string" />
<xsd:element name="Street" type="xsd:string" />
<xsd:element name="City" type="xsd:string" />
<xsd:element name="State" type="xsd:string" />
<xsd:element name="Zip" type="xsd:string" />
```

This works for defining a single address for a single use within your document. However, what if the same definition of an address is used in multiple places throughout your document? You cannot reuse the definition if you have more than one address defined in your schema unless you redefine the concept of an address multiple times in your document. For times when a simple type will not suffice, XML Schemas provide the concept of complex types to group data into manageable sections or logical chunks. Simple types cannot contain elements or attributes; they only define a single data type. Complex types, however, can contain both elements and attributes, as well as convey order of precedence for element hierarchies.

Instead of using the xsd:string type for the Address element, you can create your own addressType data type by using the xsd:complexType element.

Begin by defining what a State element would look like. A State is a simple type, so you can create a simple type called stateType. Specify its base type as xsd:string. Also, you can use a facet to specify that the state can only contain two letters by specifying a regular expression in the pattern attribute. Facets are covered in more detail in the following section.

Here's a definition of what the simple type representing a state might look like:

```
<xsd:simpleType name="stateType">
    <xsd:restriction base="xsd:string">
        <xsd:pattern value="^\w{2}$" />
    </xsd:restriction>
</xsd:simpleType>
```

Similar to the State type, you also want to create a type to describe a zip code. To do this, you can use a simple integer data type. You might want to develop a regular expression to handle an optional four-digit extension for a zip code with a hyphen as a separator. For our purposes, base your new simple type on the built-in integer data type. Also, use a facet to specify that the value can only be a five-digit numerical value, as follows:

```
<xsd:simpleType name="zipType">
    <xsd:restriction base="xsd:integer">
        <xsd:pattern value="^\d{5}$" />
    </xsd:restriction>
</xsd:simpleType>
```

Declaring XML Schemas can be somewhat of an art rather than a science. For example, you could have specified the base type for the preceding xsd:restriction element as xsd:string. This is because you specified the restriction in the regular expression to only allow five numerical digits. It is clearer to see that the value holds a five-digit number when the type is based on a numeric instead of a string, which allows for easier readability. The following section looks at different types of facets.

You can finish your address example by defining what a complete address looks like. The State and Zip elements are now based on your new simple types:

```
<xsd:complexType name="addressType">
    <xsd:sequence>
        <xsd:element name="Name" type="xsd:string" minOccurs="1"
        ↪maxOccurs="1" />
        <xsd:element name="Street1" type="xsd:string" minOccurs="1"
        ↪maxOccurs="1" />
```

```
        <xsd:element name="Street2" type="xsd:string" minOccurs="0"
        ⇒maxOccurs="1"/>
        <xsd:element name="City" type="xsd:string" minOccurs="1"
        ⇒maxOccurs="1" />
        <xsd:element name="State" type="stateType" minOccurs="1"
        ⇒maxOccurs="1" />
        <xsd:element name="Zip" type="zipType" minOccurs="1" maxOccurs="1" />
    </xsd:sequence>
</xsd:complexType>
```

Notice the use of the `minOccurs` and `maxOccurs` attributes. These specify the minimum number of times an element can occur within a given sequence. (Sequences are discussed in the section, "Sequence Groups.") A value of 1 for each element means that the element is required and is unique. A value of 0 for `minOccurs` means that the element is optional. Because you declared this as a type, it can also be reused throughout your schema document:

```
<xsd:element name="Billing" type="addressType"/>
<xsd:element name="Mailing" type="addressType"/>
```

The `xsd:element` element cannot be directly contained as a child of the `xsd:complexType` element. Instead, you must declare a *particle* for the complex type. A particle is the content within a complex type. The particle consists of one of several types of groups, such as attribute groups, choice groups, sequence groups, and all groups.

Attribute Groups

Throughout your document, you might find that a set of attributes is common for different element types. You can define them in one place and reference them by using the `xsd:attributeGroup` element so that you don't have to retype them throughout your document. This helps minimize the size of the document, which decreases the time required to parse it. Let's stop working with purchase orders and reports, and move on to something more fun. Let's work with pizzas. Listing 2.3 shows an example of specifying an attribute group to reuse some complex attribute definitions.

Listing 2.3   **A Schema Using an Attribute Group**

```
<xsd:schema id="PIZZASCHEMA"
xmlns="http://www.xmlandasp.net/pizza"
targetNamespace="http://www.xmlandasp.net/schema/pizza.xsd"
xmlns:xsd="http://www.w3.org/2001/XMLSchema"><xsd:attributeGroup
name="pizzaType">
    <xsd:attribute name="size">
        <xsd:simpleType base="xsd:string">
```

continues

```
                <xsd:enumeration value="small"/>
                <xsd:enumeration value="medium"/>
                <xsd:enumeration value="large"/>
            </xsd:simpleType>
        </xsd:attribute>
        <xsd:attribute name="method">
            <xsd:simpleType base="xsd:string">
                <xsd:enumeration value="delivery"/>
                <xsd:enumeration value="take out"/>
            </xsd:simpleType>
        </xsd:attribute>
    </xsd:attributeGroup>

    <xsd:element name="PIZZAVENDORS">
        <xsd:complexType>
            <xsd:choice>
                <xsd:element name="Dominos">
                    <xsd:complexType>
                        <xsd:attributeGroup ref="pizzaType"/>
                    </xsd:complexType>
                </xsd:element>
                <xsd:element name="PapaJohns">
                    <xsd:complexType>
                        <xsd:attributeGroup ref="pizzaType"/>
                    </xsd:complexType>
                </xsd:element>
                <xsd:element name="MellowMushroom">
                    <xsd:complexType>
                        <xsd:attributeGroup ref="pizzaType"/>
                    </xsd:complexType>
                </xsd:element>
            </xsd:choice>
        </xsd:complexType>
    </xsd:element>
</xsd:schema>
```

You can see that using attribute groups can significantly reduce the amount of code within a document. Without them, you would need to replace each line `<xsd:attributeGroup ref="pizzaType"/>` with the actual `attributeGroup`'s definition, which gives you a bloated document.

Sequence, Choice, and All Groups

The brief REPORTS example used earlier when explaining elements and attributes was basic. In fact, it's rare for an XML document to exist that only contains a single element and a single attribute. Instead, you create hierarchies of information. These hierarchies can be validated as well.

A big advantage to using XML Schemas is that it's easy to define cardinality and frequency. Suppose that you want to create an XML Schema to validate a REPORTS document that is similar to the code in Listing 2.4.

Listing 2.4 **Sample XML Document Requiring Validation**

```
<REPORTS>
    <REPORT Name="Customer Orders By Date">
        <WEBREPORT StyleSheet="CustOrdersByDate.xsl"
        ➥StoredProc="spCustOrdersDate"/>
        <PARAMETERS>
            <PARAMETER Name="@CustomerID" Description="Customer ID"
            ➥DataType="int"/>
            <PARAMETER Name="@LowDate" Description="Beginning Date
            ➥Range"/>
            <PARAMETER Name="@HighDate" Description="Ending Date Range"/>
        </PARAMETERS>
    </REPORT>
    <REPORT Name="Customer Orders">
        <CUSTOMREPORT View="vwCustOrders">
            <TABLES>
                <TABLE Name="Customer">
                    <COLUMN>CustomerID</COLUMN>
                    <COLUMN>CustomerName</COLUMN>
                </TABLE>
                <TABLE Name="Orders">
                    <COLUMN>OrderID</COLUMN>
                    <COLUMN>OrderDate</COLUMN>
                </TABLE>
            </TABLES>
        </CUSTOMREPORT>
        <PARAMETERS>
            <PARAMETER Name="@CustomerID" Description="Customer ID"
            ➥DataType="int"/>
            <PARAMETER Name="@LowDate" Description="Beginning Date Range"/>
            <PARAMETER Name="@HighDate" Description="Ending Date Range"/>
        </PARAMETERS>
    </REPORT>
</REPORTS>
```

You can easily imagine how you might use such a document to create a generic application to display reports. Two different types of reports exist: *custom reports* and *web reports*. A web report requires an associated stylesheet and is based on a stored procedure. A custom report provides a database view and details what tables and columns the user can choose to filter.

The new schema needs to validate much information that you normally might just assume. For example, the Name attribute values of each REPORT node would be required for the consuming application to work correctly. Web reports require a stylesheet, where custom reports require a set of tables and columns that can be presented to the user. A parameter element is optional because a report might not require any parameters; however, if a parameter element is defined, it must contain Name and Description attributes. Something that is also intimated is that the default value for the DataType attribute for each PARAMETER element is a string data type, unless it's explicitly stated otherwise. (This is because the default type is xsd:string.)

To perform this type of validation, XML Schemas provide the complexType element to define hierarchical relationships between elements or attributes of an element. As previously mentioned, complexType elements have particles that define what the complexType should validate. These particles contain groups that define how to validate the particle of the complexType.

Sequence Groups

A *sequence group* enables developers to define a sequence of elements that appear as a child of another element. Elements must appear in the order that they are defined in the schema. In the report schema example, the root node, REPORTS, contains child nodes called REPORT. To validate this hierarchy, create a sequence group by using the xsd:sequence element:

```
<xsd:schema id="REPORTSCHEMA"
xmlns="http://www.xmlandasp.net"
targetNamespace="http://www.xmlandasp.net/schema/reports.xsd"
xmlns:xsd="http://www.w3.org/2001/XMLSchema">

<xsd:element name="REPORTS">
    <xsd:complexType>
        <xsd:sequence minOccurs="1">
            <xsd:element name="REPORT"/>
        </xsd:sequence>
    </xsd:complexType>
</xsd:element>
</xsd:schema>
```

The sequence group is probably the most widely applicable grouping structure because it ensures that the document conforms to the structure stated explicitly.

Attribute Order Cannot Be Controlled

Schemas can specify the presence and data type of an attribute but not the order of attributes. If the order in which attributes can occur is significant, consider revising your schema to use nested elements instead of attributes.

Choice Groups

The difference between a CUSTOMREPORT and WEBREPORT in the updated REPORTS example is that a custom report requires table information for the user to be able to filter on. You can build the query on the fly from a view. A web report, on the other hand, is a static report for which the user enters parameters and is drawn from a stored procedure in the database. A report can be one or the other; it cannot be both. A *choice group* allows a choice between one element and another. To validate that the child of a REPORT element is either a CUSTOMREPORT node or a WEBREPORT node, use a choice group, as follows:

```
<xsd:schema id="REPORTSCHEMA"
    xmlns="http://www.xmlandasp.net"
    targetNamespace="http://www.xmlandasp.net/schema/reports.xsd"
    xmlns:xsd="http://www.w3.org/2001/XMLSchema">

    <xsd:element name="REPORTS">
        <xsd:complexType>
            <xsd:sequence minOccurs="1">
                <xsd:element name="REPORT">
                    <xsd:complexType>
                        <xsd:choice>
                            <xsd:element name="WEBREPORT">
                                <xsd:complexType>
                                    <xsd:attribute name="StyleSheet"
                                    ↪type="xsd:string"/>
                                    <xsd:attribute name="StoredProc"
                                    ↪type="xsd:string"/>
                                </xsd:complexType>
                            </xsd:element>
                            <xsd:element name="CUSTOMREPORT">
                                <xsd:complexType>
                                    <xsd:attribute name="View"
                                    ↪type="xsd:string"/>
                                </xsd:complexType>
                            </xsd:element>
                        </xsd:choice>
                    </xsd:complexType>
                </xsd:element>
            </xsd:sequence>
        </xsd:complexType>
    </xsd:element>
</xsd:schema>
```

All Groups

All the elements in an *all group* can be present (or none at all). You use this group to validate the PARAMETERS node, because it might or might not contain child PARAMETER nodes:

```xsd
<xsd:schema id="REPORTSCHEMA"
     xmlns="http://www.xmlandasp.net"
     targetNamespace="http://www.xmlandasp.net/schema/reports.xsd"
     xmlns:xsd="http://www.w3.org/2001/XMLSchema">

     <xsd:complexType name="parameterType">
          <xsd:all>
               <xsd:element name="PARAMETER">
                    <xsd:complexType>
                         <xsd:attribute name="Name" type="xsd:string"/>
                         <xsd:attribute name="Description"
                         ➥type="xsd:string"/>
                         <xsd:attribute name="DataType" type="xsd:string"
                         ➥default="varchar"/>
                    </xsd:complexType>
               </xsd:element>
          </xsd:all>
     </xsd:complexType>

     <xsd:element name="REPORTS">
          <xsd:complexType>
               <xsd:sequence minOccurs="1">
                    <xsd:element name="REPORT">
                         <xsd:complexType>
                              <xsd:element name="PARAMETERS"
                              ➥type="parameterType" minOccurs="1"
                              ➥maxOccurs="1"/>
                         </xsd:complexType>
                    </xsd:element>
               </xsd:sequence>
          </xsd:complexType>
     </xsd:element>
</xsd:schema>
```

You can see that a complex type named parameterType was declared that uses the xsd:all group element. We also enforced that the PARAMETERS element can only appear once as a child of each REPORT element by using the minOccurs and maxOccurs attributes. A document validated against this schema would require the PARAMETERS element, but might or might not contain any PARAMETER elements.

The following is schema-valid:

```
<REPORTS>
     <PARAMETERS/>
</REPORTS>
```

But the following is not schema-valid:

```
<REPORTS/>
```

Declaring Mixed Content

Terms you might have heard when working with XML is *data-centric* and *document-centric* modeling. The examples used here have been data-centric. They break the document into fine-grained bits of data. A document-centric view of XML would look much more like an email or a form with fields to fill in, as shown in the following code:

```
<Reminder>
    <To>Pi Kappa Alpha, Epsilon Nu Mailing List</To>
    <From>Kirk Allen Evans</From>
    <Message>Just a reminder... The <Event>Atlanta Area Alumni Charity Golf
Outing</Event> event is scheduled for <ScheduleDate>2001-08-
27</ScheduleDate>. For information, call <Contact>Keth Bunn</Contact> at
<ContactInfo>kefbum@hotmail.com</ContactInfo>.
    </Message>
</Reminder>
```

As you can see, the Message node contains mixed content. This is an example of a well-formed XML document, but how would you express this in terms of an XML Schema? The answer is to use the mixed attribute to signify that a section of data contains mixed content, as follows:

```
<?xml version="1.0" encoding="utf-8" ?>
<xsd:schema id="memo" targetNamespace="http://tempuri.org/memo.xsd"
elementFormDefault="qualified" xmlns="http://tempuri.org/memo.xsd"
xmlns:xsd="http://www.w3.org/2001/XMLSchema">
    <xsd:element name="Reminder">
        <xsd:complexType>
            <xsd:sequence>
                <xsd:element name="To" type="xsd:string" minOccurs="1"
                ➥maxOccurs="unbounded"/>
                <xsd:element name="CC" type="xsd:string" minOccurs="0"
                ➥maxOccurs="unbounded"/>
                <xsd:element name="From" type="xsd:string" minOccurs="1"
                ➥maxOccurs="1"/>
                <xsd:element name="Message">
                    <xsd:complexType mixed="true">
                        <xsd:sequence>
                            <xsd:element name="Event"
                            ➥type="xsd:string" />
                            <xsd:element name="ScheduleDate"
                            ➥type="xsd:date" />
                            <xsd:element name="Contact"
                            ➥type="xsd:string" />
                            <xsd:element name="ContactInfo"
                            ➥type="xsd:string" />
                        </xsd:sequence>
                    </xsd:complexType>
                </xsd:element>
```

```
        </xsd:sequence>
      </xsd:complexType>
    </xsd:element>
</xsd:schema>
```

The default value for the mixed attribute is false, which means that you cannot intermix character data with child elements unless it's specifically stated.

Clearing Confusion in Specifying Mixed Content Models

Earlier versions of the XML Schema working draft state that the markup for mixed content models was to use the content="mixed" attribute value, and most available online documentation still reflects this. The recommendation specifies the markup to be mixed="true".

Names and Anonymous Types

Throughout this chapter, both *anonymous types* and *named types* have been used without a real explanation of the difference. The reason is because it is fairly intuitive when you are reading a schema, but can be confusing when you sit down for the first time to manually code a schema.

A *named type* is declared with the name attribute and can be referenced using its name. Listing 2.5 shows the revised purchase order schema document from Listing 2.2.

Listing 2.5   **Revised Sample Purchase Order Schema**

```
<xsd:schema id="PURCHASEORDER"
xmlns="http://www.xmlandasp.net"
targetNamespace="http://www.xmlandasp.net"
xmlns:xsd="http://www.w3.org/2001/XMLSchema" attributeFormDefault="qualified"
elementFormDefault="qualified">
<xsd:simpleType name="emailType">
     <xsd:restriction base="xsd:string">
          <xsd:pattern value="" />
     </xsd:restriction>
</xsd:simpleType>
<xsd:complexType name="customerType">
     <xsd:sequence>
          <xsd:element name="NAME" type="xsd:string" />
          <xsd:element name="PHONE" type="xsd:string" />
          <xsd:element name="EMAIL" type="emailType" />
     </xsd:sequence>
</xsd:complexType>
<xsd:element name="PURCHASEORDER">
     <xsd:complexType>
          <xsd:choice maxOccurs="unbounded">
               <xsd:element name="CUSTOMER" type="customerType"/>
               <xsd:element name="ORDER">
```

continues

Listing 2.5   **Continued**

```
                    <xsd:complexType>
                        <xsd:sequence>
                            <xsd:element name="ITEM" minOccurs="1"
                            ⇥maxOccurs="unbounded">
                                <xsd:complexType>
                                    <xsd:sequence>
                                <xsd:element name="ITEMNAME"
                                ⇥type="xsd:string" />
                                <xsd:element name="DESCRIPTION"
                                ⇥type="xsd:string" />
                                        <xsd:element name="SIZE"
                                        ⇥type="xsd:integer" />
                                        <xsd:element name="PRICE"
                                        ⇥type="xsd:string" />
                                    </xsd:sequence>
                                </xsd:complexType>
                            </xsd:element>
                        </xsd:sequence>
                    </xsd:complexType>
                </xsd:element>
            </xsd:choice>
        </xsd:complexType>
    </xsd:element>
</xsd:schema>
```

The types `emailType` and `customerType` are examples of named types. They are referenced by using the `type` attribute of an `xsd:element` or `xsd:attribute` tag.

An anonymous type, on the other hand, is a simple or complex type declared as a child of an `xsd:element` or `xsd:attribute` tag without naming the type. For example, the child of the `PURCHASEORDER` root element in the previous code is a `complexType` containing both a `CUSTOMER` and an `ORDER` node. You don't have to explicitly declare this type and reference it by name because it is only used once in the document. If it were going to be used more than once, you'd want to create a named type to reuse the structure.

Using Annotations

A great part about XML Schemas is that you can comment them in such a way that they can document themselves. Instead of embedding comments into the document to be parsed, you can use the three annotation elements provided with schemas. The `xsd:appinfo` element can contain any well-formed XML content, so you can derive your own information to describe the schema, as shown here:

```
<xsd:annotation>
    <xsd:appinfo>
        <DocumentVersion value="1.6.7" />
        <Author>Kirk Allen Evans</Author>
        <DateCreated>2001-08-15</DateCreated>
    </xsd:appinfo>
    <xsd:documentation>
        Validates a submission memo.
    </xsd:documentation>
</xsd:annotation>
```

Child Elements

The XML Schemas documentation in Beta 2 states that any well-formed XML content is valid as a child of the appinfo or documentation element. However, at the time of this writing, the XML Schema Designer only validates elements without child elements.

Because the schema is an XML document, it can be parsed with an XML parser to determine information about the schema. You could also apply a stylesheet to the schema itself to provide automatically generated HTML help for working with your schema using the annotations to provide meaningful content.

Using Schemas in .NET

Now that you have gone through the basics of XML Schemas, you're ready to work with them. You are going to work with schemas by using the xsd.exe tool, using the System.Xml namespace in .NET, and by using the schema designer in Visual Studio .NET.

xsd.exe

The .NET Framework SDK comes with several tools that make working with XML technologies simpler. One such tool is xsd.exe. This tool makes it easy to work with a specific XSD Schema by creating a class hierarchy that matches the schema, which allows you to work with the document as a class structure programmatically rather than as an XML document. You can then serialize the class structure to an XML document. The xsd.exe utility is covered in Chapter 4, and serialization will be covered in depth in Chapter 10.

Look at an example that uses the xsd.exe utility. Save the purchase order schema from Listing 2.5 as sales.xsd because you will use xsd.exe to generate a set of classes based on this schema. Then you are able to use those classes to populate data and create a valid XML file using serialization. Open the Visual

Studio .NET command prompt (located at Start, Programs, Microsoft Visual
Studio .NET 7.0, Visual Studio .NET Tools). I changed the directory path to
the location of the XSD file and entered the following command-line prompt:

```
xsd sales.xsd /classes /language:vb /outputdir:c:\temp
```

This prompt yielded a class file with a .vb extension in the c:\temp directory
named sales.vb. Listing 2.6 shows the generated code.

Listing 2.6   **Generated Code from *xsd.exe***

```
'-----------------------------------------------------------------
' <autogenerated>
'     This code was generated by a tool.
'     Runtime Version: 1.0.2914.16
'
'     Changes to this file may cause incorrect behavior and will be lost if
'     the code is regenerated.
' </autogenerated>
'-----------------------------------------------------------------
Option Strict Off
Option Explicit On

Imports System.Xml.Serialization

'
'This source code was auto-generated by xsd, Version=1.0.2914.16.
'

<System.Xml.Serialization.XmlRootAttribute([Namespace]:="http://localhost/
➥chapters/03/xmlschemas/schemas/sales/Sales.xsd", IsNullable:=false)>
Public Class PURCHASEORDER

    <System.Xml.Serialization.XmlElementAttribute("CUSTOMER",
    ➥IsNullable:=false)> _
    Public CUSTOMER() As customerType

    <System.Xml.Serialization.XmlArrayAttribute(IsNullable:=false),
     System.Xml.Serialization.XmlArrayItemAttribute("ITEM",
    ➥GetType(itemType), IsNullable:=false)> _
    Public ORDER() As itemType
End Class

Public Class customerType

    <System.Xml.Serialization.XmlElementAttribute(IsNullable:=false)>
    Public NAME As String

    <System.Xml.Serialization.XmlElementAttribute(IsNullable:=false)>
    Public PHONE As String
```

```
    <System.Xml.Serialization.XmlElementAttribute(IsNullable:=false)>
    Public EMAIL As String

    <System.Xml.Serialization.XmlElementAttribute(IsNullable:=false)>
    Public BILLING As addressType
End Class

Public Class addressType

    <System.Xml.Serialization.XmlElementAttribute(IsNullable:=false)>
    Public Name As String

    <System.Xml.Serialization.XmlElementAttribute(IsNullable:=false)>
    Public Street1 As String

    <System.Xml.Serialization.XmlElementAttribute(IsNullable:=false)>
    Public Street2 As String

    <System.Xml.Serialization.XmlElementAttribute(IsNullable:=false)>
    Public City As String

    <System.Xml.Serialization.XmlElementAttribute(IsNullable:=false)>
    Public State As String

    <System.Xml.Serialization.XmlElementAttribute(DataType:="integer",
IsNullable:=false)>
    Public Zip As String
End Class

<System.Xml.Serialization.XmlTypeAttribute([Namespace]:="http://localhost/
➥chapters/03/xmlschemas/schemas/sales/Sales.xsd")>
Public Class itemType

    <System.Xml.Serialization.XmlElementAttribute(IsNullable:=false)>
    Public ITEMNAME As String

    <System.Xml.Serialization.XmlElementAttribute(IsNullable:=false)>
    Public DESCRIPTION As String

    <System.Xml.Serialization.XmlElementAttribute(IsNullable:=false)>
    Public SIZE As String

    Public PRICE As Decimal

    <System.Xml.Serialization.XmlIgnoreAttribute()>
    Public PRICESpecified As Boolean

    <System.Xml.Serialization.XmlAttributeAttribute()>
    Public name As String

    <System.Xml.Serialization.XmlAttributeAttribute()>
```

continues

Listing 2.6   **Continued**

```
    Public value As String

    <System.Xml.Serialization.XmlAttributeAttribute()>
    Public description As String

    <System.Xml.Serialization.XmlAttributeAttribute()>
    Public color As colorEnum

    <System.Xml.Serialization.XmlIgnoreAttribute()>
    Public colorSpecified As Boolean
End Class

Public Enum colorEnum
    Blue
    Red
    Black
    Green
End Enum
```

As with most code generators, shortcomings exist in the code. Naming things in XML documents usually differs from naming items in code, but the utility uses the names in your schema document for local variable names. The .NET Framework Design Guidelines specifies pascal casing for public properties and fields, but the generated code uses capital letters for elements and lowercase letters for attributes. I also prefer to use property procedures rather than direct field access in classes. However, the generated code serves as a good baseline for developing a set of classes to work with the XML document. Be assured that an XML document generated from this structure is generated in the proper format.

One real shortcoming of this utility is the fact that the facets for your simple types are not preserved. For example, the regular expression that you specified for emailType is not represented within the code and there is no restriction within your class hierarchy to enforce the constraints set out. Of course, this is a function of the XML schema document, but it would have been more impressive if the object hierarchy could enforce the constraints specified in the XML Schema document.

Popular Utility Development Opportunity

Although the implementation of constraining facets is not represented within generated classes, this shortcoming presents some interesting possibilities for developing your own utility that preserves the constraining facet behaviors using the CodeDom classes and System.Xml. Serialization.XmlCodeExporter to generate the code.

Another shortcoming is how you name the elements within a schema. XSD Schemas maintain different name tables for each schema component. This means that an attribute can have the same name as an element within the same class. Notice that in the itemType class in the preceding code, there are two different declarations for description: The capitalized version, DESCRIPTION, which represents the element (I use uppercase letters for elements by convention within this document), and the lowercase version that represents an attribute called description. Remember that XML is case-sensitive. But, because Visual Basic is not case-sensitive, the preceding generated code would not compile because the name description is declared twice. This would not be a limitation in C# because C# is case-sensitive. Either way, you will probably opt not to stick with the default naming within the document.

To rename the internal variables in your code but still preserve the generated XML Schema, the designers of .NET included attributes to describe exactly what the serialized XML should look like. To do this, simply rename the internal variable for the lowercase description attribute and specify the name of the attribute in the serialization attribute as follows:

```
<System.Xml.Serialization.XmlAttributeAttribute("description")>
    Public AttribDescription As String
```

After that is corrected, you can work with the generated class hierarchy. Listing 2.7 is a sample code listing for working with the new class hierarchy created in Listing 2.6. You will create a simple ASP page that will populate the typed DataSet with data and serialize the DataSet to XML. The ASP layout code is a simple interface that consists of labels and textboxes for the various properties. There are also one drop-down list box and three buttons. The UI code is unimportant, so you need to focus on the code-behind Visual Basic code.

The first section simply declares the UI elements to be used in the code-behind class.

Listing 2.7   **A Simple ASP.NET Web Application Referencing a Typed**
              DataSet

```
Imports System
Imports System.Xml
Imports System.Xml.Schema

Public Class sales
    Inherits System.Web.UI.Page
    Protected WithEvents Label1 As System.Web.UI.WebControls.Label
    Protected WithEvents Label2 As System.Web.UI.WebControls.Label
    Protected WithEvents txtPhone As System.Web.UI.WebControls.TextBox
    Protected WithEvents Label3 As System.Web.UI.WebControls.Label
```

continues

Listing 2.7 **Continued**

```
        Protected WithEvents txtEmail As System.Web.UI.WebControls.TextBox
        Protected WithEvents Label4 As System.Web.UI.WebControls.Label
        Protected WithEvents txtBillToName As System.Web.UI.WebControls.TextBox
        Protected WithEvents Label5 As System.Web.UI.WebControls.Label
        Protected WithEvents txtStreet1 As System.Web.UI.WebControls.TextBox
        Protected WithEvents Label6 As System.Web.UI.WebControls.Label
        Protected WithEvents txtStreet2 As System.Web.UI.WebControls.TextBox
        Protected WithEvents Label7 As System.Web.UI.WebControls.Label
        Protected WithEvents txtCity As System.Web.UI.WebControls.TextBox
        Protected WithEvents Label8 As System.Web.UI.WebControls.Label
        Protected WithEvents txtState As System.Web.UI.WebControls.TextBox
        Protected WithEvents Label9 As System.Web.UI.WebControls.Label
        Protected WithEvents txtZip As System.Web.UI.WebControls.TextBox
        Protected WithEvents Label10 As System.Web.UI.WebControls.Label
        Protected WithEvents txtItemName As System.Web.UI.WebControls.TextBox
        Protected WithEvents Label11 As System.Web.UI.WebControls.Label
        Protected WithEvents txtDescription As System.Web.UI.WebControls.TextBox
        Protected WithEvents Label12 As System.Web.UI.WebControls.Label
        Protected WithEvents txtSize As System.Web.UI.WebControls.TextBox
        Protected WithEvents Label14 As System.Web.UI.WebControls.Label
        Protected WithEvents txtAttribName As System.Web.UI.WebControls.TextBox
        Protected WithEvents Label15 As System.Web.UI.WebControls.Label
        Protected WithEvents txtAttribValue As System.Web.UI.WebControls.TextBox
        Protected WithEvents Label16 As System.Web.UI.WebControls.Label
        Protected WithEvents txtAttribDescription As
        ➥System.Web.UI.WebControls.TextBox
        Protected WithEvents Label17 As System.Web.UI.WebControls.Label
        Protected WithEvents DropDownList1 As
        ➥System.Web.UI.WebControls.DropDownList
        Protected WithEvents Button1 As System.Web.UI.WebControls.Button
        Protected WithEvents Button2 As System.Web.UI.WebControls.Button
        Protected WithEvents Button3 As System.Web.UI.WebControls.Button
        Protected WithEvents txtName As System.Web.UI.WebControls.TextBox

    #Region " Web Form Designer Generated Code "
        'This call is required by the Web Form Designer.
        <System.Diagnostics.DebuggerStepThrough()> Private Sub
        ➥InitializeComponent()
        End Sub

        Private Sub Page_Init(ByVal sender As System.Object, ByVal e As
        ➥System.EventArgs) Handles MyBase.Init
            'CODEGEN: This method call is required by the Web Form Designer
            'Do not modify it using the code editor.
            InitializeComponent()
        End Sub
    #End Region
```

When the page loads, you might want to add sample items to the drop-down list to work with your generated class hierarchy:

```
    Private Sub Page_Load(ByVal sender As System.Object, ByVal e As
System.EventArgs) Handles MyBase.Load
        If Not IsPostBack then
        DropDownList1.Items.Add("0 - Blue")
        DropDownList1.Items.Add("1 - Red")
        DropDownList1.Items.Add("2 - Black")
        DropDownList1.Items.Add("3 - Green")
     End if
     End Sub
```

The code for the Click event of the Button1 object populates the hierarchy with the contents of the form and serializes the hierarchy of objects to an XML file. You must look at the individual steps to achieve this. Begin by declaring the object references and creating a new object instance for each reference:

```
Private Sub Serialize(ByVal sender As System.Object, ByVal e As
System.EventArgs) Handles _
Button1.Click
        Dim po As XMLSchemas.PURCHASEORDER = New PURCHASEORDER()
        Dim cust As XMLSchemas.customerType = New customerType()
        Dim item As XMLSchemas.itemType = New XMLSchemas.itemType()
        Dim billing As XMLSchemas.addressType = New XMLSchemas.addressType()
```

So far, you have only set up the object references by using the types exposed by generated classes. To create instances of the objects, you need to create an object array to hold the object references. The generated classes support a CreateInstance method to create an instance of a class contained as a child. You can use the CreateInstance method to create instances of classes based on their type:

```
'Create a 1-element array of customerType objects
        po.CUSTOMER = po.CUSTOMER.CreateInstance(cust.GetType, 1)
        'Create a 1-element array of itemType objects
        po.ORDER = po.ORDER.CreateInstance(item.GetType, 1)
```

The first parameter to the CreateInstance method is a System.Type argument. The cust object is an object reference, not a type, so you need to get the type that it represents by using the GetType method. The second parameter to CreateInstance simply states how many elements the array will contain. For simplicity, suppose that it will hold one object.

After the containing arrays are instantiated and associated with the parent objects, you can populate the array contents, as shown here:

```
            With cust
                .EMAIL = Me.txtEmail.Text
                .NAME = Me.txtBillToName.Text
```

```
                .PHONE = Me.txtPhone.Text
            End With
            'Set the first element in the customer array to the populated
customerType object
            po.CUSTOMER(0) = cust
            With billing
                .Name = Me.txtName.Text
                .Street1 = Me.txtStreet1.Text
                .City = Me.txtCity.Text
                .State = Me.txtState.Text
                .Zip = Me.txtZip.Text
            End With
            'Set the customer's billing address property
            cust.BILLING = billing
            With item
                .color = DropDownList1.SelectedIndex
                'The color is always specified
                .colorSpecified = True
                .ITEMNAME = "Big Screen TV"
                'We did not include the price element on the UI
                .PRICESpecified = False
                .SIZE = Me.txtSize.Text
                .name = Me.txtAttribName.Text
                .value = Me.txtAttribValue.Text
            End With
            po.ORDER(0) = item
```

After the object hierarchy is completely populated, serialize the contents of the entire hierarchy to a file. We hard-coded the path to the XML file for brevity, but you probably want to use some other means of dynamically retrieving the file's name and/or contents. Again, use the GetType method to retrieve the po object's type so that the XmlSerializer knows what to serialize. The Serialize method is then called to serialize the po object to the specified XML file, as shown here:

```
        'Serialize the purchase order to an XML file.
        Dim serializer As System.Xml.Serialization.XmlSerializer
        Dim file As System.IO.FileStream = New
    System.IO.FileStream("c:\temp\xmlfromclass.xml", _
    IO.FileMode.OpenOrCreate)
        serializer = New System.Xml.Serialization.XmlSerializer(po.GetType)
        serializer.Serialize(file, po)
        file.Close()
    End Sub
```

To rehydrate the object based on the persisted XML file, do the reverse of the serialization process. Instantiate a po object to be deserialized and then populate the web form based on the contents of the hierarchy:

```
    Private Sub Deserialize(ByVal sender As System.Object, ByVal e As
    System.EventArgs) Handles Button2.Click
        Dim po As XMLSchemas.PURCHASEORDER = New XMLSchemas.PURCHASEORDER()
```

```
        Dim serializer As System.Xml.Serialization.XmlSerializer
        Dim file As System.IO.FileStream = New
System.IO.FileStream("c:\temp\xmlfromclass.xml", _
IO.FileMode.Open)

        'Open the XML file and re-hydrate the purchase order object
        serializer = New System.Xml.Serialization.XmlSerializer(po.GetType)
        po = serializer.Deserialize(file)
        file.Close()

        'Populate the web form elements' text property
        With po.CUSTOMER(0)
            txtName.Text = .NAME
            txtEmail.Text = .EMAIL
            txtPhone.Text = .PHONE
        End With
        With po.CUSTOMER(0).BILLING
            txtStreet1.Text = .Street1
            txtStreet2.Text = .Street2
            txtCity.Text = .City
            txtState.Text = .State
            txtZip.Text = .Zip
        End With
        With po.ORDER(0)
            txtItemName.Text = .ITEMNAME
            txtDescription.Text = .DESCRIPTION
            txtSize.Text = .SIZE
            txtAttribName.Text = .name
            txtAttribValue.Text = .value
            DropDownList1.SelectedIndex = .color
        End With
    End Sub

End Class
```

This example shows how easy it is to work with the generated class files and
how quick it is to generate the classes from an XSD Schema. This section also
gives a brief introduction to serialization.

Schemas in ADO.NET

You have seen that new tools in Visual Studio .NET help generate XML
Schemas, so now it's time to look at how XSD Schemas are interwoven into
.NET. XSD Schemas are tightly integrated into ADO.NET. In fact, the
DataSet in ADO.NET is structured around XSD Schemas to represent the
structure of the data. The DataSet class provides the capability to read schemas,
validate the contained data against schemas, and to infer schemas based on the
data they contain. Because a DataSet is a view of data, its structure can be represented in an XML Schema. Working with schemas and DataSets is a key

part of the ADO.NET strategy because the underlying data can easily interoperate even with non-.NET clients. Although you do not have to know much about XML or XSD Schemas to work with ADO.NET, a firm understanding of XML and schemas help you to gain mastery of .NET development.

Generating Schemas from Queries

One of the easiest operations with a DataSet is to generate a schema based on the DataSet's contents. In the following code, you read a table from a database, use the WriteXMLSchema method to write the schema to an interim stream, and return the contents of the stream to the calling function:

```
Private Function GetSchemaFromQuery(ByVal query As String, _
        ByVal connectionString As String) As String
    Dim connection As System.Data.SqlClient.SqlConnection
    Dim adapter As System.Data.SqlClient.SqlDataAdapter
    Dim mydataSet As System.Data.DataSet = New Data.DataSet()
    Dim memStream As System.IO.MemoryStream = New System.IO.MemoryStream()
    Dim writer As System.Xml.XmlTextWriter
    Dim reader As System.IO.StreamReader

    'Get the data from the database
    connection = New SqlClient.SqlConnection(connectionString)
    adapter = New SqlClient.SqlDataAdapter(query, connection)
    adapter.Fill(mydataSet)
    'Release database resources
    adapter.Dispose()
    connection.Close()
    connection.Dispose()

    'Write the schema to the memory stream
    writer = New System.Xml.XmlTextWriter(memStream, _
System.Text.Encoding.UTF8)
    mydataSet.WriteXmlSchema(writer)
    'reset the position of the stream to the beginning
    memStream.Position = 0
    'Read the data from the memory stream
    reader = New System.IO.StreamReader(memStream)
    Return reader.ReadToEnd

    'Release resources
    reader.Close()
    memStream.Close()
    mydataSet.Dispose()
End Function
```

ADO.NET provides several methods for creating a schema structure from the XML data in a DataSet. The InferXMLSchema method of the DataSet object creates a schema that's based on the contents of the XML data and allows you to specify namespaces to ignore. Similarly, the ReadXML and ReadXMLSchema both perform similar functions.

Typed DataSets in ADO.NET

One key feature of ADO.NET is its capability to work with a strongly typed DataSet. A strongly typed DataSet is a class that inherits from the `DataSet` class and uses information from an XML Schema to generate a new class as a set of first-class properties and methods (MSDN, "Introduction to DataSets"). As you saw earlier with the `xsd.exe` utility, the structure expressed in an XSD Schema file can map to the hierarchy of a `DataSet` class as a collection of tables. Figure 2.3 gives you a view of the hierarchical structure of a DataSet and the classes it contains.

DataSets are covered in more detail in Chapter 8.

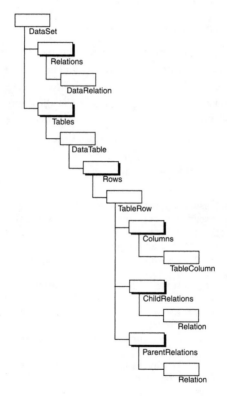

Figure 2.3   The hierarchical structure of a DataSet.

Exploring *System.Xml.Schema*

With all the integration of schemas into .NET and Visual Studio .NET, no wonder there is a mature set of classes in the .NET Framework to work with schemas. Although you can work with schemas using the `DataSet` class, the rest of this chapter focuses on working with the System.Xml.Schema classes and performing validation against schema documents.

The DataSet class enables you to work with a schema document as a set of tables, but you might find that you need to programmatically access a schema and determine its exact structure. The classes in the System.Xml.Schema namespace provide this functionality without writing custom parsing routines to parse the document simply as a raw XML document.

The designers of the framework designed a close representation of the W3C recommendation model. Class naming is relatively consistent with the recommendation model (although you need to pay attention to terms and definitions, such as particle, content, and model).

System.Xml.Schema.XmlSchema

The root node of a schema document is the schema element. The class framework provides this node through the XmlSchema class. All schema elements are children of the XmlSchema class, so they are at the top of the hierarchy. You can use the System.Xml.Schema classes to generate the following schema document shown in Listing 2.8. The output first is provided first so it's easier to reference the code that is used to create the schema document.

Listing 2.8 **Address Book Schema**

```
<?xml version="1.0" encoding="utf-8" ?>
<xsd:schema id="addressbook" targetNamespace="urn:schemas-vbdna-
net:addressbook" elementFormDefault="qualified" xmlns:tns="urn:schemas-vbdna-
net:addressbook" xmlns:xsd="http://www.w3.org/2001/XMLSchema">
    <xsd:complexType name="addressType">
        <xsd:sequence minOccurs="1" maxOccurs="1">
            <xsd:sequence>
                <xsd:element name="street1" minOccurs="1" maxOccurs="1"
                ↪type="xsd:string" />
                <xsd:element name="street2" minOccurs="0" maxOccurs="1"
                ↪type="xsd:string" />
                <xsd:element name="city" minOccurs="1" maxOccurs="1"
                ↪type="xsd:string" />
                <xsd:element name="state" minOccurs="1" maxOccurs="1"
                ↪type="xsd:string" />
                <xsd:element name="zip" minOccurs="1" maxOccurs="1"
                ↪type="tns:zipType" />
            </xsd:sequence>
        </xsd:sequence>
    </xsd:complexType>
    <xsd:simpleType name="zipType">
        <xsd:restriction base="xsd:string">
            <xsd:pattern value="\d{5}(-\d{4})?" />
```

```
        </xsd:restriction>
    </xsd:simpleType>
    <xsd:simpleType name="emailType">
        <xsd:restriction base="xsd:string">
            <xsd:pattern value="\w+([-+.]\w+)*@\w+([-.]\w+)*\.\w+([-
            ➥.]\w+)*" />
        </xsd:restriction>
    </xsd:simpleType>
    <xsd:element name="addressBook">
        <xsd:complexType>
            <xsd:sequence minOccurs="0" maxOccurs="unbounded">
                <xsd:element name="entry">
                    <xsd:complexType>
                        <xsd:sequence>
                            <xsd:element name="name" type="xsd:string" />
                            <xsd:element name="address"
                            ➥type="tns:addressType" />
                            <xsd:element name="email"
                            ➥type="tns:emailType" minOccurs="0"
                            ➥maxOccurs="unbounded" />
                        </xsd:sequence>
                    </xsd:complexType>
                </xsd:element>
            </xsd:sequence>
        </xsd:complexType>
    </xsd:element>
</xsd:schema>
```

Begin by defining the XmlSchema class object and defining the namespace that will be used as the targetNamespace in Listing 2.9. The XmlSchema class object contains an Items collection that adds items as children of the schema node.

Listing 2.9 **Using the *System.Xml.Schema* Namespace**

```
using System;
using System.Xml;
using System.Xml.Schema;

namespace XmlSchemaCS
{
    public class CustomerSchemaFunctions
    {

        public const string W3C_SCHEMA_NS =
        ➥"http://www.w3.org/2001/XMLSchema";
        private  Boolean m_IsValid = false; ///this is a comment for the
        ➥boolean variable
        private string m_targetNameSpace = "";

        //Only ctor, with parameter
```

continues

Listing 2.9 **Continued**

```
        public CustomerSchemaFunctions(string nameSpace)
        {
            m_targetNameSpace = nameSpace;
        }
     .
     .
     .

        public void WriteSchemaXml(string xsdFile)
            /// <summary>function to write the schema as xml</summary>
        {
            ///Create the schema root node with the targetNamespace
            XmlSchema schema = new XmlSchema();
            schema.TargetNamespace=m_targetNameSpace;
            schema.AttributeFormDefault = XmlSchemaForm.Unqualified;
            schema.ElementFormDefault = XmlSchemaForm.Qualified; ;
            XmlQualifiedName schemaString = new XmlQualifiedName("string",
            ↪W3C_SCHEMA_NS);

            schema.Items.Add(CreateZipType());
            schema.Items.Add(CreateEmailType());
            schema.Items.Add(CreateAddressType());
            schema.Items.Add(CreateEntryType());
     .
     .
     .

        }
    }
```

The code in Listing 2.9 is not a complete working example yet, but shows the beginnings of the complete sample (shown in Listing 2.10).

Looking at the XML Schema document, the children of the schema node are the addressBook element, the zipType, emailType simple types, and the addressType complex type. These will be added as children of the schema node. The XmlSchema class object contains an Items collection that adds items as children of the schema node.

Working with the XmlSchema classes require you to think backwards. Instead of creating a simpleType, adding a restriction, then adding the facets, you must work in reverse. Create the facet, create the restriction, add the facet to the facets collection of the restriction, and add the restriction to the simpleType. The simpleType class does not expose an Items collection like the XmlSchema object. Instead, you specify the child elements of the xsd:simpleType element by using the XmlSchemaSimpleType.Content property. The following code creates the root schema node and a simple type emailType. I split the creation of the simpleType and the schema element to better show the scope of each method:

```
private XmlSchemaSimpleType CreateEmailType()
{
    XmlSchemaSimpleTypeRestriction restriction = new
    ➥XmlSchemaSimpleTypeRestriction ();
    restriction.BaseTypeName = new
    ➥System.Xml.XmlQualifiedName("string",W3C_SCHEMA_NS);
    XmlSchemaPatternFacet pattern = new XmlSchemaPatternFacet();
    pattern.Value ="\\w+([-+.]\\w+)*@\\w+([-.]\\w+)*\\.\\w+([-
    ➥.]\\w+)*";
    restriction.Facets.Add (pattern);

    XmlSchemaSimpleType emailType = new XmlSchemaSimpleType();
    emailType.Name = "emailType";
    emailType.Content = restriction;
    return(emailType);
}
```

Notice that the `WriteSchemaXml` method in Listing 2.9 calls `schema.Items.Add()`.
This is how the `simpleType` is actually appended to the schema. Simply creating
an `XmlSchemaObject` object does not append it to the schema object; it must be
explicitly added through the `Add` method. Failure to do this results in the type
missing from the generated schema.

Creating a `complexType` is similar to creating an `XmlSchemaSimpleType`. To create a complex type, use the `Schema.XmlSchemaComplexType` object, as shown in
Listing 2.10. As with the `XmlSchemaSimpleType` object, the `XmlSchemaComplexType`
does not support an `Items` collection. To specify child content, use the `Particle`
property to specify an all, choice, or sequence group particle.

Listing 2.10 **Using Particles and SOM**

```
private XmlSchemaElement GenElement( string name, int minOccurs,
int maxOccurs)
    {
        XmlSchemaElement returnElement = new XmlSchemaElement();
        returnElement.Name = name;
        returnElement.MinOccurs = minOccurs;
        returnElement.MaxOccurs = maxOccurs;
        return (returnElement);
    }

private XmlSchemaElement GenElement(string name, int minOccurs,
    int maxOccurs, System.Xml.XmlQualifiedName qualifiedName)

    {
        XmlSchemaElement element = new XmlSchemaElement();
        element.Name = name;
        element.MinOccurs = minOccurs;
        element.MaxOccurs = maxOccurs;
```

continues

Listing 2.10 **Continued**

```
                element.SchemaTypeName = qualifiedName;
                return (element);
        }

        private XmlSchemaComplexType CreateAddressType()
        {
                System.Xml.XmlQualifiedName schemaString = new
System.Xml.XmlQualifiedName("string",W3C_SCHEMA_NS);

                XmlSchemaSequence seq = new XmlSchemaSequence();
                seq.MinOccurs=1;
                seq.MaxOccurs=1;
                seq.Items.Add (GenElement("street1",1,1,schemaString));
                seq.Items.Add (GenElement("street2",0,1,schemaString));
                seq.Items.Add (GenElement("city",1,1,schemaString));
                seq.Items.Add (GenElement("state",1,1,schemaString));
                seq.Items.Add (GenElement("zip",1,1,new
System.Xml.XmlQualifiedName("zipType",m_targetNameSpace)));

                XmlSchemaComplexType addressType = new XmlSchemaComplexType();
                addressType.Name = "addressType";
                addressType.Particle = seq;
                return(addressType);
        }
```

Rather than typing the code to create single elements, I created an overloaded helper function, GenElement (shown in Listing 2.10 as a shaded line), to facilitate the creation of elements. The overloaded version of this helper function accepts a parameter called qualifiedName: This is the QName that you can use to associate the type name (zipType) with your namespace (urn:schemas-xmlandasp-net:framework). You also created a local variable in the custom Create AddressType function called schemaString that declares the QName for the built-in string type (xsd:string).

After you're done creating each type, append it to the schema.Items collection by using the Add method. After all the types and your root element are appended to the schema, you can then retrieve the XML representation of the schema. I used an XmlTextWriter object to write the schema to a file, although you might want to store the schema as a string or keep it in memory.

Before writing the file, you need to call the Compile method. The Compile method, as shown in Listing 2.11, compiles the contents of the Schema Object Model (SOM) so that the schema can then be read or written. When you write the file, you must set up an event handler to capture errors thrown if a problem with the schema occurs.

A separate code listing for Visual Basic .NET isn't included here because the code is so similar between the two languages. The code is available on the book's website, however, which is located at www.xmlandasp.net. The main differences between the Visual Basic .NET version and the C# version is how the regular expressions look. C# requires a delimiter for \ characters, while Visual Basic .NET does not. So, the following line in C#:

```
pattern.Value ="\\w+([-+.]\\w+)*@\\w+([-.]\\w+)*\\.\\w+([-.]\\w+)*";
```

is changed to the following line in Visual Basic .NET:

```
pattern.Value = "\w+([-+.]\w+)*@\w+([-.]\w+)*\.\w+([-.]\w+)*"
```

Listing 2.11 contains the complete code listing, available for download as listing2-11.cs, for generating the schema as previously described.

Listing 2.11 **The Complete SOM Example**

```
using System;
using System.Xml;
using System.Xml.Schema;

namespace XmlSchemaCS
{
    public class CustomerSchemaFunctions
    {

        public const string W3C_SCHEMA_NS =
        ➥"http://www.w3.org/2001/XMLSchema";
        private  Boolean m_IsValid = false; ///this is a comment for the
        ➥boolean variable
        private string m_targetNameSpace = "";

        public CustomerSchemaFunctions(string nameSpace)
        {
            m_targetNameSpace = nameSpace;
        }

        public void WriteSchemaXml(string xsdFile)
            /// <summary>function to write the schema as xml</summary>
        {
            ///Create the schema root node with the targetNamespace
            XmlSchema schema = new XmlSchema();
            schema.TargetNamespace=m_targetNameSpace;
            schema.AttributeFormDefault = XmlSchemaForm.Unqualified;
            schema.ElementFormDefault = XmlSchemaForm.Qualified; ;
            XmlQualifiedName schemaString = new XmlQualifiedName("string",
            ➥W3C_SCHEMA_NS);

            schema.Items.Add(CreateZipType());
```

continues

Listing 2.11   **Continued**

```
        schema.Items.Add(CreateEmailType());
        schema.Items.Add(CreateAddressType());
        schema.Items.Add(CreateEntryType());

        XmlSchemaSequence seq = new XmlSchemaSequence();
        seq.MinOccurs=0;
        seq.MaxOccurs=1000;

        seq.Items.Add(GenElement("entry",1,1000,new
        ➥XmlQualifiedName("entryType",m_targetNameSpace)));
        XmlSchemaComplexType complexType = new XmlSchemaComplexType();
        complexType.Particle = seq;

        XmlSchemaElement addressBook = new XmlSchemaElement();
        addressBook.Name = "addressBook";
        addressBook.SchemaType = complexType;

        schema.Items.Add (addressBook);

        XmlTextWriter writer = new XmlTextWriter (xsdFile,
        ➥System.Text.Encoding.UTF8);
        schema.Compile(new
        ➥ValidationEventHandler(ValidationCallback));
        schema.Write(writer);
        writer.Close();
    }


    private XmlSchemaElement GenElement( string name, int minOccurs,
    ➥int maxOccurs)
    {
        XmlSchemaElement returnElement = new XmlSchemaElement();
        returnElement.Name = name;
        returnElement.MinOccurs = minOccurs;
        returnElement.MaxOccurs = maxOccurs;
        return (returnElement);
    }

    private XmlSchemaElement GenElement(string name, int minOccurs,
        int maxOccurs, System.Xml.XmlQualifiedName qualifiedName)

    {
        XmlSchemaElement element = new XmlSchemaElement();
        element.Name = name;
        element.MinOccurs = minOccurs;
        element.MaxOccurs = maxOccurs;
        element.SchemaTypeName = qualifiedName;
        return (element);
    }
```

```
private XmlSchemaSimpleType CreateZipType()
{
    XmlSchemaSimpleTypeRestriction restriction = new
    ↦XmlSchemaSimpleTypeRestriction ();
    restriction.BaseTypeName = new
    ↦System.Xml.XmlQualifiedName("string",W3C_SCHEMA_NS);
    XmlSchemaPatternFacet pattern = new XmlSchemaPatternFacet();
    pattern.Value ="\\d{5}(-\\d{4})?";
    restriction.Facets.Add (pattern);
    XmlSchemaSimpleType zipType = new XmlSchemaSimpleType();
    zipType.Name = "zipType";
    zipType.Content = restriction;
    return(zipType);
}

private XmlSchemaSimpleType CreateEmailType()
{
    XmlSchemaSimpleTypeRestriction restriction = new
    ↦XmlSchemaSimpleTypeRestriction ();
    restriction.BaseTypeName = new
    ↦System.Xml.XmlQualifiedName("string",W3C_SCHEMA_NS);
    XmlSchemaPatternFacet pattern = new XmlSchemaPatternFacet();
    pattern.Value ="\\w+([-+.]\\w+)*@\\w+([-.]\\w+)*\\.\\w+([-
    ↦.]\\w+)*";
    restriction.Facets.Add (pattern);

    XmlSchemaSimpleType emailType = new XmlSchemaSimpleType();
    emailType.Name = "emailType";
    emailType.Content = restriction;
    return(emailType);
}

private XmlSchemaComplexType CreateAddressType()
{
    System.Xml.XmlQualifiedName schemaString = new
    ↦System.Xml.XmlQualifiedName("string",W3C_SCHEMA_NS);

    XmlSchemaSequence seq = new XmlSchemaSequence();
    seq.MinOccurs=1;
    seq.MaxOccurs=1;
    seq.Items.Add (GenElement("street1",1,1,schemaString));
    seq.Items.Add (GenElement("street2",0,1,schemaString));
    seq.Items.Add (GenElement("city",1,1,schemaString));
    seq.Items.Add (GenElement("state",1,1,schemaString));
    seq.Items.Add (GenElement("zip",1,1,new
    ↦System.Xml.XmlQualifiedName("zipType",m_targetNameSpace)));

    XmlSchemaComplexType addressType = new XmlSchemaComplexType();
    addressType.Name = "addressType";
    addressType.Particle = seq;
    return(addressType);
```

continues

Listing 2.11   **Continued**

```
        }

        private XmlSchemaComplexType CreateEntryType()
        {
            System.Xml.XmlQualifiedName schemaString =
            ➥new System.Xml.XmlQualifiedName("string",W3C_SCHEMA_NS);

            XmlSchemaSequence seq = new XmlSchemaSequence();
            seq.MinOccurs = 1;
            seq.MaxOccurs = 1;
            seq.Items.Add (GenElement("name",1,1,schemaString));

            seq.Items.Add (GenElement("address",1,1,
            ➥new System.Xml.XmlQualifiedName("addressType",m_targetNameSpace)));

            seq.Items.Add (GenElement("email",0,4,
            ➥new System.Xml.XmlQualifiedName("emailType",m_targetNameSpace)));
            XmlSchemaComplexType entryType = new XmlSchemaComplexType();
            entryType.Name = "entryType";
            entryType.Particle = seq;
            return(entryType);
        }
    }
}
```

System.Xml.Schema.XmlSchemaCollection

Because there is no Read method on an XmlSchema object, how does someone
access a schema programmatically using System.Xml.Schema classes? The answer
is through the System.Xml.Schema.XmlSchemaCollection object. This object is a
collection of schemas that you load from a URL source or an XmlTextReader
object. You can add multiple schemas to the collection and then work with all
of them programmatically. XmlSchemaCollection is used here to read the schema
file created in the previous section and to access it programmatically.

The XmlTextReader accepts a URL for one of its constructors, so the file://
moniker is being used to load the file from the file system. You can add the
schema to the XmlSchemaCollection object to populate the SOM. You can
retrieve a reference to the populated SOM (the XmlSchema object) by using the
collection accessor foreach in C# (the same as for each in Visual Basic). After
you have a reference to the XmlSchema object, you can access its properties and
methods, as follows:

```
public void ReadSchemaXml(string xsdFile)
        {
            //Read the schema from file using the file:// moniker.
            System.Xml.XmlTextReader  reader =
            ➥new System.Xml.XmlTextReader(xsdFile);
```

```
        XmlSchemaCollection schemas = new XmlSchemaCollection();

        //Add the schema to the schemas collection
        schemas.Add(m_targetNameSpace,reader);

        foreach (XmlSchema  schema in schemas)
        {
            //We now have the schema object
            try
            {
                System.Diagnostics.Debug.WriteLine
                ➥(schema.TargetNamespace);


            .
            .
            .


            }
            catch(System.Exception e)
            {

                System.Diagnostics.Debug.WriteLine(e.ToString());
            }
        }
    }
```

This is not a complete listing, however; you still have to fill in some gaps. After
you have a reference to the schema object, you can access its properties and
child nodes the same way that you added them. You can use the for each syntax to cycle through the Items collection to look for child elements of the
schema node. Each object in the Items collection has a base type of
XmlSchemaObject, so you can test each object to see what types it supports and
cast to the appropriate type:

```
foreach ( XmlSchemaObject element in schema.Items)
{
if(element is XmlSchemaSimpleType)
    {
        XmlSchemaSimpleType simpleType = (XmlSchemaSimpleType)element;
        XmlSchemaSimpleTypeContent content = simpleType.Content ;
        if (content is XmlSchemaSimpleTypeRestriction)
        {
        XmlSchemaSimpleTypeRestriction restriction =
        ➥(XmlSchemaSimpleTypeRestriction )simpleType.Content;
        foreach(XmlSchemaFacet facet in restriction.Facets)
        {
            if (facet is XmlSchemaPatternFacet)
            {
            .
            .
            .

            }
        }
```

```
        else if(element is XmlSchemaComplexType)
        {
        }
        else

            .
            .
            .

    }
```

By using the Is operator, you can cast each object to a workable type to access the object-specific properties and methods. If you are working with a simpleType object, you need to reference its Content property. If you are working with a complexType object, you need access to its Particle property.

You can expand the simple type logic to display the XML in the debug window. You use the Is operator and a foreach loop to cycle through the facets collection and display only those facets that are *pattern facets* (facets that use regular expressions for validation):

```
foreach ( XmlSchemaObject element in schema.Items)
{
    if(element is XmlSchemaSimpleType)
    {
        XmlSchemaSimpleType simpleType = (XmlSchemaSimpleType)element;
        System.Diagnostics.Debug.WriteLine ("<xsd:simpleType name=" +
        ➥simpleType.Name );
        XmlSchemaSimpleTypeContent content = simpleType.Content ;
        if (content is XmlSchemaSimpleTypeRestriction)
        {

            XmlSchemaSimpleTypeRestriction restriction = null;
            restriction = (XmlSchemaSimpleTypeRestriction) simpletype.Content;
            System.Diagnostics.Debug.WriteLine("<xsd:restriction base=\"" +
            ➥restriction.BaseTypeName + "\">");
            foreach(XmlSchemaFacet facet in restriction.Facets)
            {
                if (facet is XmlSchemaPatternFacet)
                {
                System.Diagnostics.Debug.WriteLine("<xsd:pattern value=\"" +
                ➥facet.Value+ "\"/>");
                }
            }
            System.Diagnostics.Debug.WriteLine("<//xsd:restriction>");
        }
        System.Diagnostics.Debug.WriteLine ("<//xsd:simpleType");
    }
    else if(element is XmlSchemaComplexType)
    {
        XmlSchemaComplexType complexType = (XmlSchemaComplexType)element;
        System.Diagnostics.Debug.WriteLine (complexType.Name );
```

```
        }
        else
                System.Diagnostics.Debug.WriteLine(element.ToString());
    }
```

Notice that the Content property of the XmlSchemaSimpleType method returns an object of type XmlSchemaSimpleTypeContent. This object needs to be cast to its appropriate type (restriction, list, or union) to access the type-specific methods. You then cast the Content property's return object to an XmlSchemaSimpleType Restriction object to access the facets collection. Listing 2.12 contains the complete code to give you perspective on the logic that's used to parse out a schema using the framework classes.

Listing 2.12 **Accessing a Schema Using SOM and C#**

```
        public void ReadSchemaXml(string xsdFile)
        {
            //Read the schema from file using the file:// moniker.
            System.Xml.XmlTextReader  reader = new
System.Xml.XmlTextReader(xsdFile);
            XmlSchemaCollection schemas = new XmlSchemaCollection();

            //Add the schema to the schemas collection
            schemas.Add(m_targetNameSpace,reader);

            foreach (XmlSchema  schema in schemas)
            {
                //We now have the schema object
                try
                {

                    foreach ( XmlSchemaObject element in schema.Items)
                    {
                        if(element is XmlSchemaSimpleType)
                        {
                            XmlSchemaSimpleType simpleType =
                            ➥(XmlSchemaSimpleType)element;
                            System.Diagnostics.Debug.WriteLine
                            ➥("<xsd:simpleType name=" +
                            ➥simpleType.Name );
                            XmlSchemaSimpleTypeContent content =
                            ➥simpleType.Content ;
                            if (content is XmlSchemaSimpleType
                            ➥Restriction)
                            {

                        XmlSchemaSimpleTypeRestriction restriction =
                        ➥(XmlSchemaSimpleTypeRestriction )
```

continues

Listing 2.12   **Continued**

```
                            ➥simpleType.Content;
                                    System.Diagnostics.Debug.WriteLine("
                                    ➥<xsd:restriction base=\"" +
                                    ➥restriction.BaseTypeName + "\">");
                                    foreach(XmlSchemaFacet facet in
                                    ➥restriction.Facets)
                                    {
                            if (facet is XmlSchemaPatternFacet)
                            {
                                    System.Diagnostics.Debug.WriteLine("
                                    ➥<xsd:pattern value=\"" +
                                    ➥facet.Value+ "\"/>");
                                        }
                                    }
                                    System.Diagnostics.Debug.WriteLine("
                                    ➥</xsd:restriction>");
                                        }
                                    System.Diagnostics.Debug.WriteLine
                                    ➥("</xsd:simpleType");
                            }
                        }
                    }
                catch(System.Exception e)
                {
                        System.Diagnostics.Debug.WriteLine(e.ToString());
                }
            }
        }
    }
```

The same code in Visual Basic .NET is different regarding type conversion.
The Visual Basic .NET version of the code, shown in Listing 2.13, relies on
the Ctype function for casting and uses the TypeOf operator to determine if an
object supports a given type.

Listing 2.13   **Accessing a Schema Using SOM and Visual Basic .NET**

```
Public Sub ReadSchemaXml(ByVal xsdFile As String)

    'Read the schema from file using the file:// moniker.
    Dim reader As System.Xml.XmlTextReader = New
    ➥System.Xml.XmlTextReader(xsdFile)
    Dim schemas As XmlSchemaCollection = New XmlSchemaCollection()

    'Add the schema to the schemas collection
    schemas.Add(m_targetNameSpace, reader)
```

```
Dim schema As XmlSchema
For Each schema In schemas

    'We now have the schema object
    Try

        Dim element As XmlSchemaObject
        For Each element In schema.Items

            If TypeOf element Is XmlSchemaSimpleType Then

                Dim simpleType As XmlSchemaSimpleType =
                ⇒CType(element, XmlSchemaSimpleType)
                System.Diagnostics.Debug.WriteLine("<xsd:simple
                ⇒Typename=" + simpleType.Name)
                Dim content As XmlSchemaSimpleTypeContent =
                ⇒simpleType.Content
                If TypeOf content Is
                ⇒XmlSchemaSimpleTypeRestriction Then

                    Dim restriction As
                    ⇒XmlSchemaSimpleTypeRestriction =
                    ⇒CType(simpleType.Content, XmlSchema
                    ⇒SimpleTypeRestriction)
                    System.Diagnostics.Debug.WriteLine("
                    ⇒<xsd:restriction base=\"" +
                    ⇒restriction.BaseTypeName + " \ ">")
                    Dim facet As XmlSchemaFacet
                    For Each facet In restriction.Facets

                    If TypeOf facet Is XmlSchemaPatternFacet Then

                        System.Diagnostics.Debug.WriteLine("
                        ⇒<xsd:pattern value=\"" +
                        ⇒facet.Value+ " \ "/>")
                    End If
                    Next facet
                    System.Diagnostics.Debug.WriteLine("
                    ⇒</xsd:restriction>")
                End If

System.Diagnostics.Debug.WriteLine("</xsd:simpleType")

            End If
        Next element

    Catch errOops As System.Exception
        System.Diagnostics.Debug.WriteLine(errOops.ToString())
    End Try
```

continues

Listing 2.13 **Continued**

```
                     Next schema
              End Sub
```

The output from Listing 2.12 and Listing 2.13 yields the following:

```
urn:schemas-vbdna-net:framework
<xsd:simpleType name=zipType
    <xsd:restriction base="http://www.w3.org/2001/XMLSchema:string">
    <xsd:pattern value="\d{5}(-\d{4})?"/>
  </xsd:restriction>
</xsd:simpleType>
<xsd:simpleType name=emailType
    <xsd:restriction base="http://www.w3.org/2001/XMLSchema:string">
    <xsd:pattern value="\w+([-+.]\w+)*@\w+([-.]\w+)*\.\w+([-.]\w+)*"/>
  </xsd:restriction>
</xsd:simpleType>
```

Programmatic Validation with *XmlValidatingReader*

This section looks at programmatically validating XML documents against XML Schemas by using the XmlValidatingReader class. You must understand three main components when you're using the XmlValidatingReader: the reader, the XmlSchemaCollection object, and the ValidationEventHandler.

The *XmlValidatingReader* Class

Chapter 4 explains the concept of readers and writers in the .NET Framework in detail. That concept is introduced in this section by exploring the XmlValidatingReader class. XmlValidatingReader does precisely what its name implies: It reads XML and validates that XML against an XML Schema. XmlValidatingReader reads from a stream, so it does not actually hold the contents of the stream. It uses an instance of the XmlTextReader to read from the stream and extends the functionality of the XmlTextReader by validating the node against the specified schema(s). To associate the XmlTextReader instance with the XmlValidatingReader instance, you can use the constructor that accepts a text reader:

```
//Instantiate a reader to read the XML file
XmlTextReader textReader = new XmlTextReader(xmlFile);

//Associate the ValidatingReader with the XMLTextReader object
XmlValidatingReader validator = new XmlValidatingReader(textReader);
```

Associating a Schema with the *XmlValidatingReader*

After the `XmlTextReader` is associated with the `XmlValidatingReader`, you need to supply the schema(s) to the `XmlValidatingReader` instance. The `XmlValidating Reader` class exposes a `Schemas` collection that directs the validator to the schemas that are going to be used. The `Schemas` collection exposes an `Add` method that accepts four overloads to locate the schema(s) to be validated against. The first accepts an `XmlSchemaCollection` object, which is useful if you are working with multiple schemas:

```
XmlSchemaCollection schemas = new XmlSchemaCollection();
schemas.Add ("urn:schemas-vbdna-net:framework", new XmlTextReader(xsdFile));
validatingReader.Schemas.Add(schemas);
```

The second overload accepts a single `XmlSchema` object. As you saw earlier, using this object requires that you either build the schema on the fly or retrieve the schema from an `XmlSchemaCollection` object. The third overload accepts a namespace and an `XmlReader` abstract class. For this overload, you could specify an `XmlTextReader` because `XmlTextReader` is a concrete implementation of the `XmlReader` abstract class. This is nearly identical to the preceding usage of the `XmlSchemaCollection` object without a separate object reference:

```
validatingReader.Schemas.Add("urn:schemas-vbdna-net:customer", new
XmlTextReader(xsdFile));
```

The last overload accepts a namespace for the schema and the URL to the physical file. You'll use this overload for the example, but the third overload can also be used:

```
validatingReader.Schemas.Add("urn:schemas-xmlandasp-
net:customer","http://www.xmlandasp.net/schemas/fr.xsd");
```

Creating a *ValidationEventHandler*

As the `XmlValidatingReader` reads through the stream by using the supplied `XmlTextReader`, it validates the content in the stream to the schema specified and raises an event if the node violates the schema. This event is specified through its `ValidationEvent` property. Because the event is fired when the schema is invalid, you need a class member variable to determine, from the function containing the `ValidatingReader`, if the schema is valid or not.

To wire up the event handler and the `XmlValidatingReader`, declare a function that accepts two parameters—an `Object` type and a `ValidationEventArgs` type:

```
private void ValidationCallback ( object sender, ValidationEventArgs args )
{
```

```
System.Diagnostics.Debug.WriteLine ("Validation error: {0}" + args.Message);
isValid = false;
}
```

Inside this function, you have a simple debug output message that lets you know that a validation event occurred and what the message was. You can also set the class member variable to false to indicate that the validation was unsuccessful.

The next step is to create a `ValidationEventHandler` class that uses your created function as a callback. C# uses a delegate to wire up the event with the object, as shown here:

```
// Wire up the callback to our ValidationCallBack routine
ValidationEventHandler eventHandler = new ValidationEventHandler
(ValidationCallback);

//Wire up the event handler to the validating reader's event handler
validator.ValidationEventHandler += eventHandler;
```

In Visual Basic .NET, the same result can be accomplished by using the `AddHandler` method:

```
'Wire up the callback to our ValidationCallBack routine
AddHandler validator.ValidationEventHandler, AddressOf ValidationCallback
```

The `XmlValidatingReader` is now associated with your `callback` function and is fired when you begin the `Read` process.

Validating Using the *Read* Method

Until this point, you have set all the plumbing in place but still have not validated anything. The actual validation occurs when the `Read` method is called on each element within the XML instance document:

```
while (validator.Read())
{
//Here, you have access to each element.  We do nothing with this
//because we only want to know if the entire document is valid or not.
}
```

The `Read` method simply reads the XML instance document and validates the element against the schema. If data is invalid or missing, the event handler is called.

Listing 2.14 contains the entire example in C#.

Listing 2.14   **A Utility Class Used to Validate XML Documents Against a
Specified Schema Using C#**

```csharp
using System.Xml;
using System.Xml.Schema;

Public Class XMLFunctions
{
private Boolean isValid = false;  //Private flag to hold validation results
➥from callback

public Boolean IsXMLValid(string xsdFile, string xmlFile)
{

//Instantiate a reader to read the XML file
XmlTextReader textReader = new XmlTextReader(xmlFile);

//Associate the ValidatingReader with the XMLTextReader object
XmlValidatingReader validator = new XmlValidatingReader(textReader);
validator.ValidationType = ValidationType.Auto;

//Create the schema collection
XmlSchemaCollection schemas = new XmlSchemaCollection();
schemas.Add (null, new XmlTextReader(xsdFile));

//Add the list of schemas to validate against to the schemas collection
validator.Schemas.Add(schemas);

// Wire up the callback to our ValidationCallBack routine
ValidationEventHandler eventHandler = new ValidationEventHandler
➥(ValidationCallback);

//Wire up the event handler to the validating reader's event handler
validator.ValidationEventHandler += eventHandler;

while (validator.Read())
{
//Here, you have access to each element.  We do nothing with this
//because we only want to know if the entire document is valid or not.
}
if (isValid)
System.Diagnostics.Debug.WriteLine ("Document is valid.");
else
System.Diagnostics.Debug.WriteLine ("Document is NOT valid.");

validator.Close();
textReader.Close();

Return isValid;
}
```

continues

Listing 2.14 **Continued**

```
private void ValidationCallback ( object sender, ValidationEventArgs args )
{
System.Diagnostics.Debug.WriteLine ("Validation error: {0}" + args.Message);
isValid = false;
}
}
```

In Listing 2.15, you can see the same code in Visual Basic .NET.

Listing 2.15 **A Utility Class Used to Validate XML Documents Against a Specified Schema Using C#**

```
Imports System.Xml
Imports System.Xml.Schema

Public Class XMLFunctions
    Private isValid As Boolean = False   'Private flag to hold validation
    ↪results from callback

    Public Function IsXMLValid(ByVal xsdFile As String, ByVal xmlFile As
    ↪String) As Boolean
        'Instantiate a reader to read the XML file
        Dim textReader As XmlTextReader = New XmlTextReader(xmlFile)

        'Associate the ValidatingReader with the XMLTextReader object
        Dim validator As XmlValidatingReader = New
        ↪XmlValidatingReader(textReader)
        validator.ValidationType = ValidationType.Auto

        'Create the schema collection
        Dim schemas As XmlSchemaCollection = New XmlSchemaCollection()
        schemas.Add("urn:schemas-vbdna-net:framework", New
        ↪XmlTextReader(xsdFile))

        'Add the list of schemas to validate against to the schemas
        ↪collection
        validator.Schemas.Add(schemas)

        'Wire up the callback to our ValidationCallBack routine
        AddHandler validator.ValidationEventHandler, AddressOf
        ↪ValidationCallback

        While (validator.Read())
            'Here, you have access to each element.  We do nothing with this
            'because we only want to know if the entire document is valid or
            ↪not.
        End While
```

```
        If (isValid) Then
            System.Diagnostics.Debug.WriteLine("Document is valid.")
        Else
            System.Diagnostics.Debug.WriteLine("Document is NOT valid.")
        End If

        validator.Close()
        textReader.Close()

        Return isValid
    End Function

    Private Sub ValidationCallback(ByVal sender As Object, ByVal args As
    ➥ValidationEventArgs)
        System.Diagnostics.Debug.WriteLine ("Validation error: {0}" +
        ➥args.Message);
        isValid = False
    End Sub

End Class
```

The example in Listing 2.15 makes validating an XML document against a specified schema easy. Listing 2.16 shows a sample implementation that calls the XMLFunctions class that is defined in Listing 2.15.

Listing 2.16   **A Sample Implementation of the *XMLFunctions* Class**

```
Imports System.Xml
Imports System.Xml.Schema

Public Class WebForm1
    Inherits System.Web.UI.Page

#Region " Web Form Designer Generated Code "

    'This call is required by the Web Form Designer.
    <System.Diagnostics.DebuggerStepThrough()> Private Sub
    ➥InitializeComponent()

    End Sub

    Private Sub Page_Init(ByVal sender As System.Object, ByVal e As
    ➥System.EventArgs) Handles MyBase.Init
        'CODEGEN: This method call is required by the Web Form Designer
        'Do not modify it using the code editor.
        InitializeComponent()
    End Sub

#End Region
```

continues

Listing 2.16 **Continued**

```
    Private Sub Page_Load(ByVal sender As System.Object, ByVal e As
System.EventArgs) Handles MyBase.Load
        'Put user code to initialize the page here
        Dim test As XMLFunctions = New XMLFunctions()

        Response.Write(test.IsXMLValid(Server.MapPath("test.xsd"),
Server.MapPath("testdoc.xml")))
    End Sub

End Class
```

Note the lack of error handling in this example. Both the C# and Visual Basic .NET versions make the assumption that both the XML and XSD files already exist. You might want to expand this example to include a try..catch block to trap errors that can occur when loading the XML or XSD files fails.

The code is fairly straightforward. Again, the concept of readers and writers will be explained in more detail in Chapter 6, "Exploring the System.Xml Namespace".

Chapter Summary

In this chapter, you saw that schemas are an elegant way of validating XML instance documents. Instead of leaving developers to their own means to validate the data in an XML document, an XSD Schema can be applied to the XML instance document to validate the data if the XML document conforms to the rules agreed upon in the schema. You can validate the presence of elements and attributes, the order of elements, the cardinality of elements, and the number of times that an element can occur. You also saw how to define your types and extend those types to be used throughout your document.

You also saw that the .NET Framework classes provide access to read the structure of an XSD Schema and to programmatically create an XSD Schema. Using these classes, you can easily imagine creating a tool to display schemas graphically or to edit schemas through a utility.

Finally, you were introduced to the concept of readers and writers within the .NET Framework base classes. You used XmlValidatingReader to validate an XML document against a specified schema. Lastly, you saw how the ValidationEventHandler delegate event determines if an error occurred with the validation process.

References

Introduction to DataSets. MSDN Help, `ms-help://MS.VSCC/MS.MSDNVS/vbcon/html/vbconDataSets.htm`.

Holzner, Steven. *Inside XML.* New Riders Publishing (Indianapolis, IN), 2001. ISBN: 0-73571-020-1.

3

XML Presentation

XML IS A GREAT TOOL FOR WORKING with and structuring data. So far, this book has focused on the data. Chapter 1, "XML and ASP.NET: The Basics," showed you the basics of creating a well-formed document and gave you some practical uses for XML. Chapter 2, "XML Schemas in .NET," showed you how you can use XML to convey and validate the structure of an XML document. It also showed you why validating the data can be important. This chapter shows you some of the different mechanisms that exist for displaying data, including data islands, XML data source objects, Cascading Style Sheets (CSS), and Extensible Stylesheet Language Transformations (XSLT). You also look at Wireless Application Protocol (WAP) and Wireless Markup Language (WML) for working with a variety of devices. Finally, the benefits, tradeoffs, and differences between declarative programming with XSLT and processing information with Active Server Pages (ASP) are dicussed.

Netscape and Internet Explorer Support

Before looking at the concepts and code for XML, you first need to understand what browsers you are targeting for different uses. XML has only gained widespread acceptance in the past several years, and tool support reflects this.

Older versions of both the Netscape Navigator and Microsoft Internet Explorer browsers have limited, if any, support for XML or related technologies. Internet Explorer 5.5 is the first browser to support the XSLT 1.0 Recommendation. Version 5.0 supported an earlier working draft of the Extensible Stylesheet Language (XSL) working draft. Netscape 6.0 is the first Netscape browser to support XML, XSLT, and XML Schemas. Table 3.1 lists the compatibilities for different browser versions.

Table 3.1   **As XML Evolves, So Do Browsers and Their Support for XML**

Browser	Version	XML 1.0	XSL	XSLT	XDR	XSD	Data Islands
Netscape	4.0						
	4.5						
	6.0	X	X	X	X		
Internet Explorer	5.0	X					X
	5.5	X	X		X		X
	6.0	X	X	X	X	X	X

Data Islands

Data islands are a technology that is specific to Internet Explorer. Data islands are XML documents embedded within an HTML document. By using data islands, you can use either the client-side Document Object Model (DOM) to retrieve values from the embedded XML, or you can use Microsoft's Data Source Objects (DSO) to bind the data from the XML document to HTML objects that support data binding.

You can create an XML data island in two ways:

- Declare the XML within the HTML document
- Reference an external XML document

XML data islands are created by specifying an <XML> element within an HTML document and then either inserting the XML directly into the HTML or referencing it by using the SRC attribute of the XML element to identify the external document's source.

Creating Inline Data Islands

Listing 3.1 creates an inline data island.

Listing 3.1   **Creating an Inline Data Island**

```
<!DOCTYPE HTML PUBLIC "-//W3C//DTD HTML 4.0 Transitional//EN">
<html>
      <head>
            <title>Favorite Pitchers</title>
      </head>
      <body>
            <XML id="xmldso" async="false">
                  <Pitchers>
                        <Pitcher>
                              <Name>Tom Glavine</Name>
                              <Team>Braves</Team>
                        </Pitcher>
                        <Pitcher>
                              <Name>David Wells</Name>
                              <Team>Yankees</Team>
                        </Pitcher>
                        <Pitcher>
                              <Name>Roger Clemens</Name>
                              <Team>Yankees</Team>
                        </Pitcher>
                        <Pitcher>
                              <Name>Randy Johnson</Name>
                              <Team>Diamondbacks</Team>
                        </Pitcher>
                        <Pitcher>
                              <Name>Curt Schilling</Name>
                              <Team>Diamondbacks</Team>
                        </Pitcher>
                  </Pitchers>
            </XML>

            <table datasrc="#xmldso" width="100%" border="1">
                  <tr align="left">
                        <td><span datafld="Name"></span></td>
                        <td><span datafld="Team"></span></td>
                  </tr>
            </table>
      </body>
</html>
```

In Listing 3.1, the XML document is embedded between a pair of XML tags. The XML tag is given an ID attribute by which the data island is referenced.

Elements within Internet Explorer support binding to data source objects, such as span. Others, such as td, do not support binding directly and require a child element. Listing 3.1 shows a table that uses a data island as its data source (through the datasrc attribute), and each cell in the table is bound to an element in the data island (through the use of the datafld attribute).

Referencing External XML

Listing 3.1 used inline XML to create a data island. You can also create a data island by using the SRC attribute of the reserved <XML> element to indicate the XML file that's being referenced. Listing 3.2 shows you how an external XML file can be referenced to create a data island.

Listing 3.2   **Using an External XML File as the Source for a Data Island**

```
<!DOCTYPE HTML PUBLIC "-//W3C//DTD HTML 4.0 Transitional//EN">
<html>
    <head>
        <title>HTMLPage1</title>
    </head>
    <body>
        <XML id="xmldso" async="false" src="pitchers.xml">
        </XML>

        <table datasrc="#xmldso" width="100%" border="1">
            <tr align="left">
                <td><span datafld="Name"></span></td>
                <td><span datafld="Team"></span></td>
            </tr>
        </table>
    </body>
</html>
```

When using data islands in this manner, be aware that the entire XML document referenced is downloaded to the client. For significantly large documents, this might not be feasible. This can, however, provide an effective caching mechanism for XSLT stylesheets.

Single Record Binding

Another cool use for XML data islands is the ability to use single-record binding to create a paging effect. You can navigate through the document one record at a time. Listing 3.3 shows how you can use binding with navigation buttons to iterate through the pages.

Listing 3.3   **Using a Paging Effect with a Bound DSO**

```
<!DOCTYPE HTML PUBLIC "-//W3C//DTD HTML 4.0 Transitional//EN">
<html>
    <head>
        <title>HTMLPage1</title>
    </head>
    <body>
```

```
<XML id="xmldso" async="false">
    <Pitchers>
        <Pitcher>
            <Name>Tom Glavine</Name>
            <Team>Braves</Team>
        </Pitcher>
        <Pitcher>
            <Name>David Wells</Name>
            <Team>Yankees</Team>
        </Pitcher>
        <Pitcher>
            <Name>Roger Clemens</Name>
            <Team>Yankees</Team>
        </Pitcher>
        <Pitcher>
            <Name>Randy Johnson</Name>
            <Team>Diamondbacks</Team>
        </Pitcher>
        <Pitcher>
            <Name>Curt Schilling</Name>
            <Team>Diamondbacks</Team>
        </Pitcher>
    </Pitchers>
</XML>

<table datasrc="#xmldso" datapagesize="2" width="100%" border="1"
 id="tbl">
    <tr align="left">
        <td><span datafld="Name"></span></td>
        <td><span datafld="Team"></span></td>
    </tr>
</table>
<input type="button"  value="&lt;&lt;" onclick="tbl.firstPage();"
 ID="Button1" NAME="Button1">
<input type="button"  value="&lt;" onclick="tbl.previousPage();"
 ID="Button2" NAME="Button1">
<input type="button"  value="&gt;" onclick="tbl.nextPage();"
 ID="Button3" NAME="Button3">
<input type="button"  value="&gt;&gt;" onclick="tbl.lastPage();"
 ID="Button4" NAME="Button1">

    </body>
</html>
```

Several parts of Listing 3.3 must be noted. The table is declared with a page size, which limits the number of displayed records to two. Also, the navigation buttons are bound to the table, not directly to the data source. The result is shown in Figure 3.1.

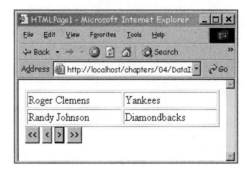

Figure 3.1   Paging through an HTML table that's bound to a data island.

Also included are several navigation buttons to navigate through the HTML table using the bound table's methods `firstPage`, `nextPage`, `previousPage`, and `lastPage`.

Multiple Record Binding

You can also bind an entire table to a data island. By simply omitting the `data-pagesize` attribute from the `table` element, you can see the entire table bound to the data island.

Working with the Client-Side DOM

Internet Explorer 5.5 and higher and Netscape 6.0 and higher support a client-side XML DOM. This DOM provides access XML documents that can populate UserInterface (UI) elements in the browser.

Let's work through an example of using XML DOM on the client. The example shows the use of the client-side DOM and DHTML to enable dynamic sorting. This section does not use any technology that's specific to .NET: It shows a mechanism for displaying XML dynamically on the client by using JavaScript, HTML, and the client-side DOM.

The files that are created for this example are shown in Table 3.2.

Table 3.2   **Explanation of Files Used to Create a Client-Side DOM Example**

Filename	Description
Pitchers.xml	Contains the data to display
PitcherStyle.xslt	Transforms the XML document into HTML
Pitchers.js	Contains the code used to perform the transformation
Pitchers.htm	Contains the UI elements

Begin by creating an XML file to hold the data that you want to dynamically display. For this example, you are displaying a list of pitchers for different baseball teams. Create a new web project called DataIslands in Visual Studio .NET. Add a new XML file called `Pitchers.xml` to the web project and paste the XML from Listing 3.4 into it.

Listing 3.4   *Pitchers.xml*

```xml
<?xml version="1.0" encoding="utf-8" ?>
<PITCHERS>
    <PITCHER>
        <FNAME>John</FNAME>
        <LNAME>Rocker</LNAME>
        <TEAM>Indians</TEAM>
        <CITY>Cleveland</CITY>
        <ERA></ERA>
    </PITCHER>
    <PITCHER>
        <FNAME>Tom</FNAME>
        <LNAME>Glavine</LNAME>
        <TEAM>Braves</TEAM>
        <CITY>Atlanta</CITY>
        <ERA></ERA>
    </PITCHER>
    <PITCHER>
        <FNAME>Greg</FNAME>
        <LNAME>Maddux</LNAME>
        <TEAM>Braves</TEAM>
        <CITY>Atlanta</CITY>
        <ERA></ERA>
    </PITCHER>
    <PITCHER>
        <FNAME>Randy</FNAME>
        <LNAME>Johnson</LNAME>
        <TEAM>Diamondbacks</TEAM>
        <CITY>Arizona</CITY>
        <ERA></ERA>
    </PITCHER>
</PITCHERS>
```

The next step to building the sample application is to add an XSLT file called `PitcherStyle.xslt`. This file transforms the XML data into HTML. XSLT transformations are discussed later in the section, "XSLT". Listing 3.5 shows the code that you enter into `PitcherStyle.xslt`.

Listing 3.5 *PitcherStyle.xslt*

```
<?xml version="1.0" encoding="UTF-8" ?>
<xsl:stylesheet version="1.0"
xmlns:xsl="http://www.w3.org/1999/XSL/Transform">
     <xsl:param name="sortBy" select="'CITY'"/>
     <xsl:template match="/">
          <xsl:apply-templates/>
     </xsl:template>
     <xsl:template match="PITCHERS">
          <TABLE border="1">
               <tr>
                    <th bgcolor="teal"><a onclick="javascript:
                    SortData('FNAME');">First Name</a></th>
                    <th bgcolor="teal"><a onclick="javascript:
                    ↦SortData('LNAME');">Last Name</a></th>
                    <th bgcolor="teal"><a onclick="javascript:
                    ↦SortData('CITY');">City</a></th>
                    <th bgcolor="teal"><a onclick="javascript:
                    ↦SortData('TEAM');">Team</a></th>
                    <th bgcolor="teal"><a onclick="javascript:
                    ↦SortData('ERA');">ERA</a></th>
               </tr>
               <xsl:for-each select="PITCHER">
                    <xsl:sort select="*[name()=$sortBy]"/>
                    <tr>
                         <td><xsl:value-of select="FNAME"/><br/></td>
                         <td><xsl:value-of select="LNAME"/></td>
                         <td><xsl:value-of select="CITY"/></td>
                         <td><xsl:value-of select="TEAM"/></td>
                         <td><xsl:value-of select="ERA"/></td>
                    </tr>
               </xsl:for-each>
          </TABLE>
     </xsl:template>
</xsl:stylesheet>
```

When this transformation is applied, a table is rendered with anchor tags in the headings. When one of the anchor tags is clicked, the table is sorted based on that column.

Next, you create the HTML that will display the data and create an XML data island on the client. Add an HTML file called pitchers.htm and enter the code from Listing 3.6 into it.

Listing 3.6 *Pitchers.htm*

```
<!DOCTYPE HTML PUBLIC "-//W3C//DTD HTML 4.0 Transitional//EN">
<html>

     <head>
          <title>HTMLPage1</title>
```

```
    <script language="javascript" src="Pitchers.js">
    </script>

</head>

<body MS_POSITIONING="GridLayout">

    <form  name="SortMethod">
        <div id="SortedPitchers"></div>
    </form>
</body>
</html>
```

The only item worth noting in Listing 3.6 is that a <DIV> element was created, called SortedPitchers. This <DIV> element will display the contents of the transformed XML. An external JavaScript file was also referenced, Pitchers.js, which will contain the functions used to work with the DOM on the client.

The final step is to create the JavaScript that will perform the sorting. In Listing 3.7, a JavaScript file is created, Pitchers.js, that contains the functions that manipulate the XML.

Listing 3.7   *Pitchers.js*

```
function SortData(strSortCol)
{
    var template = new ActiveXObject("Msxml2.XSLTemplate");
    var xslDoc = new ActiveXObject("Msxml2.FreeThreadedDOMDocument");
    var xmlDoc = new ActiveXObject("Msxml2.DOMDocument");
    var processor;

    xslDoc.async = false;
    xslDoc.load("PitcherStyle.xslt");
    template.stylesheet = xslDoc;

    processor = template.createProcessor();
    processor.addParameter("sortBy",strSortCol);
    xmlDoc.async = false;
    xmlDoc.load("pitchers.xml");

    processor.input = xmlDoc;
    processor.transform();

    SortedPitchers.innerHTML = processor.output;
}


function window.onload()
{
    SortData("TEAM");
}
```

Let's walk through the JavaScript file, beginning with the `window.onload` function.

When the browser window first loads the HTML page, the `window.onload` event fires. This function, in turn, calls the `SortData` function with a string value of `TEAM`.

The `SortData` function performs the actual transformation of data. The JavaScript file contains the code that declares the MSXML objects and instantiates them. Because the browser uses MSXML on the client, you have access to a familiar programming model. A `FreeThreadedDOMDocument` is created and loaded with the XSLT document `PitcherStyle.xslt` (refer to Listing 3.5). This document is then used as the stylesheet for the `XSLTemplate` object `template`.

The `createProcessor` method returns an `IXSLProcessor` object that performs the actual transformation over the XSLT document. The processor adds the parameter `sortBy`. (This variable is defined in the XSLT stylesheet in Listing 3.5.) Finally, the XML document is loaded and the XSL processor is invoked to perform the transformation. Finally, the HTML `div` element, named `SortedPitchers` and declared in Listing 3.6, is populated with the results of the XSLT transformation.

The cool part of this sample application is that clicking a table header causes the table to be sorted completely on the client. This is because the `SortData` method is called each time a table header is clicked. The code that specifies this is in the XSLT file itself.

Recall in Listing 3.5 that the XSLT stylesheet actually emitted the HTML that renders the HTML table. In the XSLT stylesheet, you declared the table headers with the following code:

```
<th bgcolor="teal">
      <a onclick="javascript:SortData('FNAME');">FirstName</a>
</th>
<th bgcolor="teal">
      <a onclick="javascript:SortData('LNAME');">Last Name</a>
</th>
<th bgcolor="teal">
      <a onclick="javascript:SortData('CITY');">City</a>
</th>
<th bgcolor="teal">
      <a onclick="javascript:SortData('TEAM');">Team</a>
</th>
<th bgcolor="teal">
      <a onclick="javascript:SortData('ERA');">ERA</a>
</th>
```

Notice that inside the XSLT file, you can specify the JavaScript function that is called as a result of a UI event. In this case, specify that your custom SortData function should be called when the onclick event occurs.

The results of this example are shown in Figure 3.2.

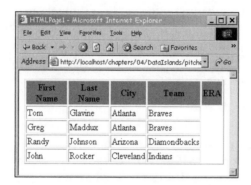

Figure 3.2   A client-side DOM example.

This example introduced many techniques. You saw how XSLT can be applied to XML to render a new format. You saw how MSXML is used to load and manipulate XML data, and how MSXML can perform transformations on the client. For more information on MSXML, see Chapter 5, "MSXML Parser." XSLT is covered in depth in the section, "XSLT."

Overview of CSS and XSLT

The common technologies for styling XML for display are CSS and XSLT. CSS enables the developer to specify HTML styles for an element, including font, weight, size, and position. XSLT is capable of styling XML and transforming XML tree structures into new structures. This section looks at the uses for each, and develops examples that use each technology.

CSS Basics

CSS is most commonly used with HTML files to generate themes for HTML sites so that changing the display of one tag does not require massive updates throughout the website to make the change consistent. You can make your HTML files leaner because they do not require as much markup to achieve the same effect, which improves overall site performance due to smaller HTML files being transferred over the network and faster parse times on the client.

For example, suppose that you want to display your company's name with a specific font every time it appears. You can use an HTML `<font>` tag to specify the font's face, color, and size, as shown here:

```
<font color="Blue" face="Tahoma" size="2">Xmlandasp.net </font>
```

Suppose that you used the preceding font tag throughout your application. Months later, your marketing department tells you that the blue color should be changed to gray to be more appealing to the eye. So, you search through your entire site to find each instance of the previous HTML code and replace the color attribute's value with Gray:

```
<font color="Gray" face="Tahoma" size="2">Xmlandasp.net </font>
```

Here's a more solid example. Suppose that you are developing a site that you want to sell to multiple vendors. Each vendor wants his own branding on the site. Instead of developing custom HTML for each vendor, you want to create a single set of HTML pages that can be used for each vendor. How do you accomplish this? The answer is CSS.

Instead of defining the layout within the HTML tag, you can separate the semantics of a layout scheme from its implementation.

Defining Element Styles

You can use CSS to define the style associated with a particular element. CSS works on the basis of rules: Rules are defined to match instances within the document being implemented. This is what each instance of the HTML `<H1>` and `<H2>` elements will look like:

```
H1
{
    font-weight: bold;
    font-size: 16pt;
    color: blue;
    font-family: Verdana, Tahoma, Arial;
    text-decoration: none;
}
H2
{
    font-weight: bold;
    font-size: 14pt;
    color: black;
    font-family: Verdana, Tahoma, Arial;
    text-decoration: none;
}
```

In each page that uses this stylesheet, any reference to an HTML `<H1>` tag is a blue, 16-point font, and an `<H2>` font is slightly smaller and black. You can use this method to define what each HTML element looks like throughout your website.

You can see that you can simply define what a particular element looks like. Now, it's time to see how to use these style rules. CSS styles are applied to HTML in several ways: linking, importing, as part of the document, or as an inline definition.

Styles can be applied by linking to an external CSS stylesheet. In an HTML file, for example, you might specify the following in the HTML `head` section:

```
<html>
<head>
<link type="text/css" rel="stylesheet" href="xmlandasp.css">
</head>
<body>
   <h1>This text is whatever is defined in "xmlandasp"</h1>
</body>
</html>
```

The `href` attribute specifies the location of the external stylesheet. This location can be a relative path or a URL.

In addition to linking to the external stylesheet, the external CSS document can also be imported by using the `@import` directive, as shown here:

```
<html>
<head>
<style type="text/css">
@import url(http://www.xmlandasp.net /styles.css);
</style>
</head>
<body>
   <h1>This text is whatever is defined in "styles.css"</h1>
</body>
</html>
```

Although external resources can be referenced, it is sometimes feasible to include styles within the current document or even inline. To define a style within the current document, again use the HTML `style` tag within the HTML `head` section:

```
<html>
<head>
<style type="text/css">
   h1 {font-family: verdana; color: green; }
</style>
</head>
<body>
   <h1>This text is a Verdana font, colored green</h1>
</body>
</html>
```

Finally, you can include style definitions inline with elements as they appear. For example, you might use an HTML span element and declare a style on the fly:

```
<html>
<head>
<style type="text/css">
   h1 {font-family: verdana; color: green; }
</style>
</head>
<body>
   <span style="color: blue; text-decoration: underline;">This is some blue
underlined text</span>
</body>
</html>
```

Typically, it is considered best to include all CSS style rules in a separate document and link them by using the link HTML element. Should a style change, there would only be a single file to update rather than all 300 HTML or .aspx pages that reference the style rule.

Note
For brevity, this chapter uses document styles using the HTML style element.

Defining Element Classes

You can use CSS to define your classes to apply to different HTML elements. A CSS class enables you to develop specific types of a broader class that are applied by using a class selector.

For example, you might declare a style rule for all H1 elements in an HTML document by using the following code:

```
h1 {font-family: verdana; color: green; }
```

After you develop your pages, you notice that you sometimes need to add several properties to this element, such as underlining and italics, but you do not need this behavior for all instances. One way to do this is to define a CSS class. A CSS class defines a more specific implementation of a broader class and is referenced by using the HTML class selector, as shown here:

```
<html>
<head>

<style type="text/css">
   h1 {font-family: verdana; color: green; }
   h1.modified {font-family: tahoma; color: blue; text-decoration:
underline;}
</style>
```

```
</head>
<body>
   <h1>This text is green in Verdana font</h1>
   <h1 class="modified">This text is blue and underlined Tahoma font</h1>

</body>
</html>
```

By now, you have probably heard of CSS and have probably seen it in use. The minute details of CSS are not covered in this book. Instead, you are urged to read the W3C Recommendation for CSS at www.w3.org/TR/REC-CSS1. What is important is the realization that you can use CSS directly with XML and HTML.

Associating XML with CSS

We briefly discussed CSS in the previous section to remind the user of the syntax of CSS and its usefulness. CSS can link directly with XML to display the XML document. The W3C recommendation (at www.w3.org/TR/xml-stylesheet/) specifies the valid ways of associating XML and CSS. One way is to use a processing instruction in the prolog (after the XML declaration and before the document element), as shown here:

```
<?xml version="1.0" encoding="utf-8" ?>
<?xml-stylesheet href="pitchers.css" type="text/css"?>

<PITCHERS>
     <PITCHER>
          <FNAME>John</FNAME>
          <LNAME>Rocker</LNAME>
          <TEAM>Indians</TEAM>
          <CITY>Cleveland</CITY>
          <ERA></ERA>
     </PITCHER>
</PITCHERS>
```

We associated the XML with a stylesheet called pitchers.css. Now build that style in the following code:

```
CITY
{
     color: blue;
}
TEAM
{
     font-weight: bold;
}
```

There's not much to it. When a CITY element is displayed, it is displayed with a blue font; when a TEAM element is displayed, it comes through as bold text.

There are many other possibilities for using CSS with XML directly. You can use CSS positioning and build complex rules to generate interesting effects. The tradeoff is that the CSS rules can become overly complex and difficult to debug.

A more popular use of CSS is to apply CSS to the HTML that is the result of an XSL transformation. The next section looks at using CSS and XSLT in more detail.

When you open an XML document in Internet Explorer, it's already styled although you did not specify any stylesheet for the XML document. This is because IE uses a default stylesheet when no stylesheet is specified. The default stylesheet for Internet Explorer is an internal resource; however, you can view it by typing the following code in the IE Address bar:

```
res://msxml3.dll/defaultss.xsl
```

Although you can view the XSL, you cannot change it because it is an internal resource. But, viewing it can give you a good idea of working with an XSLT stylesheet. This leads us into the next section.

XSL Versus CSS

CSS suffers from a number of limitations for complex documents. For example, CSS cannot render documents that do not contain display information (which is why the preceding example produced little). A good summary of these limitations can be found at www.xml.com/pub/a/w3j/s3.leventhal.html. To overcome these limitations, the W3C started a working group to address the problems of applying styles to XML. The result was XSL. XSL encompasses XSLT and XSL Formatting Objects (XSL-FO). XSLT processes documents and transforms a source document tree into another tree representation. XSL-FO applies formatting to a resultant document, such as an Adobe Acrobat PDF file.

> **Note**
>
> This book does not cover XSL-FO. IE doesn't yet support XSL-FO, and the reader should be able to apply this technology after he or she understands the base concepts of working with XSLT. For more information on XSL-FO, see the W3C's home page at www.w3c.org.

XSLT

XSLT has begun to play a vital role in the adoption of XML. We no longer think of XML simply as data. With XSLT, we begin to think how to change that data into something more usable. XSLT enables you to transform XML documents into a variety of formats, such as HTML, XHTML, PDF, other XML documents, or even other XSLT documents. The majority of this chapter focuses on XSLT and its practical uses.

XSLT processes XML documents and transforms them into other documents. The term *documents* is used here because an XML document is simply a set of well-formed XML tags (refer to Chapter 1). Recall, however, that XML does not need to be stored in a file. You can use this technique to pull XML data from a variety of sources that might or might not be file based.

The XSL recommendation also makes use of the XPath recommendation. Before jumping into using XSLT, you need to get a firm grasp on XPath. Then you can use XPath and XSLT to process XML trees.

XPath

XML is simply markup for data. That's it. XML is not a magic wand; it does not specify how data is transmitted over the wire, it does not specify how data is stored. XML simply determines the format of the data: What you do with the data is up to you. That said, the real power behind XML is not solely its ability to represent data: XML's real power lies in ancillary technologies that, when combined with XML, provide robust solutions, and XPath is one of those ancillary technologies.

Version 1.0 of the XML Path Language became a World Wide Web Consortium (W3C) recommendation on November 16th, 1999. You can view the W3C recommendation for XPath 1.0 at `http://www.w3.org/TR/xpath`. This document shows all information relating to XPath including an overview of XPath and a description of its components.

XPath grew out of efforts to share a common syntax between XSL Transformations (XSLT) and XPointer. It allows for the search and retrieval of information within an XML document structure. XPath is not an XML syntax: rather, it uses a syntax that relates to the logical structure of an XML document.

An Analogy to SQL

Consider a relational database. Is the real power of a database the ability to simply store data, index the data, and specify relations between tables of data? After all, a database is supposed to hold data, so is the capability of persisting data the real advantage behind a relational database? If so, a simple file would suffice for this. It is easy to see that the real power of a database the ability to use Structured Query Language (SQL) statements to retrieve subsets of data. To take this example one step further, the fact that SQL is an ANSI standard makes your knowledge of SQL applicable to different databases running on different platforms.

Using this same logic, XML would simply be a format for data storage without a prescribed way of retrieving that data. This is exactly what XPath is: XPath is the query language for XML documents. XPath is the common name used for XML Path Language. Using XPath statements, you can retrieve complex subsets of data from XML documents using a syntax that is universal across implementations. The same XPath statements that work within the `System.Xml` and `System.Xml.XPath` namespaces should work exactly the same as XPath statements in the MSXML Parser, and both should work exactly the same as other parsers that implement the W3C XPath recommendation.

An Analogy to a File Path

Computers are built around files and the organization of those files. To access files, you need to be able to navigate to different portions of the file system. One way to navigate a file system is to use the Uniform Naming Convention (UNC) for specifying the location of resources on a local-area network (LAN). UNC separates folders and files using a backslash (\) character. In the good ol' DOS days before point-and-click, file systems were navigated using command-line syntax. Go to the Start button on your computer; choose Run, and type **cmd** in the text box to bring up a DOS command shell window. You will see the following text:

```
Microsoft Windows 2000 [Version 5.00.2195]
(C) Copyright 1985-2000 Microsoft Corp.
C:\>
```

At the command prompt, change directories from the C: root all the way to the Program Files\Microsoft Visual studio directory.

```
C:\>cd Program Files\Microsoft Visual Studio
```

To change directories, you specified a path for the file system to navigate. More to the point, you specified a series of location steps used to navigate to a new folder based on the current folder. XPath uses a very similar syntax. Imagine your file system as an XML document.

```
<?xml version="1.0" encoding="utf-8" ?>
<C>
    <INETPUB>
        <WWWROOT>
            <ASPNET_CLIENT/>
        </WWWROOT>
    </INETPUB>
<C>
```

We could easily represent this as an XPath statement:

```
C/INETPUB/WWWROOT/ASPNET_CLIENT
```

If we are currently positioned at the very beginning of the document there are four location steps made. But what if we were currently positioned on the WWWROOT element and wanted to reposition to the ASPNET_CLIENT element? We would specify the following XPath statement:

```
./ASPNET_CLIENT
```

The period (.) at the beginning of the XPath statement represents the expression "the context node", meaning the node that we originally started from. Instead of specifying that we are navigating based on the context node, we can also use a short form of XPath that specifies a path relative to the context node:

```
ASPNET_CLIENT
```

A location path is composed of 3 parts: the axis, the node-test, and zero or more predicates.

XPath Axis

The axis component of an XPath query determines the direction of the node selection in relation to the context node. An axis can be thought of as a directional query. The axes listed in Table 3.3 are provided in XPath.

Table 3.3 **XPath Axes**

Axis	Description
ancestor	The context node's parent, the parent's parent, and so on.
ancestor-or-self	The context node as well as its ancestors.
attribute	The attributes of the context node.
child	All children of the context element (attributes cannot have children).
descendant	All descendants of the context: children, children's children, and so on.
descendant-or-self	All descendants as well as the context node.
following	All nodes in the same document as the context node that are after the context node. This does not include descendants, attribute nodes, or namespace nodes.
following-sibling	All the following siblings of the context node. A sibling is an element occurring at the same level in the tree.
namespace	The namespace nodes of the context node.
parent	The parent of the context node.

Table 3.3 **Continued**

Axis	Description
preceding	All nodes in the same document as the context node that are immediately before the context node.
preceding-sibling	Contains the preceding siblings. If the context node is either an attribute or a name-space node, the preceding-sibling axis is empty

The examples so far have used forward axes: that is, we have only navigated to nodes that are descendants of the context node. Let's look at some examples of XPath statements using reverse axes, or axes that navigate up the document hierarchy. Consider the following representation of a file system, with drives A, C, and D, and D has a backup copy of the contents of the C drive. The context node is highlighted. This document is represented in listing 3.8. Note that the line numbers are represented only for explanation and are not actually part of the XML document.

Listing 3.8 **An XML Representation of a File System**

```
1   <?xml version="1.0" encoding="utf-8" ?>
2   <FILESYSTEM>
3       <DRIVE LETTER="A" />
4       <DRIVE LETTER="C">
5         <FOLDER NAME="INETPUB">
6             <FOLDER NAME="WWWROOT">
7                 <FOLDER NAME="ASPNET_CLIENT" />
8             </FOLDER>
9         </FOLDER>
10        <FOLDER NAME="Program Files">
11            <FOLDER NAME="Microsoft Visual Studio .NET">
12                <FOLDER NAME="Framework SDK">
13                <FOLDER NAME="BIN"></FOLDER>
14                </FOLDER>
15            </FOLDER>
16        </FOLDER>
17      </DRIVE>
18      <DRIVE LETTER="D">
19        <FOLDER NAME="INETPUB">
20            <FOLDER NAME="WWWROOT">
21                <FOLDER NAME="ASPNET_CLIENT" />
22            </FOLDER>
23        </FOLDER>
24        <FOLDER NAME="Program Files">
25            <FOLDER NAME="Microsoft Visual Studio .NET"/>
26        </FOLDER>
27      </DRIVE>
28  </FILESYSTEM>
```

Working with the preceding XML structure, we introduce the following XPath statement:

```
parent::*
```

This XPath query translates to "retrieve all parent nodes of the context node", which would return the element FOLDER on line 10.

```
ancestor-or-self::*
```

This query would return a more complex structure, which is depicted in listing 3.9. The returned nodes are highlighted.

Listing 3.9 **An XML Representation of a File System**

```xml
<?xml version="1.0" encoding="utf-8" ?>
<FILESYSTEM>
    <DRIVE LETTER="A"/>
    <DRIVE LETTER="C">
        <FOLDER NAME="INETPUB">
            <FOLDER NAME="WWWROOT">
                <FOLDER NAME="ASPNET_CLIENT" />
            </FOLDER>
        </FOLDER>
        <FOLDER NAME="Program Files">
            <FOLDER NAME="Microsoft Visual Studio .NET">
                <FOLDER NAME="Framework SDK">
                    <FOLDER NAME="BIN"></FOLDER>
                </FOLDER>
            </FOLDER>
        </FOLDER>
            </DRIVE>
    <DRIVE LETTER="D">
        <FOLDER NAME="INETPUB">
            <FOLDER NAME="WWWROOT">
                    <FOLDER NAME="ASPNET_CLIENT" />
                </FOLDER>
                <FILE NAME="test.xml" size="10 Kb"/>
            </FOLDER>
            <FOLDER NAME="Program Files">
                <FOLDER NAME="Microsoft Visual Studio .NET"/>
            </FOLDER>
    </DRIVE>
</FILESYSTEM>
```

As you can see in listing 3.8, a path is depicted from the context node directly to the root node, hence the name "XPath".

Our examples of axes used an axis with an accompanying asterisk. The asterisk is considered a wildcard that translates to "all nodes within the specified path". There are several special characters in XPath syntax, listed in Table 3.4.

Table 3.4 **XPath Special Characters**

Axis	Description
/	When used at the beginning of an expression, selection begins at the root node. When used within an expression, it acts as a path separator.
//	Performs a recursive search for the matching pattern throughout the entire document.
.	The context node.
*	Wildcard operator.
@	Prefix for an attribute name.
@*	Wildcard match for attributes.
:	Namespace separator.
( )	Grouping operator, for establishing logical precedence within statements.
[ ]	Predicate container (also referred to as a filter pattern container). See the following section, "Predicates" for more information on predicates. Also used in abbreviated notation as a subscript operator.
+	Addition operator.
-	Subtraction operator.
div	Floating-point division operator.
*	Multiplication operator.
mod	Modulus operator.
=	Equality.
!=	Inequality.
<	Less than. XSLT documents typically contain the < entity reference, but this is evaluated in the XSLT parser as <.
>	Greater than. XSLT documents typically contain the > entity reference, but this is evaluated in the XSLT parser as >.
<=	Less-than or equal to.
=>	Greater-than or equal to.
and	Logical and.
or	Logical or.
not()	Boolean not.

Location paths can be relative or absolute. Relative location paths consist of one or more location paths separated by backslashes. Absolute location paths consist of a backslash optionally followed by a relative location path. In other words, relative location paths navigate relative to the context node. Absolute paths specify the *absolute position* within the document. An absolute location path would then be:

```
/FILESYSTEM/DRIVE[@LETTER='C']/FOLDER[@NAME='Program Files']
```

Using an absolute location path, the current context node is ignored when evaluating the XPath query, except for the fact that the path being searched exists in the same document.

XPath Node Test

The XPath node test does just what its name implies: it tests nodes to determine if they meet a condition. We already used one test, the asterisk character, which specified all nodes should be returned. We can limit the nodes that are returned by specifying names. Using the document in listing 1 again, we want to retrieve all ancestor elements that are named DRIVE.

```
ancestor::DRIVE
```

By specifying the node name in the node test component of the XPath statement, we limit the results so that only a single node is returned, the DRIVE element on line 4.

Besides using names for node-tests, we can also use node types. In Table 3.4, we saw that one of the axes is an attribute axis, which retrieves an attribute based on the specified node test. Again, using the document in Listing 3.8, the following node test would return the attribute NAME for the context node (highlighted in Listing 3.8):

```
attribute::NAME
```

If we wanted to select all attributes for the context node, we could also issue a wildcard node test:

```
attribute::*
```

So, the type of node returned depends partially on the axes specified. Attributes are not children of elements, so using the following XPath statement would not return any nodes:

```
child::NAME
```

This is because there is no child element of the context node that is named NAME. We can also use XPath functions as node tests to return certain nodes. The available node tests are listed in Table 3.5.

Table 3.5   **Available XPath Function Node Tests**

Axis	Description
comment()	Returns True if the matched node is a comment node.
node()	Returns True for any matched node, or False if no match was found.
processing-instruction()	Returns True if the matched node is a processing-instruction.
text()	Returns True if the matched node is a text node.

Considering the analogy of an XPath statement to a SQL statement, we have looked at the equivalent in XPath to a SQL SELECT statement. Now, let's look at the equivalent to a SQL WHERE clause in XPath: the predicate.

XPath Predicates

Predicates filter the resulting node sets of an XPath query with respect to an axis, producing a new node set. A predicate is the logical equivalent of a WHERE clause in SQL: it filters the selection based on certain criteria. A predicate can be evaluated as a Boolean or a number. When evaluated as a number, nodes matching the positional number are returned, where the index of nodes is 1-based. Listing 3.10 shows the same document as in Listing 3.8, but highlights a new context node on line 18.

Listing 3.10   **An XML representation of a file system**

```
1   <?xml version="1.0" encoding="utf-8" ?>
2   <FILESYSTEM>
3       <DRIVE LETTER="A"/>
4       <DRIVE LETTER="C">
5         <FOLDER NAME="INETPUB">
6             <FOLDER NAME="WWWROOT">
7                 <FOLDER NAME="ASPNET_CLIENT" />
8             </FOLDER>
9         </FOLDER>
10        <FOLDER NAME="Program Files">
11            <FOLDER NAME="Microsoft Visual Studio .NET">
12                <FOLDER NAME="Framework SDK">
13                    <FOLDER NAME="BIN"></FOLDER>
14                </FOLDER>
15            </FOLDER>
16        </FOLDER>
17    </DRIVE>
18    <DRIVE LETTER="D">
19        <FOLDER NAME="INETPUB" READONLY="TRUE">
20            <FOLDER NAME="WWWROOT">
```

```
21    <FOLDER NAME="ASPNET_CLIENT" />
22            </FOLDER>
23            <FILE NAME="test.xml" size="10 Kb"/>
24        </FOLDER>
25        <FOLDER NAME="Program Files">
26            <FOLDER NAME="Microsoft Visual Studio .NET"/>
27        </FOLDER>
28    </DRIVE>
29 </FILESYSTEM>
```

We can use predicates to filter results based on an expression, and the expressions allowed range from simple comparisons to complex expressions. We will begin by using simple filters and comparisons, and work up to more complex node-set functions.

Filters

Filters are a means of filtering a node set based on a condition. Filters and predicates are synonymous, except that filters provide an abbreviated syntax for node-tests. For instance, we may wish to filter based on the existence of a node within a query. An example of this is to filter based on the existence of an attribute. To do this, we simply provide the filter for the attribute:

```
child::FOLDER[@READONLY]
```

This statement retrieves only the FOLDER elements that are children of the context node (depicted on line 18) that contain an attribute named READONLY. This statement would return the FOLDER element on line 19. Similarly, we could retrieve only those children that have a specified child element:

```
child::*[FILE]
```

This statement returns only the FOLDER element on line 19: It is the only child of the context node that itself contains a child element called FILE.

Comparisons

Besides testing for the existence of nodes, we can also test the values of nodes. This statement retrieves a child element named FOLDER that contains an attribute named NAME with a value of INETPUB.

```
child::FOLDER[@NAME="INETPUB"]
```

The node returned from this statement would be the FOLDER element on line 19. Besides testing equality, we can also check for inequality:

```
child::FOLDER[@NAME != "INETPUB"]
```

This statement returns the child elements named FOLDER that do not have an attribute named NAME with a value of INETPUB.

We can also use the less-than and greater-than operators to evaluate numeric expressions. This statement queries using an absolute path from the root node to retrieve the list of drives that have no folders created in them:

```
/FILESYSTEM/DRIVE[count(FOLDER) = 0]
```

The less-than and greater-than operators are implemented for numeric use: for text comparisons, you should revert to the string XPath functions such as `con-tains()` or `substring()`.

As mentioned previously, predicates can be evaluated as a number or as a Boolean. Let's take a look at how we can use the relative position of a node within a predicate.

position()

The `position()` function returns the relative position (also referred to as an index) of the node within its parent. We can use the position function to simply retrieve a node by its ordinal position, or we can use it as a comparison.

Using the `position()` function in the XPath statement's predicate, we can return the FOLDER element on line 19 using the following XPath:

```
child::*[position() = 1]
```

The statement translates to "select all the children of the context node where the indexed position is 1". This statement simply retrieves the first child node of the context node. We can also use an abbreviated syntax to specify the same result:

```
child[1]
```

Besides using numeric position related to the context node, we can also use compound predicates to express complex Boolean results. The modulus operator is a common mechanism to test a value to see if it is even or odd. We can retrieve the even numbered child elements of the context node:

```
child::*[position() mod 2 = 0]
```

If we wanted to return only the last node, we can use the XPath function `last()` to test if the position of a node is the same as the position of the last node, returning the last node:

```
child::*[position()=last()]
```

Besides complex predicates, we can also specify complex location steps using axes, node tests, and predicates. If we wanted to find out all the drives on the current machine using the document in Listing 3.10, we could issue the following:

```
parent::FILESYSTEM/child::DRIVE
```

count()

Another common function used in predicates is the `count()` function. This function returns the count of nodes in the specified node-set.

```
FOLDER[count(child::*)=1]
```

This expression returns all `FOLDER`s that are children of the context node that have only one child element. We can use any of the axes to generate the node set used as the parameter to the `count()` function. For instance, we can retrieve the list of child `FOLDER` elements that are not the first child of the context node:

```
FOLDER[count(preceding-sibling::*)> 0]
```

Of course, there are many ways to approach the same statement: We have already seen the `position()` function can handle the equivalent statement:

```
FOLDER[position() != 1]
```

Abbreviated Location Path Syntax

Because XPath statements can become quite verbose, there also exists an abbreviated version of XPath statements. Using abbreviated syntax, the preceding XPath query is equivalent to:

```
parent::FILESYSTEM/DRIVE
```

Another abbreviation uses the backslash character to notate the root node of the document containing the context node. We saw this previously explained as an absolute location path. As an example, this XPath statement returns the `FOLDER` element on line 19.

```
/FILESYSTEM/DRIVE[@LETTER='D']/FOLDER[@NAME='INETPUB']
```

Using two backslashes successively indicates that the entire document should be searched recursively. This is a common misconception for developers used to UNC notation for working with directory paths. While useful in certain situations where an element pattern may occur anywhere in the current document, it is rarely used in this context.

```
//FOLDER[@NAME="INETPUB"]/FOLDER[@NAME="WWWROOT"]/FOLDER
```

This notation, while seemingly simple, becomes very complex when dissected. We begin by searching the entire document for an element called `FOLDER` with a child named `FOLDER` and a grandchild named `FOLDER`. We further limit the location paths by specifying the valued of the `NAME` attribute for each `FOLDER` element. Finally, we return all matching grandchild `FOLDER` elements. This example would return the `FOLDER` elements on lines 7 and 21. Note that this is not the same as the query `parent::FILESYSTEM/DRIVE`, where we limit the search to a specified path and not the entire document.

Attributes and Predicates

We have seen examples of using attributes as predicates, but have not formally addressed attributes. Attributes can be retrieved using the attribute axis or by using the abbreviated syntax, an at(@) symbol. Referring to listing 3.10 again, where the context node is represented on line 18, we can retrieve all attributes where the name of the attribute is LETTER:

```
attribute::*[name()='LETTER']
```

This syntax can be abbreviated to specify searching only the LETTER attribute and no other attributes:

```
attribute::LETTER
```

This syntax can be abbreviated further using the at symbol:

```
@LETTER
```

XPath Functions

We have mentioned Boolean expressions in the context of predicates, but let's take a look how we can leverage Boolean expressions in predicates. There are 29 different XPath functions relating to strings, numbers, node-sets, and Booleans. We will not list all 29 functions here: rather, you are encouraged to visit the W3C recommendation documentation at `http://www.w3.org/TR/xpath`.

We have already looked at two of the functions, `position()` and `count()`. Without listing all 29 XPath functions here, we will focus on the Boolean function `not()`. The `not()` function returns True if the argument is false, False if the argument is true. Let's take a look at what this really means by looking at an example. Here, we will select ourselves only if we contain an attribute named LETTER.

```
self::*[@LETTER]
```

What if we wanted to select ourselves only if we *did not* contain an attribute named LETTER? One way is to use the XPath function `not()`.

```
self::*[not(@LETTER)]
```

This statement can be misleading, so let's think about what is really being queried. It would be easy to misinterpret this statement as "return the context node's children that are not an attribute named LETTER." Recall from Table 3.3 that the self-axis returns the context node. So, we actually return the DRIVE element if the predicate matches. The `not()` function tests to see if a LETTER attribute is present. If the LETTER attribute is present, the node-test returns false, and the context node is not selected.

XPath functions cannot be used as statements themselves. For instance, the following XPath statement is not legal:

```
not(@LETTER)
```

This is because the statement must evaluate as a node-set. In other words, we omitted two parts of the location step: the axis and the node test, we skipped right to the predicate.

Logical *and*, Logical *or*

Hand-in had with the `not()` function are the logical and and logical or operators. The best way to explain logical expressions is to see examples of them.

This example returns the child FOLDER elements that contain both a FOLDER and a FILE element:

```
FOLDER[FOLDER and FILE]
```

This example selects from the root node all drives that have a drive letter of A or C:

```
/FILESYSTEM/DRIVE[@LETTER='A' or @LETTER='C']
```

Unions

We have implicitly worked with and mentioned node sets throughout this section. Working with sets implies the capability of unions to join sets of data. XPath supports the concept of unions using the pipe (|) character.

```
/FILESYSTEM/DRIVE[@LETTER='A']  |  /FILESYSTEM/DRIVE[@LETTER='D']
```

This example retrieves the union of DRIVE elements having either a drive letter A or D. Unions are very useful in XPath, and are used in many advanced XSLT operations involving keys. XSLT and keys are explained later in the section "XSLT" as well as in Appendix C.

The *stylesheet* Element

Because each XSLT document is an XML document, XSLT follows the same well-formedness rules as any other XML document. That means requiring one and only one root element. The root element for an XSLT stylesheet is the `<xsl:stylesheet>` element. This element declares the namespaces used for the document and the namespace used for the XSLT processor.

Namespaces

Namespaces are discussed in Chapters 1 and 2. This is a critical point to grasp prior to using XSLT beause the concept of namespaces is embedded throughout XSLT.

During the early working draft of XSL, Microsoft developed many products that used a technology similar to XSL. Because XSL was still a working draft and was not yet formally called XSL, Microsoft used this term to denote its implementation. This early implementation can be found in earlier versions of products such as Internet Explorer and BizTalk. The namespace associated with these early versions is the following:

```
http://www.w3.org/TR/WD-xsl
```

MSXML 4.0, which is the parser version that comes with IE 6, does not support this namespace. Instead, you can convert stylesheets by using this namespace to the W3C recommendation syntax using the XSL to XSLT Converter 1.1, which is available from Microsoft at `http://msdn.microsoft.com/downloads/sample.asp?url=/MSDN-FILES/027/000/540/msdncompositedoc.xml&frame=true`.

The correct XSLT namespace to use is `www.w3.org/1999/XSL/Transform`.

This is the namespace that's used in Visual Studio .NET and the MSXML 4.0 parser.

Using the XSL Namespace

Each XSLT stylesheet begins with the stylesheet declaration. XSLT stylesheets are also XML documents, so the `stylesheet` element is the root node of the XML document:

```
<?xml version="1.0" encoding="UTF-8" ?>
<xsl:stylesheet version="1.0"
xmlns:xsl="http://www.w3.org/1999/XSL/Transform">
.
.
.
</xsl:stylesheet>
```

> **Note**
> The `xsl:transform` element is an allowable synonym for the `xsl:stylesheet` element, but the `xsl:transform` root element is not commonly used. See Appendix C for more information on the `xsl:stylesheet` and `xsl:transform` elements.

The XSL namespace is now referenced by using the qualified element prefix `xsl`.

You might want to use other namespaces in your document. For example, you might use the XHTML namespace to create XHTML output.

XHTML is a W3C Recommendation that imposes XML well-formedness rules on HTML documents. For example, the following code is perfectly legal in HTML:

```
<p>This is some text<br>
```

With XHTML, this would not be valid because each element must have a corresponding ending element and be properly nested. The following would be required to meet XHTML's well-formedness restriction:

```
<p>This is some text<br/></p>
```

XHTML uses a specific namespace for validation, which is highlighted in this code snippet:

```
<?xml version="1.0" encoding="UTF-8" ?>
<xsl:stylesheet version="1.0"
xmlns:xsl="http://www.w3.org/1999/XSL/Transform"
xmlns:xhtml="http://www.w3.org/TR/xhtml1/strict">
.
.
.
</xsl:stylesheet>
```

You can now refer to each XHTML element using the xhtml element prefix to qualify the namespace for the element. This can lead to less-readable documents, however, so you might want to use the default namespace for the output document, as shown here:

```
<?xml version="1.0" encoding="UTF-8" ?>
<xsl:stylesheet version="1.0"
xmlns:xsl="http://www.w3.org/1999/XSL/Transform"
xmlns="http://www.w3.org/TR/xhtml1/strict">
.
.
.
</xsl:stylesheet>
```

Notice the omission of the xhtml namespace prefix. The omission of the xhtml namespace prefix associates the XHTML namespace with the default namespace. In other words, unless otherwise specified, anything in the result tree will be an XHTML element.

XSLT provides control over a multitude of different settings used for transformations. For example, you can transform XML into a variety of mediums—text, HTML, or other XML documents. You can specify this by using the <xsl:output> element as a child of the <xsl:stylesheet> element, as shown here:

```
<?xml version="1.0" encoding="UTF-8" ?>
<xsl:stylesheet version="1.0"
xmlns:xsl="http://www.w3.org/1999/XSL/Transform"
xmlns="http://www.w3.org/TR/xhtml1/strict">
```

```
<xsl:output method="html"/>
   .
   .
   .
</xsl:stylesheet>
```

Other facets that you might want to control can include what namespaces are excluded from the result document, what version of a particular namespace is used, what elements, if any, are excluded from the result tree, or even how whitespace is handled. Appendix C, "XSLT Reference," lists the different XSLT elements and provides usage for each of the elements in the form of a short example. Rather than list the different control elements here, we suggest that you browse Appendix C and look through the element listings.

Understanding Template Processing

A key concept to understand when working with XSLT is the concept of *template processing*. XSLT uses a pull method to process XML documents. The pull and push methodologies are covered in Chapter 5. Instead of the procedural approach to programming, where each function calls another function, XSLT responds to events as they occur. More appropriately, XSLT templates are actually a set of node-tests that are called when the node test applies. XSLT stylesheets usually start with a match for the root element:

```
<?xml version="1.0" encoding="UTF-8" ?>
<xsl:stylesheet version="1.0"
xmlns:xsl="http://www.w3.org/1999/XSL/Transform">
    <xsl:template match="/">
   .
   .
   .

    </xsl:template>
</xsl:stylesheet>
```

Inside this template rule, you are now pointing to the root node. In other words, you now have *context* for the root node.

As previously mentioned, XSLT is not concerned with generating text, but instead generating a result tree. As you process the source document, you output the results. Specifically, you add nodes to the result tree. Those nodes can be HTML nodes associated with the XHTML namespace. They might be structured vector graphics XML elements. The nodes can be XSL-FO elements, text, MathML elements, or a host of other outputs. The result tree might also be a combination of any of these. The point, however, is that XSLT generates result trees, not text.

Let's reuse the following `pitchers.xml` document:

```
<?xml version="1.0" ?>
<PITCHERS>
    <PITCHER>
        <FNAME>John</FNAME>
        <LNAME>Rocker</LNAME>
        <TEAM>Indians</TEAM>
        <CITY>Cleveland</CITY>
        <ERA></ERA>
    </PITCHER>
    <PITCHER>
        <FNAME>Tom</FNAME>
        <LNAME>Glavine</LNAME>
        <TEAM>Braves</TEAM>
        <CITY>Atlanta</CITY>
        <ERA></ERA>
    </PITCHER>
    <PITCHER>
        <FNAME>Greg</FNAME>
        <LNAME>Maddux</LNAME>
        <TEAM>Braves</TEAM>
        <CITY>Atlanta</CITY>
        <ERA></ERA>
    </PITCHER>
    <PITCHER>
        <FNAME>Randy</FNAME>
        <LNAME>Johnson</LNAME>
        <TEAM>Diamondbacks</TEAM>
        <CITY>Arizona</CITY>
        <ERA></ERA>
    </PITCHER>
</PITCHERS>
```

How would you logically use node-tests to work with a hierarchical document? Start by testing the root node, as you did earlier, to gain context to the document. Then set up a series of tests for the nodes in the XML document. Begin by setting up a test for the PITCHER element, as follows:

```
<?xml version="1.0" encoding="UTF-8" ?>
<xsl:stylesheet version="1.0"
xmlns:xsl="http://www.w3.org/1999/XSL/Transform">
    <xsl:template match="/">
    .
    .
    .

    </xsl:template>
    <xsl:template match="PITCHER">

    </xsl:template>
</xsl:stylesheet>
```

When this template is fired, you will have a pointer to the `<PITCHER>` element, and will have access to its related nodes through the use of XPath. Because you now have a context node of a PITCHER element, you can access the values of its children, as shown here:

```
<?xml version="1.0" encoding="UTF-8" ?>
<xsl:stylesheet version="1.0"
xmlns:xsl="http://www.w3.org/1999/XSL/Transform">
    <xsl:template match="/">
        <TABLE>
            <xsl:apply-templates/>
        </TABLE>
    </xsl:template>
    <xsl:template match="PITCHER">
        <tr>
            <td><xsl:value-of select="FNAME"/></td>
            <td><xsl:value-of select="LNAME"/></td>
            <td><xsl:value-of select="TEAM"/></td>
            <td><xsl:value-of select="CITY"/></td>
        </tr>
    </xsl:template>
</xsl:stylesheet>
```

In this example, notice the highlighted elements. Because the context node in this template rule is a PITCHER element, you can simply navigate to its child nodes without navigating from the root node.

Recursion in XSLT

Recursion is typically used with hierarchical structures and trees, so it's no wonder that XSLT makes heavy use of recursion. Recursion is the capability of a function to call itself to perform a task. The following stylesheet uses two recursive calls:

```
<?xml version="1.0" encoding="UTF-8" ?>
<xsl:stylesheet version="1.0"
xmlns:xsl="http://www.w3.org/1999/XSL/Transform">
    <xsl:template match="/">
        <TABLE>
            <xsl:apply-templates/>
        </TABLE>
    </xsl:template>

    <xsl:template match="PITCHER">
        <tr>
            <xsl:apply-templates/>
        </tr>
    </xsl:template>

    <xsl:template match="FNAME">
        <td><b><xsl:value-of select="."/></b></td>
    </xsl:template>
```

```
<xsl:template match="LNAME">
    <td><xsl:value-of select="."/></td>
</xsl:template>

<xsl:template match="TEAM">
    <td><i><xsl:value-of select="."/></i></td>
</xsl:template>

<xsl:template match="CITY">
    <td><xsl:value-of select="."/>, </td>
</xsl:template>

</xsl:stylesheet>
```

The first call is found in the template that processes the root node. After the root node is found, a TABLE element is created. A call to `<xsl:apply-templates>` is then made with no select statement. The effect of this call is that the XSLT processor then begins processing with the next node in the document, traveling the descendant axes if possible and then recursing through its parent and any descendant axes to process each node in the tree. The next node in the document is the PITCHER node because it is a child element of the context element. The PITCHER node now becomes the context element and the second template matching the PITCHER element is fired. A table row tag is emitted, and again the processor is instructed to process child nodes. This recursion allows each node in the tree to be processed, while allowing the developer to easily separate node tests for each node type.

Here's a more complex recursive example. Suppose that you are processing an XML file that contains carriage returns. You'd like to replace each instance of the carriage return with an HTML <br> tag. The input HTML looks like this:

```
<?xml version="1.0" encoding="utf-8" ?>
<DATA>
    <test>
    this,is,a,test
    this,is,another,test
    this,is,yet another,test
    hello,world,from,xslt
    </test>
    <test>
    this is
    a set of sentences
    that you want
    to preserve
    formatting on
    </test>
</DATA>
```

One way to preserve formatting in HTML is to simply use the <pre> tag, indicating that the data contained within the tag is pre-formatted. There are many situations, however, where using the <pre> tag does not suffice for formatted output and a pure HTML solution is desired. Let's look at an example of how to use recursion with string parsing to manipulate text nodes. Our example will replace each carriage-return contained in an XML document with an HTML <br> tag.

To replace each carriage-return with a line-feed, you must set up a template to match the root node. This template tells the processor to begin recursing. Because there is no select attribute for the <xsl:apply-templates> element, processing will continue recursively.

```
<?xml version="1.0" encoding="UTF-8" ?>
<xsl:stylesheet version="1.0"
xmlns:xsl="http://www.w3.org/1999/XSL/Transform">
    <xsl:template match="/">
        <xsl:apply-templates />
    </xsl:template>
```

Then declare a template rule to match the named document element. This template tells the processor to continue recursing remaining through the nodes as well:

```
<xsl:template match="DATA">
    <xsl:apply-templates />
</xsl:template>
```

The next node in the document to match is the <test> element. You can declare a template rule to handle this element as well. Because this element contains the text that you want to transform, grab the text from the element and pass it to a named template function:

```
<xsl:template match="test">
    <xsl:call-template name="replacecrwithbr">
        <xsl:with-param name="data" select="." />
    </xsl:call-template>
</xsl:template>
```

The purpose of the named template function is to grab all data up to the first carriage-return, add it to the result tree, add a <br> element to the result tree, and call itself recursively until all the text is processed. This template rule is difficult at first, but it makes a lot of sense once you break it apart. We pass in a parameter, data. We then assign a variable, this, that contains all the nodes up until the first carriage-return. We then assign all nodes from the parameter following the first carriage-return to a variable called rest.

```
<xsl:param name="data" />
<xsl:variable name="this"
        select="substring-before($data,'&#10;')" />
<xsl:variable name="rest"
        select="substring-after($data,'&#10;')" />
```

Now, we have all the nodes before the first carriage-return and all the nodes following the first carriage-return. Our next step is to test if either variable holds data, which is performed using an <xsl:if> test. We first test the this variable to see if there is any text before the first carriage-return. If there is any text, we output it and append an HTML <br /> tag to the output.

```
<xsl:if test="$this">
    <xsl:value-of select="$this" />
    <br />
</xsl:if>
```

The next step is to test if any data follows the first carriage-return. Again, we use an <xsl:if> test to determine this condition. If any data follows the first carriage-return, we recurse back into our template rule, passing the rest of the data following the first carriage-return:

```
<xsl:if test="$rest">
    <xsl:call-template name="replacecrwithbr">
        <xsl:with-param name="data" select="$rest" />
    </xsl:call-template>
</xsl:if>
```

When the template rule recurses back into itself, the operation is repeated until there is no more data following a carriage-return. The entire template rule appears as follows:

```
<xsl:template name="replacecrwithbr">
    <xsl:param name="data" />
    <xsl:variable name="this"
        select="substring-before($data,'&#10;')" />
    <xsl:variable name="rest"
        select="substring-after($data,'&#10;')" />
    <xsl:if test="$this">
        <xsl:value-of select="$this" />
        <br />
    </xsl:if>
    <xsl:if test="$rest">
        <xsl:call-template name="replacecrwithbr">
            <xsl:with-param name="data" select="$rest" />
        </xsl:call-template>
    </xsl:if>
</xsl:template>
</xsl:stylesheet>
```

Using this method, you can begin to envisage very powerful transformations. For instance, you can use this method to process comma-separated value files or fixed-length field files, simply by modifying the replacecrwithbr template rule. This is a common design pattern in XSLT that can be manipulated for a variety of tasks.

Another useful transformation pattern is the *identity transformation*. This transformation matches all attributes and a node of any type, copies it, and begins processing again with the next attribute or node:

```
<xsl:template match="@* | node()">
  <xsl:copy>
    <xsl:apply-templates select="@* | node()" />
  </xsl:copy>
</xsl:template>
```

We have looked at recursion and the identity transformation, two common (yet unintuitive) design patterns in XSLT.

A very common task in XSLT is to select a distinct set of nodes. There is no built-in mechanism in XSLT to do this. There is no distinct() function or xsl:distinct element, so we must construct a set of template rules to approach this. Because the approach includes the use of keys, we will first look at keys in XSLT.

Keys in XSLT

XSLT provides the xsl:key element to declare a named key for easier access to complex XML documents. Keys are a directory of specific nodes from a source document, identified by a friendly name. Keys must be declared as a top-level element and cannot be declared within templates.

Conceptually, keys are difficult to grasp at first. Suppose that you wanted to refer often to a list of elements within an XML document. Instead of re-querying the document each time for the nodes, you can build a list of elements and associate them with a friendly name. This is done using the <xsl:key> element.

The <xsl:key> element has 3 attributes:

- **name**—A friendly name to identify the key.
- **match**—The pattern to be matched within the document. The pattern is matched on a node-by-node basis, so global match patterns are not used. These are the nodes that we want to group.
- **use**—Provides the values of the key: The expression is matched once for each node satisfying the match pattern. This is the key's value for each matched node.

The concept of the match and use attributes seems like it is the same thing, but they are not. Think of a key as a Dictionary object, where a dictionary has a name, and the objects within the dictionary are associated name/value pairs.

One way that keys are useful is to retrieve a list of nodes that match a criteria. For instance, recall back to our PITCHERS.XML document in listing 3.4. We can define a key in an XSLT stylesheet that will return all of the pitchers on the Atlanta Braves roster:

```
<xsl:stylesheet version="1.0"
xmlns:xsl="http://www.w3.org/1999/XSL/Transform">
<xsl:output method="html"/>
<xsl:key name="Pitchers" match="PITCHER" use="TEAM"/>

<xsl:template match="/">
    <html>
        <body>
            <xsl:for-each select="key('Pitchers','Braves')">
                <xsl:value-of select="LNAME"/>
                <br/>
            </xsl:for-each>
        </body>
    </html>
</xsl:template>
</xsl:stylesheet>
```

The output for this stylesheet is as follows:

```
<html>
<body>Glavine<br>Maddux<br></body>
</html>
```

Besides matching specific values, we can also use a key to generate a list of all pitchers.

```
<xsl:stylesheet version="1.0"
xmlns:xsl="http://www.w3.org/1999/XSL/Transform">
<xsl:output method="html"/>
<xsl:key name="Pitchers" match="TEAM" use="."/>

<xsl:template match="/">
    <html>
        <body>
            <xsl:apply-templates/>
        </body>
    </html>
</xsl:template>

<xsl:template match="PITCHER">
    <xsl:for-each select="key('Pitchers',TEAM)">
        <xsl:value-of select="."/>

        <br/>
    </xsl:for-each>
</xsl:template>
</xsl:stylesheet>
```

The call to the key function indicates that the stylesheet is to retrieve nodes from the Pitchers key, passing in the child TEAM element of the context node. The TEAM element matches the pattern defined in the match attribute (defined in the <xsl:key> element), so the text node for the key is returned. This stylesheet produces the following output (formatted for readability):

```
<html>
<body>
Indians<br>
Braves<br>
Braves<br>
Braves<br>
Braves<br>
Diamondbacks<br>
</body>
</html>
```

Notice that we retrieved all teams defined in the XML document, and team names repeated. If we wanted to instead retrieve just the distinct teams, how would we accomplish this? It turns out that there are several ways to do this. We could use a template rule that uses the preceding-sibling axis to determine if the current node matches any of the nodes on the same level.

```
TEAM[not(. = preceding-sibling::TEAM)]
```

However, this type of search involves searching the preceding-sibling axis each time a TEAM node is encountered. The preceding-sibling axis can be quite expensive in terms of processing for a document of significant size once we approach the end of the document. Steve Muench, Oracle's lead XML Technical Evangelist and development lead for Oracle XSQL Pages, developed an efficient method of grouping using keys to retrieve unique items. This method is called the "Muenchian Method".

The Muenchian Method uses an XPath union, described earlier in the section on XPath. It checks to see if the union of the current node and the first node-match in the key is one node or two nodes. Node sets cannot contain repeated nodes: If the call to the count function returns 1, then the node is distinct and is returned from the XPath expression.

Here is the basic syntax:

```
<xsl:stylesheet version="1.0"
xmlns:xsl="http://www.w3.org/1999/XSL/Transform">
<xsl:output method="html"/>
<xsl:key name="distinct" match="TEAM" use="."/>

<xsl:template match="PITCHERS">
    <html><body><xsl:apply-templates/></body></html>
</xsl:template>
```

```
<xsl:template match="PITCHER">
    <xsl:for-each select="./TEAM[count(.|key('distinct',.)[1]) = 1]">
        <xsl:value-of select="."/>
        <br/>
    </xsl:for-each>
</xsl:template>
</xsl:stylesheet>
```

Remember that the (.) special character in XPath refers to the context node. So, the key matches a TEAM element and has the value of the child text node of the TEAM element. The XPath expression in the for-each loop matches the distinct child text nodes of TEAM elements. The output is as follows:

```
<html><body>Indians<br>Braves<br>Diamondbacks<br></body></html>
```

A number of common design patterns are available for using XSLT, including variations on both the identity transformation for copying nodes and using the Muenchian method for multiple levels. For more information on XSLT, visit the XSL-List mailing list archive at www.mulberrytech.com/xsl/xsl-list.

For a great description of the Muenchian Method and some of its variations, see http://www.jenitennison.com. Finally, Marrowsoft's Xselerator, available at http://www.topxml.com, has a great wizard for generating distinct groupings using the Muenchian Method.

Combining XSLT and CSS

As previously shown, XSLT is good at parsing documents, and CSS is good at defining styles within HTML documents. When XSLT is combined with CSS to produce HTML, the maintainability of a site is hugely improved. Want to change how a page is laid out? Change the XSLT. Want to change the data in a page? Change the XML. Want to change a specific font or the border for tables? Change the CSS. By abstracting the changes into separate locations, the amount of cut-and-paste coding is reduced, which yields a more efficient website.

To associate a CSS document with an XSLT stylesheet's output, simply reference the stylesheet as a result element, as shown here:

```
<?xml version="1.0" encoding="UTF-8" ?>
<xsl:stylesheet version="1.0"
xmlns:xsl="http://www.w3.org/1999/XSL/Transform"
       xmlns="http://www.w3.org/TR/xhtml1/strict">

    <xsl:template match="/">
        <html>
            <head>
                <link rel="stylesheet" type="text/css"
                ↪href="myfile.css"/>
            </head>
            <body>
```

```
        <xsl:apply-templates />
    </body>
</html>
    </xsl:template>
<xsl:stylesheet>
```

XSLT Extension Functions

While XSLT is powerful, it is a template-based language built on tests to nodes. This can be counter-intuitive to procedural programmers that are used to controlling flow of execution. As we saw in the section on keys, seemingly routine tasks can yield complex template rules. There are some tasks that can be handled in XSLT, but can be handled more efficiently using a procedural language.

Microsoft's implementation of XSLT allows for the creation of extension functions. One method of extending XSLT is through the use of JavaScript, using the `<msxsl:script>` element.

You can develop many functions by using a script extension. For example, numbering in XSLT is not intuitive for procedural programmers. Instead of using the `xsl:number` element, you might choose to implement this by using a script element. Extend the stylesheet from earlier in the chapter and call this new version `ExtendingXSLT.xslt`. Listing 3.10 shows the code for this XSLT file.

Listing 3.10 *ExtendingXSLT.xslt*

```
<?xml version="1.0" encoding="UTF-8" ?>
<xsl:stylesheet version="1.0"
xmlns:xsl="http://www.w3.org/1999/XSL/Transform"
xmlns:msxsl="urn:schemas-microsoft-com:xslt"
xmlns:tns="urn:thisnamespace:tns"
exclude-result-prefixes="tns xsl msxsl">
    <xsl:param name="sortBy" select="'CITY'"/>

    <msxsl:script language="JavaScript" implements-prefix="tns">
        var m_intVal = 0;

        function Iterate()
        {
            m_intVal += 1;
            return(m_intVal);
        }
    </msxsl:script>

    <xsl:template match="/">
        <xsl:apply-templates/>
```

```
    </xsl:template>

    <xsl:template match="PITCHERS">
        <TABLE border="1">
            <tr>
                <th bgcolor="teal">Number</th>
                <th bgcolor="teal">First Name</th>
                <th bgcolor="teal">Last Name</th>
                <th bgcolor="teal">City</th>
                <th bgcolor="teal">Team</th>
                <th bgcolor="teal">ERA</th>
            </tr>

            <xsl:for-each select="PITCHER">
                <xsl:sort select="*[name()=$sortBy]"/>
                <tr>
                    <td><xsl:value-of select="tns:Iterate()"/></td>
                    <td><xsl:value-of select="FNAME"/><br/></td>
                    <td><xsl:value-of select="LNAME"/></td>
                    <td><xsl:value-of select="CITY"/></td>
                    <td><xsl:value-of select="TEAM"/></td>
                    <td><xsl:value-of select="ERA"/></td>
                </tr>

            </xsl:for-each>
        </TABLE>
    </xsl:template>
</xsl:stylesheet>
```

The relevant parts to notice in Listing 3.10 are the additional namespaces
used, the JavaScript function addition, and the call to the Iterate function. Also
the namespace prefixes were omitted by using the `exclude-result-prefixes`
attribute of the `stylesheet` element.

Note

Using the `msxsl:script` element does not output the JavaScript in the result document. Instead,
it is a specially recognized element that the Microsoft XSL parsers recognize for extension functions. The JavaScript in Listing 3.10 is not output with the result tree. Instead, it generates the
result tree.

Call this stylsheet using `Pitchers.xml` as the input XML file. Create a new
`.aspx` page called `ExtendingXSLT.aspx`. Remove all HTML from the `.aspx` page
except the `Page` directive. In the code-behind file, enter the code shown in
Listing 3.11.

Listing 3.11   *ExtendingXSLT.aspx.vb*

```
Public Class ExtendingXSLT
    Inherits System.Web.UI.Page

#Region " Web Form Designer Generated Code "

    'This call is required by the Web Form Designer.
    <System.Diagnostics.DebuggerStepThrough()> Private Sub
    ➥InitializeComponent()

    End Sub

    Private Sub Page_Init(ByVal sender As System.Object, ByVal e As
    ➥System.EventArgs) Handles MyBase.Init
        'CODEGEN: This method call is required by the Web Form Designer
        'Do not modify it using the code editor.
        InitializeComponent()
    End Sub

#End Region

    Private Sub Page_Load(ByVal sender As System.Object, ByVal e As
    ➥System.EventArgs) Handles MyBase.Load

        If Not IsPostBack Then
            Dim xpath As System.Xml.XPath.XPathDocument = New
            ➥System.Xml.XPath.XPathDocument(Server.MapPath("pitchers.xml"))

            Dim xsl As System.Xml.Xsl.XslTransform = New
            ➥System.Xml.Xsl.XslTransform()
            xsl.Load(Server.MapPath("extendingxslt.xslt"))

            Dim args As System.Xml.Xsl.XsltArgumentList
            args = New System.Xml.Xsl.XsltArgumentList()
            args.AddParam("sortBy", "", "FNAME")
            Dim xmlWriter As System.Xml.XmlWriter =
            ➥New System.Xml.XmlTextWriter(Response.Output)

            xsl.Transform(xpath, args, xmlWriter)
            xmlWriter.Close()
        End If


    End Sub

End Class
```

The output of this extension is shown in Figure 3.3.

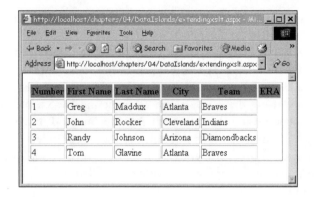

Figure 3.3   Using an extension element to number items.

Because you defined the UI using XSLT, you now have the ability to change where the XSLT transformation occurs. Listing 3.9 used MSXML to perform the transformation in the client. You might, however, decide to perform the transformation on the server to avoid browser compatibility issues, as shown in the following code:

```
private void Page_Load(object sender, System.EventArgs e)
{
    if (!IsPostBack)
    {
        XPathDocument doc = new
XPathDocument(Server.MapPath("pitchers.xml"));

        XslTransform xsl = new XslTransform();
        xsl.Load(Server.MapPath("extendingxslt.xslt"));
        XsltArgumentList args = new XsltArgumentList();
        args.AddParam("sortBy", "", "FNAME");

        XmlWriter writer = new XmlTextWriter(Response.Output);
        xsl.Transform(doc, args, writer);
        writer.Close();
    }
}
```

The server-side code began by loading the XML document, `pitchers.xml`. Then the XSLT stylesheet was loaded, `ExtendingXSLT.xslt`. Because your stylesheet uses a parameter, you can use the `XsltArgumentList` object to create a parameter and add it to the list of arguments. Finally, you can designate the output target as the response object's output stream, and perform the transformation.

The classes used in this example are dicussed in more detail in Chapter 6, "Exploring the `System.Xml` Namespace."

Although XSLT is extremely flexible, tasks can be greatly simplified by not generating a series of complex template rules. For these instances, you might want to create a simple extension function to achieve the same task. You saw how this is done using the `msxsl:script` element and JavaScript, but it is impossible to debug using this approach. Another method of extending XSLT is to create your own extensions through the use of compiled libraries that are referenced directly from XSLT. Instead of creating script code that's impossible to debug, create compiled components that are called from XSLT to generate the XSLT output.

In the following code, the XSLT stylesheet was changed only slightly by removing the JavaScript function. The MSXSL namespace was removed because it is not needed for the revised example:

```
<?xml version="1.0" encoding="UTF-8" ?>
<xsl:stylesheet version="1.0"
➥xmlns:xsl="http://www.w3.org/1999/XSL/Transform"
    xmlns:tns="urn:thisnamespace:tns">
    <xsl:param name="sortBy" select="'CITY'"/>

    <xsl:template match="/">
        <xsl:apply-templates/>
    </xsl:template>

    <xsl:template match="PITCHERS">
        <TABLE border="1">
            <tr>
                <th>Number</th>
                <th>First Name</th>
                <th>Last Name</th>
                <th>City</th>
                <th>Team</th>
                <th>ERA</th>
            </tr>

            <xsl:for-each select="PITCHER">
                <xsl:sort select="*[name()=$sortBy]"/>
                <tr>
                    <td><xsl:value-of select="tns:Iterate()"/></td>
                    <td><xsl:value-of select="FNAME"/><br/></td>
                    <td><xsl:value-of select="LNAME"/></td>
                    <td><xsl:value-of select="CITY"/></td>
                    <td><xsl:value-of select="TEAM"/></td>
                    <td><xsl:value-of select="ERA"/></td>
                </tr>
```

```
            </xsl:for-each>
        </TABLE>
    </xsl:template>
</xsl:stylesheet>
```

In the XSLT file, we added a call to a function called `tns:Iterate()`. This function is a member of the `tns` namespace. Because we declared our own function, we now must tell the XSLT processor how to handle this function. To do this, use the `XsltArgumentList` object to add an extension object and associate it with a specific namespace.

Create a new `.aspx` page called `ServerExtension.aspx` and remove all HTML from the `.aspx` page. In the code-behind file `ServerExtension.aspx.vb`, enter the following code. Listing 3.12 shows the complete code-behind for the page.

Listing 3.12 *ServerExtension.aspx.vb*

```
Imports System.Xml
Imports System.Xml.Xsl
Imports System.Xml.XPath


Public Class ServerExtension
    Inherits System.Web.UI.Page

#Region " Web Form Designer Generated Code "

    'This call is required by the Web Form Designer.
    <System.Diagnostics.DebuggerStepThrough()> Private Sub
    ➥InitializeComponent()

    End Sub

    Private Sub Page_Init(ByVal sender As System.Object, ByVal e As
    ➥System.EventArgs) Handles MyBase.Init
        'CODEGEN: This method call is required by the Web Form Designer
        'Do not modify it using the code editor.
        InitializeComponent()
    End Sub

#End Region

    Private Sub Page_Load(ByVal sender As Object, ByVal e As
    ➥System.EventArgs)

        If Not IsPostBack Then

            Dim doc As XPathDocument = New
            ➥XPathDocument(Server.MapPath("pitchers.xml"))
```

```
            Dim xsl As XslTransform = New XslTransform()
            xsl.Load(Server.MapPath("extendingxslt.xslt"))
            Dim args As XsltArgumentList = New XsltArgumentList()
            args.AddParam("sortBy", "", "FNAME")

            args.AddExtensionObject("urn:thisnamespace:tns", New Iterator())

            Dim writer As XmlWriter = New XmlTextWriter(Response.Output)
            xsl.Transform(doc, args, writer)
            writer.Close()
        End If
    End Sub
End Class

Public Class Iterator
    Private Val As Integer

    Public Function Iterate() As Integer
        Val += 1
        Return (Val)
    End Function
End Class
```

When you embedded the JavaScript extension by using the `<msxsl:script>` element, no way existed to debug the JavaScript contained within it. With compiled code on the server, however, you can set a breakpoint in the `Iterate` function and easily debug the code.

Declarative Programming with ASP.NET Versus XSLT Processing

XSLT is good for making tranformation tasks possible. But there are limitations to what it can currently do. For example, complex business logic and operations, such as transactional database processing and Microsoft Message Queue (MSMQ) manipulation, are not possible with XSLT. You can easily see, however, that many of the mundane display tasks that have polluted ASP server-side scripts in the past are greatly simplified with XSLT processing.

Declarative programming describes the way that programming is done in ASP.NET applications involving coding tasks. Within code, you declare variables and create instances of classes to perform tasks. Declarative programming involves some type of control flow, such as looping and conditional tests.

Prior to ASP.NET, web programming with ASP yielded difficult-to-maintain code. This is largely because of the presentation of data was intermingled with the logic surrounding the data. Custom COM components could be written to ease some of this maintainability, but this potentially put presentation logic in compiled code.

With the advent of ASP.NET, many of the limitations of the past are potentially removed. For example, elegant UIs can be developed using web forms controls, and the code that manipulates and interacts with the UI elements can be separated into a code-behind file. This reduces the amount of logic intermingled with presentation code, reduces complexity, and increases maintainability. In addition, ASP.NET performs many of the mundane tasks behind the scenes, such as browser compatibility and execution of script code on the client to avoid server posts.

XSLT offers a great way to separate presentation from the data. But, a great many tasks cannot be performed with XSLT, such as database updates and interaction with MSMQ. For this type of operation, custom logic must be used.

However, the two technologies are not mutually exclusive. In fact, they complement each other. The `asp:xml` web forms control, for example, provides quick access to performing transformations on a web form page.

WAP and WML

By using XSLT, you can also create WAP and WML documents on the fly from ordinary XML documents. WML is a form of markup that is specifically targeted for handheld devices that use WAP. Development with WML is similar to HTML in some respects: You designate markup for the content. But the similarities end there. In HTML, you can specify images and very complex formatting rules. In WML, you don't have this luxury because the display surface for WML browsers is extremely small. Some WAP browsers enable you to change aspects of a font, such as underlining, bold, italics, and relative size, but support for this is not standard across devices. At best, you have support for simple text.

Chapter 13, "Sample Application: Mobile Device Programming with WAP, WML, and XHTML Basic," discusses WAP, WML, and XHTML Basic and shows you how a single XML document can be rendered as HTML, WML, or XHTML Basic by applying different XSLT transformations.

Chapter Summary

In this chapter, you saw how you can use XML in the client browser in the form of data islands and external downloadable files. You explored using the client-side DOM to manipulate XML data and transform XML using XSLT stylesheets, and used the server-side DOM to transform XSLT documents. A brief discussion on XPath also served as an introduction later chapters in this book.

XPath and XSLT are rapidly becoming the building blocks of XML and are fostering XML's wide acceptance. XPath is the SQL of XML: It provides a mechanism to locate a set of nodes in an XML document. XSLT builds on XPath by providing a mechanism to transform XML documents into another form.

You also looked at extending the XSLT processor by using JavaScript functions and by using compiled code. You then looked at some of the basics of WML and saw how the same XML file used to generate HTML pages could be combined with XSLT to generate WML.

The remaining chapters build on these concepts. Chapter 5 focuses on the MSXML parser and discusses how it is still an integral part of XML development efforts. Chapter 6 discusses the XML implementation in the .NET Framework and discusses in detail how XSLT plays a significant role within the .NET Framework. Chapter 8 looks at how ADO uses XML under the seams, and shows how a set of relational tables can be queried using XPath or transformed using XSLT. Chapter 9 shows how SQL Server provides XPath and XSLT capabilities and how the .NET Framework can be used to further its capabilities.

4

XML Tool Support in Visual Studio .NET

Visual Studio .NET provides an integrated development environment with a rich set of features that greatly simplify your development efforts as an ASP.NET web applications developer. It provides a single development environment for any of the languages you choose to develop your ASP.Net applications with, such as Visual Basic.Net, C#, or JScript.Net. Several features, such as web-forms building using drag and drop for controls, Intellisense, integrated debugging tools, and templates for enterprise development, support the development life cycle. In addition, Visual Studio .NET has an enhanced support for XML integrated into the IDE. So you do not have to change your development environment in order to use other XML tools to create and edit XML files in your applications. The built-in XML editor in Visual Studio .NET eases the creation of XML and XML Schema files.

Furthermore, Visual Studio .NET significantly simplifies your job of creating, deploying, and maintaining XML Web Services. You can easily expose web services in any of the supported languages. The development is so easy that no expertise is necessary on XML and SOAP to take advantage of web services. When you compile your business objects, Visual Studio .NET automatically generates an XML file that describes the function and, when it is called, the function automatically sends and receives XML packets.

While you build a client for the web service in Visual Studio .NET, you can drag any exposed web service directly into your application. Doing so enables Visual Studio to treat the web service as a class. Calling the web service is as simple as creating a new instance of the web service class and then calling its exposed methods.

Chapter 11, "Creating and Using ASP.NET Web Services," discusses creating XML Web Services using Visual Studio .NET. In this chapter, you explore the XML editor features in Visual Studio .NET, the command-line utilities for XML available with the .NET SDK and other non-.NET Microsoft tools for XML.

Built-In XML Editor

In this section, you look at the features provided by the built-in XML editor with a few examples. To do this, it's necessary to start by creating a new ASP.NET web project. (See Figure 4.1.)

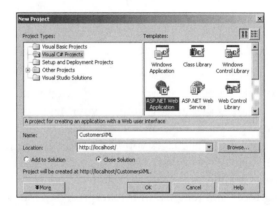

Figure 4.1   Creating a C# ASP.NET web project.

This action creates a new virtual directory with the name `CustomersXML`. Now you can add a new XML file to this project by selecting the Add New item option from the project menu and then choosing an XML file, as shown in Figure 4.2.

You can change your editor options by going to Tools, Options, as shown in Figure 4.3.

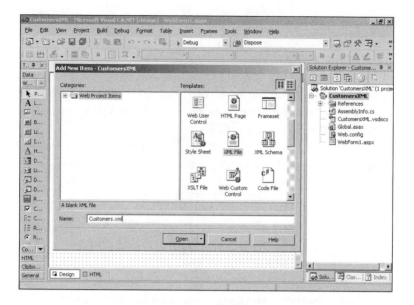

Figure 4.2 Adding an XML file to the project.

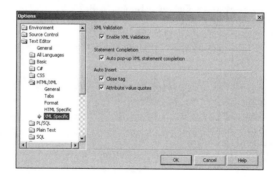

Figure 4.3 Changing your options in the text editor.

Schema, Data, and XML: The Three Views in XML Designer

The *XML Designer* provides features that enable you to create and edit XML Schema files, ADO.NET `DataSets`, XML data files, and XML source code. These features are provided in the form of the three views: Schema, Data, and XML. This section looks at each of these views individually.

The Data View

The Data view provides a datagrid that can modify .xml files. It enables you to edit the content in an XML file.

The Data Tables and Data separate this view into two areas. The Data Tables area lists relations defined in the XML file in the order of its nesting (from the outermost to the innermost). The Data area is a datagrid that displays data based on the selection in the Data Tables area.

By adding the following code to the newly created XML file and switching to Data view, you can see the datagrid that's shown in Figure 4.4:

```
<?xml version="1.0" encoding="utf-8" ?>
<Customers xmlns="http://tempuri.org/Customers.xsd">
    <Customer id="ALFKI">
        <CompanyName>Alfreds Futterkiste</CompanyName>
        <Contact>
            <FirstName>Maria</FirstName>
            <LastName>Anders</LastName>
            <Title>Sales Representative</Title>
        </Contact>
        <Em_u105 ?l>Mario@alfreds-futterkiste.com</Em_u105 ?l>
        <Phone>(703) 752-76576</Phone>
        <ShippingAddress>
            <Street>City Center Plaza 516 Main St.</Street>
            <City>Elgin</City>
            <St_u116 ?e>OR</St_u116 ?e>
            <Zip>97827</Zip>
        </ShippingAddress>
        <BillingAddress>
            <Street>12 Orchestra Terrace</Street>
            <City>Walla Walla</City>
            <St_u116 ?e>WA</St_u116 ?e>
            <Zip>99362</Zip>
        </BillingAddress>
    </Customer>
</Customers>
```

To display the Data view correctly, it's essential that the XML be well formed. The Data view generates an error message for a non-well-formed XML document. Newly created XML files contain no data and, therefore, cannot be displayed in Data view. In some cases, although the XML would be considered well formed, if it contains a structure that cannot be displayed by the Data view, trying to switch to Data view generates this message: "Although this document is well formed, it contains structure that Data view cannot display." The following XML code with the node name a repeating at different levels within the hierarchy of the data is an example:

```
<abc>
    <a><b><a>Hello</a></b></a>
</abc>
```

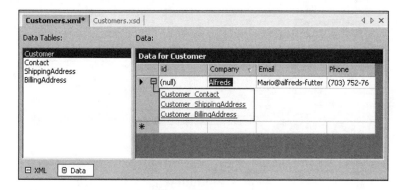

Figure 4.4   The Data view.

The XML View

The XML view provides an editor for manually editing the XML files and provides color-coding and IntelliSense, including Complete Word and List Members. The editor aligns all the elements when you save the file, so you are relieved of the pain of aligning the XML elements in the file. The file types that can be opened in this view for editing are `.xml`, `.xsd`, `.xslt`, `.wsdl`, `.web`, `.resx`, `.tdl`, `.wsf`, `.hta`, `.disco`, `.vsdisco`, and `.config`. The IntelliSense feature assists you to write well-formed and valid XML. It is available when you work with `.xsd` files and `.xml` files that have an associated schema.

To assign a schema to the XML file, first load an XML file into the XML designer by double-clicking the filename in the Solution Explorer. Then change to XML view by clicking the XML tab on the bottom of the designer. Now you can set the `targetSchema` property to the schema that's going to be associated with the XML document, as shown in Figure 4.5. The Properties window can be invoked by clicking the Properties button in the toolbar. You can also remove the reference to the schema to remove the association between the XML document and the schema.

To check if the document is well formed, you can switch from XML view to Data view. If the XML file isn't well formed, the designer shows an error message that indicates the reason and the location where the document is not well formed. Another way to see if a document is well formed is to use the validation feature provided by the IDE, which apart from the validation errors, also displays errors resulting from a non–well-formed document.

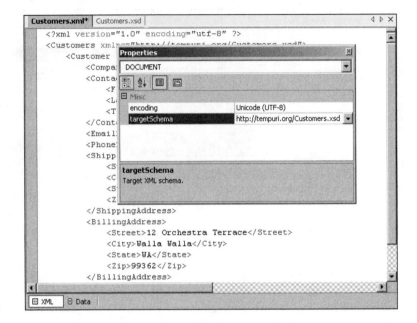

Figure 4.5   Setting the `targetSchema` property.

Validating the XML File

To validate the XML file against the associated schema, select Validate XML
Data from the XML menu. Make sure that the XML file is loaded into the
Designer and it's in XML view, as shown in Figure 4.6.

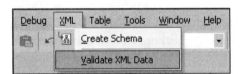

Figure 4.6   Selecting the Validate XML Data menu option.

If no errors are found in the XML file, the status bar indicates this fact with a
message similar to "No validation errors were found." If errors are encountered, the Task List gives a description of the errors with their location in the
file. Figure 4.7 shows an example of an error generated when the element
name `BillingAddress` was intentionally changed to `BillingAddress1`.

Task List - 5 Build Error tasks shown (filtered)		
☑ Description	File	Line
Click here to add a new task		
The active schema does not support the element 'BillingAddress1'.	C:\XMLTools\...\Customers.xml	18
The active schema does not support the element 'City'.	C:\XMLTools\...\Customers.xml	20
The active schema does not support the element 'State'.	C:\XMLTools\...\Customers.xml	21
The active schema does not support the element 'Street'.	C:\XMLTools\...\Customers.xml	19
The active schema does not support the element 'Zip'.	C:\XMLTools\...\Customers.xml	22

Figure 4.7   An error display in the Task List.

As you keep editing the XML file, a thread running in the background keeps validating the file. So, errors are indicated in real-time by wavy lines that underline the elements with the error(s). You can read the descriptions by hovering the mouse over the wavy line. These errors are also reflected in the Task List. (See Figure 4.8.)

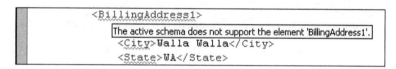

```
<BillingAddress1>
    The active schema does not support the element 'BillingAddress1'.
    <City>Walla Walla</City>
    <State>WA</State>
```

Figure 4.8   Viewing the error display in Code Editor.

IntelliSense

While you are manually editing an XML file, you, like everyone else, are prone to make mistakes. By associating an XML Schema to your XML file, Statement Completion is enabled in the XML editor. You can Type < to initiate a tag, and IntelliSense presents you with a list of elements that are valid at that location. (See Figure 4.9.)

To view a list of attributes that are supported by the element, type the element name and press the spacebar.

The Schema View

The Schema view provides a visual representation of the elements, attributes, types, and so on that make up XML Schemas and ADO.NET DataSets. Schema view allows you to visually construct schemas and ADO.NET DataSets by dropping elements on the design surface from either the XML Schema tab of the toolbox or from Server Explorer. You can create and edit relationship s between tables and edit the keys. You can generate ADO.NET DataSets from XML Schemas.

The XML Schemas in the Visual Studio .NET conform to the specification for schemas published by the World Wide Web Consortium (W3C). The next section looks into the creation of schemas and DataSets.

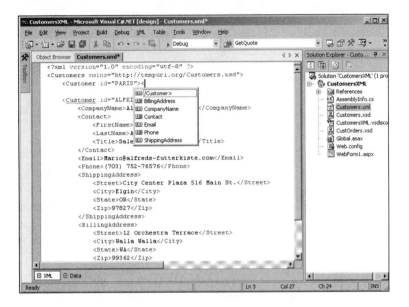

Figure 4.9   IntelliSense in the XML editor.

Creating an XML Schema with XML Designer

Chapter 2, "XML Schemas in .NET," gives you a detailed overview of schemas. In this section, you look into using Visual Studio .NET to create these schemas.

If you already have an XML file and you want to quickly create an XML Schema to represent the same data structure as this XML file, you can use the Create Schema option from the XML menu. This option adds an XML Schema (.xsd file) to the current project with the same name as the original XML file. When you create a schema with this approach, all the data types are initially set to string so you must edit the data types according to the content requirements of your XML data. To make changes to this generated schema, you can either edit the schema file or load the XML Schema into XML Designer and perform the changes visually.

Although the previous approach might appear easy and quick for simple XML files, large and complex structures can be difficult to figure out the structure generated by the IDE. Another approach is to create the XML Schema yourself from scratch. This gives you more control over the schema design. This approach is discussed next.

To add an XML Schema to the project, choose Add New Item from the Project menu, select the XML Schema icon in the Add New Item dialog box (see Figure 4.10), and rename the file (if necessary).

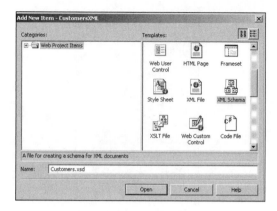

Figure 4.10   Adding a new XML Schema file.

Adding a new schema file adds the .xsd file to the project and the XML Designer appears. By switching to the XML view, you'll notice the following XML with an empty schema generated:

```
<?xml version="1.0" encoding="utf-8" ?>
<xs:schema id=" Customers" targetNamespace="http://tempuri.org/Customers.xsd"
elementFormDefault="qualified" xmlns="http://tempuri.org/Customers.xsd"
xmlns:xs="http://www.w3.org/2001/XMLSchema"></xs:schema>
```

This XML doesn't include the actual declaration part of the schema, nor does it include the actual schema tags, which are called the *root* or *document level* tags. Notice that the default namespace http://tempuri.org/ is added by Visual Studio .NET IDE whenever it generates an XML Schema. You can enter the code and replace it with your custom namespace if required.

The XML Schema Tab in the Toolbox

The Schema tab in the Toolbox provides all the elements you can add to the XML Schema and the ADO.NET DataSets. These elements appear in a form similar to visual controls that are more common to Windows GUI developers. These elements can be dragged and dropped onto the XML Designer surface. This tab is available in the Toolbox when the XML Designer is in the Schema view. The Toolbox appears by default; if it's closed but you need it, you can display the Toolbox by selecting Toolbox from the View menu. To make the Toolbox close automatically, select Autohide from the Window menu. To make it stay open, you can clear the Autohide from the Window menu or click the small pushpin that appears on the status bar on top of the ToolBox. (See Figure 4.11.)

Figure 4.11 The XML Schema tab in the ToolBox.

Take a brief look at each of the elements that appear in the Toolbox Schema tab:

- **element**—Creates an element that can be global, added to other elements, added to groups, or used to construct `complexTypes`.

- **attribute**—Creates an attribute that can be global, added to elements, or added to groups.

- **attributeGroup**—Creates an `attributeGroup` that can be global, added to elements, or used in the construction of `complexTypes`.

- **complexType**—Creates a `complexType` to which you can add elements, attributes, `attributeGroups`, anys, and `anyAttributes`.

- **simpleType**—Creates a `simpleType` to which you can add facets.

- **group**—Creates groups that can be global, added to other groups, elements, or `complexTypes`.

- **any**—Creates an any element that can be added to elements, `complexTypes`, or groups.

- **anyAttribute**—Creates an `anyAttribute` element that can be added to elements, attribute groups, or complex types.

- **Facet**—Creates a facet that can be added to a `simpleType`. A *facet* can further restrict the definition of a simple type.

- **Key**—When dragged and dropped on an existing element, launches the Edit Key dialog box that can create keys when added to an element.

Keys are the primary fields that tie relations together.

- **Relation**—Launches the Edit Relation dialog box that defines relationships between elements.

Alternatively, you can also add these elements to the designer by right-clicking the design surface and selecting Add from the pop-up menu.

Adding Simple Type Definitions

You will create a `SimpleType` element that's derived from the built-in derived type `positiveInteger` and represents a five-digit postal code. You'll use this element later to create a complex type named `usAddress`. To create a `SimpleType` element, follow these steps:

1. From the XML Schema tab of the Toolbox, drag a `simpleType` onto the design surface. The element appears on the Design surface like a datagrid control.

2. Select the default name `simpleType1` and rename this type `postalCode`.

3. Navigate to the adjacent cell on the right and click the drop-down list. You can see all the simple types built in to XML Schema. From this list, select `positiveInteger`.

4. Navigate to the next row and click the drop-down box. You can see that the only choice is facet. Simple types cannot include elements or attributes as part of their content models; therefore, only facets can be used to build simple types.

5. The drop-down list in the adjacent cell on the right lists all the constraining facets for the built-in simple type `positiveInteger` that was chosen in step 3. From this list, select Pattern.

6. In the adjacent cell to the right, type **\d{5}**. The Pattern facet allows you to enter regular expressions. The regular expression \d{5} restricts the contents of the `postalCode` type.

Figure 4.12 shows the `postalCode` simple type at the end of the preceding steps.

If you switch to XML view, you can see the following simple-type definition that's added to the schema:

```
<xs:simpleType name="postalCode">
    <xs:restriction base="xs:positiveInteger">
        <xs:pattern value="\d{5}" />
    </xs:restriction>
</xs:simpleType>
```

Now you can similarly create another simple type named `stateCode`, as shown in Figure 4.13. You'll use this during the complex type creation, which is discussed next.

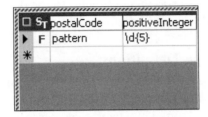

Figure 4.12   The simple type `postalCode`.

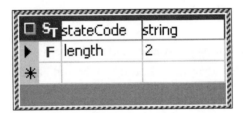

Figure 4.13   The simple type `stateCode`.

Adding Complex Type Definitions

In this section, you'll create a `ComplexType` element named `usAddress` that defines the structure of an address located in U.S.

To create a complex type, follow these steps:

1. From the XML Schema tab in the Toolbox, drag a `complexType` onto the design surface.

2. Select the default name `complexType1` and rename this type to `usAddress`. Do *not* select a data type for this element because you do not want to derive this from any other complex or simple type. Note: Selecting the data type as another simple type restricts the complex type to include only the element of type `anyAttribute`, `attribute`, `attributeGroup`, and `facet`.

3. Navigate to the next cell and click the drop-down box. You can see the many choices of elements that you can add to a complex type, as shown in Figure 4.14. You can select element. (You can even Tab over this cell because element is the default.)

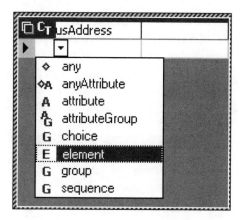

Figure 4.14   Selecting the element type.

4. In the adjacent cell on the right, type the name as `Street` and leave the type selection in the next cell as `string`, which is the default.

5. Repeat steps 3 and 4 to create the other elements, `City`, `State`, and `Zip`, as shown in Figure 4.15. For the `State` and `Zip` elements, you can select the type as the simple types that were just defined.

C_T usAddress	
E Street	string
E City	string
E State	stateCode
E Zip	postalCode

Figure 4.15   The complex type `usAddress`.

By switching to XML view, you can see the following complex type definition added to the schema:

```
<xs:complexType name="usAddress">
    <xs:sequence>
        <xs:element name="Street" type="xs:string" />
        <xs:element name="City" type="xs:string" />
        <xs:element name="State" type="stateCode" />
        <xs:element name="Zip" type="postalCode" />
    </xs:sequence>
</xs:complexType>
```

You might see the prefix `xsd:` rather than `xs:` in the rest of this chapter. This is due to a previous build of Visual Studio .NET that used `xsd` per the convention. But it is only essential that, irrespective of the name used, the namespace should be associated to the URI of `http://www.w3.org/2001/XMLSchema`.

You can create the two complex types, `contactType` and `customerType`, as shown in Figure 4.16 and Figure 4.17.

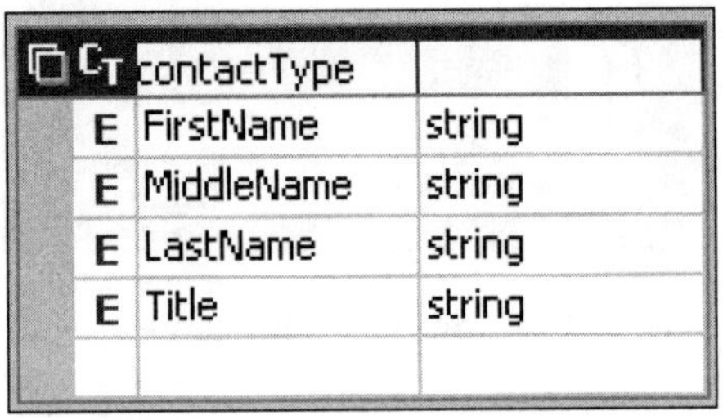

C_T contactType	
E FirstName	string
E MiddleName	string
E LastName	string
E Title	string

Figure 4.16   The complex type `contactType`.

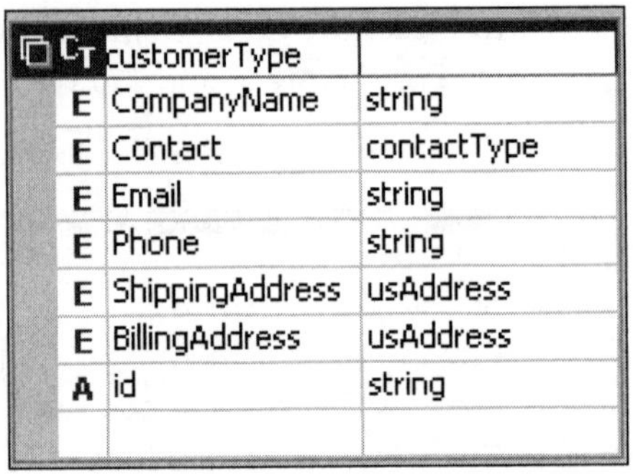

C_T customerType	
E CompanyName	string
E Contact	contactType
E Email	string
E Phone	string
E ShippingAddress	usAddress
E BillingAddress	usAddress
A id	string

Figure 4.17   The complex type `customerType`.

In the Schema Designer view, you can only set the `name` and `type` attributes of the elements in the schema definition. To set the other attributes, you can use the Properties window. In the Schema view, if you place the cursor on a specific element, the Properties window shows all the attributes conforming to the W3C Schema definition standard. This greatly eases your job because you do not have to remember these standard attributes. If you are in XML view, you must keep the cursor within the element's angular brackets to see the attributes that correspond to a specific element. Figure 4.18 shows the Properties window for the `<xsd:attribute>` element.

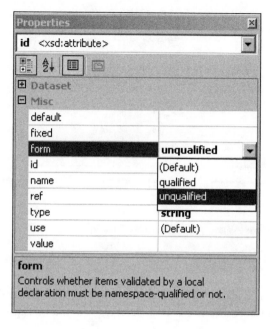

Figure 4.18   The Properties window for an `attribute` element.

Now that you have seen the creation of some simple and complex type definitions, one final step completes your schema creation. You must create the elements that will define the data. To do that, follow these steps:

1. From the XML Schema tab of the Toolbox, drag an element to the design surface.

2. Select the default name `element1` and rename this type to `Customers`.

3. Tab over the adjacent cell, leaving the default type as `Customers`, and navigate to the next row.

4. Type the name of the element in this row as `Customer`. Select the name `Customer` and, in the Properties window, set the `maxOccurs` property to unbounded.

5. In the adjacent cell on the right, select the type as `customerType`.

This finishes the schema creation. Figure 4.19 shows the relational structure in the XML Designer. You can get a clean appearance in the Schema view by clicking the Auto-Arrange option under the Schema menu. Clicking the Move symbol in the lower-right corner of the designer opens a bird's-eye view of the schema for a glance of the designer surface.

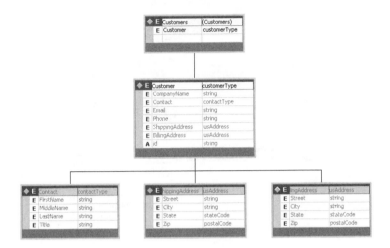

Figure 4.19 The XML Designer showing the relational structure.

The XML Designer enables you to cut or copy an element and paste it in the same designer surface, or paste it in a different schema's designer surface.

No Undo Command

The XML Designer provides the Delete option, but doesn't provide the Undo command in Schema view. Therefore, it is essential that you plan your steps and, if you are doing a more complex schema design, maintain backups at regular intervals. Doing so helps you in case you want to revert to the changes.

Editing the Generated XML

By switching to XML view, you can see the following complete code that has been added to the `Customers.xsd` file:

```
<?xml version="1.0" encoding="utf-8" ?>
<xsd:schema id="Customers" targetNamespace="http://tempuri.org/Customers.xsd"
xmlns="http://tempuri.org/Customers.xsd"
xmlns:xsd="http://www.w3.org/2001/XMLSchema" xmlns:msdata="urn:schemas-
microsoft-com:xml-msdata" attributeFormDefault="qualified"
elementFormDefault="qualified">
    <xsd:element name="Customers" >
        <xsd:complexType>
            <xsd:sequence>
                <xsd:element name="Customer" type="customerType"
                ➥maxOccurs="unbounded"/>
            </xsd:sequence>
        </xsd:complexType>
    </xsd:element>
    <xsd:complexType name="customerType">
        <xsd:sequence>
```

```
                <xsd:element name="CompanyName" type="xsd:string" minOccurs="0" />
                <xsd:element name="Contact" type="contactType" minOccurs="0" />
                <xsd:element name="Email" type="xsd:string" minOccurs="0" />
                <xsd:element name="Phone" type="xsd:string" minOccurs="0" />
                <xsd:element name="ShippingAddress" type="usAddress" minOccurs="0" />
                <xsd:element name="BillingAddress" type="usAddress" minOccurs="0" />
            </xsd:sequence>
            <xsd:attribute name="id" type="xsd:string" form="unqualified" />
        </xsd:complexType>
        <xsd:simpleType name="stateCode">
            <xsd:restriction base="xsd:string">
                <xsd:length value="2" />
            </xsd:restriction>
        </xsd:simpleType>
        <xsd:simpleType name="postalCode">
            <xsd:restriction base="xsd:positiveInteger">
                <xsd:pattern value="\d{5}" />
            </xsd:restriction>
        </xsd:simpleType>
        <xsd:complexType name="usAddress">
            <xsd:sequence>
                <xsd:element name="Street" type="xsd:string" minOccurs="0" />
                <xsd:element name="City" type="xsd:string" minOccurs="0" />
                <xsd:element name="State" type="stateCode" minOccurs="0" />
                <xsd:element name="Zip" type="postalCode" minOccurs="0" />
            </xsd:sequence>
        </xsd:complexType>
        <xsd:complexType name="contactType">
            <xsd:sequence>
                <xsd:element name="FirstName" type="xsd:string" minOccurs="0" />
                <xsd:element name="MiddleName" type="xsd:string" minOccurs="0" />
                <xsd:element name="LastName" type="xsd:string" minOccurs="0" />
                <xsd:element name="Title" type="xsd:string" minOccurs="0" />
            </xsd:sequence>
        </xsd:complexType>
    </xsd:schema>
```

You can edit this XML-generated code to add or remove any elements (if required). You can finally validate the schema by selecting Validate Schema from the Schema menu.

Creating a *DataSet* with Relational Data in XML Schemas

Now that you have created an XML Schema, it's time to create an ADO.NET typed `DataSet` from an XML Schema.

To create an ADO.NET `DataSet` from an existing schema, all you have to do is this: With the schema file loaded in Schema view, choose Generate `DataSet` from the Schema menu, as shown in Figure 4.20.

Figure 4.20   Selecting the Generate DataSet option from the Schema menu.

The XML Designer generates a DataSet Customers.cs, which has the same base name as that of the .xsd file. To see the newly generated DataSet file in the Solution Explorer, you might have to choose Show All Files from the Project menu.

When we talk about representing relational data with XML Schemas, it involves the creation of individual tables with columns and creating relationships between them based on the keys defined on the columns. We will discuss how typical database constructs, such as tables, columns, primary keys, foreign keys, unique keys, and constraint rules, are created in an XML Schema and get the corresponding DataSet that's automatically generated by the XML Designer. You'll create the two tables, Customers and Orders, with the primary keys defined on them and then create a one-to-many relationship between the Customers table (one) and the Orders table (many).

Here are the steps to complete this process:

1. Add a DataSet to the project by using the Add New Item option from the Solution Explorer (as shown in Figure 4.21). This adds a new schema file (CustOrders.xsd) and a corresponding DataSet class file, with the same name as that of the schema file, to your project.

2. In the last section, "Creating an XML Schema with XML Designer," you created complex elements in the schema by dragging from the XML Schema tab of the Toolbox. Using the same technique, you can create the following Customers element that represents a Customers table, and the subelements CustomerID to Zip that represent the columns of the table. After doing this, your table should look similar to Figure 4.22.

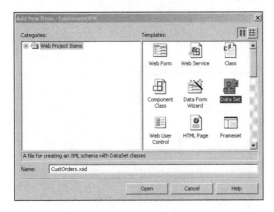

Figure 4.21   Add a new Dataset to the project.

◆ E	Customers	(Customers)
🔑E	CustomerID	string
E	CompanyNam	string
E	ContactName	string
E	Street	string
E	City	string
E	State	string
E	Zip	string

Figure 4.22   The Customers table.

Notice that the primary key is added to this table. To add the primary key, right-click to the left of the row of the element that you want to designate as a key; alternatively, drag a key element from the XML Schema tab of the Toolbox and drop it on this row. The Edit Key dialog box appears, as shown in Figure 4.23.

3. In the Name box, replace the default name with the name CustomersIDKey or anything that is appropriate for this key. If you need a multipart key, you can select additional elements in the Field area. To define a primary key, check Dataset Primary Key. If you do not check this option, the key becomes unique and null values will be allowed.

4. Follow the guidelines in step 2 to create another table, Orders, as shown in Figure 4.24. Create a primary key on the OrderID field with the name OrderIDKey.

Figure 4.23 The Edit Key dialog box.

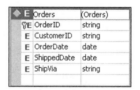

Figure 4.24 The Orders table.

This completes the creation of the two tables.

5. Now, you can create a relationship between the Customers and Orders tables by using the Relation object. Drag and drop a Relation object from the XML Schema tab of the Toolbox anywhere exactly on the Orders table. The Edit Relation dialog box appears, as shown in Figure 4.25.

Set the Parent element to Customers and the Child element to Orders. You can leave the default name CustomersOrders that appears in the Name box. Set the key to CustomersIDKey, which you defined earlier in the Customers table. In the Foreign Key Fields area, select CustomerID to match the key field in the parent Orders table. Leave the rest of the default settings as is and click OK. This creates a Relation object that appears on the designer surface, as shown in Figure 4.26.

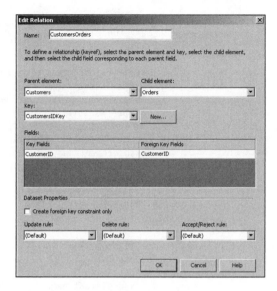

Figure 4.25   The Edit Relation dialog box.

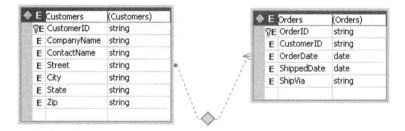

Figure 4.26   The Relation object.

6. Save the file. The XML Designer regenerates the `DataSet` class file to reflect the changes you made to the schema file since the time of creation.

By switching to XML view, you can see the following code added to the `CustOrders.xsd` file:

```
<?xml version="1.0" encoding="utf-8" ?>
<xsd:schema id="CustOrders"
targetNamespace="http://tempuri.org/CustOrders.xsd"
elementFormDefault="qualified" xmlns="http://tempuri.org/CustOrders.xsd"
xmlns:xsd="http://www.w3.org/2001/XMLSchema" xmlns:msdata="urn:schemas-
microsoft-com:xml-msdata">
    <xsd:element name="CustOrders" msdata:IsDataset="true">
        <xsd:complexType>
```

```xsd
                        <xsd:choice maxOccurs="unbounded">
                            <xsd:element name="Orders">
                                <xsd:complexType>
                                    <xsd:sequence>
                                        <xsd:element name="OrderID"
                                        ➥type="xsd:string" />
                                        <xsd:element name="CustomerID"
                                        ➥type="xsd:string" />
                                        <xsd:element name="OrderDate"
                                        ➥type="xsd:date" minOccurs="0" />
                                        <xsd:element name="ShippedDate"
                                        ➥type="xsd:date" minOccurs="0" />
                                        <xsd:element name="ShipVia"
                                        ➥type="xsd:string" minOccurs="0" />
                                    </xsd:sequence>
                                </xsd:complexType>
                            </xsd:element>
                            <xsd:element name="Customers">
                                <xsd:complexType>
                                    <xsd:sequence>
                                        <xsd:element name="CustomerID"
                                        ➥type="xsd:string" />
                                        <xsd:element name="CompanyName"
                                        ➥type="xsd:string" />
                                        <xsd:element name="ContactName"
                                        ➥type="xsd:string" minOccurs="0" />
                                        <xsd:element name="Street"
                                        ➥type="xsd:string" minOccurs="0" />
                                        <xsd:element name="City"
                                        ➥type="xsd:string" minOccurs="0" />
                                        <xsd:element name="State"
                                        ➥type="xsd:string" minOccurs="0" />
                                        <xsd:element name="Zip"
                                        ➥type="xsd:string" minOccurs="0" />
                                    </xsd:sequence>
                                </xsd:complexType>
                            </xsd:element>
                        </xsd:choice>
                    </xsd:complexType>
                    <xsd:key name="CustomersIDKey" msdata:PrimaryKey="true">
                        <xsd:selector xpath=".//Customers" />
                        <xsd:field xpath="CustomerID" />
                    </xsd:key>
                    <xsd:key name="OrderIDKey" msdata:PrimaryKey="true">
                        <xsd:selector xpath=".//Orders" />
                        <xsd:field xpath="OrderID" />
                    </xsd:key>
                    <xsd:keyref name="CustomersOrders" refer="CustomersIDKey">
                        <xsd:selector xpath=".//Orders" />
                        <xsd:field xpath="CustomerID" />
                    </xsd:keyref>
                </xsd:element>
            </xsd:schema>
```

This chapter doesn't discuss the generated `DataSet` class because you can find a detailed discussion of it in Chapter 8, "Database Access with ADO.NET and XML." Figure 4.27 shows the generated `DataSet` that's being used in the code editor.

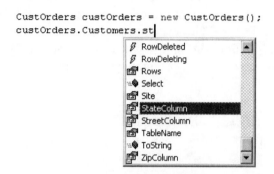

Figure 4.27   Using the auto-generated typed `DataSet`.

Creating Schemas and *DataSets* from Existing Data

XML Designer enables you to quickly create a schema based on an existing data source. This helps you when an existing source contains the desired structure for your application, and you want to use this structure without having to define each element.

Start by adding a `DataSet` to the project by using the Add New Item option from the Solutions Explorer (see Figure 4.28).

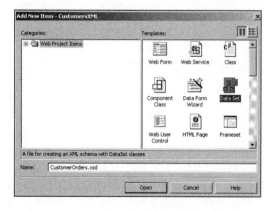

Figure 4.28   The Add New Item option.

This action adds a new, blank schema file (.xsd) and a corresponding DataSet class file, with the same name as that of the schema file, to your project. So, if you name the DataSet file CustomerOrders, you'll have both CustomerOrders.xsd and CustomerOrders.cs added to the project.

In the Server Explorer, if you do not already have the connection to the required existing data source, you can create the connection by using the Data Link Properties dialog box. This dialog box is invoked when you choose Connect to Database from the Tools menu with the Server Explorer open. Figure 4.29 shows how you can configure your connection to the desired provider on an SQL server.

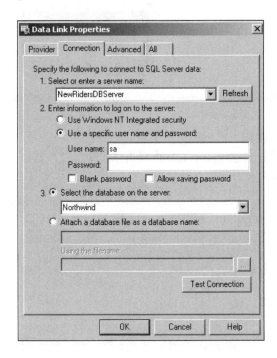

Figure 4.29 The Data Link Properties from the Server Explorer.

After you have the connection, you can see the required data source by expanding the Data Connections node and then expanding the node for the specific connection. In the Connection node, expand the node for Tables, Stored Procedures, or Views, depending on from what you want to infer the schema structure. Select the item and drag it on the XML Designer surface. Figure 4.30 shows the Schema view of the XML Designer with the two tables, Customers and Orders, dragged from the Northwind database.

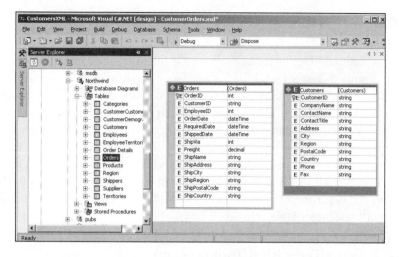

Figure 4.30   The Schema view of the XML Designer with `Customers` and `Orders` dragged from the `Northwind` database.

If you want to build the schema based on specific columns, you can expand the source node and select only the specific columns that you want before you drag it onto the designer (see Figure 4.31).

Figure 4.31   Selecting the specific columns from a table.

Now you can add a `Relation` object to the schema if you want to establish a relationship between the multiple tables you have added.

Tools Within the .NET SDK

The .NET SDK offers various tools that fall under four categories: Configuration and Deployment, Debugging, Security, and General Tools. Some command-line tools fall under the Configuration and Deployment category that you will find indispensable while you work with XML applications in the .NET Framework. These tools ease your job by performing some common tasks, such as generating code and deployment. This enables you to concentrate on the logic of your application.

All these tools are installed as part of the .NET, whether you install it as part of Visual Studio .NET or the .NET SDK. You can find the tools in the `\Program Files\Microsoft.NET\FrameworkSDK\Bin` directory. This path is added to the `PATH` system variable when you install .NET.

XML Schema Definition Tool (*xsd.exe*)

The XML Schema Definition tool generates XML Schema or common language run-time classes from XDR, XML, and XSD files, or from classes in a run-time assembly. It takes an argument to convert the input file.

Table 4.1 lists the general tool options that can be used.

Table 4.1 **General Options**

Option	Description
`/h[elp]` or `/?`	Displays command syntax and options for the tool.
`[/outputdir]:directory`	Specifies the directory for output files. This argument can appear only once. The default is the current directory.

> **Note**
> You can use shortcuts; for example, instead of typing **/outputdir**, you can type **/o**.

The following file types are accepted as input by the tool with their descriptions and syntax:

- **.xdr**—xsd.exe converts the XDR Schema file to an XSD Schema file with the same name as the XDR Schema.
  ```
  xsd filename.xdr [/outputdir:directory]
  ```

XML Data Reduced (XDR) is an early XML Schema language proposed by Microsoft. Although earlier Microsoft products and parsers supported this format, now they all provide support for the W3C XML Schema 2001 Proposed Recommendation. Therefore, this option helps you greatly when you need to convert any existing XDR Schema files to XSD files.

- **.xml**—xsd.exe infers a schema from the data in the file and produces an XSD file with the same name as the XML file:

  ```
  xsd filename.xml [/outputdir:directory]
  ```

If you have an XML file, you can quickly generate an XML Schema file to validate the XML files. Just follow the same structure as the XML file. The tool tries to infer the parent-child relationship between the complex types in the XML file and generates additional ID columns for a `Relation` to work correctly. The tool defaults all data types to `string`. So, you can edit the generated XSD file to provide the specific data types required for your application.

- **.xsd**—xsd.exe generates source code for run-time objects that correspond to the XML Schema file that is provided as input:

  ```
  xsd filename.xsd {/classes | /dataset} [/element:element]
  [/language:language] [/namespace:namespace] [/outputdir:direc-
  tory] [URI:uri]
  ```

Depending on whether you require a `DataSet` or a class, you can specify only one of the two options, /d or /c, as shown in Table 4.2.

- **.dll or .exe:** xsd.exe generates schemas for one or more types in that assembly.

  ```
  xsd {filename.dll | filename.exe} [/outputdir:directory]
  [/type:typename [...]]
  ```

Table 4.2 **Xsd Tool Options**

Option	Description
/d[ataset]	Generates a class derived from `DataSet` that corresponds to the specified schema. To read XML data into the derived class, use the `System.Data.DataSet.ReadXml` method.
/c[lasses]	Generates classes that correspond to the specified schema. To read XML data into the object, use the `System.XML.Serialization.XMLSerializer.Deserialize`r method.

continues

Table 4.2 **Continued**

Option	Description
/e[lement]:element	Specifies the element in the schema to generate code for. By default all elements are typed. You can specify this argument more than once.
/l[anguage]:language	Specifies the programming language to use. Choose from CS (default), VB, or JS. You can also specify a fully qualified name for a class by implementing `System.CodeDom.Compiler.CodeDomProvider`.
/n[amespace]:namespace	Specifies the run-time namespace for the generated types. The default namespace is `Schemas`.
/u[ri]:uri	Specifies the URI for the elements in the schema for which to generate code. This URI, if present, applies to all elements specified with the /element option.
/t[ype]:typename	Specifies the name of the `type` for which create a schema. You can specify multiple `type` arguments. If typename doesn't specify a namespace, `xsd.exe` matches all types in the assembly with the specified type. If typename specifies a namespace, only that type is matched. If typename ends with an asterisk character (*), the tool matches all types that start with the string preceding the *. If you omit the /type option, `xsd.exe` generates schemas for all types in the assembly.

You can use the /type option to specify the types for which to generate schemas. The output schemas are named `schema0.xsd`, `schema1.xsd`, and so on. Xsd.exe produces multiple schemas only if the given types specify a namespace using the XMLRoot custom attribute.

Take a look at a few simple examples of using the `xsd.exe` tool, described in the next section.

Generating XSD from an XDR File

Listing 4.1 is a simple XDR file that is passed as an input.

Listing 4.1 *Customer.xdr*

```xml
<?xml version="1.0" ?>
<Schema  xmlns = "urn:schemas-microsoft-com:xml-data"
     xmlns:dt = "urn:schemas-microsoft-com:datatypes">
    <ElementType name = "Customer" content = "eltOnly"  order = "seq"   >
         <element type = "CompanyName" minOccurs="1" maxOccurs="1"   />
         <element type = "ContactName"  minOccurs="1" maxOccurs="1"   />
```

```
      </ElementType>
      <ElementType name = "CompanyName" content = "textOnly"     order =
      ⇥"seq"    />
      <ElementType name = "ContactName" content = "textOnly"  order = "seq"
   />
   </Schema>
```

Running the `xsd.exe`, as shown in Figure 4.32, generates the `Customer.xsd` file and writes it to the current directory, which is the default. To specify a different directory, you can use the `/o[utputdir]` option.

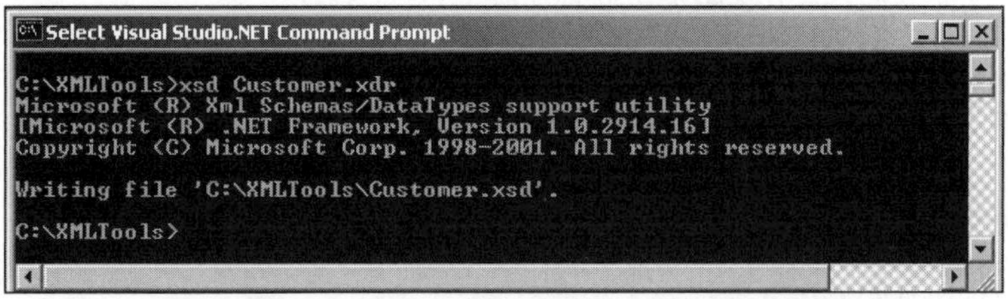

Figure 4.32 Generating XSD from an XDR file.

The screenshots in this chapter show the Visual Studio .NET command prompt. You can optionally choose to run the command-line tools in a DOS command window if you do not have the Visual Studio .NET installed. Listing 4.2 is the XSD file generated by the `xsd.exe` tool.

Listing 4.2 *Customer.xsd*

```xml
<?xml version="1.0" encoding="utf-8"?>
<xsd:schema id="NewDataset" targetNamespace="" xmlns=""
xmlns:xsd="http://www.w3.org/2001/XMLSchema" xmlns:msdata="urn:schemas-
⇥microsoft-com:xml-msdata">
  <xsd:element name="NewDataset" msdata:IsDataset="true">
    <xsd:complexType>
      <xsd:choice maxOccurs="unbounded">
        <xsd:element name="Customer">
          <xsd:complexType>
            <xsd:sequence>
              <xsd:element name="CompanyName" type="xsd:string" />
              <xsd:element name="ContactName" type="xsd:string" />
            </xsd:sequence>
          </xsd:complexType>
        </xsd:element>
      </xsd:choice>
    </xsd:complexType>
  </xsd:element>
</xsd:schema>
```

Generating XSD from an XML File

Listing 4.3 is a simplified form of the `Customers.xml` file.

Listing 4.3   **Source XML File** *Customers.xml*

```xml
<?xml version="1.0" encoding="utf-8" ?>
<Customers>
    <Customer id="ALFKI">
        <CompanyName>Alfreds Futterkiste</CompanyName>
        <Contact>
            <FirstName>Maria</FirstName>
            <LastName>Anders</LastName>
            <Title>Sales Representative</Title>
        </Contact>
    </Customer>
</Customers>
```

Running the `xsd.exe` tool as follows generates an XSD file with the name `Customers.xsd`:

```
Xsd Customers.xml
```

Listing 4.4 is the XSD file that is generated.

Listing 4.4   **The Generated** *Customers.xsd* **File**

```xml
<?xml version="1.0" encoding="utf-8"?>
<xs:schema id="Customers" xmlns=""
xmlns:xs="http://www.w3.org/2001/XMLSchema" xmlns:msdata="urn:schemas-
➥microsoft-com:xml-msdata">
  <xs:element name="Customers" msdata:IsDataset="true">
    <xs:complexType>
      <xs:choice maxOccurs="unbounded">
        <xs:element name="Customer">
          <xs:complexType>
            <xs:sequence>
              <xs:element name="CompanyName" type="xs:string" minOccurs="0"
              ➥msdata:Ordinal="0" />
              <xs:element name="Contact" minOccurs="0" maxOccurs="unbounded">
                <xs:complexType>
                  <xs:sequence>
                    <xs:element name="FirstName" type="xs:string"
                    ➥minOccurs="0" />
                    <xs:element name="LastName" type="xs:string"
                    ➥minOccurs="0" />
                    <xs:element name="Title" type="xs:string" minOccurs="0" />
                  </xs:sequence>
                </xs:complexType>
              </xs:element>
            </xs:sequence>
            <xs:attribute name="id" type="xs:string" />
          </xs:complexType>
```

```
      </xs:element>
        </xs:choice>
      </xs:complexType>
    </xs:element>
  </xs:schema>
```

Generating *DataSet* and Classes from an XSD File

The following command generates a `DataSet` from the XSD file
`Customers.xsd` that was generated from `Customers.xml` (refer to Listing 4.4):

```
Xsd Customers.xsd /d /l:VB
```

This generates the source code for the `DataSet` with the filename
`Customers.vb`. Refer to Chapter 8 for a detailed discussion on `DataSet`. Figure
4.33 shows the `DataSet` class `Customers` as viewed in the Object browser of a
Visual Basic .NET class library project. Note that, for the reason of space, the
`Customers.vb` file was converted into assembly to provide a quick view of the
`Customers` class.

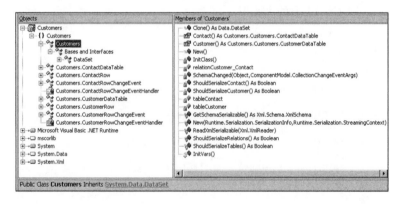

Figure 4.33   The generated `DataSet` class, as viewed in the Object browser.

The tool can only process schemas, which reference the www.w3.org, March
16, 2001, XML Schema Specification. Chapter 2, "XML Schemas in .NET,"
provides more detailed samples of generating classes from an XSD file.

Generating an XSD File from a Type or Types in a Run-Time Assembly File

Consider Listing 4.5, which contains the code in the C# file `class1.cs`.
Compile this to have the assembly `OrderInvoice.dll`. Alternatively, you can
create an executable for this example. The following command compiles the
`class1.cs` file into the assembly `OrderInvoice.dll`:

```
csc /out:OrderInvoice.dll /target:library class1.cs
```

Listing 4.5 **The C# File** *class1.cs* **in the Class Library** *OrderInvoice*

```csharp
using System;
using System.Xml.Serialization;


    /* Applying the XmlTypeAttribute to a class instructs the xsd.exe tool
    about the XML type's namespace, the XML type name, and whether to
    include the type in the XML schema document.
     */
     [XmlType(Namespace = "http://www.mydomain.com",
         TypeName = "USAddress")]
    public class Address
    {
        /* Setting the IsNullable property to false instructs the
        xsd.exe tool to in turn set the 'nillable' property of the element
         to false in the generated schema*/
        [XmlElementAttribute(IsNullable = false)]
        public string Street;
        [XmlElementAttribute(IsNullable = false)]
        public string City;
        [XmlElementAttribute(IsNullable = false)]
        public string State;
        [XmlElementAttribute(IsNullable = false)]
        public string Zip;
    }


    public class Invoice
    {
        [XmlElementAttribute(IsNullable = false)]
        public Person Customer;
        [XmlElementAttribute(IsNullable = false)]
        public Address       ShippingAddress;
        [XmlElementAttribute(IsNullable = false)]
        public Order[] Orders;
    }

    public class Person
    {
        [XmlElementAttribute(IsNullable = false)]
        public string FirstName;
        [XmlElementAttribute(IsNullable = false)]
        public string LastName;
    }

    public class Order
    {
        /* The XmlAttribute instructs the xsd.exe tool to generate the Qty
        field as an XML attribute instead of an XML element (the default
        ↩behavior).
```

```
        Secondly, explicitly setting the AttributeName to 'Quantity'
        ↵specifies that the Qty field should be encoded with the name
        ↵Quantity*/
        [XmlAttribute (AttributeName = "Quantity")]
        public int Qty;
        [XmlElement (ElementName = "ProductName", IsNullable = false)]
        public string ItemName;
        [XmlElementAttribute(IsNullable = false)]
        public string ShipDate;
    }
```

The comments in the preceding code explain how you can use the different attributes of the System.Xml.Serialization namespace to give some hints to the xsd.exe tool about the schema generation. These attributes are the same that you would use to instruct the XmlSerializer on how objects are encoded into XML. You can find a more detailed discussion on XML serialization and the System.Xml.Serialization. XmlSerializer class in Chapter 10, "XML Serialization."

Pass this assembly file to the xsd.exe tool and the tool generates two schema files, schema0.xsd and schema1.xsd, as shown in Figure 4.34.

Figure 4.34   Generating an XSD file from a type or types in a run-time assembly file.

Listing 4.6 and Listing 4.7 contain the code for the generated schema files.

Listing 4.6   *Schema0.xsd*

```
<?xml version="1.0" encoding="utf-8"?>
<xs:schema elementFormDefault="qualified"
xmlns:xs="http://www.w3.org/2001/XMLSchema">
  <xs:import namespace="http://www.mydomain.com" />
  <xs:element name="USAddress" nillable="true"
xmlns:q1="http://www.mydomain.com" type="q1:USAddress" />
  <xs:element name="Invoice" nillable="true" type="Invoice" />
  <xs:complexType name="Invoice">
    <xs:sequence>
```

continues

Listing 4.6 *Continued*

```
        <xs:element minOccurs="0" maxOccurs="1" name="Customer" type="Person" />
        <xs:element minOccurs="0" maxOccurs="1" name="ShippingAddress"
        xmlns:q2="http://www.mydomain.com" type="q2:USAddress" />
        <xs:element minOccurs="0" maxOccurs="unbounded" name="Orders"
        type="Order" />
      </xs:sequence>
    </xs:complexType>
    <xs:complexType name="Person">
      <xs:sequence>
        <xs:element minOccurs="0" maxOccurs="1" name="FirstName"
        type="xs:string" />
        <xs:element minOccurs="0" maxOccurs="1" name="LastName"
        type="xs:string" />
      </xs:sequence>
    </xs:complexType>
    <xs:complexType name="Order">
      <xs:sequence>
        <xs:element minOccurs="0" maxOccurs="1" name="ProductName"
        type="xs:string" />
        <xs:element minOccurs="0" maxOccurs="1" name="ShipDate"
        type="xs:string" />
      </xs:sequence>
      <xs:attribute name="Quantity" type="xs:int" />
    </xs:complexType>
    <xs:element name="Person" nillable="true" type="Person" />
    <xs:element name="Order" nillable="true" type="Order" />
</xs:schema>
```

Listing 4.7 *Schema1.xsd*

```
<?xml version="1.0" encoding="utf-8"?>
<xs:schema xmlns:tns="http://www.mydomain.com" elementFormDefault="qualified"
targetNamespace="http://www.mydomain.com"
xmlns:xs="http://www.w3.org/2001/XMLSchema">
  <xs:complexType name="USAddress">
    <xs:sequence>
      <xs:element minOccurs="0" maxOccurs="1" name="Street" type="xs:string" />
      <xs:element minOccurs="0" maxOccurs="1" name="City" type="xs:string" />
      <xs:element minOccurs="0" maxOccurs="1" name="State" type="xs:string" />
      <xs:element minOccurs="0" maxOccurs="1" name="Zip" type="xs:string" />
    </xs:sequence>
  </xs:complexType>
</xs:schema>
```

Web Services Discovery Tool (*Disco.exe*)

Web service discovery is the process of locating and interrogating web service descriptions. You can read more about web services and the web services description and discovery process in Chapter 11. Potential web-service clients can learn that a web service exists and how to interact with it by performing a discovery. When you are creating a web service client, this web services discovery tool (`Disco.exe`) helps you to discover these URLs of web services located on a web server and save the documents related to each web service on the local disk. Then you can also use the `.wsdl`, `.xsd`, `.disco`, and `.discomap` files produced by this tool as input to the web services description language tool (`Wsdl.exe`) to create web-service clients.

This syntax is for use of this command-line tool:

```
disco [options] URL
```

The `URL` in the argument is the discovery document (`.wsdl`, `.xsd`, `.disco`, and `.discomap` files) for which the tool needs to discover and produce published discovery documents.

Table 4.3 lists the available options for this tool.

Table 4.3   *Disco.exe* **Options**

Option	Description
/d[omain]:domain	Specifies the domain name to use when connecting to a proxy server that requires authentication.
/nosave	Does not save the discovered documents or results (`.wsdl`, `.xsd`, `.disco`, and `.discomap` files) to disk. The default is to save these documents.
/nologo	Suppresses the Microsoft start-up banner display.
/o[ut]:directoryName	Specifies the output directory in which to save the discovered documents. The default is the current directory.
/p[assword]:password	Specifies the password to use when connecting to a proxy server that requires authentication.
/proxy:URL	Specifies the URL of the proxy server to use for HTTP requests. The default is to use the system proxy setting.
/proxydomain:domain or /pd:domain	Specifies the domain to use when connecting to a proxy server that requires authentication.
/proxypassword:password or /pp:password	Specifies the password to use when connecting to a proxy server that requires authentication.

continues

Table 4.3 **Continued**

Option	Description
/proxyusername:username or /pu:username	Specifies the username to use when connecting to a proxy server that requires authentication.
/u[sername]:username	Specifies the username to use when connecting to a proxy server that requires authentication.
/?	Displays command syntax and options for the tool.

Using the *disco.exe* Tool

Assume that your web server exposes the two web services: a news update service described by the Web Services Description Language (WSDL) document available at http://localhost/MyWebServices/NewsService.asmx?wsdl and a stock quote service described by the WSDL document at http://localhost/MyWebServices/StockQuoteService.asmx?wsdl.

Listing 4.8 is an example of a .disco file that contains the links to the preceding two web service descriptions.

Listing 4.8 **A Sample Disco File (*MyWebServices.disco*)**

```
<?xml version="1.0" encoding="utf-8" ?>
<disco:discovery xmlns:disco="http://schemas.xmlsoap.org/disco/"
xmlns:scl="http://schemas.xmlsoap.org/disco/scl/">
    <scl:contractRef
ref="http://localhost/MyWebServices/NewsService.asmx?wsdl"
docRef="http://localhost/MyWebServices/NewsService.asmx" />
    <scl:contractRef
ref="http://localhost/MyWebServices/StockQuoteService.asmx?wsdl"
docRef="http://localhost/MyWebServices/StockQuoteService.asmx" />
</disco:discovery>
```

Running the tool, as shown in the following code line, generates and saves the four documents, StockQuoteService.wsdl, NewsService.wsdl, MyWebservices.disco, and results.discomap, to a subfolder named DISCO-FOLDER:

```
disco /o:DISCOFOLDER http://localhost/MyWebServices/MyWebServices.disco
```

Figure 4.35 shows the tool in action.

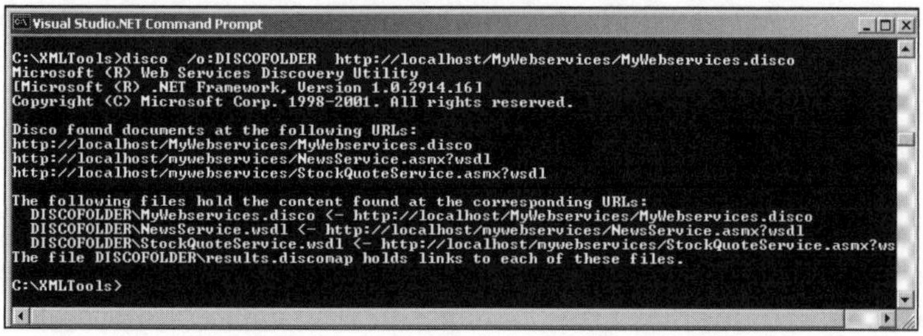

Figure 4.35   Running the disco.exe tool.

If the tool cannot find discoverable resources at the specified URL, you see an error message displayed in the Command window.

Of the four XML documents generated, the `MyWebservices.disco` is a copy of the `MyWebservices.disco` that was provided as an input to the tool; the files `StockQuoteService.wsdl` and `NewsService.wsdl` are the WSDL contract files that you will use with the `wsdl.exe` tool to generate the client proxies for the web service; finally, `results.discomap` is generated by the tool and contains the mapping between the files saved on the local disk and the original documents on the web server. Listing 4.9 contains the contents of the `results.discomap` file.

Listing 4.9   *results.discomap*

```
<?xml version="1.0" encoding="utf-8"?>
<DiscoveryClientResultsFile
  xmlns:xsi="http://www.w3.org/2001/XMLSchema-instance"
  xmlns:xsd="http://www.w3.org/2001/XMLSchema">
  <Results>
      <DiscoveryClientResult
        referenceType="System.Web.Services.Discovery.
        DiscoveryDocumentReference"
        url="http://localhost/MyWebservices/MyWebservices.disco"
        filename="MyWebservices.disco" />
      <DiscoveryClientResult
        referenceType="System.Web.Services.Discovery.ContractReference"
        url="http://localhost/mywebservices/NewsService.asmx?wsdl"
        filename="NewsService.wsdl" />
      <DiscoveryClientResult
        referenceType="System.Web.Services.Discovery.ContractReference"
        url="http://localhost/mywebservices/StockQuoteService.asmx?wsdl"
        filename="StockQuoteService.wsdl" />
  </Results>
</DiscoveryClientResultsFile>
```

A `.discomap` file is similar to a `.disco` file published by the web service and contains links to other resources that describe the web service. You can only specify the file path and not a URL to a `.discomap` discovery document with the Wsdl.exe tool. The document results.discomap, generated by the tool, can only be used on the client as an input to the Wsdl.exe to create web-service clients.

If you have created a web service project using Visual Studio .NET, you can see the <Web Sevice Name>.vsdisco auto-generated by the IDE. You can get the same results by using this file with the disco.exe as an alternative to the .disco file. You can use this on the server to get the .disco file generated for you and publish it for the clients. Listing 4.10 is a sample .vsdisco file that's generated by the IDE.

Listing 4.10   *My WebServices.vsdisco*

```
<?xml version="1.0" ?>
<dynamicDiscovery xmlns="urn:schemas-dynamicdiscovery:disco.2000-03-17">
<exclude path="_vti_cnf" />
<exclude path="_vti_pvt" />
<exclude path="_vti_log" />
<exclude path="_vti_script" />
<exclude path="_vti_txt" />
<exclude path="Web References" />
</dynamicDiscovery>
```

When a client requests this file, the server dynamically checks for the available web services and returns the discovery information rather than returning the preceding file contents. This contains the list of web services in the current folder and any .disco files available in the subfolders. You can see the results by typing the URL in the address location of a web browser, as shown in Figure 4.36.

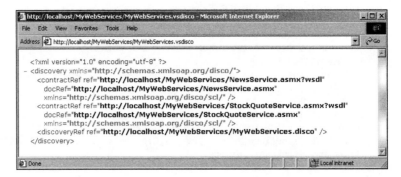

Figure 4.36   Viewing the .vsdisco file in the browser.

If you are aware of the web service URL and you want the corresponding disco file, you can get it simply by appending ?disco, just as you did to get the WSDL file for a web service.

Making the Name of the Discovery Document Transparent to the Clients

If you want prospective consumers of your web service to not have to know the name of any discovery documents during the discovery process, you can do so by adding a link to the default page for the Internet Information Server (IIS) application. First, set a default page for the IIS application in the Properties dialog box from the IIS Microsoft Management Console (MMC) snap-in (see Figure 4.37).

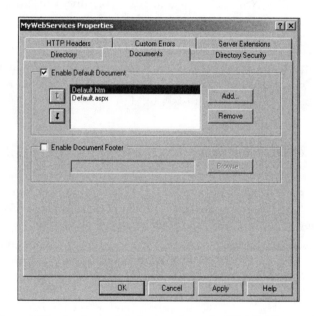

Figure 4.37   Setting a default page from the IIS MMC snap–in.

You can then add a link to the discovery document in the <HEAD> tag of the default web page for the web server, as shown in the following code:

```
<HTML>
    <HEAD>
        <LINK type='text/xml' rel='alternate' href='MyWebServices.disco' />
    </HEAD>
    <BODY>    <H1>My Web Services Default Page</H1>    </BODY>
</HTML>
```

Now it is possible for the clients to provide the URL input to the `disco.exe` tool:

```
disco http://localhost/MyWebServices
```

If you set the default page for the web application as an XML document, you need to place the following code at the top of this document:

```
<?xml-stylesheet type="text/xml" alternate="yes" href="MyWebServices.disco" ?>
```

Web Services Description Language Tool (*WSDL.exe*)

The WSDL tool generates code for web services and web-service clients from WSDL contract files, XSD Schemas, and `.discomap` discovery documents. The following is the syntax to run the `wsdl.exe` tool:

```
wsdl [options] {URL | path}
```

The URL or path can be a WSDL contract file (.wsdl), XSD schema file (.xsd), or discovery document (.disco). A `.discomap` discovery document can be specified only as a path and not as a URL. Table 4.4 lists the available options.

Table 4.4 **WSDL Tool Options**

Option	Description
`/appsettingurlkey:key` or `/urlkey:key`	Specifies the configuration key to use in order to read the default value for the URL property when generating code.
`/appsettingbaseurl:baseurl` or `/baseurl:baseurl`	Specifies the base URL to use when calculating the URL fragment. The tool calculates the URL fragment by converting the relative URL from the `baseurl` argument to the URL in the WSDL document. You must specify the `/appsettingurlkey` option with this option.
`/d[omain]:domain`	Specifies the domain name to use when connecting to a server that requires authentication.
`/l[anguage]:language`	Specifies the language to use for the generated proxy class. You can specify CS (C#; default), VB (Visual Basic), or JS (JScript) as the `language` argument. You can also specify the fully qualified name of a class that implements the `System.CodeDom.Compiler.CodeDomProvider` class.

Option	Description
/n[amespace]:namespace	Specifies the namespace for the generated proxy or template. The default namespace is the global namespace.
/nologo	Suppresses the Microsoft start-up banner display.
/o[ut]:filename	Specifies the file in which to save the generated proxy code. The tool derives the default filename from the web service name. The tool saves generated `DataSets` in different files.
/p[assword]:password	Specifies the password to use when connecting to a server that requires authentication.
/protocol:protocol	Specifies the protocol to implement. You can specify `SOAP` (default), `HttpGet`, `HttpPost`, or a custom protocol specified in the configuration file.
/proxy:URL	Specifies the URL of the proxy server to use for HTTP requests. The default is to use the system proxy setting.
/proxydomain:domain or /pd:domain	Specifies the domain to use when connecting to a proxy server that requires authentication.
/proxypassword:password or /pp:password	Specifies the password to use when connecting to a proxy server that requires authentication.
/proxyusername:username or /pu:username	Specifies the username to use when connecting to a proxy server that requires authentication.
/server	Generates an abstract class for a web service based on the contracts. The default is to generate client `proxy` classes.
/u[sername]:username	Specifies the username to use when connecting to a server that requires authentication.
/?	Displays command syntax and options for the tool.

The following is an example of generation of the source file, `StockQuote.cs`, by running the `wsdl.exe` tool from the command prompt with the Microsoft logo suppressed:

```
wsdl /o:StockQuote.cs  /nologo
http://localhost/MyWebServices/StockQuoteService.asmx?WSDL
```

Figure 4.38 shows the source file StockQuote.cs being generated by using the wsdl.exe tool.

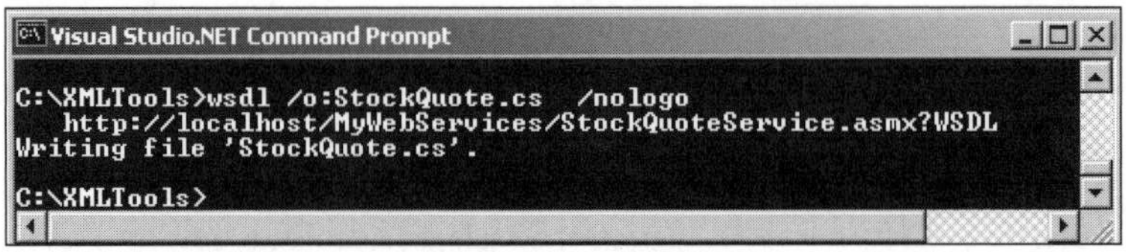

Figure 4.38 Generating source file using the wsdl.exe tool.

Listing 4.11 is the source for the file StockQuote.cs.

Listing 4.11 *StockQuote.cs*

```
//
// This source code was auto-generated by wsdl, Version=1.0.2914.16.
//
using System.Diagnostics;
using System.Xml.Serialization;
using System;
using System.Web.Services.Protocols;
using System.Web.Services;


[System.Web.Services.WebServiceBindingAttribute(Name="Service1Soap",
Namespace="http://tempuri.org/")]
public class Service1 : System.Web.Services.Protocols.SoapHttpClientProtocol
{

    [System.Diagnostics.DebuggerStepThroughAttribute()]
    public Service1() {
        this.Url = "http://localhost/MyWebServices/StockQuoteService.asmx";
    }

    [System.Diagnostics.DebuggerStepThroughAttribute()]

[System.Web.Services.Protocols.SoapDocumentMethodAttribute("http://tempuri.org/
➥GetQuote", Use=System.Web.Services.Description.SoapBindingUse.Literal,
➥ParameterStyle=System.Web.Services.Protocols.SoapParameterStyle.Wrapped)]
    public System.Double GetQuote(string symbol) {
        object[] results = this.Invoke("GetQuote", new object[] {
                    symbol});
        return ((System.Double)(results[0]));
    }

    [System.Diagnostics.DebuggerStepThroughAttribute()]
    public System.IAsyncResult BeginGetQuote(string symbol,
```

```
System.AsyncCallback callback, object asyncState) {
        return this.BeginInvoke("GetQuote", new object[] {
                        symbol}, callback, asyncState);
    }

    [System.Diagnostics.DebuggerStepThroughAttribute()]
    public System.Double EndGetQuote(System.IAsyncResult asyncResult) {
        object[] results = this.EndInvoke(asyncResult);
        return ((System.Double)(results[0]));
    }
}
```

Notice in the source that the class `Service1` does not belong to any name-space. If you want this class to be added to a namespace, you can manually edit the source or alternatively use the `namespace` option with the `wsdl.exe` tool. Do not worry if you do not understand the details of the source generated. These are the low-level details for making the SOAP calls to the web ser-vice—all wrapped up as objects. You are only required to use the `GetQuote()` method in your client application.

The language defaults to C#, so if you want a Visual Basic .NET source file generated, you must run the tool by setting the language option to Visual Basic, as shown here:

```
wsdl o/StockQuote.vb /l:vb
http://localhost/MyWebServices/StockQuoteService.asmx?WSDL
```

Listing 4.12 is the source for the auto-generated `StockQuote.vb` file.

Listing 4.12 **StockQuote.vb**

```
Option Strict Off
Option Explicit On

Imports System
Imports System.Diagnostics
Imports System.Web.Services
Imports System.Web.Services.Protocols
Imports System.Xml.Serialization

'
'This source code was auto-generated by wsdl, Version=1.0.2914.16.
'

<System.Web.Services.WebServiceBindingAttribute(Name:="Service1Soap",
[Namespace]:="http://tempuri.org/")>  _
Public Class Service1
    Inherits System.Web.Services.Protocols.SoapHttpClientProtocol
```

continues

Listing 4.12   *Continued*

```
<System.Diagnostics.DebuggerStepThroughAttribute()>
Public Sub New()
    MyBase.New
    Me.Url = "http://localhost/MyWebServices/StockQuoteService.asmx"
End Sub

<System.Diagnostics.DebuggerStepThroughAttribute(),

System.Web.Services.Protocols.SoapDocumentMethodAttribute("http://tempuri.org
/GetQuote", Use:=System.Web.Services.Description.SoapBindingUse.Literal,
ParameterStyle:=System.Web.Services.Protocols.SoapParameterStyle.Wrapped)> _
    Public Function GetQuote(ByVal symbol As String) As Double
        Dim results() As Object = Me.Invoke("GetQuote", New Object()
        {symbol})
        Return CType(results(0),Double)
    End Function

<System.Diagnostics.DebuggerStepThroughAttribute()> _
Public Function BeginGetQuote(ByVal symbol As String, ByVal callback As
System.AsyncCallback, ByVal asyncState As Object) As System.IAsyncResult
    Return Me.BeginInvoke("GetQuote", New Object() {symbol}, callback,
    asyncState)
End Function

<System.Diagnostics.DebuggerStepThroughAttribute()> _
Public Function EndGetQuote(ByVal asyncResult As System.IAsyncResult) As
Double
    Dim results() As Object = Me.EndInvoke(asyncResult)
    Return CType(results(0),Double)
End Function
End Class
```

You can compile this into a .NET library assembly for use in your client
applications. We use the VBC.EXE command-line compiler, as shown here:

```
vbc /t:library /out:StockClient\bin\VBStockQuote.dll  /r:System.dll
/r:System.Xml.dll /r:System.Web.dll /r:System.Web.Services.dll  StockQuote.vb
```

This command creates the assembly file VBStockQuote.dll and places it in the
\bin directory of your client application so you can create in the \StockClient
directory. You can use the following command for the C# source file
StockQuote.cs to create the assembly file CSStockQuote.dll:

```
csc /t:library /out:StockClient\bin\CSStockQuote.dll  /r:System.dll
/r:System.Xml.dll /r:System.Web.dll /r:System.Web.Services.dll  StockQuote.cs
```

Soapsuds (*soapsuds.exe*)

The Soapsuds tool helps you compile client applications that communicate with web services using a technique called *.NET Remoting*. .NET Remoting provides a framework for objects in different application domains or processes to seamlessly communicate with each other. This infrastructure offers a powerful, yet simple, programming model and run-time support for making these interactions transparent. You can read more about .NET Remoting in Chapter 11, "Creating and Using ASP.NET Web Services."

The Soapsuds tool can be used in the following two ways:

- **On the server**—.NET Remoting server objects (managed classes and COM objects) use this tool to generate WSDL files or XML Schemas that can serve as metadata, describing the services exposed in a common language run-time assembly. Any client that can read and generate SOAP requests corresponding to the WSDL file can invoke this object and communicate to it by using SOAP.

- **On the client**—.NET Remoting uses metadata to dynamically create proxy objects on the client (for example, using the Activator.GetObject() method call). The proxy objects that are created at the client side have the same members as the original server class. In the client application, after an instance of the proxy object is handed over to the client, the client application makes method calls on the Remote Object through this local proxy object. The rest of the code assumes that the methods and properties of the Remote Object are available locally on the proxy object. So, the client needs to reference the assembly while he or she compiles the client object.

The following code snippet is from an example in Chapter 11. This first statement gets the proxy object for the Remote Object named AddressEntries dynamically from the GetObject() method. The second statement calls the GetCount() on this proxy.

```
AddressEntries addrEntires  =    (AddressEntries)Activator.GetObject(
typeof( RemotingAddressBookService.AddressEntries),
"http://localhost:8085/AddressEntries.soap");


divAddrCount.InnerHtml = "<B>Total number of Addresses in the"
+ " Address Book: </B>" + addrEntires.GetCount();
```

For this code to compile properly, the information about the method name GetCount, which is actually a method exposed by the Remote Object, must be locally available to the compiler on the client.

.NET clients use the Soapsuds tool to download the XML schema from the server (generated on the server) to generate source files or an assembly that contains only metadata, no code. This assembly can be used to compile the client. Note that, alternatively, the clients can use the metadata assembly that is generated on the server and distribute it to the clients.

In addition, Soapsuds can create a static `proxy` object that wraps up the calls to the remote server object.

This is the syntax for running the `Soapsuds.exe` tool:

```
soapsuds {-url:schemaUrl | -types:type1,assemblyname[,serviceEndpoint]
[;type2,assemblyname][...]] | -is:schemafile | -ia:assemblyfile} [options]
```

Table 4.5 lists the available options.

Table 4.5 **Soapsuds Tool Options**

Option	Description
domain:domain or -d:domain	Specifies the domain name to use when connecting to a server that requires a domain name for authentication.
generatecode or -gc	Generates code. This option is equivalent to using -od:., where the additional period indicates that the code should be placed in the current directory.
Httpproxyname:name or -hpn:name	Specifies the HTTP proxy name to use when connecting to a server through an HTTP proxy server.
Httpproxyport:number or -hpp:number	Specifies the HTTP proxy port number to use when connecting to a server through an HTTP proxy server.
-inputassemblyfile: assemblyfile or -ia:assemblyfile	Specifies the input assembly file. The tool imports all types from the assembly. When you specify an input assembly, do not include the .exe or .dll extension.
-inputdirectory:directory or -id:directory	Specifies the directory location of input dynamic link library (DLL) files.
-inputschemafile:schemafile or -is:schemafile	Specifies the input XML schema file.
-nowrappedproxy or -nowp	Does not create a wrapped proxy. If you do not specify this option, the tool creates a wrapped proxy by default.

Option	**Description**

`-outputassemblyfile:`
`assemblyfile`
or
`-oa:assemblyfile`
	Saves output to the specified assembly file. `Soapsuds.exe` always generates source code when it generates an assembly.

`outputdirectory:output`
`directory`
or
`-od:outputdirectory`
	Saves output to the specified output directory.

`-outputschemafile:schemafile`
or
`-os:schemafile`
	Saves output to the specified XML Schema file.

`-password:password`
or
`-p:password`
	Specifies the password to use when connecting to a server that requires authentication.

`-proxynamespace:namespace`
or
`-pn`
	Specifies the namespace for the code in the generated proxy.

`-serviceendpoint:URL`
or
`-se:URL`
	Specifies the URL or the path to the URL for the service endpoint to place in the WSDL file.

`-strongnamefile:filename`
or
`-sn:filename`
	Signs the assembly being generated with the key pair found in filename. You can generate this file by using the Strong Name tool (`Sn.exe`).

`-types: type1,assemblyname`
`[,serviceEndpoint] [;type2,`
`assemblyname[,serviceEndpoint]`
`] [...]`
	Specifies the input type list.

`-urltoschema:schemaURL`
or
`-url:schemaURL`
	Specifies the URL from which to retrieve the XML schema.

`-username:username`
or
`-u:username`
	Specifies the username to use when connecting to a server that requires authentication.

`-wrappedproxy`
or
`-wp`
	Creates a wrapped proxy. This is the default.

`-wsdl`	Generates WSDL schema. This is the default.

The following sections contain a few sample commands that show the use of the Soapsuds tool with the different options listed in Table 4.5.

Downloading the XML Schema for the Web Service

The following command downloads a schema from a URL and saves it to an XML file:

```
soapsuds -url:http://localhost/Service/MyService.soap?wsdl -os:MyService.xml
```

The following command downloads a schema from a URL and generates code:

```
soapsuds -url:http://localhost/Service/MyService.soap?wsdl -gc
```

The following command downloads a schema from a URL, generates code, compiles, and generates an assembly:

```
soapsuds -url:http://localhost/Service/MyService.soap?wsdl -oa:StockQuote.dll
```

Converting a Type to a Schema

The following command converts a type to a schema and saves it to a file:

```
soapsuds -types:MyClass.MyMethod,Service -os:StockQuote.xml
```

The following command converts a type to a schema and generates code:

```
soapsuds -types:MyClass.MyMethod,Service -gc
```

Other Microsoft XML Tools

Now that you're comfortable with most .NET tools for XML, let's complete the discussion with a brief overview of a few non .NET XML tools available from Microsoft.

XML Notepad

Microsoft XML Notepad application enables you to create and edit XML documents quickly and easily. The tool displays the structure of your XML data in an intuitive and simple user interface that graphically represents it in a tree structure. The interface presents two panes: The one on the left represents the structure with a tree control; the one on the right displays the values. You can add elements, attributes, comments, and text to the XML document by creating the tree structure in the left pane and entering values in the right pane's corresponding text boxes.

Figure 4.39 shows XML Notepad with an XML document loaded into it. The following features can be useful when you create and edit your documents with XML Notepad:

- **New, open, save and exit**—The File menu option provides these standard options that are common to text editors, such as creating new documents, opening existing documents, saving documents, and exiting the XML Notepad application.

- **Inserting an XML node**—To insert a new XML node, you can highlight the node relative to which you want to insert the new node. Then select the appropriate node type that you want to insert. Figure 4.40 shows a new child element being added to the Customer node.

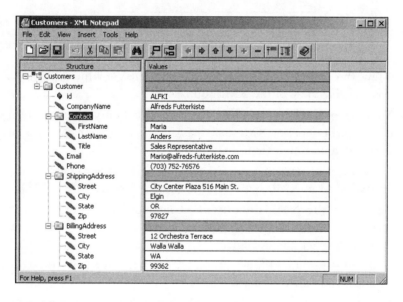

Figure 4.39 An XML document loaded into the XML Notepad.

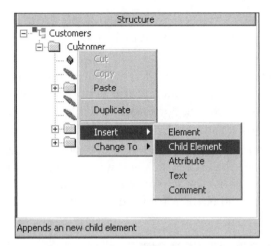

Figure 4.40   Inserting an XML node.

- **View the source**—Selecting Source from the View menu displays a non-editable view of the XML source.

- **Validating XML**—If you have IE 5.*x* installed on your computer, you can perform DTD or XML Schema validation on your files by enabling the validation option from the options.

- **Creating a schema**—You can create an XML schema because schemas are expressed in XML syntax. You cannot, however, create a DTD.

- **Searching the XML document**—Clicking Find from the Edit menu makes the Find dialog box appear. From here, you can provide your criteria to search the document.

- **Options**—Selecting Options from the Tools menu allows you to enable or disable the XML Notepad options.

- **Converting a node's type**—To change the type of a leaf node, you can highlight the node to change and then select Change To from the Tools menu.

Apart from the preceding list, you might also find some interesting features, such as Dragging and Dropping Nodes, Duplicating a Subtree, and so on.

Downloading the XML Notepad Tool
You can download the XML Notepad tool from this URL on Microsoft's MSDN site:
`http://msdn.microsoft.com/xml/notepad/intro.asp`

Command-Line Transformation Utility (*MSXSL.EXE*)

Imagine that, in a staging environment, you want to merge two XML documents into one before you push it to the production environment, or say that you want to filter out a large XML document into a smaller one. You would surely choose to write an XSL stylesheet because the declarative nature of XSL saves you from having to write code using any specific language or an XML parser implementation. But, if you want to perform the transformation using the Microsoft XSL processor, you must write code to load the source document and the stylesheet, followed by the calls to the methods that perform the transformation. But what if you want to perform all the transformation in an off-the-shelf manner? One workaround is to use the IE 5.*x* browser to perform a transformation and copy the results from the browser and paste it to a new file.

MSXSL command-line utility lets you perform off-the-shelf XSL transformations by invoking `MSXML3.DLL` or `MSXML4.DLL`. To use this tool, you must install MSXML 2.6 or later on your computer. The following is the syntax for running the tool from the command prompt:

```
MSXSL source stylesheet [options] [param=value...] [xmlns:prefix=uri...]
```

Here, `param` indicates the XSL Transformations (XSLT) parameters that conform to the XML QName syntax. There can be any number of parameters—a white space needs to separate a parameter value from the next parameter name.

`xmlns:prefix=uri` indicates the prefix part that the parameter names and the start mode name can contain. This prefix is a convenience alias for a namespace Uniform Resource Identifier (URI) that fully qualifies the name.

Table 4.6 lists the options available.

Table 4.6 **MSXSL Tool Options**

Options	Description
-?	Shows this message.
-o filename	Writes output to a named file. Absence of this makes MSXSL dump the result of the transformation directly to the console window.
-m startMode	By default, template rules are grouped within the empty mode. However, they can be explicitly grouped within another mode by specifying the mode attribute on the `xsl:template` element. The -m option allows you to specify this mode.
-xw	Instructs MSXSL to strip non-significant white space from the input XML document during the load phase.

continues

Table 4.6   **Continued**

Options	Description
-xe	Instructs MSXSL to not resolve external definitions during the parse phase. By default, MSXSL instructs the parser to resolve external definitions, such as document type definition (DTD), external subsets, or external entity references, when parsing the source and stylesheet documents.
-v	By default, MSXSL turns off document validation. This option instructs MSXSL to turn on validation during the parse phase.
-pi	If this option is specified instead of a stylesheet argument, MSXSL uses the href attribute from the XML stylesheet PI in the source document as the name of the stylesheet.
-u version	By default, MSXSL uses the latest version of MSXML that it can locate on the machine. This option lets you use a specific version of MSXML: 2.6, 3.0, 4.0, and so on.
-t	Instructs MSXSL to show load and transformation timings. This helps to measure the relative speed of various transformations.
-	Dash used as source argument loads XML from stdin.
-	Dash used as stylesheet argument loads XSL from stdin.

The following example transforms the source XML file Customers.xml by using the stylesheet format.xsl to the output file out.xml:

```
MSXSL Customers.xml format.xsl -o out.xml
```

If the arguments contain white spaces, you can use single or double quotes, as shown here:

```
MSXSL -o out.xml "C:\XML Tools\MSXSL\Customers.xml" format.xsl
```

Downloading the MSXSL.EXE Tool

You can download the MSXSL.EXE tool from this URL on the MSDN site:

http://download.microsoft.com/download/xml/Utility/2.0/NT5XP/EN-US/msxsl.exe.

For a detailed discussion of all the available options with the tool, visit this page on the MSDN online library: http://msdn.microsoft.com/library/en-us/Dnxslgen/html/msxsl.asp.

Chapter Summary

In this chapter, you explored the XML editor features in Visual Studio .NET, the command-line utilities, xsd.exe, disco.exe, wsdl.exe, and soapsuds.exe, available with the .NET SDK and the non-.NET Microsoft tools, XML Notepad and MSXSL.EXE.

II

XML on the Server

5

MSXML Parser

Now that you've learned the basics of XML and its related technologies, you can begin working with XML documents. The .NET platform introduced the System.XML namespace to work with XML documents. The .NET Framework System.XML classes were modeled after Microsoft's XML Parser, MSXML 3.0, but several improvements were added, such as better standards compliance, extensible APIs, and a simpler programming model. The MSXML Parser still continues to be the cornerstone for native COM applications that use XML (such as Microsoft Internet Explorer, Dynamic HTML applications, Microsoft Office, Visual Basic 6.0, and so on).

In this chapter, you learn how to work with XML documents with the two Application Programming Interfaces (APIs), *Document Object Model (DOM)* and the *Simple API for XML (SAX2)*, as implemented in the high-performance MSXML COM component. This chapter discusses the use of DOM in the client-side and how to continue using MSXML with ASP.NET on the server-side by using the COM Interop services provided in .NET.

Push Versus Pull Models

To understand the differences in the two APIs, it is important to first understand the differences between the push and the pull models. In a *pull model*, the application queries the parser for document contents. With this model, it is possible for the consumer (the application) to pull document contents one at a time and even perform selective processing by skipping over elements of no interest. The parser can make all the document contents available to the application by completing one task: The parser loads the entire document into memory. Because the parser constructs an internal tree structure that allows the application to access the tree structure through the API, the API is also referred to as *tree-based API*.

In the *push model*, the parser notifies the application of the document contents as it encounters them (when it parses through the stream of documents in a forward-only fashion). The parser does this through a sequence of callback methods, or events, fired into the application. These events are similar to the more common events in a graphical user interface (GUI). The application developer must provide the event handlers with the knowledge to handle the events that correspond to the start and end of each tag in the document, the start and end of the document, and the occurrence of a block of text. At any given time, the parser holds only a small part of the document in memory, which is equal to the currently encountered tag and its attributes (in the case of an element or the block of text). The application has to implement the event listeners, which expose a standard set of events. This model is known as an *event-driven interface*. The API is referred as an *event-based API*.

The DOM is an example of the pull model. This standard was produced by the World Wide Web Consortium (W3C). W3C released the first DOM recommendation, the DOM Level 1, in 1998. On November 13, 2000, it released the DOM Level 2 Specification. (You can view this specification at `www.w3.org/TR/2000/REC-DOM-Level-2-Core-20001113/`). At the time of this writing, the DOM Level 3 specification was being drafted (visit `www.w3.org/TR/2001/WD-DOM-Level-3-Core-20010605/` or, for an updated version, visit `www.w3.org/TR/DOM-Level-3-Core/`).

Building Push and Pull Models

Both push and pull models can be built one over the other. To build a push model over a pull model, generate the events by traversing an in-memory data structure constructed by the pull model. On the other hand, you can generate a tree data structure similar to the one in a pull model through the event handlers in the push model.

The DOM is a platform-neutral specification that declares a set of interfaces. These interfaces define how a DOM-compliant parser might allow us to load, access, manipulate, and serialize XML documents. Various DOM implementations are available today for various platforms. Because we are discussing the integration of the ASP.NET and XML technologies, we need to discuss Microsoft's implementation of the DOM interface. This chapter discusses the MSXML implementation that all the ASP and IE 5.x developers currently use.

The *SAX* implementation model uses a push model for document parsing. Although the DOM provides a powerful set of interfaces to access and manipulate the document structure, it has some inherent limitations when it works with large documents. It consumes an enormous amount of memory and it slows down the process during loading because it creates the in-memory representation of the large document. SAX evolved in response to these limitations in the DOM approach discussed by the members of the xml-dev mailing list. David Megginson, who released a specification on May 11, 1998, led this group. He also provided the implementations for several popular XML parsers, including Microsoft's MSXML. The SAX specification, although not backed by any consortia like the W3C, is widely accepted by the XML development community and several parser developers have included support for SAX. Megginson released the latest SAX2 specification with support for namespaces in May of 2000.

Understanding DOM and SAX is easy when you compare them to database cursors. The DOM is similar to the scrollable and updateable cursors, whereas the SAX is similar to the read-only, forward-only cursors.

The .NET Reader and Writer Classes

The .NET `System.XML` assembly provides a combination of stream-based API, such as the SAX model, with a forward-only cursor and pull model, such as the DOM. This is an innovative change in XML document parsing because the SAX model gives us the "best of both the worlds" approach. Chapter 6, "Exploring the System.XML Namespace," looks into the abstract XMLReader and XMLWriter base classes and their concrete implementations. The streaming nature of the classes eliminates the need to create the in-memory representation of the entire document.

One of the most significant benefits in the DOM model is its provision for the random accessing of nodes to insert, delete, or update the nodes. As long as you are working with smaller documents and with the use of permissible resources, you cannot forgo the DOM model. The `System.XML` assembly provides the classes implementing the DOM interfaces. These are similar to the implementation found in MSXML 4.0 (with a few changes).

The MSXML parser is written with COM technology, whereas the classes in the System.XML namespace are written using managed code. Although neither share common code, they are tested using the same suite of regression tests. Furthermore, the same teams at Microsoft were used to design and implement each of the libraries, and large parts of each library are built on the W3C DOM specification. Therefore, both libraries contain similar objects and methods.

New Features and Changes in MSXML 4.0

Over the years, the MSXML component has grown to provide more functionality than just parsing. With the release of MSXML 4.0, the original name MSXML Parser has been changed to Microsoft XML Core Services. The following features and changes in MSXML 4.0 are new compared to MSXML 3.0:

- **Extended support for the final W3C XML Schema (XSD) Recommendation**—Earlier versions of MSXML used the XML data-reduced schema language. Version 4.0 supports validation against W3C XSD schemas (proposed recommendation: March 30, 2001). It's possible to activate XSD validation by using the schemaLocation attribute instead of loading a schema independently and setting it to use a schema cache. Schema type information is accessible in DOM by using additional Schema Object Model (SOM) APIs.

- **Extended support for SAX**—You can use the MXXMLWriter object to generate SAX events out of a DOM tree and, likewise, build a DOM tree out of SAX events. A new object, MXHTMLWriter, enables you to output HTML using a stream of SAX events. It is possible to track namespace declarations through a newly added IMXNamespaceManager interface. A SaxAppWizard utility for Microsoft Visual Studio simplifies C++-based SAX components' development.

- **SAX-based XSD validation and type discovery**—Support for XSD validation using the SAX parser is added through the IMXSchemaDeclHandler extension handler interface according to the SAX2 standard.

- **New and faster parser**—By setting the NewParser property to True, you can use the new and faster XML parser.

- **Removal of Replace mode**—Until MSXML 3.0, you could use Replace mode to make the latest MSXML component simulate MSXML 2.0. But this feature has been completely removed from

MSXML 4.0 to avoid the application-maintenance problems. For the same reason, the version-independent ProgIDs were removed. You must use the version-dependent ProgID MSXML2.DOM Document.4.0 to instantiate the MSXML 4.0 parser.

- **Removal of legacy code**—The Replace mode was intended to support old code while using the newer version of the parser. This made the size of the MSXML component much bigger than it would have normally been. Some of the legacy features that were removed include the old non-conformant XSL (in favor of XSLT 1.0), XSLPattern language (replaced by XPath 1.0), and XDR rudimentary uuid: namespaces.

- **Separate WinHTTP Version 5.0 component**—Functionality of the ServerHTTPRequest component is now provided by a separate WinHTTP 5.0 component, which is shipped and installed with MSXML 4.0. This is a new server-side component that provides reliable HTTP stack functionality.

- **Faster XSLT engine**—An XSLT engine that is at least 4 times faster except for a known serious performance bug with the xsl:key.

DOM and the MSXML Interfaces

The DOM models the documents by using objects, and this model encompasses not only the structure of a document, but also the behavior of a document and the objects of which it is composed. The DOM model identifies these objects and interfaces, their semantics, relationships, and collaborations among them. You can access and manipulate parsed XML content by using the set of interfaces exposed by these objects.

These objects in the DOM tree are referred to as *nodes*. Nodes implement other, more specialized interfaces. The DOM treats nodes as generic objects, which makes it possible for you to load a document and then traverse and manipulate all the nodes. The node types can be found in the *XML DOM Enumerated Constants*, which also defines valid parent and children nodes for each node type. MSXML DOM handles this with four interfaces: DOMDocument, IXMLDOMNode, IXMLDOMNodeList and IXMLDOMNamedNodeMap. This manner of manipulation through the Node interface is referred to as the *simplified* or *flattened view* by the DOM specification. Alternatively, DOM also allows an *object-oriented* interface to a document with a hierarchy of inheritance. This approach requires casts (in Java and other C languages) or queries interface calls in COM environments. These operations are expensive.

The MSXML DOM Interfaces

The DOM Specification defines the *DOM Core API*, which is a set of objects and interfaces used to access and manipulate document objects. These interfaces are broken down into *fundamental interfaces* and *extended interfaces*. Fundamental interfaces must be fully implemented by all conforming implementations of the DOM, including all HTML DOM implementations. The extended interfaces do not need to be implemented by DOM implementations that deal only with HTML, but are only required with the implementations that deal with XML. The MSXML DOM implements both fundamental and extended interfaces. The MSXML objects/interfaces include Microsoft extensions to support namespaces, data types, XML schemas, Extensible Stylesheet Language (XSL), XSL Transformations (XSLT) operations, asynchronous loading, and saving documents. The approach of providing extensions in the same API enables developers to work with a single consistent API for document processing and transformations.

Table 5.1 lists the fundamental interfaces.

Table 5.1 **Fundamental Interfaces**

W3C Interface	MSXML Interface	Description
Node	IXMLDOMNode	Represents a single node in the document tree; the base interface for accessing data in the XML object model. Valid node types are defined in the XML DOM Enumerated Constants. IXMLDOMNode includes support for data types, namespaces, document type definitions (DTDs), and XML schemas.
Document	DOMDocument	Represents the top node of the XML DOM tree.
	IXMLDOMDocument2	Extension of DOMDocument that supports schema caching, runtime validation, and a way to switch on XML Path Language (XPath) support.

W3C Interface	MSXML Interface	Description
DOM Implementation	IXMLDOMImplementation	Provides methods that are independent of any particular instance of the DOM. Useful for finding out whether a specific version of the MSXML parser implementation supports a specified feature.
Document Fragment	IXMLDOMDocumentFragment	Represents a lightweight object that is useful for tree insert operations.
NodeList	IXMLDOMNodeList	Supports iteration and indexed access operations on the live collection of IXMLDOMNode.
Element	IXMLDOMElement	Represents the element object.
Named NodeMap	IXMLDOMNamedNodeMap	Provides iteration and access by name to the collection of attributes. IXMLDOMNamedNodeMap includes support for namespaces.
Attr	IXMLDOMAttribute	Represents an attribute of the IXMLDOMElement. Valid and default values for the attribute are defined in a DTD or schema.
CharacterData	IXMLDOMCharacterData	Provides text manipulation methods used by several objects.
Text	IXMLDOMText	Represents the text content of an element or attribute.
Comment	IXMLDOMComment	Represents the content of an XML comment.

The DOMException, defined in the DOM specification, is raised when a requested operation cannot be performed either because the data is lost or the implementation has become unstable. For languages and object systems that do not support the concept of exceptions, error conditions can be indicated by using native error-reporting mechanisms. MSXML supports parse error reporting through the XMLDOMParseError object, which holds information about the most recent parse error. It returns detailed information about the last error, including the error number, line number, character position, and a text description.

Table 5.2 contains the extended interfaces with their corresponding COM equivalents in MSXML 4.0.

Table 5.2   **Extended Interfaces**

W3C Interface	MSXML Interface	Description
CDATASection	IXMLDOMCDATASection	Quotes or escapes blocks of text so that text is not interpreted as markup language.
DocumentType	IXMLDOMDocumentType	Contains information associated with the document type declaration.
Notation	IXMLDOMNotation	Contains a notation declared in the DTD or schema.
Entity	IXMLDOMEntity	Represents a parsed or unparsed entity in the XML document.
EntityReference	IXMLDOMEntityReference	Represents an entity reference node.
Processing Instruction	IXMLDOMProcessing Instruction	Represents a processing instruction that XML defines to keep processor-specific information in the text of the document.

Microsoft–Specific Interfaces

The objects/interfaces listed in Table 5.3 include Microsoft extensions to support namespaces, data types, XML schemas, XSL, and XSL Transformations (XSLT) operations.

Table 5.3   **Microsoft Extensions**

MSXML Interface	Description
XMLSchemaCache	Represents a set of namespace Uniform Resource Identifiers (URIs). Used by the schemas and namespaces properties on IXMLDOMDocument2.
IXMLDOMSchemaCollection	Represents a SchemaCache object.
IXSLProcessor	Used for transformations with compiled stylesheets.
IXSLTemplate	Represents a cached XSL stylesheet.
IXMLDOMSelection	Represents the list of nodes that match a given XSL Pattern or XML Path Language (XPath) expression.
IXTLRuntime	Implements methods that can be called from XSLT stylesheets.

The two objects/interfaces in Table 5.4 are provided for communication with HTTP servers.

Table 5.4 **The Object/Interfaces for Establishing HTTP Connection to Web Servers**

MSXML Interface	Description
IXMLHTTPRequest	Provides client-side protocol support for communication with HTTP servers.
IServerXMLHTTPRequest/ServerXMLHTTP	Provides methods and properties that enable you to establish an HTTP connection between files or objects on different web servers.

The DOM interfaces model the entire XML document structure, which allows you to work with all the nodes in the document tree. Look at the sample XML document that's shown in Listing 5.1 and see how the information items in the XML document are modeled by the DOM interfaces.

Listing 5.1 **A Sample XML Document**

```
<?xml version="1.0" encoding="utf-8" ?>
<!DOCTYPE customers SYSTEM "customers.dtd">
<Customers>
    <Customer id="ALFKI">
        <CompanyName>Alfreds Futterkiste</CompanyName>
        <Contact>
            <FirstName>Maria</FirstName>
            <LastName>Anders</LastName>
            <Title>Sales Representative</Title>
        </Contact>
    </Customer>
<!--insert the new customer here-->
    <Customer id="THEBI">
        <CompanyName>The Big Cheese</CompanyName>
        <Contact>
            <FirstName>Liz</FirstName>
            <LastName>Nixon</LastName>
            <Title>Marketing Manager</Title>
        </Contact>
    </Customer>
</Customers>
```

After loading this document into the MSXML DOM, it builds an in-memory representation (see Figure 5.1). Each of the informational items in the document is modeled by the interfaces shown in the boxes beside them. The interfaces on the top denote the collection of the objects. The IXMLDOMNamedNodeMap represents the collection of the attribute nodes and the `IXMLDOMNodeList` represents the collection of the nodes.

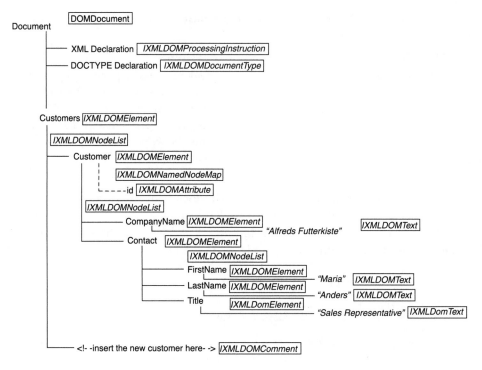

Figure 5.1 The document modeled as tree nodes and
the corresponding MSXML interfaces.

Now that you have an overview of the MSXML DOM interfaces, it's time find out how to use these interfaces to access and manipulate the XML documents. You will see examples of this manipulation on the client-side using HTML and JavaScript in IE browsers (version 5.0 and later) and then on the server-side using ASP.NET.

Instantiating the Parser

The following code shows how you create an instance of the MSXML `DOMDocument` object in JavaScript with MSXML 3.0. All other objects are accessed or created from this object:

```
var objXML = new ActiveXObject("MSXML2.DOMDocument")
```

MSXML 3.0 is designed to exist in *side-by-side* mode with the current version of MSXML on your system. So the old MSXML-related entries in the registry keep pointing to MSXML.dll even after you install MSXML3.dll. You are required to be explicit when you provide the ProgID.

MSXML2.DOMDocument is the version-independent ProgID for a rental-threaded component. If your application requires caching the component into an application or session scope variable, you must create an instance of the *free-threaded model* with the ProgID as MSXML2.FreeThreadedDOMDocument. Rental-threaded documents exhibit better performance because the parser doesn't need to manage concurrent access among threads. You might want to use the free-threaded model when you use cached documents, which is discussed in the section, "Caching Compiled Stylesheets Using `IXMLDOMXSLTemplate` and `IXSLProcessor`."

MSXML 3.0 is backwards compatible with earlier versions, so if you want your old code to start using this version so that you can take advantage of the new features and the performance enhancements, use the `xmlinst.exe` utility to run MSXML 3.0 in *replace mode*. The utility also provides an option to roll back to side-by-side mode.

The following code shows you how to create an instance of the MSXML `DOMDocument` object using the version-dependent ProgID with MSXML 4.0:

```
var objXML = new ActiveXObject("MSXML2.DOMDocument.4.0")
```

Note

Because IE 6.0 ships with MSXML 3.0, we use the MSXML 3.0 version for all client-side examples, in this chapter.

Document Loading States and Validation

This section discusses an application that loads an XML document asynchronously and validates it against a DTD. Listing 5.2 shows the XML document `manycustomers.xml`, which contains 225 customer elements. This document also contains an internal DTD because you will validate this document against the DTD.

Note

For the sake of brevity, Listing 5.2 shows a single `customer` element.

Listing 5.2 **A Customer's XML Document That Contains 255 *Customer* Elements**

```
<?xml version="1.0" encoding="utf-8" ?>
<!DOCTYPE Customers [
    <!ELEMENT Customers (Customer)* >
    <!ELEMENT Customer (CompanyName,Contact)  >
    <!ATTLIST Customer
              id  CDATA  #REQUIRED >
    <!ELEMENT CompanyName (#PCDATA)  >
    <!ELEMENT Contact (FirstName , LastName , Title  )  >
    <!ELEMENT FirstName (#PCDATA)  >
    <!ELEMENT LastName (#PCDATA)  >
    <!ELEMENT Title (#PCDATA)  >
]>
<Customers>
    <Customer id="ALFKI">
        <CompanyName>Alfreds Futterkiste</CompanyName>
        <Contact>
            <FirstName>Maria</FirstName>
            <LastName>Anders</LastName>
            <Title>Sales Representative</Title>
        </Contact>
    </Customer>
    .
    .
    .
</Customers>
```

Listing 5.3 shows the JavaScript code that sets the event handlers for the events onreadystatechange and ondataavailable. You can do this by setting the corresponding properties onreadystatechange and ondataavailable respectively of the DOMDocument object.

Listing 5.3 **The HTML Page for the Loading (*parseevents.htm*)**

```
<html>
    <head>
        <title>Parser Events</title>
    </head>
    <body>
        <div id="state">
        </div>
        <div id="data">
        </div>
    </body>
</html>
<script language="javascript">
```

```
var LOADING       = 1;
var LOADED        = 2;
var INTERACTIVE = 3;
var COMPLETED   = 4;

state.innerHTML = "<B>Data Loading State</B><BR>";
data.innerHTML = "<B>Data Available State</B><BR>";
var objXML = new ActiveXObject("MSXML2.DOMDocument.4.0") ;
objXML.async = true;
objXML.validateOnParse= true;


objXML.onreadystatechange = readyStateChangeHandler;
objXML.ondataavailable        =       dataAvailableHandler ;
objXML.load("manycustomers.xml");

function getTime(currDate)
{
var time =  currDate.getMinutes()
     + ":" + currDate.getSeconds()
     + "." + currDate.getMilliseconds();
return time;
}

function  readyStateChangeHandler()
{
     var  currDate = new Date();
     var time = getTime(currDate);

     state.innerHTML += "Time: " + time + " State: ";

     switch(objXML.readyState)
     {
          case LOADING :
               state.innerHTML += "The loading is in progress.<BR>";
               break;
          case LOADED :
               state.innerHTML += "The document is loaded.<BR>";
               break;
          case INTERACTIVE :
               state.innerHTML +=  "The object model is available as read-
               only.<BR>";
               break;
          case COMPLETED:
               state.innerHTML +=  "The document has been " +
                    "completely loaded, successfully or unsuccessfully.<BR>";
               if (objXML.parseError.errorCode != 0)
               {
                    state.innerHTML += getErrorMsg(objXML.parseError);
               }
               else
```

continues

Listing 5.3 **Continued**

```
              {
                    state.innerHTML += "<BR><B>The XML document was loaded "
                          + "successfully</B><BR><BR>";
              }
              break;
        }
    }

    function getErrorMsg( objError)
    {
        var strError = "";
        strError +=   "<BR><B>The XML document was not loaded "
              + "successfully...</B><BR> ";
        strError +=      "The URL  '"+ objError.url  + "' contained "
              + "the following error <BR>";
        strError +=        "<B>" + objError.reason +      "Line "
              + objError.line + ", Position "
              + objError.linepos + ".</B><BR>";
        strError +=  objError.srcText + "<BR>";
        return strError;
    }

    function dataAvailableHandler()
     {
        var currDate = new Date();
        var time = getTime(currDate);

        data.innerHTML += "Time: " + time + "     Data Available :" +
              objXML.documentElement.childNodes.length + " nodes. <BR>";
     }
    </script>
```

The DOM specification leaves the approach of loading and saving the document to the DOM implementations. MSXML provides two extensions to the DOM API: the `load` method and the `async` property (which loads a document into the DOM). Setting the `async` property to true forces the `load` method to return the control to the caller before the document is completely downloaded. This enables you to do other things while the document loads. This feature is called *asynchronous loading* because, if you set it to false, the control returns only after the document finishes loading.

In this example, you set the `async` property to true so that you can examine the parser events. You attached an `onreadystatechange` event handler called `readyStateChangeHandler` that gets called when the parser's ready state changes. The parser can be in one of the four ready states: *loading*, *loaded*, *interactive*, or *completed*. The method `readyStateChangeHandler()` checks these parser states from the `readyState` property and displays them to the browser by using the DHTML `innerHTML` property.

After the parser is in the completed state, it does not mean that document loading was successful. The `ParseError` object holds information about the most recent parse error that might have occurred during the loading. You must check this property to find out whether the document was loaded successfully and display the error messages, if any, through the `getErrorMsg` method. You set the `validateOnParse` property to true before calling the `load` method. This makes the parser validate the document against a DTD and report any errors through the `ParseError` object.

The loading states and the error message are displayed, as shown in Figure 5.2.

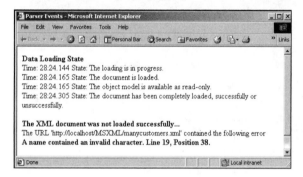

Figure 5.2 The parser ready states and error notification.

Now look at the `ondataavailable` event handler that I repeated in the following code:

```
function dataAvailableHandler()
{
    var currDate = new Date();
    var time = getTime(currDate);

    data.innerHTML += "Time: " + time + "    Data Available :" +
        objXML.documentElement.childNodes.length + " nodes. <BR>";
}
```

The method `dataAvailableHandler()` is the event handler for the `ondataavailable` event. This method is called when the data becomes available to the parser. This allows you to work with the data or display it to the client as soon as it is available. This saves the wait time for the client, in the case of large XML documents using the *synchronous* loading technique. In this example, the number of nodes loaded is displayed with the time shown. Figure 5.3 shows the output after all the 225 nodes are loaded.

Notice that, from the time the ready state is interactive to the time it is complete, almost all the data becomes available to the parser. So you don't have to wait for the entire document to load before you start working with the data. Therefore, in the case of large documents, by setting the async property to false, the user must wait until the entire file downloads to the client machine. The transformation to HTML using XSLT or through the JavaScript program adds more waiting time for the user. On the other hand, with asynchronous download, the user can see the display immediately after data is available to the parser.

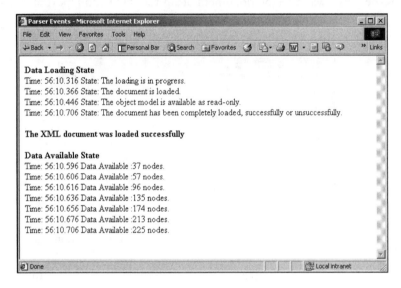

Figure 5.3   The parser ready states and the stages in which data is available after a document is successfully loaded.

Validating the Documents Against Cached Schemas

You saw the validation against DTD in the last section's example; now it's time to see the validation against the *XML Data Reduced (XDR)* schema supported in MSXML 3.0. The IXMLDOMSchemaCollection interface enables you to cache parsed XDR schema definitions in memory and reuse them with different instances of the documents. This leads to improved efficiency and better performance because you do not have to load the XDR file each time you want to perform a validation. Listing 5.4 shows the two XDR files, Customers.xdr and Customer.xdr, the XML file Custdoc.xml, and the HTML file valschema.htm. Running the valschema.htm file in the browser shows you the validation against cached schemas in action.

Listing 5.4 *Customers.xdr*

```
<?xml version="1.0" ?>
<Schema     xmlns = "urn:schemas-microsoft-com:xml-data"
      xmlns:dt = "urn:schemas-microsoft-com:datatypes"
      xmlns:cus="urn:my-Customer">
      <ElementType name = "Customers" content="eltOnly" order="seq" >
            <element type="cus:Customer"     />
      </ElementType>
</Schema>
```

Customer.xdr

```
<?xml version="1.0" ?>
<Schema  xmlns = "urn:schemas-microsoft-com:xml-data"
      xmlns:dt = "urn:schemas-microsoft-com:datatypes">

      <ElementType name="Customer" content="eltOnly"       order="seq">
                  <element type="CompanyName" minOccurs="1" maxOccurs="1"/>
                  <element type="ContactName"  minOccurs="1" maxOccurs="1"/>
      </ElementType>
      <ElementType name="CompanyName" content="textOnly"       order="seq"/>
      <ElementType name="ContactName" content="textOnly"  order="seq"/>
</Schema>
```

Custdoc.xml

```
<?xml version="1.0" encoding="utf-8" ?>
<Customers xmlns="urn:my-Customers" xmlns:cus="urn:my-Customer">
      <cus:Customer>
            <cus:CompanyName>Alfreds Futterkiste</cus:CompanyName>
            <cus:ContactName>Maria Anders</cus:ContactName>
      </cus:Customer>
</Customers>
```

valschema.htm

```
<html>
      <head>
            <title>Schema Validation</title>
      </head>
      <body onload="schemaValidate()">
      </body>
</html>
<script language="javascript">
function schemaValidate()
{
      var objXML = new ActiveXObject("MSXML2.DOMDocument");
      var schemas = new ActiveXObject("MSXML2.XMLSchemaCache");
```

continues

Listing 5.4 *Continued*

```
      schemas.add("urn:my-Customer", "customer.xdr");
      schemas.add("urn:my-Customers", "customers.xdr");
      objXML.schemas=schemas;
      objXML.validateOnParse = false;
      objXML.async = false;
      objXML.load("custdoc.xml");
      var parseError = objXML.validate();

      if(  parseError.errorCode !=0 )
      {
          alert("The document is invalid. " + parseError.reason);
      }
      else
      {
          alert("The document is valid.");
      }
  }
  </script>
```

You can populate the schema collection with some schemas and attach it to the document through the schemas property—defined in the IXMLDOMDocument2 interface. As shown in Listing 5.4 , the validate() method defined in the IXMLDOMDocument2 interface also allows you to perform run-time validation on the currently loaded document. Note that you can use this schema cache in another document's load method.

The MSXML 4.0 supports validation against W3C XSD schemas (Proposed Recommendation: March 30, 2001). Support for XDR will continue so that it is kept backwards compatible. So MSXML 4.0 supports validation using all the three validation types: DTD, XDR, and XSD.

Displaying the Node Details in an XML Document

One of the most common programming tasks you must perform when working with the DOM document is navigating through the nodes in the document. In this section, you look at a simple example that recursively traverses through all the nodes in the document and displays the name, value, and type properties of the nodes. This example introduces you to the IXMLDOMNamedNodeMap and the IXMLDOMNodeList interfaces and gives you a feel of the *flattened view* (the "everything-is-a-node" approach), as discussed earlier in the "DOM and the MSXML Interfaces" section. You use an XML document that's similar to Listing 5.1. It is repeated here with an inline DTD and the comments removed (the file is named `displayNodes.xml`):

```xml
<?xml version="1.0" encoding="utf-8" ?>
<!DOCTYPE Customers [
    <!ELEMENT Customers (Customer)* >
    <!ELEMENT Customer (CompanyName,Contact)  >
    <!ATTLIST Customer
                id  CDATA  #REQUIRED >
    <!ELEMENT CompanyName (#PCDATA)  >
    <!ELEMENT Contact (FirstName , LastName , Title  )  >
    <!ELEMENT FirstName (#PCDATA)  >
   <!ELEMENT LastName (#PCDATA)  >
    <!ELEMENT Title (#PCDATA)  >
]>
<Customers>
    <Customer id="ALFKI">
        <CompanyName>Alfreds Futterkiste</CompanyName>
        <Contact>
            <FirstName>Maria</FirstName>
            <LastName>Anders</LastName>
            <Title>Sales Representative</Title>
        </Contact>
    </Customer>
    <Customer id="THEBI">
        <CompanyName>The Big Cheese</CompanyName>
        <Contact>
            <FirstName>Liz</FirstName>
            <LastName>Nixon</LastName>
            <Title>Marketing Manager</Title>
        </Contact>
    </Customer>
</Customers>
```

Listing 5.5 shows the `DisplayNode.htm` file.

Listing 5.5   **Displaying Node Details in the Document (*DisplayNode.htm*)**

```html
<html>
    <head>
        <title>Nodes Display</title>
    </head>
    <body>
        <div id="customers">
        </div>
    </body>
</html>
<script language="javascript">
var NODE_ELEMENT                = 1;
var NODE_ATTRIBUTE               = 2;
var NODE_TEXT                    = 3;
var NODE_CDATA                    = 4;
var NODE_ENTITY_REFERENCE       = 5;
```

continues

Listing 5.5   **Continued**

```
var NODE_ENTITY                    = 6;
var NODE_PROCESSING_INSTRUCTION = 7;
var NODE_COMMENT                = 8;
var NODE_DOCUMENT               = 9;
var NODE_DOCUMENT_TYPE          = 10;
var NODE_DOCUMENT_FRAGMENT      = 11;
var NODE_NOTATION               = 12;

var objXML = new ActiveXObject("MSXML2.DOMDocument.4.0");
objXML.async = false;
objXML.load("displayNodes.xml");
var objDocElement = objXML.documentElement;
var indent1 = "        ";
var indent2 = indent1 + indent1;

displayNode( objXML ,"" );

function displayNode(node , strSpaces)
{
    customers.innerHTML  +=  strSpaces + indent1 +
        "<B><I>Name</I></B>: " + node.nodeName +
        " <B><I>Value</I></B>: " +
        node.nodeValue +  " <B><I>Type</I></B>: " +
        node.nodeTypeString + "<BR>"
    if( node.nodeType == NODE_ELEMENT )
    {
        var namedNodeMap = node.attributes;
        for (var attr = namedNodeMap.nextNode(); attr != null; attr =
        ⇒namedNodeMap.nextNode())
      {
            displayNode(attr, strSpaces + indent2);
      }
    }
    if(node.nodeType == NODE_DOCUMENT || node.nodeType == NODE_ELEMENT)
    {
        var nodeList = node.childNodes;
        for(var childNode = nodeList.nextNode(); childNode != null;
        ⇒childNode = nodeList.nextNode())
        {
            displayNode(childNode , strSpaces + indent1);
        }
    }
}
</script>
```

You pass the DOM document's object to the `displayNode` method. The first statement in the method displays the node properties. In the case of an element node, you get the `NamedNodeMap` collection that enables you to navigate through the attributes in the element. For each occurrence of an attribute, this method calls itself recursively to display the properties of the attribute node. But, in the case of an attribute node, the method exits after the node properties are displayed. In the case of the document object or an element node, you navigate through the `NodeList` collection to find the child nodes of the current node and call the `displayNode` method recursively until you reach the leaf nodes under each node.

The `nodeType` values used in this example are defined by the `IXMLDOMNodeType` enumerations that specify valid settings for the DOM node type. Table 5.5 lists these enumerations.

Table 5.5 **XML DOM Enumerated Constants (*IXMLDOMNodeType* Enumerations)**

IXMLDOMNodeType Enumerations	*IXMLDOMNode nodeType*	*IXMLDOMNode nodeTypeString*
NODE_ELEMENT	1	element
NODE_ATTRIBUTE	2	attribute
NODE_TEXT	3	Text
NODE_CDATA_SECTION	4	cdatasection
NODE_ENTITY_REFERENCE	5	entityreference
NODE_ENTITY	6	entity
NODE_PROCESSING_INSTRUCTION	7	processinginstruction
NODE_COMMENT	8	Comment
NODE_DOCUMENT	9	Document
NODE_DOCUMENT_TYPE	10	documenttype
NODE_DOCUMENT_FRAGMENT	11	documentfragment
NODE_NOTATION	12	Notation

Figure 5.4 shows the display from the call to `displayNode` with proper indentation using the   entity reference in HTML.

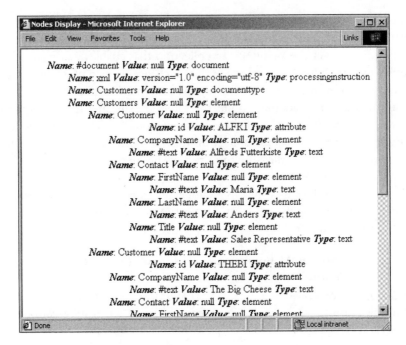

Figure 5.4 Displaying the node details.

Inserting, Updating, Deleting, and Cloning Nodes

This section discusses how to use the most helpful features in the DOM API: creating content, inserting, updating, and deleting the nodes into the DOM document structure.

In this section, you create a new project, called CSMSXML, that you use for the next few examples in this chapter. Figure 5.5 shows the creation of this new project.

Rename the default file that was created with the name webform1.aspx to saveXML.aspx. Then, after adding the two files (customers.xml and editCustomer.htm), the Solution Explorer will look like Figure 5.6. Look at the saveXML.aspx in the next section to see the code for the customers.xml and editCustomer.htm files.

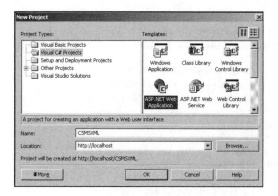

Figure 5.5   Creating the CSMSXML project.

Figure 5.6   The Solution Explorer for the CSMSXML project.

In this example, you use the following `customers.xml` document with three customer elements:

```
<?xml version="1.0" encoding="utf-8" ?>
<!DOCTYPE Customers [
    <!ELEMENT Customers (Customer)* >
    <!ELEMENT Customer (CompanyName,Contact)  >
    <!ATTLIST Customer
             id   CDATA  #REQUIRED >
    <!ELEMENT CompanyName (#PCDATA)  >
    <!ELEMENT Contact (FirstName , LastName , Title  )  >
    <!ELEMENT FirstName (#PCDATA)  >
    <!ELEMENT LastName (#PCDATA)  >
    <!ELEMENT Title (#PCDATA)  >
]>
```

continues

```
<Customers>
    <Customer id="ALFKI">
        <CompanyName>Alfreds Futterkiste</CompanyName>
        <Contact>
            <FirstName>Maria</FirstName>
            <LastName>Anders</LastName>
            <Title>Sales Representative</Title>
        </Contact>
    </Customer>
    <Customer id="THEBI">
        <CompanyName>The Big Cheese</CompanyName>
        <Contact>
            <FirstName>Liz</FirstName>
            <LastName>Nixon</LastName>
            <Title>Marketing Manager</Title>
        </Contact>
    </Customer>
    <Customer id="EASTC">
        <CompanyName>Eastern Connection</CompanyName>
        <Contact>
            <FirstName>Ann</FirstName>
            <LastName>Devon</LastName>
            <Title>Sales Agent</Title>
        </Contact>
    </Customer>
</Customers>
```

Listing 5.6 shows the HTML file editCustomer.htm that sequentially performs the tasks of inserting, updating, and deleting nodes from an XML document loaded into the DOM. This is achieved by making calls to separate methods that implement respective functionality. These calls are interspersed with calls to a method that displays the current state of the documents in the DOM so that you can see the results after each operation. Note that we will discuss each part in Listing 5.6 separately instead of providing a continuous listing, which makes it too difficult to follow.

Listing 5.6 **Inserting, Updating, and Deleting Nodes** *(editCustomer.htm)*

```
<html>
    <head>
        <title>Insert, Update, Delete</title>
    </head>
    <body>
        <form name="modify" method="post" ID="Form1">
            <div id="customers">
            </div>
            <INPUT type="hidden" name="customerData" value=""
            ➥ID="Hidden1"> <INPUT type="button" value="Save XML"
            ➥onclick="saveXML()" ID="Button1" NAME="Button1">
        </form>
    </body>
</html>
```

```
<script language="javascript">
var objXML = new ActiveXObject("MSXML2.DOMDocument");
objXML.async = false;
objXML.load("customers.xml");

var objDocElement = objXML.documentElement;

displayCustomers("After Loading");
var newCustNode = createCustomerNode("PARIS","Paris
spécialités","Marie","Bertrand","Owner");

insertNewCustomer(newCustNode, "THEBI");
displayCustomers("After insertion");
updateContact(findCustomer("ALFKI" ),"Mario","Pontes","Accounting Manager");
displayCustomers("After Updating");
deleteCustomer("EASTC");
displayCustomers("After Deletion");


function displayCustomers( strHeading )
 {
    var custNode;
    var contactNode;
    var nodeList =   objXML.getElementsByTagName("Customer");
    var strHTML = "<B>" + strHeading + "...</B>";
    strHTML += "<table border='1'><thead><th>CustomerID</th><th>
➡Company Name</th>" +
                "<th>Contact Name</th><th>Contact Title
                ➡</th></thead><tbody>";

    for (var i=0; i< nodeList.length ; i++)
    {
        custNode = nodeList.item(i);
        strHTML += "<tr>" ;
        strHTML += "<td>" + custNode.getAttribute("id") + "</td>" ;
        strHTML += "<td>" + custNode.childNodes.item(0).text + "</td>";
        contactNode = custNode.childNodes.item(1);
        strHTML += "<td>" + contactNode.childNodes.item(0).text  ;
        strHTML += " "    + contactNode.childNodes.item(1).text + "</td>";
        strHTML += "<td>" + contactNode.childNodes.item(2).text + "</td>" ;
        strHTML += "</tr>";
    }
    customers.innerHTML += strHTML + "</tbody></table>" ;
 }

function createCustomerNode( customerID , companyName , contactFirstName ,
            contactLastName , contactTitle )
 {
    var custNode    = objXML.createElement( "Customer" );
    var idAttr        = objXML.createAttribute( "id" );
    idAttr.value    = customerID;
    custNode.setAttributeNode(idAttr);
    custNode.appendChild(createElement("CompanyName", companyName));
    var contactNode = objXML.createElement("Contact");
    contactNode.appendChild( createElement("FirstName", contactFirstName));
    contactNode.appendChild( createElement("LastName", contactLastName));
    contactNode.appendChild( createElement("Title", contactTitle));
```

continues

Listing 5.6   **Continued**

```
        custNode.appendChild(contactNode);
        return custNode;
 }

function insertNewCustomer(custNode, beforeID)
{
        var nextCustNode = objXML.selectSingleNode( "/Customers/Customer[@id='"
        ➥+ beforeID + "']");
        if( nextCustNode==null)
        {
              alert("The Customer node with the id '"+ beforeID +"' was not found");
              return;
        }
        objXML.documentElement.insertBefore( custNode , nextCustNode ) ;
        //performing runtime validation of the document to handle the error
        ➥resulting out of the insertion of new node
        var parseError = objXML.validate();
        if( parseError != 0  )
        {
              alert(     parseError.reason  );
              //roll back on the latest insertion
              objXML.documentElement.removeChild( custNode    );
        }
}

function createElement( elementName , text )
{
        var elementNode = objXML.createElement( elementName );
        var textNode = objXML.createTextNode( text );
        elementNode.appendChild(textNode);
        return elementNode;
}

function createClonedNode( customerID , companyName , contactFirstName ,
          contactLastName , contactTitle )
{
        var custNode      = objDocElement.firstChild.cloneNode(true);
        //make deep copy
        custNode.setAttribute( "id" , customerID );
        custNode.firstChild.text = companyName;
        updateContact( custNode , contactFirstName , contactLastName ,
        ➥contactTitle );
        return custNode;
}

function findCustomer( customerID )
{
        var custNode =    objDocElement.firstChild;
        while( custNode!=null )
        {
              if( custNode.getAttribute("id")== customerID )
              {
                    return custNode;
              }
              custNode = custNode.nextSibling;
```

```
        }
    }

    function updateContact( custNode , contactFirstName , contactLastName ,
    ⇔contactTitle )
    {
        if( custNode == null  )
        {
            alert("The Customer node with the id '"+ customerID +"' was not
            ⇔found");
            return;
        }
        contactNode = custNode.getElementsByTagName("Contact").item(0);
        contactNode.childNodes.item(0).text = contactFirstName;
        contactNode.childNodes.item(1).text = contactLastName;
        contactNode.childNodes.item(2).text = contactTitle;
    }

    function deleteCustomer(  customerID )
    {
        var custNode = findCustomer( customerID );
        if( custNode == null  )
        {
            alert("The Customer node with the id '"+ customerID +"' was not
            ⇔found");
            return;
        }
        objDocElement.removeChild(custNode);
    }

    function saveXML()
    {
        document.modify.customerData.value = objXML.xml;
        document.modify.action = "saveXML.aspx";
        document.modify.submit();
    }

</script>
```

We then call a sequence of methods to insert a new Customer node, update a node, delete a node, and intermittently call the method displayCustomers(), which displays the latest state of the document. The following code shows the implementation of the method displayCustomers():

```
    function displayCustomers( strHeading )
    {
        var custNode
        var contactNode
        var nodeList =   objXML.getElementsByTagName("Customer")
        var strHTML = "<B>" + strHeading + "...</B>"
        strHTML += "<table border='1'><thead><th>CustomerID</th><th>Company
        ⇔Name</th>" +
                    "<th>Contact Name</th><th>Contact Title
                    ⇔</th></thead><tbody>"
```

```
for (var i=0; i< nodeList.length ; i++)
{
    custNode = nodeList.item(i)
    strHTML += "<tr>" ;
    strHTML += "<td>" + custNode.getAttribute("id") + "</td>" ;
    strHTML += "<td>" + custNode.childNodes.item(0).text + "</td>";
    contactNode = custNode.childNodes.item(1) ;
    strHTML += "<td>" + contactNode.childNodes.item(0).text  ;
    strHTML += " "    + contactNode.childNodes.item(1).text + "</td>";
    strHTML += "<td>" + contactNode.childNodes.item(2).text + "</td>" ;
    strHTML += "</tr>";
}
customers.innerHTML += strHTML + "</tbody></table>" ;
}
```

The displayCustomers method shows how to transform XML into HTML by using DOM. You see how to do this same transformation using XSLT and SAX later in this chapter.

You can use the getElementsByTagName method of the DOMDocument object. This returns an IXMLDOMNodeList object, a collection of elements that have the name Customer in the document. The IXMLDOMElement interface exposes the same method, but it only returns descendant elements, not all the elements that were encountered in the document (see the updateContact method shown in the following code). Navigate through this collection by using the ordinal index. Because you are aware of the document's structure, use the index to find the appropriate child nodes of the Customer node. You find the text of the elements by using the text property, which is an MSXML extension of the DOM.

The remaining code shows the implementation of the different operations:

```
function createCustomerNode( customerID , companyName , contactFirstName ,
                            contactLastName , contactTitle )
{
        var custNode    = objXML.createElement( "Customer" )
        var idAttr      = objXML.createAttribute( "id" )
        idAttr.value    = customerID
        custNode.setAttributeNode(idAttr)
        custNode.appendChild(   createElement( "CompanyName" , companyName
        ➥)   )
        var contactNode = objXML.createElement( "Contact" )
        contactNode.appendChild( createElement( "FirstName" ,
        ➥contactFirstName ))
        contactNode.appendChild( createElement( "LastName" ,
        ➥contactLastName ))
        contactNode.appendChild( createElement( "Title" , contactTitle))
        custNode.appendChild(     contactNode )
        return custNode
}

function insertNewCustomer( custNode , beforeID   )
{
    var nextCustNode = objXML.selectSingleNode( "/Customers/Customer[@id='"
    ➥+ beforeID + "']"   )
```

```
    if( nextCustNode==null)
    {
        alert("The Customer node with the id '"+ beforeID +"' was not
        ⇥found")
        return;
    }
    objXML.documentElement.insertBefore( custNode , nextCustNode  )
     //performing runtime validation of the document to handle the error
     //resulting out of
     //the insertion of new node
     var parseError = objXML.validate()
     if(  parseError != 0  )
     {
         alert(  parseError.reason  )
         //roll back on the latest insertion
         objXML.documentElement.removeChild( custNode   )
     }
}

function createElement( elementName , text )
{
        var elementNode = objXML.createElement( elementName )
        var textNode = objXML.createTextNode( text )
        elementNode.appendChild(textNode)
        return elementNode
}

function createClonedNode( customerID , companyName , contactFirstName ,
                    contactLastName , contactTitle )
{
        var custNode = objDocElement.firstChild.cloneNode(true)
        //make deep copy
        custNode.setAttribute( "id" , customerID )
        custNode.firstChild.text = companyName
        updateContact( custNode , contactFirstName , contactLastName ,
        ⇥contactTitle )
        return custNode

}

function findCustomer( customerID )
{
        var custNode =   objDocElement.firstChild
        while( custNode!=null )
        {
            if( custNode.getAttribute("id")== customerID )
            {
                return custNode
            }
            custNode = custNode.nextSibling
        }
}

function updateContact( custNode , contactFirstName , contactLastName ,
⇥contactTitle )
{

        if( custNode == null  )
        {
```

```
                    alert("The Customer node with the id '"+ customerID +"' was
                    ⏎not found")
                    return
              }
            contactNode = custNode.getElementsByTagName("Contact").item(0)
            contactNode.childNodes.item(0).text = contactFirstName
            contactNode.childNodes.item(1).text = contactLastName
            contactNode.childNodes.item(2).text = contactTitle
      }

      function deleteCustomer( customerID )
      {
              var custNode = findCustomer( customerID )
              if( custNode == null  )
              {
                  alert("The Customer node with the id '"+ customerID +"' was
                  ⏎not found")
                  return
              }
              objDocElement.removeChild(custNode)
      }

      function saveXML()
      {
          document.modify.customerData.value = objXML.xml
          document.modify.action = "saveXML.aspx"
          document.modify.submit()
      }

      </script>
```

The `createCustomerNode` method demonstrates the creation of new content by
using a set of the `createXXX` methods on the `DOMDocument` object. Alternatively,
you can call the `createClonedNode()` method, which is mentioned in the previous code, to create the new node. This method clones an existing node by
making a detailed copy of it and then updates the values of the created node to
make a new node. This method is more efficient than the `createXXX` methods.

The `insertNewCustomer` method inserts the newly created node before the
`customer` element with a specified value for the `id` attribute. It uses the
`selectSingleNode` to search the specified node. This method takes an XSL
query and performs the pattern-matching operation to the content of the
node that's specified by the query and returns the first matching node. You will
see how to use the XPath query language with this method in the section,
"Selecting Nodes with XPath 1.0." Next, the `insertNewCustomer` method performs runtime validation on the document to handle the errors resulting from
the insertion of new nodes.

You can extend the functionality that you saw in `createCustomerNode` to
build an entire XML document from scratch. The following code shows how
to start creating this document:

```
      var rootElement = objXML.createElement( "Customers" );
```

```
objXML.documentElement =  rootElement;
var  pi = objXML.createProcessingInstruction("xml",
↪"version=\"1.0\"");
objXML.insertBefore(pi, objXML.childNodes.item(0));
```

The previous code will be complete as you append the customer nodes that are returned to the documentElement by the createCustomerNode function.

The updateContact method updates the values of the node passed to it. The deleteCustomer deletes the node from the DOM by using the removeChild method on the documentElement. Figure 5.7 shows the state of the document before and after each of the operations on the document.

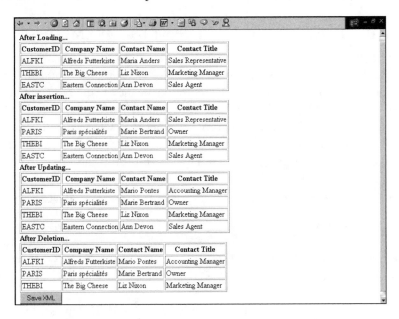

Figure 5.7 The document's state before and after the insert, update, and delete operations.

Clicking the Save button posts the XML data to the saveXML.aspx page in the form of a string that's assigned to a hidden variable. The next section looks at the saveXML.aspx page and how you can save this XML data to the web server.

So far, you have seen the workings of MSXML in the client browser using JavaScript. From this point on, the focus shifts to the server-side use of MSXML with ASP.NET.

Working with MSXML 4.0 on the Server-Side with ASP.NET

You can continue using MSXML in the .NET Framework. If you already have much ASP code that uses the COM component MSXML, as you migrate to the .NET, you cannot afford to delete all your existing code only to forego all the learning, time, and resources you spent on it. If you are contemplating importing the code to ASP.NET, this section helps you do that by using the COM Interop services provided in .NET. Some new features in MSXML are also discussed.

Using the *TlbImp.exe* Utility to Import the MSXML Type Library into a .NET Application

.NET and COM components conform to different compiled standards. It is impossible to directly import a COM component into your .NET application and start using it. Microsoft provides a utility called `TlbImp.exe` with the .NET SDK, which aids in this process. This utility imports a COM type library into a proxy .NET assembly (called a Run-time Class Wrapper) that your .NET clients can reference through early binding. To run this utility from the command prompt, type the following:

```
tlbimp msxml4.dll /out: Interop.MSXML2_4_0.dll  /namespace:MSXML2   /silent
```

The first argument is the name of the COM type library, the `/out` argument specifies the name of the output file, assembly, and namespace in which to write the metadata definitions, the `/namespace` specifies the namespace in which to produce the assembly, and `/silent` suppresses the display of success messages.

You can examine the imported assembly with the MSIL Disassembler (`Ildasm.exe`) tool. The MSIL Disassembler tool provides a default GUI to view the metadata and disassembled code of any existing portable executable (PE) file in a hierarchical tree view. To use the GUI, type **ildasm** at the command line without supplying the `PEfilename` argument or any options. From the File menu, you can navigate to the PE file, the imported `MSXML2_4_0.dll` file in this case, to load `Ildasm.exe`. Figure 5.8 shows the imported assembly as viewed from the MSIL Disassembler tool.

Creating this wrapper by using Visual Studio .NET makes things much simpler. All you need to do is this:

1. In the Add Reference window, select the COM tab and browse to Microsoft XML, v4.0 component.

2. Select the v4.0 component and click OK.

The IDE creates a wrapper and copies it to the bin directory of your project. (See Figure 5.9.)

Figure 5.8   Using the MSIL Disassembler tool to view the imported assembly.

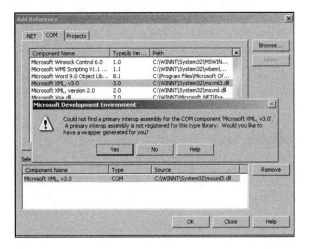

Figure 5.9   Using `tlbimp.exe` from Visual Studio .NET.

You can follow the same procedure to create a wrapper for your existing COM components using MSXML. The utility automatically creates the wrapper for MSXML, so you don't need to do it separately.

The *saveXML.aspx* Page

You can look into using ASP.NET and C# to produce more elegant code by using the *WebControls* and *HTMLControls.* You can save the XML data that was posted in the previous example to a file on the server hard disk. You will also see how you can perform XSL Transformation using MSXML. Listing 5.7 shows the webform that displays a message after saving the XML data and the data in the form of an HTML table. (Skip to Listing 5.9 to see the code behind this webform.)

Listing 5.7 **Saving XML Data to the Disk and XSLT Transformation** *(saveXML.aspx)*

```
<%@ Page language="c#" Codebehind="saveXML.aspx.cs" AutoEventWireup="false"
        Inherits="CSMSXML.SaveXML" %>
<HTML>
    <body>
        <form id="Form1" Runat="server">
            <table>
                <tr>
                    <td align="middle">
                        <asp:Label ID="SaveMessage" Runat="server"
Font-Bold="True"></asp:Label>
                    </td>
                </tr>
                <tr>
                    <td>
                        <div ID="tblCustomers" Runat="server">
                        </div>
                    </td>
                </tr>
                <tr>
                    <td align="middle">
                        <asp:Button Text="Reload" Runat="server"
id="Button1"></asp:Button>
                    </td>
                </tr>
            </table>
        </form>
    </body>
</HTML>
```

This aspx page creates the HTML interface using the *Label* and *Button* web controls and the *DIV* HTML controls.

Transformation

The HTMLControl tblCustomers in Listing 5.7's webform contains the XML data that's transformed into an HTML table. We perform this transformation using an XSLT stylesheet, Customers.xslt, shown in Listing 5.8.

Listing 5.8 **Stylesheet for Transforming XML to a HTML Table**
(Customers.xslt)

```
<?xml version="1.0" encoding="UTF-8" ?>
<xsl:stylesheet version="1.0"
xmlns:xsl="http://www.w3.org/1999/XSL/Transform">
    <xsl:template match="/">
        <xsl:apply-templates />
    </xsl:template>
    <xsl:template match="Customers">
        <table border="1">
            <thead>
                <th>CustomerID</th>
                <th>Company Name</th>
                <th>Contact Name</th>
                <th>Contact Title</th>
            </thead>
            <tbody>
                <xsl:for-each select="Customer">
                    <tr>
                        <td>
                            <xsl:value-of select="@id" />
                        </td>
                        <td>
                            <xsl:value-of select="CompanyName" />
                        </td>
                        <xsl:apply-templates select="Contact" />
                    </tr>
                </xsl:for-each>
            </tbody>
        </table>
    </xsl:template>
    <xsl:template match="Contact">
        <td>
            <xsl:value-of select="FirstName" />
            <xsl:text disable-output-
            ➥escaping='yes'><![CDATA[ ]]></xsl:text>
            <xsl:value-of select="LastName" />
        </td>
        <td>
            <xsl:value-of select="Title" />
        </td>
    </xsl:template>
</xsl:stylesheet>
```

The "Code Behind" Class in C#

In the code behind file saveXML.aspx.cs, you can see the class saveXML that does the job of saving the XML string data that was posted to the saveXML.aspx page from the editCustomers.htm page as the value of a hidden HTML form field named customerData. This XML string data is saved into the XML file customers1.xml that is created on the first request. This class also transforms the XML data into a HTML table by using XSL transformation and displays it within the HTMLControl named tblCustomers by setting the controls innerHTML property. Listing 5.9 shows the code behind the file saveXML.aspx.cs.

> **Note**
>
> This file is generated by the Visual Studio .NET with empty code when the corresponding webform saveXML.aspx is created.

Listing 5.9   **The Code Behind *saveXML.aspx.cs***

```
using System;
using MSXML2;

namespace CSMSXML
{
    public class SaveXML : System.Web.UI.Page
    {
        private DOMDocument40  objXML = new DOMDocument40 ();
        private DOMDocument40  objXSL = new DOMDocument40 ();
        protected System.Web.UI.WebControls.Label SaveMessage;
        protected System.Web.UI.HtmlControls.HtmlGenericControl
        ➥tblCustomers;
        protected System.Web.UI.WebControls.Button Button1;


        public SaveXML()
        {
            Page.Init += new System.EventHandler(Page_Init);
        }

        private void Page_Load(object sender, System.EventArgs e)
        {
            string  xslPath = Server.MapPath(".") + "\\customers.xslt" ;
            string destXMLPath = Server.MapPath(".") + "\\customers1.xml" ;

            objXML.async = false;

            if (! Page.IsPostBack )
            {
                objXML.loadXML( Request.Form.Get("customerData") );
```

```
                    objXML.save( destXMLPath );
                    SaveMessage.Text = "The updated Customers XML file was
                    ⤶saved on the server";
            }
            else
            {
                    objXML.load(destXMLPath);
                    SaveMessage.Text = "The saved file was reloaded into
                    ⤶DOM.";
            }

            objXSL.async = false;
            objXSL.load(xslPath);

            tblCustomers.InnerHtml = objXML.transformNode( objXSL );
        }

        private void Page_Init(object sender, EventArgs e)
        {
            InitializeComponent();
        }

        private void InitializeComponent()
        {
            this.Load += new System.EventHandler(this.Page_Load);
        }

    }
}
```

Listing 5.9 uses the save method of the DOMDocument to save the loaded document to a new destination, the customers1.xml file. This method is an extension of DOM because, as mentioned earlier, DOM doesn't provide any specifications for the documents. Optionally, you can provide the Response object as a parameter to the save method to send the document back to the client browser. In the case of a postback, which can be generated by using the Reload button, the document is loaded from the newly created file.

This example also shows you how server-side transformation works with MSXML 4.0, which is close to compliance with the XSLT Recommendation. You load the XSLT in Listing 5.9 into another instance of the MSXML DOM. Then perform the transformation using the transformNode() method, which processes the Document node and its children using the supplied XSLT. This enables you to apply an XSL template without explicitly having to define the link within the XML document; thus leaving you the flexibility to have multiple XSLT files for the same XML and provide multiple views. Figure 5.10 shows the output from the aspx page.

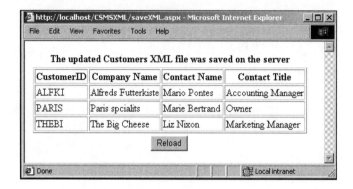

Figure 5.10   Saving XML and server-side transformation in ASP.NET.

Caching Compiled Stylesheets Using *IXMLDOMXSLTemplate* and *IXSLProcessor*

In the last section's example, you saw the XSL transformation using the `transformNode` method. But this is not practical for enormous sites that require a large number of XSL transformations because the stylesheet must be compiled every time you call the `transformNode()` method. The `IXMLDOMXSLTemplate` and the `IXSLProcessor` interfaces solve this problem by enabling you to cache compiled stylesheets, as shown in Listing 5.10. Listing 5.10 shows the code for the webform `XSLTemplate.aspx` that displays the results of transformation and the code behind file `XSLTemplate.aspx.cs` that demonstrates the use of `IXMLDOMXSLTemplate` and `IXSLProcessor`.

> **Note**
> These two files are derived with small modifications from our preceding sample, `saveXML.aspx` and the code behind file `saveXML.aspx.cs`.

Listing 5.10   *XSLTemplate.aspx*

```
<%@ Page language="c#" Codebehind="XSLTemplate.aspx.cs"
AutoEventWireup="false"
Inherits="CSMSXML.MyXSLTemplate" %>
<HTML>
    <body>
        <form id="Form1" Runat="server">
            <table>
                <tr>
                    <td align="middle">
                        <asp:label id="HeadingMessage" Runat="server"
                        ➥Font-Bold="True"></asp:label>
                    </td>
                </tr>
```

```
                <tr>
                    <td>
                        <div id="tblCustomers" Runat="server">
                        </div>
                    </td>
                </tr>
            </table>
        </form>
    </body>
</HTML>
```

Caching Compiled Stylesheets *(XSLTemplate.aspx.cs)*

```csharp
using System;
using MSXML2;

namespace CSMSXML
{

    public class MyXSLTemplate : System.Web.UI.Page
    {

        private FreeThreadedDOMDocument40  objXML = new
        ➥FreeThreadedDOMDocument40 ();
        private FreeThreadedDOMDocument40  objXSL = new
        ➥FreeThreadedDOMDocument40 ();
        private XSLTemplate40  objXSLTemplate ;
        private IXSLProcessor  processor;
        protected System.Web.UI.WebControls.Label HeadingMessage;
        protected System.Web.UI.HtmlControls.HtmlGenericControl
        ➥tblCustomers;



        public MyXSLTemplate()
        {
            Page.Init += new System.EventHandler(Page_Init);
        }

        private void Page_Load(object sender, System.EventArgs e)
        {

            string  xslPath = Server.MapPath(".") + "\\customers.xslt" ;
            string destXMLPath = Server.MapPath(".") + "\\customers.xml" ;
            objXML.async = false;
            try
            {
                objXSLTemplate = (XSLTemplate40
                ➥)Application.Get("custProcessor" );
                if( objXSLTemplate==null)
                {
                    throw  new NullReferenceException() ;
```

```
              }
          }
          catch(     Exception  ) //InvalidCastException OR
          ➥NullReferenceException
          {
              objXSLTemplate = CreateCachedXSL(xslPath);
          }
          processor = objXSLTemplate.createProcessor();

          objXML.load(destXMLPath);
          HeadingMessage.Text = "Caching compiled stylesheets using
          ➥IXMLDOMXSLTemplate "
          + "and IXSLProcessor.";

          processor.input = objXML;
          processor.transform();
          tblCustomers.InnerHtml = processor.output.ToString() ;

      }

      private  XSLTemplate40  CreateCachedXSL(string  xslPath)
      {
          objXSL.async = false;
          objXSL.load(xslPath);
          objXSLTemplate = new XSLTemplate40 ();
          objXSLTemplate.stylesheet =  objXSL ;
      //cache the template object into an Application variable for future
      ➥use
          Application.Lock();
          Application.Add("custProcessor", objXSLTemplate );
          Application.UnLock();
          return objXSLTemplate;
      }

      private void Page_Init(object sender, EventArgs e)
      {
          InitializeComponent();
      }


      private void InitializeComponent()
      {
          this.Load += new System.EventHandler(this.Page_Load);

      }


  }


}
```

The XSLTemplate is a free-threaded component that compiles stylesheets. We create an instance of the free-threaded version of the DOMDocument to load the XSLT and assign it to the stylesheet property of the XSLTemplate object. The template is created and stored in the Application object. To perform the transformation, obtain a template in the form of the XSL processor component by calling the createProcessor method on the template. Finally, before the call to the transform method, you must specify the input to the template as the target XML document loaded into another instance of the free-threaded version of DOMDocument.

Adding Objects and Params into a Stylesheet Using the *addObject* and *addParam* Method

MSXML 4.0 enables you to extend the capabilities of the XSLT language through custom script libraries and COM components or classes. You will add a class called Customer to the last example. This class supports a GetCompanyName method and a ContactFirstName property. Listing 5.11 shows you how you can make use of them in a transformation by using the appropriate namespace qualifier.

Listing 5.11   **Stylesheet Using an Object** *(custAddObject.xslt)*

```xml
<?xml version="1.0" encoding="UTF-8" ?>
<xsl:stylesheet version="1.0"
xmlns:xsl="http://www.w3.org/1999/XSL/Transform"
➥xmlns:Customer="urn:Customer">
    <xsl:output method="xml" indent="yes" />
    <xsl:param name="id" />
    <xsl:template match="/">
        <xsl:element name="Customer">
            <xsl:attribute name="id">
                <xsl:value-of select="$id" />
            </xsl:attribute>
            <xsl:element name="CompanyName">
                <xsl:value-of select="Customer:GetCompanyName()" />
            </xsl:element>
            <xsl:element name="ContactFirstName">
                <xsl:value-of select="Customer:get-ContactFirstName()" />
            </xsl:element>
        </xsl:element>
    </xsl:template>
</xsl:stylesheet>
```

The code behind file addObject.aspx.cs shows the class Customer, which represents the Customer object that is referenced by the namespace Customer in the XSLT file custAddObject.xslt. Also, this Customer class exposes the method GetCompanyName() and the property ContactFirstName that are being used in the

XSLT file `custAddObject.xslt`. The rest of the code in this file is similar to the one shown in the `XSLTemplate.aspx.cs` file in Listing 5.10, except for the calls to the `addObject()` and the `addParameter()` methods on the object of type `IXSLProcessor`.

The `Customer` class represents the `customer` node in the DOM that corresponds to the ID passed to its constructor. Listing 5.12 shows the code for the `addObject.aspx` page followed by the code behind the file `addObject.aspx.cs`.

Listing 5.12   *addObject.aspx*

```
<%@ Page language="c#" Codebehind="addObject.aspx.cs" AutoEventWireup="false"
Inherits="CSMSXML.addObject" %>
<HTML>
    <body>
        <form id="Form1" Runat="server">
            <table>
                <tr>
                    <td align="middle">
                        <asp:label id="HeadingMessage" Runat="server"
                        ▪Font-Bold="True"></asp:label>
                    </td>
                </tr>
                <tr>
                    <td>
                        <div id="tblCustomers" Runat="server">
                        </div>
                    </td>
                </tr>
            </table>
        </form>
    </body>
</HTML>
```

Adding Objects and Params *(addObject.aspx.cs)*

```
using System;
using MSXML2;

namespace CSMSXML
{

    public class addObject : System.Web.UI.Page
    {

        private FreeThreadedDOMDocument40  objXML = new
        FreeThreadedDOMDocument40 ();
        private FreeThreadedDOMDocument40  objXSL = new
        FreeThreadedDOMDocument40 ();
        private XSLTemplate40  objXSLTemplate ;
        private IXSLProcessor  processor;
        protected System.Web.UI.WebControls.Label HeadingMessage;
```

```
        protected System.Web.UI.HtmlControls.HtmlGenericControl
        tblCustomers;



        public addObject()
        {
            Page.Init += new System.EventHandler(Page_Init);
        }

        private void Page_Load(object sender, System.EventArgs e)
        {

            string  xslPath = Server.MapPath(".") + "\\custAddObject.xslt" ;
            string destXMLPath = Server.MapPath(".") + "\\customers.xml" ;
            objXML.async = false;
            objXML.load(destXMLPath);
            objXSL.async = false;
             objXSL.load(xslPath);
             objXSLTemplate = new XSLTemplate40 ();
             objXSLTemplate.stylesheet =  objXSL ;

             processor = objXSLTemplate.createProcessor();
             processor.input = objXML;


             Customer customer = new Customer("THEBI" ,objXML);
             processor.addParameter( "id" , "THEBI", "" );
             processor.addObject( customer, "urn:Customer");
             processor.transform();
HeadingMessage.Text = "Adding Objects and params Into a Stylesheet using the
➥" +"addObject and addParam method.";
             tblCustomers.InnerHtml = Server.HtmlEncode(
             ➥processor.output.ToString()) ;
        }

        private void Page_Init(object sender, EventArgs e)
        {
            InitializeComponent();
        }


        private void InitializeComponent()
        {
            this.Load += new System.EventHandler(this.Page_Load);

        }


    }
```

continues

Listing 5.12 **Continued**

```
public class Customer
{
    private string contactFirstName    ;
    private string companyName    ;
    public string ContactFirstName
    {
        get
        {
            return contactFirstName;
        }
    }
    public Customer(string customerID , FreeThreadedDOMDocument40
    ⇒objXML )
    {
        IXMLDOMNode custNode =
        ⇒objXML.documentElement.selectSingleNode(
            "/Customers/Customer[@id='" + customerID + "']"   );
        companyName          = custNode.childNodes[0].text ;
        contactFirstName = custNode.childNodes[1].firstChild.text    ;
    }
    public string GetCompanyName()
    {
        return companyName ;
    }
}

}
```

The code in Listing 5.12 also shows the parameter value being added through
the addParameter method to the XSLT param named "id". The transformation
outputs the following string to the browser:

```
<?xml version="1.0" encoding="UTF-16"?>
<Customer  id="THEBI">
    <CompanyName>The Big Cheese</CompanyName>
    <ContactFirstName>Liz</ContactFirstName>
</Customer>
```

The addParameter method can be called between transform calls (in asynchronous processing), and further processing will use the updated parameter. Added
parameters are referenced by <xsl:param> within the stylesheet.

Selecting Nodes with XPath 1.0

Listing 5.6 showed you node searching using XSL query passed to the
selectSingleNode method. XPath 1.0 offers a more flexible processing model as
compared to its precursor XSL Patterns, which was first supported in MSXML
2.0. The most significant change in XPath is the location path, which consists

of an axis that establishes a tree relationship between the context and the nodes selected by the query. MSXML 4.0 provides support for the legacy XSL Patterns syntax and XPath 1.0. To maintain backward compatibility with existing code, the default selection language is XSL Patterns.

To change the current selection language to XPath, set the SelectionLanguage property to XPath through the setProperty method that's available from the IXMLDOMDocument2 interface. To revert back to the XSL Patterns, reset the property value to XSLPatterns. You can read the SelectionLanguage property through the getProperty method. The IXMLDOMSelection interface represents the list of nodes that match a given XSL Pattern or XPath expression. Listing 5.13 shows a simple example for using IXMLDOMSelection to find the number of nodes that match a specified XPath expression with two different contexts.

Listing 5.13 **Stylesheet for Transforming XML to a HTML Table (DOMSelection.aspx)**

```
<%@ Page language="c#"    %>
<%@ Import Namespace = "MSXML2"    %>
<script language="c#" runat="server">

void Page_Load(Object Sender, EventArgs E)
{
string  lf = "<BR>";
DOMDocument40  objXML = new DOMDocument40 ();
IXMLDOMSelection selection ;
string xmlPath = Server.MapPath(".") + "\\customers.xml" ;
objXML.async = false;
objXML.load(xmlPath);
//default section for MSXML3 is "SDLPattern"
//XSLPattern is no longer supported in MSXML4
objXML.setProperty( "SelectionLanguage", "XPath" );
IXMLDOMNode rootNode =      objXML.documentElement;
selection = (IXMLDOMSelection) rootNode.selectNodes(
"child::Customer/Contact/*");
Response.Write("Expression: " + selection.expr + lf );
//prints child::Customer/Contact/*
Response.Write( "Length with the root node: " + selection.length + lf
➥);//prints 9

IXMLDOMNode custNode =      rootNode.childNodes[1];
IXMLDOMNode contactNode = custNode.selectSingleNode( "child::Contact/*");
IXMLDOMNode  context =     selection.matches( contactNode );

if( context == null) //false
{
    Response.Write("contactNode is not contained in the selected
    ➥collection." + lf );
}
```

continues

Listing 5.13   **Continued**

```
else if (context.Equals( rootNode ) ) //true
{
    Response.Write("contactNode is contained in the selected collection." +
    ⇒lf   );
}
selection.context = objXML ;
Response.Write( "Length with the  second customer node: " + selection.length
⇒+ lf );//prints 0

}


</script>
```

The specified `context` node might even come from a different document as
long as it shares the same threading model as the document that created the
`selection` object. The `selectNodes` method returns an object that implements
both the `IXMLDOMNodeList` interface and the new `IXMLDOMSelection` interface. So,
apart from traversing the node list like the `IXMLDOMNodeList`, the
`IXMLDOMSelection` provides other useful methods such as `peekNode` (to peek at
the current node), `removeAll`, `removeNext` (to remove nodes from the collection), and `clone` (to clone the entire collection).

ServerXMLHTTP

The `IXMLHTTPRequest` interface provides methods and properties to establish
communication with remote HTTP servers. The `XMLHTTP` implementation was
designed to work on the clients and not on a web server, which has higher
scalability requirements. You can create the object of `XMLHTTP` and use it in a
browser client with JavaScript:

```
var objXMLHTTP = Server.CreateObject("MSXML2.XMLHTTP.4.0")
```

The drawback to this implementation is that it was built around WinInet control and is not capable of handling multiple threads. This prevented it from
being a scalable solution on the server-side when large numbers of requests
must be serviced. When used from a page in the client browser, the requests to
a web server other than the one the page is hosted on will perform poorly or
give incorrect results. You might notice a similar problem with the `load` method
of `XMLDOMDocument` as you attempt to load XML documents from other servers.

  MSXML 4.0 provides another object, `ServerXMLHTTP`. This object is an
implementation of the `IServerXMLHTTPRequest` interface that inherits from
`IXMLHTTPRequest` and extends it with the following four new methods:
`getOption`, `setOption`, `waitForResponse`, and `setTimeouts`.

The following C# code in the `ServerXMLHTTP.aspx` opens a connection to a HTTP server and displays the response as XML. This example sends a request to another page, `GetCustXML.aspx`, which is on the same server. (This can be a page on any other web server.)

```
<%@ Page language="c#"    %>
<%@ Import Namespace = "MSXML2"    %>
<script language="c#" runat="server">
void Page_Load(Object Sender, EventArgs E)
{
        string url =
"http://localhost/CSMSXML/GetCustXML.aspx?customerid=THEBI";
        try
        {
              ServerXMLHTTP40    objXMLHTTP = new ServerXMLHTTP40 ();
              objXMLHTTP.open( "GET" , url , false , "" , "" );

              objXMLHTTP.send("");
              if( objXMLHTTP.status == 200)
              {
                    Response.Write( ( (IXMLDOMNode ) objXMLHTTP.responseXML
                    ➡).xml );
              }
        }
        catch( Exception exception)
        {
                Response.Write("Error: " + exception.Message );
        }

}
</script>
```

The following code is for the `GetCustXML.aspx` page that receives the `customerid` as a query string, formats the `customerid` into XML, and writes it to the response stream:

```
<%@ Page language="c#"   %>
<%
Response.ContentType = "text/xml";
Response.Write("<?xml version='1.0' encoding='utf-8' ?> ");
Response.Write("<Customers><CustomerID>"+  Request["customerid"]
➡+"</CustomerID></Customers>");
%>
```

Running the `ServerXMLHTTP.aspx` page from the browser displays the following in the browser window:

```
<?xml version="1.0" ?>
<Customers>
  <CustomerID>THEBI</CustomerID>
</Customers>
```

The following code line shows the syntax for the `open` method of the `ServerXMLHTTP` object:

```
oServerXMLHTTPRequest.open(bstrMethod, bstrUrl, bAsync, bstrUser,
bstrPassword);
```

`bstrUser` and `bstrPassword` are optional parameters of the `open` method and enable users to log on to web servers secured with basic authentication. The third `varAsync` parameter is similar to the `async` property of the `DOMDocument` object. The `open` method also enables you to post data to the target URL. This is required if you want to post data to an `aspx` page that will dynamically build an XML based on the submitted data. You might also want to post data to an XML template file that's kept on a SQL XML virtual directory of a SQL Server 2000.

The following code is for the `ServerXMLHTTP_POST.aspx` page that uses the `POST` method to send a request to the `GetCustXML.aspx` page:

```
<%@ Page language="c#"     %>
<%@ Import Namespace = "MSXML2"    %>
<script language="c#" runat="server">
void Page_Load(Object Sender, EventArgs E)
{
        string url = "http://localhost/CSMSXML/getCustXML.aspx?
        ~contname=Liz";
        try
        {
          ServerXMLHTTP40    objXMLHTTP = new ServerXMLHTTP40 ();

          objXMLHTTP.open("POST", url , false , "" , "" );
          objXMLHTTP.setRequestHeader("Content-Type", "application/x-www-
          ~form-urlencoded" );
          objXMLHTTP.send("customerid=THEBI&count=2");

          if( objXMLHTTP.status == 200)
            {
              Response.Write( ( (IXMLDOMNode ) objXMLHTTP.responseXML ).xml );
          }

        }
        catch( Exception exception)
        {
                Response.Write("Error: " + exception.Message );
        }

}
</script>
```

Running the `ServerXMLHTTP_POST.aspx` page from the browser produces the same result that the `ServerXMLHTTP.aspx` page produced.

```
<?xml version="1.0" ?>
```

```
<Customers>
  <CustomerID>THEBI</CustomerID>
</Customers>
```

Another application area where ServerXMLHTTP is exploited is with building *Simple Object Access Protocol (SOAP)* clients, where you can use this object to send a SOAP request to a remote server and receive the SOAP response. The following code snippet shows sending a SOAP request to a web service and getting the SOAP body sent as part of the SOAP response into an XMLDOMNode object:

```
objXMLHTTP.open("POST", "http://localhost/CSMSXML/SOAPListener.aspx" , false
➥, "" , "" );
  objXMLHTTP.setRequestHeader("SOAPAction","http://newriders.com/
  ➥GetCustomerDetail" );
  objXMLHTTP.setRequestHeader("Content-Type", "text/xml" );

  objXMLHTTP.send(strSOAPRequest);
  IXMLDOMDocument soapEnvelope = (IXMLDOMDocument) objXMLHTTP.responseXML;
  IXMLDOMNode     soapBody  = soapEnvelope.selectSingleNode("//SOAP-
  ➥ENV:Body");
```

The strSOAPRequest that's passed to the send() method contains the string that represents an XML SOAP request. SOAP requests are discussed in greater detail in Chapter 11, "Creating and Using ASP.NET Web Services." You can read the response data in a specific format by using one of the four following properties: responseBody, responseStream, responseText, and responseXML. The responseXML property that you saw in the previous code represents the response entity body as parsed by the MSXML Parser. The responseStream property represents the response entity body as Istream; this offers considerable performance benefits when moving data through the HTTP protocol.

Using the *ServerHTTPRequest* Property to Load XML Documents

The following code shows you how to load XML documents with the load method of XMLDOMDocument in a thread-safe manner:

```
DOMDocument40  objXML = new DOMDocument40 ();
objXML.async = false;
objXML.setProperty ("ServerHTTPRequest", true);
objXML.load ("http://localhost/CSMSXML/customers.xml");
Response.ContentType = "text/xml";
Response.Write (objXML.xml);
```

The code takes advantage of the ServerHTTPRequest property flag, which indicates that the parser needs to use the server-safe ServerXMLHTTP object instead of the DOMDocument object to synchronously load an XML document from a server.

Things You Need to Know Before You Work with *ServerXMLHTTP*

For cases where a proxy server exists, you must install and run the WinHTTP Proxy Configuration Utility (`Proxycfg.exe`) that enables you to configure WinHTTP to access HTTP and HTTPS servers through a proxy server. After installing and running the utility, restart IIS to get `ServerXMLHTTP` working.

`ServerXMLHTTP` support is only available on computers that have Microsoft Windows 2000 installed or have Microsoft Windows NT 4.0 with Microsoft Internet Explorer 5.01 (or later) installed. For Microsoft Windows 95 and Microsoft Windows 98, `XMLHTTP` is the only alternative and it is well suited for single-user desktop applications. `XMLHTTP` also offers some advantages, such as URL caching and auto-discovery of proxy settings support, that are available with WinInet. The `ServerXMLHTTP` component has a limitation: The maximum number of instances existing simultaneously within a single process must not exceed 5,460.

Benefits of Using DOM

Before we move on to discuss SAX2 implementation in the MSXML Parser, you must understand when you should choose the DOM API to parser XML in your applications. The following lists the benefits of using DOM:

- **Easy to understand object-based implementation**—The DOM represents the XML document as a set of interfaces defined by the W3C DOM Recommendation. These interfaces model the contents of the XML document structure. This allows the programmer to think of the document contents as objects and use the properties and invoke methods on the objects to work with the document.

- **Maps closely with XML Infoset**—XML Information Set (Infoset) is an abstract data set that describes the available information from an XML document. For many applications, this way of looking at an XML document is more useful than analyzing and interpreting XML syntax. The DOM API closely maps to this XML Infoset recommendation.

- **Better XSLT transformations and XPath filtering**—The DOM works better for XSL transformations where the source XML document is transformed based on the XSLT template applied. DOM allows complex XPath filtering and automatically retains complex data structures that hold context information. With SAX, you must devise mechanisms to retain the context information yourself.

- **Easy to modify and save XML**—The DOM enables you to create or modify a document in memory and save the changed document to the hard disk. SAX is preferred for reading, not editing, the documents.

- **Provides random access to data**—It is possible to move back and forth in the document and randomly move to any part or node of the DOM tree. You do not have to worry about maintaining the context information, which is required by SAX.

- **Easy to implement push model on top of pull model**—After you have the entire document loaded into memory, it's easy to invoke the events in the push interfaces as you navigate through the DOM tree from top to bottom. This builds a push layer on top of the pull model.

Drawbacks of Using DOM

The following lists the drawbacks of using DOM:

- **Loads entire document in memory**—A document loaded in memory by the DOM parser in the MSXML might take up one to four times its original size in RAM. This can lead to a performance bottleneck when you work with large documents of 2MB or more on a web server.

- **Different parser versions**—As the MSXML parser tries to keep pace with the latest W3C specifications, you will find newer parser versions. You might need to update your code that uses an earlier parser version to make it compatible to a newer version; some methods or properties depreciate after newer versions are released, or you might want to take advantage of some newly added features.

- **Not extensible**—The DOM implementations cannot be extended to provide new implementations. The DOM Level 2 Core is defined in terms of interfaces, not implementations. To provide some extensions to DOM, you must use interface inheritance with DOM interfaces. Mathematical Markup Language (MathML), Synchronized Multimedia Integration Language (SMIL), and Scalable Vector Graphics (SVG) are examples of specifications that define some DOM extensions. The interfaces they define are inherited from the interfaces in Core DOM.

SAX2 and MSXML Interfaces

Previously, you saw how to work with the MSXML 4.0 DOM implementation with ASP.NET by using the .NET's COM Interop services. In this section, you look at how to implement the SAX2 Visual Basic interfaces in Visual Basic .NET. SAX defines a set of interfaces that model the Infoset. MSXML 4.0 offers C++ and Visual Basic-based support to SAX. The names of the interfaces in MSXML mirror what was originally defined in the Java

Language, but prefixed with ISAX for C++ and IVBSAX for Visual Basic. Table 5.6 maps the MSXML SAX2 COM Visual Basic interfaces to the original Java interfaces.

Table 5.6   **SAX Interfaces**

Java Interfaces	MSXML COM and Visual Basic	Description
ContentHandler	IVBSAXContentHandler	Primary SAX interface that models the Infoset's core information items.
ErrorHandler	IVBSAXErrorHandler	Models fatal errors, errors, and warnings (per XML 1.0).
DTDHandler	IVBSAXDTDHandler	Models unparsed entities and notations.
EntityResolver	IVBSAXEntityResolver	Allows an application to perform custom resolution of external entity identifiers.
LexicalHandler	IVBSAXLexicalHandler	Models non-core lexical information (such as comments, CDATA sections, and entity references).
DeclHandler	IVBSAXDeclHandler	Models element and attribute declarations.
XMLReader	IVBSAXXMLReader	Makes it possible to tie together the previously listed interfaces in order to process a complete document information item.
Attributes	IVBSAXAttributes	Models a collection of attributes.
Locator	IVBSAXLocator	Provides contextual information about the caller.

SAX is essentially comprised of three basic components:

- The *XML Parser*, the implementation of the XMLReader interface {SAXXMLReader in MSXML}, streams the document from top to bottom and notifies the content handler when it encounters different items in the document, such as the start and the end tags of an element. For example, when it encounters the start of an element, it calls the startElement method that's defined in the ContentHandler interface.

- In the *Event Handlers*, you need to provide the code to process the document. The Event Handlers are the classes that implement one or more of the SAX interfaces that model the Infoset's information items. The

`ContentHandler` interface models the core items, and the `DTDHandler`, `LexicalHandler`, and the `DeclHandler` model the rest. The `ErrorHandler` interface supports error handling, and models fatal errors and warnings.

- The *Application* creates an instance of the `XMLReader` and creates instances of one or more handler classes that together represent the Document Handler. It then registers the different handler objects with the reader by setting the respective properties of the reader. Finally, it starts the process by calling the `parse()` method of the XML Parser.

Transforming XML to HTML Using SAX

In the examples discussed earlier in this chapter, we transformed the Customers XML document to HTML by using node traversal in DOM and by using an XSLT stylesheet. Let's see how we can accomplish the same result by implementing the SAX interfaces. Start by creating a new Visual Basic project for an ASP.NET web application and name this project VBSAX, as shown in Figure 5.11. We use this project for the remaining examples in this chapter.

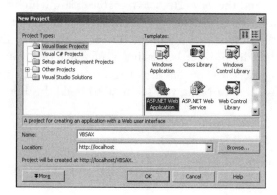

Figure 5.11   Creating the VBSAX ASP.NET web application.

The following is the `customers.xml` file that you need to add to the VBSAX project and use for the transformation:

```xml
<?xml version="1.0" encoding="utf-8" ?>
<Customers>
    <Customer id="ALFKI">
        <CompanyName>Alfreds Futterkiste</CompanyName>
        <Contact>
            <FirstName>Maria</FirstName>
            <LastName>Anders</LastName>
            <Title>Sales Representative</Title>
```

continues

```
        </Contact>
    </Customer>
    <Customer id="THEBI">
        <CompanyName>The Big Cheese</CompanyName>
        <Contact>
            <FirstName>Liz</FirstName>
            <LastName>Nixon</LastName>
            <Title>Marketing Manager</Title>
        </Contact>
    </Customer>
    <Customer id="EASTC">
        <CompanyName>Eastern Connection</CompanyName>
        <Contact>
            <FirstName>Ann</FirstName>
            <LastName>Devon</LastName>
            <Title>Sales Agent</Title>
        </Contact>
    </Customer>
</Customers>
```

Rename the `webform1.aspx` that was created by default to `SAXTransform.aspx`.
Listing 5.14 shows the code for the `SAXTransform.aspx` page that instantiates the
`SAXXMLReader` class and the `VBSAXLIB.CSAXTransform` class, which you see in
Listing 5.15. While you instantiate the `CSAXTransform` class, you can choose
either to write the output to a file on the server, as shown by the commented
code, or directly to the browser by passing a reference of the `Response` object
to the `transform` object. To run this `aspx` page, you must add a reference to the
VBSAXLIB Class Library. Next, you see how to build this library.

Listing 5.14   **Transforming XML to HTML Using SAX**
              (*SAX Transform.aspx*)

```
<%@ Page language="VB"    %>
<%@ Import Namespace = "VBSAXLIB"   %>
<%@ Import Namespace = "MSXML2"    %>
<%
        'write the output to file
        'Dim htmlFilePath as String
        'htmlFilePath =  Server.MapPath(".") & "\customers.html"
        'Dim transform As New VBSAXLIB.CSAXTransform(htmlFilePath)
        'write the output to the browser
        Dim transform As New VBSAXLIB.CSAXTransform(Response)
        Dim reader As New MSXML2.SAXXMLReader40 ()

        reader.contentHandler = transform
        reader.errorHandler = transform
        On Error Resume Next
        reader.parseURL("http://localhost/VBSAX/customers.xml")
%>
```

The `contentHandler` and the `errorHandler` properties are set to the `transform` object so that the reader notifies it of the corresponding events after the `parseURL` method is invoked.

To create the VBSAXLIB Class Library, you need to create a Visual Basic project, as shown in Figure 5.12.

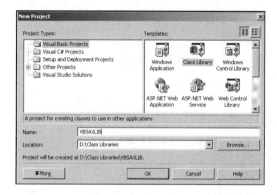

Figure 5.12 Creating the VBSAXLIB Class Library.

The next step is to add a class to the project by using the Add New Item menu item from the Project menu. Name the file `CSAXTransform.vb`, as shown in Figure 5.13.

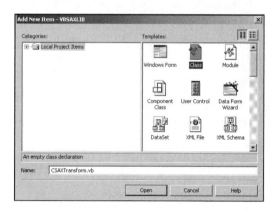

Figure 5.13 Adding the CSAXTransform class.

The `CSAXTransform` class requires a reference to the System.web assembly and the MSXML2 wrapper (discussed in the section, "Working with MSXML 4.0 on the Server-Side with ASP.NET"). After you add these references the Solution Explorer, it looks close to what's shown in Figure 5.14.

Figure 5.14   The Solution Explorer after adding the
assembly references and the CSAXTransform class.

The CSAXTransform class implements the IVBSAXContentHandler and the
IVBSAXErrorHandler interfaces. This class provides two constructors: One allows
you to send the data to the browser through the HTTP Response stream, and
the other provides you with an option to alternatively write the output to an
HTML file on the file system. The second option is a common scenario when
you need to generate HTML in a staging environment before you push it to
the production environment. Also, this option allows you to use this Class
Library in a desktop-based Windows application. Listing 5.15 shows the code
for the CSAXTransform class that performs the job of transforming the XML
into HTML for use in the VBSAX ASP.NET application. (Listing 5.15 is split
with some explanation introduced along with the subheadings at important
steps.)

Listing 5.15   **Implementing the *ContentHandler* and the *ErrorHandler***
   Interfaces in Visual Basic .NET *(CSAXTransform.vb)*

```
Imports System.IO
Imports MSXML2

Public Class CSAXTransform
    Implements IVBSAXContentHandler, IVBSAXErrorHandler

    Private custCount As Integer
    Private Response As System.Web.HttpResponse
    Private file As StreamWriter

    Private bHTTPStream As Boolean

    '***************** constructors ****************************
    Sub New(ByRef Response As System.Web.HttpResponse)
```

```
      Me.Response = Response
      bHTTPStream = True
End Sub

Sub New(ByVal filePath As String)
      bHTTPStream = False
      Dim fs As FileStream = New FileStream(filePath, FileMode.Create, _
             FileAccess.Write)
      file = New StreamWriter(fs)
      ' Set the file pointer to the beginning.
      file.BaseStream.Seek(0, SeekOrigin.Begin)
End Sub

Private Sub writeHTML(ByVal str As String)
      If bHTTPStream Then
          Response.Write(str)
      Else
          file.Write(str)
      End If
End Sub
```

Implementing the *IVBSAXContentHandler* Interface

When you implement an interface, it's mandatory to provide an implementation for all the methods and properties in the interface, as shown in the following code. Otherwise, you might find some methods contain code that does not perform any functions.

```
Private Sub startDocument() Implements IVBSAXContentHandler.startDocument
      writeHTML("<HTML><HEAD><TITLE>Customers</TITLE></HEAD>"
      ⇒& vbCrLf & "<BODY>")
End Sub

Private Sub startElement(ByRef strNamespaceURI As String, ByRef
⇒strLocalName As String, _
             ByRef strQName As String, ByVal oAttributes As
             ⇒MSXML2.IVBSAXAttributes) _
             Implements IVBSAXContentHandler.startElement

      Select Case strLocalName
          Case "Customers"
              writeHTML("<TABLE border='1'><THEAD>
              <TH>CustomerID</TH><TH>Company Name</TH>" & _
                        "<TH>Contact Name</TH><TH>Contact
                        ⇒Title</TH></THEAD><TBODY>")
          Case "Customer"
              writeHTML("<TR><TD>")
              If oAttributes.length > 0 Then
                  writeHTML(oAttributes.getValue(0))
```

continues

Listing 5.15   **Continued**

```
                End If
                custCount = custCount + 1
        Case "CompanyName", "Title"
                writeHTML("</TD><TD>")
        Case "FirstName"
                writeHTML("</TD><TD>")
    End Select
End Sub
Private Sub processingInstruction(ByRef target As String, ByRef data As String) _
                Implements IVBSAXContentHandler.processingInstruction
End Sub

Private Sub startPrefixMapping(ByRef strPrefix As String, ByRef strURI As String) _
                Implements IVBSAXContentHandler.startPrefixMapping
End Sub

Private Sub endPrefixMapping(ByRef strPrefix As String) _
                Implements IVBSAXContentHandler.endPrefixMapping
End Sub

Private Sub endElement(ByRef strNamespaceURI As String, ByRef strLocalName As
▬String, _
                ByRef strQName As String) Implements
                ▬IVBSAXContentHandler.endElement
    Select Case strLocalName
        Case "Customers"
            writeHTML("</TABLE> " & vbCrLf & _"<BR><P><B>Found "
                    & custCount & " customer(s) </B></P>")
        Case "Customer"
            writeHTML("</TD>" & vbCrLf & "</TR>")
    End Select
End Sub

Private Sub ignorableWhitespace(ByRef strChars As String) _
                Implements IVBSAXContentHandler.ignorableWhitespace
End Sub

Private Sub characters(ByRef strChars As String) _
                Implements IVBSAXContentHandler.characters
            writeHTML(removeNewline(strChars))
End Sub

Private Sub skippedEntity(ByRef strName As String) Implements
▬IVBSAXContentHandler.skippedEntity
End Sub

Private WriteOnly Property documentLocator() As MSXML2.IVBSAXLocator _
                Implements IVBSAXContentHandler.documentLocator
    Set(ByVal Value As MSXML2.IVBSAXLocator)
```

```
        End Set
    End Property

    Private Sub endDocument() Implements IVBSAXContentHandler.endDocument
        writeHTML(vbCrLf & "</BODY></HTML>")
        If Not bHTTPStream Then
            file.Flush()
            file.Close()
        End If
    End Sub
    Private Function removeNewline(ByVal strChars As String) As String
        Select Case strChars
            Case vbCrLf, vbCr, vbLf
                strChars = ""
        End Select
        removeNewline = strChars
    End Function
End Class
```

The preceding code is simple to follow. The startDocument method starts by writing the HTML syntax. The startElement method starts a TABLE tag on the occurrence of the root element and increments the counter to count the number of customers it encounters. On the occurrence of other elements, it closes and starts the TD tags. The characters method simply writes out all the PCDATA the parser encounters. The endElement method writes out the closing tags and also writes the final count of the customers when the end of the root tag is encountered. The endDocument method closes the BODY and HTML tags and closes the stream writer in the case of a file stream.

In this example, you are writing the data to the output stream as you find it. Notice that, to keep track of the number of customers, a counter variable is maintained, whereas in the case of DOM, you could easily find that value from the length property of a NodeList object. In a more complex application where you need to do some processing based on the previously found data, you need to create your state-handling mechanism using data structures, such as Stacks and Collections, in the ContentHandler implementation. This retains the state as the parser reads the document from start to finish. For example, if you want to calculate the sum of the three items purchased from an inventory document and display them in alphabetical order, you need to retain the state of all the items until you encounter the last item purchased.

Implementing the *IVBSAXErrorHandler* Interface

The current SAX2 implementation in MSXML treats all types of errors as fatal errors, so we must provide implementation for the fatalError() method alone. We write the error message to the output stream and log the message to a file. The following code shows how you can implement the IVBSAXErrorHandler interface.

```
Public Sub localError(ByVal oLocator As MSXML2.IVBSAXLocator, ByRef
➥strErrorMessage As String, _
    ByVal nErrorCode As Integer) Implements IVBSAXErrorHandler.error
End Sub

Public Sub fatalError(ByVal oLocator As MSXML2.IVBSAXLocator, ByRef
➥strErrorMessage As String, _
    ByVal nErrorCode As Integer) Implements IVBSAXErrorHandler.fatalError
    writeHTML("<BR><B>Error  <BR>Error Code: " & _
                    nErrorCode & " Error: " & strErrorMessage & "
                    ➥Line:" & oLocator.lineNumber & _
                    ", Position " & oLocator.columnNumber & "</B><BR>")
    Log(" Error Code: " & nErrorCode & " Error: " & strErrorMessage & "
                    ➥Line: " & oLocator.lineNumber & _
                    ", Position " & oLocator.columnNumber)
End Sub

Public Sub ignorableWarning(ByVal oLocator As MSXML2.IVBSAXLocator, ByRef
➥strErrorMessage As String, _
                        ByVal nErrorCode As Integer) Implements
                        ➥IVBSAXErrorHandler.ignorableWarning
End Sub
```

You might notice a slight difference in the name used for the error() method. This is because Visual Basic .NET does not allow you to use the keyword error for a method name.

Log Errors to a File

The following code is a simple subroutine to write out the error messages to a log file:

```
Public Shared Sub Log(ByVal logMessage As String)
    Dim fs As FileStream = New FileStream("log.txt",
    ➥FileMode.OpenOrCreate, _
        FileAccess.Write)
    Dim w As New StreamWriter(fs)
    ' Set the file pointer to the end.
    w.BaseStream.Seek(0, SeekOrigin.End)
    w.Write(vbCrLf + "Log Entry : ")
    w.WriteLine("{0} {1}", DateTime.Now.ToLongTimeString(), _
        DateTime.Now.ToLongDateString())
    w.WriteLine(" {0}", logMessage)
    w.WriteLine("--------------------------------------------------------")
    w.Flush()
    w.Close()
End Sub
```

The subroutine logs the error message that's passed to it as an argument into the log.txt file with the current time and date. The subroutine then closes the file stream.

Although this example parses an XML document of a small size, it shows you how to implement the SAX interfaces and use SAX in an ASP.NET application. This example converts all the data available in the XML document into HTML. However, in the case of XML documents of large sizes, you can change the code to display only a summary of the data by filtering some elements. We look at an alternative way of doing this in the next section, as we learn about SAX filters.

SAX Filters

The XMLFilter interface enables you to include additional transparent interceptors between the XMLReader and the ContentHandler class. This lets you create a chain or a pipeline of filters and gives each one a specific processing responsibility. Each of these filters intercept the calls to the final content handler, do some processing themselves, and delegate the call to the next content handler in the chain.

This can be slightly confusing when you look at it for the first time, so here's a simple explanation: The first filter in the chain behaves as a content handler for the base XMLReader class and it behaves as an XMLReader for the second filter (or the content handler) in the chain. This dual behavior is possible for the filter class because it must implement both the XMLReader and the ContentHandler interfaces. Figure 5.15 shows a visual representation of the chain of filters.

> **Note**
> The current example does not include the second level, represented by FILTER2 in Figure 5.15, but it's been added here to show a possible intermediate filter in the chain.

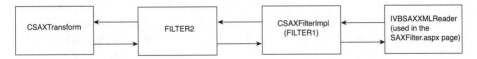

Figure 5.15   The flow of methods.

Next, you see how to include a filter in between the Reader class and the CSAXTransform class that you saw in the last example. The responsibility of the CSAXTransform class was to count the number of customers and transform the XML syntax into HTML. This class ignores what is present in the XML document; instead, it simply responds to the calls by the Reader class. We utilize this fact to add some searching capability into the same application. An implementation of the XMLFilter interface intercepts the calls, reviews all the customer elements, but passes to the CSAXTransform instance only those customer elements whose ID attribute value starts with a specified search string.

We need to add a new ASP.NET page, SAXFilter.aspx, to the VBSAX web project and the corresponding Visual Basic .NET class CSAXFilterImpl to the VBSAXLIB Class Library.

The SAXFilter.aspx ASP.NET page in Listing 5.16 is almost identical to the SAXTransform.aspx page in the previous example with the exception for the inclusion of the CSAXFilterImpl class, which implements the IVBSAXXMLFilter interface.

Listing 5.16   *SAXFilter.aspx*

```
<%@ Page language="VB"    %>
<%@ Import Namespace = "VBSAXLIB"    %>
<%@ Import Namespace = "MSXML2"    %>
<%
    Dim reader As IVBSAXXMLReader
        reader = New SAXXMLReader40 ()
        Dim filterImpl As New CSAXFilterImpl("AL")// provide "AL" as the
                                                  //search string
        Dim filter As MSXML2.IVBSAXXMLFilter
        filter = filterImpl
        filter.parent = reader
        Dim transform As New CSAXTransform(Response)
        reader = filterImpl
        reader.contentHandler = transform
        reader.errorHandler = transform
        On Error Resume Next
        reader.parseURL("http://localhost/VBSAX/customers.xml")
%>
```

The constructor for CSAXFilterImpl takes a string parameter, which is the search string for the ID attribute. The filter sets an instance of the XMLReader as its parent. Then the reader variable is set to the filter implementation. This is possible because the CSAXFilterImpl implements the XMLReader interface. This reader sets its Content Handler and Error Handler to an instance of the CSAXTransform class. Notice that the Filter implementation class keeps a reference to these handlers in instance variables (these variables are prefixed with m_ in the CSAXFilterImpl example class), so that it can call methods on them when required. Finally, the application calls the parseURL() method. CSAXFilterImpl, in turn, passes this call of parseURL() to its parent XMLReader (m_parent in the CSAXFilterImpl class), to which it had received a reference in the beginning through its parent property.

This class is lengthy because it must provide an implementation for the four interfaces and must account for all the handler types a parent XMLReader might set. (Look at the most significant part of this code in Listing 5.17.)

Listing 5.17 **The *CSAXFilterImpl* Class (*VBSAXLIB.CSAXFilterImpl*)**

```
Imports MSXML2

Public Class CSAXFilterImpl
    Implements IVBSAXXMLFilter, IVBSAXXMLReader, IVBSAXContentHandler,
IVBSAXErrorHandler

    Private m_parent As IVBSAXXMLReader
    Private m_contentHandler As IVBSAXContentHandler
    Private m_dtdHandler As IVBSAXDTDHandler
    Private m_entityResolver As IVBSAXEntityResolver
    Private m_errorHandler As IVBSAXErrorHandler
    Private m_lexicalHandler As IVBSAXLexicalHandler
    Private m_declHandler As IVBSAXDeclHandler

    Private m_secureBaseURL As String
    Private m_baseURL As String
    Private bSkipCustomer As Boolean
    Private customerID As String


    Sub New(ByVal customerID As String)
        Me.customerID = customerID
        bSkipCustomer = False
    End Sub
```

The initParse() method sets the contentHandler and the errorHandler properties of the parent XMLReader class to itself. We mentioned that the filter behaves as the Content Handler to the base XMLReader class. That is exactly what the initParse() method configures.

The following code shows the initparse() method and the IVBSAXXMLFilter and IVBSAXXMLReader interface implementations:

```
    Public Sub initParse()
        m_parent.contentHandler = Me
        m_parent.errorHandler = Me
    End Sub
    .
    .
    Private Sub parseURL(ByVal strURL As String) _
                                Implements IVBSAXXMLReader.parseURL
        initParse()
        m_parent.parseURL(strURL)
    End Sub
```

```
    .
'IVBSAXXMLFilter  interface implementation
    Public Property parent() As MSXML2.IVBSAXXMLReader _
                                     Implements IVBSAXXMLFilter.parent
        Set(ByVal Value As MSXML2.IVBSAXXMLReader)
            m_parent = Value
        End Set
        Get
            Return m_parent
        End Get
    End Property
' IVBSAXXMLReader  interface implementation
Public Property contentHandler() As MSXML2.IVBSAXContentHandler _
                                    Implements IVBSAXXMLReader.contentHandler
        Set(ByVal Value As MSXML2.IVBSAXContentHandler)
            m_contentHandler = Value
        End Set
        Get
            Return m_contentHandler
        End Get
    End Property

    .
Public Property errorHandler() As MSXML2.IVBSAXErrorHandler _
                                      Implements IVBSAXXMLReader.errorHandler
        Set(ByVal Value As MSXML2.IVBSAXErrorHandler)
            m_errorHandler = Value
        End Set
        Get
            Return m_errorHandler
        End Get
End Property
```

The *ContentHandler* Implementation

As previously mentioned, the `filter` class behaves like the `XMLReader` for the filter or the Content Handler that appears next in the chain. The `filter` class accomplishes this by performing the necessary processing when it receives information through a `parse` event by the parent `XMLReader`. It passes the event down the chain to the next Content Handler, `m_contentHandler` in this case, which has a reference to the `CSAXTransform` instance.

```
'IVBSAXContentHandler interface implementation
Private Sub startElement(ByRef strNamespaceURI As String, ByRef strLocalName
➥As String, _
                ByRef strQName As String, ByVal oAttributes As
                ➥MSXML2.IVBSAXAttributes) _
                Implements IVBSAXContentHandler.startElement
        Select Case strLocalName
            Case "Customer"
                If Mid(oAttributes.getValue(0), 1, Len(customerID)) =
                ➥customerID Then
                    bSkipCustomer = False
```

```
                    m_contentHandler.startElement(strNamespaceURI,
                    ➥strLocalName, strQName, oAttributes)
                Else
                    bSkipCustomer = True
                End If
            Case "Customers"
                m_contentHandler.startElement(strNamespaceURI, strLocalName,
                ➥strQName, oAttributes)
            Case Else
                If Not bSkipCustomer Then
                    m_contentHandler.startElement(strNamespaceURI,
                    ➥strLocalName, strQName, oAttributes)
                End If
        End Select
    End Sub

    Private Sub endElement(ByRef strNamespaceURI As String, ByRef
strLocalName As String, _
                    ByRef strQName As String) Implements
                    ➥IVBSAXContentHandler.endElement
        If strLocalName = "Customers" Or Not bSkipCustomer Then
            m_contentHandler.endElement(strNamespaceURI, strLocalName,
            ➥strQName)
        End If
    End Sub

    .

    ,
Private WriteOnly Property documentLocator() As MSXML2.IVBSAXLocator _
                            Implements IVBSAXContentHandler.documentLocator
        Set(ByVal Value As MSXML2.IVBSAXLocator)
            m_contentHandler.documentLocator = Value
        End Set

    End Property

    .
    .
  Private Sub characters(ByRef strChars As String) _
                            Implements IVBSAXContentHandler.characters
        If Not bSkipCustomer Then
            m_contentHandler.characters(strChars)
        End If
    End Sub
    Private Sub endDocument() Implements IVBSAXContentHandler.endDocument
        m_contentHandler.endDocument()
    End Sub

    .
'IVBSAXErrorHandler interface implementation
Public Sub fatalError(ByVal oLocator As MSXML2.IVBSAXLocator, ByRef
strErrorMessage As String, _
                            ByVal nErrorCode As Integer) Implements
                            ➥IVBSAXErrorHandler.fatalError
```

```
        m_errorHandler.fatalError(oLocator, strErrorMessage, nErrorCode)
    End Sub
```

The methods of the ContentHandler interface pass the events to the CSAXTransform instance to do the processing only if the ID attribute matches the search criteria. The Error Handler simply passes the events to the next Error Handler to take necessary action. Figure 5.16 shows the output that's produced by the CSAXTransform class.

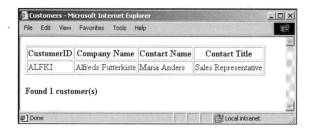

Figure 5.16   Using XMLFilter to filter XML documents.

Using *SAXFilter* to Update and Create New Elements

The preceding SAXFilter example shows you how to call the methods of a Content Handler selectively. In a way, it simulates the events when required. We can make use of this technique to modify the existing content or create new content in the XML documents. Although using SAX, it is not possible to modify the contents of the original document and save it as you can with DOM; you can only make it appear to be modifying the content by creating a new document. For example, as the events are being intercepted by the filter, you can pass a new parameter value to the characters() method of the Content Handler. As the handler writes the document to a new location, the new document will contain the modified values. Similarly, you can add new elements to the document by manually invoking methods of the ISAXContentHandler in an appropriate order that's similar to the old location, in case an element already exists.

Abort Processing

When an implementation finds the content it's looking for in a document (take the Customer example, for instance), if you are searching for a specific customer, you can stop processing if you find a customer with a specified ID. The SAXXMLReader object doesn't have a method that can interrupt parsing. Instead, you must stop parsing by raising an application-specific exception. The

`ContentHandler` implementations can accomplish this by indicating to the `XMLReader` that it wants to abort processing. The following code shows how this is done:

```
Private Sub endElement(ByRef strNamespaceURI As String, ByRef strLocalName As
String, _
                    ByRef strQName As String) Implements
                    ➥IVBSAXContentHandler.endElement
        If bFound Then
            Err.Raise(vbObjectError + errAbort , "endElement", "Abort
            ➥processing")
        End If
    End Sub
```

MXXMLWriter

The `CSAXTransform` class transforms the XML syntax to HTML. Assume that we required an implementation of a Content Handler who handles the details of building another XML document from the events passed to it by the `XMLReader` class. This class allows you to specify the output as a string or an implementation of the IStream interface. It allows you to control the output by specifying whether indentation is required, omitting the XML declaration, setting the encoding, and so on. If this is the requirement, the `MXXMLWriter` class does all this for you when it's connected to `SAXXMLReader`. Listing 5.18 shows you how to use the `MXXMLWriter` in conjunction with the `SAXXMLReader` class. This application writes the output XML string (string is the default output; this can be set to an implementation of IStream) created by the `MXXMLWriter` class. Setting the `omitXMLDeclaration` property to true filters out the XML declaration part in the output.

Listing 5.18 **Using** *MXXMLWriter (MXXMLWriter.aspx)*

```
<%@ Page language="VB"    %>
<%@ Import Namespace = "MSXML2"    %>
<%
        Dim reader As New SAXXMLReader()
        Dim writer As New MXXMLWriter()

        reader.contentHandler = writer
        reader.dtdHandler = writer
        reader.errorHandler = writer
        reader.putProperty("http://xml.org/sax/properties/declaration-
        ➥handler", writer)
        reader.putProperty("http://xml.org/sax/properties/lexical-handler",
        ➥writer)
        writer.omitXMLDeclaration = True
        reader.parseURL("http://localhost/VBSAX/customers.xml")
```

continues

Listing 5.18   **Continued**

```
%>
<html>
    <body>
        <PRE>
            <%= Server.HTMLEncode(writer.output)%>
        </PRE>
    </body>
</html>
```

You can also manually build an XML document by using the MXXMLWriter class, and by invoking methods of the ISAXContentHandler, ISAXDTDHandler, ISAXDeclHandler, and ISAXLexicalHandler interfaces. To make your life simpler, a new object, MXHTMLWriter in MSXML 4.0, allows you to output HTML using a stream of SAX events, similar to what we did in the CSAXTransform class.

Benefits of Using SAX

Now that you have seen the DOM and the SAX APIs at work and you have seen the benefits of using DOM, take a look at the benefits of using SAX so that you can make a well-balanced decision between the two APIs when you develop your applications using XML:

- **Can parse large documents efficiently**—With SAX, memory consumption does not increase with the size of the file. If you need to process large documents of the order of 2MB and more, SAX is the better alternative, as long as you want the document for read-only access.

- **Allows you to abort parsing**—SAX allows you to abort processing at any time. You can use it to create applications that fetch particular data. After data is retrieved, you can stop processing.

- **Can retrieve small amounts of information**—If you want to scan the document for a small subset of data, it's inefficient to read the unnecessary data into memory. With SAX, it's possible to ignore the data that doesn't interest you.

- **Creating a new document structure is efficient**—In cases where you might want to create a new document structure by filtering out some elements in the original document, SAX allows you to do this more efficiently and quickly.

Drawbacks of Using SAX

The following are the drawbacks of the SAX API:

- **Requires state handling mechanisms**—As the SAX parses through the documents and raises the events, it does not retain any state of the previous elements and even the relationships between two elements. You might want to maintain some context and do further processing based on the previous values. To accomplish this, you need to include state handling mechanisms in your code. You have to create data structures, which can become complex for documents with complex structures.

- **Difficult to implement pull model on top of push model**—It is a challenge when you want to build a pull model on top of the push model. The pull model is consumer driven and it allows the consumer to navigate to the content it desires to process. But with a push model, everything must be passed through the application. To simulate the pull behavior, the content handlers require building complex state machines that involve working with many variables. The document might have to be parsed more than once, because navigating back and forth is not possible in a single pass with the SAX model.

With the .NET Framework, you might choose to work with XMLReader classes as the pull model offers a more familiar programming model along with several performance benefits. If you still find yourself comfortable with SAX, it's possible to layer a set of push-style interfaces on top of the XMLReader pull model, but the reverse is not true.

MSXML Versions Shipped with Microsoft Products

Table 5.7 lists some of the more recent MSXML versions to help you find out the version that's available to you.

Table 5.7 **MSXML Versions Shipped with Microsoft Products**

Operating System or Program	Internet Explorer	MSXML Version / Filename
Office 2000	Internet Explorer 5.0	2.0a / msxml.dll
Windows 95, Windows 98, or Windows NT 4.0	Internet Explorer 5.01	2.5a / msxml.dll
Windows 2000	Internet Explorer 5.01	2.5 / msxml.dll

continues

Table 5.7   **MSXML Versions Shipped with Microsoft Products**

Operating System or Program	Internet Explorer	MSXML Version / Filename
Windows 2000	Internet Explorer 5.01, Service Pack 1 (SP1)	2.5 Service Pack 1 (SP1) / `msxml.dll`
Windows 95, Windows 98, Windows NT 4.0, Windows 2000, or Windows 2000 Service Pack 1 (SP1)	Internet Explorer 5.5	2.5 Service Pack 1 f(SP1) / `msxml.dll`
Microsoft SQL Server 2000		2.6 / `msxml2.dll`
Windows XP Home Edition, Windows XP Professional	Internet Explorer 6	3.0 / `msxml3.dll`

Downloading Microsoft XML Core Services 4.0

You can download MSXML 4.0 from the Microsoft download center at `http://msdn.microsoft.com/downloads/default.asp?url=/downloads/sample.asp?url=/msdn-files/027/001/766/msdncompositedoc.xml`.

Chapter Summary

In this chapter, you learned about the DOM and the SAX models of document parsing. You saw how to work with these models using the MSXML 4.0 component and also the extended features provided by this parser. The classes in the `System.XML` namespace are explored in Chapter 6, "Exploring the `System.XML` Namespace."

6

Exploring the *System.Xml* Namespace

Admittedly, structuring this book has been difficult. We wanted to cover XML and its concepts, discuss Microsoft's implementation of those concepts in the MSXML Parser and the .NET Framework classes, and introduce design patterns to make these concepts useful in your everyday application development. Each of the recommendations for XML Schemas, XPath, and XSLT could easily make, and have made, excellent books without covering a vendor's implementation of those technologies.

We decided to take another approach: Cover the individual technologies while giving glimpses of how to implement those technologies in .NET. Realizing that cursory examples won't paint a complete-enough picture, this chapter serves to cover those technologies in depth, from the perspective of how they are implemented in .NET.

We begin by looking at the abstract base classes, XmlReader and XmlWriter, and how they support working with XML in .NET. We then move on to working with those classes in creating a familiar DOM-style document. We then cover validation, modifying documents, transforming documents, and handling exceptions. Finally, we revisit XPath and its functions by tying in more advanced XSLT transformations and a custom XML reader implementation.

The Abstract Base Classes

As we saw in Chapter 5, "MSXML Parser," the MSXML Parser provides two models for working with XML data: push and pull models. A pull model queries a document, and a push model involves notifications from the parser. A pull model typically requires the entire XML document to be loaded, and a push model allows for forward-only reading of a document. In MSXML, the push model is implemented by using the SAX interfaces, and the pull model is implemented by using the DOM interfaces.

The DOM implementation of a pull model loads the entire document into memory so that it can be navigated and updated easily. The problem with loading the entire document into memory is that it is not scalable: Loading a large document in its entirety requires significant memory. Multiply the memory consumption for one large document by potentially tens of thousands of users, and you can see why you want to reduce the memory footprint as much as possible. The DOM, however, is a great choice for working with smaller documents that require updating. The DOM model is retained in .NET through the XmlDocument class.

Because a push model doesn't require the entire document to be loaded, it uses less memory and is better suited for parsing large documents. The downside of the push model is that it is difficult to add and update nodes in the document. Constant maintenance of state information is required to know with what node you are working. In .NET, SAX is not supported. Rather, the designers of the System.Xml classes developed a new forward-only, stream-based model that mixes the document-based approach of the DOM with the forward-only nature of SAX. The classes that form the foundation of this model are the XmlReader and XmlWriter classes. Both classes are abstract, which means that they require an implementation class to create a new instance. Figure 6.1 shows you the available implementation classes.

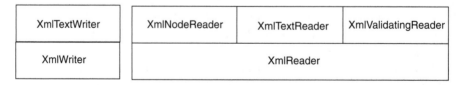

Figure 6.1   The available implementations of XmlReader and XmlWriter in the .NET Framework.

XmlReader

As its name implies, the XmlReader class enables you to read an XML document. More specifically, the XmlReader provides a forward-only, non-cached mechanism to read XML data. This is most analogous to an ActiveX Data Objects (ADO) firehose cursor.

The XmlReader is an abstract class, so let's look at its implementation classes: XmlTextReader, XmlNodeReader, and XmlValidatingReader.

XmlTextReader

The XmlTextReader class is a concrete implementation of the XmlReader class. It's one of the classes that you are going to frequently work with in your XML and ASP.NET applications.

The DOMDocument class in MSXML provides a loadXML() method that accepts a string representation of the XML document and works with it. The XmlTextReader class in .NET does not provide such a method. Instead, it provides 14 different overloaded New() methods to instantiate an XmlTextReader.

Populating an **XmlReader**

Let's load an XmlTextReader with data by loading the XML from a string. We display a table that shows each node in the document and some properties of each node. Listing 6.1 shows the code that is used to build the XML document as a string in memory, load the document into an XmlReader, and interrogate the document's nodes.

Listing 6.1 **Interrogating the Nodes in an** *XmlReader*

```
<%@ Import Namespace="System.Xml"%>
<%@ Import Namespace="System.Text"%>
<!DOCTYPE HTML PUBLIC "-//W3C//DTD HTML 4.0 Transitional//EN">
<html>
  <head>
    <title>WebForm1</title>
  </head>
<LINK rel="stylesheet" type="text/css"
href="http://localhost/chapters/SystemXML/Styles.css">
  <body MS_POSITIONING="GridLayout">

 <script language="vb" runat="server">

    Private Sub Page_Load(ByVal sender As System.Object, ByVal e As
System.EventArgs) Handles MyBase.Load
        Dim sb As StringBuilder
        Dim reader As XmlTextReader
```

continues

Listing 6.1 **Continued**

```
        sb = New StringBuilder()
        With sb
            .Append("<DATA xmlns=""urn:foo:bar"">")
            .Append("<PERSON name=""Carson Allen Evans""/>")
            .Append("<PERSON name=""Deanna Evans"">Hello, Wife</PERSON>")
            .Append("</DATA>")
        End With
        reader = New XmlTextReader(sb.ToString, XmlNodeType.Document,
        ➥Nothing)
        writeTable(reader)
    End Sub

    Private Sub writeTable(ByVal reader As XmlReader)
        With Response
            .Write("<TABLE border=""1"">")
            .Write("<TR>")
            .Write("<TH>Name</TH><TH>NodeType</TH><TH>NodeValue</TH>")

.Write("<TH>Depth</TH><TH>NamespaceURI</TH><TH>BaseURI</TH><TH>LocalName</TH>")
            .Write("<TH>IsStartElement</TH><TH>IsEmptyElement</TH>")
            .Write("</TR>")

            Do While reader.Read()
                .Write("<TR>")
                .Write(getTableData(reader.Name))
                .Write(getTableData(reader.NodeType.ToString))
                .Write(getTableData(reader.Value))
                .Write(getTableData(reader.Depth))
                .Write(getTableData(reader.NamespaceURI))
                .Write(getTableData(reader.BaseURI))
                .Write(getTableData(reader.LocalName))
                .Write(getTableData(reader.IsStartElement))
                .Write(getTableData(reader.IsEmptyElement))
                .Write("</TR>")
            Loop
            .Write("</TABLE>")
        End With
    End Sub

    Private Function getTableData(ByVal data As String) As String
        getTableData = String.Concat("<TD>", data, "</TD>")
    End Function

</script>
  </body>
</html>
```

The Abstract Base Classes 265

The output for Listing 6.1 is depicted in Figure 6.2.

Name	NodeType	NodeValue	Depth	NamespaceURI	BaseURI	LocalName	IsStartElement	IsEmptyElement
DATA	Element		0	urn:foo:bar		DATA	True	False
PERSON	Element		1	urn:foo:bar		PERSON	True	True
PERSON	Element		1	urn:foo:bar		PERSON	True	False
	Text	Hello, Wife	2				False	False
PERSON	EndElement		1	urn:foo:bar		PERSON	False	False
DATA	EndElement		0	urn:foo:bar		DATA	False	False
Name	NodeType	NodeValue	Depth	NamespaceURI	BaseURI	LocalName	IsStartElement	IsEmptyElement
DATA	Element		0	urn:foo:bar		DATA	True	False
PERSON	Element		1	urn:foo:bar		PERSON	True	True
PERSON	Element		1	urn:foo:bar		PERSON	True	False
	Text	Hello, Wife	2				False	False
PERSON	EndElement		1	urn:foo:bar		PERSON	False	False
DATA	EndElement		0	urn:foo:bar		DATA	False	False

Figure 6.2 Each node in the `XmlTextReader` is interrogated for its properties.

Listing 6.1 shows the use of a `StringBuilder` object to build an XML string, but could have easily concatenated the strings together to form the input document.

Another method to load an `XmlReader` without using a file or database involves using a `Stream` object. Let's use a `MemoryStream` object to create a reader based on a stream of data held in memory. The updated code is shown in Listing 6.2.

Listing 6.2 **Reading XML Data From a** *MemoryStream*

```
<%@ Import Namespace="System.Xml"%>
<%@ Import Namespace="System.Text"%>
<!DOCTYPE HTML PUBLIC "-//W3C//DTD HTML 4.0 Transitional//EN">
<html>
  <head>
    <title>WebForm1</title>
  </head>
<LINK rel="stylesheet" type="text/css"
href="http://localhost/chapters/SystemXML/Styles.css">
  <body MS_POSITIONING="GridLayout">

 <script language="vb" runat="server">

    Private Sub Page_Load(ByVal sender As System.Object, ByVal e As
    ➥System.EventArgs) Handles MyBase.Load
        Dim sb As StringBuilder
        Dim reader As XmlTextReader
```

continues

Listing 6.2 **Continued**

```
Dim memStream As IO.MemoryStream
Dim memStreamWriter As IO.StreamWriter

sb = New StringBuilder()
With sb
    .Append("<DATA xmlns=""urn:foo:bar"">")
    .Append("<PERSON name=""Carson Allen Evans""/>")
    .Append("<PERSON name=""Deanna Evans"">Hello, Wife</PERSON>")
    .Append("</DATA>")
End With

memStream = New IO.MemoryStream()
memStreamWriter = New IO.StreamWriter(memStream,
➥System.Text.Encoding.UTF8)
memStreamWriter.Write(sb.ToString)
memStreamWriter.Flush()
memStream.Position = 0

reader = New XmlTextReader(memStream)
writeTable(reader)

On Error Resume Next

memStreamWriter.Close()
memStream.Close()

reader.Close()
End Sub

Private Sub writeTable(ByVal reader As XmlReader)
    With Response
        .Write("<TABLE border=""1"">")
        .Write("<TR>")
        .Write("<TH>Name</TH><TH>NodeType</TH><TH>NodeValue</TH>")

.Write("<TH>Depth</TH><TH>NamespaceURI</TH><TH>BaseURI</TH><TH>LocalName</TH>")
        .Write("<TH>IsStartElement</TH><TH>IsEmptyElement</TH>")
        .Write("</TR>")

        Do While reader.Read()
            .Write("<TR>")
            .Write(getTableData(reader.Name))
            .Write(getTableData(reader.NodeType.ToString))
            .Write(getTableData(reader.Value))
            .Write(getTableData(reader.Depth))
            .Write(getTableData(reader.NamespaceURI))
            .Write(getTableData(reader.BaseURI))
            .Write(getTableData(reader.LocalName))
            .Write(getTableData(reader.IsStartElement))
```

```
                .Write(getTableData(reader.IsEmptyElement))
                .Write("</TR>")
            Loop
            .Write("</TABLE>")
        End With
    End Sub

    Private Function getTableData(ByVal data As String) As String
        getTableData = String.Concat("<TD>", data, "</TD>")
    End Function

  </script>
  </body>
</html>
```

The output for Listing 6.2 is identical to what's depicted in Figure 6.2.

In the highlighted code in Listing 6.2, we created a `MemoryStream` object and used a `StreamWriter` object to write data to the stream. We called the `Flush()` method of the `StreamWriter` class to commit the changes to the underlying stream and then reset the stream's internal pointer to the beginning of the stream by using the `Position()` property. Resetting the stream's internal pointer to the beginning of the stream is important. Otherwise, no data can be read from the stream. The last line of highlighted text shows that we created the `XmlTextReader` class by using the `MemoryStream` object and then called our `writeXML` function by using `XmlReader`.

Retrieving External Data

The `XmlTextReader` accepts a URL as a parameter for one of its overloaded `New()` functions:

```
        reader = New
XmlTextReader("http://www.xmlandasp.net/examples/xmlfile1.xml")
```

This allows you to access resources over the Internet or within your intranet. Several of the overloaded versions of the `New()` function accepts a URL for resolving external resources. The `XmlTextReader` accepts a `XmlResolver` property for resolving these external resources. This property accepts an object of type, you guessed it, `XmlResolver`. By specifying the URL for the external resource in the URL parameter of the overloaded function and providing an `XmlResolver`, you can work with external resources and resolve only those resources that you want to retrieve remotely.

For example, suppose that you are working with an XML Schema file that's located on a remote server. You want to retrieve the entire XML Schema to ensure that it is up to date. To do this, use this code:

```
Private Sub getdata()

    Dim resolver As XmlUrlResolver = New XmlUrlResolver()
    Dim baseURI As Uri = New Uri("http://www.sample.com/sample.xsd")
    Dim relativeURI As Uri = resolver.ResolveUri(baseURI, "Customer.xsd")
    Dim inputStream As IO.Stream = resolver.GetEntity(relativeURI,
    ➥Nothing, GetType(IO.Stream))

    Dim reader As XmlTextReader = New XmlTextReader(inputStream)
    Do While reader.Read
        Response.Write(reader.ReadOuterXml())
    Loop

    On Error Resume Next
    inputStream.Close()
    reader.Close()

End Sub
```

But what if those external resources are secured and require authentication that's different than the currently logged-in user? Traditional means for solving this problem included developing a service to run as a specific user for the request, or calling Win32 APIs to log into a resource with specific credentials.

The designers of the XmlReader class provided the Credentials property of the XmlResolver class. Using the CredentialCache and NetworkCredential classes found in the System.Net namespace, you can specify authentication to external resources, as shown here:

```
Private Sub getdata()

    Dim credentials As Net.CredentialCache = New Net.CredentialCache()
    credentials.Add(New Uri("http://www.xmlandasp.net/"), "Basic", New
    ➥Net.NetworkCredential("kirke", "mypass"))
    credentials.Add(New Uri("http://www.xmlandasp.net/schemas/auth"),
    ➥"Digest", New Net.NetworkCredential("kirke", "mypass"))

    Dim resolver As XmlUrlResolver = New XmlUrlResolver()
    Dim baseURI As Uri = New Uri("http://www.xmlandasp.net/schemas/auth")

    resolver.Credentials = credentials

    Dim relativeURI As Uri = resolver.ResolveUri(baseURI, "Customer.xsd")
    Dim inputStream As IO.Stream = resolver.GetEntity(relativeURI,
    ➥Nothing, GetType(IO.Stream))
```

```
        Dim reader As XmlTextReader = New XmlTextReader(inputStream)
        Do While reader.Read
            Response.Write(reader.ReadOuterXml())
        Loop

        On Error Resume Next
        inputStream.Close()
        reader.Close()
    End Sub
```

Accessing Data in the **XmlReader**

Listings 6.1 and 6.2 both used a custom function called writeTable that interrogates an XMLReader implementation object. You can load the reader prior to calling the function and then pass the populated reader to the writeTable function to display its results. Each call to the Read() method within the writeTable function advances the pointer and returns if the method call was successful. If the call was successful, another node must be processed. Otherwise, you're at the end of the XML document. This can be counter-intuitive to developers who are used to checking for an End of File (EOF) marker that signals the end of processing. When the Read() method returns a Boolean false, this is the equivalent of an EOF condition.

Using a Do..While loop and accessing the reader's properties inside the loop is the typical design pattern for working with the various stream-based readers in .NET, such as the TextReader object and StreamReader object.

Referring to Figure 6.1, you can see that the elements and text nodes are displayed in the output, but the attributes are not. This is an important point to remember when working with the XmlTextReader: The attributes are not output unless the code retrieves them. Otherwise, they are skipped. This ability to skip nodes unless otherwise requested adds to the efficiency of the XmlReader implementation.

To iterate the attributes for the current node, you can use the MoveToFirstAttribute method and the MoveToNextAttribute method. If you know the name or index of an attribute, you can also use the GetAttribute method to return the specific attribute.

As of this writing, a bug exists when you call MoveToNextAttribute and then pass the XmlTextReader reference to another function. The bug causes the pointer to be set back on the first attribute. For example, the following code causes an endless loop because the pointer is always positioned on the first attribute and never advances:

```
While (reader.MoveToNextAttribute())
                Diagnostics.Debug.WriteLine(reader.Name & " " &
                ⮑reader.Value)
                writeData(reader)
        End While
```

One way around this is to use the AttributeCount property of the XmlTextReader to use its indexer. The internal attribute collection is 0-based, so you need to offset the indexer by subtracting the count to get the correct upper index (see Listing 6.3).

Listing 6.3 **Iterating the Attributes of an** *XmlReader*

```
<%@ Import Namespace="System.Xml"%>
<%@ Import Namespace="System.Text"%>
<%@ Import Namespace="System.Xml"%>
<!DOCTYPE HTML PUBLIC "-//W3C//DTD HTML 4.0 Transitional//EN">
<html>
  <head>
    <title>WebForm1</title>
  </head>
<LINK rel="stylesheet" type="text/css"
href="http://localhost/chapters/SystemXML/Styles.css">
  <body MS_POSITIONING="GridLayout">

 <script language="vb" runat="server">

    Private Sub Page_Load(ByVal sender As System.Object, ByVal e As
    ➥System.EventArgs) Handles MyBase.Load
        Dim sb As StringBuilder
        Dim reader As XmlTextReader
        Dim memStream As IO.MemoryStream
        Dim memStreamWriter As IO.StreamWriter

        sb = New StringBuilder()
        With sb
            .Append("<DATA xmlns=""urn:foo:bar"">")
            .Append("<PERSON name=""Carson Allen Evans""/>")
            .Append("<PERSON name=""Deanna Evans"">Hello, Wife</PERSON>")
            .Append("</DATA>")
        End With

        memStream = New IO.MemoryStream()
        memStreamWriter = New IO.StreamWriter(memStream,
        ➥System.Text.Encoding.UTF8)
        memStreamWriter.Write(sb.ToString)
        memStreamWriter.Flush()
        memStream.Position = 0

        reader = New XmlTextReader(memStream)
        writeTable(reader)

        On Error Resume Next

        memStreamWriter.Close()
        memStream.Close()

        reader.Close()
```

```vb
        End Sub

    Private Sub writeTable(ByVal reader As XmlTextReader)
        With Response
            .Write("<TABLE border=""1"">")
            .Write("<TR>")
            .Write("<TH>NodeType</TH><TH>Name</TH><TH>NodeValue</TH>")

.Write("<TH>Depth</TH><TH>NamespaceURI</TH><TH>BaseURI</TH><TH>LocalName</TH>")

.Write("<TH>IsStartElement</TH><TH>IsEmptyElement</TH><TH>XmlSpace</TH>")
            .Write("</TR>")

            Do While reader.Read()
                getTableRow(reader)
                If reader.HasAttributes Then
                    Dim loopVar As Integer
                    For loopVar = 0 To reader.AttributeCount - 1
                        reader.MoveToAttribute(loopVar)
                        getTableRow(reader)
                    Next
                    reader.MoveToElement()
                End If
            Loop
            .Write("</TABLE>")
        End With

    End Sub

    Private Function getTableRow(byval reader as XmlReader) as string
        With Response
            .Write("<TR>")
            .Write(getTableData(reader.Name))
            .Write(getTableData(reader.NodeType.ToString))
            .Write(getTableData(reader.Value))
            .Write(getTableData(reader.Depth))
            .Write(getTableData(reader.NamespaceURI))
            .Write(getTableData(reader.BaseURI))
            .Write(getTableData(reader.LocalName))
            .Write(getTableData(reader.IsStartElement))
            .Write(getTableData(reader.IsEmptyElement))
            .Write("</TR>")
        end with
    End Function

    Private Function getTableData(ByVal data As String) As String
        getTableData = String.Concat("<TD>", data, "</TD>")
    End Function

    </script>
   </body>
</html>
```

The output of Listing 6.3 is shown in Figure 6.3. Notice that this listing is similar to what's shown in Figure 6.2, but adds the document's attributes and their properties to the table.

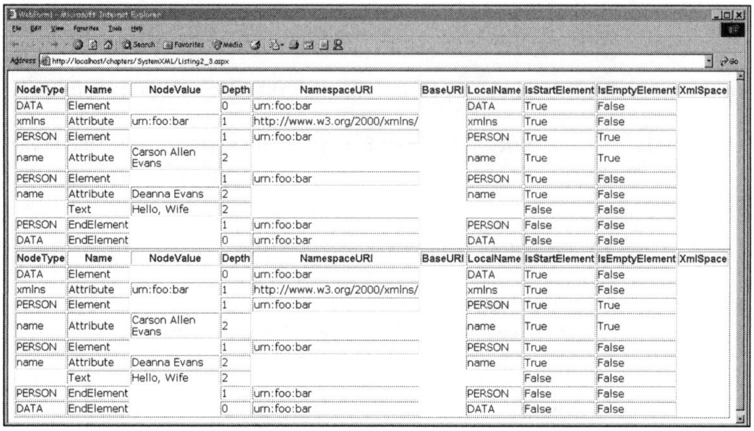

NodeType	Name	NodeValue	Depth	NamespaceURI	BaseURI	LocalName	IsStartElement	IsEmptyElement	XmlSpace
DATA	Element		0	urn:foo:bar		DATA	True	False	
xmlns	Attribute	urn:foo:bar	1	http://www.w3.org/2000/xmlns/		xmlns	True	False	
PERSON	Element		1	urn:foo:bar		PERSON	True	True	
name	Attribute	Carson Allen Evans	2			name	True	True	
PERSON	Element		1	urn:foo:bar		PERSON	True	False	
name	Attribute	Deanna Evans	2			name	True	False	
	Text	Hello, Wife	2				False	False	
PERSON	EndElement		1	urn:foo:bar		PERSON	False	False	
DATA	EndElement		0	urn:foo:bar		DATA	False	False	
NodeType	Name	NodeValue	Depth	NamespaceURI	BaseURI	LocalName	IsStartElement	IsEmptyElement	XmlSpace
DATA	Element		0	urn:foo:bar		DATA	True	False	
xmlns	Attribute	urn:foo:bar	1	http://www.w3.org/2000/xmlns/		xmlns	True	False	
PERSON	Element		1	urn:foo:bar		PERSON	True	True	
name	Attribute	Carson Allen Evans	2			name	True	True	
PERSON	Element		1	urn:foo:bar		PERSON	True	False	
name	Attribute	Deanna Evans	2			name	True	False	
	Text	Hello, Wife	2				False	False	
PERSON	EndElement		1	urn:foo:bar		PERSON	False	False	
DATA	EndElement		0	urn:foo:bar		DATA	False	False	

Figure 6.3 Displaying the attributes of an XML document using `XmlReader`.

Suppose that you didn't want to grab all the attributes, but only wanted a single attribute. The `MoveToElement` method enables you to move back to the element to which the current attribute node belongs.

```
reader.MoveToAttribute("CustomerID")
writeData(reader)
reader.MoveToElement()
writeData(reader)
```

Table 6.1 details the properties of the `XmlTextReader` class and Table 6.2 details its methods.

Table 6.1 **Properties of the *XmlTextReader* Class**

Property Name	Description
`AttributeCount`	The integer count of attribute nodes for the current node.
`BaseURI`	Returns the URI location from where the node was loaded as a string. This will be blank if the node was loaded from a stream or a string.
`CanResolveEntity`	Gets a value indicating if this reader can parse and resolve entities.
`Depth`	The depth of the current node in the XML document.
`Encoding`	The encoding of the document.

Property Name	Description
EOF	Indicates whether the reader is positioned at the end of the stream.
HasAttributes	Boolean that indicates whether the current node has any attributes.
HasValue	Indicates if the current node can have a value. Nodes with `NodeType` of `EndElement` cannot have a value.
IsDefault	Boolean that tells if the current node is an attribute that was defined as a default in a schema or DTD.
IsEmptyElement	Returns a Boolean that specifies if the current element is empty.
Item	Gets the value of the attribute at the specified index.
LineNumber	The current line number.
LinePosition	The current line position.
LocalName	The local name of the current node. The `localname` is the element or attribute name without a namespace prefix.
Name	The qualified name of the current node, including the name of the element or attribute and any associated namespace prefix. If the node is in the default namespace, it returns the local name.
Namespaces	Gets or sets a Boolean that indicates whether its namespaces are supported. The default is true.
NamespaceURI	The namespace URI of the current node. Refer to Figure 6.2 for an example.
NameTable	Gets the `XmlNameTable` associated with the `XmlReader`.
NodeType	The type of the current node. Corresponds to the `XmlNodeType` enumeration. Using the `ToString` method on the enumeration returns the string representation instead of the numeric value.
Normalization	Gets or sets a value that indicates whether to normalize white space and attribute values.
Prefix	Gets the namespace prefix for the current node. If the node is in the default namespace, it returns an empty string.
QuoteChar	Gets the quotation character that's used to enclose an attribute value. Valid values are single quote (') or double quote (").

continues

Table 6.1 **Continued**

Property Name	Description
ReadState	One of the ReadState enumeration values that indicate the state of the reader.
Value	The text value of the current node.
WhitespaceHandling	One of the WhitespaceHandling enumeration values that indicate how whitespace should be handled.
XmlLang	Gets the current xml:lang scope.
XmlResolver	Gets or sets the XmlResolver that's used to resolve external resources, such as entities, DTDs, or schemas.
XmlSpace	One of the XmlSpace enumeration values that indicate the current xml:space scope.

Table 6.2 **Methods of the *XmlTextReader* Class**

Method Name	Description
Close	Changes the ReadState to ReadState.Closed and releases any resources held. If the reader is based on a stream, it also closes the underlying stream.
GetAttribute	Gets an attribute for the specified index or name.
GetRemainder	Returns a TextReader that contains the remainder of the buffered XML and sets EOF to True.
GetType	Gets the System.Type of the current instance.
IsName	Returns a Boolean that indicates if the string argument is a valid XML name. See www.w3.org/TR/2000/REC-xml-20001006#NT-Name. (Inherited from XmlReader.)
IsNameToken	Returns a Boolean that indicates if the string argument is a valid XML name token. See www.w3.org/TR/2000/REC-xml-20001006#NT-NmToken.
IsStartElement	Calls MoveToContent and tests if the current content node is a start tag or an empty element tag.
LookupNamespace	Resolves a namespace prefix for the current element's scope.
MoveToAttribute	Moves to the attribute with the specified index or name.

Method Name	Description
MoveToContent	Checks whether the current node is a content node. Content nodes are non-whitespace Text, CDATA, Element, EndElement, EntityReference, or EndEntity nodes. If the current node isn't a content node, the method skips ahead to the next content node or to the end of the file (EOF).
	The node types that are skipped include ProcessingInstrucution, DocumentType, Comment, Whitespace, SignificantWhitespace.
MoveToElement	Moves to the element that contains the current attribute node. Use after GetAttribute, MoveToAttribute, MoveToFirstAttribute, or MoveToNextAttribute.
MoveToFirstAttribute	Moves to the first attribute node. Returns true if an attribute exists and positions the cursor on the attribute node; otherwise, returns false and doesn't move the cursor.
MoveToNextAttribute	Moves to the next attribute node. Returns true if an attribute exists and positions the cursor on the attribute node; otherwise, it returns false and doesn't move the cursor.
Read	Reads the next node from the stream. Returns true if the next node was read successfully; otherwise, it returns false.
ReadAttributeValue	Parses the attribute value into one or more Text, EntityReference, or EndEntity nodes. Returns true if there are nodes to return, false if the reader is not positioned on an attribute node or if all attributes have been read. An empty attribute, such as CustomerID="", returns true with a single node having the value String.Empty.
ReadBase64	Decodes Base64 and returns the decoded binary bytes.
ReadBinHex	Decodes BinHex and returns the decoded binary bytes.
ReadChars	Reads the textual contents of an element into a character buffer. Designed to read large streams of embedded text by calling it successively.
ReadElementString	Reads a text-only element.

continues

Table 6.2   **Continued**

Method Name	Description
ReadEndElement	Checks that the current content node is an end tag and advances the reader to the next node.
ReadInnerXml	Reads all the content, including markup, as a string.
ReadOuterXml	Reads the content, including markup, representing this node and all its children.
ReadStartElement	Checks that the current node is an element and advances the reader to the next node.
ReadString	Reads the content of an element or a text node as a string.
ResetState	Resets the state of the reader to ReadState.Initial.
ResolveEntity	Resolves the entity reference for EntityReference nodes.
Skip	Skips the children of the current node.

XmlNodeReader

The XmlNodeReader class is another concrete implementation class based on the XmlReader abstract class. This class reads the given node in a forward-only, non-cached manner. Because it inherits from XmlReader, the members of the class are the same as the XmlReader class. The following code snippet uses an XmlNodeReader to read a DOM document in almost the same way as the other reader implementations:

```
Public Sub getNodeReader()
        Dim document As XmlNode = New XmlDocument()
        document.InnerXml = "<TEST><DATA>testing</DATA></TEST>"
        Dim nr As XmlNodeReader = New XmlNodeReader(document)
        While nr.Read
            Response.Write(nr.Name + "<br>")
        End While
    End Sub
```

You can also mix implementations of the XmlTextReader and XmlNodeReader. For example, you can return an XmlNode back from the XmlTextReader and read it by using the XmlNodeReader. You can also mix implementations of the XmlNodeReader and XmlDocument or XmlDataDocument, working with an in-memory DOM structure as a stream. This provides efficiency because only one entire copy of the DOM is in memory.

One way that this might be used is with an XmlDocument that's held in the Cache object, as shown here:

```
Dim dom As XmlDocument = New XmlDocument()
dom.Load(Server.MapPath("XmlFile1.xml"))
Cache.Insert("XMLDataFile", dom, New
CacheDependency(Server.MapPath("XmlFile1.xml")))
```

Because the entire document is already stored in memory, you don't want to copy its contents and create a new in-memory copy of the document just to read its contents. Instead, you can use the XmlNodeReader object to read its contents as a stream, as shown here:

```
Dim nodeReader As XmlNodeReader = New
XmlNodeReader(Cache.Get("XMLDataFile"))
    While nodeReader.Read()
        response.Write ("<h1>" & nodereader.Name & "</h1>")
    End While
```

XmlValidatingReader

This section discusses programmatically validating XML documents against XML Schemas by using the XmlValidatingReader class. You need to understand three main components when using the XmlValidatingReader: the actual reader, the XmlSchemaCollection object, and the ValidationEventHandler.

XmlValidatingReader is inherited from XmlReader just as the XmlTextReader class is, Therefore, they share most of the same properties and methods. XmlValidatingReader adds several methods to the mix. These methods and properties are described in Tables 6.3, 6.4, and 6.5.

Table 6.3 **Properties Added by *XmlValidatingReader***

Property Name	Description
Encoding	Gets the encoding attribute for the entire document.
EntityHandling	Specifies if the reader handles entities by expanding general or character entity references.
Namespaces	Indicates if the reader supports namespaces.
Reader	Gets the XmlReader that's used to construct the XmlValidatingReader instance.
Schemas	Returns the XmlSchemaCollection object to use with the XmlValidatingReader.
SchemaType	Gets a SchemaType object for the current node.

continues

Table 6.3 **Continued**

Property Name	Description
ValidationType	Gets or sets the validation type, specified in the ValidationType enumeration (XDR, DTD, XSD, or None) and must be set prior to the first call to the Read() method.
XmlResolver	Sets the XmlResolver object that's used to resolve external resources and XML Schema import and include elements.

Table 6.4 **Methods Added by** *XmlValidatingReader*

Method Name	Description
ReadTypedValue	Gets a System.Xml.Schema.XmlSchemaType object for the current node.

Table 6.5 **Events Added by** *XmlValidatingReader*

Event Name	Description
ValidationEventHandler	Sets the error handler for receiving information from validation errors. Typically, this event contains code to set a module-level Boolean variable to false.

The ValidationType enumeration is fairly straight forward: Use DTD, XDR, or schema when you're validating against a DTD, XDR schema, or XSD Schema, respectively. If None is specified, no validation is performed and any validation errors that occur are not thrown. The Auto member implicitly checks what type of validation to perform. This is the default validation type if no type is specified. However, some specific behaviors for each validation type exist. Refer to the .NET SDK documentation, "Validation Types of the XmlValidatingReader" for a detailed explanation of each type.

The XmlValidatingReader does precisely what its name implies: It reads XML and validates that XML against an XML Schema. The XmlValidatingReader reads from a stream so it does not actually hold the contents of the stream. It uses an instance of the XmlTextReader to read from the stream, and extends the functionality of the XmlTextReader by validating the node against the schema(s) specified. To associate the XmlTextReader instance with the XmlValidatingReader instance, use the constructor that accepts a text reader:

```
//Instantiate a reader to read the XML file
XmlTextReader textReader = new XmlTextReader(xmlFile);

//Associate the ValidatingReader with the XMLTextReader object
XmlValidatingReader validator = new XmlValidatingReader(textReader);
```

Associating a Schema with the XmlValidatingReader

After the XmlTextReader is associated with the XmlValidatingReader, you
need to supply the schema(s) to the XmlValidatingReader instance. The
XmlValidatingReader class exposes a Schemas collection that directs the validator
to the schemas that are going to be used. The Schemas collection exposes an
Add method that accepts four overloads to locate the schema(s) to be validated
against. The following first overload accepts an XmlSchemaCollection object,
which is useful if you are working with multiple schemas:

```
XmlSchemaCollection schemas = new XmlSchemaCollection();
schemas.Add ("urn:schemas-/xmlandasp-net:framework", new
XmlTextReader(xsdFile));
validatingReader.Schemas.Add(schemas);
```

The second overload accepts a single XmlSchema object. As you saw earlier, using
this object requires that you either build the schema on the fly or retrieve the
schema from an XmlSchemaCollection object. The third overload accepts a namespace and an XmlReader abstract class. For this overload, you could specify an
XmlTextReader because XmlTextReader is a concrete implementation of the
XmlReader abstract class. This is nearly identical to the previous usage of the
XmlSchemaCollection object, but without a separate object reference:

```
validatingReader.Schemas.Add("urn:schemas-/xmlandasp-net:customer", new
XmlTextReader(xsdFile));
```

The last overload accepts a namespace for the schema and the URL to the
physical file. This last overload is used for the example, but the third overload
could've been used just as easily:

```
validatingReader.Schemas.Add("urn:schemas-/xmlandasp-
net:customer","http://www.xmlandasp.net/schemas/fr.xsd");
```

Creating a ValidationEventHandler

As the XmlValidatingReader reads through the stream using the supplied
XmlTextReader, it validates the content in the stream to the schema specified and
raises an event if the node violates the schema. This event is specified through
its ValidationEvent property. Because the event is fired when the schema is
invalid, you need a class member variable to determine through the function
containing ValidatingReader if the schema was valid.

To wire up the event handler and the XmlValidatingReader, begin by declaring a function that accepts two parameters: an Object type and a ValidationEventArgs type:

```
private void ValidationCallback ( object sender, ValidationEventArgs args )
{
System.Diagnostics.Debug.WriteLine ("Validation error: {0}" + args.Message);
isValid = false;
}
```

Inside this function is a simple debug output message that lets you know that a validation event occurred and what the message was. You also set the class member variable to false to indicate that the validation was not successful.

The next step is to create a ValidationEventHandler class that uses the previously created function as a callback. C# uses a delegate to wire up the event with the object, as shown here:

```
// Wire up the callback to our ValidationCallBack routine
ValidationEventHandler eventHandler = new ValidationEventHandler
(ValidationCallback);

//Wire up the event handler to the validating reader's event handler
validator.ValidationEventHandler += eventHandler;
```

In Visual Basic .NET, the same can be accomplished by using the AddHandler method:

```
'Wire up the callback to our ValidationCallBack routine
AddHandler validator.ValidationEventHandler, AddressOf ValidationCallback
```

The XmlValidatingReader is now associated with the callback function and is fired when the Read process begins.

Validating Using the Read *Method*

Until this point, all the plumbing has been set in place, but you still haven't validated anything. The actual validation occurs when the Read method is called on each element within the XML instance document, as shown here:

```
while (validator.Read())
{
//Here, you have access to each element.  We do nothing with this
//because we only want to know if the entire document is valid or not.
}
```

The Read method simply reads the XML instance document and validates the element against the schema. If invalid or missing data exists, the event handler is called.

Because the code differs significantly in Visual Basic and C#, both language implementations are shown. Listing 6.4 shows the full example in C#.

Listing 6.4 **Creating a Utility Class of XML Functions in C#**

```
Public Class XMLFunctions
{
private Boolean isValid = false;  //Private flag to hold validation results
                               ↳from callback

public Boolean IsXMLValid(string xsdFile, string xmlFile)
{

//Instantiate a reader to read the XML file
XmlTextReader textReader = new XmlTextReader(xmlFile);

//Associate the ValidatingReader with the XMLTextReader object
XmlValidatingReader validator = new XmlValidatingReader(textReader);
validator.ValidationType = ValidationType.Auto;

//Create the schema collection
XmlSchemaCollection schemas = new XmlSchemaCollection();
schemas.Add (null, new XmlTextReader(xsdFile));

//Add the list of schemas to validate against to the schemas collection
validator.Schemas.Add(schemas);

// Wire up the callback to our ValidationCallBack routine
ValidationEventHandler eventHandler = new ValidationEventHandler
(ValidationCallback);

//Wire up the event handler to the validating reader's event handler
validator.ValidationEventHandler += eventHandler;

while (validator.Read())
{
//Here, you have access to each element.  We do nothing with this
//because we only want to know if the entire document is valid or not.
}
if (isValid)
System.Diagnostics.Debug.WriteLine ("Document is valid.");
else
System.Diagnostics.Debug.WriteLine ("Document is NOT valid.");

validator.Close();
textReader.Close();

Return isValid;
}

private void ValidationCallback ( object sender, ValidationEventArgs args )
{
System.Diagnostics.Debug.WriteLine ("Validation error: {0}" + args.Message);
isValid = false;
}
}
```

Listing 6.5 shows the same code in Visual Basic .NET.

Listing 6.5   **Creating a Utility Class of XML Functions in Visual Basic.NET**

```vb.net
Imports System.Xml
Imports System.Xml.Schema

Public Class XMLFunctions
    Private isValid As Boolean = False   'Private flag to hold validation
    ➥results from callback

    Public Function IsXMLValid(ByVal xsdFile As String, ByVal xmlFile As
    ➥String) As Boolean
        'Instantiate a reader to read the XML file
        isValid = True
        Dim textReader As XmlTextReader = New XmlTextReader(xmlFile)

        'Associate the ValidatingReader with the XMLTextReader object
        Dim validator As XmlValidatingReader = New
        ➥XmlValidatingReader(textReader)
        validator.ValidationType = ValidationType.Auto

        'Create the schema collection
        Dim schemas As XmlSchemaCollection = New XmlSchemaCollection()
        schemas.Add("urn:schemas-vbdna-net:framework", New
        ➥XmlTextReader(xsdFile))

        'Add the list of schemas to validate against to the schemas
        ➥collection
        validator.Schemas.Add(schemas)

        'Wire up the callback to our ValidationCallBack routine
        AddHandler validator.ValidationEventHandler, AddressOf
        ➥ValidationCallback

        While (validator.Read())
            'Here, you have access to each element.  We do nothing with this
            'because we only want to know if the entire document is valid or
            ➥not.
        End While

        If (isValid) Then
            System.Diagnostics.Debug.WriteLine("Document is valid.")
        Else
            System.Diagnostics.Debug.WriteLine("Document is NOT valid.")
        End If

        validator.Close()
        textReader.Close()
```

```
        Return isValid
    End Function

    Private Sub ValidationCallback(ByVal sender As Object, ByVal args As
    ▬ValidationEventArgs)
        System.Diagnostics.Debug.WriteLine ("Validation error: {0}" +
        ▬args.Message);
        isValid = False
    End Sub

End Class
```

Take a look at how you might use this sample class. An XML document, sample.xml, and an XML Schema document, validsample.xsd, are used to perform validation by using the sample class. First, list the schema document that's used for validation:

```
<?xml version="1.0" encoding="utf-8" ?>
<xsd:schema id="xmlfunctions"
                targetNamespace="urn:schemas-/xmlandasp-net:framework"
                elementFormDefault="qualified"
                xmlns="urn:schemas-/xmlandasp-net:framework"
                xmlns:tns="urn:schemas-/xmlandasp-net:framework"
                xmlns:xsd="http://www.w3.org/2001/XMLSchema">

    <xsd:element name="root">
        <xsd:complexType>
            <xsd:sequence>
                <xsd:element name="child1"/>
                <xsd:element name="child2"/>
                <xsd:element name="child3"/>
            </xsd:sequence>
        </xsd:complexType>
    </xsd:element>
</xsd:schema>
```

Now that you have seen the schema document, it's time to look at the .aspx page that contains the code that's used to call the function. Listing 6.6 shows the .aspx page in its entirety.

Listing 6.6 **A Sample** *.aspx* **Page that Calls the** *XMLFunctions* **Class**

```
<%@Import Namespace="SystemXml"%>
<!DOCTYPE HTML PUBLIC "-//W3C//DTD HTML 4.0 Transitional//EN">
<HTML>
    <HEAD>
        <title>Listing6_4</title>
        <script language="vb" runat="server">
```

continues

Listing 6.6   **Continued**

```
Private Sub Button1_Click(ByVal sender As System.Object, ByVal e As
➥System.EventArgs)
     Dim xmlLib As XMLFunctions = New XMLFunctions()
     Dim retValid As Boolean = False

     retValid = xmlLib.IsXMLValid(Server.MapPath("validsample.xsd"),
               Server.MapPath(TextBox1.Text))

     Label2.Text = "xmlLib.IsValid = " + retValid.ToString()
End Sub

    </script>
</HEAD>
<body>
    <form runat="server">
        <P>
            <asp:Label id="Label1" runat="server" Width="115px"
            ➥Height="16px">XML File:</asp:Label>
            <asp:TextBox id="TextBox1" runat="server"
            ➥Width="196px"></asp:TextBox></P>
        <P>
            <asp:Label id="Label2" runat="server" Width="224px"
            ➥Height="21px"/></P>
        <P>
            <asp:Button id="Button1" runat="server"
            ➥OnClick="Button1_Click" Width="106px" Height="29px"
Text="Button"></asp:Button></P>
    </form>
</body>
</HTML>
```

When you run the sample, you're prompted for an XML document name. If you enter a valid document, you should see the label's text as `xmlLib.IsValid = True`. For example, the following XML document is schema-valid:

```
<?xml version="1.0" encoding="utf-8" ?>
<root xmlns="urn:schemas-/xmlandasp-net:framework">
    <child1/>
    <child2/>
    <child3/>
</root>
```

The following code, however, is not schema-valid and produces a different result. Save the following as `badxml.xml` in the same directory as the code in Listing 6.6:

```
<?xml version="1.0" encoding="utf-8" ?>
<root xmlns="urn:schemas-/xmlandasp-net:framework">
```

```
    <badnodename/>
</root>
```

Figure 6.4 shows how the page looks when it's run. You can see that the class correctly returns the fact that the XML document is not schema-valid.

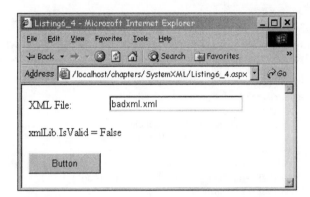

Figure 6.4   A sample using a utility class for validation.

Note the lack of error handling in this example. Both the C# and Visual Basic .NET versions make the assumption that both the XML and XSD files already exist. You might want to extend this example to include a `try..catch` block to trap errors that might occur when loading the XML or XSD files fails.

XmlWriter

The `XmlWriter` abstract class has only one concrete implementation class: `XmlTextWriter`. Using this class is straight forward. It simply writes out each node in a forward-only, non-cached manner. This is a useful class for creating new XML documents.

Rather than detail each method and property of this class, the following simple example suffices. Listing 6.7 shows an example of using the `XmlTextWriter` class to create an XML document.

Listing 6.7   **Creating an XML Document by Using *XmlWriter***

```
<%@ Import Namespace="System.Xml"%>
<!DOCTYPE HTML PUBLIC "-//W3C//DTD HTML 4.0 Transitional//EN">
<HTML>
    <HEAD>
        <title>Listing6_7</title>
        <script language="vb" runat="server">
```

continues

Listing 6.7   **Continued**

```
Private Sub Button1_Click(ByVal sender As System.Object, ByVal e As
➥System.EventArgs)
    CreateXmlDocument("c:\myxmldoc.xml")

End Sub

Public Sub CreateXmlDocument(ByVal fileToCreate As String)
    Dim writer As XmlTextWriter = New XmlTextWriter(fileToCreate,
    ➥System.Text.Encoding.UTF8)

    With writer
        .Formatting = Formatting.Indented
        .WriteStartDocument()
        .WriteStartElement("", "COLLEGES",
        ➥"http://tempuri.org/XMLFile1.xsd")
        .WriteStartElement("COLLEGE")
        .WriteElementString("NAME", "University of Georgia")
        .WriteElementString("MASCOT", "Bulldog")
        .WriteEndElement()
        .WriteEndElement()
        .WriteEndDocument()
        .Flush()
        .Close()
    End With

End Sub

        </script>
    </HEAD>
    <body>
        <form id="Form1" method="post" runat="server">
            <asp:TextBox id="TextBox1" runat="server"></asp:TextBox>
            <asp:Button OnClick="Button1_Click" id="Button1"
runat="server" Text="Button"></asp:Button>
        </form>
    </body>
</HTML>
```

It's specified that the XmlTextWriter should create an XML document that is indented by using the Formatting property. Then the actual document is created by using the WriteStartDocument method. This outputs the XML declaration and encoding. The next method call, WriteStartElement, writes an element with no namespace prefix but belongs to the default namespace. The next method call is another call to WriteStartElement. This nests the elements properly. The output of this function creates an XML file with the following data:

```
<?xml version="1.0" encoding="utf-8"?>
```

```
<COLLEGES xmlns="http://tempuri.org/XMLFile1.xsd">
  <COLLEGE>
    <NAME>University of Georgia</NAME>
    <MASCOT>Bulldog</MASCOT>
  </COLLEGE>
</COLLEGES>
```

XmlNode

Remember that, in XML, everything is a node. A processing instruction in an XML document is a node, just as an element or an attribute is. Even text contained in an element is referred to as a text node. While working with these various components of XML, it is helpful that they all share a common set of attributes that forms the basis for all the components of an XML document. That basis is realized through the XmlNode class.

Figure 6.5 illustrates that everything in XML is a node, even the document itself.

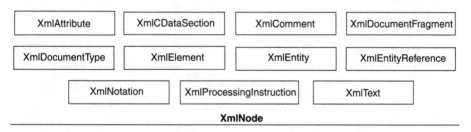

Figure 6.5   Everything in XML is considered a node.

Before the implementation of XmlNode is defined within the .NET Framework, remember what an XML document is. At first glance, an XML document is nothing more than tags and text. Consider this example:

```
<?xml version="1.0" encoding="utf-8" ?>
<customers>
    <customer id="kaevans">
        <name>Kirk Allen Evans</name>
        <topics>
            <topic>Georgia Bulldogs</topic>
            <topic>Atlanta Thrashers</topic>
        </topics>
    </customer>
</customers>
```

This document can be represented visually, as shown in Figure 6.6.

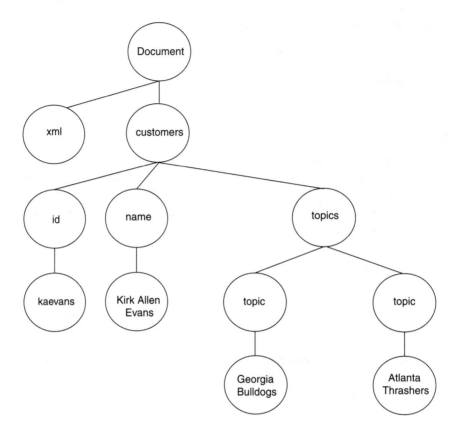

Figure 6.6 An XML document can be represented as a set of nodes.

To make this type of structure navigable, everything contained in the structure must share a common interface or be inherited from the same base class. The base class that all the components of an XML document in .NET inherit from is XmlNode.

This is similar to working with the MSXML parser, where all components share the IXMLDomNode interface to make the document navigable.

To demonstrate how Figure 6.6 arose, look at the following code snippet. We simply move through all the nodes and report what node type was found:

```
Public Sub displayTree(ByVal fileToOpen As String)
    Dim doc As XmlDocument = New XmlDocument()
    Dim child As XmlNode

    doc.Load(fileToOpen)
    For Each child In doc.ChildNodes
        traverseTree(child, 0)
```

```
    Next
End Sub


Private Sub traverseTree(ByVal node As XmlNode, ByVal indent As Integer)
    Dim tempNode As XmlNode

    Dim indentChars As String = New String(" ", indent)
    Debug.WriteLine(String.Concat(indentChars, node.Name, vbTab,
    ➥node.NodeType))
    If Not node.Attributes Is Nothing Then
        If node.Attributes.Count > 0 Then
            For Each tempNode In node.Attributes
                '*****RECURSIVE CALL
                traverseTree(tempNode, indent + 4)
            Next
        End If
    End If
    If node.HasChildNodes Then
        For Each tempNode In node.ChildNodes
            '*****RECURSIVE CALL
            traverseTree(tempNode, indent + 4)
        Next
    End If
End Sub
```

You can see that each node supports the XmlNode base class when using methods, such as SelectSingleNode, that return an XmlNode object, or SelectNodes that returns a collection of XmlNode objects. You see this in more detail in the section, "Document Navigation."

The Document Object Model Implementation

The *Document Object Model (DOM)* is the representation of an XML document as a set of objects that can manipulate the structure and contents of the document. By now, you should be aware of this concept. Chapter 2 introduced the DOM, Chapter 3 gave examples of how to work with the DOM, and Chapter 5 went into detail about the DOM and how it is used with MSXML. This section details how the DOM is represented in .NET.

The DOM implementation in .NET is like the MSXML parser. The entire structure is loaded into memory, and the document's parts can be accessed as a set of linked nodes. These nodes are manipulated by using the XmlNode class and its derived classes. Refer to Figure 6.5, which shows the different implementations of the XmlNode abstract class. Notice that one of the classes derived from XmlNode is the XmlDocument class: This class forms the basis for the DOM implementation in .NET.

The *XmlDocument* Class

Loading the entire document into memory provides many benefits. For example, it's easy to navigate through the DOM, adding, updating, and removing nodes within it. We discussed how this functionality comes at a price: Loading the entire document requires more memory than reading the document as a stream, compounded by the fact that each user accessing the document creates their own object instance in memory. However, this is an acceptable tradeoff for most scenarios where the XML being loaded is relatively small.

> **Consider the Usage in Your Designs**
>
> As with all distributed application designs, you need to consider whether you need the flexibility of updating, adding, and removing nodes with the XmlDocument class, or if you only need to read the document with an XmlReader class.

Looking at the XmlDocument class shows that the methods and properties of the class are similar to those of the MSXML parser. Table 6.6 shows the properties of the XmlDocument class, Table 6.7 shows its methods, and Table 6.8 shows its events.

Table 6.6   **Properties of the *XMLDocument* Class**

Property Name	Description
Attributes	Gets an XmlAttributeCollection that contains the attributes of this node.
BaseURI	Gets the base URI of the current node. Indicates from where the node was loaded.
ChildNodes	Gets all the children of the current node.
DocumentElement	Retrieves the root element of the XML document as an XmlElement object.
DocumentType	Gets the <!DOCTYPE..> declaration, if one exists as an XmlDocumentType object.
FirstChild	Gets the first child of the current node.
HasChildNodes	Returns a Boolean that indicates if the current node has child nodes.
Implementation	Returns the XmlImplementation object for the XML document.
InnerText	Gets or sets the concatenated values of the node and all its children.

Property Name	Description
InnerXml	Gets or sets the markup that represents the children of the current node.
IsReadOnly	Returns a Boolean that indicates whether the current node is read only.
Item	Returns the specified child element. This is the indexer in C# for the XmlDocument class.
LastChild	The last child of the node.
LocalName	Gets the name of the node without the namespace prefix.
Name	Gets the qualified name of the node.
NamespaceURI	Returns the namespace URI of the current node.
NameTable	Returns the XmlNameTable associated with this implementation.
NextSibling	Returns the node following this node at the same level in the document hierarchy.
NodeType	Returns an XmlNodeType enumeration member that represents this node's type.
OuterXml	Gets the XML markup that represents the current node and its children. This is similar to InnerXml, except the current node is also returned.
OwnerDocument	Gets the XmlDocument to which the current node belongs.
ParentNode	Gets the parent of the current node. If the node has been created but not added to the tree, this returns a null reference in C#, or nothing in Visual Basic .NET.
Prefix	Gets or sets the namespace prefix for the current node.
PreserveWhitespace	Gets or sets a Boolean that indicates if white space would be preserved or stripped.
PreviousSibling	Gets the node previous to this node at the same level in the document hierarchy.
Value	Gets or sets the value of the current node.
XmlResolver	Sets the XmlResolver to use for resolving external resources.

Table 6.7 **Methods of the *XMLDocument* Class**

Method Name	Description
AppendChild	Adds the specified node to the end of the list of children of the current node.
Clone	Creates a duplicate of the current node.
CloneNode	Similar to Clone, but accepts a deep Boolean parameter that indicates if the subtree should be duplicated also.
CreateAttribute	Creates an XmlAttribute node with the specified name.
CreateCDATASection	Creates an XmlCDATASection that contains the specified data.
CreateComment	Creates an XmlComment that contains the data specified.
CreateDocumentFragment	Creates an empty XmlDocumentFragment used for tree inserts.
CreateDocumentType	Creates an XmlDocumentType object.
CreateElement	Creates an empty XmlElement. Uses the Value property to specify text data for the element or append an XmlTextNode as the element's child.
CreateEntityReference	Creates an XmlEntityReference with the specified name.
CreateNavigator	Creates an XpathNavigator for navigating this object as a DOM structure.
CreateNode	Creates an XmlNode object with the specified XmlNodeType.
CreateProcessingInstruction	Creates an XmlProcessingInstruction that contains the specified target and data. To work with the <?xml version="1.0"?> xml declaration, use the CreateXmlDeclaration method.
CreateSignificantWhitespace	Creates an XmlSignificantWhitespace node that contains only the characters &#20;,
, , and 	.
CreateTextNode	Creates an XmlTextNode with the passed in text.
CreateWhitespace	Creates an XmlWhitespace node containing only the characters &#20;,
, , and 	.
CreateXmlDeclaration	Creates an XmlDeclaration object with the specified values. Accepts parameters for version, encoding, and standalone.

Method Name	Description
GetElementByID	Gets the XmlElement with the specified ID attribute. If multiple matches are found, returns only the first match.
GetElementsByTagName	Returns an XmlNodeList that contains all the descendant elements with the specified name.
GetEnumerator	Enables For Each enumerations on the object.
GetHashCode	Serves as a hash function for a particular type, suitable for use in hashing algorithms and data structures, such as a hash table.
GetNamespaceOfPrefix	Retrieves the namespace URI in the closest XMLNS declaration for the given prefix.
GetPrefixOfNamespace	Retrieves the prefix in the closest XMLNS declaration for the given URI.
GetType	Gets the type of the current instance.
ImportNode	Imports a node from an external document to the current document.
InsertAfter	Inserts the node immediately after the specified reference node.
InsertBefore	Inserts the node immediately before the specified reference node.
Load	Loads the XML data. Sources for the XML data include a URL, a stream, a text reader, and an XmlReader.
LoadXml	Loads the XML document from the string parameter.
Normalize	Puts all XmlText nodes in the full depth of the subtree underneath this XmlNode into a normal form where only markup (for example, tags, comments, processing instructions, CDATA sections, and entity references) separates XmlText nodes; that is, no adjacent XmlText nodes exist.
PrependChild	Adds the specified node as the first child of the current node.
ReadNode	Creates an XmlNode object based on the information in the XmlReader. The reader must be positioned on a node or attribute. If positioned on an element node, it advances the reader to the next position. If positioned on an attribute, it does not advance the reader.

continues

Table 6.7　**Continued**

Method Name	Description
RemoveAll	Removes all children and/or attributes of the current node.
RemoveChild	Removes the specified child node associated with the current node.
ReplaceChild	Removes the old child node and replaces it with the new child node.
Save	Saves the XML document to the specified location.
SelectNodes	Selects an XmlNodeList of nodes that match the specified XPath expression.
SelectSingleNode	Selects an XmlNode that matches the specified XPath expression. If more than one match is found, only the first match is returned.
Supports	Tests if the DOM implementation supports a specific feature.
ToString	Returns a string that represents the current object.
WriteContentTo	Saves the contents of the XmlDocument node to the specified XmlWriter.
WriteTo	Saves the XmlDocument node to the specified XmlWriter.

Table 6.8　**Events of the *XMLDocument* Class**

Event Name	Description
NodeChanged	The value of a node belonging to this document has been changed.
NodeChanging	The value of a node belonging to this document is about to change.
NodeInserted	A node belonging to this document has been inserted into another node.
NodeInserting	A node belonging to this document is about to be inserted into another node.
NodeRemoved	A node belonging to this document has been removed.
NodeRemoving	A node belonging to this document is about to be removed.

Populating an *XmlDocument*

Several methods for loading an XmlDocument object with data exist. You've already seen examples of using a file to load the XmlDocument earlier in this chapter. You can also specify a string to populate it with data, as shown here:

```
<%@ Import Namespace="System.Xml"%>
<%@ Import Namespace="System.Text"%>
<!DOCTYPE HTML PUBLIC "-//W3C//DTD HTML 4.0 Transitional//EN" >
<HTML>
    <HEAD>
        <title>WebForm1</title>
        <script language="C#" runat="server">
        private void Page_Load(object sender, System.EventArgs e)
        {
            StringBuilder sb = new StringBuilder();

            sb.Append("<DATA xmlns=\"urn:foo:bar\">");
            sb.Append("<PERSON name=\"Carson Allen Evans\"/>");
                sb.Append("<PERSON name=\"Deanna Evans\">Hello,
                ➥Wife</PERSON>");
                sb.Append("</DATA>");

                XmlDocument doc = new XmlDocument();
                doc.LoadXml(sb.ToString());

                TextBox1.Text = doc.OuterXml;

        }
        </script>
    </HEAD>
    <body>
        <form runat="server">
        <asp:TextBox id="TextBox1" runat="server" TextMode="MultiLine"
        ➥Width="473px" Height="447px"></asp:TextBox>
        </form>
    </body>
</HTML>
```

This example uses a StringBuilder to build a string representation of the XML document. The XmlDocument object is then populated by calling the LoadXml method. You could also use an XmlTextReader to populate the XmlDocument because an XmlTextReader is an implementation of the XmlReader class.

Recall that you can use the XmlTextReader to access secured documents on external resources. Using the XmlTextReader as the source for the XmlDocument is a good choice in this situation.

Now that you have seen how to get data into the XmlDocument, take a look at how to navigate through its contents.

Document Navigation

One of the primary benefits of the XmlDocument class is that you can easily navigate through its contents. Whereas the XmlReader implementations are forward only and non-cached, the XmlDocument allows forward and reverse navigation, as well as querying.

Navigating with *XmlNode*

The XmlNode object provides methods for navigating the document. As you saw in the section, "XmlNode," you can navigate the nodes in the DOM by using the ChildNodes collection, and you can iterate the attributes using a For Each loop with the Attributes collection. You can also use NextSibling, FirstChild, ParentNode, and PreviousSibling properties in a similar manner. Listing 6.8 demonstrates using these properties to navigate through a document.

Listing 6.8   **The Use of Context Nodes and Navigation**

```
private void Page_Load(object sender, System.EventArgs e)
{
    StringBuilder sb = new StringBuilder();

sb.Append("<BULLDOGS xmlns=\"urn:uga:bulldogs\">");
sb.Append("<NICKNAME>Hairy Dawgs</NICKNAME>");
sb.Append("<ANNOUNCER>Larry Munson</ANNOUNCER>");
    sb.Append("</BULLDOGS>");

    XmlDocument doc = new XmlDocument();
    doc.LoadXml(sb.ToString());

    DisplayContext(doc);                        //Document node
    XmlNode node = doc.DocumentElement;
    DisplayContext(node);                       //BULLDOGS
    node = node.ChildNodes[0];
    DisplayContext(node);                       //NICKNAME
    node = node.NextSibling;
    DisplayContext(node);                       //ANNOUNCER
    node = node.ChildNodes[0];
    DisplayContext(node);                       //#Text - Larry
                                                ➥Munson
    node = node.ParentNode.ParentNode;
    DisplayContext(node);                       //BULLDOGS

}
private void DisplayContext(XmlNode node)
{
    Response.Write("Context node is " + node.Name + " with type "
    ➥+ node.NodeType );
```

```
        if (node.Value != null)
        {
            Response.Write( " and value " + node.Value);
        }
        Response.Write("<br>");
    }
```

Besides navigating by using the preceding methods, the XmlDocument class also supports XPath queries through the SelectNodes and SelectSingleNode methods. In Listing 6.9, we alter the Bulldogs example to show querying using XPath. The code shows how you can use XPath to navigate through an XML document.

Listing 6.9   **Using XPath to Navigate Through an XML Document**

```
<%@ Page language="c#" Debug="true"%>
<%@ Import Namespace="System.Xml"%>
<%@ Import Namespace="System.Text"%>
<!DOCTYPE HTML PUBLIC "-//W3C//DTD HTML 4.0 Transitional//EN" >

<html>
  <head>
    <title>WebForm1</title>
    <meta name="GENERATOR" Content="Microsoft Visual Studio 7.0">
    <meta name="CODE_LANGUAGE" Content="C#">
    <meta name=vs_defaultClientScript content="JavaScript">
    <meta name=vs_targetSchema
    ➥content="http://schemas.microsoft.com/intellisense/ie5">
    <link rel="stylesheet" href="SystemXML.css" >
  </head>
  <body MS_POSITIONING="GridLayout">

    <script language="C#" runat="server" >
        private void Page_Load(object sender, System.EventArgs e)
        {
            StringBuilder sb = new StringBuilder();

          sb.Append("<BULLDOGS>");
          sb.Append("<NICKNAME>Hairy Dawgs</NICKNAME>");
          sb.Append("<ANNOUNCER>Larry Munson</ANNOUNCER>");
          sb.Append("<HIGHLIGHTS>");
          sb.Append("<GAME DESCRIPTION=\"Beat Tennessee at Tennessee\"/>");
          sb.Append("<GAME DESCRIPTION=\"Comeback versus Kentucky\"/>");
          sb.Append("</HIGHLIGHTS>");
            sb.Append("</BULLDOGS>");

            XmlDocument doc = new XmlDocument();
            doc.LoadXml(sb.ToString());
```

continues

Listing 6.9 **Continued**

```
                        String expression = "";
                        expression = "descendant-or-self::*";
                        DisplayXPathResults(expression,doc.SelectNodes(expression));

                        expression = "BULLDOGS/NICKNAME";

DisplayXPathResults(expression,doc.SelectSingleNode(expression));

                        expression = "BULLDOGS/HIGHLIGHTS/GAME/@DESCRIPTION";
                        DisplayXPathResults(expression,doc.SelectNodes(expression));

                        expression = "BULLDOGS/HIGHLIGHTS/GAME[@DESCRIPTION='Beat
                     ➥Tennessee at Tennessee']";

DisplayXPathResults(expression,doc.SelectSingleNode(expression));
            }

            private void DisplayXPathResults(string expression, XmlNodeList
            ➥nodeList)
            {
                Response.Write("<h3>" + expression + " yields: </h3>");
                foreach(XmlNode node in nodeList)
                {
                        Response.Write(node.Name + " (" + node.NodeType + ")");
                        if (node.Value != null)
                        {
                                Response.Write( " = " + node.Value);
                        }
                        Response.Write("<br>");

                }
            }
            private void DisplayXPathResults(string expression, XmlNode node)
            {
                        Response.Write("<h3>" + expression + " yields: </h3>");
                        Response.Write(node.Name + " (" + node.NodeType + ")");
                        if (node.Value != null)
                        {
                                Response.Write( " = " + node.Value);
                        }
                        Response.Write("<br>");


            }
            </script>
        </body>
    </html>
```

Notice that both the `SelectNodes` and `SelectSingleNode` methods are being used to retrieve data based on the XPath expression. The `DisplayXPathResults` method is overloaded: When using the `SelectNodes` method, the first overload is called. When using `SelectSingleNode` to query the document, the second overload is called instead.

Navigating Using *SelectNodes* and *SelectSingleNode*

When you use a namespace in your document, the nodes within the scope of the namespace need to be qualified when using the `SelectNodes` and `SelectSingleNode` methods.

For example, look at the following XML document, `xmlfile1.xml`:

```
<?xml version="1.0" encoding="utf-8"?>
<COLLEGES xmlns="urn:schools:universities">
    <COLLEGE STATE="Georgia">
        <NAME>University of Georgia</NAME>
        <NAME xmlns="urn:schools:abbreviations">UGA</NAME>
        <MASCOT xmlns="urn:schools:data">Bulldog</MASCOT>
    </COLLEGE>
</COLLEGES>
```

If you attempt the following code using the `xmlfile1.xml` previously shown, it does *not* output the text UGA to the debug window as expected. In fact, it throws an error because the `XmlNode` object returned from the `SelectSingleNode` method is a null reference (nothing in Visual Basic):

```
Imports System.Xml
    Imports System.Diagnostics

    Public Class XmlDocNamespaces

        Inherits System.Web.UI.Page

        Private Sub Page_Load(ByVal sender As System.Object, ByVal e As
        ➥System.EventArgs) Handles MyBase.Load
            Dim doc As XmlDocument = New XmlDocument()
            doc.Load(Server.MapPath("xmlfile1.xml"))


            Dim node As XmlNode = doc.SelectSingleNode
            ➥("COLLEGES/COLLEGE/NAME/text()")
            Debug.WriteLine(node.Value)
        End Sub

    End Class
```

Why is this? Blame it on your use of namespaces. Three namespaces are represented in `xmlfile1.xml`, and no namespace prefixes are associated with any of them. To query this document, you must specify the namespaces and a prefix that you can use to identify each namespace URI within the XPath expression. Do this by using the `XmlNamespaceManager` object.

The `XmlNamespaceManager` object simply manages a list of namespaces that is associated with a given document. It atomizes the namespace prefix and namespace URI to be used in comparison with the namespaces in the document itself, as shown in the following code:

```
Imports System.Xml
Imports System.Diagnostics

Public Class XmlDocNamespaces

    Private Sub Page_Load(ByVal sender As System.Object, ByVal e As
    ➥System.EventArgs) Handles MyBase.Load
        Dim doc As XmlDocument = New XmlDocument()
        doc.Load(Server.MapPath("xmlfile1.xml"))

        Dim nsmgr As XmlNamespaceManager = New
        ➥XmlNamespaceManager(doc.NameTable)
        nsmgr.AddNamespace("univ", "urn:schools:universities")
        nsmgr.AddNamespace("abbrev", "urn:schools:abbreviations")
        nsmgr.AddNamespace("data", "urn:schools:data")
```

By using the `XmlNamespaceManager` class, you add the namespace URIs to the class and associate a prefix with each namespace. Then, the XPath query is changed in the `SelectSingleNode` to use the new prefix that's associated with each namespace URI, and the namespace manager is passed in as well, like this:

```
        Dim node As XmlNode =
    doc.SelectSingleNode("univ:COLLEGES/univ:COLLEGE/abbrev:NAME/text()", nsmgr)
        Debug.WriteLine(node.Value)
    End Sub

End Class
```

Again, using `xmlfile1.xml`, this code returns the proper text node, and outputs the string UGA to the output window as expected.

Navigating with *XmlNavigator*

Besides the methods exposed by the `XmlNode` class (and inherited by the `XmlDocument` class), you can use the `XPathNavigator` class to navigate the `XmlDocument` class.

The XPathNavigator class provides the ability to use XPath queries over any data store. It uses a read-only cursor over the data store, so you cannot use the XPathNavigator class to update nodes. However, the class provides an efficient means of querying data. Besides issuing XPath queries (as you can already do with the XmlDocument class' SelectSingleNode and SelectNodes methods), XPathNavigator provides the means to test whether the current node matches an XPath query, to execute compiled queries, and to compare the current navigator against another.

To navigate an XML document, create an XPathNavigator and iterate over its results by using an XPathNodeIterator. You need to create an XML file, samples.xml, in the same directory to make the code for this sample work correctly. Listing 6.10 shows the code used to iterate the results.

Listing 6.10   **Using *XPathNodeIterator* and *XPathNavigator***

```
<%@ Page language="c#" Debug="true"%>
<%@ Import Namespace="System.Xml"%>
<%@ Import Namespace="System.Xml.XPath"%>
<%@ Import Namespace="System.Text"%>
<!DOCTYPE HTML PUBLIC "-//W3C//DTD HTML 4.0 Transitional//EN" >

<html>
  <head>
    <title>WebForm1</title>
    <meta name="GENERATOR" Content="Microsoft Visual Studio 7.0">
    <meta name="CODE_LANGUAGE" Content="C#">
    <meta name=vs_defaultClientScript content="JavaScript">
    <meta name=vs_targetSchema
    ➥content="http://schemas.microsoft.com/intellisense/ie5">
    <link rel="stylesheet" href="SystemXML.css" >
  </head>
  <body MS_POSITIONING="GridLayout">

    <script language="C#" runat="server" >
        private void Page_Load(object sender, System.EventArgs e)
        {
            XmlDocument doc = new XmlDocument();
            doc.Load(Server.MapPath("sample.xml"));

            XPathNavigator nav = doc.CreateNavigator();
            XPathNodeIterator iterator =
            ➥nav.SelectDescendants(XPathNodeType.All, true);

            Response.Write("<table>");
            Response.Write("<tr>");
            Response.Write("<th>NodeType</th>");
            Response.Write("<th>LocalName</th>");
```

continues

Listing 6.10   **Continued**

```
                Response.Write("<th>Prefix</th>");
                Response.Write("<th>NamespaceURI</th>");
                Response.Write("<th>Value</th>");
                Response.Write("</tr>");
                while (iterator.MoveNext())
                {
                    WriteNavigator(iterator.Current);
                }
                Response.Write("</table>");
        }

        private void WriteNavigator(XPathNavigator current)
        {
                Response.Write("<tr>");

                WriteTD(current.NodeType.ToString());
                WriteTD(current.LocalName);
                WriteTD(current.Prefix);
                WriteTD(current.NamespaceURI);
                WriteTD(current.Value);

                Response.Write("</tr>");
        }
        private void WriteTD(String cellData)
        {
                Response.Write(String.Concat("<td>", cellData , "</td>"));
        }
        </script>
    </body>
</html>
```

This example begins by using the CreateNavigator method of the XmlDocument class to create the navigator class. This method is exposed through the IXPathNavigable interface, which has only the CreateNavigator method as a member. This interface is implemented by the XmlNode object, from which the XmlDocument object inherits. The implication of this is that any object inheriting from XmlNode, such as what we saw in Figure 6.3, supports the CreateNavigator method. The XpathDocument object also supports the IXPathNavigable interface, which means it supports the CreateNavigator method as well.

This example uses the SelectDescendants method with a Boolean true, which indicates that you want a deep query. This has the same effect as issuing the following XPath query:

```
descendant-or-self::*
```

The `SelectDescendants` method of the `XPathNavigator` returns an `XPathNodeIterator` object. This class is optimized to iterate over a set of nodes. It also provides a set of methods to navigate further through the returned nodes.

You can use the `MoveNext` method of the `XPathNodeIterator` to iterate through the node set returned by the XPath query. For each accessed node, you use the `Current` method to return a new `XPathNavigator` object to access the properties of the current node. Table 6.9 shows the properties of the `XPathNavigator` class.

Table 6.9 **Properties of the *XPathNavigator* Class**

Property Name	Description
BaseURI	Retrieves the base URI of the node, which indicates from where the node was loaded.
HasAttributes	Retrieves a Boolean that indicates if the current node has any attributes.
HasChildren	Returns a Boolean that indicates if the current node has any child nodes.
	The root can have element, comment, or processing instruction child nodes.
	An element can have element, text, comment, whitespace, or significant whitespace child nodes.
	Any other node type cannot have child nodes.
IsEmptyElement	Indicates if the current node is an empty element, such as `<Customers/>`.
LocalName	Gets the name of the current node without a namespace prefix.
Name	Gets the qualified name of the current node.
NamespaceURI	Gets the namespace URI of the current node.
NameTable	Gets the `XmlNameTable` associated with this implementation.
NodeType	Returns the `XmlNodeType` of the current node. Use the `ToString` method to return its text representation.
Prefix	Gets the namespace prefix associated with the current node.
Value	Gets the value of the current node. If the current node is an element whose child elements have child text nodes, the text of the descendant nodes is returned as a concatenated string.
XmlLang	Gets the `xml:lang` scope for the current node.

Look at the HasChildren property description in Table 6.9. Attribute nodes are not considered child nodes. The example in Listing 6.10 does not return the attributes for the current node. For this reason, you have to explicitly retrieve the attributes from the XPathNavigator by using the MoveToFirstAttribute method to move to the first attribute, then iterate through the attributes using the MoveToNextAttribute method, like this:

```
private void Page_Load(object sender, System.EventArgs e)
{
    XmlDocument doc = new XmlDocument();
    doc.Load(Server.MapPath("sample.xml"));

    XPathNavigator nav = doc.CreateNavigator();
    XPathNodeIterator iterator =
nav.SelectDescendants(XPathNodeType.All, true);

    Response.Write("<table>");
    Response.Write("<tr>");
    Response.Write("<th>NodeType</th>");
    Response.Write("<th>LocalName</th>");
    Response.Write("<th>Prefix</th>");
    Response.Write("<th>NamespaceURI</th>");
    Response.Write("<th>Value</th>");
    Response.Write("</tr>");
    while (iterator.MoveNext())
    {
        WriteNavigator(iterator.Current);
        if (iterator.Current.MoveToFirstAttribute())
        {
            WriteNavigator(iterator.Current);
            while(iterator.Current.MoveToNextAttribute())
            {
                WriteNavigator(iterator.Current);
            }
            iterator.Current.MoveToParent();
        }
    }
    Response.Write("</table>");
}
```

The MoveToParent method was used to move from the attributes back to the parent element. This seems to contradict the fact that attributes are not considered child nodes, yet elements are parent nodes of elements. But, you need to call the MoveToParent method to navigate back to the element; otherwise, you can not properly access all the nodes.

Table 6.10 details the MoveToParent method and the other methods of the XPathNavigator class.

Table 6.10 **Methods of the *XPathNavigator* Class**

Method Name	Description
Clone	Creates a new XPathNavigator positioned at the same node as this XPathNavigator.
ComparePosition	Compares the position of the current XPathNavigator with the position of the specified XPathNavigator. Returns XmlNodeOrder enumeration member (Before, After, Same, Unknown).
Compile	Compiles the XPath string expression and returns an XpathExpression object.
Equals	Determines if two object instances are equal.
Evaluate	Evaluates the given expression and returns the typed result. Use this to return strongly typed values (numbers such as integer or double, Boolean, string, or node set).
GetAttribute	Returns the value of the attribute specified by the local name and namespace URI. If no namespace is associated with the attribute, specify String.Empty. The current node must be an element node that contains the attribute, or String.Empty is returned.
GetHashCode	Serves as a hash function for a particular type, suitable for use in hashing algorithms and data structures such as a hash table.
GetNamespace	Returns the value of the namespace node corresponding to the specified local name.
GetType	Gets the Type of the current instance.
IsDescendant	Returns a Boolean that indicates if the specified XPathNavigator is a descendant of the current XPathNavigator.
IsSamePosition	Returns a Boolean that indicates if the specified XPathNavigator is positioned the same as the current XPathNavigator.
Matches	Determines whether the current node matches the specified XSLT pattern.
MoveTo	Moves to the same position as the specified XPathNavigator.
MoveToAttribute	Moves to the attribute of the current node that has the local name and namespace URI specified.

continues

Table 6.10 **Continued**

Method Name	Description
MoveToFirst	Moves to the first sibling of the current node.
MoveToFirstAttribute	Moves to the first attribute.
MoveToFirstChild	Moves to the first child node. Refer to the HasChildren property description in Table 6.9 for information on child nodes.
MoveToFirstNamespace	Moves to the first namespace node with the specified local name.
MoveToId	Moves to the node with an ID attribute that has a value matching the specified string.
MoveToNamespace	Moves the XPathNavigator to the namespace node with the specified local name.
MoveToNext	Moves to the next sibling of the current node. Similar to the following-sibling XPath axis.
MoveToNextAttribute	Moves to the next attribute for the current node.
MoveToNextNamespace	Moves to the next namespace node.
MoveToParent	Moves to the parent node of the current node. Use this when accessing attributes to return to the containing element.
MoveToPrevious	Moves to the previous sibling of the current node. Similar to the preceding-sibling XPath axis.
MoveToRoot	Moves to the current node's root node.
Select	Returns an XPathNodeIterator that is used to iterate over the nodes returned by the given XPath expression.
SelectAncestors	Returns an XPathNodeIterator that is used to iterate over the ancestor nodes of the current node with the specified XmlNodeType. Accepts a Boolean parameter that indicates if the current node is also matched. Similar to the ancestor or ancestor-or-self XPath axis.
SelectChildren	Returns an XPathNodeIterator that is used to iterate over the child nodes of the current node with the specified XmlNodeType. Similar to the child XPath axis.

Method Name	Description
SelectDescendants	Returns an XPathNodeIterator that is used to iterate over the descendant nodes of the current node with the specified XmlNodeType. Accepts a Boolean parameter that indicates if the current node is also matched. Similar to the descendant or descendant-or-self XPath axis.
ToString	Gets the text value of the current node. Equivalent to calling the Value property.

The *XPathDocument* Object

At the beginning of this section, we mentioned the XPathDocument class and the IXPathNavigable interface. XPathDocument provides yet another means of working with and querying XML data. The XPathDocument class is a fast, read-only cache for document processing using XSLT. It can, however, also be used to take advantage of its extremely fast XPath capabilities. In fact, according to Fadi Fakhouri, the Microsoft Core XML Framework project manager, the XPathDocument class gives an order of magnitude performance gain over other XPath implementations, such as XmlDocument.SelectSingleNode.

The XPathDocument object has few members. But, it is optimized for XPath querying and highly performant because it does not maintain node identity (notice that it has no properties, unlike the XmlReader and XmlDocument classes) and does not perform rule checking that is required for the DOM implementation specified by the W3C.

Table 6.11 lists the methods of the XPathDocument class.

Table 6.11 **Methods of the *XPathDocument* Class**

Method Name	Description
CreateNavigator	Creates a new XPathNavigator for this document.
Equals	Determines whether two object instances are equal.
GetHashCode	Serves as a hash function for a particular type, suitable for use in hashing algorithms and data structures, such as a hash table.
GetType	Gets the Type of the current instance.
ToString	Returns a String that represents the current Object.

Looking at the available methods for the class, only one method is notable: the CreateNavigator method. This method simpy creates an XPathNavigator object for the data contained in the current document. This is so useful because of the way that the XPathDocument can be instantiated.

Remember that the XmlReader class supports forward-only access to its underlying data; it does not support random access to its nodes. Using XmlReader as the source of the XpathNavigator, however, allows you to run random-access queries against an XmlReader, the following example shows.

For this example, let's use a lengthy XML document called sample.xml, which is shown in Listing 6.11.

Listing 6.11 **The** *sample.xml* **File**

```xml
<?xml version="1.0" encoding="utf-8" ?>
<Customers xmlns="urn:foo:bar">
    <Customer id="ALFKI">
        <CompanyName>Alfreds Futterkiste</CompanyName>
        <Contact>
            <FirstName>Maria</FirstName>
            <LastName>Anders</LastName>
            <Title>Sales Representative</Title>
        </Contact>
    </Customer>
    <Customer id="LOWES">
        <CompanyName>Lowe&apos;s</CompanyName>
        <Contact>
            <FirstName>Keth</FirstName>
            <LastName>Bunn</LastName>
            <Title>Assistant Manager</Title>
        </Contact>
    </Customer>
    <Customer id="VELVE">
        <CompanyName>The Velvet Room</CompanyName>
        <Contact>
            <FirstName>Rodney</FirstName>
            <LastName>Wade</LastName>
            <Title>Bar Manager</Title>
        </Contact>
    </Customer>
    <Customer id="GABST">
        <CompanyName>Georgia&apos;s Best Pressure and Stain</CompanyName>
        <Contact>
            <FirstName>Steve</FirstName>
            <LastName>Durling</LastName>
            <Title>Owner</Title>
        </Contact>
    </Customer>
```

```
    <Customer id="VBDNA">
        <CompanyName>Kirk Allen Evans Consulting, Inc.</CompanyName>
        <Contact>
            <FirstName>Kirk Allen</FirstName>
            <LastName>Evans</LastName>
            <Title>Owner</Title>
            </Contact>
    </Customer>

</Customers>
```

You probably recognize much of this data: It comes from the Northwinds data-base that ships with Access and SQL Server. Now that you have a base document, look at how you can query this document. Listing 6.12 shows how to navigate the document by using XPathNavigator.

Listing 6.12   **Navigating with *XPathNavigator***

```
<%@ Page Language="vb" Debug="true"%>
<%@ Import Namespace="System.Xml"%>
<%@ Import Namespace="System.Xml.XPath"%>
<!DOCTYPE HTML PUBLIC "-//W3C//DTD HTML 4.0 Transitional//EN">
<html>
  <head>
    <title>WebForm3</title>
    <meta name="GENERATOR" content="Microsoft Visual Studio.NET 7.0">
    <meta name="CODE_LANGUAGE" content="Visual Basic 7.0">
    <meta name=vs_defaultClientScript content="JavaScript">
    <meta name=vs_targetSchema
    ⮑content="http://schemas.microsoft.com/intellisense/ie5">
    <link rel="stylesheet" href="SystemXML.css">
  </head>
  <body MS_POSITIONING="GridLayout">

<script language="visualbasic" runat="server" >
    Private Sub Page_Load(ByVal sender As System.Object, ByVal e As
    ⮑System.EventArgs) Handles MyBase.Load
        Dim file As IO.FileStream = New
        ⮑IO.FileStream(Server.MapPath("sample.xml"), IO.FileMode.Open)
        Dim reader As XmlTextReader = New XmlTextReader(file)

        Dim xpathdoc As XPathDocument = New XPathDocument(reader,
        ⮑XmlSpace.Preserve)

        Dim nav As XPathNavigator = xpathdoc.CreateNavigator()
        Dim expression As XPathExpression =
        ⮑nav.Compile("Customers/Customer/Contact")
```

continues

Listing 6.12   **Continued**

```
        Dim iterator As XPathNodeIterator = nav.Evaluate(expression)

        Response.Write("<table>")
        Response.Write("<tr>")
        Response.Write("<th>NodeType</th>")
        Response.Write("<th>LocalName</th>")
        Response.Write("<th>Prefix</th>")
        Response.Write("<th>NamespaceURI</th>")
        Response.Write("<th>Value</th>")
        Response.Write("</tr>")
        While (iterator.MoveNext())

            WriteNavigator(iterator.Current)
            If (iterator.Current.MoveToFirstAttribute()) Then

                WriteNavigator(iterator.Current)
                While (iterator.Current.MoveToNextAttribute())

                    WriteNavigator(iterator.Current)
                End While
                iterator.Current.MoveToParent()
            End If

        End While
        Response.Write("</table>")

        reader.Close()
        file.Close()

    End Sub

    Private Sub WriteNavigator(ByVal current As XPathNavigator)

        Response.Write("<tr>")

        WriteTD(current.NodeType.ToString())
        WriteTD(current.LocalName)
        WriteTD(current.Prefix)
        WriteTD(current.NamespaceURI)
        WriteTD(current.Value)

        Response.Write("</tr>")
    End Sub

    Private Sub WriteTD(ByVal cellData As String)
        Response.Write(String.Concat("<td>", cellData, "</td>"))
    End Sub
</script>

  </body>
</html>
```

This example almost mirrors the preceding example using the XPathNavigator object. The difference is how you create the XPathNavigator object using the XPathDocument.CreateNavigator method. The XPathDocument is created with an XmlTextReader as its source, which enables you to access nodes using XPath syntax over an XmlReader object.

Using the sample.xml file shown in Listing 6.11, the results of this example are shown in Figure 6.7.

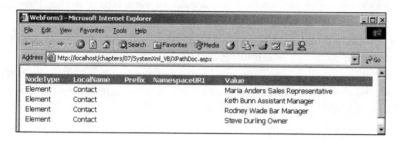

Figure 6.7   The sample output shown when using the XPathNavigator.

The Evaluate method was used to retrieve the node list from the XPath expression. However, you could also use the Evaluate method to return a strongly-typed value, as shown here:

```
Private Sub Page_Load(ByVal sender As System.Object, ByVal e As
System.EventArgs) Handles MyBase.Load
        Dim file As IO.FileStream = New IO.FileStream
        ➥(Server.MapPath("sample.xml"), IO.FileMode.Open)
        Dim reader As XmlTextReader = New XmlTextReader(file)

        Dim xpathdoc As XPathDocument = New XPathDocument(reader,
        ➥XmlSpace.Preserve)

        Dim nav As XPathNavigator = xpathdoc.CreateNavigator()
        Dim expression As XPathExpression = nav.Compile
        ➥("count(Customers/Customer/Contact)")

        Dim contactCount as Integer = CType(nav.Evaluate(expression),Integer)

        Response.write ("The count of Contact nodes is " &
        ➥contactCount.ToString())

        reader.Close()
        file.Close()

End Sub
```

Here's the part that is really worth mentioning: You are not limited to a single expression evaluation. The following code is also legal:

```
Dim expression As XPathExpression = nav.Compile
➥("count(Customers/Customer/Contact)")
Dim contactCount as Integer = CType(nav.Evaluate(expression),Integer)
Dim expression As XPathExpression = nav.Compile
➥("Customers/Customer/Contact")
Dim iterator As XPathNodeIterator = nav.Evaluate(expression)
```

Notice that the evaluate expression was called twice, where the underlying data is provided by a forward-only XmlTextReader. This means that random access is provided to stream-based implementations, providing lightweight and performant operations for querying large XML documents.

You've seen how to populate an XmlDocument with data and how to navigate through the document. Now it's time to see how to manipulate the document's contents.

Inserting, Updating, and Deleting Nodes

A frequently asked question on various XML mailing lists is "How do I insert a node into an XML document using an API?" The answer is surprisingly easier than what you'd think.

To update documents, you need to return to the XmlNode and XmlDocument classes. Table 6.7 shows that the XmlDocument class contains methods for creating nodes, such as CreateAttribute and CreateElement. You can use these methods in the same way that they are used with the MSXML Parser.

The .NET XML classes differ slightly from the MSXML classes. For example, text nodes can be created as children of elements simply by setting the Text property of the IXMLDOMElement interface. In the XmlDocument class in .NET, a text node must be specifically created and appended as a child of the element.

The following example loads an existing XML document and appends XML to the document:

```
<%@ Page Language="vb" %>
<%@ Import Namespace="System.Xml" %>
<script language="visualbasic" runat="server">
    Private Sub Page_Load(ByVal sender As System.Object, ByVal e As
    ➥System.EventArgs) Handles MyBase.Load
        'Put user code to initialize the page here
        Dim doc As XmlDocument = New XmlDocument()
        doc.Load(Server.MapPath("sample.xml"))
```

```
        Dim root As XmlElement = doc.DocumentElement
        Dim customer As XmlNode = root.AppendChild
        ➥(doc.CreateElement("Customer"))
        Dim attrib As XmlAttribute = doc.CreateAttribute("id")
        attrib.Value = "VBDNA"
        customer.Attributes.SetNamedItem(attrib)
        Dim companyName As XmlElement = customer.AppendChild
        ➥(doc.CreateElement("CompanyName"))
        companyName.AppendChild(doc.CreateTextNode
        ➥("Kirk Allen Evans Consulting, Inc"))
        Dim contact As XmlElement = customer.AppendChild
        ➥(doc.CreateElement("Contact"))
        Dim tempNode As XmlElement = contact.AppendChild
        ➥(doc.CreateElement("FirstName"))
        tempNode.AppendChild(doc.CreateTextNode("Kirk Allen"))
        tempNode = contact.AppendChild(doc.CreateElement("LastName"))
        tempNode.AppendChild(doc.CreateTextNode("Evans"))
        tempNode = contact.AppendChild(doc.CreateElement("Title"))
        tempNode.AppendChild(doc.CreateTextNode("President"))

        Response.ContentType = "text/xml"
        Response.Clear()
        doc.Save(Response.OutputStream)
    End Sub
</script>
```

The output from this example is shown in Figure 6.8.

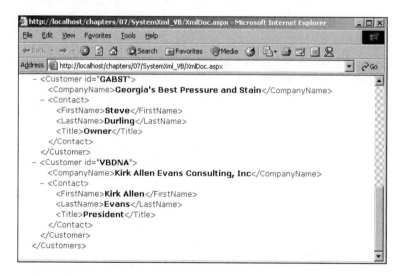

Figure 6.8 Outputting an XML document directly to the HTTP response.

As you can see, the code for creating XML from scratch is straightforward, but not as straightforward as using the XmlTextWriter class. The XmlTextWriter is more useful to create XML documents from scratch, while the XmlDocument class is better suited to update the contents of a document.

However, you can mix the implementations. In the following code, you are using the XmlTextWriter to write to a stream in memory. Then the contents of the stream are used to form a new DOM document that contains only the newly created XML nodes. This DOM document is then imported into the new DOM document and appended to the document element:

```vb
<%@ Page Language="vb" Debug="true"%>
<%@ Import Namespace="System.Xml" %>
<script language="visualbasic" runat="server">
    Private Sub Page_Load(ByVal sender As System.Object, ByVal e As
    ⇒System.EventArgs) Handles MyBase.Load

        Dim memStream As IO.MemoryStream = New IO.MemoryStream()

        Dim writer As XmlTextWriter
        writer = New XmlTextWriter(memStream, System.Text.Encoding.UTF8)

        writer.Formatting = Formatting.Indented

        writer.WriteStartElement("Customer")
        writer.WriteAttributeString("id", "VBDNA")
        writer.WriteElementString("Companyname", "Kirk Allen Evans
        ⇒Consluting, Inc.")
        writer.WriteStartElement("Contact")
        writer.WriteElementString("FirstName", "Kirk Allen")
        writer.WriteElementString("Lastname", "Evans")
        writer.WriteElementString("Title", "President")
        writer.WriteEndElement()
        writer.WriteEndElement()
        writer.Flush()
        memStream.Position = 0

        'Load a DOM document using the contents of the memory stream
        Dim sourceDoc As XmlDocument = New XmlDocument()
        sourceDoc.Load(memStream)

        dim targetDoc as XmlDocument = New XmlDocument()
        targetDoc.Load(Server.MapPath("sample.xml"))

        Dim node As XmlNode = targetDoc.ImportNode
        ⇒(sourceDoc.DocumentElement,True)
        targetDoc.DocumentElement.AppendChild(node)

        Response.ContentType = "text/xml"
        Response.Clear()
```

```
        targetDoc.Save(Response.OutputStream)
        On Error Resume Next
        memStream.Close()
        writer.Close()
    End Sub
</script>
```

The output from this example is the same as what's shown in Figure 6.6, but the code is cleaner and easier to understand.

Now that you have seen how to read documents, navigate through them, and change their contents, look at transforming an XML structure into a new structure. XSLT was examined in Chapter 3, "XML Presentation," from the perspective of using the XSLT elements. The next section looks at the objects in the System.Xml namespace that facilitate XSLT transformations.

XSLT Transformations

As discussed in Chapter 3, XSLT can be used to transform a source XML document into a different result tree. This result tree can be a variety of XML formats, which makes XSLT such an exciting technology. The .NET classes used to perform the transformations are not concerned with the format of the output—rather, they're concerned with performing the transformation.

You've already seen the XPathDocument object and examined using it with XPath queries. Recall that the XPathDocument object contains only one method specific to XML—the CreateNavigator method. The real power behind the XPathDocument object is how it is instantiated: It can read over stream object implementations, such as MemoryStream and FileStream, reader implementations, such as XmlReader and TextReader, or accept a path to a file.

You can use the XPathDocument object to read XML data from one of these sources and then use this document as the source of the XML transformation.

Now let's walk through the XSLT stylesheet to confirm your understanding of it. Begin by creating the XSLT stylesheet node in the following code. The example XML file uses a namespace with a URI of urn:foo:bar, so add that namespace to the XSLT document as well. You can use a prefix of tns to distinguish the namespace URI from the xsl namespace prefix. You can also specify that the output method for this stylesheet is XML:

```
<?xml version="1.0" encoding="UTF-8" ?>
<xsl:stylesheet version="1.0"
xmlns:xsl="http://www.w3.org/1999/XSL/Transform" xmlns:tns="urn:foo:bar">
    <xsl:output method="xml"/>
    .
    .
    .
</xsl:stylesheet>
```

The next step: Add some template rules to the document. The first template rule matches the Customers element that has a namespace URI that matches the namespace URI associated with the prefix tns. It creates the root result element called DATA and then tells the parser to continue processing, as shown here:

```
<xsl:template match="tns:Customers">
    <xsl:element name="DATA">
        <xsl:apply-templates />
    </xsl:element>
</xsl:template>
```

The second template rule matches the Customer element because it also has a namespace URI that matches the namespace URI associated with the tns prefix. It creates an element called Company with an ID attribute. The CompanyID attribute in the result tree receives the same value as the ID attribute in the source tree. It then tells the processor to continue processing the template rules using a specific set of nodes:

```
<xsl:template match="tns:Customer">
    <xsl:element name="Company">
        <xsl:attribute name="CompanyID">
            <xsl:value-of select="@id"/>
        </xsl:attribute>
        <xsl:apply-templates select="tns:CompanyName"/>
        <xsl:apply-templates select="tns:Contact"/>
    </xsl:element>
</xsl:template>
```

The final template rules to add both act the same way. They simply add attributes to the result document, like this:

```
<xsl:template match="tns:CompanyName">
    <xsl:attribute name="CompanyName">
        <xsl:value-of select="."/>
    </xsl:attribute>
</xsl:template>

<xsl:template match="tns:Contact">
    <xsl:attribute name="FirstName">
        <xsl:value-of select="tns:FirstName"/>
    </xsl:attribute>
    <xsl:attribute name="LastName">
        <xsl:value-of select="tns:LastName"/>
    </xsl:attribute>
    <xsl:attribute name="Title">
        <xsl:value-of select="tns:Title"/>
    </xsl:attribute>
</xsl:template>
```

The following output from this transformation contains the same data as the input tree, but with a different structure than the input document. The XSLT document and the results are shown here (the code to perform the transformation is explained in the next section):

```
<?xml version="1.0" encoding="utf-8" ?>
<DATA>
    <Company CompanyID="ALFKI" CompanyName="Alfreds Futterkiste"
FirstName="Maria" LastName="Anders" Title="Sales Representative"></Company>
    <Company CompanyID="LOWES" CompanyName="Lowe's" FirstName="Keth"
LastName="Bunn" Title="Assistant Manager"></Company>
    <Company CompanyID="VELVE" CompanyName="The Velvet Room"
FirstName="Rodney" LastName="Wade" Title="Bar Manager"></Company>
    <Company CompanyID="GABST" CompanyName="Georgia's Best Pressure and
Stain" FirstName="Steve" LastName="Durling" Title="Owner"></Company>
    <Company CompanyID="VBDNA" CompanyName="Kirk Allen Evans Consulting,
Inc." FirstName="Kirk Allen" LastName="Evans" Title="Owner"></Company>
</DATA>
```

Now that your memory about template processing and the difference between input and result trees has been refreshed, take a closer look at the code that performs the transformations.

The *XslTransform* Class

The XslTransform class is specifically designed to perform XSLT transformations in .NET. It supports XSLT 1.0 and can be extended with the <msxsl:script> element or through custom XSLT extension functions (recall the discussion in Chapter 3 about the XSLT extension functions). It has two main methods worth noting: the Load and the Transform methods.

Using the *Load* Method of the *XslTransform* Class

The Load method of the XslTransform class loads a stylesheet into memory. The Load method supports a variety of data sources to load the stylesheet. It also accepts an XmlResolver class that can specify credentials for external resources (refer to the section, "Retrieving External Data" for a refresher on how to use the XmlResolver abstract class).

Table 6.12 shows the overloads for the Load method.

Table 6.12 **Constructors for the *XslTransform* Class**

Overloaded *Load()* Method	Description
Load(IXPathNavigable)	Loads the stylesheet contained in the object that implements the IXPathNavigable interface.
Load(string)	Loads the stylesheet located at the specified URL.
Load(XmlReader)	Loads the stylesheet contained in the specified XmlReader (XmlTextReader or XmlNodeReader).
Load(XPathNavigator)	Loads the stylesheet contained in the XPathNavigator.
Load(IXPathNavigable, XmlResolver)	Loads the stylesheet contained in the object that implements the IXPathNavigable interface. Resolves external resources by using the XmlResolver object specified.
Load(string, XmlResolver)	Loads the XSLT stylesheet located at the specified URL. Uses the XmlResolver object to resolve external resources.
Load(XmlReader,XmlResolver)	Loads the stylesheet contained in the specified XmlReader by using the XmlResolver to resolve external resources.
Load(XPathNavigator,XmlResolver)	Loads the stylesheet contained in the specified XPathNavigator by using the XmlResolver to resolve external resources.

Recall that the XmlNode object supports the IXPathNavigable interface so all nodes that inherit from XmlNode can be passed in as arguments to the Load method. This includes an XmlDocument object. You can also pass an XmlReader object, reading the entire contents of the reader into the XslTransform object.

Using the *Transform* Method of the *XslTransform* Class

Just as the Load method accepts multiple overloads, the Transform method also accepts multiple overloads. The simplest version of the overloaded transform accepts two string arguments: the path for the input XML document and the path for the output result document. You can, however, perform more complicated transformations by using a variety of sources. For example, it's been stated multiple times throughout this chapter that each XmlNode object also supports the IXPathNavigable interface. So, you can pass in an XmlDocument object to the `Transform` method and an `XPathDocument` object. Recall, however, that the `XPathDocument` object doesn't perform the same rule checking that the `XmlDocument` class does, so the `XPathDocument` is faster by an order of magnitude or more.

Listing 6.13 creates an `XmlTextReader` object based on an XML file and then creates an `XPathDocument` based on the reader's XML contents.

Listing 6.13   **A Sample Transformation**

```
<%@ Page language="c#" Debug="true"%>
<%@ Import Namespace="System.Xml"%>
<%@ Import Namespace="System.Xml.XPath"%>
<%@ Import Namespace="System.Text"%>
<%@ Import Namespace="System.Xml.Xsl"%>

<script language="C#" runat="server">
          private void Page_Load(object sender, System.EventArgs e)
          {
              XmlTextReader reader = new
XmlTextReader(Server.MapPath("sample.xml"));
              XPathDocument doc = new XPathDocument(reader);
              reader.Close();

              reader = new
XmlTextReader(Server.MapPath("sampletransform.xslt"));

              XslTransform transform = new XslTransform();
              transform.Load(reader);
              transform.Transform(doc,null,Response.OutputStream);
              reader.Close();
          }
</script>
```

Because the contents of the reader were already loaded into the `XPathDocument`, it's safe to close the reader and reload it with the XSLT stylesheet. The transform method is then called using the input file, with no argument list, and the contents are specified so that they're written to the `Response` object's content stream.

You have seen examples of loading all the object types and have used `XmlResolver` to add `NetworkCredentials` for a specified URI. These concepts are used later in this section. In Listing 6.13, you specified null for the `XsltArgumentList` parameter. But what if you want to pass a parameter to the stylesheet? Suppose, for example, that you want to sort your document based on the parameter that's passed in.

The *XsltArgument* Class

The XsltArgument class is predominately used to pass parameters to an XSLT stylesheet. As you saw in Chapter 3, it can also be used to add extension functions to the XSLT processor.

Listing 6.14 reconstructs the Pitchers.xml example XML document from Chapter 3.

Listing 6.14   *Pitchers.xml*

```
<?xml version="1.0" encoding="utf-8" ?>
<PITCHERS>
    <PITCHER>
        <FNAME>John</FNAME>
        <LNAME>Rocker</LNAME>
        <TEAM>Indians</TEAM>
        <CITY>Cleveland</CITY>
        <ERA></ERA>
    </PITCHER>
    <PITCHER>
        <FNAME>Tom</FNAME>
        <LNAME>Glavine</LNAME>
        <TEAM>Braves</TEAM>
        <CITY>Atlanta</CITY>
        <ERA></ERA>
    </PITCHER>
    <PITCHER>
        <FNAME>Greg</FNAME>
        <LNAME>Maddux</LNAME>
        <TEAM>Braves</TEAM>
        <CITY>Atlanta</CITY>
        <ERA></ERA>
    </PITCHER>
    <PITCHER>
        <FNAME>Randy</FNAME>
        <LNAME>Johnson</LNAME>
        <TEAM>Diamondbacks</TEAM>
        <CITY>Arizona</CITY>
        <ERA></ERA>
    </PITCHER>
</PITCHERS>
```

The stylesheet in Listing 6.15 is used to process the XML document.

Listing 6.15   *Pitcherstyle.xslt*

```
<?xml version="1.0" encoding="UTF-8" ?>
<xsl:stylesheet version="1.0"
xmlns:xsl="http://www.w3.org/1999/XSL/Transform">
```

```
<xsl:param name="sortBy" select="'CITY'"/>
<xsl:template match="/">
      <xsl:apply-templates/>
</xsl:template>
<xsl:template match="PITCHERS">
      <TABLE border="1">
            <tr>
                  <th><a onclick="javascript:SortData('FNAME');">First
                  ➥Name</a></th>
                  <th><a onclick="javascript:SortData('LNAME');">Last
                  ➥Name</a></th>
                  <th><a onclick="javascript:SortData('CITY');
                  ➥">City</a></th>
                  <th><a onclick="javascript:SortData('TEAM');
                  ➥">Team</a></th>
                  <th><a onclick="javascript:SortData('ERA');">ERA</a></th>
            </tr>
            <xsl:for-each select="PITCHER">
                  <xsl:sort select="*[name()=$sortBy]"/>
                  <tr>
                        <td><xsl:value-of select="FNAME"/><br/></td>
                        <td><xsl:value-of select="LNAME"/></td>
                        <td><xsl:value-of select="CITY"/></td>
                        <td><xsl:value-of select="TEAM"/></td>
                        <td><xsl:value-of select="ERA"/></td>
                              </tr>
            </xsl:for-each>
      </TABLE>
</xsl:template>
</xsl:stylesheet>
```

You can use the sortBy parameter to specify the element that you want to sort
on. The default is the CITY element, which occurs if no parameter is passed in.
Otherwise, the value passed in is used. To pass the parameter to the stylesheet,
use XsltArgumentList to add parameters that are passed to the stylesheet, as
shown here:

```
private void Page_Load(object sender, System.EventArgs e)
{
      XmlTextReader reader = new
XmlTextReader(Server.MapPath("pitchers.xml"));
      XPathDocument doc = new XPathDocument(reader);
      reader.Close();

      reader = new
XmlTextReader(Server.MapPath("pitcherstyle.xslt"));
      XslTransform transform = new XslTransform();
      transform.Load(reader);
```

```
XsltArgumentList args = new XsltArgumentList();
args.AddParam("sortBy",string.Empty,"TEAM");
transform.Transform(doc,args,Response.OutputStream);
reader.Close();
    }
```

This example was slightly changed to include the `XsltArgumentList` object reference. You can add a parameter that's not associated with a specific namespace, and specify its value as the string `TEAM`. Then, you can pass the `XsltArgumentList` object to the `Transform` method to pass the parameters to the stylesheet, which causes the stylesheet to sort based on the `TEAM` element.

The XML Web Control

As you have just seen, performing an XSL transformation does not require a large amount of code after you have the XML document and XSLT template ready. With ASP.NET, however, Microsoft has supplied a control that makes XSL transformations even easier. In many cases, you can accomplish the same transformation with as little as a single tag, using the `<asp:Xml>` control:

```
<asp:Xml id="PitcherDisplay" runat="server"
    DocumentSource="pitchers.xml"
    TransformSource="pitcherstyle.xslt" />
```

If both your XML and XSLT are located in local files and you don't need to pass any arguments to your XSLT, a single `<asp:Xml>` tag is all you need to apply the transformation and output it to the browser. However, what if your needs are more complicated? Perhaps you need to pull the XML data from a remote server or a database—or perhaps you simply need to pass an argument or two to your XSLT stylesheet. You're in luck because the `<asp:Xml>` control was designed to accommodate those needs. The control has additional properties that accept an `XmlDocument` object (which can be loaded from anywhere) for the XML data, an `XslTransform` object for the XSL transformation, and an `XsltArgumentList` object for any arguments that your XSLT template might require. The properties are called `Document`, `Transform`, and `TransformArgumentList`, respectively. These properties expect live objects so they cannot be set declaratively in the tag, but must be set in the code for the page.

You might have noticed that the single tag listed previously duplicates the last example almost perfectly, with the exception that we haven't told the stylesheet what sort-order we'd like. Let's complete the duplication of the last example so that you can compare the amount of effort required for each method. First, create a new Web Form in Visual Studio, and add an XML control from the Toolbox to the page. Call it `PitchersDisplay` and add values for the DocumentSource and TransformSource properties, as you just saw in the preceding sample tag.

Now switch to the code view for the page. You need to add some using (or Imports, if you're working with Visual Basic) statements to the top of the page—one for System.Xml and one for System.Xml.Xsl. In the Page_Load event handler, add the code shown in Listing 6.16.

Listing 6.16 **Transforming Using the *asp:xml* Control**

```
using System;
using System.Collections;
using System.ComponentModel;
using System.Data;
using System.Drawing;
using System.Web;
using System.Web.SessionState;
using System.Web.UI;
using System.Web.UI.WebControls;
using System.Web.UI.HtmlControls;
using System.Xml;
using System.Xml.XPath;
using System.Xml.Xsl;

namespace XSLT
{
    /// <summary>
    /// Summary description for pitch.
    /// </summary>
    public class pitch : System.Web.UI.Page
    {
        protected System.Web.UI.WebControls.Xml PitchersDisplay;

        private void Page_Load(object sender, System.EventArgs e)
        {
            XmlTextReader reader = new
XmlTextReader(Server.MapPath("pitchers.xml"));
            XPathDocument doc = new XPathDocument(reader);
            reader.Close();

            reader = new
XmlTextReader(Server.MapPath("pitcherstyle.xslt"));
            XslTransform transform = new XslTransform();
            transform.Load(reader);

            XsltArgumentList args = new XsltArgumentList();
            args.AddParam("sortBy", string.Empty, "TEAM");

            PitchersDisplay.TransformArgumentList = args;
        }
```

Listing 6.16   **Transforming Using the *asp:xml* Control**

```
#region Web Form Designer generated code
override protected void OnInit(EventArgs e)
{
    //
    // CODEGEN: This call is required by the ASP.NET Web Form
    // Designer.
    //
    InitializeComponent();
    base.OnInit(e);
}

/// <summary>
/// Required method for Designer support - do not modify
///  the contents of this method with the code editor.
/// </summary>
private void InitializeComponent()
{
this.Load += new System.EventHandler(this.Page_Load);

}
#endregion
        }
    }
```

And there you have it. You've done an XSLT transformation, complete with arguments, using a single tag and three lines of code. Using the Document and Transform properties of this control is equally straightforward; simply create your XmlDocument or XslTransform objects as you would if you were performing the transformation yourself, and pass them to the appropriate property of the XML Web Control.

Catching Parsing Exceptions

Throughout this chapter, we have shown little error handling for brevity. In your production applications, you might want to include error handling for a variety of situations. For example, if you're working with files, you might want to trap errors indicating the file was not found.

There might also be a case where the input document could not be parsed. Some instances might be where XML data was dynamically generated and did not generate well-formed XML data.

For example, the following XML document, badxml.xml, is not well formed because it has multiple root elements:

```
<?xml version="1.0" encoding="utf-8" ?>
<multiple>
</multiple>
```

```
<multiple>
</multiple>
```

The following code would trap the parse error after successfully loading the file:

```vb
<%@ Page language="vb" Debug="true"%>
<%@ Import Namespace="System.Xml"%>
<script language="vb" runat="server">
    Private Sub Page_Load(ByVal sender As Object, ByVal e As
    ►System.EventArgs) Handles MyBase.Load
        Dim doc As XmlDocument = New XmlDocument()
        Try
            doc.Load(Server.MapPath("badxml.xml"))
        Catch parseError As System.Xml.XmlException
            Response.write(parseError.ToString())
        End Try
    End Sub
</script>
```

Remember that stream-based resources, such as XmlReader and XmlWriter, support a Close method so that you can ensure that resources are appropriately closed. Always include a test in your error handlers to ensure that you properly closed all resources.

Chapter Summary

You have seen many of the various classes in the System.Xml and System.Xml.XPath namespaces. A number of different approaches of working with XML were provided, each with its own unique benefits.

The XmlDocument class loads all its data into memory. This makes updating the XML contained in it easy, and enables random access to any of its nodes. This flexibility comes at a price: Loading a large XML document can consume plenty of memory, causing a server-side application to be less scalable. Using this class is best suited for making many updates to an existing XML document.

When using the XmlDocument class' SelectSingleNode or SelectNodes methods, remember that you need to use an XmlNamespaceManager class to create namespace prefixes associated with the URIs in the document, or the results won't be the same as what you expect.

The XmlReader class performs fast forward-only, non-cached reading of XML data. The tradeoff for its speed capabilities is that you cannot navigate through the ancestor axis (parents, parents' parents, and so on). This class is best suited for reading an entire existing XML document.

The XPathDocument class is an extremely performant class that provides random, read-only access to XML documents. This class can be used over any data store (such as a file, stream, or DOM document), and can be customized to navigate over custom stores.

Finally, you learned that you can use the XsltArgument class to pass parameters to an XsltTransform class.

7

ASP.NET Extensibility With XML

THROUGHOUT THIS BOOK, IT'S BEEN SHOWN that .NET incorporates XML into key areas of the .NET Framework, as well as into technologies, such as ADO.NET. This chapter discusses how XML is integrated with the configuration of Windows Forms and Web Forms applications.

A Word on the Metabase

The process for configuring the operating system and applications that run on it has evolved since MS-DOS' inception. To configure MS-DOS, `AUTOEXEC.BAT` and `CONFIG.SYS` files were used, and applications running on top of the operating system used their own proprietary configuration files. Back in the days of Windows 3.1, people were introduced to `.INI` files that stored configuration information. A set of simple APIs were included to work with `.INI` files in a standard fashion (remember `GetProfileString` and `GetProfileSection`?). A simple tool called *sysedit* provided easy access to edit the `SYSTEM.INI`, `WIN.INI`, `CONFIG.SYS`, and `AUTOEXEC.BAT` files by simply loading all of them into a *Multiple Document Interface (MDI)* window.

When Windows NT 3.5 was released, everyone became more familiar with the registry. It wasn't until Windows 95 was released, however, that people saw the true ability to control the operating system, expecially with the release of *PowerToys*, an application designed to customize the Windows 95 UI. The registry allowed for easier development of hierarchical structures that could contain both text and binary data in several formats. The registry became favored over .INI files.

The release of Windows NT 4.0 increased the use of the registry. But when the Option Pack for Windows NT 4.0 was released (including IIS 3.0), developers quickly became intimately familiar with tweaking the registry to manipulate IIS for capabilities such as ADO connection pooling and connection timeouts. Microsoft's integration of some of these registry settings into the Microsoft Mangement Console (MMC) snap-in eased the developer's research time, but it was soon realized that using the registry for IIS management was not an optimal solution because of speed and complexity issues.

The solution to using the registry is provided by the *metabase*. The metabase is a binary file that provides hierarchical configuration information for Internet Information Services (IIS). It is located at %windir%\system32\inetsrv\ MetaBase.bin. Several utilities are available for working with the metabase, including the Internet Services Manager MMC snap-in.

In ASP.NET, configuration information is stored in XML configuration files. These XML files can be modified while the server is running, and changes take effect without rebooting the web server. If you have ever had to go back to work at 3 a.m. to reboot the web server, you'll appreciate this new feature. The managed code configuration system reads the values and applies them without restarting the server. The exception to this case is the processModel section—it's read directly by aspnet_isapi.dll. Changes do not take effect in this section until IIS is restarted.

Several configuration files are available that you can use with the .NET Framework: security configuration files, the machine configuration file (machine.config), and application configuration files.

Security Configuration Files

Security configuration files manage the permissions associated with a policy level and the code group hierarchy. These settings need to be modified using only the .NET Configuration MMC snap-in (mscorcfg.msc) or by using the Code Access Security Policy tool (caspol.exe).

machine.config

The machine configuration file, machine.config, specifies machine-wide settings. It contains settings for machine-wide ASP.NET, as well as assembly binding and built-in remoting channels. You can also specify custom settings in its `appSettings` section (described in the section, "Walk-Through of `web.config`'s Hierarchical Structure"). It's recommended that application-specific settings be placed in their associated application configuration files unless they pertain to all applications on the machine.

Application Configuration Files

A benefit to using configuration files at the application level is that each application can configure the environment for its own use. For example, one of the settings available in a configuration file is the `requiredRuntime` setting in the `startup` section. It defines what version of the run-time to use. For machines with multiple versions of the common language run-time installed, this key can be used to manage on which version the application depends.

Two types of application configuration files exist: executable-hosted configuration files and web application configuration files (`web.config`).

Executable Configuration Files

Executable configuration files manage the configuration settings for the executable environment. The application configuration file is not compiled into the executable file as a resource file is. Rather, the configuration file is external to the application and uses the same name as the application with a `.config` extension. For example, an application named `WindowsApplication.exe` would have a single configuration file in its `bin` directory when it's compiled as `WindowsApplication.exe.config`. Unless this setting matches the executable name, the configuration file is not found.

web.config

When the application to be configured is a web application, the configuration file used is called `web.config`. When you create a new ASP.NET web application project in Visual Studio .NET, a `web.config` file is included in the list of files that is automatically generated.

Not only can the application's virtual root have a `web.config` file, but each subdirectory in the virtual directory can also have its own `web.config` file. Each `web.config` file applies its settings to its own virtual directory and its virtual subdirectories. If a conflict in settings occurs between a directory and a subdirectory, the settings in the subdirectory take precedence over the parent directory's settings. For example, look at the virtual directory structure in Figure 7.1.

Configuration Files Are Secured in ASP.NET

ASP.NET configuration files are secured and are not viewable through a browser: An attempt to access the `web.config` file causes an HTTP error, 403 (Forbidden).

Figure 7.1   Each subdirectory in the virtual directory
might have its own `web.config` file.

The `Public` directory doesn't have its own `web.config` file: Settings are inherited from the parent `Application` directory.

The `Secure` directory, which represents the set of web pages that require authentication, uses its own `web.config` file separately from the parent `Application` directory. In this model, a conflicting setting in the `Secure` directory's `web.config` file would be used. Any settings not specifically overridden in the child directory would be inherited from the parent directory. This enables the developer to require a different authentication model for each subdirectory if desired, or to use the settings for the parent directory. This also prevents the user from duplicating custom application settings for each virtual subdirectory.

Take a look at the components of the `web.config` file and see what configuration options are available.

Configuration Settings Are URL Specific
Settings are inherited by subdirectories according to the URL, not the physical disk path.

Walk-Through of *web.config*'s Hierarchical Structure

The `web.config` file's schema contains the sections defined in Table 7.1.

Table 7.1   **Overview of the *web.config* Sections**

Configuration Section Element	Description
configuration	Provides custom configuration. This is where custom `appSetting` keys are defined.
mscorlib	Specifies mapping of configuration algorithm monikers to implementation classes.
remoting	Provides customization for remoting.

Configuration Section Element	Description
runtime	Specifies how garbage collection is handled and the version assembly for configuration files.
startup	Defines what version of the run-time is required to run the application.
system.diagnostics	Configures tracing and debugging options and handlers.
system.net	Defines how the .NET Framework connects to the Internet.
system.web	Customizes ASP.NET application behavior.

A sample web.config section is shown in Listing 7.1.

Listing 7.1   A sample *web.config* File

```
<?xml version="1.0" encoding="utf-8" ?>
<configuration>
    <appSettings>
        <add key="connectionString"
value="User ID=sa;Password=;Initial Catalog=Northwind;Data Source=AT1LT-3165-
➥03"/>
        <add key="startupTable"
            value="Customers"/>
    </appSettings>
    <system.web>
        <processModel enable="true"
            idleTimeout="00:30:00"
            pingFrequency="00:01:00"
            pingTimeout="00:00:30"
            logLevel="Errors"
            webGarden="true"/>
        <compilation defaultLanguage="vb"
                debug="true"
                explicit="true"
                strict="true"/>

        <customErrors mode="RemoteOnly" >
            <error statusCode="404" redirect="FileNotFound.aspx" />
            <error statusCode="500" redirect="Oops.aspx" />
        </customErrors>

        <authentication mode="Forms" >
            <forms name="OrderForm" loginUrl="/login.aspx">
                <credentials passwordFormat="Clear">
                    <user name="deanna" password="wife"/>
                    <user name="lilbit" password="son"/>
                    <user name="teenybit" password="unborn"/>
```

continues

Listing 7.1 Continued

```
                    </credentials>
                </forms>
            </authentication>

            <authorization>
                <allow users="Admin" />
                <deny users="?" />
            </authorization>

            <trace enabled="true"
                    requestLimit="10"
                    pageOutput="true"
                    traceMode="SortByTime"
                    localOnly="true" />
            <sessionState mode="InProc"
                    stateConnectionString="tcpip=127.0.0.1:42424"
                    sqlConnectionString="data source=127.0.0.1;user
                    ↩id=sa;password="
                    cookieless="false" timeout="20" />
            <globalization requestEncoding="utf-8" responseEncoding="utf-8" />
        </system.web>
    </configuration>
```

The `web.config` file in Listing 7.1 demonstrates the use of two configuration sections: `appSettings` and `system.web`. This chapter looks at these sections in detail.

Configuration Files Are Extensive

Many more elements in other sections are out of the scope of this book. For more information on the sections in the configuration file, see the .NET General Framework Reference in the .NET SDK documentation at `ms-help://MS.VSCC/MS.MSDNVS/cpgenref/html/gngrfaspnetconfigurationsectionschema.htm`.

The *appSettings* Configuration Section

The `appSettings` configuration section defines custom application settings. This section is useful for static configuration information, such as database connection strings. This information can then be easily accessed by using the classes in the `System.Configurations` namespace (discussed in the section, "`System.Configuration` and `System.Web.Configuration` Namespaces").

The *system.web* Configuration Section

The system.web configuration section allows customization of nearly any aspect of the current application's environment at run-time. ASP.NET builds a collection of settings by using the hierarchy rules illustrated in Figure 7.2 and caches them for subsequent requests for the URL.

Figure 7.2 shows a logical grouping of the sections in the system.web section.

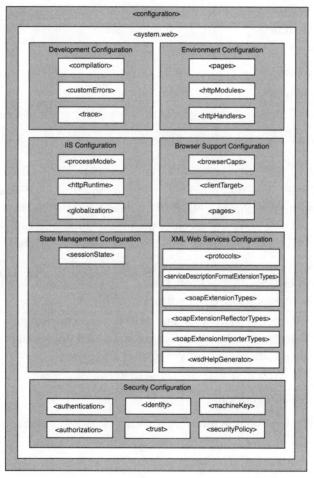

Figure 7.2   A logical grouping of the system.web subsections.

The following subsections in the `system.web` section are the focus of this chapter:

- `<authentication>`
- `<authorization>`
- `<browserCaps>`
- `<compilation>`
- `<customErrors>`
- `<globalization>`
- `<pages>`
- `<processModel>`
- `<sessionState>`
- `<trace>`

Let's take a look at each section in more detail.

authentication

The `authentication` section provides configuration settings for how authentication is performed in the ASP.NET environment.

The required `mode` attribute specifies the default authentication mode for the application. The `mode` attribute supports the following values:

- **Windows**—Windows authentication is used. Use this mode if you're using any form of IIS authentication: Basic, Digest, Integrated Windows Authentication (NTLM/Kerberos), or certificates.
- **Forms**—ASP.NET forms authentication is used. This authentication mode occurs when application-specified credentials are used rather than server-level authentication, such as Windows NT accounts.
- **Passport**—Microsoft Passport is used.
- **None**—No authentication support is provided.

The `authentication` section also supports the `forms` and `passport` child elements.

forms

The `forms` element specifies the configuration for an application using forms-based authentication. Table 7.2 lists the attributes of the `forms` element.

Table 7.2 **Attributes of the *forms* Element**

Attribute Name	Description
name	(Required). Specifies the HTTP cookie to use for authentication. The default value is `.ASPXAUTH`. You must configure the cookie name for each application on a server requiring a unique cookie in each application's `web.config` file.
loginUrl	Specifies the URL to redirect the user to if no valid authentication cookie is found. The default value is `default.aspx`.
protection	Specifies how the cookie is protected. The valid values are the following: • **None**—Encryption and validation are disabled. Use this option for sites with weak security requirements but that require cookies for personalization. • **Encryption**—The cookie is encrypted using Triple-DES or DES, but data validation is not performed on the cookie. • **Validation**—Validates that the cookie has not been altered. • **All** (default)—The cookies for this application are protected by both encryption and validation.
timeout	The number of minutes since the last request received, after which the authentication cookie expires. (The default is 30 minutes.)
path	The path used for cookies issued by the application. (The default is \.)

The `forms` element supports the `credentials` subelement that contains the user IDs and associated passwords, as well as how the passwords as encrypted. The `credentials` element supports a single attribute, `passwordFormat`, which describes the password encryption algorithm used. The `passwordFormat` attribute supports the following values:

- **Clear**—No encryption is performed on the password. The password is stored as clear text.

- **MD5**—The password has been encrypted using the MD5 hash algorithm. The user's password is encrypted and the hashed values are compared to determine authentication.

- **SHA1**—The password has been encrypted using the SHA1 hash algorithm. The user's password is encrypted and the result is compared to the stored password hash value.

The credentials element supports a child element, user, which stores the name of the user and the password using the encryption technique specified by the passwordFormat attribute. The user element supports two attributes:

- **name**—The user ID of an authorized user of the system.
- **password**—The password encrypted using the algorithm specified in the passwordFormat attribute.

passport

The passport element configures authentication by using Microsoft Passport. It supports a single attribute, redirectUrl. This attribute specifies the login page where the user is redirected if he or she hasn't signed on with Passport authentication. (The default redirect URL is default.aspx.)

authorization

The authorization element specifies client access to URL resources by explicitly allowing or denying user access to a specific resource. This is done through the allow and deny subelements. These elements share the same attributes and possible values:

- **users**—Comma separated list of users. A question mark (?) is used for anonymous users and an asterisk (*) denotes all users.
- **roles**—Comma separated list of roles explicitly allowed or denied access to the URL resource.
- **verbs**—Comma separated list of HTTP transmission methods that are allowed or denied access to the resource (GET, POST, HEAD, and DEBUG).

Recall that settings are inherited from the machine.config file unless they're overridden. The default value in the machine.config file is the following:

```
<allow users="*"/>
```

This implies that all users are authorized for a URL resource unless otherwise configured. The sample web.config file in Listing 7.2 shows how to use forms authentication that denies unauthenticated users to the URL resource.

Listing 7.2 Sample *web.config* File that Uses Forms Authentication and Denies Unauthenticated Users

```
<?xml version="1.0" encoding="utf-8" ?>
<configuration>
    <system.web>
        <authentication mode="Forms">
            <forms loginUrl="/sitelogin.aspx">
                    <credentialspasswordFormat="Clear">
                      <user name="deanna"password="wife"/>
                      <user name="lilbit"password="son"/>
                      <user name="teenybit"password="unborn"/>
                    </credentials>
            </forms>
        </authentication>
        <authorization>
            <allow users="Users" />
            <deny users="?" />
        </authorization>
    </system.web>
</configuration>
```

browserCaps

The browserCaps element controls the settings for the browser capabilities component. The browser capabilities component is similar to its predecessor, browscap.ini, which determines capabilities of browsers based on their User_Agent header value.

By defining new browser capabilities within this section, you can take advantage of newly released browsers and their capabilities. The browserCaps element supports three child elements: filter, result, and use.

filter

The filter element evaluates the case child element to evaluate the first rule to be applied.

The filter element supports the following optional attributes:

- **match**—A regular expression tested against the value resulting from the expression in the with attribute.

- **with**—A regular expression or string to be searched. If this attribute is not present, the value in the use element is used.

In case multiple rules need to be evaluated, the filter element also supports the child case element, which supports the match and with elements to provide conditional rule processing where only the first match is evaluated.

result

The `result` element specifies the `HttpCapabilitiesBase`, which is a derived class that holds the results from parsing this section. This element supports a single attribute called `Type`. `Type` represents the fully qualified name of the class responsible for parsing the section and providing the results.

use

The use element specifies the server variables that evaluates the `filter` and case statements in this section and the value assignments.

The use element supports two optional attributes:

- **var**—The IIS server variable that is parsed to evaluate browser compatibility settings. The default is `HTTP_USER_AGENT`.

- **as**—A name that can be referenced in the child `filter` and `case` elements, as well as in variable expressions and assignments.

A Browser Capabilities Example

Listing 7.3 shows an example of how to define settings in the `browserCap` section of the `web.config` file that parses the `HTTP_USER_AGENT` server variable to determine the various browsers' capabilities. Here's an example of the `HTTP_USER_AGENT` server variable string:

```
Mozilla/4.0 (compatible; MSIE 6.0; Windows NT 5.0; .NET CLR 1.0.2914)
```

Listing 7.3   **Sample *web.config* File Showing the *browserCaps* Section and Nested Filters**

```
<?xml version="1.0" encoding="UTF-8" ?>
<configuration>
    <system.web>
        <browserCaps>
            <result type="System.Web.HttpBrowserCapabilities" />
            <use var="HTTP_USER_AGENT" />
            browser=Unknown
            version=0.0
            majorversion=0
            minorversion=0
            frames=false
            tables=false
            cookies=false
            backgroundsounds=false
            vbscript=false
            javascript=false
            javaapplets=false
            activexcontrols=false
            win16=false
            win32=false
            beta=false
```

```
ak=false
sk=false
aol=false
crawler=false
cdf=false
gold=false
authenticodeupdate=false
tagwriter=System.Web.UI.Html32TextWriter
ecmascriptversion=0.0
msdomversion=0.0
w3cdomversion=0.0
platform=Unknown
clrVersion=0.0
css1=false
css2=false
xml=false

<filter>
    <case match="COM\+¦\.NET CLR (?'clrVersion'[0-9\.]*)">
        clrVersion=${clrVersion}
    </case>
</filter>

<filter>
    <case match="^Microsoft Pocket Internet Explorer/0.6">
        browser=PIE
        version=1.0
        majorversion=1
        minorversion=0
        tables=true
        backgroundsounds=true
        platform=WinCE
    </case>
    <case match="^Mozilla[^(]*\(compatible; MSIE
(?'version'(?'major'\d+)(?'minor'\.\d+)(?'letters'\w*))(?'extra'.*)">
        browser=IE
        version=${version}
        majorversion=${major}
        minorversion=${minor}

        <case match="[5-9]\." with="${version}">
            frames=true
            tables=true
            cookies=true
            backgroundsounds=true
            vbscript=true
            javascript=true
            javaapplets=true
            activexcontrols=true
            tagwriter=System.Web.UI.HtmlTextWriter
            ecmascriptversion=1.2
            msdomversion=${major}${minor}
```

continues

Listing 7.3   **Continued**

```
                                w3cdomversion=1.0
                                css1=true
                                css2=true
                                xml=true

                                <filter with="${letters}" match="^b">
                                beta=true
                                </filter>
                        </case>
                    </case>
                </filter>
            </browserCaps>
        </system.web>
    </configuration>
```

The example in Listing 7.3 begins by defining the default browser capabilities. By default, you can assume that no features are supported, so you can set numeric values to 0 and Boolean values to false. Evaluate the HTTP_USER_AGENT string and turn capabilities as you see that they are supported. The HTTP_USER_AGENT string value is then parsed and applied to any filters that are present.

The first filter (using the regular expression COM\+|\.NET CLR (?'clrVersion'[0-9\.]*)) parses the string to see if the client has the .NET Common Language Run-time (CLR) installed; if it does, it assigns the CLR version to the browser capability property, clrVersion.

The second filter uses the regular expression, ^Microsoft Pocket Internet Explorer/0.6, to see if the browser is a mobile device running Microsoft Pocket Internet Explorer. If a match occurs, the only supported attributes for the browser are tables and background sounds. Cookies, VBScript, JavaScript, JavaApplets, and other browser functions are not supported.

The third filter uses a long and complex regular expression:

```
^Mozilla[^(]*\(compatible; MSIE
(?'version'(?'major'\d+)(?'minor'\.\d+)(?'letters'\w*))(?'extra'.*)
```

In effect, this regular expression looks to see if the HTTP_USER_AGENT string contains the string Mozilla(compatible; MSIE. If the substring is found, the major version, minor version, and any trailing letters are stored in the major, minor, and letters variables, respectively. So, given this HTTP_USER_AGENT string,

```
Mozilla/4.0 (compatible; MSIE 6.0; Windows NT 5.0; .NET CLR 1.0.2914)
```

the variables would be populated as

- **version**—MSIE 6.0
- **major**—6

- **minor**—0
- **letters**—{empty}

Now that you understand how to define browser capabilities and why you'd
want to do this, look at how you can leverage the `browserCaps` section in the
ASP.NET and XML code.

Recall that the `result` element defined the type of object that is returned
from interrogating browser capabilities. The type of object must be derived
from the `HttpCapabilitiesBase` class, which is found in the
`System.Web.Configuration` namespace. This class provides the various properties needed to interrogate the browser's capabilities. The
`HttpBrowserCapabilities` class in the `System.Web` namespace derives from this
class, so you'll need to use this class to interrogate the class' properties.

Listing 7.4 demonstrates the use of the `HttpBrowserCapabilities` class to
detect the browser version and apply the appropriate XSLT stylesheet. Note
the use of the `Browser` property to determine if the browser is IE compatible.

Listing 7.4 **Sample Application to Determine Browser Capabilities**

```
<%@ Import Namespace="System.Web.Configuration"%>
<!DOCTYPE HTML PUBLIC "-//W3C//DTD HTML 4.0 Transitional//EN">
<HTML>
    <HEAD>
        <title>Browscap Demo</title>
        <script language="vb" runat="server">
            Private Sub Page_Load(ByVal sender As System.Object, ByVal e
            ➥As System.EventArgs) Handles MyBase.Load
                Dim browsCap As HttpBrowserCapabilities
                browsCap = Request.Browser
                Xml1.DocumentSource = "source.xml"
                If browsCap.Browser = "IE" Then
                    Xml1.TransformSource = "ie.xslt"
                Else
                    Xml1.TransformSource = "non_ie.xslt"
                End If
            End Sub
        </script>
    </HEAD>
    <body MS_POSITIONING="GridLayout">
        <form id="Form1" method="post" runat="server">
            <asp:Xml id="Xml1" runat="server"></asp:Xml></TD>
        </form>
    </body>
</HTML>
```

Besides the browser's name, other properties can be determined by using the
`HttpBrowserCapabilities` class. These properties are discussed in the section,
"`System.Configuration` and `System.Web.Configuration` Namespaces."

compilation

The compilation section configures how ASP.NET compiles the application. Table 7.3 shows the acceptable attributes of the compilation section.

Table 7.3 **Attributes of the *compilation* Section**

Attribute Name	Description
debug	Indicates if the debug version of the code needs to be compiled. The default is false.
defaultLanguage	Specifies the default language to use in dynamic compilation files. The default is vb.
explicit	Specifies the Visual Basic explicit compile option, requiring variable declaration when enabled. The default is true.
batch	Indicates if batching is supported.
batchTimeout	The time-out period, in seconds, for batch compilation.
maxBatchGeneratedFileSize	The maximum size (KB) of the generated source files per batched compile.
maxBatchFileSize	The maximum number of pages per batch compile.
numRecompilesBeforeApprestart	The number of dynamic recompiles before the application is restarted.
strict	Specifies the Visual Basic strict compile option, where only widening implicit conversions are allowed. (For example, long to integer is disallowed, but integer to long is okay.)
tempDirectory	Specifies the temporary directory used for compilation.

customErrors

The customErrors element supports custom error messages for an ASP.NET application. It specifies if custom error messages are enabled and custom redirect pages are associated with an HTTP status code, as well as if custom error messages are visible to local developers.

The required `mode` attribute specifies how custom error messages are handled and supports the following values:

- **On**—Custom error messages are enabled.
- **Off**—Custom error messages are disabled and detailed errors are displayed.
- **RemoteOnly**—Custom error messages are shown to remote clients only; the local host still receives detailed error messages.

The optional `defaultRedirect` attribute specifies the default URL to redirect to if an error occur.

The `error` subelement defines the error page that's associated with an HTTP status code. It supports the following attributes:

- **statusCode**—The HTTP status code that causes the display of the redirect page.
- **redirect**—The page to redirect to as a result of the HTTP status code.

globalization

The `globalization` element supports encoding attributes for globalization of the application. The `globalization` element supports the attributes shown in Table 7.4.

Table 7.4 **Attributes of the *globalization* Element**

Attribute Name	Description
culture	The default culture for processing incoming requests. Valid values are ISO 639 country codes and subcodes (en-US and en-GB).
uiCulture	The default culture for processing locale-dependent resource searched. Valid values are ISO 639 country codes and subcodes.
requestEncoding	Specifies the assumed encoding of the incoming request. If request encoding is not specified, the locale of the server is used. (The default is UTF-8.)
responseEncoding	Specifies the content encoding of responses. (The default is UTF-8.)
fileEncoding	Specifies the default encoding for `.aspx`, `.asmx`, and `.asax` file parsing.

identity

The `identity` element specifies if impersonation is used for the application. It supports the following required attributes:

- **`impersonate`**—Client impersonation is used.
- **`userName`**—The username to use if impersonation is used.
- **`password`**— The password to use if impersonation is used.

pages

The `pages` element controls page-specific configuration settings. Table 7.5 shows the optional attributes of the `pages` section.

Table 7.5   **Optional Attributes of the *pages* Element**

Attribute Name	Description
autoEventWireup	Indicates if page events are automatically enabled.
buffer	Specifies if response buffering is used.
enableSessionState	Indicates if session state handling is enabled. The following values are accepted: • `true`—Session state management is enabled. • `false`—Session state management is disabled. • `readOnly`—An application can read session variables but cannot modify them.
enableViewState	Indicates if the page and its controls should persist view state after page processing is complete.
pageBaseType	Specifies a code-behind class that `.aspx` pages inherit from by default.
smartNavigation	Indicates if IE 5.0 smart history navigation is enabled.
userControlBaseType	Specifies a code-behind class that user-control inherits from by default.

processModel

The `processModel` element represents a process model configuration for the IIS web server. The `processModel` element supports the following optional attributes, as shown in Table 7.6.

Table 7.6 **Optional Attributes of the *processModel* Element**

Attribute Name	Description
clientConnectedCheck	How long a request is left in the queue until IIS performs a check to see if the client is still connected.
comAuthenticationLevel	Indicates the level of DCOM security.
comImpersonationLevel	Specifies the authentication level for DCOM security.
cpuMask	Defines what CPUs on a multiprocessor server are eligible to run ASP.NET processes.
enable	Indicates if this process model is enabled.
idleTimeout	Specifies the period of inactivity after which ASP.NET ends the worker process.
logLevel	Specifies event types to be logged to the event log.
maxWorkerThreads	The maximum number of threads to be allocated on a per CPU basis.
maxIoThreads	The maximum number of threads to be allocated on a per CPU basis.
memoryLimit	The maximum percentage of total system memory before ASP.NET launches a new worker process and enqueues existing processes.
password	Specifies the worker process to run as the specified username with the specified password.
pingFrequency	The time interval at which ASP.NET pings the worker process to see if it is still running.
pingTimeout	The time after which a nonresponsive worker process is restarted.
requestLimit	The number of requests allowed before a new process is spawned to replace the current one.
requestQueueLimit	Specifies the number of requests allowed in the queue before ASP.NET begins returning 503—Server Too Busy errors to new requests. The default is 5,000.
serverErrorMessageFile	Specifies the file to use in place of the Server Unavailable message.
shutdownTimeout	The number of minutes the worker process is allowed to shut itself down.
timeout	Number of minutes before a new process is spawned to replace the current one.
userName	Specifies the worker process to run as the specified username with the specified password.
webGarden	Controls CPU affinity.

sessionState

The `sessionState` section controls how session management is handled in the application. The `sessionState` element requires a `mode` attribute that supports the following values:

- `Inproc`—Session state is stored locally in memory (in process).
- `StateServer`—Session state is stored on a remote server.
- `SQLServer`—Session state is stored on the specified SQL Server.
- `Off`—Session state is disabled.

The optional attributes shown in Table 7.7 are also supported by the `sessionState` element.

Table 7.7 **Optional Attributes of the *sessionState* Element**

Attribute Name	Description
cookieless	Indicates if sessions without cookies are used. If cookies are not used, an identifier is used in the querystring.
timeout	The number of minutes a session can be idle before it times out.
stateConnectionString	Specifies the address of the remote server when the mode is `StateServer`.
sqlConnectionString	Specifies the SQL connection string to use when the mode is `SQLServer`.

trace

The `trace` section configures the ASP.NET trace service. The optional attributes, shown in Table 7.8, are supported.

Table 7.8 **Optional Attributes of the *trace* Element**

Attribute Name	Description
enabled	Indicates if tracing is enabled for an application. This setting can be overridden at the page level.
localOnly	Specifies that only the local host can see `trace` information.
pageOutput	Specifies if `trace` information is included with each page output. If false, `trace` information is viewable only through the `trace` viewer `trace.axd`.

Attribute Name	Description
requestLimit	The number of trace requests to store on the server. If the limit is reached, `trace` is automatically disabled.
traceMode	Indicates how tracing information is to be sorted. Supports the following values:
	▪ SortByTime—Trace information is displayed on the order it is processed.
	▪ SortByCategory—Trace information is displayed alphabetically.

System. Configuration and *System. Web. Configuration* Namespaces

Because the configuration files are XML, you probably have already envisioned different ways to access the files and work with the settings in them. It just so happens that you don't have to start coding a custom configuration file reader yet because a rich API already exists for working with the configuration system files.

The .NET Framework supplies classes for working with configuration files in the System.Configuration and System.Web.Configuration namespaces. As you can infer from their names, the System.Web.Configuration namespace is designed to support the web.config file, and the System.Configuration namespace contains classes that support the configuration system as a whole. Take a look at the classes that are available in these namespaces and the methods they provide.

System. Configuration

The System.Configuration namespace contains the classes that are used to programmatically access .NET Framework configuration files. It also supplies objects for providing custom section handlers and handling errors in configuration files. The System.Configuration namespace provides the classes that are shown in Table 7.9.

Table 7.9 **Classes of the *System. Configuration* Namespace**

Class Name	Description
AppSettingsReader	Provides a single method for reading a value from the appSettings section.

continues

Table 7.9   **Continued**

Class Name	Description
ConfigurationException	Represents the exception thrown due to an error in a configuration file section. Provides methods for serializing the exception and determining the source configuration file and the source line number of the section node in the file.
ConfigurationSettings	Provides access to the configuration settings in a specified section.
DictionarySectionHandler	Reads key-value pair information for a section.
IgnoreSectionHandler	Provides a section handler for sections read and handled by systems other than System.Configuration.
NameValueSectionHandler	Defines a section handler for providing name-value section information.
SingleTagSectionHandler	Defines a section handler for providing access to attributes in a section.

In addition to the classes defined, the System.Configuration namespace also includes a single interface definition, IConfigurationSectionHandler. This interface is required for defined section handlers. The following classes support this interface:

- DictionarySectionHandler
- IgnoreSectionHandler
- NameValueSectionHandler
- SingleTagSectionHandler

Reading Custom Settings

The configuration file API provides a set of APIs for retrieving settings that are defined in the appSettings section, as well as for retrieving settings from custom sections. Two main methods of retrieving custom values from the appSettings section exist: using the AppSettingsReader class and using the ConfigurationSettings class.

The AppSettingsReader class supports one basic method, GetValue, which gets a single value based on its key from the configuration system.

The ConfigurationSettings class exposes two methods:

- **AppSettings**—Retrieves a custom setting from the appSettings section.
- **GetConfig**—Retrieves a custom setting from a custom section.

The code for retrieving application settings using the
`ConfigurationSettings.AppSettings` class is similar to the code that uses the
`AppSettingsReader` class. However, there's one main difference: If the key is not
found in the configuration file using the `ConfigurationSettings.AppSettings`
class, no error is thrown. This contrasts the `AppSettingsReader`, which throws
an error if the specified key doesn't exist.

Listing 7.5 demonstrates how each method can easily be used by using the
sample `web.config` file that was defined in Listing 7.1.

Listing 7.5   Reading Values from *appSettings*

```
<%@ Import Namespace="System.Configuration"%>
<!DOCTYPE HTML PUBLIC "-//W3C//DTD HTML 4.0 Transitional//EN">
<HTML>
    <HEAD>
        <title>Custom appSettings</title>
        <script language="vb" runat="server" >
            Private Sub Button_Click(ByVal sender As System.Object, ByVal
            ➥e As System.EventArgs)
                Try
                        If Me.optConfigurationSettings.Checked Then
                            lblResults.Text = "The startup table value is:
                            ➥" & ConfigurationSettings.AppSettings
                            ➥(txtKey.Text)
                        Else
                            Dim reader As AppSettingsReader = New
                            ➥AppSettingsReader()

                            lblResults.Text = "The value is: " &
                            ➥reader.GetValue(txtKey.Text, GetType(String))
                        End If
                Catch generalExcep As System.Exception
                    lblResults.Text = generalExcep.ToString()
                End Try
            End Sub
        </script>
    </HEAD>
    <body>
        <form runat="server">
            <asp:textbox
                    id="txtKey" style="LEFT: 150px; POSITION: absolute;
                    TOP: 14px" runat="server" />
            <asp:label
                    id="lblKey" style="LEFT: 10px; POSITION: absolute;
                    TOP: 15px" runat="server">
                    Enter the value key:</asp:label>
            <asp:radiobutton
                    id="optConfigurationSettings"
                    style="LEFT: 41px; POSITION: absolute; TOP: 63px"
```

continues

Listing 7.5   Reading Values from *appSettings*

```
                          runat="server" Width="186px"
                          Text="ConfigurationSettings.AppSettings"
                          Checked="True"
                          GroupName="method"></asp:radiobutton>
            <asp:radiobutton
                          id="optAppSettingsReader"
                          style="LEFT: 41px; POSITION: absolute; TOP: 89px"
                          runat="server" Width="186px"
                          Text="AppSettingsReader.GetValue"
                          GroupName="method"></asp:radiobutton>
            <asp:button
                          id="Button1"
                          style="LEFT: 55px; POSITION: absolute; TOP: 138px"
                          runat="server" Width="103px"
                          Text="Button" Height="29px" OnClick="Button_Click">
                          </asp:button>
            <asp:Label id="lblResults" runat="server"
                          Width="360px" Height="37px"
                          style="LEFT: 13px; POSITION: absolute; TOP: 203px">
            </asp:Label>
        </form>
    </body>
</HTML>
```

Run the code in Listing 7.5 and enter the value startupTable in the text box. Choose either access method and click the button: You will receive the value Customers. Next, enter a value of foo in the textbox and try this value with each method. The ConfigurationSettings.AppSettings option does not generate an error, while the AppSettingsReader method shows that an error occurred.

Creating Configuration Sections

Instead of defining many single tags, you can find that you need to persist a more complex structure. The web.config file also supports the creation of custom tags and groups by using the configSections element.

The configSections element defines the section names that appear in the configuration system. Open your machine.config file and look at the configSections section: Look familiar? This is where the sections discussed throughout this chapter are defined. Take a look at the components of the configSections section and its child elements.

The configSections element supports the following child elements:

- **section**—Defines a configuration section. This element is discussed in more detail in the following section.

- **sectionGroup**—Defines a grouping or namespace of configuration sections. Can contain other sectionGroup or section elements. Each sectionGroup element must have a name attribute that defines it.

- **remove**—Removes a section or group defined higher in the configuration hierarchy. For example, if a section was defined in machine.config, it can be suppressed at the application level by using the remove element in web.config. Has the same effect as clear, but suppresses only a single element.

- **clear**—Clears all predefined sections and groups. If the section or group was defined in machine.config, it can be suppressed at the application level by using the clear element. clear the same effect as remove, but it works on multiple elements at once.

section

The section defines a section within the configuration hierarchy. The section element supports the attributes listed in Table 7.10.

Table 7.10 **Attributes of the *section* Element**

Attribute Name	Use	Description
name	Required	Specifies the name for the configuration section.
type	Required	Specifies the type of section handler used to read the settings for the section.
allowDefinition	Optional	Specifies which configuration file the section can be used in. Possible values are - Everywhere (default)—Allows the section to be used in any configuration file. - MachineOnly—The section can only be used in the machine.config file. - MachineToApplication—The section can appear in machine.config or the application configuration file (web.config).
allowLocation	Optional	Determines if the section can be used within the location element (true by default).

In Table 7.10, one of the required attributes for the section element is the type attribute. type follows this form:

```
configuration section handler class, assembly [, Version, Culture,
PublicKeyToken]
```

The configuration section handler portion of the value is any class that implements the IConfigurationSectionHandler interface. As previously mentioned, the System.Configuration namespace provides a set of classes that support this interface (DictionarySectionHandler, IgnoreSectionHandler, NameValueSection Handler, or SingleTagSectionHandler).

The assembly is the managed assembly to which the handler belongs. For example, the DictionarySectionHandler class is part of the System assembly. This can be verified by going to the Object browser and viewing the hierarchy to which the class belongs.

If the Global Assembly Cache manages the assembly, you also need to include the Version, Culture, and PublicKeyToken values. You can find these settings by going to the .NET Configuration MMC snap-in, double-clicking the assembly name, and copying the values from the dialog box. You can also determine this information by going to the .NET command prompt and running the gacutil.exe utility.

Listing 7.6 demonstrates how to define a custom group and section.

Listing 7.6 **A Sample** *config.web* **File with Custom Sections Defined**

```
<?xml version="1.0" encoding="utf-8" ?>
<configuration>

    <configSections>
      <sectionGroup name="databases">
          <section name="SQLServer"
              type="System.Configuration.NameValueSectionHandler, System,
              ➥Version=1.0.3300.0, Culture=neutral, PublicKeyToken=
              ➥b77a5c561934e089" />
      </sectionGroup>
    </configSections>

    <databases>
        <SQLServer>
            <add key="Northwind"
                value="User ID=sa;Password=;Initial
                ➥Catalog=Northwind;Data Source=localhost" />
            <add key="Pubs"
                value="User ID=sa;Password=;Initial Catalog=pubs;Data
                ➥Source=localhost" />
        </SQLServer>
    </databases>
    <system.web>
        <compilation defaultLanguage="vb" debug="true" />
    </system.web>
</configuration>
```

Backup your `web.config` file and save the sample file from Listing 7.6 as `web.config` in your local project. Then add the web form that's found in Listing 7.7.

Listing 7.7 **Reading Custom Configuration Sections**

```
<%@Import Namespace="System.Collections.Specialized"%>
<!DOCTYPE HTML PUBLIC "-//W3C//DTD HTML 4.0 Transitional//EN">
<html>
  <head>
    <title>Custom Sections Demo</title>
     <script language="vb" runat="server">
          Private Sub Page_Load(ByVal sender As System.Object, ByVal e As
          ➥System.EventArgs)
                Dim config As NameValueCollection =
                ➥ConfigurationSettings.GetConfig("databases/SQLServer")
                Response.Write("The Northwind connection string: " &
                ➥config("Northwind") & "<br>")
                Response.Write("The Pubs connection string: " & config("Pubs")
                ➥& "<br>")
          End Sub
     </script>
  </head>
  <body>

  </body>
</html>
```

Again, make sure to check the value of the `PublicKeyToken` property in the `type` attribute to ensure that it matches the value found in your Global Assembly Cache.

System. Web. Configuration

The primary class in the `System.Web.Configuration` namespace is the `HttpBrowserCapabilities` class. As you saw in Listing 7.5, this class determines browser capabilities. Table 7.11 details the additional properties available for this class.

Table 7.11 **Properties of the *System. Web. HttpBrowserCapabilities* Class**

Property Name	Description
ActiveXControls	Indicates if the browser supports ActiveX controls.
AOL	Determines if the user is an AOL client.
BackgroundSounds	Indicates if the browser supports background sounds.
Beta	Indicates if the browser is a beta release.

continues

Table 7.11 **Continued**

Property Name	Description
Browser	Gets the browser string (if any) transmitted in the User-Agent header.
CDF	Indicates if the browser supports Channel Definition Format (CDF) for webcasting.
ClrVersion	Gets the CLR version number installed on the client.
Cookies	Indicates if the browser supports cookies.
Crawler	Indicates if the browser is a web crawler search engine.
EcmaScriptVersion	Gets the number of the ECMA script version supported by the client.
Frames	Indicates if the browser supports HTML frames.
Item	Gets the value of the specified browser capability.
JavaApplets	Indicates if the browser supports Java applets.
JavaScript	Indicates if the browser supports JavaScript.
MajorVersion	Gets the major version number of the browser.
MinorVersion	Gets the minor version number of the browser.
MSDomVersion	Gets the number of the Microsoft HTML DOM version supported by the client.
Platform	Gets the name of the client platform.
Tables	Indicates if the browser supports HTML tables.
Type	Gets the name and major version number of the browser.
VBScript	Indicates if the browser supports Visual Basic Scripting (VBScript).
Version	Gets the full version number for the browser.
W3CDomVersion	Gets the number of the World Wide Web Consortium (W3C) XML DOM version supported by the client.
Win16	Indicates if the client is a Win16-based computer.
Win32	Indicates if the client is a Win32-based computer.

Take a look at a practical use for storing custom configuration settings for the application and for creating custom sections. One way that this configuration system is useful is by allowing you to alter a site's look, feel, and content for different customers that use the same application.

For example, suppose that you have one base application being used by two companies simultaneously. Instead of coding the same application twice or hosting the same application in two separate locations, they can share the same set of servers. Additionally, you have the capability of moving their site content around your server without requiring extensive search and replace operations throughout the source code.

Here's a sample web.config file that uses the appSettings section to define application-wide settings (here, it is a shared database). You can also create a custom section, customers, that stores grouped information per customer. Listing 7.8 shows the necessary entries in the web.config file.

Listing 7.8   A Sample *web.config* File that Shows Custom Settings

```
<?xml version="1.0" encoding="utf-8" ?>
<configuration>
   <configSections>
      <sectionGroup name="customers">
              <section name="ALFKI"
                      type="System.Configuration.NameValueSectionHandler,
                      ➥System, Version=1.0.3300.0, Culture=neutral,
                      ➥PublicKeyToken=b77a5c561934e089"/>
              <section name="ANATR"
                      type="System.Configuration.NameValueSectionHandler,
                      ➥System, Version=1.0.3300.0, Culture=neutral,
                      ➥PublicKeyToken=b77a5c561934e089" />
       </sectionGroup>
   </configSections>
    <appSettings>
        <add key="connectionString" value="User ID=sa;Password=;Data
        ➥Source=localhost;" />
    </appSettings>

<customers>
     <ALFKI>
             <add key="Initial Catalog"
                    value="Northwind" />
             <add key="Styles"
                    value="futterkiste.css" />
             <add key="XSLT"
                    value="main.xslt" />
             <add key="Directory"
                    value="Alfreds" />
      </ALFKI>
      <ANATR>
             <add key="Initial Catalog"
                    value="Northwind" />
             <add key="Styles"
                    value="trujilio.css" />
             <add key="XSLT"
                    value="layout.xslt"      />
             <add key="Directory"
                    value="Trujilio" />
      </ANATR>
   </customers>
```

continues

Listing 7.8   **Continued**

```
    <system.web>
        <compilation defaultLanguage="vb" debug="true" />
    </system.web>
</configuration>
```

This `web.config` file contains the custom sections `ALFKI` and `ANATR` within the `customers` namespace. Within each one of these tags, the following keys are defined:

- **Initial Catalog**—Defines the initial catalog for the SQL Server database.
- **Styles**—Defines the cascading stylesheet filename this customer uses for site colorization.
- **XSLT**—Defines the XSLT stylesheet filename this customer uses for site layout.
- **Directory**—Defines the directory where the customer's files reside, relative to the current path.

You then create subdirectories for each customer that contains the files. These folder names must match the names specified in the `Directory` key. We also create the CSS and XSLT files specified for each customer. Listing 7.9 shows the CSS file used for customer ID `ALFKI` in the `Northwinds` database, and Listing 7.10 shows the XSLT file.

Listing 7.9   **Contents of** *alfreds/futterkiste.css*

```
body
{
    color: black;
    font-family: Verdana, Tahoma, Sans-Serif;
    border-collapse: collapse;
    background-color: white;
}

.contactHeader
{
    font-weight: bold;
    font-size: 10pt;
    color: blue;
    font-family: 'Comic Sans MS';
    border-collapse: collapse;
}
```

Listing 7.10   Contents of *alfreds/main.xslt*

```
<xsl:stylesheet version="1.0"
xmlns:xsl="http://www.w3.org/1999/XSL/Transform">
    <xsl:output method="html" encoding="ISO-8859-1"
    doctype-public="-//W3C//DTD HTML 4.0 Transitional//EN" />
    <xsl:param name="css" select="'styles.css'"/>
    <xsl:template match="/">
        <link rel="stylesheet" type="text/css">
            <xsl:attribute name="href">
                    <xsl:value-of select="$css"/>
                    </xsl:attribute>
        </link>
        <h1>
            <xsl:value-of select="Customers/CompanyName" />
        </h1>
        <xsl:apply-templates />
        <br/>
        <br/>
        <br/>
        <a href="choose.htm">Click here to choose again</a>
    </xsl:template>
    <xsl:template match="Customers">
        <table border="0">
            <tr>
                <th>Customer ID</th>
                <th>Contact Name</th>
                <th>Contact Title</th>
                <th>Phone</th>
            </tr>
            <tr>
                <td class="contactHeader">
                    <xsl:value-of select="CustomerID" />
                </td>
                <td class="contactHeader">
                    <xsl:value-of select="ContactName" />
                </td>
                <td class="contactHeader">
                    <xsl:value-of select="ContactTitle" />
                </td>
                <td class="contactHeader">
                    <xsl:value-of select="Phone" />
                </td>
            </tr>
        </table>
    </xsl:template>
</xsl:stylesheet>
```

In Listing 7.10, you use a parameter for the stylesheet to dynamically locate the stylesheet file. Remember: The context page is the page that performs the transformation, so the path will be relative to this page (this is revisited in a moment).

Listing 7.11 shows the CSS file that's used for `customerID ANATR`, while Listing 7.12 shows the XSLT file for the customer.

Listing 7.11   **Contents of** *trujilio/trujilio.css*

```
body
{
    font-size: smaller;
    color: black;
    font-family: Verdana, Tahoma, Sans-Serif;
    border-collapse: collapse;
    background-color: gray;
}

.contactHeader
{
    font-weight: bold;
    font-size: 10pt;
    color: white;
    font-family: 'Comic Sans MS' , Verdana, Tahoma, Sans-Serif;
    border-collapse: collapse;
}
```

Listing 7.12   **Contents of** *trujilio/layout.xslt*

```
<xsl:stylesheet version="1.0"
xmlns:xsl="http://www.w3.org/1999/XSL/Transform">
    <xsl:output method="html" encoding="ISO-8859-1" doctype-public="-
➥//W3C//DTD HTML 4.0 Transitional//EN" />
    <xsl:param name="css" select="'styles.css'"/>
    <xsl:template match="/">
        <link rel="stylesheet" type="text/css">
            <xsl:attribute name="href">
                <xsl:value-of select="$css"/>
                </xsl:attribute>
        </link>

        <h1>
            <xsl:value-of select="Customers/CompanyName" />
        </h1>
        <xsl:apply-templates />
        <br/>
        <br/>
        <br/>
        <a href="choose.htm">Click here to choose again</a>
    </xsl:template>
    <xsl:template match="Customers">
        <table border="0">
            <tr>
                <td class="contactHeader">Customer ID:</td>
                <td><xsl:value-of select="CustomerID" /></td>
```

```
                    </tr>
                    <tr>
                        <td class="contactHeader">Contact Name:</td>
                        <td><xsl:value-of select="ContactName" /></td>
                    </tr>
                    <tr>
                        <td class="contactHeader">Contact Title:</td>
                        <td><xsl:value-of select="ContactTitle" /></td>
                    </tr>
                    <tr>
                        <td class="contactHeader">Phone:</td>
                        <td><xsl:value-of select="CustomerID" /></td>
                    </tr>
                </table>
            </xsl:template>
        </xsl:stylesheet>
```

Now that you have seen the XSLT and CSS files associated with each customer, you can build a generic page that displays the contents for each customer based on their customer ID. Listing 7.13 lists the .aspx code that's used to generically display pages for different customers.

Listing 7.13   *WebForm2.aspx*: **A Generic Page Display Application that Leverages the** *web.config* **File**

```
<%@ Import Namespace="System.Collections.Specialized"%>
<%@ Import Namespace="System.Data"%>
<%@ Import Namespace="System.Data.SqlClient"%>
<%@ Import Namespace="System.Xml"%>
<%@ Import Namespace="System.Xml.Xsl"%>
<!DOCTYPE HTML PUBLIC "-//W3C//DTD HTML 4.0 Transitional//EN">
<HTML>
    <HEAD>
        <title>CoBranding Sample</title>
        <script language="vb" runat="server">
            Private Sub Page_Load(ByVal sender As System.Object, ByVal e
            ➥As System.EventArgs)
                Dim customerID As String
                customerID = Request.Form.Item("customer")

                Dim config As NameValueCollection =
                ➥ConfigurationSettings.GetConfig("customers/" +
                ➥customerID)

                Dim args As XsltArgumentList = New XsltArgumentList()
                args.AddParam("css", String.Empty,
                ➥config.Item("Directory") + "/" + config.Item("Styles"))
```

continues

Listing 7.13   **Continued**

```
                        Dim appReader As AppSettingsReader = New
                        ↝AppSettingsReader()
                        Dim connectionString As String =
                        ↝appReader.GetValue("connectionString",
                        ↝GetType(System.String))

                        connectionString += "Initial Catalog=" +
                        ↝config.Item("Initial Catalog")

                        Dim connection As SqlClient.SqlConnection = New
                        ↝SqlClient.SqlConnection()
                        connection.ConnectionString = connectionString

                        Dim command As SqlClient.SqlCommand = New
                        ↝SqlClient.SqlCommand()
                        connection.Open()
                        command.Connection = connection
                        command.CommandText = "SELECT * FROM Customers WHERE
                        ↝CustomerID='" + customerID + "' FOR XML AUTO,ELEMENTS"
                        command.CommandType = CommandType.Text

                        Dim reader As XmlTextReader
                        reader = command.ExecuteXmlReader()

                        Dim strXML As String

                        Do While reader.Read()
                              strXML += reader.ReadOuterXml()
                        Loop

                        reader.Close()
                        connection.Close()
                        connection.Dispose()
                        command.Dispose()

                        Xml1.TransformArgumentList = args
                        Xml1.DocumentContent = strXML
                        Xml1.TransformSource = config.Item("Directory") + "/" +
                        ↝config.Item("XSLT")
                  End Sub
            </script>
      </HEAD>
      <body MS_POSITIONING="GridLayout">
            <form id="Form1" method="post" runat="server">
                  <asp:xml id="Xml1" runat="server" />
            </form>
      </body>
</HTML>
```

Let's walk through the sample application. When the page is loaded, the `Page_Load` event is fired. You retrieve the customer ID value from the `customer` form element and use that value as the basis for retrieving the custom configuration section. You then read from that section to find the CSS file location and add that value as a parameter for the XSLT transformation. The database connection string is read from the `appSettings` section, and the customer's individual initial catalog is applied to the connection string.

XML is retrieved from SQL Server using the `FOR XML` clause (see Chapter 9, "SQL Server 2000 and XML," for more information on the `FOR XML` clause). The returned XML string is used as the source for the `<asp:xml>` control on the form, and the list of parameters is added to the control. Finally, you locate the XSLT file for the particular customer, and the page is displayed.

To test the application, build a simple driver HTML page to call the test application. Listing 7.14 shows the sample driver page.

Listing 7.14   *Choose.htm*: **A Simple Driver Page Used to Test the Application**

```
<!DOCTYPE HTML PUBLIC "-//W3C//DTD HTML 4.0 Transitional//EN">
<html>
<head>
<title>Choose Customer</title>
</head>
<body MS_POSITIONING="GridLayout">
    <form action="webform2.aspx" method="post">
        <select name="customer">
            <option value="ALFKI">Alfreds Futterkiste</option>
            <option value="ANATR">Ana Trujilio</option>
        </select>
        <br/>
        <input type="submit" value="Load CoBranding">
    </form>

</body>
    </html>
```

This sample driver file simply posts the customer ID to the page described in Listing 7.13. Compare the results in Figures 7.3 and 7.4 to see that the XSLT file is applied differently per customer ID.

Figure 7.3   Using customer ID ALFKI, you can apply the XSLT and CSS files to the
XML data for the customer based on the settings in the web.config file.

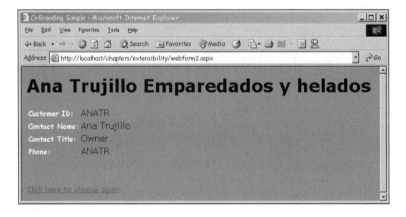

Figure 7.4   Viewing data for customer ID ANATR displays the same data, but using a
different stylesheet and CSS file as specified in the web.config file.

Accessing *web.config* Using *System.Xml*

As a web developer, you might have been called late in the evening (or
extremely early in the morning) to support a failing web application. At those
times, genius can strike: What if I had a tool that I could look at the configuration information?

Alas, the `web.config` file is not viewable by directly navigating to it. However, it isn't difficult to develop a quick application that displays the contents of the `web.config` file through the browser.

Because `web.config` is simply an XML file, it's easy to use the classes found in the `System.Xml` class to load the document and read or manipulate its contents. Listing 7.15 shows the code that is used to develop a simple viewer utility to view the contents of the `web.config` file.

Potential Security Risk

Exposing the `web.config` file externally could pose security risks. Be sure to thoroughly examine your security policy before implementing this example.

Listing 7.15   **Viewing *web.config* Using the *System.Xml* Classes**

```
Imports System.Xml
Public Class configviewer
    Inherits System.Web.UI.Page

#Region " Web Form Designer Generated Code "

    'This call is required by the Web Form Designer.
    <System.Diagnostics.DebuggerStepThrough()> Private Sub
    ➥InitializeComponent()

    End Sub

    Private Sub Page_Init(ByVal sender As System.Object, ByVal e As
    ➥System.EventArgs) Handles MyBase.Init
        'CODEGEN: This method call is required by the Web Form Designer
        'Do not modify it using the code editor.
        InitializeComponent()
    End Sub

#End Region

    Private Sub Page_Load(ByVal sender As System.Object, ByVal e As
    ➥System.EventArgs) Handles MyBase.Load

        Dim reader As XmlTextReader
        reader = New XmlTextReader(Server.MapPath("web.config"))

        Dim doc As XmlDocument = New XmlDocument()
        doc.Load(reader)

        Dim writer As XmlTextWriter = New
        ➥XmlTextWriter(Response.OutputStream, System.Text.Encoding.UTF8)
        doc.WriteTo(writer)
```

continues

Listing 7.15 **Continued**

```
        writer.Flush()

        writer.Close()
        reader.Close()
    End Sub

End Class
```

This example uses the `Server.MapPath` method to map the physical path to the `web.config` file found in the same directory as the `.aspx` source code file. The `XmlTextReader` class loads the contents into an `XmlDocument` object, which then writes its contents to an `XmlTextWriter` class. The `XmlTextWriter` writes directly to the `Response` stream, and the XML is displayed in the browser.

For more information on using `System.Xml`, see Chapter 6, "Exploring the `System.XML` Namespace."

Chapter Summary

This chapter focused on the configuration system in the .NET Framework and paid particular attention to the settings for ASP.NET `web.config` files. The various sections of the `system.web` configuration section were discussed, and you learned how to store and retrieve custom settings in the configuration files by using the framework classes.

Also discussed was the hierarchy of settings within the configuration files. Settings in an application configuration file generally take precedence over settings in a machine configuration file, with the exception of settings in the `appSettings` section.

Finally, you looked at some practical applications of the configuration system. For simple configuration information that's relatively static (such as directory structures and database connection strings), the configuration files are favored over other storage mechanisms (such as custom files or the database). Because the configuration system provides a structured and uniform means of accessing and configuring data, it also aids in maintenance tasks that would otherwise require significant documentation.

8

Database Access with ADO.NET and XML

O NE OF THE MOST COMPELLING ASPECTS of web development is the ability to dynamically create web pages based on data from a database. Most web applications involve retrieving, displaying, manipulating, and updating data contained in a database. Because you have likely done some ASP programming, this chapter assumes that you have some experience working with a database and that you are at least casually familiar with ADO. If you are not, read on anyway: Much of the material actually has little to do with database programming and has everything to do with XML. This chapter describes much of ADO.NET by comparing it to classic ADO, but works with XML under the covers and using ADO.NET for an abstraction of the underlying XML.

Database programming is a broad category, with concepts such as structured query language, transactions, and indexing and the performance of each easily comprises its own book. This chapter doesn't completely cover ADO.NET. There is so much material to cover in ADO.NET that it can (and likely will) be the subject of entire books on its own. Instead, this chapter focuses on the following:

- ADO's evolution to ADO.NET
- Some of the .NET classes used to work with data retrieved from a database

- Creating typed `DataSets`
- Binding a `DataSet` to a data-aware control

This chapter refers to classic ADO simply as ADO, and it refers to the ADO implementation in the .NET Framework SDK as ADO.NET.

So far, you have seen different ways of working with XML documents through the use of data islands in Internet Explorer, client-side DOM, MSXML Parser, `System.Xml` classes, and `<asp:>` server controls.

An Introduction to ADO.NET

Many developers are excited about the changes to ASP and the increased support for XML, but have reservations about learning a new data access strategy. It seems that every new version of Visual Basic brings another data-access strategy. The release of VB 3.0 brought forth Data Access Objects (DAO), Visual Basic 4.0 created a new release of DAO and introduced developers to Remote Data Objects (RDO), and Visual Basic 5.0 included a new release of RDO. Around the release of Visual Basic 5.0, Microsoft introduced its Universal Data Access strategy and its key component, ActiveX Data Objects (ADO). Since Visual Basic 5.0's release, developers have seen ADO versions 1.5, 2.0, 2.1, 2.5, 2.6, and recently released version 2.7. Besides ADO releases, developers have also seen interfaces for working with the Data Definition Language (DDL) in the form of ADO Extensions for DDL and Security (ADOX) for versions 2.1 and 2.5. With so many revisions (and updates to existing code), it's understandable that many developers dread yet another data access strategy.

Why so many changes? More importantly, what makes ADO.NET a compelling technology to migrate code to or adopt for new development? The simple answer is evolution: Because the way that developers work with data has changed over the years, so have the interfaces that developers use to gain access to the underlying data. DAO was built to facilitate forms-based development with local access databases where a constant, open connection to the database is feasible. RDO was built to provide fast access for forms-based applications to remote SQL server databases. ADO was built to provide access to disparate data sources with the added design goal of working in a disconnected server environment. As web development gained maturity, lessons learned have yielded a new programming model that best serves the disconnected environment.

ADO Versus ADO.NET

One of the reasons that ADO has been so successful is its ability to work with different data sources and still expose the same programming model without concern of the specific features of the given provider. ADO.NET builds on the past success of ADO as a tool for working with disparate data sources. The term ADO is an acronym for ActiveX Data Objects. ActiveX is the marketing name that replaced Object Linking and Embedding (OLE), and the name ActiveX was surpassed by Component Object Model (COM) and Distributed COM (DCOM). As you can recall from Chapter 1, .NET is not built on COM and does not rely on COM, so the term ADO.NET is actually somewhat of a misnomer. As you'll see throughout this chapter, using XML as the underlying support mechanism in ADO.NET is a key factor in the expansion of the ADO vision.

OLE DB and Managed Providers

OLE DB is a Microsoft specification that provides an open standard for accessing disparate data sources. It is a set of COM interfaces that provide universal access to data, whether the data source is a relational database, a mainframe, or an Excel spreadsheet. Microsoft eased the developer's burden by providing a set of wrapper classes and helper methods in the form of ADO. Using ADO, the developer is able to focus on the business problem rather than the low-lying APIs.

ADO is traditionally associated with databases. Its primary function is to provide database support with an easy-to-understand, common API that can be applied to a variety of databases, such as SQL Server, Access, Sybase, or Oracle. It can also be applied to other nonrelational data stores, such as ADSI or Excel. It achieves this by abstracting exposed APIs from the underlying implementation through the concept of providers. Data retrieved from a database is received in streams, and working with these streams is simplified through the use of the Recordset object. How the streams are read and updated depends on from where the data came. For example, working with data in an Excel spreadsheet is different than working with data in an Oracle database. The abstraction that ties the two data sources together is known as a *data provider*.

OLE DB Providers

The notion of universal data access was first introduced through the Open Database Connectivity (ODBC) specification, where different data providers could access ODBC data sources through a standard API. The problem with ODBC is that it brings all implementors down to the lowest-common

denominator by requiring a minimum level of support. Requiring all implementors to adhere to certain behaviors doesn't easily enable the individual data
providers to extend their support base.

ADO supports ODBC as a lowest-common denominator approach, but also
introduces the concept of using existing data providers and creating custom
data providers using OLE DB data providers. OLE DB data providers enable
the use of the common ADO programming model while accessing vendor-
specific implementations and features.

Figure 8.1 shows the additional ODBC layer that accesses data stores using
ODBC and ensures ODBC compliance, whereas Figure 8.2 shows that using a
specific provider for data access reduces the number of layers needed and
enables direct access to vendor-specific features.

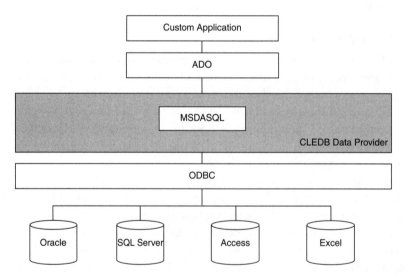

Figure 8.1 An additional ODBC layer is needed
to access data stores using ODBC connectivity.

A *data provider* owns its own data and exposes it in tabular form to your application[1]. Many different data providers are available that provide optimizations
for each type of data store. In ADO, the `Provider` property of the `Connection`
object or using the `Provider` argument in a connection string specified which
data provider was to be used. Examples of provider arguments for ADO are
SQLOLEDB (Microsoft OLE DB Provider for SQL server), MSDAORA
(Microsoft OLE DB Provider for Oracle), and MSDASQL (Microsoft OLE
DB Provider for ODBC).

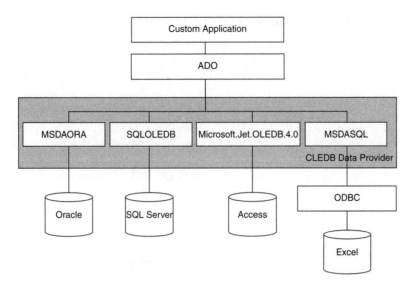

Figure 8.2   Direct provider access reduces overhead while allowing implementors to extend functionality.

Using an OLE DB provider directly instead of going through the additional ODBC layer provides several benefits, such as the following:

- Bypassing the additional ODBC layer increases performance by reducing the amount of executed code
- Accessing vendor-specific implementations increases flexibility and potentially performance
- Creating custom providers to custom data stores reduces duplication of effort and code continuity

Managed Providers in .NET

Data access in .NET builds on the concept of abstracting data sources, data providers, and the interfaces used to interact with the underlying data by introducing managed providers. A managed provider is used to connect to a database, execute commands, and retrieve results. It's designed to create a minimal layer between the data source and your code, which increases performance without sacrificing functionality[2]. Currently three choices of managed providers are available, which are listed in Table 8.1.

Table 8.1 **Managed Data Providers in ADO.NET**

Data Provider	Description
SQL Server .NET Data Provider	Recommended for middle-tier applications using Microsoft SQL server 7.0 or later or single-tier applications using MSDE or SQL Server 7.0 or later.
OLEDB .NET Data Provider	Recommended for middle-tier applications using Microsoft SQL server 6.5 or earlier, or any OLEDB provider that supports the OLEDB interfaces. Does not support OLEDB Provider for ODBC.
ODBC .NET Data Provider	Provides access to ODBC data sources. This provider is not part of the .NET Framework SDK, and is obtained through a separate download at `http://msdn.microsoft.com/downloads`.

The main difference between providers is depicted in Figure 8.3.

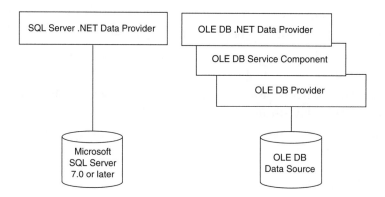

Figure 8.3   The difference between providers in the .NET Framework.

`ms-help://MS.VSCC/MS.MSDNVS/cpguide/html/cpconadonetproviders.htm`.

OLEDB providers are built using the COM programming model, so they rely on the IUnknown interface's AddRef and Release methods. Again, .NET is not built on COM, so a new programming model is needed for data interaction that takes advantage of managed code in .NET, which takes advantage of the Common Language Run-time's garbage collection mechanism. Therefore, a layer of abstraction is needed to take care of the COM reference counting necessary for OLEDB providers.

The four core types of objects used in a managed provider are `Connection`, `Command`, `DataReader`, and `DataAdapter`. Table 8.2 explains these object types.

Table 8.2   **Core Objects in ADO.NET Data Providers**

Type	SQL Server .NET Managed Provider Implementation	OLEDB .NET Managed Provider Implementation	Description
Connection	SqlConnection	OleDbConnection	Similar to the ADO Connection object. Provides connectivity to the specified data store.
Command	SqlCommand	OleDbCommand	Similar to the ADO Command object. Issues commands to the database.
DataReader	SqlDataReader	OleDbDataReader	Reads a forward-only stream of rows from the database.
DataAdapter	SqlDataAdapter	OleDbDataAdapter	Fills a DataSet and updates a database.

It is also worth mentioning that it is possible to create your own managed provider. No example is provided here, but refer you to the SDK documentation. Figure 8.4 depicts some of the interfaces used to create your own provider. This is helpful in understanding how the different implementations use interfaces to create their individual implementations while retaining a common API.

Because providers use common interfaces, it is possible to work with interfaces to create a provider-agnostic implementation, as shown in the following code:

```
IDbConnection connection =
Activator.CreateInstance("System.Data","System.Data.SqlClient.SqlConnection")
;
```

This chapter focuses on using the SQL server .NET Managed Provider classes.

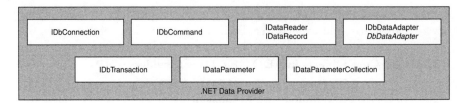

Figure 8.4   Interfaces to implement to create your provider.

Namespaces in .NET

Currently, five different namespaces comprise ADO.NET. The namespace that nearly all ADO.NET implementations utilize is System.Data. This namespace contains the base classes and interfaces used to retrieve data in a tabular format. Table 8.3 describes the different namespaces that comprise ADO.NET.

Table 8.3   **Namespaces in ADO.NET**

.NET Namespace	Description
System.Data	Contains the base classes and interfaces for ADO.NET, such as DataSet, DataView, and DataTable.
System.Data.Common	Contains classes shared by the .NET data providers, such as DataAdapter and DbDataAdapter.
System.Data.OLEDB	Contains classes that comprise the OLEDB .NET Data Provider, such as OleDbConnection and OleDbCommand.
System.Data.SqlClient	Contains classes that comprise the OLEDB .NET Data Provider, such as SqlConnection and SqlCommand.
System.Data.SqlTypes	Provides the classes for native data types within SQL server.

OLEDB .NET Data Provider

The SQL server .NET Data Provider is implemented through the classes in the System.Data.OLEDB namespace. As mentioned in Table 8.1, this provider is used for connectivity to OLEDB data sources other than SQL Server 7.0 or later. It contains classes similar to ADO. The code in Listing 8.1 is similar to code you have likely done in the past with ADO. For example, look at the following class that provides data connectivity to an OLEDB data source.

Listing 8.1   **The *OLEDBSample* Class**

```csharp
using System;
using System.Data.OleDb;
using System.Collections;

namespace ADOSamples
{
    /// <summary>
    /// Summary description for OLEDB.
    /// </summary>
    public class OLEDBSample
    {
        private string m_connectionString = "";

        public OLEDBSample(string connectionString)
        {
            m_connectionString = connectionString;
        }

        public void ExecuteCommand(string commandString,
        ⇥System.Data.CommandType commandType)
        {
            string errorString = string.Empty;

            OleDbCommand command = new OleDbCommand(commandString);
            command.CommandType = commandType;
            try
            {
                _execute(command);
            }
            catch(System.Exception e)
            {
                errorString = e.ToString();
            }
            finally
            {
                command.Dispose();
                if (errorString != string.Empty)
                    throw ( new System.Data.DataException(errorString));
            }
        }

        private void _execute(OleDbCommand command)
        {
            string errorString = string.Empty;

            OleDbConnection connection = null;
            try
            {
                connection = new OleDbConnection(m_connectionString);
```

continues

Listing 8.1 **Continued**

```
                    command.CommandTimeout = 30;
                    command.Connection = connection;
                    command.Connection.Open();
                    command.ExecuteNonQuery();
            }
            catch(System.Exception  e)
            {
                    errorString = e.ToString();
            }
            finally
            {
                    if(connection != null)
                    {
                            if (connection.State !=
System.Data.ConnectionState.Closed )
                            {
                                    connection.Close();
                            }
                            connection.Dispose();
                    }
                    if (errorString != string.Empty)
                            throw(new System.Data.DataException(errorString));
            }
        }
    }

    }
}
```

The preceding code provides the ability to issue a command to the database
that does not return a rowset. Common instances of commands that do not
return a rowset are INSERT, UPDATE, and DELETE statements. The method to concentrate on in this example is the private _execute() method of our
OLEDBSample class. This is where you actually create a database connection, set
the length of time the query should be able to execute in, and execute the
query. Notice that you explicitly close your database connection and call the
Dispose() method. The rationale for explicitly closing and disposing of database
resources is discussed in the section, "Disconnected Designs."

To call this method, simply pass a connection string to the class' constructor
and call the ExecuteCommand method, as shown here:

```
    Try
            Dim connectionString As String
            connectionString = "Provider=Microsoft.Jet.OLEDB.4.0;Data
            ⇒Source=C:\Program Files\Microsoft Office\Office\Samples\
            ⇒Northwind.mdb;Persist Security Info=False"
            Dim con As ADOSamples.OLEDBSample = New
```

```
ADOSamples.OLEDBSample(connectionString)
            con.ExecuteCommand("INSERT INTO CUSTOMERS(CustomerID,CompanyName)
            ►VALUES ('VBDNA','Kirk Allen Evans')", CommandType.Text)
        Catch errOops As System.Exception
            Console.WriteLine(errOops.ToString())
        End Try
```

This code inserts a new row in the Customers table in the Northwind sample
database for Access 2000 using the Jet OLEDB 4.0 data provider.

SQL Server .NET Data Provider

The SQL server .NET Data Provider is implemented through the classes in
the System.Data.SqlClient namespace, and is used for connectivity to SQL
Server 7.0 or later. Listing 8.2 shows that the code changes between the two
implementations in are minimal.

Listing 8.2   **The *SqlClientExample* Code**

```
Imports System
Imports System.Data.SqlClient
Imports System.Collections

Namespace ADOSamples

    Public Class SqlClientExample

        Private m_connectionString As String = ""

        Public Sub New(ByVal connectionString)
            m_connectionString = connectionString
        End Sub

        Public Sub ExecuteCommand(ByVal commandString As String, ByVal
        ►commandType As System.Data.CommandType)

            Dim errorString As String = String.Empty
            Dim command As SqlCommand = New SqlCommand(commandString)

            command.CommandType = commandType
            Try

                _execute(command)

            Catch e As System.Exception

                errorString = e.ToString()

            Finally
```

continues

Listing 8.2 **Continued**

```
            command.Dispose()
            If errorString <> String.Empty Then
                Throw (New System.Data.DataException(errorString))
            End If
        End Try
    End Sub

    Private Sub _execute(ByVal command As SqlCommand)

        Dim errorString As String = String.Empty
        Dim connection As SqlConnection = Nothing

        Try

            connection = New SqlConnection(m_connectionString)
            command.CommandTimeout = 30
            command.Connection = connection
            command.Connection.Open()
            command.ExecuteNonQuery()

        Catch e As System.Exception

            errorString = e.ToString()

        Finally

            If Not connection Is Nothing Then

                If connection.State <> System.Data.ConnectionState.Closed
                ➥Then

                    connection.Close()
                End If

                connection.Dispose()
            End If
            If errorString <> String.Empty Then
                Throw (New System.Data.DataException(errorString))
            End If
        End Try
    End Sub
End Class
End Namespace
```

C# was used in the previous OLEDB example and Visual Basic in this
`SqlClient` example, but if you look at the two versions, they are nearly identical. The only real change to the code is to search for `OleDb` and replace it with
`SqlClient`.

The code to call the class does change slightly, however. The difference is in the connection string used:

```
<%@Import Namespace="ADOSamples"%>

<script language="vb" runat="server">
    Private Sub Page_Load(ByVal sender As System.Object, ByVal e As
    ➥System.EventArgs) Handles MyBase.Load
        Try
            Dim connectionString As String
            connectionString = "Integrated Security=SSPI;Persist Security
            ➥Info=False;Initial Catalog=Northwind;Data Source=at1lt-3165-03"
            Dim con As ADOSamples.SqlClientExample = New
            ➥ADOSamples.SqlClientExample(connectionString)
            con.ExecuteCommand("INSERT INTO
            ➥CUSTOMERS(CustomerID,CompanyName) VALUES ('VBDNA','Kirk
            ➥Allen Evans')", CommandType.Text)
            Response.Write ("Successfully inserted the record into the
            ➥database!")
        Catch errOops As System.Exception
            Response.Write (errOops.ToString())
        End Try
    End Sub
</script>
```

Notice the lack of a `Provider` argument in the connection string. This argument isn't necessary when working with the class in the `SqlClient` namespace because the provider is implied through the use of the SQL-server specific implementation classes.

Now that you have seen how to make a basic connection and issue a simple text command, it's time to look at how to use parameterized queries with ADO.NET.

Parameterized Queries and Stored Procedures in .NET

Just as in ADO, you can specify the type of command being issued through the `Command` object's `CommandType` property. The `CommandType` in ADO.NET accepts a member of the `CommandType` enumeration. Table 8.4 lists the members of the `CommandType` enumeration.

Table 8.4 **Members of the *CommandType* Enumeration**

Member Name	Description
Text	Executes a text command. An example is SELECT * FROM AUTHORS. This is the default setting.
StoredProcedure	Executes a stored procedure. This is used for SQL Server, Sybase, and Oracle stored procedures, as well as saved queries in Access.

continues

Table 8.4 **Continued**

Member Name	Description
TableDirect	Accesses a table directly. When an Execute method is called, all columns and rows of the table are returned. Not currently supported. To work with tables directly, see the DataAdapter class and the SourceTable argument description.

In the previous examples, you simply issued a non-parameterized text command. In the May 2000 issue of *Visual Basic Programmer's Journal*, I wrote an article called "Minimize Cache Thrash" (also available in MSDN) that explains why the use of stored procedures and parameterized queries can be essential for a database-intensive application.

Using parameters in ADO.NET is just as simple as it was in ADO; in fact, it looks similar, with a few exceptions.

The syntax for representing parameters in the SQL command text has changed since ADO classic. I have seen posts in newsgroups where users wanted to know how to reference a parameter by its name within the SQL command text. Until ADO.NET, parameters were represented as question marks (?). In ADO.NET, parameters are represented by using their parameter name preceded by an at (@) symbol.

The API for ADO.NET is familiar, but also has some slight variations. You can either instantiate an ADO.NET Parameter object, or you can use the CreateParameter method of the Command object to return an unpopulated Parameter object. After the object is created and available, use Command.Parameters.Add to add the parameter.

For practice, create a stored procedure in SQL Server. Open Query Analyzer (located in the SQL Server programs group on your Start menu, if the client tools for SQL Server are installed) and connect to the Northwind database. Enter the instructions in Listing 8.3 into the code pane and press the F5 button.

Listing 8.3 **Creating a Procedure Called *AddCustomer* in the *Northwinds* Database**

```
create procedure AddCustomer(@CustomerID char(5), @CompanyName varchar(40))
as

insert into Customers(CustomerID, CompanyName) VALUES
➥(@CustomerID,@CompanyName)
if (@@ERROR <> 0) goto errorhandler
```

```
cleanup:
     return(0)
errorhandler:
     return(1)
```

These steps created a stored procedure in the Northwind database called AddCustomer. To execute this stored procedure, you need two input parameters. Optionally, you can also use a return value parameter to inspect the return value, as shown in Listing 8.4.

Listing 8.4 **Familiar Code for Database Access**

```vb
<%@Page Language="vb" Debug="true"%>
<%@Import Namespace="System.Data.SqlClient"%>
<%@Import Namespace="System.Data"%>
<%@Import Namespace="System.Data.Common"%>
<!DOCTYPE HTML PUBLIC "-//W3C//DTD HTML 4.0 Transitional//EN">
<HTML>
    <HEAD>
        <title>WebForm3</title>
        <script language="vb" runat="server" >

    Private Sub Button1_Click(ByVal sender As System.Object, ByVal e As
    ➥System.EventArgs)
        Dim customerID As String = String.Empty
        Dim companyName As String = String.Empty
        'Retrieve the Customer ID from the form element "CustomerID"
        customerID = TextBox1.Text
        companyName = TextBox2.Text

        Dim command As SqlCommand = New SqlCommand("AddCustomer")
        command.CommandType = System.Data.CommandType.StoredProcedure
        Dim tempParam As SqlParameter

        'Create the input parameter for the CustomerID parameter
        tempParam = New SqlParameter("@CustomerID", SqlDbType.Char)
        tempParam.Direction = ParameterDirection.Input
        tempParam.Size = customerID.Length
        tempParam.Value = customerID
        'Add the parameter directly to the collection
        command.Parameters.Add(tempParam)

        'Create the parameter using the Add method and return the parameter
        tempParam = command.Parameters.Add("@CompanyName", SqlDbType.VarChar,
        ➥companyName.Length)
        'Access the parameter object directly
        tempParam.Direction = ParameterDirection.Input
        tempParam.Value = companyName
```

continues

Listing 8.4 **Continued**

```
                'Create the input parameter for the return value
                tempParam = command.Parameters.Add(New SqlParameter("@RetVal",
                ↩SqlDbType.Int))
                tempParam.Direction = ParameterDirection.ReturnValue

                Dim connection As SqlConnection = New SqlConnection("Initial
                ↩Catalog=Northwind;User ID=sa;Password=;Data Source=at1lt-3165-03")
                command.Connection = connection
                command.Connection.Open()
                command.ExecuteNonQuery()

                Dim retVal As Int32 = 0
                retVal = CType(command.Parameters("@RetVal").Value, Int32)
                If (0 <> retVal) Then
                    Response.Write("The insert failed")
                Else
                    Response.Write("The insert succeeded.")
                End If
                command.Dispose()
                connection.Close()
                connection.Dispose()

        End Sub
            </script>

    </HEAD>
    <body>
            <form id="Form1" method="post" runat="server">
                <asp:Label id="Label1" runat="server" Width="152px"
                ↩Height="16px">CustomerID:</asp:Label>
                <asp:TextBox id="TextBox1" runat="server" Width="200px"
                ↩Height="21px"></asp:TextBox>
                <p/>
                    <asp:Label id="Label2" runat="server" Width="152px"
                    ↩Height="16px">Company Name:</asp:Label>
                    <asp:TextBox id="TextBox2" runat="server"
                    ↩Width="200px"></asp:TextBox>
                <p/>
                    <asp:Button OnClick="Button1_Click" id="Button1"
                    ↩runat="server" Text="Button"></asp:Button>
            </form>
            </P>
        </body>
</HTML>
```

Another option to using stored procedures is using parameters in inline SQL text:

```
private void Page_Load(object sender, System.EventArgs e)
{
    String customerID = string.Empty;
```

```
String companyName = string.Empty;
//Retrieve the Customer ID from the form element "CustomerID"
customerID = Request.Form.Get("CustomerID");
companyName = Request.Form.Get("CompanyName");

SqlCommand command = new SqlCommand("AddCustomer");

command.CommandText="INSERT INTO CUSTOMERS (CustomerID,CompanyName)
➥VALUES (@CustomerID,@CompanyName)";
command.CommandType = System.Data.CommandType.Text;
SqlParameter tempParam = null;

//Create the input parameter for the CustomerID parameter
tempParam = new SqlParameter ("@CustomerID", SqlDbType.Char);
tempParam.Direction = ParameterDirection.Input;
tempParam.Size = customerID.Length;
tempParam.Value = customerID;
//Add the parameter directly to the collection
command.Parameters.Add(tempParam);

//Create the parameter using the Add method and return the parameter
tempParam = command.Parameters.Add
➥("@CompanyName",SqlDbType.VarChar,companyName.Length);
//Access the parameter object directly
tempParam.Direction = ParameterDirection.Input;
tempParam.Value = companyName;

SqlConnection connection = new SqlConnection("Integrated
➥Security=SSPI;Persist Security Info=False;Initial
➥Catalog=Northwind;Data Source=at1lt-3165-03");
command.Connection = connection;
command.Connection.Open();
command.ExecuteNonQuery();

command.Dispose();
connection.Close();
connection.Dispose();
}
```

You are now able to use named parameters instead of using question marks for parameter placeholders. These examples are similar to ADO coding, with the notable exception of the new ExecuteNonQuery method and using constructors for objects.

Now that you have seen how to execute stored procedures and can use parameterized queries, you're ready to work with the real "meat" of ADO.NET—returning data.

Disconnected Designs

One of the key differences between ADO and ADO.NET development is the concept of *disconnected development*. Disconnected development has everything to do with how you retrieve data.

The term *disconnected* refers to the fact that you do not maintain an open connection with the database while the data is in use. It is essentially a snapshot of the data. Using disconnected designs in web applications can be crucial to the success or failure of an application because maintaining open connections to a database can be expensive: More open connections means more memory that needs to be managed both by SQL Server and the Internet Information Services (IIS) server. By disconnecting the data, you can relinquish the database connection back to a pool of available connections where they might be reused again, which increases performance on high-volume websites.

ADO introduced developers to disconnected development by enabling them to set the `ActiveConnection` property of a `Recordset` object to `Nothing`. By setting the connection to `Nothing`, the underlying data is retained while the connection can be returned to the connection pool. The problem is that properly disconnecting a recordset requires using a client-side, static cursor with batch optimistic locking (say that five times fast!) The default behavior of ADO was not to use client-side static cursors. Instead, ADO provides read-only server-side cursors as a default. Failure to set the properties correctly yields a recordset that did not disconnect when it was instructed to do so. This was a common bug in many web applications, and its results could be catastrophic to an otherwise healthy web application.

Many ADO web developers have been developing with Visual Basic for years, and learned to access databases by using DAO. The DAO development model urged the developer to update resultsets directly and call the `Update` method to commit the underlying changes. Developers that were familiar with this model applied the same design patterns in ASP applications by using ADO. This action is an expensive operation in server-side applications because it keeps the connection to the database open for a longer period of time than necessary. Again, the result was applications that were not as scalable as they could be.

You've no doubt heard the term *stateless* repeatedly with respect to web-application development. The concept of disconnecting goes hand-in-hand with stateless design. The goal is to create and connect to resources as late as possible, perform a small unit of work, and release resources as soon as possible. By using disconnected designs, you can increase server scalability as the number of connections open at any given time is reduced.

Relational Versus Hierarchical Models

The release of ADO 2.5 introduced limited XML support for ADO, but it does not use XML natively. It supports exposing hierarchical data through the Data Shaping Service for OLEDB, persisting relational data as XML through the Recordset object's Save method, and accessing XML through the Stream object. None of these features were available in ADO until version 2.5, which shows how development with ADO has evolved since its inception.

It is possible to create XML from an ADO Recordset, but the underlying XML is riddled with namespaces and an inline XDR Schema that proves difficult for novices. As previously mentioned, XML support was an afterthought, so ADO did not use XML natively—the native data format for ADO was Advanced Data Tablegram (ADTG).

ADO was not particularly good at delivering hierarchical data. The MSDataShape provider was a useful tool, but developing useful applications using it proved difficult in the middle-tier. Providing parameterized queries as the basis for the shaped data meant that the underlying data could not be persisted by using XML. Restricting the amount of data returned required elaborate WHERE clauses and RELATE operations in the shaped statement.

ADO is good at working with Data Manipulation Language (DML), such as INSERT or DELETE statements, but has limited support for providing information regarding its underlying schema. For example, determining which columns comprise a composite primary key is not possible using ADO without querying the database's system tables for the information. ADOX was introduced to provide this type of information, but required yet another library reference to maintain.

As you'll see, ADO.NET addresses these limitations by using XML as its underlying store. XML is returned natively from the DataSet, DataRelations define relations between DataTables contained in a DataSet, and XML Schemas define the underlying structures. Other important benefits of using XML are also notable: XML can be passed through firewalls, so security risks of passing ADO Recordsets remotely no longer exist. XML is also inherently disconnected and persistent, which gives increased asynchronous support for your applications.

The Key Components of ADO.NET

Now that you're familiar with the Connection and Command objects in ADO.NET, now it's time to address the second pair of core component types: DataReader and DataAdapter.

The *DataReader* Class

The DataReader class is implemented like the other reader classes found in .NET. It provides forward-only, read-only access to an underlying stream of data. The DataReader can increase scalability in your applications because only one row of data at a time is ever in memory[3].

Chapter 7, "ASP.NET Extensibility with XML," introduced you to XmlTextReader and XmlNodeReader classes. Recall that the primary design pattern for reading data was to use a While loop:

```
While(reader.Read())
{
    //Inspect the reader's exposed properties here
}
```

DataReader classes are used in the same manner. This example selects everything from the Northwinds database and outputs it as an HTML table. Create a new Visual Basic web form called WebForm1. Open the code view for webform1.aspx.vb and paste the code in Listing 8.5.

Listing 8.5   **A Sample Application Using the *SqlDataReader***

```
Imports System
Imports System.Data.SqlClient
Imports System.Collections

Public Class WebForm1
  Inherits System.Web.UI.Page

#Region " Web Form Designer Generated Code "

  'This call is required by the Web Form Designer.
  <System.Diagnostics.DebuggerStepThrough()> Private Sub
  ➥InitializeComponent()

  End Sub

  Private Sub Page_Init(ByVal sender As System.Object, ByVal e As
  ➥System.EventArgs) Handles MyBase.Init
    'CODEGEN: This method call is required by the Web Form Designer
    'Do not modify it using the code editor.
    InitializeComponent()
  End Sub

#End Region

  Private Sub Page_Load(ByVal sender As System.Object, ByVal e As
  ➥System.EventArgs) Handles MyBase.Load
    DumpTable("SELECT * FROM Customers", "User ID=sa;password=;Persist
    ➥Security Info=False;Initial Catalog=Northwind;Data Source=p450")
```

```
    End Sub

    Public Sub DumpTable(ByVal query As String, ByVal connectionString As
String)
        Dim connection As SqlConnection = New SqlConnection(connectionString)
        Dim command As SqlCommand = New SqlCommand(query)
        command.CommandType = CommandType.Text
        command.Connection = connection
        command.Connection.Open()
        Dim reader As SqlDataReader = command.ExecuteReader
        ⇒(CommandBehavior.CloseConnection)
        Response.Write("<table border=""1"" cellpadding=""1""
        ⇒cellspacing=""1"">")
        If Not reader.IsClosed() Then
          While (reader.Read())
            'We now have an entire row to interrogate
            Dim loopVar As Integer
            Response.Write("<tr>")
            For loopVar = 0 To reader.FieldCount - 1
              If reader.IsDBNull(loopVar) Then
                Response.Write("<td></td>")
              Else
                Response.Write("<td>" & reader.GetValue(loopVar) & "</td>")
              End If
            Next loopVar
            Response.Write("</tr>")
          End While
        End If
        Response.Write("</table>")
        reader.Close()
        command.Dispose()
        connection.Close()
        connection.Dispose()
    End Sub

End Class
```

Inside the `While` loop, you have access to a variety of properties and methods. You can also access individual columns instead of relying on their ordinal position:

```
        While (reader.Read())
            Response.Write("<tr>")
            Response.Write("<td>" & reader("CustomerID").ToString() &
            ⇒"</td>")
            Response.Write("</tr>")
        End While
```

Handling Database Nulls

A key difference between working with ASP and ASP.NET is how database nulls are handled. Using `Response.Write()` to output a null value was not a problem in ASP. In ASP.NET, nulls are not allowed to be output. You can deal with nulls in several ways: One way is to explicitly test for a null by using the `IsDbNull` method of the `Reader`.

```
Dim idx As Integer = reader.GetOrdinal("CompanyName")
While (reader.Read())
    Response.Write("<tr>")
    If reader.IsDBNull(idx) Then
        Response.Write("<td>IsDbNull</td>")
    Else
        Response.Write("<td>" & reader("CompanyName").ToString() &
        "</td>")
    End If
    Response.Write("</tr>")
End While
```

Another method for handling database null values is to use the `GetString` method of the `Reader`. It automatically converts the null value to an empty string:

```
Dim idx As Integer = reader.GetOrdinal("CompanyName")
While (reader.Read())
    Response.Write("<tr>")
    Response.Write("<td>" & reader.GetString(idx) & "</td>")
    Response.Write("</tr>")
End While
```

The `DataReader` class can generate XML on the fly. In this example, an HTML table was generated but this could easily be adapted to create XML data. As you see in the next section, there are better ways to get at the underlying XML data.

The *DataSet* Class

By now, you're probably wondering when we will be getting to the XML material. Well, we're almost there. We're at the right class level, but we still have a bit to go to show how to read, write, and update XML using the `DataSet` class.

The `DataSet` class is one of the key parts of XML integration in ADO.NET. In fact, it is a key feature of ADO.NET as a whole. This section shows you that it is one of several objects that make working with XML and ADO.NET so easy.

Figure 8.5 shows the hierarchy of classes in the `DataSet` class. For brevity, the `ExtendedParameters` collections of the `DataTable` and `DataColumn` classes were left out. As you can see, the class hierarchy is complex. But after you work with the `DataSet`, you'll realize that it's intuitive.

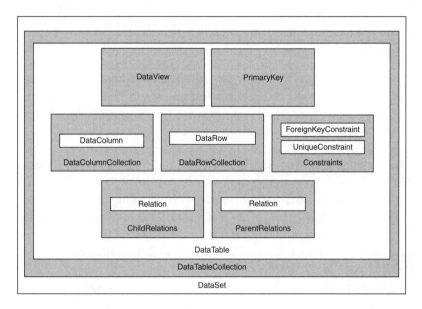

Figure 8.5   The hierarchy of classes within the `DataSet` class.

So, what are you looking at? It looks like an object representation of a database. In fact, that is the best analogy for the `DataSet` class: an in-memory database. The `DataSet` class is central to ADO.NET's support of disconnected and distributed development. Unlike the `ADODB.Recordset` class that holds a single tabular representation of data, the `DataSet` class holds multiple tables from potentially different sources in memory. It is a container for a collection of `DataTable` classes that can manage the relations between the tables it contains.

Look at this example of filling a `DataSet` with data:

```
Public Function GetDS(ByVal connectionString As String) As DataSet

    Dim connection As SqlConnection = New SqlConnection(connectionString)
    Dim command As SqlCommand = New SqlCommand()
    command.CommandText = "SELECT CustomerID, CompanyName FROM Customers"
    command.CommandType = CommandType.Text
    command.Connection = connection

    Dim adapter As SqlDataAdapter = New SqlDataAdapter()
    Dim ds As DataSet = New DataSet()
```

```
adapter.SelectCommand = command
connection.Open()
adapter.Fill(ds, "Customers")

connection.Close()
connection.Dispose()
adapter.Dispose()

Return (ds)
End Function
```

This example starts out by using a `Connection` and a `Command` object, which is similar to previous examples. Then an `Adapter` object is used to fill a `DataTable`, called `Customers`, in the `DataSet` class. Because the `DataSet` has already been filled with data, it is safe to close the open connection to the database.

A `DataSet` contains at least one `DataTable`. When the `Adapter.Fill()` method is called, you are specifying which `DataTable` inside the `DataSet` to fill with data.

This is an obvious source of confusion for many ADO programmers. You aren't really filling the `DataSet` with data—you are filling a table *contained* in the `DataSet` with data. Furthermore, the name of the `DataTable`, `Customers`, has nothing to do with the source of the data itself. This is just a name that the programmer uses to keep track of the different tables contained.

Rewrite your `GetDS` function in the previous example to help clarify this point. This time, fill two tables in the `DataSet` and name them to show that the name of the underlying table in the `DataSet` has no bearing on the name of the database table—it is simply a naming convenience:

```
Public Function GetDS(ByVal connectionString As String) As DataSet

    Dim connection As SqlConnection = New SqlConnection(connectionString)
    Dim command As SqlCommand
    Dim customerAdapter As SqlDataAdapter
    Dim orderAdapter As SqlDataAdapter
    Dim ds As DataSet = New DataSet()

    'Create the Command object to select from the Customers database
    'table and append it to the adapter.
    command = New SqlCommand()
    With command
        .CommandText = "SELECT CustomerID, CompanyName FROM Customers"
        .CommandType = CommandType.Text
        .Connection = connection
    End With
    customerAdapter = New SqlDataAdapter()
    customerAdapter.SelectCommand = command

    'Create the Command object to select from the Orders database
    'table and append it to the adapter.
    command = New SqlCommand()
    With command
```

```
                .CommandText = "Orders"
                .CommandType = CommandType.TableDirect
                .Connection = connection
            End With
            orderAdapter = New SqlDataAdapter()
            orderAdapter.SelectCommand = command

            connection.Open()
            customerAdapter.Fill(ds, "NorthwindCustomers")
            orderAdapter.Fill(ds, "NorthwindOrders")
            connection.Close()

            connection.Dispose()
            customerAdapter.Dispose()
            orderAdapter.Dispose()

            Return (ds)
        End Function
```

This revision of the `GetDS` uses two different `Adapters`; each has its own associated `SelectCommand`.

DataSet *Support for XML*

Now for the XML material. Once filled with data, you can use the methods of the `DataSet` to read, expose, and manipulate XML data. Several key methods exposed by the `DataSet` class facilitate working with XML data. Table 8.5 lists the methods that facilitate working with XML data in the `DataSet` class.

Table 8.5 **XML Support Methods of the *DataSet* Class**

Method Name	Description
GetXml	Returns the XML representation of the data stored in the `DataSet`.
GetXmlSchema	Returns the XSD Schema for the XML representation of the data stored in the `DataSet`.
InferXmlSchema	Infers the XML Schema from the XML data into the `DataSet`.
ReadXml	Reads XML data and schema into the `DataSet`.
ReadXmlSchema	Reads the XML Schema into the `DataSet`.
WriteXml	Writes the XML Schema and data from the `DataSet`.
WriteXmlSchema	Writes an XML Schema representation of the structure of the `DataSet`.

So far, you have only retrieved tabular data from a database. Using the XML support methods of the `DataSet` makes reading and writing XML simple.

Start by using your GetDS example method to populate a DataSet with data
from a database and then output the contents as XML.

Create a new C# web application project and create a C# web form called
WebForm1.aspx. Paste the code found in Listing 8.6 into the WebForm1.aspx page.

Listing 8.6   **Extracting XML from the *DataSet***

```
<%@ Page language="c#" Debug="true"%>
<%@ Import Namespace="System.Data"%>
<%@ Import Namespace="System.Data.SqlClient"%>
<%@ Import Namespace="System.Xml"%>
<%@ Import Namespace="System.Configuration"%>
<script language="C#" runat="server" >

    public DataSet GetDS(String connectionString)
    {
        SqlConnection connection = new SqlConnection(connectionString);
        SqlCommand command;
        SqlDataAdapter customerAdapter;
        SqlDataAdapter orderAdapter;
        DataSet ds  = new DataSet();

        //Create the Command object to select from the Customers database
        //table and append it to the adapter.
        command = new SqlCommand();

        command.CommandText = "SELECT CustomerID, CompanyName FROM
        ➥Customers";
        command.CommandType = CommandType.Text;
        command.Connection = connection;

        customerAdapter = new SqlDataAdapter();
        customerAdapter.SelectCommand = command;

        //Create the Command object to select from the Orders database
        //table and append it to the adapter.
        command = new SqlCommand();

        command.CommandText = "SELECT * FROM Orders";
        command.CommandType = CommandType.Text;
        command.Connection = connection;

        orderAdapter = new SqlDataAdapter();
        orderAdapter.SelectCommand = command;

        connection.Open();
        customerAdapter.Fill(ds, "NorthwindCustomers");
        orderAdapter.Fill(ds, "NorthwindOrders");
        connection.Close();
```

```
            connection.Dispose();
            customerAdapter.Dispose();
            orderAdapter.Dispose();

            return (ds);
            }

        private void Page_Load(object sender, System.EventArgs e)
        {
            String connectionString = "User ID=sa;Password=;Data
            ➥Source=localhost;Initial Catalog=Northwind";
            DataSet ds = GetDS(connectionString);

            Response.ContentType = "text/xml";

            ds.WriteXml(Response.OutputStream,XmlWriteMode.IgnoreSchema);
            ds.Dispose();
        }
    </script>
```

The results are structured similar to the following:
```
<NewDataSet>
  <NorthwindCustomers>
    <CustomerID>WOLZA</CustomerID>
    <CompanyName>Wolski  Zajazd</CompanyName>
  </NorthwindCustomers>
  <NorthwindOrders>
    <OrderID>10248</OrderID>
    <CustomerID>VINET</CustomerID>
    <EmployeeID>5</EmployeeID>
    <OrderDate>1996-07-04T00:00:00.0000000-04:00</OrderDate>
    <RequiredDate>1996-08-01T00:00:00.0000000-04:00</RequiredDate>
    <ShippedDate>1996-07-16T00:00:00.0000000-04:00</ShippedDate>
    <ShipVia>3</ShipVia>
    <Freight>32.38</Freight>
    <ShipName>Vins et alcools Chevalier</ShipName>
    <ShipAddress>59 rue de l'Abbaye</ShipAddress>
    <ShipCity>Reims</ShipCity>
    <ShipPostalCode>51100</ShipPostalCode>
    <ShipCountry>France</ShipCountry>
  </NorthwindOrders>
</NewDataSet>
```

You can specify how each column is output from the DataSet by using the
DataColumn object's ColumnMapping property to indicate if the column should be
output as an attribute, element, text, or not at all (hidden):
```
ds.Tables["NorthwindCustomers"].Columns["CustomerID"].ColumnMapping =
➥MappingType.Attribute;
ds.Tables["NorthwindCustomers"].Columns["CompanyName"].ColumnMapping =
➥MappingType.Attribute;
```

This changes the XML output of the `NorthwindCustomers` data table to output the following:

```
<NewDataSet>
  <NorthwindCustomers CustomerID="WOLZA" CompanyName="Wolski  Zajazd"/>
<NewDataSet>
```

You can also specify your XML Schema and table mappings. This is discussed in depth later in this section.

Another means of working with XML and the `DataSet` object is through the `ReadXml` method. This method reads an XML representation of the data and optional inline schema to populate all the tables in the `DataSet`.

Reuse the `sample.xml` file from Chapter 7:

```xml
<?xml version="1.0" encoding="utf-8" ?>
<Customers xmlns="urn:foo:bar">
    <Customer id="ALFKI">
        <CompanyName>Alfreds Futterkiste</CompanyName>
        <Contact>
            <FirstName>Maria</FirstName>
            <LastName>Anders</LastName>
            <Title>Sales Representative</Title>
        </Contact>
    </Customer>
    <Customer id="LOWES">
        <CompanyName>Lowe&apos;s</CompanyName>
        <Contact>
            <FirstName>Keth</FirstName>
            <LastName>Bunn</LastName>
            <Title>Assistant Manager</Title>
        </Contact>
    </Customer>
    <Customer id="VELVE">
        <CompanyName>The Velvet Room</CompanyName>
        <Contact>
            <FirstName>Rodney</FirstName>
            <LastName>Wade</LastName>
            <Title>Bar Manager</Title>
        </Contact>
    </Customer>
    <Customer id="GABST">
        <CompanyName>Georgia&apos;s Best Pressure and Stain</CompanyName>
        <Contact>
            <FirstName>Steve</FirstName>
            <LastName>Durling</LastName>
            <Title>Owner</Title>
        </Contact>
    </Customer>
    <Customer id="VBDNA">
        <CompanyName>Kirk Allen Evans Consulting, Inc.</CompanyName>
        <Contact>
```

```
                        <FirstName>Kirk Allen</FirstName>
                        <LastName>Evans</LastName>
                        <Title>Owner</Title>
                    </Contact>
                </Customer>
            </Customers>
```

By using this XML file, you can load the XML data into a `DataSet`. Note that you do not load the XML into a specific table. Rather, the XML represents all the data contained in the different `DataTable` objects contained in the `DataSet`:

```csharp
<%@ Page language="c#" %>
<%@ Import Namespace="System.Data"%>
<%@ Import Namespace="System.Xml"%>
    <link rel="stylesheet"  type="text/css" href="ADOSamples.css">

<script language="C#" runat="server">
        private void Page_Load(object sender, System.EventArgs e)
        {
            System.Xml.XmlTextReader reader = new
            ➥XmlTextReader(Server.MapPath("sample.xml"));
            DataSet ds = new DataSet("Northwind Data");
            ds.ReadXml(reader,XmlReadMode.InferSchema );
            reader.Close();

            DumpTable(ds);
            ds.Dispose();
        }

        public void DumpTable(DataSet ds)
        {
            foreach(DataTable table in ds.Tables)
            {
                Response.Write("<h1>" + table.TableName + "</h1>");
                Response.Write("<table border=\"1\" cellpadding=\"2\"
                ➥cellspacing=\"2\">");
                Response.Write("<tr>");
                foreach(DataColumn column in table.Columns)
                {
                    Response.Write("<th>" + column.ColumnName +
                    ➥"</th>");
                }
                Response.Write("</tr>");
                foreach(DataRow row in table.Rows)
                {
                    Response.Write("<tr>");
                    foreach(DataColumn column in table.Columns)
                    {
                        Response.Write("<td>" + row[column].ToString()
                        ➥+ "</td>");
                    }
```

```
                    Response.Write("</tr>");
            }
            Response.Write("</table>");
        }


    }

</script>
```

The output shown in Figure 8.6 shows that two data tables were created with the names Customer and Contact.

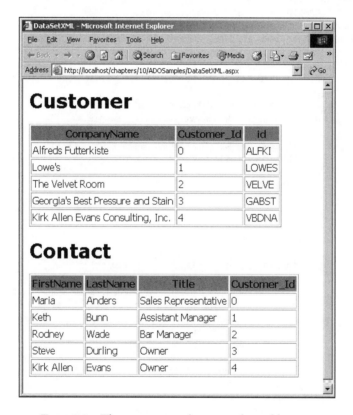

Figure 8.6 The Customer and Contact data tables are created by using an XML document as the data source.

The previous example told ADO.NET to guess at the schema based on the XML's contents by specifying the XmlReadMode.InferSchema parameter of the ReadXml() method. You can inspect the schema created by ADO.NET by using the WriteXml method and specifying the write mode as WriteSchema, as shown here:

```
<%@ Page language="c#" %>
<%@ Import Namespace="System.Data"%>
<%@ Import Namespace="System.Xml"%>
<script language="C#" runat="server">
        private void Page_Load(object sender, System.EventArgs e)
        {
            System.Xml.XmlTextReader reader = new
XmlTextReader(Server.MapPath("sample.xml"));
            DataSet ds = new DataSet("Northwind Data");
            ds.ReadXml(reader,XmlReadMode.InferSchema );
            reader.Close();

            Response.ContentType = "text/xml";
            ds.WriteXml(Response.OutputStream,XmlWriteMode.WriteSchema);
            ds.Dispose();
        }
</script>
```

Figure 8.7 shows the output schema.

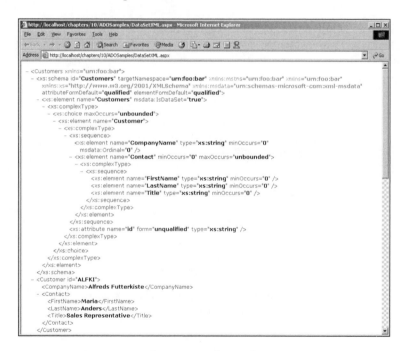

Figure 8.7   The output schema from a `DataSet`.

The problem with inferring a schema is that the inference depends on the data. This is not always a desirable side effect, so you want to specify your own schema prior to loading the XML data. By specifying the XML Schema, you can control what the DataSet looks like. Table 8.6 shows how the elements in XSD Schemas are mapped to DataSet objects.

Table 8.6 **Mappings of Schemas to *DataSet* Objects**

XML Schema Element	***DataSet* Mapping**
ComplexType	DataTable
Nested complexTypes	DataTables with DataRelations
key or unique	UniqueConstraint
KeyRef	ForeignKeyConstraint

Take a look at how to read a schema into a DataSet. The example begins in Listing 8.7 by creating another version of the GetDS method. This version loads a schema into a DataSet from a file by using DataSet.ReadXmlSchema and then loads the DataSet with data by using the LoadXml method.

Listing 8.7 **The *GetDS* Method Reading into a *DataSet***

```
public DataSet GetDS(String connectionString, String schemaFilePath, String
➥xmlFilePath)
        {

            DataSet ds = new DataSet();

            ds.ReadXmlSchema(schemaFilePath);
            ds.ReadXml(xmlFilePath, XmlReadMode.IgnoreSchema);
            ds.AcceptChanges();
            try
            {
                ds.EnforceConstraints = true;
            }
            catch(Exception e)
            {
                Response.Write("<h1>The input file failed
                ➥validation.</h1>");
                foreach(DataTable table in ds.Tables)
                {
                    DataRow [] errorRows = table.GetErrors();
                    if (errorRows != null)
                    {
                        Response.ContentType = "text/html";
                        Response.Clear();
                        Response.Write("<h3>Error in " +
                        ➥table.TableName + "</h3>");
                        foreach(DataRow row in errorRows)
                        {
                            Response.Write ("<i>" + row.RowError +
                            ➥"</i><br/>" );
```

```
DataColumn [] errorColumns =
↳row.GetColumnsInError();
if (errorColumns.Length > 0)
{
    Response.Write ("The following columns
    ↳are in error:");
    Response.Write("<ul>");
    foreach(DataColumn column in
    ↳errorColumns)
    {
        Response.Write("<li>" +
        ↳column.ColumnName + "</li>");
    }
    Response.Write("</ul>");
}
                }
            }

        }
        ds.Dispose();
        throw (new System.Xml.Schema.XmlSchemaException("One or
        ↳more tables in the DataSet failed validation.",e));
    }
    return(ds);
}
```

This example loads an XML Schema into the DataSet, loads the XML data into the DataSet, and applies the changes to the DataSet by using the AcceptChanges() method. When the data is loaded into the DataSet, you specified the XmlReadMode.IgnoreSchema parameter value. This value tells the processor to ignore the layout of the XML data being read. You can use this setting so that the schema populated using the ReadXmlSchema method is not overwritten. The EnforceConstraints property is then set to true, which tells the DataSet to validate the XML data against the underlying schema.

After data is contained in a DataSet, you can also output its contents as XML by using the WriteXml method. While you output the XML, you might want to control how it is structured. For example, you might read the XML as all elements, and easily output the XML as all attributes. To accomplish this task without using ADO.NET requires either a small but unintuitive XSLT transformation (as described in Chapter 3) or a looping algorithm, but ADO.NET makes this task very simple.

Look at an example of how to load XML data and an XML Schema file to populate a DataSet. By specifying the schema, you can specify what the schema should look like rather than have it inferred based on the XML data that's being read. The XML Schema is shown in Listing 8.8.

Listing 8.8 **The *sample1.xsd* Schema**

```
<?xml version="1.0"?>
<xs:schema id="Customers" targetNamespace="http://tempuri.org/sample1.xsd"
➥xmlns:mstns="http://tempuri.org/sample1.xsd"
➥xmlns="http://tempuri.org/sample1.xsd"
➥xmlns:xs="http://www.w3.org/2001/XMLSchema" xmlns:msdata="urn:schemas-
➥microsoft-com:xml-msdata" attributeFormDefault="qualified"
➥elementFormDefault="qualified">
    <xs:complexType name="contactType">
        <xs:sequence>
        <xs:element name="FirstName" type="xs:string" minOccurs="0" />
        <xs:element name="LastName" type="xs:string" minOccurs="0" />
        <xs:element name="Title" type="xs:string" minOccurs="0" />
        </xs:sequence>
        </xs:complexType>

    <xs:element name="Customers" msdata:IsDataSet="true"
➥msdata:EnforceConstraints="False">
     <xs:complexType>
       <xs:choice maxOccurs="unbounded">
         <xs:element name="Customer">
          <xs:complexType>
           <xs:sequence>
             <xs:element name="CompanyName" type="xs:string" minOccurs="0"
             ➥msdata:Ordinal="0" />
             <xs:element name="Contact" minOccurs="0" maxOccurs="unbounded"
             ➥type="contactType">
             </xs:element>
           </xs:sequence>
           <xs:attribute name="id" form="unqualified" type="xs:string" />
          </xs:complexType>
         </xs:element>
       </xs:choice>
     </xs:complexType>
    </xs:element>
</xs:schema>
```

The data to load into the DataSet comes from an XML file, sample.xml. This XML file is valid against the schema depicted in Listing 8.8 and uses an element-dominant form. The XML file sample.xml is shown in Listing 8.9.

Listing 8.9 *sample.xml*

```
<?xml version="1.0" encoding="utf-8"?>
<Customers xmlns="http://tempuri.org/sample1.xsd">
    <Customer id="ALFKI">
        <CompanyName>Alfreds Futterkiste</CompanyName>
        <Contact>
```

```
                <FirstName>Maria</FirstName>
                <LastName>Anders</LastName>
                <Title>Sales Representative</Title>
            </Contact>
        </Customer>
        <Customer id="LOWES">
            <CompanyName>Lowe's</CompanyName>
            <Contact>
                <FirstName>Keth</FirstName>
                <LastName>Bunn</LastName>
                <Title>Assistant Manager</Title>
            </Contact>
        </Customer>
        <Customer id="VELVE">
            <CompanyName>The Velvet Room</CompanyName>
            <Contact>
                <FirstName>Rodney</FirstName>
                <LastName>Wade</LastName>
                <Title>Bar Manager</Title>
            </Contact>
        </Customer>
        <Customer id="GABST">
            <CompanyName>Georgia's Best Pressure and Stain</CompanyName>
            <Contact>
                <FirstName>Steve</FirstName>
                <LastName>Durling</LastName>
                <Title>Owner</Title>
            </Contact>
        </Customer>
        <Customer id="VBDNA">
            <CompanyName>Kirk Allen Evans Consulting, Inc.</CompanyName>
            <Contact>
                <FirstName>Kirk Allen</FirstName>
                <LastName>Evans</LastName>
                <Title>Owner</Title>
            </Contact>
        </Customer>
    </Customers>
```

With a simple routine using a `DataSet`, you can load the XML using the schema from Listing 8.8 and the XML from Listing 8.9 to alter its structure to an attribute-dominant form. Notice also that you are reusing the `GetDS` method from Listing 8.5. To run this example, create a new Visual Basic .NET web application called `ADOVB` and create a new web form called `Listing8_10.aspx`. Remove all HTML code from the `.aspx` page, leaving only the `Page` directive:

```
<%@ Page Language="vb" AutoEventWireup="false"
➥Codebehind="Listing8_10.aspx.vb" Inherits="ADOVB.Listing8_10"%>
```

Open the code-behind file, `Listing8_10.aspx.vb`, and enter the code from Listing 8.10 into it.

Listing 8.10 **A Working Example of Transforming an XML Document From Element-Centric Form to Attribute-Centric Form**

```vb
Imports System.Data
Imports System.Data.SqlClient

Public Class Listing8_10
    Inherits System.Web.UI.Page

#Region " Web Form Designer Generated Code "

    'This call is required by the Web Form Designer.
    <System.Diagnostics.DebuggerStepThrough()> Private Sub
InitializeComponent()

    End Sub

    Private Sub Page_Init(ByVal sender As System.Object, ByVal e As
➥System.EventArgs) Handles MyBase.Init
        'CODEGEN: This method call is required by the Web Form Designer
        'Do not modify it using the code editor.
        InitializeComponent()
    End Sub

#End Region

    Public Function GetDS(ByVal schemaFilePath As String, ByVal xmlFilePath
➥As String) As DataSet

        Dim ds As DataSet = New DataSet()

        ds.ReadXmlSchema(schemaFilePath)
        ds.ReadXml(xmlFilePath, XmlReadMode.IgnoreSchema)
        ds.AcceptChanges()
        Try
            ds.EnforceConstraints = True
        Catch e As System.Exception

            Response.Write("<h1>The input file failed validation.</h1>")
            Dim table As DataTable
            For Each table In ds.Tables

                Dim errorRows() As DataRow = table.GetErrors()
                If errorRows Is Nothing Then

                    Response.ContentType = "text/html"
                    Response.Clear()
                    Response.Write("<h3>Error in " + table.TableName + "</h3>")
                    Dim row As DataRow
```

```
            For Each row In errorRows

                Response.Write("<i>" + row.RowError + "</i><br/>")

                Dim errorColumns() As DataColumn =
                ➥row.GetColumnsInError()
                If errorColumns.Length > 0 Then

                    Response.Write("The following columns are in
                    ➥error:")
                    Response.Write("<ul>")
                    Dim column As DataColumn
                    For Each column In errorColumns

                        Response.Write("<li>" + column.ColumnName +
                        ➥"</li>")
                    Next column
                    Response.Write("</ul>")
                End If
            Next row
        End If
    Next table
    ds.Dispose()
    Throw (New System.Xml.Schema.XmlSchemaException("One or more
    ➥tables in the DataSet failed validation.", e))
    End Try
    ds.Dispose()
    Return (ds)
End Function


Private Sub Page_Load(ByVal sender As System.Object, ByVal e As
➥System.EventArgs) Handles MyBase.Load
    'Put user code to initialize the page here

    Dim ds As DataSet = GetDS(Server.MapPath("sample1.xsd"),
    ➥Server.MapPath("sample.xml"))
    Dim table As DataTable
    For Each table In ds.Tables
        Dim column As DataColumn
        For Each column In table.Columns
            column.ColumnMapping = MappingType.Attribute
        Next
    Next

    Response.ContentType = "text/xml"
    ds.WriteXml(Response.OutputStream)
    table.Dispose()
    ds.Dispose()

End Sub

End Class
```

Run the application. When the Page_Load event fires, each column in each table in the DataSet is changed from element-dominant form to attribute-dominant form by changing the ColumnMapping to MappingType.Attribute. The results are as follows:

```
<Customers xmlns="http://tempuri.org/sample1.xsd">
  <Customer CompanyName="Alfreds Futterkiste" id="ALFKI" Customer_Id="0">
    <Contact FirstName="Maria" LastName="Anders" Title="Sales Representative"
    ➥Customer_Id="0" />
  </Customer>
  <Customer CompanyName="Lowe's" id="LOWES" Customer_Id="1">
    <Contact FirstName="Keth" LastName="Bunn" Title="Assistant Manager"
    ➥Customer_Id="1" />
  </Customer>
  <Customer CompanyName="The Velvet Room" id="VELVE" Customer_Id="2">
    <Contact FirstName="Rodney" LastName="Wade" Title="Bar Manager"
    ➥Customer_Id="2" />
  </Customer>
  <Customer CompanyName="Georgia's Best Pressure and Stain" id="GABST"
  ➥Customer_Id="3">
    <Contact FirstName="Steve" LastName="Durling" Title="Owner"
    ➥Customer_Id="3" />
  </Customer>
  <Customer CompanyName="Kirk Allen Evans Consulting, Inc." id="VBDNA"
  ➥Customer_Id="4">
    <Contact FirstName="Kirk Allen" LastName="Evans" Title="Owner"
    ➥Customer_Id="4" />
  </Customer>
</Customers>
```

With a small amount of code, you can easily change the structure of the XML representation of a DataSet simply by changing the ColumnMapping property of the DataColumn. This code also introduces the concept of multiple DataTables within a DataSet and demonstrates looping through the DataColumns of a table.

As you can see, support for XML and XML Schemas plays a large role in ADO.NET. You are able to validate data against a specified XML Schema, infer a schema based on the data in the DataSet, and extract the XML Schema and XML data from a populated DataSet.

You have seen that a DataSet contains one or more DataTable objects, and you've gotten a glimpse at how using XML and XSD Schemas can facilitate loading a DataSet object's underlying DataTables. So, what is a DataTable object? Read on to find out.

The *DataTable* Class

The DataTable class is the closest representation of an ADODB.Recordset class in ADO.NET. A better analogy is a table in a database. A DataTable provides structure to its data through the use of DataRow and DataColumn objects, enforces data integrity through a collection of `Constraints`, and manages how it is related to other `DataTable` objects through its `ParentRelations` and `ChildRelations` collections.

When the `DataSet` is populated using the `Adapter.Fill()` method, you can optionally specify the name of the `DataTable` to fill with data. If the `DataTable` does not already exist, it is created and appended to the collection of tables.

The `ADODB.Recordset` class does not have a mechanism to return an entire row of data, but instead returns individual `Field` objects. The model for the ADO.NET `DataSet` accesses entire `DataRows`, which are indexed using `DataColumn` objects to access individual column values.

DataRows

A `DataRow` represents a single row of data contained in a `DataTable`. `DataRow` objects can be added to a `DataSet` by using several different methods. Look at an example.

You will use an application setting variable from the `web.config` file to store the database connection string. Application settings are discussed in detail in Chapter 7, "ASP.NET Extensibility With XML."

Creating an Application Setting

To create an application setting, add an `appSettings` element as a child of the configuration element in the `web.config` file:

```
<configuration>
    <appSettings>
        <add key="connectionString" value="User ID=sa;Password=;Initial
Catalog=Northwind;Data Source=localhost" />
    </appSettings>
    .
    .
    .
</configuration>
```

After the `web.config` file is altered to include your connection string, you can create a new version of the `GetDS` method from Listing 8.7 to read from the database instead of from an XML file. Listing 8.11 shows several methods for adding rows of data to a `DataSet`. Add a new web form to your ADOVB application, called `Listing8_11.aspx`. Add a `DataGrid` control to the web form called `DataGrid1`, and add the code from Listing 8.11 in the code-behind file, `listing8_11.aspx.vb`:

Listing 8.11 **Adding Rows of Data to a *DataSet***

```
Imports System.Data
Imports System.Data.SqlClient
Imports System.Configuration


Public Class Listing8_11
    Inherits System.Web.UI.Page
    Protected WithEvents DataGrid1 As System.Web.UI.WebControls.DataGrid

#Region " Web Form Designer Generated Code "

    'This call is required by the Web Form Designer.
    <System.Diagnostics.DebuggerStepThrough()> Private Sub
    ➥InitializeComponent()

    End Sub

    Private Sub Page_Init(ByVal sender As System.Object, ByVal e As
    ➥System.EventArgs) Handles MyBase.Init
        'CODEGEN: This method call is required by the Web Form Designer
        'Do not modify it using the code editor.
        InitializeComponent()
    End Sub

#End Region

    Private Sub Page_Load(ByVal sender As System.Object, ByVal e As
    ➥System.EventArgs) Handles MyBase.Load
        'Put user code to initialize the page here
        Dim connectionString As String =
        ➥ConfigurationSettings.AppSettings.Item("connectionString")
        Dim ds As DataSet = GetDS(connectionString)
        Dim row As DataRow

        'Directly manipulate the DataRow object
        row = ds.Tables("NorthwindCustomers").NewRow()
        row.Item("CustomerID") = "HLZNR"
        row.Item("CompanyName") = "Inside XML"
        ds.Tables("NorthwindCustomers").Rows.Add(row)

        'Add a row using an array of values
        Dim values() As String = Array.CreateInstance(GetType(String), 2)
        values.SetValue("WORLY", 0)
        values.SetValue("Inside ASP.NET", 1)
        row = ds.Tables("NorthwindCustomers").Rows.Add(values)

        values.SetValue("EVANS", 0)
        values.SetValue("XML and ASP.NET", 1)
        row = ds.Tables("NorthwindCustomers").LoadDataRow(values, True)

        Dim dv As DataView = New DataView(ds.Tables("NorthwindCustomers"))
        dv.RowStateFilter = DataViewRowState.Added
```

```
        DataGrid1.DataSource = dv
        DataGrid1.DataBind()
        ds.Dispose()
    End Sub

    Public Function GetDS(ByVal connectionString As String) As DataSet

        Dim connection As SqlConnection = New SqlConnection(connectionString)
        Dim command As SqlCommand
        Dim customerAdapter As SqlDataAdapter
        Dim orderAdapter As SqlDataAdapter
        Dim ds As DataSet = New DataSet()

        'Create the Command object to select from the Customers database
        'table and append it to the adapter.
        command = New SqlCommand()
        With command
            .CommandText = "SELECT CustomerID, CompanyName FROM Customers"
            .CommandType = CommandType.Text
            .Connection = connection
        End With
        customerAdapter = New SqlDataAdapter()
        customerAdapter.SelectCommand = command

        'Create the Command object to select from the Orders database
        'table and append it to the adapter.
        command = New SqlCommand()
        With command
            .CommandText = "Select * from Orders"
            .CommandType = CommandType.Text
            .Connection = connection
        End With
        orderAdapter = New SqlDataAdapter()
        orderAdapter.SelectCommand = command

        connection.Open()
        customerAdapter.Fill(ds, "NorthwindCustomers")
        orderAdapter.Fill(ds, "NorthwindOrders")
        ds.Relations.Add("CustomerOrders",
        ↪ds.Tables("NorthwindCustomers").Columns("CustomerID"),
        ↪ds.Tables("NorthwindOrders").Columns("CustomerID"))

        connection.Close()

        connection.Dispose()
        customerAdapter.Dispose()
        orderAdapter.Dispose()

        Return (ds)

    End Function
End Class
```

In Listing 8.11, you can see three different ways to add a row of data to a `DataTable`. First, the `DataTable.NewRow()` method was used to create a new `DataRow` and set the values for the specified columns. Next, you create a string array and add a `DataRow` to the `DataTable` by using the array to specify the values being added, positionally. Finally, you use the `DataTable.LoadDataRow()` method to search for a particular `DataRow` based on the values specified. If the `DataRow` is found, it is updated. If the `DataRow` is not found, it is created with the specified values.

Interestingly enough, when the `LoadDataRow` method is called, a row is added to the `DataSet`, but its `RowState` is unchanged. `RowStates` are explained in the section, "Versioning in the DataSet." The output of the code is shown in Figure 8.8.

Figure 8.8   The output from Listing 8.11 shows the two newly added rows.

The `ADODB.Recordset` object does not have the capability to return an entire row of data. Instead, it exposes methods such as `MoveNext()` and `MoveLast()`. The `DataRows` collection in ADO.NET can be iterated over, which is another improvement over ADODB:

```
Dim connectionString As String = AppSettings.Item("connectionString")
    Dim ds As DataSet = GetDS(connectionString)
    Dim row As DataRow

    Response.Write("<table>")
    For Each row In ds.Tables("NorthwindCustomers").Rows
        Response.Write("<tr>")
        Response.Write("<td>" & row.Item("CustomerID") & "</td>")
        Response.Write("<td>" & row.Item("CompanyName") & "</td>")
        Response.Write("</tr>")
    Next
    Response.Write("</table>")
```

A useful feature of the ADODB.Recordset and its predecessors was the ability to locate data based on conditions. For example, DAO supplied the Seek() method, and ADO supplied a Filter property. ADO.NET achieves the same means through a Select() method, as shown here:

```
Dim connectionString As String = AppSettings.Item("connectionString")
        Dim ds As DataSet = GetDS(connectionString)
        Dim row As DataRow

Dim foundRows() As DataRow =
➥ds.Tables("NorthwindCustomers").Select("CustomerID LIKE 'TEST%'")
        For Each row In foundRows
            Response.Write("<tr>")
            Response.Write("<td>" & row.Item("CustomerID") & "</td>")
            Response.Write("<td>" & row.Item("CompanyName") & "</td>")
            Response.Write("</tr>")
        Next
```

This example retrieved an array of DataRow objects that matched the Select criteria. Notice the use of wildcards in the Select criteria. Unlike ADO, ADO.NET supports complex expressions in the Select criteria.

DataColumns

Unlike the DataRow object, a DataColumn object does not contain data. A DataColumn object only contains schema information for a column in the DataTable. Table 8.7 lists the properties of the DataColumn class.

Table 8.7 **Properties of the *DataColumn* Class**

Member Name	Description
AllowDBNull	Boolean that indicates if the column is nullable.
AutoIncrement	Boolean that indicates if this column should be incremented for each new row added.
AutoIncrementSeed	Gets or sets the starting value for a field with a true value for its AutoIncrement property.
AutoIncrementStep	Gets or sets the increment step for a field with a true value for its AutoIncrement property.
Caption	Gets or sets the caption for the column when used in controls that support displaying DataSet captions.
ColumnMapping	Gets or sets the MappingType of the column. Specifies how the column will appear when written as XML (Element, Attribute, Hidden, or SimpleContent (text)).
ColumnName	The name for the column.
Container	Gets the container for the component.

continues

Table 8.7 **Continued**

Member Name	Description
DataType	Gets or sets the base .NET Framework data type of data stored in the column. Read-only after a DataRow having the specified index column contains data.
DefaultValue	Gets or sets the default value when creating a new DataRow.
DesignMode	Gets a value that indicates whether the component is currently in design mode.
Expression	Gets or sets the expression used to filter rows, calculate values in a column, or create an aggregate column.
ExtendedProperties	Gets a collection of custom user information. Each property must be of type String to emit the property as XML.
MaxLength	Gets or sets the maximum length of a text column.
Namespace	Gets or sets the namespace for the XML representation of the column.
Ordinal	Gets the position of the column in the DataColumnCollection.
Prefix	Gets or sets the namespace prefix for the XML representation of the column.
ReadOnly	Gets or sets a Boolean that indicates if the column is read-only once an associated DataRow is populated with data.
Site	Gets or sets the site of the component.
Table	Gets or sets the DataTable to which the column belongs.
Unique	Gets or sets a Boolean that indicates if the values in the column must be unique. Adds a UniqueConstraint object to the DataTable.Constraints collection.

Working with DataColumn objects is similar to working with DataRow objects. The columns can be iterated over, and are indexed on ordinal position and column name:

```
Dim connectionString As String = AppSettings.Item("connectionString")
    Dim ds As DataSet = GetDS(connectionString)
Dim table As DataTable
    Dim column As DataColumn

    table = ds.Tables("NorthwindCustomers")
    Response.Write("<h1>Columns of " & table.TableName & "</h1>")
    Response.Write("<table>")
```

```
Response.Write("<tr>")
Response.Write("<th>ColumnName</th>")
Response.Write("<th>Nullable</th>")
Response.Write("<th>Data Type</th>")
Response.Write("<th>Unique?</th>")
Response.Write("<th>ColumnName</th>")
Response.Write("<th>MaxLength</th>")
Response.Write("</tr>")
For Each column In table.Columns
    Response.Write("<tr>")
    Response.Write("<td>" & column.ColumnName & "</td>")
    Response.Write("<td>" & column.AllowDBNull & "</td>")
    Response.Write("<td>" & column.DataType.ToString() & "</td>")
    Response.Write("<td>" & column.Unique & "</td>")
    Response.Write("<td>" & column.MaxLength & "</td>")
    Response.Write("</tr>")
Next
Response.Write("</table>")
```

You can use the `DataRows` and `DataColumns` collections to iterate through the entire `DataSet`. You can create a new version of the `DumpTable` method that was introduced at the beginning of this chapter. This new version emits an HTML table for each `DataTable` in the `DataSet`:

```
Public Sub DumpTable(ByVal ds As DataSet)
        Dim table As DataTable
        Dim column As DataColumn
        Dim row As DataRow

        For Each table In ds.Tables
            Response.Write("<h1>" & table.TableName & "</h1>")
            Response.Write("<table>")
            For Each row In table.Rows
                Response.Write("<tr>")
                For Each column In table.Columns
                    Response.Write("<td>")
                    Response.Write(row.Item(column.Ordinal))
                    Response.Write("</td>")
                Next
                Response.Write("</tr>")
            Next
            Response.Write("</table>")
        Next
    End Sub
```

Versioning in the *DataSet*

Each row has an associated state. These states are as follows:

- **Added**—The row has been added to a `DataRowCollection`, and `AcceptChanges` has not been called.

- **Deleted**—The row was deleted by using the `Delete` method of the `DataRow`.
- **Detached**—The row has been created but is not part of any `DataRowCollection`. A `DataRow` is in this state immediately after it is created and before it is added to a collection, or if it has been removed from a collection.
- **Modified**—The row has been modified and `AcceptChanges` has not been called.
- **Unchanged**—The row has not changed since `AcceptChanges` was last called.

In addition to having a state, each row can also have a version. To check if a row has a version, use the `HasVersion` method of the `DataRow` object. The `DataSet` object does not commit changes to the underlying data until the `AcceptChanges` method is called. This means that changes to a row can be undone and the values in the row can be returned to their original value.

To do this, the `DataRow` class maintains versions of its data. This is similar to the `ADODB.Field` object's `Value`, `OriginalValue`, and `UnderlyingValue` properties.

The valid versions are as follows:

- `Current`—The row contains current values.
- `Default`—The row contains its default values.
- `Original`—The row contains its original values.
- `Proposed`—The row contains proposed values.

The `DataRow`'s version is affected by using the `BeginEdit`, `CancelEdit`, `EndEdit`, and `AcceptChanges` methods of the `DataRow`. Table 8.8 describes what happens when data in a data row is edited.

Table 8.8   **Effects on *DataRowVersion***

Called Method Name	Effect
`DataRow.BeginEdit`	Changing a value of a column in the row makes the `Current` and `Proposed` values available.
`DataRow.CancelEdit`	The `Proposed` value is deleted.
`DataRow.EndEdit`	The `Proposed` value becomes the `Current` value.
`DataRow.AcceptChanges`	The `Proposed` value becomes the `Current` value; the `Original` value remains.
`DataTable.AcceptChanges`	`Original` value is set to the `Current` value.
`DataRow.RejectChanges`	Version becomes `Current`. `Proposed` value is discarded.

DataViews

The data in a `DataTable` can be queried by using a `Select` method that supports SQL syntax. The array of `DataRow` objects returned from this method are static; that is, if the underlying `DataTable` changes, the array of `DataRow` objects returned from the `Select` method do not reflect the changes made. Requerying, rebuilding, and displaying these changes can be a time-consuming process. This problem is addressed by using the `DataView` object.

Simliar to views in a database, a `DataView` object represents a particular view of the underlying `DataTable` object. Changes made to the `DataTable` include changes to content, membership, and ordering[4]. Unlike a view in a database, `DataViews` cannot span multiple tables, exclude columns in the source table, or include columns not present in the source table.

Creating a **DataView**

To create a `DataView`, use the overloaded constructor to create a reference to a `DataView` object:

```
Dim connectionString as String = AppSettings.Item("connectionString")
Dim ds as DataSet = GetDS(connectionString)
Dim table as DataTable = ds.Tables("NorthwindCustomers")

Dim view as DataView
view = New DataView(table, "CustomerID = 'ALFKI')", "CompanyName",
➥DataViewRowState.CurrentRows)
```

This version of the constructor accepts the `DataTable` to create a view over, the filter condition for the rows, the column to sort on, and the `DataViewRowState`, respectively.

The `DataViewRowState` parameter indicates what rows are to be included in the view. Table 8.9 lists the different enumeration members and their descriptions.

Table 8.9 **Members of the *DataViewRowState* Enumeration**

Member Name	Description
CurrentRows	The current row version of all `Unchanged`, `Added`, and `Modified` rows. This is the default.
Added	The current row version of all `Added` rows.
Deleted	The original row version of all `Deleted` rows.
ModifiedCurrent	The current row version of all `Modified` rows.
ModifiedOriginal	The original row version of all `Modified` rows.
None	No rows.
OriginalRows	The original row version of all `Unchanged`, `Modified`, and `Deleted` rows.
Unchanged	The current row version of all `Unchanged` rows.

By using DataViews, you can create separate views of the same table. You use DataViews in the next section, "Binding to Controls."

Binding to Controls

DataViews are typically used for binding to controls. In .NET, controls that support the IBindingList interface can bind to a control such as the <asp:DataGrid> control. Neither the DataSet nor the DataTable classes support this interface, so neither can be directly bound to a control. The DataTable class, however, exposes a method called DefaultView that returns a DataView. The DataView supports IBindingList, so it can be bound to a control.

You can bind a DataView to a control in several ways. In Listing 8.12, you create a DataView using the same table for three different views: added rows, changed rows, and unchanged rows. Note that all three use the same underlying table. The only difference is the RowStateFilter that uses one of the values from Table 8.9 to indicate which version of the rows should be shown in each data grid. Create a new web form called Listing8_12.aspx. Replace the Page directive and paste the code form Listing 8.12 into Listing8_12.aspx.

Listing 8.12   **Working with Versioning in the *DataSet***

```vb
<%@ Page Language="vb" %>
<%@Import Namespace="System.Xml"%>
<%@Import Namespace="System.Data"%>
<%@Import Namespace="System.Data.SqlClient"%>
<%@Import Namespace="System.Configuration"%>

<script language="visualbasic" runat="server">
Public Function GetDS(ByVal connectionString As String) As DataSet

        Dim connection As SqlConnection = New SqlConnection(connectionString)
        Dim command As SqlCommand
        Dim customerAdapter As SqlDataAdapter
        Dim orderAdapter As SqlDataAdapter
        Dim ds As DataSet = New DataSet()

        'Create the Command object to select from the Customers database
        'table and append it to the adapter.
        command = New SqlCommand()
        With command
            .CommandText = "SELECT CustomerID, CompanyName FROM Customers"
            .CommandType = CommandType.Text
            .Connection = connection
        End With
        customerAdapter = New SqlDataAdapter()
        customerAdapter.SelectCommand = command

        'Create the Command object to select from the Orders database
        'table and append it to the adapter.
```

```
command = New SqlCommand()
With command
    .CommandText = "Select * from Orders"
    .CommandType = CommandType.Text
    .Connection = connection
End With
orderAdapter = New SqlDataAdapter()
orderAdapter.SelectCommand = command

connection.Open()
customerAdapter.Fill(ds, "NorthwindCustomers")
orderAdapter.Fill(ds, "NorthwindOrders")
ds.Relations.Add("CustomerOrders",
➥ds.Tables("NorthwindCustomers").Columns("CustomerID"),
➥ds.Tables("NorthwindOrders").Columns("CustomerID"))

connection.Close()

connection.Dispose()
customerAdapter.Dispose()
orderAdapter.Dispose()

Return (ds)

End Function

Private Function GetRow(ByVal table as DataTable, ByVal customerID as
➥string, ByVal companyName as String) as DataRow
    dim row as DataRow = table.NewRow()
    row("CustomerID") = customerID
row("CompanyName") = companyName
    return(row)
End Function

Private Sub Page_Load(ByVal sender As System.Object, ByVal e As
➥System.EventArgs) Handles MyBase.Load
    Dim connectionString As String =
    ➥ConfigurationSettings.AppSettings.Item("connectionString")

    Dim ds As DataSet = GetDS(connectionString)
    Dim table As DataTable = ds.Tables("NorthwindCustomers")

    'Add some new rows
    table.Rows.Add(GetRow(table,"STLTH","Charles Townsend"))
    table.Rows.Add(GetRow(table,"JAMES","James Townsend"))
    table.Rows.Add(GetRow(table,"MRRYK","Linda Evans"))
    table.Rows.Add(GetRow(table,"RTIRD","Bob Evans"))

    'Change some rows
    Dim foundRows() As DataRow = table.Select("CustomerID in
    ➥('ALFKI','BLAUS','OCEAN','BOLID','BONAP')")
```

continues

Listing 8.12   **Continued**

```
            Dim row as DataRow
        For Each row In foundRows
                select case row("CustomerID")
                    case "ALFKI"
                        row("CompanyName") = "Michelle Schultz"
                    case "BLAUS"
                        row("CompanyName") = "John Schultz"
                    case "OCEAN"
                        row("CompanyName") = "Madison Schultz"
                    case "BOLID"
                        row("CompanyName") = "Janice Hickey"
                    case "BONAP"
                        row("CompanyName") = "George Hickey"
                end select
        Next

        'Bind the 3 grids to the same DataTable, using different views
        Dim view As DataView
        view = New DataView(table)

        view.Sort = "CompanyName"
        view.RowStateFilter = DataViewRowState.Added
        AddedRows.DataSource = view
        AddedRows.DataBind()

        ChangedRows.DataSource = New DataView(table, String.Empty,
        ➥"CustomerID", DataViewRowState.ModifiedCurrent)
        ChangedRows.DataBind()

        OriginalRows.DataSource = New DataView(table, String.Empty,
        ➥"CustomerID", DataViewRowState.Unchanged)
        OriginalRows.DataBind()
    End Sub
</script>

<!DOCTYPE HTML PUBLIC "-//W3C//DTD HTML 4.0 Transitional//EN">
<HTML>
    <HEAD>
        <title>DataViewExample</title>
        <meta name="GENERATOR" content="Microsoft Visual Studio.NET 7.0">
        <meta name="CODE_LANGUAGE" content="Visual Basic 7.0">
        <meta name="vs_defaultClientScript" content="JavaScript">
        <meta name="vs_targetSchema"
        ➥content="http://schemas.microsoft.com/intellisense/ie5">
    </HEAD>

    <body MS_POSITIONING="GridLayout">

        <form id="Form1" method="post" runat="server">
```

```
        <h3>Added Rows</h3>
        <asp:DataGrid id="AddedRows" runat="server" Font-
        ↪Names="Verdana,Tahoma,Arial" Width="500" BackColor="silver"
        ↪BorderColor="#000000" EnableViewState="False">
            <HeaderStyle BackColor="black" ForeColor="white" Font-
            ↪Bold="True" Font-Names="Verdana,Tahoma,Arial" Font-
            ↪Size="10pt" />
        </asp:DataGrid>
        <h3>Changed Rows</h3>
        <asp:DataGrid   id="ChangedRows" runat="server" Font-
        ↪Names="Verdana,Tahoma,Arial" Width="500" BackColor="silver"
        ↪BorderColor="#000000" EnableViewState="False">
            <HeaderStyle BackColor="black" ForeColor="white" Font-
            ↪Bold="True" Font-Names="Verdana,Tahoma,Arial" Font-
            ↪Size="10pt" />
        </asp:DataGrid>
        <h3>Original Rows</h3>
        <asp:DataGrid   id="OriginalRows" runat="server" Font-
        ↪Names="Verdana,Tahoma,Arial" Width="500" BackColor="silver"
        ↪BorderColor="#000000" EnableViewState="False">
            <HeaderStyle BackColor="black" ForeColor="white" Font-
            ↪Bold="True" Font-Names="Verdana,Tahoma,Arial" Font-
            ↪Size="10pt" />
        </asp:DataGrid>
        <br/>

    </form>
  </body>
</HTML>
```

The *DataAdapter* Class

The different managed providers supply a Command object that supports the IDbCommand interface. The base IDbCommand interface by itself doesn't really provide you with a means of working with XML natively, so working with XML using an OLEDB Provider and the OleDbCommand object requires you to create your own XML. It is great for giving you access to stored procedures and issuing SQL UPDATE commands. But, the Command object suffers from limitations that are solved by using the DataAdapter class.

The DataAdapter class provides the ability to control what happens behind the scenes. It is also used as a bridge to pass data back and forth using a DataSet object and a database connection.

As previously stated, ADO supports the notion of disconnected recordsets and batch updates. When batch updates occur, the data updated in the database depends on from where the data was retrieved. For example, you select data from two different tables using a SQL JOIN. After you update several values in different rows, you issue an UpdateBatch statement. Which table gets updated, the table to the left of the JOIN, or both tables? More often than not, you receive an error similar to "Insufficient key column information," which can be a difficult bug to correct in your application. Suppose that you retrieved the data from a complex stored procedure or view. Properly updating the underlying data becomes fallible and risky.

The DataAdapter class solves this issue by allowing you to define your own operations to respond to individual rows being manipulated. Suppose that you select using inline text, but want to call your own stored procedures when the underlying data is changed. This is impossible in ADO, but easy in ADO.NET. In addition to the previous AddCustomer stored procedure from Listing 8.3, you create several new stored procedures for use with the Northwinds database in SQL Server. Open Query Analyzer, connect to the Northwinds database, and enter the following code into the code pane:

```
create procedure UpdateCustomerCompanyName(@CustomerID char(5), @CompanyName
➥varchar(40))
as

update Customers set CompanyName = @CompanyName where CustomerID =
➥@CustomerID
if (@@ERROR <> 0) goto errorhandler

cleanup:
     return(0)
errorhandler:
     return(1)

GO
create procedure DeleteCustomer(@CustomerID char(5))
as

delete from  Customers where CustomerID = @CustomerID
if (@@ERROR <> 0) goto errorhandler

cleanup:
     return(0)
errorhandler:
     return(1)

GO
```

Click the F5 button, and the stored procedures are created.

Next, create a new .aspx page called Listing8_13.aspx and enter the code from Listing 8.13 into the .aspx page.

Listing 8.13   **By Using the *SqlDataAdapter*, You Can Control Update Operations for a *DataSet***

```vb
<%@ Import Namespace="System.Data"%>
<%@ Import Namespace="System.Data.SqlClient"%>
<%@ Import Namespace="System.Configuration"%>
<script language="vb" runat="server">

Public Function GetDS(ByVal connectionString As String) As DataSet

        Dim connection As SqlConnection = New SqlConnection(connectionString)
        Dim command As SqlCommand
        Dim customerAdapter As SqlDataAdapter
        Dim orderAdapter As SqlDataAdapter
        Dim ds As DataSet = New DataSet()

        'Create the Command object to select from the Customers database
        'table and append it to the adapter.
        command = New SqlCommand()
        With command
            .CommandText = "SELECT CustomerID, CompanyName FROM Customers"
            .CommandType = CommandType.Text
            .Connection = connection
        End With
        customerAdapter = New SqlDataAdapter()
        customerAdapter.SelectCommand = command

        'Create the Command object to select from the Orders database
        'table and append it to the adapter.
        command = New SqlCommand()
        With command
            .CommandText = "SELECT * FROM Orders"
            .CommandType = CommandType.Text
            .Connection = connection
        End With
        orderAdapter = New SqlDataAdapter()
        orderAdapter.SelectCommand = command

        connection.Open()
        customerAdapter.Fill(ds, "NorthwindCustomers")
        orderAdapter.Fill(ds, "NorthwindOrders")
        connection.Close()

        connection.Dispose()
        customerAdapter.Dispose()
        orderAdapter.Dispose()

        Return (ds)
    End Function

    Public Sub UpdateDS(ByVal connectionString As String, ByVal ds As
    ➥DataSet)
```

continues

Listing 8.13   **Continued**

```
        Dim adapter As SqlDataAdapter = New SqlDataAdapter()
        Dim connection As SqlConnection = New SqlConnection(connectionString)

        Dim parm As SqlParameter

        With adapter

            .InsertCommand = New SqlCommand("AddCustomer", connection)
            .InsertCommand.CommandType = CommandType.StoredProcedure
            parm = .InsertCommand.Parameters.Add("@CustomerID",
            ➥SqlDbType.Char, 5)
            parm.SourceColumn = "CustomerID"
            parm = .InsertCommand.Parameters.Add("@CompanyName",
            ➥SqlDbType.VarChar, 40)
            parm.SourceColumn = "CompanyName"

            .UpdateCommand = New SqlCommand("UpdateCustomerCompanyName",
             ➥connection)
            .UpdateCommand.CommandType = CommandType.StoredProcedure
            parm = .UpdateCommand.Parameters.Add("@CustomerID",
            ➥SqlDbType.Char, 5)
            parm.SourceColumn = "CustomerID"
            parm = .UpdateCommand.Parameters.Add("@CompanyName",
            ➥SqlDbType.VarChar, 40)
            parm.SourceColumn = "CompanyName"

            .DeleteCommand = New SqlCommand("DeleteCustomer", connection)
            .DeleteCommand.CommandType = CommandType.StoredProcedure
            parm = .DeleteCommand.Parameters.Add("@CustomerID",
            ➥SqlDbType.Char, 5)
            parm.SourceColumn = "CustomerID"

            connection.Open()
            .Update(ds, "NorthwindCustomers")
        End With
    End Sub

    Public Sub DumpTable(ByVal ds As DataSet)
        Dim table As DataTable
        For Each table In ds.Tables

            Response.Write("<h1>" + table.TableName + "</h1>")
            Response.Write("<table border=""1"" cellpadding=""2""
            ➥cellspacing=""2"">")
            Response.Write("<tr>")
            Dim column As DataColumn
            For Each column In table.Columns

                Response.Write("<th>" + column.ColumnName + "</th>")
            Next column
            Response.Write("</tr>")
            Dim row As DataRow
```

```
        For Each row In table.Rows

            Response.Write("<tr>")
            For Each column In table.Columns
                Response.Write("<td>" + row(column).ToString() + "</td>")
            Next column
            Response.Write("</tr>")
        Next row
        Response.Write("</table>")
    Next table

End Sub


Private Sub Page_Load(ByVal sender As System.Object, ByVal e As
System.EventArgs)
    'Get the connection string from web.config
    Dim connectionString As String =
ConfigurationSettings.AppSettings.Item("connectionString")
    'Get a populated DataSet object
    Dim ds As DataSet = GetDS(connectionString)
    Dim table As DataTable = ds.Tables("NorthwindCustomers")
    Dim row As DataRow

    'Use an array to add a single row to the table.
    Dim values() As String = Array.CreateInstance(GetType(String), 2)
    values.SetValue("VBDNA", 0)
    values.SetValue("Kirk Allen Evans", 1)
    row = table.Rows.Add(values)

    'Use the NewRow method to add a new row to the table
    row = ds.Tables("NorthwindCustomers").NewRow()
    row.Item("CustomerID") = "CARSN"
    row.Item("CompanyName") = "Carson Allen Evans"

    'The LoadDataRow method will update the row if it is found,
    'otherwise it will create a row with the values
    values.SetValue("DEANA", 0)
    values.SetValue("Deanna Evans", 1)
    row = table.LoadDataRow(values, True)

    Dim foundRows() As DataRow = table.Select("CustomerID LIKE 'TEST%'")
    For Each row In foundRows
        row.Delete()
    Next

    UpdateDS(connectionString, ds)

    'Get a new copy of the underlying data
    ds = GetDS(connectionString)
    DumpTable(ds)
End Sub

</script>
```

The DataAdapter exposes properties for performing SQL SELECT, INSERT, UPDATE, and DELETE operations. These are shown in the UpdateDS method in Listing 8.13.

The Command object was used in previous examples throughout this chapter, so this object is nothing new. Separate Command objects perform the data manipulation and are specified by using the respective InsertCommand, UpdateCommand, and DeleteCommand properties. But here is what is really cool: You can use the SourceColumn property of the Parameter object to specify the column in the DataSet to read the value from. You can then call the Update method of the DataAdapter, specifying the DataSet and its DataTable that you want to modify, and call a single Update method. Any inserted rows will call the InsertCommand to perform the insertion, any deleted rows will call the DeleteCommand to perform the deletion, and updated rows will call the UpdateCommand to perform the update. It's all done in one shot. (Pretty cool, huh?)

To test this, insert some fake data into the Northwinds database. Open Query Analyzer again, connect to the Northwinds database, and enter the following code into the code pane:

```
INSERT INTO Customers (CustomerID, CompanyName) VALUES ('TEST1','Testing 1')
INSERT INTO Customers (CustomerID, CompanyName) VALUES ('TEST2','Testing 2')
INSERT INTO Customers (CustomerID, CompanyName) VALUES ('TEST3','Testing 3')
INSERT INTO Customers (CustomerID, CompanyName) VALUES ('TEST4','Testing 4')
INSERT INTO Customers (CustomerID, CompanyName) VALUES ('TEST5','Testing 5')
INSERT INTO Customers (CustomerID, CompanyName) VALUES ('TEST6','Testing 6')
```

Press the F5 button, and the data is inserted into the database. Finally, run your sample project by opening listing8_13.aspx in your browser.

The end result of this example is that all the data in all the tables for the DataSet is displayed as individual HTML tables, which shows you that three rows were successfully added to the database and the six test rows were deleted.

DataRelations

DataSets can represent data as a hierarchical set of relational views and an XML view. This is achieved through the DataRelation object, as follows:

```
ds.Relations.Add("CustomerOrders",
ds.Tables("NorthwindCustomers").Columns("CustomerID"),
ds.Tables("NorthwindOrders").Columns("CustomerID"))
```

Those familiar with the MSDataShape provider can see the vast improvement in this method. This allows you to relate the data in the parent table with the data in the child table. We can see this in use in the sections, "Binding to Controls," and "XmlDataDocument."

The *SqlDataCommand* Class Revisited

The `SqlDataCommand` class provides several methods in addition to the `DataSet` class for working with XML. These methods are contained in the `SqlDataCommand` class and are not part of the base `IDbDataCommand` interface because returning XML from a database is a SQL Server-specific implementation not found in most data stores. Listing 8.14 uses the `ExecuteXmlReader` method of the `SqlDataCommand` object to return XML data from SQL Server.

Listing 8.14 **Using the *ExecuteXmlReader* Method**

```
Imports System.Xml
Imports System.Data.SqlClient
Public Class WebForm1
  Inherits System.Web.UI.Page

#Region " Web Form Designer Generated Code "

  'This call is required by the Web Form Designer.
  <System.Diagnostics.DebuggerStepThrough()> Private Sub
  ⇒InitializeComponent()

  End Sub

  Private Sub Page_Init(ByVal sender As System.Object, ByVal e As
  ⇒System.EventArgs) Handles MyBase.Init
    'CODEGEN: This method call is required by the Web Form Designer
    'Do not modify it using the code editor.
    InitializeComponent()
  End Sub

#End Region

  Private Sub Page_Load(ByVal sender As System.Object, ByVal e As
  ⇒System.EventArgs) Handles MyBase.Load
    Call GetXMLFromDb("Server=p450;Database=Northwind;User ID=sa;Password=;")

  End Sub

  Public Sub GetXMLFromDb(ByVal connectionString)
    Dim connection As SqlConnection = New SqlConnection(connectionString)
    Dim command As SqlCommand = New SqlCommand("SELECT TOP 5 CustomerID,
    ⇒CompanyName FROM CUSTOMERS FOR XML AUTO")
    command.CommandType = CommandType.Text
    command.Connection = connection
    connection.Open()
    'Fill the XmlTextReader with the XML returned from the database
    Dim reader As System.Xml.XmlTextReader = command.ExecuteXmlReader()
    Response.ContentType = "text/xml"
```

continues

Listing 8.14   **Continued**

```
Dim writer As System.Xml.XmlWriter = New
➥System.Xml.XmlTextWriter(Response.OutputStream,
➥System.Text.Encoding.UTF8)

writer.WriteStartDocument(True)
writer.WriteStartElement("DATA")
While reader.Read()

  Select Case reader.NodeType
    Case XmlNodeType.Element
      writer.WriteStartElement(reader.LocalName)
      If reader.HasAttributes() Then

        writer.WriteAttributes(reader, True)
      End If
      If reader.IsEmptyElement Then
        writer.WriteEndElement()
      End If
    Case XmlNodeType.EndElement
      writer.WriteEndElement()
  End Select
End While

writer.WriteEndElement()
writer.WriteEndDocument()
writer.Close()
reader.Close()
connection.Close()
connection.Dispose()
command.Dispose()

  End Sub

End Class
```

You look at how SQL Server generates XML data in Chapter 9. But you can see here that the SQL Server implementation of the IDbDataCommand interface extends support for returning XML data from the database.

Another function to note is the WriteAttributes method of the XmlWriter. This method writes all the attributes for the current node of an XmlReader. The output of this method is shown here:

```
<?xml version="1.0" encoding="utf-8" ?>
<DATA>
    <CUSTOMERS CustomerID="ALFKI" CompanyName="Alfreds Futterkiste" />
    <CUSTOMERS CustomerID="ANATR" CompanyName="Ana Trujillo Emparedados y
    ➥helados" />
```

```
      <CUSTOMERS CustomerID="ANTON" CompanyName="Antonio Moreno Taquería" />
      <CUSTOMERS CustomerID="AROUT" CompanyName="Around the Horn" />
      <CUSTOMERS CustomerID="BERGS" CompanyName="Berglunds snabbköp" />
  </DATA>
```

The *XmlDataDocument* Class

Throughout this book, you have seen many different methods for working with XML data. You have used stream-based readers and writers, in-memory DOM representations, IXPathNavigable documents, and now the ADO.NET DataSet and SqlCommand objects. As you are already aware, each of these approaches to working with XML can usually be mixed with another approach. The DataSet class is no exception.

A DataSet object can easily be represented either as XML or as a relational object view, as you saw earlier using relations.

```
ds.Relations.Add("CustomerOrders",
    ds.Tables("NorthwindCustomers").Columns("CustomerID"),
    ds.Tables("NorthwindOrders").Columns("CustomerID"))
```

The flexibility of the DataSet comes with several drawbacks. When loading the XML into a DataSet, only the data that is meaningful to the relational view is preserved. Element ordering can change, white space is not preserved, and content not mapped to the DataSet's schema is discarded. These are rational limitations to working with XML in a relational view. If you must preserve document fidelity, consider using the XmlDataDocument class instead.

The XmlDataDocument class is flexible and is designed for working with the DataSet and its XML capabilities.

Besides preserving the source XML document's original structure, using the XmlDataDocument class provides several benefits. Because the DataSet provides hierarchy and supports XML, it is possible to use tools such as XPath and XSLT with the XML it provides.

Preserving Document Fidelity

If you want to preserve the original XML document when working with XML data using a DataSet, use the XmlDataDocument class.

Another key benefit of using the XmlDataDocument with the DataSet is that changes between each associated object can be automatically synchronized (see Figure 8.9). This means that changes in the DataSet are reflected in the XmlDataDocument instance associated with the DataSet. Because the DataSet is only concerned with data that fits within its relational view, however, nodes added to the XML document that do not fit within the DataSet's schema are not synchronized.

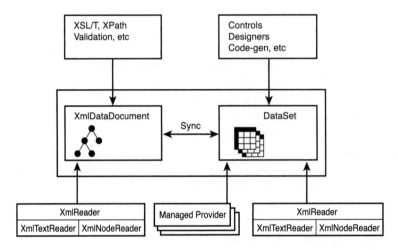

Figure 8.9 The synchronization between XmlDataDocument and the DataSet.

The XmlDataDocument class is inherited from XmlDocument. Tables 7.6 and 7.7 in Chapter 7 show the properties and methods of the XmlDocument class. The XmlDataDocument class adds several properties and methods to the XmlDocument class, which are shown in Tables 8.10 and 8.11.

Table 8.10 **Properties Added by** *XmlDataDocument*

Member Name	Description
DataSet	Gets a DataSet that can access the data in the XmlDataDocument by using a relational model.

Table 8.11 **Methods Added by** *XmlDataDocument*

Member Name	Description
GetElementFromRow	Returns the XmlElement that contains an XML representation of the specified DataRow.
GetRowFromElement	The inverse of the GetElementFromRow method, returns a DataRow associated with the specified XmlElement.

Listing 8.7 introduced you to working with XML and the DataSet class and introduced a new version of the GetDS method that returns a DataSet that was populated from an XML file and an XSD schema. This example is again utilized here:

```
public DataSet GetDS(String connectionString, String
➥schemaFilePath, String xmlFilePath)
{

    DataSet ds = new DataSet();

    ds.ReadXmlSchema(schemaFilePath);
    ds.ReadXml(xmlFilePath, XmlReadMode.IgnoreSchema);
    ds.AcceptChanges();
    try
    {
        ds.EnforceConstraints = true;
    }
    catch(Exception e)
    {
        Response.Write("<h1>The input file failed
        ➥validation.</h1>");
        foreach(DataTable table in ds.Tables)
        {
            DataRow [] errorRows = table.GetErrors();
            if (errorRows != null)
            {
                Response.ContentType = "text/html";
                Response.Clear();
                Response.Write("<h3>Error in " +
                ➥table.TableName + "</h3>");
                foreach(DataRow row in errorRows)
                {
                    Response.Write ("<i>" + row.RowError +
                    ➥"</i><br/>" );

                    DataColumn [] errorColumns =
                    ➥row.GetColumnsInError();
                    if (errorColumns.Length > 0)
                    {
                        Response.Write ("The following
                        ➥columns are in error:");
                        Response.Write("<ul>");
                        foreach(DataColumn column in
                        ➥errorColumns)
                        {
                            Response.Write("<li>" +
                            ➥column.ColumnName + "</li>");
                        }
                        Response.Write("</ul>");
```

```
                                    }
                                }
                            }

                        }
                        ds.Dispose();
                        throw (new System.Xml.Schema.XmlSchemaException("One or
                        ➥more tables in the DataSet failed validation.",e));
                    }
                    return(ds);
                }
```

The next step is to set up more versions of the DumpTable to output the results as an HTML table:

```
                public void DumpTable(XPathNodeIterator iterator)
                {

                    Response.Write("<table border=\"1\"");
                    Response.Write("<tr>");
                    Response.Write("<td>Name</td>");
                    Response.Write("<td>BaseURI</td>");
                    Response.Write("<td>LocalName</td>");
                    Response.Write("<td>NamespaceURI</td>");
                    Response.Write("<td>Prefix</td>");
                    Response.Write("</tr>");

                    while(iterator.MoveNext())
                    {
                        Response.Write("<tr>");
                        Response.Write("<td>" + iterator.Current.Name + "</td>");
                        Response.Write("<td>" + iterator.Current.BaseURI  +
                        ➥"</td>");
                        Response.Write("<td>" + iterator.Current.LocalName   +
                        ➥"</td>");
                        Response.Write("<td>" + iterator.Current.NamespaceURI
                        ➥+ "</td>");
                        Response.Write("<td>" + iterator.Current.Prefix      +
                        ➥"</td>");
                        Response.Write("</tr>");

                    }
                    Response.Write("</table>");
                }

                public void DumpTable(XmlElement element)
                {
                    Response.Write("<table border=\"1\"");
                    Response.Write("<tr>");
                    Response.Write("<td>Name</td>");
                    Response.Write("<td>BaseURI</td>");
```

```
        Response.Write("<td>LocalName</td>");
        Response.Write("<td>NamespaceURI</td>");
        Response.Write("<td>Prefix</td>");
        Response.Write("</tr>");

        Response.Write("<tr>");
        Response.Write("<td>" + element.Name + "</td>");
        Response.Write("<td>" + element.BaseURI   + "</td>");
        Response.Write("<td>" + element.LocalName    + "</td>");
        Response.Write("<td>" + element.NamespaceURI    + "</td>");
        Response.Write("<td>" + element.Prefix       + "</td>");
        Response.Write("</tr>");

        Response.Write("</table>");
    }

    public void DumpTable(DataRow row)
    {
        //Outputs a single DataRow as an HTML table
        Response.Write("<h4>Table:" + row.Table.TableName + "</h4>");
        Response.Write("<table border=\"1\" cellpadding=\"2\"
        ⇒cellspacing=\"2\">");
        Response.Write("<tr>");
        foreach(DataColumn column in row.Table.Columns)
        {
            Response.Write("<th>" + column.ColumnName + "</th>");
        }
        Response.Write("</tr>");

        Response.Write("<tr>");
        foreach(DataColumn column in row.Table.Columns)
        {
            Response.Write("<td>" + row[column].ToString() +
            ⇒"</td>");
        }
        Response.Write("</tr>");

        Response.Write("</table>");
    }
```

The overloaded version of the DumpTable method that accepts a DataRow uses
the Table method to retrieve the DataTable that the DataRow belongs to. This
enables you to retrieve the TableName of the table and output it. Each DataRow
object is indexed on its columns. To retrieve the list of columns, you must
resort back to the Columns collection of the Table object the current DataRow
belongs to.

The following sample.xml file from Listing 8.9 and the sample1.xsd file from
Listing 8.8 are used here.

Create a new web form called Listing8_15.aspx and paste the code from Listing 8.15 into the code-behind view.

Listing 8.15 **Navigating a *DataSet* Using *XmlDataDocument* and XPath**

```
Imports System.Xml
Imports System.Xml.XPath
Imports System.Data
Imports System.Data.SqlClient


Public Class Listing8_15
    Inherits System.Web.UI.Page

#Region " Web Form Designer Generated Code "

    'This call is required by the Web Form Designer.
    <System.Diagnostics.DebuggerStepThrough()> Private Sub
    ➥InitializeComponent()

    End Sub

    Private Sub Page_Init(ByVal sender As System.Object, ByVal e As
    ➥System.EventArgs) Handles MyBase.Init
        'CODEGEN: This method call is required by the Web Form Designer
        'Do not modify it using the code editor.
        InitializeComponent()
    End Sub

#End Region

    Public Function GetDS(ByVal schemaFilePath As String, ByVal xmlFilePath
    ➥As String) As DataSet

        Dim ds As DataSet = New DataSet()

        ds.ReadXmlSchema(schemaFilePath)
        ds.ReadXml(xmlFilePath, XmlReadMode.IgnoreSchema)
        ds.AcceptChanges()
        Try
            ds.EnforceConstraints = True
        Catch e As System.Exception

            Response.Write("<h1>The input file failed validation.</h1>")
            Dim table As DataTable
            For Each table In ds.Tables

                Dim errorRows() As DataRow = table.GetErrors()
                If errorRows Is Nothing Then
```

```vb
            Response.ContentType = "text/html"
            Response.Clear()
            Response.Write("<h3>Error in " + table.TableName +
            ➥"</h3>")
            Dim row As DataRow
            For Each row In errorRows

                Response.Write("<i>" + row.RowError + "</i><br/>")

                Dim errorColumns() As DataColumn =
                ➥row.GetColumnsInError()
                If errorColumns.Length > 0 Then

                    Response.Write("The following columns are in
                    ➥error:")
                    Response.Write("<ul>")
                    Dim column As DataColumn
                    For Each column In errorColumns

                        Response.Write("<li>" + column.ColumnName +
                        ➥"</li>")
                    Next column
                    Response.Write("</ul>")
                End If
            Next row
        End If
    Next table
    ds.Dispose()
    Throw (New System.Xml.Schema.XmlSchemaException("One or more
    ➥tables in the DataSet failed validation.", e))
    End Try
    ds.Dispose()
    Return (ds)
End Function

Private Sub Page_Load(ByVal sender As Object, ByVal e As
➥System.EventArgs) Handles MyBase.Load

    Dim connectionString As String =
    ➥ConfigurationSettings.AppSettings.Get("connectionString")
    Dim ds As DataSet
    Dim writer As XmlWriter = New XmlTextWriter(Response.OutputStream,
    ➥System.Text.Encoding.UTF8)
    Try

        ds = GetDS(Server.MapPath("sample1.xsd"),
        ➥Server.MapPath("sample.xml"))
        Response.ContentType = "text/html"
        Dim doc As XmlDataDocument = New XmlDataDocument(ds)
```

continues

Listing 8.15 **Continued**

```
                        Dim ns As XmlNamespaceManager = New
                    ⇒XmlNamespaceManager(doc.NameTable)
                        ns.AddNamespace("bar", "http://tempuri.org/sample1.xsd")
                        'Select a Customer element
                        Dim query As String = "bar:Customers/bar:Customer[@id='ALFKI']"
                        Dim element As XmlElement = CType(doc.SelectSingleNode(query,
                    ⇒ns), XmlElement)
                        Dim row As DataRow = doc.GetRowFromElement(element)

                        Response.Write("<h3>Results Using SelectSingleNode</h3>")
                        DumpTable(row)

                        Dim foundRows() As DataRow =
                    ⇒ds.Tables("Customer").Select("id='VBDNA'")
                        Response.Write("<h3>Results Using GetElementFromRow</h3>")
                        Dim foundRow As DataRow

                        For Each foundRow In foundRows
                            element = doc.GetElementFromRow(foundRow)
                            DumpTable(element)
                        Next foundRow

                        'Select a Contact element
                        query = "bar:Customers/bar:Customer[@id='ALFKI']/bar:Contact"
                        'Use the XPathNavigator class for XPath queries from DataSet
                        Dim nav As XPathNavigator = doc.CreateNavigator()
                        Dim expression As XPathExpression = nav.Compile(query)
                        expression.SetContext(ns)
                        Dim iterator As XPathNodeIterator =
                    ⇒CType(nav.Evaluate(expression), XPathNodeIterator)
                        Response.Write("<h3>Results Using XPathNavigator</h3>")
                        DumpTable(iterator)

                    Catch oops As Exception

                        Response.Write(oops.ToString())

                    Finally

                        writer.Close()
                        If Not ds Is Nothing Then ds.Dispose()
                    End Try
                End Sub



    Public Sub DumpTable(ByVal iterator As XPathNodeIterator)
```

```
    Response.Write("<table border=""1""")
    Response.Write("<tr>")
    Response.Write("<td>Name</td>")
    Response.Write("<td>BaseURI</td>")
    Response.Write("<td>LocalName</td>")
    Response.Write("<td>NamespaceURI</td>")
    Response.Write("<td>Prefix</td>")
    Response.Write("</tr>")

    While (iterator.MoveNext())

        Response.Write("<tr>")
        Response.Write("<td>" + iterator.Current.Name + "</td>")
        Response.Write("<td>" + iterator.Current.BaseURI + "</td>")
        Response.Write("<td>" + iterator.Current.LocalName + "</td>")
        Response.Write("<td>" + iterator.Current.NamespaceURI + "</td>")
        Response.Write("<td>" + iterator.Current.Prefix + "</td>")
        Response.Write("</tr>")

    End While
    Response.Write("</table>")
End Sub

Public Sub DumpTable(ByVal element As XmlElement)

    Response.Write("<table border=""1""")
    Response.Write("<tr>")
    Response.Write("<td>Name</td>")
    Response.Write("<td>BaseURI</td>")
    Response.Write("<td>LocalName</td>")
    Response.Write("<td>NamespaceURI</td>")
    Response.Write("<td>Prefix</td>")
    Response.Write("</tr>")

    Response.Write("<tr>")
    Response.Write("<td>" + element.Name + "</td>")
    Response.Write("<td>" + element.BaseURI + "</td>")
    Response.Write("<td>" + element.LocalName + "</td>")
    Response.Write("<td>" + element.NamespaceURI + "</td>")
    Response.Write("<td>" + element.Prefix + "</td>")
    Response.Write("</tr>")

    Response.Write("</table>")
End Sub

Public Sub DumpTable(ByVal row As DataRow)

    'Outputs a single DataRow as an HTML table
    Response.Write("<h4>Table:" + row.Table.TableName + "</h4>")
    Response.Write("<table border=""1"" cellpadding=""2""
    ➥cellspacing=""2"">")
```

continues

Listing 8.15 **Continued**

```
        Response.Write("<tr>")
        Dim column As DataColumn

        For Each column In row.Table.Columns

            Response.Write("<th>" + column.ColumnName + "</th>")
        Next column
        Response.Write("</tr>")

        Response.Write("<tr>")
        For Each column In row.Table.Columns
            Response.Write("<td>" + row(column).ToString() + "</td>")
        Next column
        Response.Write("</tr>")

        Response.Write("</table>")
    End Sub

End Class
```

The cool part of this example is in the Page_Load event handler. You are able to create an XmlDataDocument based on the DataSet and then run XPath queries against the XmlDataDocument class itself. This enables you to create robust solutions using XPath to query relational data such as tables in a mainframe where XPath is not supported.

The output from this example is shown in Figure 8.10.

Recall from Chapter 7 that the XmlDocument class supports the IXPathNavigable interface, which exposes a CreateNavigator method that can be used with the XPathNavigator and XsltTransform classes. Because the XmlDataDocument class inherits from XmlDocument, you can (by proxy) use these classes with the XmlDataDocument class. Use the CreateNavigator method to retrieve an XPathNavigator.

The XML sample that you are using contains namespaces. Recall from Chapter 7 that you use the XmlNamespaceManager object to express the namespaces for the XML document so that you can prefix them for XPath queries. You associated the namespace URI urn:foo:bar with the prefix bar. You can now use the prefix in your XPath queries, as shown here:

```
string expression = "bar:Customers/bar:Customer[@id='ALFKI']/bar:Contact";
```

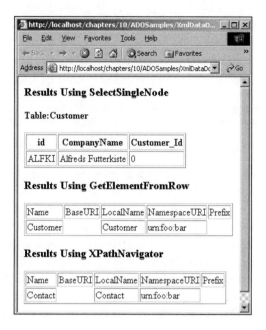

Figure 8.10   The output from Listing 8.15 shows the results
of querying the XmlDataDocument using XPath.

Use the XmlNamespaceManager to query the XmlDataDocument, retrieving an
XmlNode object that you cast to XmlElement. You can now use the element to
retrieve a DataRow from the DataSet, as shown here:

```
XmlElement element = (XmlElement)doc.SelectSingleNode(query,ns);
DataRow row = doc.GetRowFromElement(element);
```

Earlier in this chapter, you used the Select method of the DataTable object to
select rows matching the selection criteria. Use this method again in the following code to retrieve rows, iterate through each DataRow, and retrieve an
XmlElement that's output as HTML:

```
DataRow [] foundRows = ds.Tables["Customer"].Select("id='VBDNA'");
Response.Write("<h3>Results Using GetElementFromRow</h3>");
foreach(DataRow foundRow in foundRows)
{
    element = doc.GetElementFromRow(foundRow);
    DumpTable(element);
}
```

Just as with the SelectSingleNode example, you must associate a namespace with a prefix by using the XmlNamespaceManager class to run XPath queries against XML that uses namespaces. Do this by using the SetContext method of the XPathExpression object, as follows:

```
//Select a Contact element
query = "bar:Customers/bar:Customer[@id='ALFKI']/bar:Contact";
//Use the XPathNavigator class for XPath queries from DataSet
XPathNavigator nav = doc.CreateNavigator();
XPathExpression expression = nav.Compile(query);
expression.SetContext(ns);
XPathNodeIterator iterator = (XPathNodeIterator)nav.Evaluate(expression);
Response.Write("<h3>Results Using XPathNavigator</h3>");
DumpTable(iterator);
```

The return from the Evaluate method returns an Object, so you have to explicitly cast the Object as an XPathNodeIterator. After you have the iterator, you can output its contents as HTML.

Another option that the XmlDataDocument gives you is the ability to apply an XSLT transformation directly to a DataSet. Although it is possible to use this ability to output HTML from a DataSet, it would probably be more practical to bind the DataSet directly to a DataGrid control or other web control. Instead, the ability to apply an XSLT transformation to a DataSet can be incredibly useful any time you need to convert relational data (probably coming from a database) into XML. For example, you might have a business partner that needs periodic dumps of part of your relational database, but he needs the data to conform to a particular XML Schema, or he just finds XML to be the easiest format to import. Microsoft SQL Server 2000 has the ability to output relational data as XML directly, but the DataSet method has the advantage that it can work with any database at all (or any data source that can be loaded into a DataSet, database or not).

As an example, complete the following steps:

1. Load some data from the Northwind sample database that comes with SQL Server into a DataSet, and produce a hierarchical XML file from that data.

2. To produce a single XML file with one entry for each customer, containing all the orders for that customer, load both the Customers and the Orders tables from the Northwind database into a single DataSet, and set up a relation within the DataSet (each order is placed by a customer).

3. Wrap the DataSet in an XmlDataDocument object, and transform that object with an XSLT stylesheet and the XML web control, streaming the resulting XML to the browser.

4. Create a new Web Application Project in Visual Studio .NET and call the project "XSLT".

5. Add a new web form to the project; call it DSTransform.aspx.

6. Add a new XML web control from the toolbox to the page, and make its ID OrderOutput. The HTML view should look similar to this:

```
<%@ Page language="c#" Codebehind="DSTransform.aspx.cs"
➥AutoEventWireup="false" Inherits="XSLT.DSTransform" %>
<asp:Xml id="OrderOutput" runat="server"/>
```

There's not much to it, really. The remainder of the code goes into the code-behind file for this page, in the Page_Load event handler.

7. Add a using or Imports statement for the System.Xml namespace. The Page_Load method looks like this:

```
protected System.Web.UI.WebControls.Xml OrderOutput;

private void Page_Load(object sender, System.EventArgs e)
{
    string connectionString = "Data Source=localhost;Initial
    ➥Catalog=Northwind;Integrated Security=SSPI;";
    SqlConnection myConnection = new SqlConnection(connectionString);
    SqlDataAdapter customerAdapter = new SqlDataAdapter("SELECT *
    ➥FROM Customers", myConnection);
    SqlDataAdapter orderAdapter = new SqlDataAdapter("SELECT *
    ➥FROM Orders", myConnection);

    DataSet myDataSet = new DataSet("CustomerOrders");

    try
    {
        myConnection.Open();
        customerAdapter.Fill(myDataSet, "Customers");
        orderAdapter.Fill(myDataSet, "Orders");
    }
    finally
    {
        if (myConnection.State == ConnectionState.Open)
            myConnection.Close();
    }

    DataRelation custOrderRelation = new
    ➥DataRelation("CustomerOrderXREF",
```

```
                        myDataSet.Tables["Customers"].Columns["CustomerID"],
                        myDataSet.Tables["Orders"].Columns["CustomerID"]);
            custOrderRelation.Nested = true;

            myDataSet.Relations.Add(custOrderRelation);

            XmlDataDocument xmlDoc = new XmlDataDocument(myDataSet);

            OrderOutput.Document = xmlDoc;
            OrderOutput.TransformSource = "CustomerOrders.xslt";

            Response.Clear();
            Response.ContentType = "text/xml";
        }
```

As you can see in this code, you begin by creating one `SqlDataAdapter` for each table from which you're selecting. Select all records from each table into separate tables with the same names in the `DataSet` that you create. Then set up a `DataRelation` that joins the `CustomerID` in the `Orders` table to the `CustomerID` in the `Customers` table. Then add the `DataRelation` to the `DataSet`, and create a new `XmlDataDocument` from the `DataSet`, and pass the `XmlDataDocument` to the `Document` property of the `OrderOutput` object (remember that `OrderOutput` is the XML web control that you added to the page previously). Then set the `TransformSource` of the `OrderOutput` object, and set the `ContentType` of the page to `text/xml`.

At this point, it is necessary to examine the XSLT stylesheet in Listing 8.16, which you use to do the transformation. You did not start with the stylesheet because much of it depends on the names used in creating the `DataSet` in the code that was just examined.

Listing 8.16   *CustomerOrders.xslt*

```
<?xml version="1.0" encoding="UTF-8" ?>
<xsl:stylesheet version="1.0"
xmlns:xsl="http://www.w3.org/1999/XSL/Transform">

    <xsl:template match="CustomerOrders">
        <Customers>
            <xsl:apply-templates select="Customers"/>
        </Customers>
    </xsl:template>

    <xsl:template match="Customers">
        <Customer>
            <CustomerID><xsl:value-of select="CustomerID"/></CustomerID>
            <CompanyName><xsl:value-of
```

```
    ➥select="CompanyName"/></CompanyName>
    <Contact>
        <Name><xsl:value-of select="ContactName"/></Name>
        <Title><xsl:value-of select="ContactTitle"/></Title>
        <Phone><xsl:value-of select="Phone"/></Phone>
        <Fax><xsl:value-of select="Fax"/></Fax>
        <Address>
            <Street><xsl:value-of select="Address"/></Street>
            <City><xsl:value-of select="City"/></City>
            <Region><xsl:value-of select="Region"/></Region>
            <PostalCode><xsl:value-of
            ➥select="PostalCode"/></PostalCode>
            <Country><xsl:value-of select="Country"/></Country>
        </Address>
    </Contact>
    <Orders>
        <xsl:apply-templates select="Orders"/>
    </Orders>
    </Customer>
</xsl:template>

<xsl:template match="Orders">
    <Order>
        <OrderID><xsl:value-of select="OrderID"/></OrderID>
        <OrderDate><xsl:value-of select="OrderDate"/></OrderDate>
        <Shipping>
            <Name><xsl:value-of select="ShipName"/></Name>
            <Address><xsl:value-of select="ShipAddress"/></Address>
            <City><xsl:value-of select="ShipCity"/></City>
            <Region><xsl:value-of select="ShipRegion"/></Region>
            <PostalCode><xsl:value-of
            ➥select="ShipPostalCode"/></PostalCode>
            <Country><xsl:value-of select="ShipCountry"/></Country>
        </Shipping>
    </Order>
</xsl:template>

</xsl:stylesheet>
```

This stylesheet consists basically of three templates. It is important to note which XML tags are being matched on for these templates, and compare those names to the code you just wrote for the code-behind of DSTransform.aspx. Because the data you intend to feed to this stylesheet does not come from an XML file, the tag names you must use are derived from the the column names in the source database and from the names that you give to the DataSet, and each of the tables it contains.

The first template matches on a tag called CustomerOrders. If you look for that name in the code-behind file, you'll find it on this line:

```
DataSet myDataSet = new DataSet("CustomerOrders");
```

That tells you that the root element of the virtual XML document created from the DataSet is the name that you give to the DataSet when you create it. If you do not assign a name to the DataSet, a default name, such as NewDataSet, is assigned.

The next template matches on a tag called Customers. This is taken from the name of the Customers table in the DataSet, created on the following line:

```
customerAdapter.Fill(myDataSet, "Customers");
```

Likewise, the template that matches on the Orders tag uses the name of the Orders table in the same DataSet. This stylesheet then produces an XML document with a root element called Customers. This element contains a series of Customer elements, which, in turn, contain customer details and a series of Order elements that contain details of each order that a particular customer has placed. After you compile the project and open the page in a browser, the resulting XML file looks something like Figure 8.11. The result is a database-independent and simple way of turning relational data into hierarchical XML.

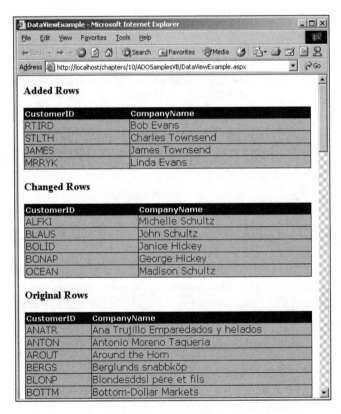

Figure 8.11   Hierarchical XML can be easily produced from any relational database.

Chapter Summary

ADO.NET certainly has brought many changes with it. Sadly, there is only so much room in a book to cover such a broad subject. We have tried to cover the most important concepts, focusing on ASP.NET development and ADO.NET's XML capabilities.

As you have seen, ADO.NET adds much in the way of XML support. You can use XML Schemas to define the structure of a `DataSet`, validate its contents, and validate data that is added or changed.

The `DataSet` class provides great flexibility compared to the `ADODB.Recordset` class that we have all grown to love so much. The `DataSet` can also work with an `XmlDataDocument` to provide extremely flexible solutions.

This chapter focused on ADO.NET and accessing databases. Chapter 9 focuses on what XML support SQL Server provides natively and how you can merge ADO.NET and SQL Server's XML support together to develop robust custom solutions.

References

[1] Appendix A: ADO Programmer's Reference, version 2.7.
ms-help://MS.VSCC/MS.MSDNVS/ado270/htm/mdrefadoprovinfo.htm
[2] .NET Data Providers: .NET Framework Developer's Guide.
ms-help://MS.VSCC/MS.MSDNVS/cpguide/html/cpconadonetproviders.htm
[3] Retrieving Data Using the `DataReader`: .NET Framework Developer's Guide.
ms-help://MS.VSCC/MS.MSDNVS/cpguide/html/cpcontheadonetdatareader.htm
[4] Creating and Using DataViews: .NET Framework Developer's Guide.
ms-help://MS.VSCC/MS.MSDNVS/cpguide/html/cpconcreatingusingdataviews.htm

9

SQL Server 2000 and XML

SQL SERVER 2000 HAS SEVERAL KEY FEATURES right out of the box that enable support for XML. Combining these features with ADO.NET and the XML Framework classes provide a broad range of options for working with data, which simplifies data access over the web.

In addition to the XML support that an out-of-the-box installation of SQL Server provides, Microsoft has also released SQLXML 3.0, a service pack to SQL Server that provides additional features to those already present in SQL Server 2000. The installation executable can be obtained from `www.microsoft.com/sqlserver`.

The first portion of this chapter deals with XML support in a base installment of SQL Server 2000. The additional features SQLXML 3.0 adds is covered later in this chapter.

SQL Server 2000 XML Support

As you will see throughout this chapter, SQL Server 2000 provides several important options for reading XML data from SQL Server. You can explicitly query the database and request XML data back using the `FOR XML` clause. You can also query SQL Server over HTTP, which enables you to create XML views of relational data that can be queried by using XPath syntax.

SQL Server 2000 added a set of reserved words that extract data with an XML representation. These reserved words are associated with the FOR XML and OPENXML clauses.

FOR XML

Suppose that you want to represent all the rows in the Customers table in the Northwind database as XML. What is the best approach to solving this problem? One way to do this is to fill an ADO.NET DataSet object, loop through the rows and columns of its Table object, and add each column to an XmlDocument object. You have already seen better ways to handle this problem because the DataSet object provides rich XML support.

Another approach, then, is to simply fill the DataSet object and use the ReadXml method to extract XML from the DataSet object. Both approaches solve the problem by loading all the data into memory and creating an XML representation. As you see repeatedly throughout this chapter, SQL Server's XML support provides you with a range of options for working with data as XML.

One way that SQL Server 2000 adds XML support is through the addition of the FOR XML clause. Using this new clause, you can query the database and have the results returned as XML rather than as a tabular resultset. Providing XML bypasses the need to load the tabular data into an interim object, such as ADO.NET, and loop through the records to create an XML representation. Using the FOR XML clause in a SQL statement causes the results to be returned as XML data rather than as tabular data.

FOR XML Returns Multiple Rows When Not Streamed

Behind the scenes, a single column resultset is returned. The results of the XML query are broken up into strings, where each row consists of up to 8,192 characters (the upper limit for the number of characters that a row can contain). But because you receive the entire resultset using a stream, breaking the XML into different rows makes no difference.

The XML returned as a result of a FOR XML query does not contain a root node; it only represents the rows that are returned. When outputting the results from an XML query, add your own root element to make the XML well formed.

By default, elements map to a table or view, and attributes map to the table or view's columns. The FOR XML clause, however, provides several options for returning data that has other structures. The complete syntax of the FOR statement in transact SQL is represented with the following production:

```
[ FOR { BROWSE | XML { RAW | AUTO | EXPLICIT }
        [ , XMLDATA ]
        [ , ELEMENTS ]
        [ , BINARY BASE64 ]
    }
]
```

The parts of this production are described in Table 9.1.

Table 9.1 **Arguments of the *FOR XML* Clause**

Member Name	Description
RAW	Each row in the returned rowset is represented as a <row> element in the return string.
AUTO	Results are returned as a nested XML tree. The structure depends on the order in which the columns appear in the SELECT list.
EXPLICIT	Results are returned as a nested XML tree where the structure is explicitly stated.
XMLDATA	Indicates that an inline XDR Schema needs to be included with the results.
ELEMENTS	All columns in the SELECT list need to be returned as elements. If not specified, columns are returned as attributes. Used in conjunction with AUTO.
BINARYBASE64	Indicates that binary data is returned and will be encoded using Base64-encoding.

Take a look at the FOR XML clause in detail.

FOR XML RAW

Using FOR XML RAW is the simplest form of returning data from SQL Server. Each row in the returned rowset is represented as an empty <row> element with attributes that represent the columns in the resultset. Listing 9.1 shows the query using FOR XML RAW.

Listing 9.1 **A Sample *FOR XML RAW* Query**

```
SELECT  c.CustomerID, c.ContactName,
    o.ShipCity, e.FirstName + ' ' + e.LastName as EmployeeName, e.Region
FROM Customers c INNER JOIN
    Orders o ON c.CustomerID = o.CustomerID INNER JOIN
    Employees e ON o.EmployeeID = e.EmployeeID
WHERE (c.CustomerID IN ('ALFKI', 'TRAIH'))
FOR XML RAW
```

To execute this query, open up Query Analyzer for SQL Server, connect to the Northwind sample database, and paste the code from Listing 9.1 into the query window. Press the F5 key to run the query and see the results in the results pane.

The result of this query is shown in Listing 9.2. No white space is present in the actual output: It is formatted for readability.

Listing 9.2 **Abbreviated Output of the Query Shown in Listing 9.1**

```
<row CustomerID="ALFKI" ContactName="Maria Anders" ShipCity="Berlin"
➥EmployeeName="Michael Suyama" />
<row CustomerID="ALFKI" ContactName="Maria Anders" ShipCity="Berlin"
EmployeeName="Margaret Peacock" Region="WA" />
    .
    .
    .

<row CustomerID="TRAIH" ContactName="Helvetius Nagy" ShipCity="Kirkland"
➥EmployeeName="Margaret Peacock" Region="WA" />
<row CustomerID="TRAIH" ContactName="Helvetius Nagy" ShipCity="Kirkland"
➥EmployeeName="Anne Dodsworth" />
<row CustomerID="TRAIH" ContactName="Helvetius Nagy" ShipCity="Kirkland"
➥EmployeeName="Michael Suyama" />
```

No root element is returned, so this is not well-formed XML. This issue is addressed later in this section when you use the XML classes in .NET to retrieve the data. Also notice the lack of the Region attribute in the highlighted rows. This is because the value is Null in the database: Null values simply are not returned in XML representation.

FOR XML AUTO

The AUTO argument of the FOR XML clause is a flexible means of generating XML data. It structures the XML hierarchy depending on the order of the columns in the SELECT list. This means that the order of the items in the SELECT list is imperative to the structure of the XML query. Listing 9.3 shows a sample query that uses FOR XML AUTO.

Listing 9.3 **A Sample FOR XML AUTO Query**

```
SELECT Customers.CustomerID, Customers.ContactName,
    Orders.ShipCity, Employees.FirstName + ' ' + Employees.LastName as
    ➥EmployeeName, Employees.Region
FROM Customers INNER JOIN
    Orders ON Customers.CustomerID = Orders.CustomerID INNER JOIN
    Employees ON Orders.EmployeeID = Employees.EmployeeID
WHERE (Customers.CustomerID IN ('ALFKI',  'TRAIH'))
FOR XML AUTO
```

This query produces output, as shown in Listing 9.4. Again, no white space is present in the actual output for formatting and indention. This is provided for readability only.

Listing 9.4 **Output of Listing 9.3**

```
<Customers CustomerID="ALFKI" ContactName="Maria Anders">
    <Orders ShipCity="Berlin" EmployeeName="Michael Suyama">
        <Employees />
    </Orders>
    <Orders ShipCity="Berlin" EmployeeName="Margaret Peacock">
        <Employees Region="WA" />
        <Employees Region="WA" />
    </Orders>
    <Orders ShipCity="Berlin" EmployeeName="Nancy Davolio">
        <Employees Region="WA" />
        <Employees Region="WA" />
    </Orders>
    <Orders ShipCity="Berlin" EmployeeName="Janet Leverling">
        <Employees Region="WA" />
    </Orders>
</Customers>
<Customers CustomerID="TRAIH" ContactName="Helvetius Nagy">
    <Orders ShipCity="Kirkland" EmployeeName="Margaret Peacock">
        <Employees Region="WA" />
    </Orders>
    <Orders ShipCity="Kirkland" EmployeeName="Anne Dodsworth">
        <e />
    </Orders>
    <Orders ShipCity="Kirkland" EmployeeName="Michael Suyama">
        <Employees />
    </Orders>
</Customers>
```

The structure of the document was inferred from the order of columns in the SELECT list. Had you reordered the SELECT list, the output would look different. For example, change the SELECT list from what was shown in Listing 9.3 to what's shown in Listing 9.5.

Listing 9.5 **Reordering the *SELECT* List in a Query Using *FOR XML AUTO* Produces Different Output Results**

```
SELECT Orders.ShipCity, Employees.FirstName + ' ' + Employees.LastName as
EmployeeName, Employees.Region, Customers.CustomerID, Customers.ContactName
.
.
.
FOR XML AUTO
```

Although the order of JOINs is the same, the document is reordered. Listing 9.6 differs from Listing 9.4 because the hierarchical order of elements is reversed.

Listing 9.6 **The Hierarchical Order of Document Nodes Is Affected by the Order of Columns Within the *SELECT* List Shown in Listing 9.5**

```
<Orders ShipCity="Berlin" EmployeeName="Michael Suyama">
    <Employees>
        <Customers CustomerID="ALFKI" ContactName="Maria Anders" />
    </Employees>
</Orders>
<Orders ShipCity="Berlin" EmployeeName="Margaret Peacock">
    <Employees Region="WA">
        <Customers CustomerID="ALFKI" ContactName="Maria Anders" />
        <Customers CustomerID="ALFKI" ContactName="Maria Anders" />
    </Employees>
</Orders>
<Orders ShipCity="Berlin" EmployeeName="Nancy Davolio">
    <Employees Region="WA">
        <Customers CustomerID="ALFKI" ContactName="Maria Anders" />
        <Customers CustomerID="ALFKI" ContactName="Maria Anders" />
    </Employees>
</Orders>
<Orders ShipCity="Berlin" EmployeeName="Janet Leverling">
    <Employees Region="WA">
        <Customers CustomerID="ALFKI" ContactName="Maria Anders" />
    </Employees>
</Orders>
<Orders ShipCity="Kirkland" EmployeeName="Margaret Peacock">
    <Employees Region="WA">
        <Customers CustomerID="TRAIH" ContactName="Helvetius Nagy" />
    </Employees>
</Orders>
<Orders ShipCity="Kirkland" EmployeeName="Anne Dodsworth">
    <Employees>
        <Customers CustomerID="TRAIH" ContactName="Helvetius Nagy" />
    </Employees>
</Orders>
<Orders ShipCity="Kirkland" EmployeeName="Michael Suyama">
    <Employees>
        <Customers CustomerID="TRAIH" ContactName="Helvetius Nagy" />
    </Employees>
</Orders>
```

By retrieving XML in AUTO mode with the ELEMENTS argument, you can change the default behavior to return elements instead of attributes. You can change the query, as shown in Listing 9.7.

Listing 9.7   **Specifying the *ELEMENTS* Argument in a Query Using**
              FOR XML AUTO

```
SELECT  Customers.CustomerID, Customers.ContactName,
    Orders.ShipCity, Employees.FirstName + ' ' + Employees.LastName as
    ➥EmployeeName, Employees.Region
FROM Customers INNER JOIN
    Orders ON Customers.CustomerID = Orders.CustomerID INNER JOIN
    Employees ON Orders.EmployeeID = Employees.EmployeeID
WHERE (Customers.CustomerID = 'TRAIH')
FOR XML AUTO, ELEMENTS
```

The result of this query is now changed from using attribute-centric form to
element-centric form. Listing 9.8 shows that no attributes are used in the output; rather, the document is composed solely of elements.

Listing 9.8   **Output of Listing 9.7**

```
<Customers>
    <CustomerID>TRAIH</CustomerID>
    <ContactName>Helvetius Nagy</ContactName>
    <Orders>
        <ShipCity>Kirkland</ShipCity>
        <EmployeeName>Margaret Peacock</EmployeeName>
        <Employees>
            <Region>WA</Region>
        </Employees>
    </Orders>
    <Orders>
        <ShipCity>Kirkland</ShipCity>
        <EmployeeName>Anne Dodsworth</EmployeeName>
        <Employees />
    </Orders>
    <Orders>
        <ShipCity>Kirkland</ShipCity>
        <EmployeeName>Michael Suyama</EmployeeName>
        <Employees />
    </Orders>
</Customers>
```

The table names were used as the names of the XML elements up to this
point. The names of the database tables used in the queries are in plural form.
This usually indicates a collection of items rather than a grouping of a single
item for XML developers. You can rename the output columns by aliasing the
tables. Listing 9.9 shows a SQL query where the tables are aliased with uppercase names.

Listing 9.9   **Aliasing the Table Names Within the *SELECT* List Affects the Element Names in the Resulting XML**

```
SELECT  CUSTOMER.CustomerID, CUSTOMER.ContactName,
    [ORDER].ShipCity, EMPLOYEE.FirstName + ' ' + EMPLOYEE.LastName as
    ↩EmployeeName, EMPLOYEE.Region
FROM Customers CUSTOMER INNER JOIN
    Orders [ORDER] ON CUSTOMER.CustomerID = [ORDER].CustomerID INNER JOIN
    Employees EMPLOYEE ON [ORDER].EmployeeID = EMPLOYEE.EmployeeID
WHERE (CUSTOMER.CustomerID = 'TRAIH')
FOR XML AUTO, ELEMENTS
```

Listing 9.9 produces the results shown in Listing 9.10. Notice that the element names are now capitalized and in singular form.

Listing 9.10   **Output of Listing 9.9**

```
<CUSTOMER>
    <CustomerID>TRAIH</CustomerID>
    <ContactName>Helvetius Nagy</ContactName>
    <ORDER>
        <ShipCity>Kirkland</ShipCity>
        <EmployeeName>Margaret Peacock</EmployeeName>
        <EMPLOYEE>
            <Region>WA</Region>
        </EMPLOYEE>
    </ORDER>
    <ORDER>
        <ShipCity>Kirkland</ShipCity>
        <EmployeeName>Anne Dodsworth</EmployeeName>
        <EMPLOYEE />
    </ORDER>
    <ORDER>
        <ShipCity>Kirkland</ShipCity>
        <EmployeeName>Michael Suyama</EmployeeName>
        <EMPLOYEE />
    </ORDER>
</CUSTOMER>
```

An interesting inference that SQL Server makes when structuring the hierarchy is how it handles aliased or computed columns. It simply adds them as an attribute of the last table to which a column belonged. In Listing 9.10, the EmployeeName column was represented in the XML as a child of the ORDER element even though its data was retrieved from the Employees database table. You could move the column later in the SELECT list, but it turns out that there is another way of controlling the XML output and its structure.

FOR XML EXPLICIT

You saw that the AUTO mode query depends on the order of the columns in the select list. This yields a difficult to track bug in your application. Instead of relying on SQL Server's interpretation of the data's structure, you also have the capability of explicitly stating the document's structure by using EXPLICIT mode queries. To control the structure, you must use a specific syntax to control the hierarchy.

Tag *and* **Parent** *Columns*

The first step in creating an XML document explicitly with SQL Server is to use two special meta data columns in your queries:

- **Tag**—Stores the tag number of the current element.
- **Parent**—Specifies the Tag number of the element that will be this element's parent. If null, the element is placed at the top of the hierarchy.

The Tag and Parent combination defines how the data is hierarchically related.

Column Naming

The second step of using EXPLICIT mode is to specify the column names in the SELECT list. Column names have the following syntax:

```
ElementName!TagID!AttributeName!Directive
```

The parts of the column name are described in Table 9.2.

Table 9.2 **Parts of Explicit Mode Column Name**

Part	Description
ElementName	Names the output element name that is associated with the tag ID.
TagID	The number of the tag element. One TagID is used for exactly one ElementName.
AttributeName	The name of the output attribute if no directive is specified, or the name of the containing element if a directive is specified.
Directive	The directive for output. Directives are discussed later in the section, "Specifying Directives."

The sample SQL statement in Listing 9.11 produces a single level in the hierarchy.

Listing 9.11   **A Simple Query Using *EXPLICIT* Mode XML Querying**

```
SELECT
    1                   as Tag,
    NULL                as Parent,
    CustomerID          as [Customer!1!CustomerID],
    ContactName         as [Customer!1!ContactName]
FROM Customers
WHERE CustomerID IN ('ALFKI','TRAIH')
FOR XML EXPLICIT
```

This produces the XML output in Listing 9.12.

Listing 9.12   **Output of Listing 9.11**

```
<Customer CustomerID="ALFKI" ContactName="Maria Anders" />
<Customer CustomerID="TRAIH" ContactName="Helvetius Nagy" />
```

This approach can seem strange at first, but you really haven't done anything outstanding. If you execute the statement without the FOR XML EXPLICIT clause at the end, you'd have a resultset that looks similar to what's shown in Figure 9.1.

Tag	Parent	Customer!1!CustomerID	Customer!1!ContactName
1	NULL	ALFKI	Marla Anders
1	NULL	TRAIH	Helvetius Nagy

Figure 9.1   A sample resultset that shows the levels of a FOR XML EXPLICIT query.

The examples have been basic so far because you have only queried a single level in the hierarchy. Let's add another level.

Use the UNION operator with the ALL argument to create the levels in the hierarchy. Also use the Tag meta data column to specify the element's tag, and the Parent meta data column to specify which tag ID this element will be a child of. Listing 9.13 shows an explicit mode query that uses two levels of nesting to control the output XML hierarchy.

Listing 9.13   **An Explicit Mode Query with Two Levels**

```
SELECT
    1                   as Tag,
    NULL                as Parent,
```

```
        CustomerID              as [Customer!1!CustomerID],
        ContactName              as [Customer!1!ContactName],
        NULL              as [Order!2!OrderID],
        NULL              as [Order!2!ShipCity]
FROM Customers
WHERE CustomerID IN ('ALFKI','TRAIH')

UNION ALL

SELECT
    2,
    1,
    c.CustomerID,
    NULL,
    o.OrderID,
    o.ShipCity

FROM Customers c INNER JOIN Orders o
    ON c.CustomerID = o.CustomerID
WHERE c.CustomerID IN ('ALFKI','TRAIH')

ORDER BY [Customer!1!CustomerID],[Order!2!OrderID]
FOR XML EXPLICIT
```

The first change you made was to add two new columns to the SELECT list. The new element, <Order>, references tag ID 2 and contains the attributes OrderID and ShipCity.

The second level in the hierarchy (which is highlighted) declares the tag ID of 2 and specifies that the element with tag ID of 1 is its parent in the hierarchy. This element level does not use column aliases: The first section in the UNION ALL operator specifies what the output columns are, the other sections in the UNION must provide the same number of columns for the UNION.

We specified the ContactName attribute to have a Null value in the second part of the UNION operation. Think about this for a second: The second level in the hierarchy does not include this in its data. You only need a column from its parent to specify which columns form the hierarchy.

Finally, using EXPLICIT mode requires an ORDER BY clause to determine how the columns should be related. The tabular relation is represented in Figure 9.2.

Tag	Parent	Customer!1!CustomerID	Customer!1!ContactName	Order!2!OrderID	Order!2!ShipCity
1	NULL	ALFKI	Maria Anders	NULL	NULL
2	1	TRAIH	NULL	10643	Berlin
2	1	ALFKI	NULL	10692	Berlin
2	1	TRAIH	NULL	10702	Berlin
2	1	ALFKI	NULL	10835	Berlin
2	1	TRAIH	NULL	10952	Berlin
2	1	ALFKI	NULL	11011	Berlin
1	NULL	TRAIH	Helvetius Nagy	NULL	NULL
2	1	TRAIH	NULL	10574	Kirkland
2	1	ALFKI	NULL	10577	Kirkland
2	1	TRAIH	NULL	10822	Kirkland

Figure 9.2   The tabular relation of columns in an EXPLICIT mode query.

In Figure 9.2, you can see the level of the hierarchy represented. The XML representation in Listing 9.14 is then easier to see.

Listing 9.14   **Output of Listing 9.13**

```
<Customer CustomerID="ALFKI" ContactName="Maria Anders">
    <Order OrderID="10643" ShipCity="Berlin" />
    <Order OrderID="10692" ShipCity="Berlin" />
    <Order OrderID="10702" ShipCity="Berlin" />
    <Order OrderID="10835" ShipCity="Berlin" />
    <Order OrderID="10952" ShipCity="Berlin" />
    <Order OrderID="11011" ShipCity="Berlin" />
</Customer>
<Customer CustomerID="TRAIH" ContactName="Helvetius Nagy">
    <Order OrderID="10574" ShipCity="Kirkland" />
    <Order OrderID="10577" ShipCity="Kirkland" />
    <Order OrderID="10822" ShipCity="Kirkland" />
</Customer>
```

Specifying Directives

After you have created the basic hierarchical structure of the document, you can further refine the structure by using directives, as shown in Table 9.3.

Table 9.3   **Directives for Column Naming**

Directive	Description
ID	The output attribute will be an ID type attribute based on the W3C Extensible Markup Language (XML) 1.0 Recommendation. Used with XMLDATA directive.

Directive	Description
IDREF	Specifies a reference to an ID type attributes. Used with XMLDATA directive.
IDREFS	Specifies references to multiple ID type attributes. Used with XMLDATA directive.
hide	This attribute is not output. Useful for sorting columns, not output, in the document.
element	The value from the SELECT list is represented as an element. The value is enclosed in an element with the specified tag name. Provides encoding for data (& becomes &, < becomes <).

element (continued):

Take this example:

```
select 1 as tag,
       null as parent,
       CompanyName     as [Customer!1!CompanyName!element]
from Customers where CustomerID = 'TRAIH'
for XML explicit
```

This yields the following XML output:

```
<Customer>
   <CompanyName>Trail&apos;s Head Gourmet
Provisioners</CompanyName>
</Customer>
```

Directive	Description
xml	Similar to the element directive, but no encoding is performed (& stays &). The AttributeName portion of the column name can be omitted.

Take this example:

```
select 1 as tag,
       null as parent,
       '<MYTAG />'              as [CustomTags!1!!xml]
for XML explicit
```

This example yields the following:

```
<CustomTags><MYTAG /></CustomTags>
```

Directive	Description
xmltext	Wraps the column's contents with a single XML tag. Used with OPENXML queries (discussed in the section, "OPENXML").

continues

Table 9.3   **Continued**

Directive	Description
CDATA	The contents are wrapped in a CDATA section. The AttributeName portion of the column name is left empty because CDATA sections cannot be named.

Take this example:

```
select 1 as tag,

null as parent,

    CompanyName            as [Customer!1!!cdata]
from Customers where CustomerID = 'TRAIH'
for XML explicit
```

This example yields the following:

```
<Customer>

    <![CDATA[Trail's Head Gourmet Provisioners]]>

</Customer>
```

Putting It Together

Listing 9.15 shows a full example of a stored procedure that returns XML from an EXPLICIT mode XML query.

Listing 9.15   **Example of an *EXPLICIT* Mode XML Query in SQL Server**

```
create procedure GetCustomerXML(@CustomerID char(5))
as

select
    1           as Tag,
    NULL        as Parent,
    CustomerID      as [Customer!1!CustomerID],
    CompanyName      as [Customer!1!CompanyName],
    NULL         as [Order!2!OrderID!id],
    NULL         as [Order!2!ShipVia],
    NULL         as [Order!2!ShippedDate],
    NULL         as [Order!2!ShipName],
    NULL        as [OrderDetails!3!OrderID!idref],
    NULL        as [OrderDetails!3!ProductID!idref],
    NULL        as [OrderDetails!3!UnitPrice!element],
    NULL        as [OrderDetails!3!Quantity!element],
    NULL        as [OrderDetails!3!Discount!element],
    NULL            as [Product!4!ProductID!id],
    NULL            as [Product!4!ProductName],
```

```
     NULL                    as [Product!4!Category],
     NULL                    as [Product!4!QuantityPerUnit]
from Customers where CustomerID = @CustomerID

UNION ALL

select
     2,
     1,
     CustomerID,
     NULL,
     o.OrderID,
     s.CompanyName,
     o.ShippedDate,
     o.ShipName,
     NULL,
     NULL,
     NULL,
     NULL,
     NULL,
     NULL,
     NULL,
     NULL,
     NULL
FROM Orders o INNER JOIN Shippers s ON o.ShipVia = s.ShipperID
WHERE o.CustomerID = @CustomerID

UNION ALL

select
     3          as Tag,
     2          as Parent,
     o.CustomerID,
     NULL,
     d.OrderID,
     NULL,
     NULL,
     NULL,
     d.OrderID,
     d.ProductID,
     d.UnitPrice,
     d.Quantity,
     str(d.Discount,4,2),
     NULL,
     NULL,
     NULL,
     NULL
FROM       [Order Details] d INNER JOIN
                    Orders o ON d.OrderID = o.OrderID
WHERE o.CustomerID = @CustomerID
```

continues

Listing 9.15 **Continued**

```
UNION ALL

select
      4               as Tag,
      3               as Parent,
      o.CustomerID,
      NULL,
      o.OrderID,
      NULL,
      NULL,
      NULL,
      o.OrderID,
      p.ProductID,
      NULL,
      NULL,
      NULL,
      p.ProductID,
      p.ProductName,
      c.CategoryName,
      p.QuantityPerUnit
FROM          dbo.[Order Details] d INNER JOIN
                  dbo.Orders o ON d.OrderID = o.OrderID INNER JOIN
                  dbo.Products p ON d.ProductID = p.ProductID INNER
JOIN
                  dbo.Categories c ON p.CategoryID = c.CategoryID
      WHERE o.CustomerID = @CustomerID

ORDER BY
[Customer!1!CustomerID],[Order!2!OrderID!id],[OrderDetails!3!OrderID!idref],[
➥OrderDetails!3!ProductID!idref],[Product!4!ProductID!id]
FOR XML EXPLICIT,XMLDATA
```

Listing 9.15 is available on the book's website as GetCustomerXML.sql.

Note several points about Listing 9.15. Directives specify id type attributes for Orders.OrderID and Products.ProductID. We also used idref directives to refer to these attributes (see OrderDetails.OrderID and OrderDetails.ProductID). The id type attribute speficies the value is unique, while the idref type refers to a specified unique id. You also specificed that the UnitPrice, Quantity, and Discount columns should be output as elements rather than as attributes. Finally, you used the XMLDATA argument to the FOR XML clause to specify that an inline schema should be generated.

To retrieve the XML results, you can load the data into a **DataSet** or you can use the **ExecuteXmlReader** method of the **SqlCommand** object, as shown in Listing 9.16.

Listing 9.16   **Using the *SqlCommand.ExecuteXmlReader* to Retrieve XML Data from SQL Server**

```csharp
<%@ Import Namespace="System.Configuration"%>
<%@ Import Namespace="System.Xml"%>
<%@ Import Namespace="System.Data.SqlClient"%>
<%@ Import Namespace="System.Data"%>

<script language="C#" runat="server">
        private void Page_Load(object sender, System.EventArgs e)
        {
            Response.ContentType="text/xml";

            string customerID = Request.QueryString.Get("CustomerID");

        if (customerID == null )
        {
            Response.Write ("<ERROR><![CDATA[The CustomerID parameter
            ➥was not specified.]]></ERROR>");
        }
        else
        {
            string connectionString =
            ➥ConfigurationSettings.AppSettings["connectionString"];
            XmlReader reader = null;
            XmlTextWriter writer = null;
            SqlConnection connection = new
            ➥SqlConnection(connectionString);
            SqlCommand command = new
            ➥SqlCommand("GetCustomerXML",connection);
            command.CommandType = CommandType.StoredProcedure ;
            SqlParameter param =
            ➥command.Parameters.Add("@CustomerID",SqlDbType.Char,5);
            param.Direction = ParameterDirection.Input;
            param.Value = customerID;
            try
            {
                connection.Open();
                reader = command.ExecuteXmlReader();
                writer = new XmlTextWriter
                ➥(Response.OutputStream,System.Text.Encoding.UTF8);
                writer.WriteStartDocument(true);
                writer.WriteStartElement("DATA");

                while(reader.Read())
                {
                    switch(reader.NodeType)
                    {
                        case XmlNodeType.Element:
```

continues

Listing 9.16 **Continued**

```
writer.WriteStartElement(reader.Prefix,reader.LocalName,reader.NamespaceURI);
                                if (reader.HasAttributes)
                                {
                                    writer.WriteAttributes(reader,true);
                                    reader.MoveToElement();
                                }
                                if (reader.IsEmptyElement)
                            writer.WriteEndElement();
                                break;
                                    case XmlNodeType.EndElement:
                                    writer.WriteEndElement();
                                break;
                                    case XmlNodeType.Text:
                                    writer.WriteString
                                    (reader.Value);
                                break;
                                    case XmlNodeType.CDATA:
                                    writer.WriteCData
                                    (reader.Value);
                                break;
                    }
                }
                writer.WriteEndDocument();
            }
            catch(Exception oops)
            {
                Response.Write ("<ERROR><![CDATA[" + Server.HtmlEncode
                ➥(oops.ToString()) + "]]></ERROR>");
            }
            finally
            {

                if (writer != null)
                    writer.Close();
                        if (reader != null)
                    reader.Close();
                        connection.Close();
                        command.Dispose();
                        connection.Dispose();
            }
        }
    }
</script>
```

This page was executed by creating a new web form called
CustomerOrders.aspx in the current project, pasting the preceding C# code

into the `CustomerOrders.aspx` file, building the project, and typing the following URL into the browser: `http://localhost/chapters/10/SQLServerXMLCS/CustomerOrders.aspx?CustomerID=ALFKI`.

The results of this example are shown in Listing 9.17.

Listing 9.17 **Output Results of an *EXPLICIT* Mode Query that Specified the *XMLDATA* Option**

```
<?xml version="1.0" encoding="utf-8" standalone="yes"?>
<DATA>
<Schema name="Schema1"
    xmlns="urn:schemas-microsoft-com:xml-data"
    xmlns:dt="urn:schemas-microsoft-com:datatypes">
  <ElementType name="Customer" content="mixed" model="open">
    <AttributeType name="CustomerID" dt:type="string" />
    <AttributeType name="CompanyName" dt:type="string" />
    <attribute type="CustomerID" />
    <attribute type="CompanyName" />
  </ElementType>
  <ElementType name="Order" content="mixed" model="open">
    <AttributeType name="OrderID" dt:type="id" />
    <AttributeType name="ShipVia" dt:type="string" />
    <AttributeType name="ShippedDate" dt:type="dateTime" />
    <AttributeType name="ShipName" dt:type="string" />
    <attribute type="OrderID" />
    <attribute type="ShipVia" />
    <attribute type="ShippedDate" />
    <attribute type="ShipName" />
  </ElementType>
  <ElementType name="OrderDetails" content="mixed" model="open">
    <AttributeType name="OrderID" dt:type="idref" />
    <AttributeType name="ProductID" dt:type="idref" />
    <attribute type="OrderID" />
    <attribute type="ProductID" />
    <element type="UnitPrice" />
    <element type="Quantity" />
    <element type="Discount" />
  </ElementType>
  <ElementType name="UnitPrice" content="textOnly" model="closed"
  ➥dt:type="fixed.14.4" />
  <ElementType name="Quantity" content="textOnly" model="closed"
  ➥dt:type="i2" />
  <ElementType name="Discount" content="textOnly" model="closed"
  ➥dt:type="string" />
  <ElementType name="Product" content="mixed" model="open">
    <AttributeType name="ProductID" dt:type="id" />
    <AttributeType name="ProductName" dt:type="string" />
    <AttributeType name="Category" dt:type="string" />
    <AttributeType name="QuantityPerUnit" dt:type="string" />
    <attribute type="ProductID" />
```

continues

Listing 9.17 **Continued**

```
        <attribute type="ProductName" />
        <attribute type="Category" />
        <attribute type="QuantityPerUnit" />
    </ElementType>
</Schema>
<Customer xmlns="x-schema:#Schema1" CustomerID="ALFKI" CompanyName="Alfreds
Futterkiste">
    <Order OrderID="10643" ShipVia="Speedy Express" ShippedDate="1997-09-
02T00:00:00" ShipName="Alfreds Futterkiste">
      <OrderDetails OrderID="10643" ProductID="28">
        <UnitPrice>45.6000</UnitPrice>
        <Quantity>15</Quantity>
        <Discount>0.25</Discount>
        <Product ProductID="28" ProductName="Rössle Sauerkraut"
Category="Produce" QuantityPerUnit="25 - 825 g cans" />
      </OrderDetails>
      <OrderDetails OrderID="10643" ProductID="39">
        <UnitPrice>18.0000</UnitPrice>
        <Quantity>21</Quantity>
        <Discount>0.25</Discount>
        <Product ProductID="39" ProductName="Chartreuse verte"
Category="Beverages" QuantityPerUnit="750 cc per bottle" />
      </OrderDetails>
      <OrderDetails OrderID="10643" ProductID="46">
        <UnitPrice>12.0000</UnitPrice>
        <Quantity>2</Quantity>
        <Discount>0.25</Discount>
        <Product ProductID="46" ProductName="Spegesild" Category="Seafood"
QuantityPerUnit="4 - 450 g glasses" />
      </OrderDetails>
    </Order>
    .
    .
    .
  </Customer>
</DATA>
```

Notice that the generated schema reflects the structure of the individual
SELECT statements instead of the overall structure of all UNION operations. This
inline schema can be useful for quickly creating DataSets in ADO.NET. This
flexibility comes at a price: Creating schemas on the server introduces overhead and impacts performance. Consider creating your own schema against
the expected results of a FOR XML query and caching it for validation or specifying schemas for DataSets, as you saw in Chapter 7, "ASP.NET Extensibility
with XML."

The ability to generate XML directly from SQL Server yields some interesting design patterns and system architectures. For example, you can generate

web reports by using XSLT stylesheets directly against the XML data that's returned from SQL Server, which enables dynamic filtering, sorting, and a range of interactive DHTML capabilities.

OPENXML

Besides using the FOR XML clause to return XML data, Microsoft SQL Server 2000 also provides the OPENXML function to shred an XML document and provide a rowset representation of the XML data.

As with many Win32 API calls, a function must be called to obtain a handle to an internal resource. You then work with the handle reference instead of the actual resource, then release the resource with a separate API call. Figure 9.3 depicts the steps required to shred an XML document.

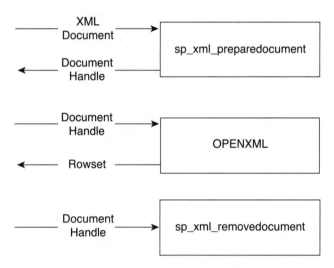

Figure 9.3   Shredding an XML document by using OPENXML.

To shred an XML document using OPENXML, a handle to a DOM representation of the document is obtained using sp_xml_preparedocument. After the rowset has been obtained using the OPENXML function, sp_xml_removedocument needs to be called to remove the document from memory.

The OPENXML function accepts three parameters:

- A handle to an open document in memory
- An XPath pattern dictating the rowset to return
- A flag that specifies the data structure

The following sections address obtaining the resource handle and supported XPath queries. But first, look at the flags that are available for OPENXML.

The flags argument of OPENXML specifies if the document is modeled as attribute-centric or element-centric, or both. Table 9.4 describes these flags in detail.

Table 9.4 **Flags Argument of *OPENXML***

Flag Name	Bit Value	Description
XML_DEFAULT	0	Defaults to attribute-centric mapping.
XML_ATTRIBUTES	1	Specifies attribute-centric mapping. If combined with XML_ELEMENTS, attribute-centric mapping is applied first and then element-centric mapping is used for unhandled columns.
XML_ELEMENTS	2	Specifies element-centric mapping. If combined with XML_ATTRIBUTES, attribute-centric mapping is applied first and then element-centric mapping is used for unhandled columns.
XMLTEXT_OVERFLOW	8	Specifies that any consumed data is not copied to the overflow property @mp:xmltext. Can be combined with XML_ELEMENTS or XML_ATTRIBUTES by using a logical OR.

To obtain the handle to the in-memory resource, two system stored procedures are used: sp_xml_preparedocument and sp_xml_removedocument.

sp_xml_preparedocument

In order to represent an XML document as a rowset, the input XML is first parsed and loaded into an internal DOM object. The DOM is retained in memory, and a handle to the open DOM is returned as an OUTPUT parameter.

Because the entire document is retained in memory, it is advisable to limit the size of documents used with OPENXML.

sp_xml_removedocument

Because the DOM document is retained in memory, its memory must be explicitly deallocated. Calling `sp_xml_removedocument` is a crucial step in successfully deploying applications that use OPENXML. Failure to do so leaves the document in memory. For example, the following code creates an in-memory DOM representation of the XML and outputs the handle to the created resource. Simply enter this code into the query window in Query Analyzer and run the query:

```
DECLARE @idoc int
DECLARE @doc varchar(1000)
SET @doc ='<data>
    <customers>
        <CustomerID>ALFKI</CustomerID>
        <CompanyName>Alfreds Futterkiste</CompanyName>
    </customers>
</data>'
EXEC sp_xml_preparedocument @idoc OUTPUT, @doc
select @idoc
```

Run this code several times. Note the number that is output each time.

Now execute the following statement in Query Analyzer using a number that was output by executing the preceding `sp_xml_preparedocument` procedure:

```
exec sp_xml_removedocument 79
```

Executing `sp_xml_removedocument` deallocates the memory used to represent the DOM in memory. You can see how failure to deallocate copies of each DOM representation can add up to much wasted memory. Unless you retain a running list of handles to open DOM documents, they cannot be retrieved for later removal.

WITH Clause

After the handle to the open DOM resource is obtained from `sp_xml_pre-paredocument`, it is shredded by using the OPENXML function, as shown in Listing 9.18. The WITH clause specifies the elements in the document that are used to satisfy the SELECT list.

Listing 9.18 **Using the *sp_xml_preparedocument* and *sp_xml_removedocument* System Procedures**

```
DECLARE @idoc int
DECLARE @doc varchar(1000)
SET @doc ='<data>
    <customers>
        <CustomerID>ALFKI</CustomerID>
```

continues

Listing 9.18 **Continued**

```
                <CompanyName>Alfreds Futterkiste</CompanyName>
                <ContactName>Maria Anders</ContactName>
                <ContactTitle>Sales Representative</ContactTitle>
                <Address>Obere Str. 57</Address>
                <City>Berlin</City>
                <PostalCode>12209</PostalCode>
                <Country>Germany</Country>
                <Phone>030-0074321</Phone>
                <Fax>030-0076545</Fax>
        </customers>
        <customers>
                <CustomerID>AROUT</CustomerID>
                <CompanyName>Around the Horn</CompanyName>
                <ContactName>Thomas Hardy</ContactName>
                <ContactTitle>Sales Representative</ContactTitle>
                <Address>120 Hanover Sq.</Address>
                <City>London</City>
                <PostalCode>WA1 1DP</PostalCode>
                <Country>UK</Country>
                <Phone>(171) 555-7788</Phone>
                <Fax>(171) 555-6750</Fax>
        </customers>
</data>'
--Create an internal representation of the XML document.
EXEC sp_xml_preparedocument @idoc OUTPUT, @doc
-- Execute a SELECT statement that uses the OPENXML rowset provider.
SELECT    *
FROM      OPENXML (@idoc, 'data/customers[CustomerID=''AROUT'']',2)
              WITH (CustomerID nchar(5),
              CompanyName nvarchar(20))
exec sp_xml_removedocument @idoc
```

Executing this query causes a rowset to be returned:

```
CustomerID CompanyName
---------- --------------------
AROUT      Around the Horn
```

Querying an XML document to return a rowset cannot seem that functional.
You can, however, use OPENXML to perform INSERT, UPDATE, and DELETE statements. This enables you to specify an XML document to be used in mass
insertions or updates to multiple tables. Listing 9.19 shows you how a table is
inserted into an XML document.

Listing 9.19 **Using an XML Document as the Basis for Inserting Records into a Table**

```
DECLARE @idoc int
DECLARE @doc varchar(1000)
SET @doc ='<data>
    <customers>
        <CustomerID>VBDNA</CustomerID>
        <CompanyName>Kirk Allen Evans</CompanyName>
    </customers>
</data>'
EXEC sp_xml_preparedocument @idoc OUTPUT, @doc

INSERT INTO Customers (CustomerID, CompanyName)
SELECT   *
FROM     OPENXML (@idoc, 'data/customers[CustomerID=''VBDNA'']',2)
            WITH (CustomerID nchar(5),
         CompanyName nvarchar(20))

exec sp_xml_removedocument @idoc
```

Because the OPENXML function returns a rowset, you can easily combine it with other clauses, such as EXISTS and IN, to dynamically modify data in the database. For example, you can create a stored procedure that accepts an XML document as a parameter, where the XML document contains the data to be modified. This capability, combined with the ability to access SQL Server over HTTP, provides some clever possibilities.

If the input XML document contains more data than there are columns defined, OPENXML enables you to store the overflow data in a column so that it can be retrieved later.

Querying SQL Server over HTTP

SQL Server 2000 introduced the ability to query the database over HTTP by leveraging virtual directories in IIS. Because the results are delivered as XML over the web, data can be consumed over disparate platforms and from remote locations. This reduces the complexity of your applications by reducing the amount of coding necessary to produce the XML data and provide error handling.

Configuring SQL XML Support in IIS

To support XML over HTTP, SQL Server provides a Microsoft Management Console (MMC) snap-in that configures SQL XML support in IIS.

To use this snap-in, select Configure SQL XML Support in IIS from the Start menu. When you open the snap-in, expand the nodes to display the default website. Right-click the Default website and from the Context menu, click New, Virtual Directory. This brings up a property sheet with several tabs.

The General Tab

On the General tab, set the virtual directory name as `Northwind`, and set the local path to a file path that you have access to. For example, I used a local folder on my D: drive:

```
D:\projects\New Riders\chapters\SQL Server
```

The Security Tab

The Security Tab enables you to specify the security used when working with SQL Server over HTTP. For example, you can be accessing the website using the `IUSR_MachineName` account because you are allowing anonymous access to the website. You don't want to add the `IUSR_MachineName` account as a user of the SQL Server database. Instead, you can specify what security model is used when accessing the database. Table 9.5 shows you explanations of this tab's options.

Table 9.5 **Security Tab Options**

Security Option	Description
Always Log On As	Each time the virtual web directory is accessed, the specified user is used to log onto SQL Server. This is the least secure form of authentication because you rely on the user to be authenticated only to the website.
Use Windows Integrated Authentication	Uses the currently logged-on user's windows authentication token. Requires the user to be running Windows and to have a valid user account with permissions to access SQL Server.
Use Basic Authentication	Use this mode with anonymous authentication because it prompts the user for a valid SQL Server user ID and password.

The Data Source Tab

The Data Source tab specifies the server that you are querying and the database on that server that is to be queried. These settings are the same server and database used when accessing a database by using an ADO.NET connection string. I used my local server and specified the Northwind database, which is used for the examples throughout this chapter.

The Settings Tab

The Settings tab enables you to specify what actions can be performed for this virtual directory. Valid application concerns exist for why you would not want the users to perform certain actions. For example, the Allow POST option specifies that the user can use an HTTP POST to post his own template files (explored later in the section, "Executing Template Files") and enables restrictions on what size those template files can be.

You can also want to restrict the capability of the user to run ad-hoc queries against the database using the URL Queries option. Figure 9.4 shows that we are going to check all the options for demonstration purposes.

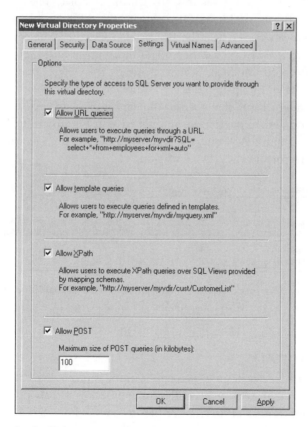

Figure 9.4 Check all the options on the Settings tab for demonstration purposes.

> **Uncheck Options That Are not in Use**
> In a production system, it is advised that you uncheck options that are not used. This prevents hackers from attempting to access various parts of your database that were not intentionally exposed.

The Virtual Names Tab

The Virtual Names tab specifies a virtual name that's part of the URL. Three different types of virtual names are used: a database object, a schema file, or a template file. The virtual name enables you to associate a subdirectory name with a specific type of access. The use of virtual names is discussed in detail later in this chapter. (Using SQL Server to access database objects over HTTP is discussed in the section, "Accessing Database Objects," and the use of template files is discussed in the section, "Executing Template Files.")

SQL Server Books Online (BOL) explains the different tabs and settings in the snap-in. However, only use the IIS Virtual Directory Management for SQL Server utility to modify virtual directories that expose SQL Server: Special permissions for accessing SQL Server are set by this MMC snap-in that the more familiar MMC snap-in for IIS does not provide.

The remainder of this chapter uses the Northwind database. The virtual directory is also named Northwind, and permission is granted for URL access, template access, and XPath queries. Figure 9.5 depicts the finished version of the virtual directory in the MMC snap-in.

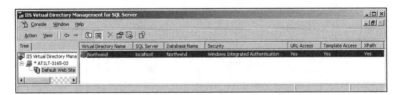

Figure 9.5 The properties of the sample Northwind virtual directory in the SQL Server MMC snap-in for virtual directory management.

Querying over HTTP

A common task in developing web applications is providing data that can be consumed from remote sources. Different approaches to solving this problem can range from using FTP to transfer files to embedding data in an HTML page that is to be screen-scraped. As you will see in Chapter 11, "Creating and Using ASP.NET Web Services," you can use XML to access methods remotely using SOAP.

Another method for providing data to remote clients is to provide XML data over the web through an HTTP request. This section discusses how SQL Server provides a rich mechanism for providing XML data over the web, while allowing secure access to server resources.

After a virtual directory is created with the properties shown in Figure 9.5, you can begin to query SQL Server over HTTP. There are several ways to do this:

- Include URL-encoded SQL in the URL
- Access database objects directly
- Execute templates

Encoding SQL in the URL

When sending SQL Data Modification Language (DML) commands in a URL, such as INSERT, UPDATE, or DELETE statements, the SQL string is represented in a QueryString item named sql. Remember that query results returned from FOR XML queries might not be well-formed XML. You can optionally provide a root element to contain the results of the query by specifying a QueryString item named root that indicates the name of the root element.

We named the virtual directory Northwind and made it a child of the root web so that we can open a browser and type the following:

```
http://localhost/northwind?sql=select%20*%20from%20customers%20for%20xml%20au
➥to,elements&root=DATA
```

This query produces the following XML in the browser:

```
<?xml version="1.0" encoding="utf-8" ?>
<DATA>
    <customers>
        <CustomerID>ALFKI</CustomerID>
        <CompanyName>Alfreds Futterkiste</CompanyName>
    </customers>
</DATA>
```

Think about what happened here. You entered a SQL query into a URL. The URL was parsed by an Internet Information Services API (ISAPI) filter that recognized the reserved QueryString elements sql and root. The ISAPI filter then forwarded the request to SQL Server by using the specified authentication (we leveraged "Windows Integrated Authentication" in the example), which returned the results of the query back to the browser over HTTP. This tremendous amount of flexibility is provided with a few simple settings.

Take a closer look at what was actually sent to SQL Server. We talked about the `sql` and `root` QueryString variables at the beginning of this section. Notice the `%20` between each word in the `sql` QueryString variable. Because the SQL is part of the URL, the complete URL string must still conform to URL encoding specifications. As you will see throughout the remainder of this chapter, we use the convenient `Server.URLEncode` method to return an encoded URL string.

Another interesting point is that no file is specified to retrieve in the URL; we only specified a root directory to navigate to. There is no file with a `.html` extension or a `.aspx` extension: The ISAPI filter responds to requests to access the virtual directory.

You can see that any query that is valid for SQL Server is also valid to use within the URL. For example, the following code uses a `WHERE` clause and names individual column names in the `SELECT` list:

```
http://localhost/northwind?sql=select%20CustomerID,CompanyName%20from%20
➥customers%20where%20customerid='ALFKI'%20for%20xml%20auto,elements&root=
➥Customers
```

Calling Stored Procedures

Because any query is valid, you can also access stored procedures through a URL. Let's create a stored procedure called `GetCustomersXML`. Open SQL Query Analyzer from the SQL Server program group in your Start menu. Connect to the `Northwind` database and enter the text from Listing 9.20 into the text window.

Listing 9.20   **Create a Stored Procedure to Return XML**

```
CREATE procedure GetCustomersXML(@CustID varchar(5))
as
declare @SearchVar varchar(6)

select @SearchVar = @CustID + '%'
SELECT * FROM Customers WHERE CustomerID LIKE @SearchVar for XML
AUTO,ELEMENTS
```

This stored procedure enables you to enter up to five characters to search for a customer by `CustomerID` and display the results as XML. Press the F5 key to create the stored procedure. You can test the stored procedure by entering the following text into the query pane, highlighting the text, and pressing F5:

```
GetCustomersXML 'ALFKI'
```

You should see an XML string in the results window that contains the data for `CustomerID "ALFKI"`. Now that you have a stored procedure to test with, you can execute the procedure through a URL in the browser:

```
http://localhost/northwind?sql=GetCustomersXML+'ALFKI'&root=DATA
```

Another interesting capability is the ability to call system stored procedures or Database Console Commands (`dbcc` commands) through the URL, provided that you have obtained authentication as specified in the MMC snap-in for administering XML support for SQL Server. As long as you have the privileges to invoke it, it is perfectly legal to issue `dbcc` commands using the URL. The following example executes the `dbcc` command `freeproccache`, which clears the system cache in the database:

```
http://localhost/northwind?sql=dbcc%20freeproccache
```

This example does not provide a return or `recordset`, so it is easy to call. However, suppose that you want to call a system stored procedure or a dbcc command that returns a recordset. This issue is addressed in the following sections.

Accessing Database Objects

Because SQL Server adds XML support to its database, you also have the option of querying database objects, such as tables or views, directly through the URL by using XPath syntax. This adds flexibility that users unfamiliar with T-SQL or SQL syntax can use to access and navigate your database.

To access a database object directly through the URL, a virtual name must be added to your virtual directory that enables access to database objects.

Follow these steps to create a virtual name through which you can access a database object over HTTP:

1. Go into the IIS Virtual Directory Management for SQL Server MMC snap-in and choose the `Northwind` virtual directory that was created at the beginning of this section.

2. Right-click and choose Properties to show the property sheet for the virtual directory.

3. Click the Virtual Names tab, click the New button, and enter a name for the new virtual name. For example, I chose `myvirt` as a name.

4. Select `dbobject` from the type drop-down list and click Save. This enables access to database objects through the virtual name `myvirt`.

By using this virtual name, you can specify the database object to be queried using XPath syntax. The following code selects the `CompanyName` column from the `Customers` table where the `CustomerID` column's value is `'ALFKI'`:

```
http://localhost/northwind/myvirt/Customers[@CustomerID='ALFKI']/@CompanyName
```

You should receive the following code in your browser:

```
Alfreds Futterkiste
```

This code retrieved only one column. What about retrieving multiple columns? Recall that SQL Server uses a single-column `resultset` when providing XML using `FOR XML` queries. Because there is only one column, no column delimiters are needed in the result. This makes streaming individual rows simpler. When accessing database objects directly through the URL, you have to structure your XPath query to only retrieve a single-column result, or else SQL Server cannot provide a stream representation. To better understand this process, try retrieving multiple columns using an XPath query. The following XPath statement attempts to retrieve all columns for the `Customers` table:

```
http://localhost/northwind/myvirt/Customers[@CustomerID='ALFKI']/@*?root=data
```

Instead of retrieving all columns, you receive an error similar to the following:

```
<?xml version="1.0" encoding="utf-8" ?>
<data>
        <?MSSQLError HResult="0x80004005" Source="Microsoft XML Extensions to
    ➥SQL Server" Description="Streaming not supported over multiple column
    ➥result"?>
</data>
```

Accessing database objects directly through the URL provides limited functionality. There is also not a mechanism to select which database objects are exposed through the URL and which are not without relying on the security scheme (SQL Server or Windows authentication, which is set up on the Security tab in the SQL Server XML MMC snap-in). SQL Server provides a more attractive mechanism for exposing your database through templates.

Executing Template Files

Allowing users to execute queries through the URL is useful, but can also have adverse effects on your database. Nothing prevents the user from entering the following query:

```
SELECT c.*, o.*, p.*
from customers c, orders o, products p
```

The result of this query is an extremely large `resultset` that puts a large burden on SQL Server to generate the results, IIS to deliver the results, and the client browser to parse and display the results. If many users ran this query within a short period of time, it would bring the database and, likely, the web servers to a screeching halt.

Instead of providing direct query access through the URL, you can create predefined queries and store them in template files on the server. A template file is an XML file that includes certain elements outlined in this section. This XML file can contain one or more SQL statements and XPath queries. The benefit to using template files is that you can provide predefined queries that return XML over the web, which enables you to have more control over what users can access over the web.

One way to think of a template file is like a database view—it's a predefined way to query the database. A better analogy might be a *stored procedure*. A stored procedure can contain multiple queries that are to be executed. Template files can also contain multiple SQL statements, but they add the capability to work with the SQL Server database like a set of XML documents using XPath syntax.

Creating Templates

Before you create a template file, make sure that the option to execute templates is checked in the SQL Server Virtual Directory Management MMC snap-in, as shown in Figure 9.4. Unless this option is checked, you'll receive HTTP error 400, `Bad Request`.

Listing 9.21 shows what a template file looks like.

Listing 9.21 **Syntax for Creating Template Files for Use with SQL Server Virtual Directories**

```
<ROOT xmlns:sql="urn:schemas-microsoft-com:xml-sql"
      sql:xsl='XSL FileName' >
  <sql:header>
    <sql:param>..</sql:param>
    <sql:param>..</sql:param>...n
  </sql:header>
  <sql:query>
    sql statement(s)
  </sql:query>
  <sql:xpath-query mapping-schema="SchemaFileName.xml">
    XPath query
  </sql:xpath-query>
</ROOT>
```

Break up the template example into its individual parts. Table 9.6 shows an explanation of the elements and attributes that might appear in an XML template file.

Table 9.6 **Elements and Attributes of a Template File**

Element Name	Description
`<ROOT>`	A tag providing the root element name. Can have any name and namespaces are supported.
`<sql:header>`	Reserved for header items. Currently only `<sql:param>` items are supported as header items.

continues

Table 9.6 **Continued**

Element Name	Description
`<sql:param>`	Provides parameters for the template file. Each `<sql:param>` element defines a single parameter, and multiple parameters are supported in the `<sql:header>` section.
`<sql:query>`	Each `<sql:query>` element represents a single SQL query, and multiple queries are supported in a template.
`<sql:xpath-query>`	Specifies an XPath query against the XDR Schema specified in the `mapping-schema` attribute.

Attribute Name	Description
`sql:xsl`	Specifies an XSL stylesheet that will be applied to the XML results of the template query. This location pertains to an XSL stylesheet file stored on the server, and supports both absolute and relative paths.
`mapping-schema`	Identifies an annotated XDR Schema that describes the mapping of table and column names to an XML document.

Now that you have seen how to construct a template file, let's walk through an example. First, you need to set up your virtual directory to support templates and specify where the files are physically located.

When you set up the virtual name to access database objects in the preceding section, you were given a choice of a type of virtual name when configuring a new virtual name. This is how the MMC snap-in enables you to specify where the template files physically reside.

Follow these steps to create a virtual name to access your template files over HTTP:

1. Open the MMC snap-in for SQL Server virtual directory management.

2. Open the properties for the `Northwind` virtual directory.

3. Click the Virtual Names tab to see the list of virtual names that are already defined.

4. Click the New button and a dialog box titled Virtual Name Configuration.

5. Type the virtual name as **mytemplates**, the Type is **template**, and the path as a valid path on your server's file system that holds the template files. For example, I used a relative path called templates that would be a subdirectory of the directory specified when creating the SQL Server virtual directory.

6. On the General tab for the virtual directory's property sheet, specify the local path for the virtual directory. When I originally created the virtual directory, I used a local path on my D: drive:

```
D:\projects\New Riders\Chapters\SQL Server
```

After specifying a relative path for your template files, the physical location of the template files translates to the following:

```
D:\projects\New Riders\Chapters\SQL Server\templates
```

By using a relative path, you are basically going one level deeper in the physical path.

The URL to your virtual directory is `http://localhost/Northwind`. Append the virtual name to the end of the URL for your virtual directory. For example, I used the new virtual name, `mytemplates`, so I can append this virtual name to the SQL Server virtual directory to access the virtually named object:

```
http://localhost/Northwind/mytemplates
```

At this point, you have only named the location where your template files will be stored, but we have not yet created a template.

Create a simple template file that consists of two queries: one that selects a row from the `Customers` table, and one that selects a row from the `Products` table. Also specify the root element to be named `Data` instead of `ROOT` to demonstrate that the name of the root node does not matter; it only needs to be a valid XML name. Listing 9.22 shows the finished result.

Listing 9.22 **A Sample Query Template File**

```
<Data xmlns:sql="urn:schemas-microsoft-com:xml-sql">
  <sql:query>
    SELECT CustomerID, CompanyName
    FROM Customers
    WHERE CustomerID = 'AROUT'
    FOR XML AUTO, ELEMENTS
  </sql:query>
  <sql:query>
    SELECT ProductID, ProductName
    FROM Products
    WHERE ProductID = 1
    FOR XML AUTO, ELEMENTS
  </sql:query>
</Data>
```

Because the template specified that the root element would be named `Data`, all data returned from within the template's body will be contained within the root `Data` element. The data from the `Customers` table will be a sibling with the data from the `Products` table.

Save this template file as `sampleselect.xml` into the templates folder specified earlier. The full path to the sample file on my directory is the following:

```
D:\projects\New Riders\Chapters\SQL Server\templates\sampleselect.xml
```

To execute this template, use the URL to the template file by using the virtual
name that you set up at the beginning of this section:

```
http://localhost/Northwind/mytemplates/sampleselect.xml
```

By entering this URL into the browser window, the XML document in
Listing 9.23 is displayed in the browser.

Listing 9.23   **Output for Listing 9.22**

```
<Data xmlns:sql="urn:schemas-microsoft-com:xml-sql">
    <Customers>
        <CustomerID>AROUT</CustomerID>
        <CompanyName>Around the Horn</CompanyName>
    </Customers>
    <Products>
        <ProductID>1</ProductID>
        <ProductName>Chai</ProductName>
    </Products>
</Data>
```

In Table 9.6, you saw that you can specify parameters to templates by using the
`<sql:query>` element. You will create a new template in Listing 9.24 that will
call the stored procedure you created in Listing 9.20.

Listing 9.24   **Using a Parameter Within a Template File**

```
<?xml version="1.0" encoding="utf-8" ?>
<Data xmlns:sql="urn:schemas-microsoft-com:xml-sql">
  <sql:header>
    <sql:param name="CustomerID">ALFKI</sql:param>
  </sql:header>
  <sql:query>
    exec GetCustomersXML @CustomerID
  </sql:query>
</Data>
```

Save this file as `sampleparameter.xml` in the `templates` directory. After the
XML file is saved, you can then execute the template file by entering the
URL to the file in the browser, as shown here:

```
http://localhost/northwind/mytemplates/sampleparameter.xml
```

The results are shown in Listing 9.25.

Listing 9.25   **Output of Listing 9.24**

```
<?xml version="1.0" encoding="utf-8" ?>
<Data xmlns:sql="urn:schemas-microsoft-com:xml-sql">
    <Customers>
        <CustomerID>ALFKI</CustomerID>
        <CompanyName>Alfreds Futterkiste</CompanyName>
        <ContactName>Maria Anders</ContactName>
        <ContactTitle>Sales Representative</ContactTitle>
        <Address>Obere Str. 57</Address>
        <City>Berlin</City>
        <PostalCode>12209</PostalCode>
        <Country>Germany</Country>
        <Phone>030-0074321</Phone>
        <Fax>030-0076545</Fax>
    </Customers>
</Data>
```

As you can see, specifying SQL queries using XML templates is significantly easier and less error prone than entering the URL-encoded equivalent in the Address bar of a browser. This also enables you, as the site administrator, to control access to the database through such an open mechanism as the web.

Posting Templates

Suppose that you want to execute a set of queries and the amount of text in the URL makes the query cumbersome, error prone, and difficult to debug. Instead of asking the site's administrator to add a custom template file for you, you can have him grant you permission to post template files to the virtual directory to be processed. The ability to use HTTP POST to send templates to SQL Server to be processed enables the user to dynamically construct queries and execute them on the database without having to resort to using the URL or having static template files on the server. By using this feature, you can give ad-hoc access to your users to query any combination of data. Just as with the URL, be forewarned that your users have the capability to execute extremely long-running queries.

To post a template, simply use an HTTP POST to send the template as a stream to the virtual directory.

For simplicity, generate an HTTP POST using HTML. In Listing 9.26, you use client-side HTML to post the contents of the TEXTAREA to the Northwind virtual directory directly. Inside the TEXTAREA, you specify the template that's to be posted to the virtual directory. You also specify the name of the text box as CustomerID to match the parameter specified in the query template.

Listing 9.26 **Example of Using *HTTP POST* to Execute Templates**

```
<HTML>
    <HEAD>
        <title>TemplatePost</title>
    </HEAD>
    <body MS_POSITIONING="GridLayout">
        <form id="TemplatePost" method="post" action=
        ➥"http://localhost/northwind">
              <input type="text" name="CustomerID" value="ALFKI"
            ➥style="Z-INDEX: 101; LEFT: 187px; POSITION: absolute;
            ➥TOP: 52px">
            <input type="hidden" name="contenttype" value="text/xml"
            ➥style="Z-INDEX: 102; LEFT: 188px; POSITION: absolute;
            ➥TOP: 17px">  
            <TEXTAREA name="template" rows="12" cols="51" style="Z-
            ➥INDEX: 103; LEFT: 44px; WIDTH: 428px; POSITION: absolute;
            ➥TOP: 91px; HEIGHT: 190px">
&lt;Data xmlns:sql="urn:schemas-microsoft-com:xml-sql"&gt;
&lt;sql:header&gt;
    &lt;sql:param name="CustomerID"&gt;ALFKI&lt;/sql:param&gt;
&lt;/sql:header&gt;
&lt;sql:query&gt;
    exec GetCustomersXML @CustomerID
&lt;/sql:query&gt;
&lt;/Data&gt;
            </TEXTAREA> <input type="submit" name="submitform"
            ➥value="Submit Query" style="Z-INDEX: 104; LEFT: 339px;
            ➥POSITION: absolute; TOP: 302px">
            <DIV style="DISPLAY: inline; Z-INDEX: 105; LEFT: 45px;
            ➥WIDTH: 130px; POSITION: absolute; TOP: 54px; HEIGHT: 21px"
            ➥ms_positioning="FlowLayout">Customer
                ID:</DIV>
        </form>
    </body>
</HTML>
```

Using Stylesheets With Templates

You can also associate a stylesheet with a template. This enables you to control the formatting and output, which lets you build a truly data-driven website. Suppose that you have a website that's mostly an interface to research data. It is easy, then, to create a set of XSLT stylesheets that drive the flow of the site.

Use a stylesheet to display an HTML table of Customers. This stylesheet is depicted in Listing 9.27.

Listing 9.27 **A Stylesheet Applied to a SQL Server Template File**

```
<?xml version="1.0" encoding="UTF-8" ?>
<xsl:stylesheet
    xmlns:xsl="http://www.w3.org/1999/XSL/Transform"
    xmlns:sql="urn:schemas-microsoft-com:xml-sql"
    version="1.0" >

    <xsl:output method="html" version="4.0"/>
    <xsl:template match="/">
        <html>
            <body>
                <xsl:apply-templates />
            </body>
        </html>
    </xsl:template>
    <xsl:template match="Data">
        <table border="1">
            <xsl:for-each select="Customers">
                <tr>
                    <td><xsl:value-of select="CustomerID"/></td>
                    <td><xsl:value-of select="CompanyName"/></td>
                </tr>
            </xsl:for-each>
        </table>
    </xsl:template>
</xsl:stylesheet>
```

Save the stylesheet from Listing 9.27 as `Customers.xslt` in the templates direc-
tory with the query templates you have generated throughout this section.
You can then edit the `sampleparameter.xml` template that you created in
Listing 9.25 to use a stylesheet for its output.

```
<?xml version="1.0" encoding="utf-8" ?>
<Data xmlns:sql="urn:schemas-microsoft-com:xml-sql" sql:xsl="customers.xslt">
  <sql:header>
    <sql:param name="CustomerID">ALFKI</sql:param>
  </sql:header>
  <sql:query>
    exec GetCustomersXML @CustomerID
  </sql:query>
</Data>
```

The result of executing this query is shown in the following code snippet:

```
<table border="1" xmlns:sql="urn:schemas-microsoft-com:xml-sql">
<tr>
<td>ALFKI</td>
<td>Alfreds Futterkiste</td>
</tr>
</table>
```

Creating XML Views

You have seen that you can retrieve XML from SQL Server and query the returned XML document by using the .NET managed classes. You have also seen that you can return transformed XML from SQL Server by specifying XSLT files that reside in a SQL Server virtual directory. Suppose that you want to query the database as an XML document. One way to do this would be to execute a FOR XML clause and return the XML to the client so it can be queried using XPath. But constructing complex FOR XML clauses can be tedious and difficult to maintain.

Yet another way that SQL Server 2000 supports XML is through its representation of the database as an XML document, called an *XML view*. To provide an XML view, SQL Server uses a mapping between the physical database item and an XML representation of that item. This mapping is provided through annotations to an XDR Schema. SQL Server 2000 supports only XDR Schemas, but you can also use XSD Schemas by installing the SQLXML 3.0 add-on, which is discussed in the section, "SQLXML 3.0."

XML views are used for other technologies within SQL Server. For example, you can use XML views in conjunction with XPath statements to provide XPath querying over the database on the server rather than pulling the data back to the client to be queried. You can also use XML views with Updategrams to perform updates to the database using XML syntax.

The best analogy for an XML view is a database view. A database view does not actually contain data; it only contains pointers to where the data is physically stored and how it is represented. The same is true with an XML view: It simply serves as a set of pointers to where the physical data resides and describes how the XML representation should appear.

There are two ways to structure a schema to develop the mappings between database objects and XML: by using default mappings, and creating explicit mappings using SQL Server 2000 annotations to the XDR Schema.

Using Default Mappings

By default, elements map to a table or view having the same name and attributes map to the columns within that table or view. For example, the database table Customers in the Northwind database would map to an XML element named Customers, and the database column CustomerID in the Customers table would map to an attribute named CustomerID in its XML representation.

Let's walk through a simple example that uses default mappings. You will query the Customers table in Northwind by using XPath. Listing 9.28 shows a simple XDR Schema that does not use annotations.

Listing 9.28 **An Example of an XDR Schema Without Annotations**

```
<?xml version="1.0" ?>
<Schema xmlns="urn:schemas-microsoft-com:xml-data"
        xmlns:dt="urn:schemas-microsoft-com:datatypes"
        xmlns:sql="urn:schemas-microsoft-com:xml-sql">

<ElementType name="Customers" >
    <AttributeType name="CustomerID" />
    <AttributeType name="CompanyName" />
    <AttributeType name="ContactName" />

    <attribute type="CustomerID" />
    <attribute type="CompanyName" />
    <attribute type="ContactName" />
</ElementType>
</Schema>
```

To test this example, create a virtual name for schemas by following these steps:

1. Open the IIS Virtual Directory Management for SQL Server MMC snap-in.
2. Choose the Northwind virtual directory and open its property sheet.
3. On the Virtual Names tab, click the New button.
4. Enter the virtual name as **myschemas**, the type as **schema**, and the path as **schemas**.

You specified a relative path, so now you need to save the preceding file to the schemas folder in your local path for the virtual directory. The full path on my machine is

```
D:\projects\New Riders\Chapters\SQL Server\schemas\customers.xdr
```

You also need to ensure that your virtual directory enables XPath queries. Go to the Settings tab for the virtual directory in the SQL Server MMC snap-in and make sure the Allow XPath option is checked. After you configure the virtual name, you can execute the following XPath query through a URL:

```
http://localhost/northwind/myschemas/customers.xdr/Customers[@CustomerID=
➥'AROUT']?root=Data
```

The result of this XPath query is shown in Listing 9.29.

Listing 9.29 **Results of a Sample XPath Query Using Default Mappings**

```
<?xml version="1.0" encoding="utf-8" ?>
<Data>
     <Customers CustomerID="AROUT" CompanyName="Around the Horn"
ContactName="Thomas Hardy"/>
</Data>
```

Using Explicit Mappings

Cases can arise when using default mappings simply will not suffice. The table name can have a space in it, so you need to provide an XML element without a space in the name and map that to the table. Or you can have an XPath query that spans multiple tables. A variety of reasons exist for why you can want to tweak the mappings of a schema to the database to provide an XML view that can be queried using XPath.

Take a closer look at how you can use XPath syntax within a query template. To use XPath syntax, you must map the tables and columns using annotations to a schema. The current release of SQL Server only supports XDR schemas; however, you will see later in the section, "SQLXML 3.0," that XSD Schemas are supported as well. The annotations provide control over what the mapping from XML Schemas to the database will look like, but still enable you to stay within the realm of XML and schemas for configuration of that mapping. Table 9.7 lists the annotations provided for XDR schemas and describes each XML component.

Table 9.7 **The SQL Server 2000 XDR Annotations**

Annotation	Description
sql:relation	Maps an attribute or element to a database table or view.
sql:field	Maps an element or attribute to a specific field within a database table or view.
sql:is-constant	Creates an output element that does not map to a table or table item.
sql:map-field	Excludes items from the output result.
sql:relationship	Specifies relationships between XML elements. The key, key-relation, foreign-key, and foreign-relation attributes establish the relationship.
sql:limit-field	Filters fields based on value.
sql:limit-value	Filters fields based on value.
sql:key-fields	Specifies the column(s) to act as a unique key for the table.
sql:target-namespace	Places output items into a namespace separate from the default namespace.
sql:id-prefix	Creates valid ID, IDREF, and IDREFS, prepending the ID, IDREF, and IDREFS with a string, creating a valid named token from numerics and ensuring uniqueness.
sql:use-cdata	Specifies an item is a CDATA type.
sql:url-encode	URL encodes the information item, typically pertaining to BLOB fields.
sql:overflow-field	Specifies the column that's used for data overflow.

Take a look at the most popular example from the Northwind database, representing Customers and their Orders. You will extend the previous example from Listing 9.19 to use roughly the same hierarchy, making some minor adjustments for further explanation. Listing 9.30 shows the finished XDR Schema.

Listing 9.30   **Sample XDR Schema Using Annotations**

```xml
<?xml version="1.0" ?>
<Schema xmlns="urn:schemas-microsoft-com:xml-data" xmlns:dt="urn:schemas-
➥microsoft-com:datatypes" xmlns:sql="urn:schemas-microsoft-com:xml-sql">

    <ElementType name="Order" sql:relation="Orders" sql:key-
➥fields="OrderID">
        <AttributeType name="OrdID" dt:type="id" sql:id-prefix="Orders-" />
        <AttributeType name="ShipMethod"  />
        <AttributeType name="ShippedDate"  />
        <AttributeType name="ShipName"  />

        <attribute type="OrdID" sql:field="OrderID" />
        <attribute type="ShipMethod" sql:field="ShipVia" />
        <attribute type="ShippedDate" sql:field="ShippedDate" />
        <attribute type="ShipName" sql:field="ShipName" />
        <element type="OrderDetail" >
            <sql:relationship
                key-relation="Orders"
                key="OrderID"
                foreign-relation="[Order Details]"
                foreign-key="OrderID" />
        </element>
    </ElementType>

    <ElementType name="Price" sql:relation="[Order Details]" />
    <ElementType name="Qty" sql:relation="[Order Details]" />
    <ElementType name="Disc" sql:relation="[Order Details]" />

    <ElementType name="OrderDetail" sql:relation="[Order Details]" sql:key-
➥fields="OrderID ProductID">
        <AttributeType name="OrdID" dt:type="idref" sql:id-prefix="Orders-" />
        <AttributeType name="ProdID" dt:type="idref" sql:id-
➥prefix="Products-" />

        <attribute type="ProdID" sql:field="ProductID" />
        <attribute type="OrdID" sql:field="OrderID" />
        <element type="Price" sql:field="UnitPrice" />
        <element type="Qty" sql:field="Quantity" />
        <element type="Disc" sql:field="Discount" />
        <element type="Product" sql:relation="Products">
```

continues

Listing 9.30   **Continued**

```
                    <sql:relationship
                            key-relation="[Order Details]"
                            key="ProductID"
                            foreign-relation="Products"
                            foreign-key="ProductID" />
            </element>
    </ElementType>


    <ElementType name="Product" sql:relation="Products" sql:key-
    ➥fields="ProductID">
        <AttributeType name="ProductID" dt:type="id" sql:id-
        ➥prefix="Products-" />
        <AttributeType name="ProdName"  />
        <AttributeType name="Category" />
        <AttributeType name="QtyPerUnit" />

        <attribute type="ProductID" />
        <attribute type="ProdName" sql:field="ProductName" />
        <attribute type="Category" sql:field="CategoryID" />
        <attribute type="QtyPerUnit" sql:field="QuantityPerUnit" />
    </ElementType>

    <ElementType name="Customer" sql:relation="Customers">
        <AttributeType name="CustID" dt:type="id" />
        <AttributeType name="CompanyName" />
        <AttributeType name="CustomerOrders"
                dt:type="idrefs"
                sql:id-prefix="Orders-" />

        <attribute type="CustID" sql:field="CustomerID" />
        <attribute type="CompanyName" sql:field="CompanyName" />
        <attribute type="CustomerOrders" sql:relation="Orders"
        ➥sql:field="OrderID">
            <sql:relationship
                    key-relation="Customers"
                    key="CustomerID"
                    foreign-relation="Orders"
                    foreign-key="CustomerID" />
        </attribute>
        <element type="Order">
            <sql:relationship
                    key-relation="Customers"
                    key="CustomerID"
                    foreign-relation="Orders"
                    foreign-key="CustomerID" />
        </element>
    </ElementType>
</Schema>
```

The most notable portion of the schema is the `OrderDetail` element type definition. This highlighted section shows how to use several key annotations. For example, you can alias a table name by using the `sql:relation` annotation, as you did by renaming the `Order Details` table as `OrderDetail`. You also aliased column names by using the `sql:field` annotation to designate to which column in the table the element or attribute belongs. You also used `idref` attributes to reference `id` fields from other tables, as seen with the `OrdID` and `ProdID` attributes. Finally, this section shows you how to build relationships to other tables to represent a hierarchy using the `sql:relation` annotation.

If you are not familiar with XDR syntax, you will see the more familiar XSD Schema syntax later in the section, "XML Views Using Annotated XSD Schemas."

Save this template to the schemas directory as `ExplicitMapping.xdr` and run the following XPath query in your browser:

```
http://localhost/northwind/myschemas/ExplicitMapping.xdr/Customer/Order
➥[@OrdID='Orders-10308']?root=data
```

The result of this query is shown in Listing 9.31.

Listing 9.31 **Sample XDR Schema Using Annotations**

```
<?xml version="1.0" encoding="utf-8" ?>
<data>
    <Order OrdID="Orders-10308" ShipMethod="3" ShippedDate="1996-09-
    ➥24T00:00:00" ShipName="Ana Trujillo Emparedados y helados">
        <OrderDetail>
            <Price>28.8</Price>
            <Qty>1</Qty>
            <Disc>0</Disc>
            <Product ProductID="Products-69" ProdName="Gudbrandsdalsost"
            ➥Category="4" QtyPerUnit="10 kg pkg." />
        </OrderDetail>
        <OrderDetail>
            <Price>12</Price>
            <Qty>5</Qty>
            <Disc>0</Disc>
            <Product ProductID="Products-70" ProdName="Outback Lager"
            ➥Category="1" QtyPerUnit="24 - 355 ml bottles" />
        </OrderDetail>
    </Order>
</data>
```

Using XPath Queries

Now that you have defined your schema as a view of the database, you can look further at using XPath with SQL Server. Several benefits exist to using XPath instead of SQL. For example, developers not familiar with SQL, but familiar with XML, can develop complex queries quickly. Because SQL is a relational language, it is sometimes difficult to hierarchically represent data. Using XML, it becomes easy to see hierarchical relationships between tables.

Limitations exist to what can be expressed using XPath in SQL Server, however, because SQL Server only supports a subset of the XPath specification. Table 9.8 shows the unsupported features.

Table 9.8 **Unsupported XPath Features in SQL Server**

Unsupported Feature	Unsupported XPath Item
Root queries	`/`
Axes	`ancestor, ancestor-or-self, descendant, descendant-or-self` (`//`), `following, following-sibling, namespace, preceding, preceding-sibling`
Numeric-valued predicates	Example: `[count(myNode)=1]`
Arithmetic operators	`Mod`
Node functions	`ancestor, ancestor-or-self, descendant, descendant-or-self` (`//`), `following, following-sibling, namespace, preceding, preceding-sibling`
String functions	`string(), concat(), starts-with(), contains(), substring-before(), substring-after(), substring(), string-length(), normalize(), translate()`
Boolean functions	`lang()`
Numeric functions	`sum(), floor(), ceiling(), round()`
Union operator	`|`

Now that you know what the limitations are, look at a few examples.

One way to issue XPath queries is by providing XPath statements in the URL in a browser. Simply type the following URL in the browser, taking care to refer to an actual order ID for customer ID ANTON:

```
http://localhost/Northwind/myschemas/ExplicitMapping.xdr/Customer[@Cust
➥ID='ANTON']/Order[@OrdID='Orders-10308']
```

Besides issuing XPath statements in the browser URL, you can also include them in template files. Recall that template files can contain one or more XPath statements and/or one or more SQL statements. The template containing the XPath query is shown in Listing 9.32. Save the template file to your templates directory and adjust the `mapping-schema` attribute value to match your directory structure.

Listing 9.32   **Sample Template File Containing XPath Queries**

```
<?xml version="1.0" encoding="utf-8" ?>
<Data xmlns:sql="urn:schemas-microsoft-com:xml-sql">
    <sql:xpath-query mapping-schema="../schemas/ExplicitMapping.xdr">
        Customer/Order[@OrdID='Orders-10308']
    </sql:xpath-query>
</Data>
```

Because of the current limitations on XPath syntax, it is difficult to write complex XPath statements that take advantage of the node-set querying abilities of XPath. As this technology continues to mature, watch for added support in the form of service packs and add-ons.

Using Updategrams is discussed in depth in the section, "XML Views Using Annotated XSD Schemas."

SQLXML 3.0

One stride towards advancing SQL Server's XML capabilities is the release of SQLXML 3.0. This add-on, which is available from www.microsoft.com/downloads, enhances SQL Server's out-of-the-box XML functionality by providing annotations and support for creating XML views using XSD Schemas, Updategrams, DiffGrams, and a new .NET Managed Provider in the form of SQLXML Managed Classes. SQLXML 3.0 also introduced the concept of client-side XML formatting, allowing a rowset to be formatted as XML on the client rather than on the server, which saves processing time.

This section focuses on creating annotated XSD Schemas and introduces the SQLXML 3.0 managed provider classes.

Improvements to Virtual Directory Management

SQLXML 3.0 introduces a new MMC snap-in that manages virtual directories for SQL Server. This snap-in should be used in place of the snap-in that ships with SQL Server 2000. It provides new capabilities, such as upgrading existing directories to use the version 2 library and managing caching of templates and schemas.

Virtual directories created with the MMC snap-in that ships with SQL Server can be upgraded to use SQLXML 3.0 by using the snap-in that comes with SQLXML 3.0. Simply click the virtual directory that you want to upgrade using the SQLXML 3.0 MMC snap-in and the tabbed dialog appears to manage the virtual directory as before. A new tab, "Upgrade to Version 3", is added to the dialog. Click the "Upgrade to Version 3" tab to upgrade the virtual directory so that it can use the latest features. Figure 9.6 shows the dialog.

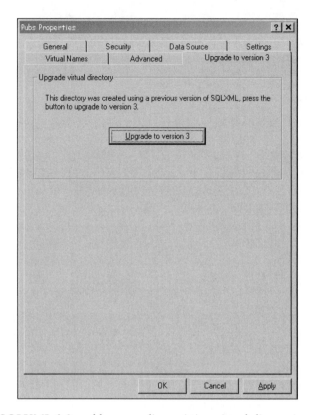

Figure 9.6   SQLXML 3.0 enables upgrading existing virtual directories to version 3.

After the virtual directory is upgraded, you can work with SQLXML 3.0's new features.

XML Views Using Annotated XSD Schemas

As mentioned in Chapters 3 and 4, XDR Schemas were implemented prior to the W3C's recommendation release for XSD Schemas. While existing products, such as BizTalk, currently support XDR Schemas, they do not have wide acceptance throughout the developer community, where XSD Schemas are typically favored. Because one of the main goals of XML development is platform-independence and data interchange, it makes sense that SQL Server would support this concept by supporting the W3C's recommendation.

To use XSD Schemas with SQL Server, you must change the namespaces used with the schema to reference the W3C XML Schema namespace (www.w3.org/2001/XMLSchema) and the new Microsoft mapping schema namespace (urn:schemas-microsoft-com:mapping-schema).

Default Mappings

Just as with XDR Schemas, XSD schemas can be used with SQL Server 2000 annotations to create explicit mappings of data, or default mappings may be used as well. Listing 9.33 shows an XML view using default mappings where an element is named the same as a table, and attributes directly map to column names within that table.

Listing 9.33   **SQL Server 2000 XSD Schema Using Default Mappings**

```
<?xml version="1.0" encoding="utf-8" ?>
<xsd:schema xmlns:xsd="http://www.w3.org/2001/XMLSchema"
            xmlns:sql="urn:schemas-microsoft-com:mapping-schema">

    <xsd:element name="Customers">
        <xsd:complexType>
            <xsd:attribute name="CustomerID" type="xsd:string"/>
            <xsd:attribute name="CompanyName" type="xsd:string"/>
            <xsd:attribute name="ContactName" type="xsd:string"/>
        </xsd:complexType>
    </xsd:element>
</xsd:schema>
```

Explicit Mappings

Just as with SQL Server 2000 XDR Annotations, the SQLXML 3.0 XSD Annotation supports annotations to provide mappings to the database. Although most of the functionality remains the same, a few changes exist. Table 9.9 indicates the changed or new items that appear in SQLXML 3.0.

Table 9.9   **Changes and Additions to SQL Server 2000 Annotations**

Change or Addition	Description	Comparative in SQL Server 2000 XDR Annotations
sql:mapped	Enables exclusion of schema items from the output. Literal values are 0, 1, true, and false, where 0 = false and 1 = true.	map-field
sql:relationship	Defines relationships between elements using attributes parent, parent-key, child, and child-key.	key-relation, foreign-relation, key, foreign-key
sql:encode	Creates a URI to be used with BLOB data. Literal values are url or default.	url-encode

continues

Table 9.9 **Continued**

Change or Addition	Description	Comparative in SQL Server 2000 XDR Annotations
`sql:inverse`	Inverses the relationship defined using `sql:relationship` for use with Updategrams. Literal values are `0`, `1`, `true`, and `false`, where `0` = `false` and `1` = `true`.	N/A
`sql:hide`	Hides the element from the output. Literal values are `0`, `1`, `true`, and `false`, where `0` = `false` and `1` = `true`.	N/A
`sql:identity`	Specifies how IDENTITY columns in the database are updated. Values are `ignore` and `useValue`.	N/A
`sql:guid`	Indicates how GUIDs are to be handled for diffgrams. Literal values are `generate` and `useValue`.	N/A
`sql:max-depth`	Defines a maximum depth for recursive relationships.	N/A

The XDR Schema in Listing 9.30 will be changed to use XSD Schema notation. Listing 9.34 shows the finished result.

Listing 9.34 **XML View Using SQLXML 3.0 Annotations**

```
<xsd:schema xmlns:xsd="http://www.w3.org/2001/XMLSchema"
➥xmlns:sql="urn:schemas-microsoft-com:mapping-schema">
    <xsd:annotation>
        <xsd:appinfo>
        <sql:relationship
                    name="CustomerOrders"
                    parent="Customers"
                    parent-key="CustomerID"
                    child="Orders"
                    child-                    <sql:relationship
                    name="OrderDetails"
                    parent="Orders"
                    parent-key="OrderID"
                    child="[Order Details]"
                    child-key="OrderID" />
        </xsd:appinfo>
    </xsd:annotation>
    <xsd:complexType name="OrderDetailType">
        <xsd:attribute name="OrderID" type="xsd:int" />
```

```
            <xsd:attribute name="ProductID" type="xsd:int" />
            <xsd:attribute name="Quantity" type="xsd:decimal" />
        </xsd:complexType>
        <xsd:complexType name="OrderType">
            <xsd:sequence>
                <xsd:element
                        name="OrderDetails"
                        sql:relation="[Order Details]"
                        sql:relationship="OrderDetails"
                        type="OrderDetailType" />
            </xsd:sequence>
            <xsd:attribute
                        name="OrderID"
                        type="xsd:int"
                        sql:field="OrderID"
                        sql:identity="ignore" />
            <xsd:attribute name="CustomerID" type="xsd:string" />
        </xsd:complexType>
        <xsd:element name="Customer" sql:relation="Customers">
            <xsd:complexType>
                <xsd:sequence>
                    <xsd:element name="CustID" type="xsd:string"
                    ➥sql:field="CustomerID" />
                    <xsd:element name="CompName" type="xsd:string"
                    ➥sql:field="CompanyName" />
                    <xsd:element name="ContactName" type="xsd:string" />
                    <xsd:element
                        name="Order"
                        type="OrderType"
                        sql:relation="Orders"
                        sql:relationship="CustomerOrders" />
                </xsd:sequence>
            </xsd:complexType>
        </xsd:element>
    </xsd:schema>
```

To test this XML view, save the schema as `CustomersOrders.xsd` into the schemas directory that you have been using throughout this chapter. Open a browser window and type the following URL into it: `http://localhost/Northwind/myschemas/CustomersOrders.xsd/Customer[CustID='ALFKI']?root=Data`.

Notice that, unlike XDR Schemas, XSD Schemas enable the use of named relationships. This helps segment the code more cleanly because relationships can be defined in one area, types in another, and finally, the implementation of types in yet another. Notice that the `sql:identity` column was used in the example with a value of `ignore` (you'll see why this value was chosen in the following section, "Updategrams").

XSD Schemas provide a flexible means of providing a static view, known as XML views, of a database that can easily be queried using XPath notation. XML views can also be used in conjunction with other SQL Server XML tools, such as Diffgrams and Updategrams.

Updategrams

As previously mentioned, XML views are also useful in conjunction with Updategrams. Updategrams provide a means to perform INSERT, UPDATE, or DELETE statements using an XML document. The syntax for an Updategram is as follows:

```
<ROOT xmlns:updg="urn:schemas-microsoft-com:xml-Updategram">
  <updg:sync [mapping-schema= "AnnotatedSchemaFile.xml"] >
    <updg:before>
        ...
    </updg:before>
    <updg:after>
        ...
    </updg:after>
  </updg:sync>
</ROOT>
```

The mapping-schema attribute specifies the XML view to use for mapping. If this is omitted, SQL Server defaults to using default mappings where each element corresponds to a table and attributes correspond to the table's columns. The updg:before block represents what the data should look like before the operation, and the updg:after block represents what the data should look like after the operation. The type of operation depends on the structure of the data:

- If data appears in the updg:before block and not in the updg:after block, a DELETE is performed.

- If data appears in the updg:after block and not in the updg:before block, an INSERT is performed.

- If data appears in both the updg:before and updg:after blocks, an UPDATE is performed.

The updg:sync element determines the bounds of transactional scope. Multiple statements can be contained in each updg:sync block, and if one fails, all statements are rolled back. Each updg:sync block is autonomous: If statements in one updg:sync block fail, other updg:sync statements are not affected.

Inserting Data Using Updategrams

To modify data in a database, different considerations tat need to be made that you already take for granted. For example, how do you handle IDENTITY columns in a table? If you want to provide the value for the identity column, you need to first suppress the creation of the IDENTITY column in the database. If you have the server create the value, you need a way to retrieve the value. These are common tasks that you likely already perform with SQL. To perform these tasks using XML, SQL Server provides several annotations that aid in updating and inserting data in a database. Table 9.10 shows the annotations.

Table 9.10 **SQL Server Updategram Annotations**

Annotation	Description
updg:id	Enables linking of rows in the updg:before and updg:after blocks when multiple rows are being modified.
updg:at-identity	Stores the value of a newly inserted IDENTITY column for use in subsequent tasks.
updg:guid	Generates a uniqueidentifier value.
updg:returned	Returns the value created for an IDENTITY or uniqueidentifier column.

Look at an example of how to perform an INSERT into the database strictly using XML. Create a new XML file, insertupdategram.xml, and insert the code from Listing 9.35 into it.

Listing 9.35 **Example of an *INSERT* Updategram**

```
<?xml version="1.0" encoding="utf-8" ?>
<ROOT xmlns:updg="urn:schemas-microsoft-com:xml-updategram">
<updg:sync mapping-schema="../schemas/CustomersOrders.xsd">
  <updg:before>
  </updg:before>
  <updg:after updg:returnid="NewOrderID" >
    <Customer>
        <CustID>VBDNA</CustID>
        <CompName>Kirk Allen Evans Consulting, Inc.</CompName>
        <ContactName>Kirk Allen Evans</ContactName>
        <Order updg:at-identity="NewOrderID" CustomerID="VBDNA">
            <OrderDetails OrderID="NewOrderID" ProductID="3"
            ↪Quantity="10.0"/>
        </Order>
    </Customer>
  </updg:after>
</updg:sync>
</ROOT>
```

We are referencing the schema from Listing 9.35 as the mapping schema. No data is in the `updg:before` block, and the data in the `updg:after` block conforms to the mapping schema, so an `INSERT` is performed. The following operations are performed in this Updategram:

- A new `Customer` record is created for `CustomerID VBDNA`.

- A new `Order` record is created for `CustomerID VBDNA`. The generated `IDENTITY` value is stored into a variable, `NewOrderID`.

- A new `Order Details` record is created by using the value of the variable `NewOrderID`.

- The value of the variable `NewOrderID` is returned.

To test this result, execute the following URL:

`http://localhost/northwind/mytemplates/insertupdategram.xml`.

The record can already exist in your database from past examples. If so, simply go into the database and delete the record, and try the example again.

The output of this Updategram is shown in Figure 9.7.

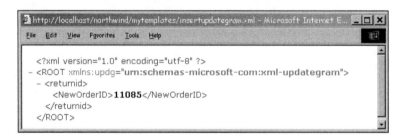

Figure 9.7   Output of an Updategram.

Deleting Data Using Updategrams

In the previous section, you inserted a new customer, order, and order detail record into the `Northwind` database. Because this is test data, say that you would like to delete it. Instead of going through each table and deleting the records, wouldn't it be great to delete them all at once? Using Updategrams, this task is simple.

Again, the schema from Listing 9.35 is referenced. The delete Updategram looks similar to the version that performed an `INSERT`, with one notable exception: The data only appears in the `updg:before` section and not the `updg:after` section. Figure 9.8 shows that the previous example created an `Orders` record with an `OrderID` of 11085. This value is referenced to delete the created records. Listing 9.36 shows the Updategram.

The OrderID value can be different on your database. Before deleting orders, check the database for clarification on the order ID that is to be deleted before executing this code.

Listing 9.36 **Example of a *DELETE* Updategram**

```xml
<?xml version="1.0" encoding="utf-8" ?>
<ROOT xmlns:updg="urn:schemas-microsoft-com:xml-updategram">
<updg:sync mapping-schema="../schemas/CustomersOrders.xsd">
  <updg:before>
    <Customer>
        <CustID>VBDNA</CustID>
        <Order OrderID="11085">
            <OrderDetails OrderID="11085"/>
        </Order>
    </Customer>
  </updg:before>
  <updg:after>

  </updg:after>
</updg:sync>
</ROOT>
```

Save the Updategram as deleteupdategram.xml to the templates directory that you created earlier in this chapter and execute the following URL: http://localhost/northwind/mytemplates/deleteupdategram.xml.

Figure 9.8   A sample Updategram using a DELETE operation.

Diffgrams

Diffgrams follow the same logic as Updategrams, with some syntax differences. Records use both a Before and an After snapshot to determine what action is performed, although the names of the sections are changed. The general Diffgram format is as follows:

```xml
<?xml version="1.0"?>
<diffgr:diffgram
        xmlns:msdata="urn:schemas-microsoft-com:xml-msdata"
        xmlns:diffgr="urn:schemas-microsoft-com:xml-diffgram-v1"
```

```
        xmlns:xsd="http://www.w3.org/2001/XMLSchema">
    <DataInstance>
      ...
    </DataInstance>
    [<diffgr:before>
      ...
    </diffgr:before>]

    [<diffgr:errors>
      ...
    </diffgr:errors>]
  </diffgr:diffgram>
```

Because the use of Diffgrams so closely resembles that of Updategrams, no further explanations of them are given.

The SQLXML Managed Classes

Notice that, throughout this chapter, we have not covered any new managed code—we only covered querying SQL Server and updating it through the URL or templates. Although you can certainly use URLs and templates through the `System.Xml` classes, SQLXML 3.0 also provides a set of managed classes, referred to as the *SQLXML managed classes*. These classes make working with SQL Server's different technologies, such as templates and Updategrams, simple and easy to understand.

Because these classes use the same model as a data provider (data providers are discussed at length in Chapter 8, "Database Access With ADO.NET and XML"), they are familiar to use. There are three objects in the SQLXML managed classes object model: `SqlXmlAdapter`, `SqlXmlParameter`, and `SqlXmlCommand`.

SqlXmlAdapter

Similar to the `Adapter` objects in the `System.Data.SqlClient` and `System.Data.OleDb` namespaces, the `SqlXmlAdapter` class provides the capability to fill a `DataSet` object and update its datasource. In fact, these are the only two methods it provides:

- `Fill()`—Fills a `DataSet` with the contents specified by the `SqlXmlCommand` object
- `Update()`—Updates the data source specified by the `SqlXmlCommand` object.

SqlXmlParameter

The `SqlXmlParameter` object is equally unexciting, as it only provides a `Name` and `Value` property. As seen in Chapter 8, you can use parameters for stored procedures or as variables within a query.

SqlXmlCommand

The "meat" of the SQLXML 3.0 managed classes is the `SqlXmlCommand` class. It provides methods for retrieving and modifying data in SQL Server strictly through its XML interfaces.

Table 9.11 lists the properties of the `SqlXmlCommand` object.

Table 9.11 **Properties of the *SqlXmlCommand* Class**

Property	Description
BasePath	Returns the directory path associated with a virtual name, used to resolve relative paths between different virtual name types (schema, `dbobject`, or template).
ClientSideXml	A Boolean that indicates if XML transformation should occur on the client.
CommandStream	The command stream to execute, such as from a memory stream or file stream.
CommandText	The text to execute on the server.
CommandType	One of the `SqlXmlCommandType` enumerated values, this property indicates the type of command being executed. When used in conjunction with the `CommandStream` property, acceptable values are `Template`, `TemplateFile`, `UpdateGram`, and `DiffGram`.
Namespaces	Enables XPath queries that use namespaces.
OutputEncoding	Specifies the encoding of the output resulting from executing the command.
RootTag	Specifies the root element used for the output.
SchemaPath	The path to the schema file, either absolute or relative.
XslPath	The path to the XSLT file, either absolute or relative.

In table 9.12, we discuss the values for the `CommandType` property of the `SqlXmlCommand` class. The values `Template` and `TemplateFile` bear additional explanation. We use the `Template` value when we are specifying a template within code that is to be executed. If we are executing a template file that resides on the server, then use the value `TemplateFile`. This is demonstrated in listing 9.37.

Table 9.12 shows the available methods of the `SqlXmlCommand` class.

Table 9.12 **Methods of the *SqlXmlCommand* Class**

Method	Description
ClearParameters	Clears the SqlXmlParameter objects for the command object.
CreateParameter	Creates a SqlXmlParameter object.
ExecuteNonQuery	Executes a command that does not return a result, such as an INSERT command.
ExecuteStream	Executes the command and returns the results in a Stream object.
ExecuteToStream	Executes the command and writes the results to the specified Stream object.
ExecuteXmlReader	Executes the command and returns the results in an XmlReader object.

Let's walk through an example to see how the managed classes work. We begin by defining the interface for the web form. Listing 9.37 shows the interface code.

Listing 9.37 **User Interface Code for SQLXML Managed Classes Demonstration**

```
<%@ Page language="c#" Codebehind="SqlXmlManagedClasses.aspx.cs"
AutoEventWireup="false" Inherits="sqlserverxml_cs1.SqlXmlManagedClasses" %>
<!DOCTYPE HTML PUBLIC "-//W3C//DTD HTML 4.0 Transitional//EN" >
<HTML>
    <HEAD>
        <title>SqlXmlManagedClasses</title>
        <meta name="GENERATOR" Content="Microsoft Visual Studio 7.0">
        <meta name="CODE_LANGUAGE" Content="C#">
        <meta name="vs_defaultClientScript" content="JavaScript">
        <meta name="vs_targetSchema" content=
        ➥"http://schemas.microsoft.com/intellisense/ie5">
    </HEAD>
    <body MS_POSITIONING="GridLayout">
        <form id="SqlXmlManagedClasses" method="post" runat="server">
            <asp:DataGrid id="CustomersGrid" runat="server" Width="700px"
            ➥BackColor="LightGray" BorderColor="Black" Font-
            ➥Names="Tahoma" Font-Size="Smaller">
                <HeaderStyle ForeColor="White"
                ➥BackColor="Black"></HeaderStyle>
            </asp:DataGrid>
            <asp:DataGrid id="OrdersGrid" runat="server" Width="700px"
            ➥BackColor="LightGray" BorderColor="Black" Font-
            ➥Names="Tahoma" Font-Size="Smaller">
```

```
              <HeaderStyle ForeColor="White"
              ⇒BackColor="Black"></HeaderStyle>
          </asp:DataGrid>
      </form>
  </body>
</HTML>
```

Now that we have defined the interface code, take a look at the code-behind code for Listing 9.37. Listing 9.38 shows the code-behind code.

Listing 9.38   **Code-Behind Code for SQLXML Managed Classes Demonstration**

```
using System;
using System.Collections;
using System.ComponentModel;
using System.Data;
using System.Drawing;
using System.Web;
using System.Web.SessionState;
using System.Web.UI;
using System.Web.UI.WebControls;
using System.Web.UI.HtmlControls;
using Microsoft.Data.SqlXml;

namespace sqlserverxml_cs1
{
    public class SqlXmlManagedClasses : System.Web.UI.Page
    {
        protected System.Web.UI.WebControls.DataGrid CustomersGrid;
        protected System.Web.UI.WebControls.DataGrid OrdersGrid;
        protected System.Web.UI.WebControls.DataGrid OrderDetailsGrid;

        private string ConnectionString = " Provider=SQLOLEDB;User
        ⇒ID=sa;Password=;Initial Catalog=Northwind;Data Source=at1lt
        ⇒-3165-03";
        //Change this location to point to your local path
        private string BasePath = "d:/projects/new riders/chapters/
        ⇒sql server";

        private void Page_Load(object sender, System.EventArgs e)
        {
            SqlXmlCommand command = new SqlXmlCommand(ConnectionString);
            DataSet ds = new DataSet();
            if (!IsPostBack)
            {
                //Execute a stored procedure that returns the data as XML
                command.CommandType =
                ⇒Microsoft.Data.SqlXml.SqlXmlCommandType.TemplateFile;
```

continues

Listing 9.38 **Continued**

```
                                command.CommandText = BasePath +
                                ➥"/templates/sampleselect.xml";
                                command.RootTag = "Data";
                                SqlXmlParameter param  = command.CreateParameter();
                                param.Name = "CustomerID";
                                param.Value = "AROUT";

                                //Fill a DataSet by executing the template
                                SqlXmlAdapter adapter = new SqlXmlAdapter(command);
                                adapter.Fill(ds);

                                //Populate the DataGrids with the XML data
                                CustomersGrid.DataSource = new
                                ➥DataView(ds.Tables["Customers"]);
                                CustomersGrid.DataBind();
                                OrdersGrid.DataSource = new
                                ➥DataView(ds.Tables["Products"]);
                                OrdersGrid.DataBind();
                        }

                }

                #region Web Form Designer generated code
                override protected void OnInit(EventArgs e)
                {
                        //
                        // CODEGEN: This call is required by the ASP.NET Web Form
                        // Designer.
                        //
                        InitializeComponent();
                        base.OnInit(e);
                }

                /// <summary>
                /// Required method for Designer support - do not modify
                /// the contents of this method with the code editor.
                /// </summary>
                private void InitializeComponent()
                {
                        this.Load += new System.EventHandler(this.Page_Load);

                }
                #endregion
        }
}
```

The pertinent section is in the Page_Load event code. We executed a template
file using the SQLXML managed classes, loaded a DataSet, and displayed the
contents of the DataGrid in the browser.

As you can see, the `SqlXmlCommand` is the workhorse of the SQLXML managed classes object model. By using this set of classes, it's easy to execute templates, XPath statements, and `FOR XML` queries using the object model.

Exposing SQL Server as a Web Service

Another new feature in SQLXML 3.0 is the capability to expose SQL Server 2000 as a web service. This capability enables you to send SOAP HTTP requests to the server to execute stored procedures, user-defined functions, and templates. These web services can then be consumed using the SOAP Toolkit or by leveraging .NET's web service capabilities (these are discussed in detail in chapter 11).

Let's walk through the steps necessary to configure SQL Server as a web service. We will continue to use the `Northwind` virtual directory created earlier in the section, "Configuring SQL XML Support in IIS". To configure SQL Server as a web service:

- Open the Cofigure IIS Support MMC snap-in that was installed with SQLXML 3.0.

- Locate the `Northwind` virtual directory. Right-click this virtual directory and select Properties.

- Click the Virtual Names tab.

- Enter a name for the new web service virtual directory. Our example will use `mysoap`.

- Choose soap in the type drop-down list. This tells SQL Server that this virtual name defines a SOAP web service directory.

- Enter a path to a valid directory on the database server. Our example uses `d:\projects\sql` soap.

- Enter a web service name for the virtual name. Our example uses `sqlsoap` as the web service name.

- Enter a domain name for the web service. This can be the name of your web server.

- Click the Save button. The configure button is now enabled. Click the configure button. A new property window appears.

- In the SOAP Virtual Name Configuration window, choose the type of mapping (template or stored procedure). Our example will execute a template, so choose the Template option.

- Enter a method name for this operation. Our example uses `GetSampleSelect` as the method name.

- In the SP/Template read-only textbox, choose the ellipsis button to locate either the stored procedure or template file. We are using the `sampleselect.xml` template file from listing 9.22.

- Click Save to save the new method. Click OK to exit the property window.

Behind the scenes, the configuration of the SOAP virtual name actually created a WSDL file in the path specified. After completing the above steps for the `sampleselect.xml` template file, a new file was created as D:\projects\sql soap\sqlsoap.wsdl.

We will create a small test harness to call our sample web service. In Visual Studio .NET, click the References node in the Solution Explorer window. Right-click the References node and choose Add Web Reference. A dialog window is displayed, prompting for the location of the WSDL file.

Configuring our sample created a virtual name called `mysoap` in the `Northwind` virtual directory as well as its corresponding WSDL file. To access the WSDL for the web service, we enter the full URL with `wsdl` as a single querystring in the address bar:

```
http://localhost/Northwind/mysoap?wsdl
```

Click the Add Reference button to add the web reference. Now that the web reference is configured and the web service enabled, we can now develop a quick client application to test our service.

Create a new web form called `soapTest`, and enter the following code in `soapTest.aspx`:

```
<%@ Page language="c#" Codebehind="soapTest.aspx.cs" AutoEventWireup="false"
Inherits="WebApplication1.soapTest" %>
<HTML>
    <HEAD>
        <title>Calling a SQL Server Web Service</title>
    </HEAD>

    <body MS_POSITIONING="GridLayout">
        Results from SQL Web Service Call:
        <br/>
        <div id="templateHolder" runat="server">
        </div>
    </body>
</HTML>
```

This code simply creates an HTML server DIV control called `templateHolder`. We then look at the code-behind for `soapTest.aspx`, depicted in Listing 9.38:

Listing 9.38 Code-Behind Code for SQLXML Web Service Demonstration

```
using System;
using System.Collections;
using System.ComponentModel;
using System.Data;
using System.Drawing;
using System.Web;
using System.Web.SessionState;
using System.Web.UI;
using System.Web.UI.WebControls;
using System.Web.UI.HtmlControls;


namespace WebApplication1
{
    public class soapTest : System.Web.UI.Page
    {
        protected System.Web.UI.HtmlControls.HtmlGenericControl
        ↦templateHolder;

        private void Page_Load(object sender, System.EventArgs e)
        {
            System.Xml.XmlElement returnVal;

            localhost.sqlsoap proxy = new localhost.sqlsoap();

            object[] results;
            results = proxy.GetSampleSelect("ANTON");
            returnVal = (System.Xml.XmlElement)results[0];
            templateHolder.InnerText = returnVal.OuterXml;
        }

        #region Web Form Designer generated code
        override protected void OnInit(EventArgs e)
        {
            //
            // CODEGEN: This call is required by the ASP.NET Web Form
            // Designer.
            //
            InitializeComponent();
            base.OnInit(e);
        }

        /// <summary>
        /// Required method for Designer support - do not modify
        /// the contents of this method with the code editor.
        /// </summary>
        private void InitializeComponent()
        {
            this.Load += new System.EventHandler(this.Page_Load);
```

Listing 9.38 **Continued**

```
        }
        #endregion
    }
}
```

When run, this sample emits an XML representation similar to that found in Listing 9.23.

Chapter Summary

This chapter introduced many different ways that SQL Server 2000 provides XML support, both out-of-the box and through the SQLXML 3.0 add-on.

A convenient tool that SQL Server provides is the FOR XML clause to retrieve data from the database as XML. This provides many possibilities, including the ability to generate web reports quickly by combining SQL Server's generated XML with XSLT stylesheets.

Querying SQL Server over the web has traditionally required custom software to be written to act as a broker between the client and database. SQL Server 2000 also significantly reduces the amount of code necessary to provide data over the web through virtual directories. Within virtual directories, virtual names can be associated for different types of objects: database objects, schemas, and templates.

Template files provide a mechanism to store queries and XPath statements so they may be executed multiple times. By providing only template files and not allowing direct access to the database, you are able to reduce the risk of exposing data directly over the web.

Schemas also play an important role in SQL Server's XML strategy. Special annotations within the schemas create XML views of data on the server. These views are used to map XPath queries, Diffgrams, and Updategrams to the physical data locations on the database.

10

XML Serialization

So far in this book, you've examined many different ways of working with XML *explicitly* within the .NET Framework. That is to say, nearly everything that's been covered focused on working directly with XML and the various ways in which you can create, manipulate, and transform XML. In this chapter, we're going to examine an *implicit* method that the .NET Framework provides for working with XML. XML serialization provides a nearly transparent way of persisting object data as XML, and recreating the original objects from the XML data without the complexities of working directly with the XML Document Object Model (DOM) or XSLT transformations.

What Is Serialization?

Serialization is the process of converting an object to a form that can be readily transported. Generally, this means saving the object's data in a way that makes it easy to recreate the object later, through a process called *deserialization*. Serialization does not save any of the methods of an object—it is assumed that the object's code will be available during the deserialization process, and that the data unique to the object is all that is necessary to recreate the object. The serialized data can take many formats, but they all have one thing in common:

the serialized data is not tied to the originating object or system, and the data contains all the information necessary to recreate an object that's identical to the original.

Different Types of Serialization

The Microsoft .NET Framework provides an almost bewildering variety of ways to serialize an object. This chapter focuses on XML serialization, but before we get into the details, I'd like to briefly examine and compare the various serialization methods offered.

XML Serialization

XML serialization allows the public properties and fields of an object to be reduced to an XML document that describes the publicly visible state of the object. This method serializes only public properties and fields—private data will not be persisted, so XML serialization does not provide full fidelity with the original object in all cases. However, because the persistence format is XML, the data being saved can be read and manipulated in a variety of ways and on multiple platforms.

The benefits of XML serialization include the following:

- Allows for complete and flexible control over the format and schema of the XML produced by serialization.

- Serialized format is both human-readable and machine-readable.

- Easy to implement. Does not require any custom serialization-related code in the object to be serialized.

- The XML Schema Definition tool (`xsd.exe`) can generate an XSD Schema from a set of serializable classes, and generate a set of serializable classes from an XSD Schema, making it easy to programmatically consume and manipulate nearly any XML data in an object-oriented (rather than XML-oriented) fashion.

- Objects to be serialized do not need to be explicitly configured for serialization, either by the `SerializableAttribute` or by implementing the `ISerializable` interface.

The restrictions of XML serialization include the following:

- The class to be serialized must have a default (parameterless) public constructor.

- Read-only properties are not persisted.

- Only public properties and fields can be serialized.

SOAP Serialization

SOAP serialization is similar to XML serialization in that the objects being serialized are persisted as XML. The similarity, however, ends there. The classes used for SOAP serialization reside in the `System.Runtime.Serialization` namespace rather than the `System.Xml.Serialization` namespace used by XML serialization. The run-time serialization classes (which include both the `SoapFormatter` and the `BinaryFormatter` classes) use a completely different mechanism for serialization than the `XmlSerializer` class.

The benefits of SOAP serialization include the following:

- Produces a fully SOAP-compliant envelope that can be processed by any system or service that understands SOAP.
- Supports either objects that implement the `ISerializable` interface to control their own serialization, or objects that are marked with the `SerializableAttribute` attribute.
- Can deserialize a SOAP envelope into a compatible set of objects.
- Can serialize and restore non-public and public members of an object.

The restrictions of SOAP serialization include the following:

- The class to be serialized must either be marked with the `SerializableAttribute` attribute, or must implement the `ISerializable` interface and control its own serialization and deserialization.
- Only understands SOAP. It cannot work with arbitrary XML schemas.

Binary Serialization

Binary serialization allows the serialization of an object into a binary stream, and restoration from a binary stream into an object. This method can be faster than XML serialization, and the binary representation is usually much more compact than an XML representation. However, this performance comes at the cost of cross-platform compatibility and human readability.

The benefits of binary serialization include the following:

- It's the fastest serialization method because it does not have the overhead of generating an XML document during the serialization process.
- The resulting binary data is more compact than an XML string, so it takes up less storage space and can be transmitted quickly.
- Supports either objects that implement the `ISerializable` interface to control its own serialization, or objects that are marked with the `SerializableAttribute` attribute.
- Can serialize and restore non-public and public members of an object.

The restrictions of binary serialization include the following:

- The class to be serialized must either be marked with the SerializableAttribute attribute, or must implement the ISerializable interface and control its own serialization and deserialization.

- The binary format produced is specific to the .NET Framework and it cannot be easily used from other systems or platforms.

- The binary format is not human-readable, which makes it more difficult to work with if the original program that produced the data is not available.

Other Forms of Serialization

A number of other forms of serialization are available in the .NET Framework that are either not intended to be used directly or are specific to a problem domain, which is outside the scope of this book. These other serialization methods include the LosFormatter, which is used to serialize and deserialize page view state in ASP.NET, the CodeDomSerializer, which is used to serialize an object graph representing dynamically generated source code, the binary serialization used in .NET Remoting, and others.

How Is Serialization Used in ASP.NET?

Now that you have a good idea of what serialization is and what types of serialization are offered by the .NET Framework, let's take a brief tour of the various ways that serialization is used behind-the-scenes in ASP.NET. Most of the serialization that is built-in to ASP.NET requires no direct interaction with the average ASP.NET developer; however, having a good understanding of what is going on behind the scenes helps you make an informed decision when it comes to certain performance and scalability issues. As you will see, the ASP.NET run-time uses many different types of serialization, depending on what type is best-suited for any given situation.

Session State

As you might or might not be aware, ASP.NET offers three different storage mechanisms for session state:

- In-process
- Out-of-process as a Windows service
- Out-of-process in a SQL server database

The default method of session state storage is in-process, which uses no serialization. Instead, objects that are stored in session state using this method are simply held in memory in the same process that the ASP.NET application in question is running in.

With the out-of-process as a Windows service method, session state is stored in memory by the ASP.NET State service. This service can run on the same physical server as the ASP.NET application that uses it, or it can run on a separate server that is accessed over a Local Area Network (LAN) by ASP.NET whenever it needs to store or retrieve session state data. The support for remote session state servers allows for a dedicated session state server to be shared by all the servers in a web farm, for example.

Because it is problematic at best to move a live object instance between processes on the same machine, and impossible to move a live object instance across the network to a different machine, the session state service cannot take the easy way out that the in-process method does by simply storing a reference to an already-in-memory object. Instead, when this storage method is selected (in the `Web.config` file), ASP.NET uses the `BinaryFormatter` object to serialize the object placed in session state to a binary stream that is sent to the session state service under the `SessionID` key for the current user. The binary serialization allows for quick and memory-efficient storage of an object, but the serialization process obviously takes more time and processing power than simply storing a reference to an object that is already in memory. Therefore, you should carefully consider which session state storage is right for your situation.

Similar to the previous method, the out-of-process in a SQL server database method also uses binary serialization to store session data, but in this case, the data is stored in a table in the SQL server's `tempdb` database. This adds both the extra overhead and the extra reliability of SQL server over the session state service previously mentioned.

View State

If you've done any ASP.NET development, you might have noticed a hidden form field called `__VIEWSTATE` embedded in the HTML generated by most web forms. This field contains a compact text serialization of the state of the server controls on that web form. ASP.NET uses the view state to compare a control's state to its previous state to see if it needs to raise any events for that control (due to the text property being changed, for example). The contents of the `__VIEWSTATE` field are generated by the `LosFormatter`, which is specifically designed to produce an extremely compact ASCII serialization that's suitable to include in web forms while taking up a minimum amount of bandwidth. The LosFormatter is intended only for internal use during the lifetime of a web request; it is not recommended to persist the serialization produced by this object for any significant length of time.

XML Web Services

XML Web Services use shallow serialization, involving only the public read/write properties of an object, much like XML serialization. However, the result is specific to the SOAP standard, which is an agreed-upon standard for data transport and method calls using XML. Some SOAP-related attributes in the System.XML.Serialization namespace allow customization of the generated code.

What About Configuration Files?

As you learned more about XML serialization, you might have wondered whether the XML-based configuration files in the .NET Framework (such as Web.config) use XML serialization. The answer appears to be no. Configuration files in .NET are read by a series of *configuration section handlers* that are each responsible for their own section of the configuration file (sessionState is one such section in the Web.config file). Unless Microsoft decides to release the source code to the .NET Framework, there's no way of being 100 percent certain whether the built-in section handlers use XML serialization or not. However, each section handler must implement the IConfigurationSectionHandler interface, which specifies a single method, Create. The Create method accepts an XmlNode object that is not friendly to the XmlSerializer, causing namespace errors whenever it is used as the source for deserialization. It might be possible to get a custom configuration section handler to work with XML serialization, but it appears to be more work than just using the XmlNode object directly.

An Overview of XML Serialization

The main class used in XML serialization is the XmlSerializer class, with its Serialize and Deserialize methods. Nearly everything else in the System.Xml.Serialization namespace has to do with modifying the behavior or output of the XmlSerializer. XML serialization persists only public read-write properties and fields. It does not save methods, private fields or properties, read-only properties, or indexers.

Basic XML Serialization

How do you actually serialize an object to XML? First, you need to create an object to serialize; for the purposes of this demonstration, let's create a class that can hold all the information associated with a particular link in a web-based menu. We'll need to store the URL itself, of course, and a title for the link (the text to display for the link). In addition, we'll include a ToolTip property to provide an extra description of the link when the user hovers over it, and a flag that indicates whether the link is external to the current site. This "IsExternal" flag enables us to treat external links differently from links to other pages in the same site, whether it's displaying a graphic next to external links (as Microsoft does) or opening external links in a different browser window.

Creating an Object to Serialize

Start by creating a new C# Console application project in Visual Studio .NET. Then add a new class to the project called MenuLink.cs. Recall that the restrictions specific to XML serialization state that you need a default (or parameterless) constructor and that only public read/write properties and fields are serialized. With the four properties we've already defined, the code for the MenuLink class looks like this:

```
public class MenuLink
{
    private string _Url, _Title, _ToolTip;
    private bool _IsExternal;

    public MenuLink()
    {
        _Url = "";
        _Title = "";
        _ToolTip = "";
        _IsExternal = false;
    }

    public string Url
    {
        get { return _Url; }
        set { _Url = value; }
    }

    public string Title
    {
        get { return _Title; }
        set { _Title = value; }
    }
}
```

```
    public string ToolTip
    {
        get { return _ToolTip; }
        set { _ToolTip = value; }
    }

    public bool IsExternal
    {
        get { return _IsExternal; }
        set { _IsExternal = value; }
    }
}
```

This class does not contain any extra code or attributes that have to do with XML serialization. This characteristic of XML serialization makes it so easy to use. Because it works with only public read/write properties and fields, it can be used with virtually any object without modifying the object.

Serializing an Object to XML

Now that you have an object to serialize, you can begin the process of converting an instance of that object to its XML representation:

1. Switch back to the default `Class1.cs` file that was created for you when you opened the project.

2. Add a few `using` statements to the file:
   ```
   using System;
   using System.IO;
   using System.Xml;
   using System.Xml.Serialization;
   ```

3. Inside the `Main` method, create an instance of the `MenuLink` object and populate it with some data:
   ```
   // create and populate a new MenuLink object
   MenuLink link = new MenuLink();
   link.Title = "GotDotNet";
   link.Url = "http://www.gotdotnet.com/";
   link.ToolTip = "Click here for Microsoft's GotDotNet developer
   ►site.";
   link.IsExternal = true;
   ```

Now that you have an object with data in it, you can serialize the object to an XML file in the current directory.

4. Create an instance of the `XmlSerializer` object. The `XmlSerializer` constructor takes a `Type` object that gives it the information on the public properties and fields that it needs to perform the serialization.

```
Console.WriteLine("Serializing link to XML...");
XmlSerializer serializer = new XmlSerializer(typeof(MenuLink));
```

In this example, you're using the C# `typeof` keyword to get the `Type` object for the `MenuLink`. This could also be accomplished by calling the `GetType` method on the existing `MenuLink` instance, `link`.

5. If you look at the MSDN documentation on the `XmlSerializer.Serialize` method, you can see that it accepts a `Stream`, a `TextWriter`, or an `XmlWriter` as the object to which to serialize. This allows for a great deal of flexibility because the output stream could be pointing to a text file, to a database, to a location in memory, to the ASP.NET `Response.Output` object (allowing serialization directly to the browser), or quite a few other locations. In this case, write the XML to a text file:

```
// serialize the object to a file
string path = ".\\link.xml";
FileStream fs = File.OpenWrite(path);
```

You could just stop here and pass the `FileStream` object directly to the overload of `XmlSerializer.Serialize` that accepts a `Stream` object, but that writes an unformatted mass of XML to the text file. With just two more lines of code, you can have nicely formatted and indented XML written to the text file—this gives the XML better readability.

6. Create an `XmlTextWriter` object that points to the `FileStream`. Set the `Formatting` property to `Indented`, and pass the `XmlTextWriter` to the `XmlSerializer` instead of passing the `FileStream` directly.

```
XmlTextWriter writer = new XmlTextWriter(fs,
System.Text.Encoding.UTF8);
writer.Formatting = Formatting.Indented;
```

7. You're ready to perform the serialization. Wrap the call to `Serialize` in a try block and close the `XmlTextWriter` in the `finally` block so that you can ensure that the file isn't held open if something unforeseen happens.

```
try
{
    // perform the XML serialization
    serializer.Serialize(writer, link);
}
```

```
finally
{
    // close the writer, which closes the underlying
FileStream
    writer.Close();
}

Console.WriteLine("Serialization Complete!");
```

8. Compile and run the project. You've successfully serialized the MenuLink object to an XML file! Here's what the generated link.xml file looks like:

```
<?xml version="1.0" encoding="utf-8"?>
<MenuLink xmlns:xsi="http://www.w3.org/2001/XMLSchema-instance"
xmlns:xsd="http://www.w3.org/2001/XMLSchema">
  <Url>http://www.gotdotnet.com/</Url>
  <Title>GotDotNet</Title>
  <ToolTip>Click here for Microsoft's GotDotNet developer
site.</ToolTip>
  <IsExternal>true</IsExternal>
</MenuLink>
```

Deserializing an Object from XML

You've created an XML file from a live object, but what about deserialization? How do you get a live object back from that XML file? The XmlSerializer makes this task just as easy, if not easier. It starts the same way:

1. Create an instance of the XmlSerializer and initialize it with the Type object for the MenuLink class. For the purposes of this demonstration, you can comment out the serialization code that you've just been through in the Main routine and insert the deserialization code in its place. You create the XmlSerializer object in exactly the same way that you did for serializing the MenuLink.

   ```
   Console.WriteLine("Deserializing link from XML...");
   XmlSerializer serializer = new XmlSerializer(typeof(MenuLink));
   ```

2. Open the XML file for reading:

   ```
   string path = ".\\link.xml";
   FileStream fs = File.OpenRead(path);
   ```

3. Declare a new MenuLink instance and perform the actual deserialization. Again, you're going to wrap the action in a try block and close the FileStream in the corresponding finally block.

   ```
   MenuLink loadedLink;
   try
   ```

```
    {
        loadedLink = (MenuLink)serializer.Deserialize(fs);
    }
    finally
    {
        fs.Close();
    }
```

As you can see, you're passing the `FileStream` object to the `Deserialize` method as the source from which to deserialize. Again, this allows for flexibility because the stream's source could be many things—including, in this case, a simple local file. The `Deserialize` method always returns an `object` type, which must then be cast to the correct destination type before it's used.

4. Finally, you can output the properties of the newly loaded `MenuLink` to verify that everything was correctly deserialized:

```
    Console.WriteLine("Link information:");
    Console.WriteLine("Title: {0}", loadedLink.Title);
    Console.WriteLine("URL: {0}", loadedLink.Url);
    Console.WriteLine("ToolTip: {0}", loadedLink.ToolTip);
    Console.WriteLine("IsExternal: {0}", loadedLink.IsExternal);
```

That's it. With a relative handful of code, you serialized an arbitrary object to XML and restored it to its original state from that XML.

Using Attributes to Control XML Serialization

If the operation illustrated in the previous example were all that XML serialization could do, it would be a useful tool for many developers. However, closer examination reveals that the `System.Xml.Serialization` namespace contains a number of *attribute classes* that can control the format of the XML generated during serialization of any given object. These attributes, when applied to a class or its properties, enable you to control whether a given item is serialized as an XML element or an attribute on an existing element, what the name of the element or attribute should be, what XSD data type is specified in the XML, and many other aspects of serialization over which you might want fine-grained control. This can be useful if you need your serialized XML to conform to a certain schema, as we discover in the next section. This level of control can also be useful for simply making the serialized output look a certain way.

Returning to the serialized `MenuLink` object, take a closer look at the default XML generated by the serialization process:

```
<?xml version="1.0" encoding="utf-8"?>
<MenuLink xmlns:xsi="http://www.w3.org/2001/XMLSchema-instance"
xmlns:xsd="http://www.w3.org/2001/XMLSchema">
  <Url>http://www.gotdotnet.com/</Url>
  <Title>GotDotNet</Title>
  <ToolTip>Click here for Microsoft's GotDotNet developer site.</ToolTip>
  <IsExternal>true</IsExternal>
</MenuLink>
```

As you can see, the `MenuLink` class becomes the root element of the XML document, with an element name that matches the name of the class. Each property becomes a subelement, with a name that exactly matches the name of the property. This is the method that the `XmlSerializer` object follows when it is not given any special instructions on how to format a class. It's good enough for many situations, but say that you have a requirement that the root element of a link should be named simply "`Link`" instead of "`MenuLink`". In addition, you might be required to make the `IsExternal` property serialize as an attribute of the new `Link` element, but this attribute should be named simply "`External`" rather than "`IsExternal`".

To change the name of the root element in this case, go back to the `MenuLink` class in `MenuLink.cs`:

1. Add a new `using` statement so that you have easy access to the attribute classes in the `System.Xml.Serialization` namespace:
   ```
   using System.Xml.Serialization;
   ```

2. Because the class itself becomes the root element of the XML document, you need to add an `XmlRootAttribute` to the class definition, like this:
   ```
   [XmlRootAttribute()]
   public class MenuLink
   {
   ...
   }
   ```

   You might have noticed that attributes have their own special syntax that is not shared by any other programming element. Because of this, many people find that typing the word "Attribute" on an attribute to be redundant, especially when working with items such as the `XmlAttributeAttribute` attribute class (say that quickly three times). For this reason, the .NET Framework accepts either the full name of the attribute class, or an abbreviated version that leaves off the word "Attribute" from the end of the class name. For example, `XmlRootAttribute` becomes simply `XmlRoot` and `XmlAttribteAttribute` becomes `XmlAttribute`. The shortened version is used for the remainder of this chapter.

3. You've attached an XmlRoot attribute to the MenuLink class, but because the class is already rendered as the XML root element, you really haven't changed much yet. To change the name of the root element, modify the ElementName property of the XmlRoot attribute that we're using:

```
[XmlRoot(ElementName = "Link")]
public class MenuLink
{
...
}
```

4. To make the IsExternal property into an attribute rather than an element, a similar application of the XmlAttribute attribute to the property declaration is needed:

```
[XmlAttribute(AttributeName = "External")]
public bool IsExternal
{
    get { return _IsExternal; }
    set { _IsExternal = value; }
}
```

The XmlAttribute attribute tells the XML serializer to serialize the property it is applied to as an attribute of the parent tag, rather than as its own element. If the AttributeName property is set, that value is used for the XML attribute name instead of the name of the property.

5. Return to the Class1.cs file and comment out the deserialization code. Then uncomment the original serialization code that you used to generate the first version of the link.xml file.

You might need to delete the existing link.xml file before you can overwrite it. Compile the project and run it.

With those two attributes applied and no other changes to the program, the following serialized XML now looks exactly like you want it to look. The root element is now called Link, and it has an attribute called External that stores the value of the IsExternal property:

```
<?xml version="1.0" encoding="utf-8"?>
<Link xmlns:xsi="http://www.w3.org/2001/XMLSchema-instance"
xmlns:xsd="http://www.w3.org/2001/XMLSchema" External="true">
  <Url>http://www.gotdotnet.com/</Url>
  <Title>GotDotNet</Title>
  <ToolTip>Click here for Microsoft's GotDotNet developer
site.</ToolTip>
</Link>
```

Using XSD Schemas for Strongly Typed XML Serialization

The uses for XML serialization that you've examined so far work best when you have control over the XML structures involved, but what if you needed to write a program to consume and/or produce XML that conforms to a particular schema? You could always use the classes in the `System.Xml` namespace to manually manipulate the XML, and rely on your own understanding of the XSD Schema in question to make sure that you produce valid XML. Perhaps you've realized that it is possible to create some classes that, through the use of XML serialization attributes, can be automatically serialized to an XML structure that conforms to the XSD Schema, allowing you to work with the XML data in a purely object-oriented fashion.

Creating serializable classes manually is certainly possible, but might become tedious when you work with a large or complicated schema. This again relies on your thorough understanding of the requirements of the XSD Schema in question to ensure that your classes never serialize to a nonconformant XML structure. Fortunately, Microsoft provided a better solution in the form of a command-line utility called `xsd.exe`, which is provided with the .NET Framework SDK. This utility has numerous uses that are beyond the scope of this chapter. What we're interested in is its ability to take an XSD Schema as input and produce the source code to a set of classes that can deserialize from any XML that conforms to the XSD Schema, and serialize into XML that can be understood by any other tool that expects the format specified in the schema. The generated source code can be in any language you specify, as long as you specify C#, Visual Basic .NET, or JScript .NET.

This ability has tremendous potential. It makes it almost trivial to exchange data with a business partner in an industry-standard XML format without ever having to touch the XML directly in your code. Here's an example: Let's go to the source of the XSD standard, the World Wide Web Consortium (W3C). We'll use the canonical Purchase Order Schema sample found in Section 2.1 at www.w3.org/TR/xmlschema-0/.

For those of you who aren't sitting in front of a computer as you read this, the Purchase Order Schema is reproduced in full in Listing 10.1.

Listing 10.1 **The Purchase Order Schema**

```
<xsd:schema xmlns:xsd="http://www.w3.org/2001/XMLSchema">

 <xsd:annotation>
  <xsd:documentation xml:lang="en">
   Purchase order schema for Example.com.
   Copyright 2000 Example.com. All rights reserved.
```

```xsd
    </xsd:documentation>
  </xsd:annotation>

  <xsd:element name="purchaseOrder" type="PurchaseOrderType"/>

  <xsd:element name="comment" type="xsd:string"/>

  <xsd:complexType name="PurchaseOrderType">
   <xsd:sequence>
    <xsd:element name="shipTo" type="USAddress"/>
    <xsd:element name="billTo" type="USAddress"/>
    <xsd:element ref="comment" minOccurs="0"/>
    <xsd:element name="items"  type="Items"/>
   </xsd:sequence>
   <xsd:attribute name="orderDate" type="xsd:date"/>
  </xsd:complexType>

  <xsd:complexType name="USAddress">
   <xsd:sequence>
    <xsd:element name="name"   type="xsd:string"/>
    <xsd:element name="street" type="xsd:string"/>
    <xsd:element name="city"   type="xsd:string"/>
    <xsd:element name="state"  type="xsd:string"/>
    <xsd:element name="zip"    type="xsd:decimal"/>
   </xsd:sequence>
   <xsd:attribute name="country" type="xsd:NMTOKEN"
      fixed="US"/>
  </xsd:complexType>

  <xsd:complexType name="Items">
   <xsd:sequence>
    <xsd:element name="item" minOccurs="0" maxOccurs="unbounded">
     <xsd:complexType>
      <xsd:sequence>
       <xsd:element name="productName" type="xsd:string"/>
       <xsd:element name="quantity">
        <xsd:simpleType>
         <xsd:restriction base="xsd:positiveInteger">
          <xsd:maxExclusive value="100"/>
         </xsd:restriction>
        </xsd:simpleType>
       </xsd:element>
       <xsd:element name="USPrice"  type="xsd:decimal"/>
       <xsd:element ref="comment"   minOccurs="0"/>
       <xsd:element name="shipDate" type="xsd:date" minOccurs="0"/>
      </xsd:sequence>
      <xsd:attribute name="partNum" type="SKU" use="required"/>
     </xsd:complexType>
    </xsd:element>
   </xsd:sequence>
  </xsd:complexType>
```

continues

Listing 10.1   **Continued**

```
<!-- Stock Keeping Unit, a code for identifying products -->
<xsd:simpleType name="SKU">
 <xsd:restriction base="xsd:string">
  <xsd:pattern value="\d{3}-[A-Z]{2}"/>
 </xsd:restriction>
</xsd:simpleType>

</xsd:schema>
```

Generating Classes from an XSD Schema

Creating a set of classes from this schema is easy:

1. Create a text file on your hard drive with the XSD Schema as the contents. (It's easiest to copy and paste from the W3C website.)
2. Rename the text file to `PurchaseOrder.xsd`.
3. Open a command prompt and navigate to the directory where you
   placed this file.

In order to use `xsd.exe` from the command prompt, the directory containing
`xsd.exe` must be in your Path environment variable. If you have Visual Studio
.NET installed, the Visual Studio .NET Command Prompt link located in the
Visual Studio .NET Tools folder in your Start menu takes care of setting the
proper environment variables for you. Enter the following command at the
prompt:

```
xsd.exe PurchaseOrder.xsd /classes
```

This command generates a set of classes from the XSD file in the default language (C#). The generated classes are created in a file called `PurchaseOrder.cs`
and looks something like what's shown in Listing 10.2.

Listing 10.2   **C# Code Generated from *PurchaseOrder.xsd***

```
using System.Xml.Serialization;

[System.Xml.Serialization.XmlRootAttribute("purchaseOrder", Namespace="",
➥IsNullable=false)]
public class PurchaseOrderType
{
    public USAddress shipTo;

    public USAddress billTo;

    public string comment;
```

```
    [System.Xml.Serialization.XmlArrayItemAttribute("item",
    ⇒IsNullable=false)]
    public ItemsItem[] items;

    [System.Xml.Serialization.XmlAttributeAttribute(DataType="date")]
    public System.DateTime orderDate;

    [System.Xml.Serialization.XmlIgnoreAttribute()]
    public bool orderDateSpecified;
}

public class USAddress
{
    public string name;

    public string street;

    public string city;

    public string state;

    public System.Decimal zip;

    [System.Xml.Serialization.XmlAttributeAttribute(DataType="NMTOKEN")]
    [System.ComponentModel.DefaultValueAttribute("US")]
    public string country = "US";
}

public class ItemsItem
{
    public string productName;


[System.Xml.Serialization.XmlElementAttribute(DataType="positiveInteger")]
    public string quantity;

    public System.Decimal USPrice;

    public string comment;

    [System.Xml.Serialization.XmlElementAttribute(DataType="date")]
    public System.DateTime shipDate;

    [System.Xml.Serialization.XmlIgnoreAttribute()]
    public bool shipDateSpecified;

    [System.Xml.Serialization.XmlAttributeAttribute()]
    public string partNum;
}
```

Using these classes, you can take any XML document that conforms to the Purchase Order Schema, such as the sample purchase order on the same page that the XSD Schema came from, and deserialize it into a `PurchaseOrderType` object by using the techniques introduced in the previous section. You can then manipulate the object and its properties just like you would with any other object, and serialize it to a new XML document that conforms to the original XSD Schema. You do this without ever touching the XML directly in your code. Let's do exactly that.

Manipulating XML Using Schema-Generated Classes

You are going to use the classes that `xsd.exe` just generated for you from `PurchaseOrder.xsd` to read and modify the sample purchase order listed on the same page of the W3C site that we got the XSD file from. This purchase order is reproduced in Listing 10.3.

Listing 10.3   **The Purchase Order,** *po.xml*

```xml
<?xml version="1.0"?>
<purchaseOrder orderDate="1999-10-20">
    <shipTo country="US">
        <name>Alice Smith</name>
        <street>123 Maple Street</street>
        <city>Mill Valley</city>
        <state>CA</state>
        <zip>90952</zip>
    </shipTo>
    <billTo country="US">
        <name>Robert Smith</name>
        <street>8 Oak Avenue</street>
        <city>Old Town</city>
        <state>PA</state>
        <zip>95819</zip>
    </billTo>
    <comment>Hurry, my lawn is going wild!</comment>
    <items>
        <item partNum="872-AA">
            <productName>Lawnmower</productName>
            <quantity>1</quantity>
            <USPrice>148.95</USPrice>
            <comment>Confirm this is electric</comment>
        </item>
        <item partNum="926-AA">
            <productName>Baby Monitor</productName>
            <quantity>1</quantity>
            <USPrice>39.98</USPrice>
            <shipDate>1999-05-21</shipDate>
        </item>
    </items>
</purchaseOrder>
```

Use the classes generated for you by xsd.exe to programmatically add a new item to the purchase order:

1. Start by creating a new Console application called PurchaseOrder. Add a new XML file to the project called po.xml and enter the contents of Listing 10.3 into the file (or copy and paste the listing from the W3C website referenced earlier, if you can).

2. Add an existing item to the project and browse to the location where you saved the PurchaseOrder.cs file that was generated earlier by xsd.exe. If you want, create a new class file and enter the code from Listing 10.2 instead.

3. Open the Class1.cs file that was created for you with the project, and add the following using statements:

```
using System.IO;
using System.Xml;
using System.Xml.Serialization;
```

4. Inside the Main routine, enter the code to deserialize po.xml into a set of objects:

```
// deserialize the existing purchase order
XmlSerializer serializer = new
XmlSerializer(typeof(PurchaseOrderType));
FileStream fs = File.OpenRead(".\\po.xml");

PurchaseOrderType order;

try
{
    order = (PurchaseOrderType)serializer.Deserialize(fs);
}
finally
{
    fs.Close();
}
```

Referring back to Listing 10.2, you can see that the first class listed is PurchaseOrderType. It has an XmlRoot attribute attached to it that tells you that this class will serialize to (and deserialize from) an XML root element called purchaseOrder. Because this class corresponds to the XML root element, it is the class that you pass to the XmlSerializer constructor. The rest of the deserialization code should look pretty familiar to you: You open the po.xml file, declare an instance of the PurchaseOrderType object, and fill it with the object returned from the XmlSerializer's Deserialize method.

5. Create a new item to add to the purchase order. Referring back to Listing 10.2, you see that the generated class for holding items is called ItemsItem.

```
ItemsItem newItem = new ItemsItem();
newItem.partNum = "352-AA";
newItem.productName = "Hedge Trimmer";
newItem.quantity = "1";
newItem.USPrice = 27.95m;
```

The m suffix on the value you're passing to newItem.USPrice simply tells the C# compiler to treat a literal number as a decimal data type because that's the type defined for the USPrice field of the ItemsItem class.

6. You need to add the newly created item to the list of items in the purchase order. Referring back to Listing 10.2, you see that the items are held in an array of type ItemsItem in the PurchaseOrderType class. What you must do is create a new ItemsItem array that's the same size as the original array, plus one. Then you must copy the current array into the new array and fill the empty slot with the newly created item.

```
// create a new array of type ItemsItem to hold the current
items plus the new one
ItemsItem[] allItems = new ItemsItem[order.items.Length + 1];

// copy the current items into the new array
Array.Copy(order.items, allItems, order.items.Length);

// add our new item to the array
allItems[allItems.Length - 1] = newItem;

// set the order's item array to our new array
order.items = allItems;
```

The last line in the previous code simply replaces the list of items in the purchase order with the new list.

7. All you need to do is serialize the modified PurchaseOrderType object back to XML. Create a new file so the original file is not overwritten.

```
// serialize the modified purchase order
fs = File.Open(".\\po_new.xml", FileMode.OpenOrCreate);
XmlTextWriter writer = new XmlTextWriter(fs,
System.Text.Encoding.UTF8);
writer.Formatting = Formatting.Indented;

try
```

```
    {
        serializer.Serialize(writer, order);
    }
    finally
    {
        // close the XmlTextWriter, which closes the underlying
        // stream
        writer.Close();
    }

    Console.WriteLine("Purchase order modified!");
```

8. You must do one more thing before you can compile the project and run it. The code you wrote expects to find po.xml in the current directory, but the directory that the code will be running from is actually the PurchaseOrder\bin\Debug subdirectory of the Project directory. Use Windows Explorer to copy po.xml into this directory. If the directory doesn't exist, you can click Build Solution in the Build menu to create it.

9. After everything is ready, compile and run the project. You should find a file called po_new.xml in the same \bin\Debug directory into which you just copied po.xml. Open it; the contents should match what's shown in Listing 10.4.

Listing 10.4   **The Modified Purchase Order**

```
<?xml version="1.0" encoding="utf-8"?>
<purchaseOrder xmlns:xsd="http://www.w3.org/2001/XMLSchema"
xmlns:xsi="http://www.w3.org/2001/XMLSchema-instance" orderDate="1999-10-20">
  <shipTo>
    <name>Alice Smith</name>
    <street>123 Maple Street</street>
    <city>Mill Valley</city>
    <state>CA</state>
    <zip>90952</zip>
  </shipTo>
  <billTo>
    <name>Robert Smith</name>
    <street>8 Oak Avenue</street>
    <city>Old Town</city>
    <state>PA</state>
    <zip>95819</zip>
  </billTo>
  <comment>Hurry, my lawn is going wild!</comment>
  <items>
    <item partNum="872-AA">
      <productName>Lawnmower</productName>
```

continues

Listing 10.4 **Continued**

```
        <quantity>1</quantity>
        <USPrice>148.95</USPrice>
        <comment>Confirm this is electric</comment>
      </item>
      <item partNum="926-AA">
        <productName>Baby Monitor</productName>
        <quantity>1</quantity>
        <USPrice>39.98</USPrice>
        <shipDate>1999-05-21</shipDate>
      </item>
      <item partNum="352-AA">
        <productName>Hedge Trimmer</productName>
        <quantity>1</quantity>
        <USPrice>27.95</USPrice>
      </item>
    </items>
  </purchaseOrder>
```

As you can see, the new hedge trimmer has been added to the purchase order, but at no time did we manipulate any XML, or even the Document Object Model, directly.

Another feature of the `xsd.exe` utility bears mentioning—it works in reverse as well. You can pass it a compiled assembly and the name of a type located in that assembly, and `xsd.exe` generates an XSD Schema from that class that conforms to any public properties or fields of the class, and any XML serialization-related attributes that have been applied to the class. The utility is described in the .NET Framework documentation if you're interested in this functionality.

XML Serialization at Work in ASP.NET

Demonstrations and examples can only remain interesting for so long before most people start looking for something more substantial. In this section, we put XML serialization to work in a tool that some of our readers might find useful in their own ASP.NET projects.

Creating and Modifying an XML-Based Menu Using Serialization

Now that you're familiar with what's involved in XML serialization, you can make something useful out of the `MenuLink` class that was introduced earlier in this chapter. Specifically, you'll build an XML-based menuing system for ASP.NET that uses XML serialization to both edit and display the menu.

Requirements for a Menuing System

Before you begin, let's examine the requirements for the menuing system:

- The menu data should be stored in XML so that the menu contents are independent of the menu format and to allow for easy editing of the menu, either manually or with a tool.

- The menu data must be cached in memory to improve performance, but any changes to the underlying XML data needs to be reflected immediately in the menu.

- We want to be able to read and modify the menu data in an object-oriented fashion without touching the XML directly.

- The menu itself must allow for internal links that open in the same browser window, external links that open in a new browser window, and separators to allow for grouping of menu items.

Getting Started

If you're coding along as you read, the remainder of this chapter assumes that you're working with a single solution that contains two projects: a C# class library project called XMLMenu and a C# web application called XMLSerialization. The web application project needs to have a reference to the class library project. To save space, we cover the important classes and techniques involved, but will not offer a step-by-step walk-through for creating every single file. You're welcome to code as you read, but you might want to retrieve the full source code for this section from this book's website, located at www.xmlandasp.net, and follow along with that instead. If you do code while you read, most of the listings in this section focus on the code rather than on the framework around the code, and omit many repetitive elements, such as the using statements, that are required to compile the code as listed.

Creating the *MenuItems*

Let's start with the last bulleted item in the section, "Requirements for a Menuing System": We need internal and external links and separators for grouping menu items. The MenuLink class that you used at the beginning of this chapter already has an IsExternal property that you'll be able to make good use of later, but it has no provisions for a menu separator. Rather than add this to the existing MenuLink class, you'll create a MenuSeparator class that you can use to mark the location of a separator in the menu. However, it would be helpful to treat both classes the same way and, because both links and separators are types of menu items, our first step is to create a MenuItem base class from which both MenuLink and MenuSeparator can inherit. In just a bit, you'll see what this inheritance structure gives us.

The first step to creating the MenuItems is an easy one. Add a new class file to our XMLMenu class library project and name the file MenuItem.cs. The class definition should look like this:

```
public abstract class MenuItem
{
}
```

That's all there is to the MenuItem class at this point. It's an abstract class, which means that you cannot create an instance of the class itself. Its only purpose is to serve as a common base class for both MenuLink and MenuSeparator. If MenuLink and MenuSeparator had any properties in common, you would define them in this class to ensure that all classes that inherit from MenuItem implement those properties; in this case, you can see that none are necessary.

Now you can define the MenuSeparator, which is almost as simple as MenuItem because its only role is to serve as a placeholder. You'll implement it as an empty class that inherits from MenuItem.

Simply add a class file, called MenuSeparator, to the XMLMenu project. The class definition should look like this:

```
public class MenuSeparator : MenuItem
{
}
```

Now you can focus on the MenuLink class. This class is almost identical to the version used earlier in this chapter, but it inherits from MenuItem and includes some additional overloads to the constructor to make creating new menu links more convenient. Add a new class file, called MenuLink, to the XMLMenu project. The class definition is shown in Listing 10.5.

Listing 10.5 **The *MenuLink* Class**

```
public class MenuLink : MenuItem
{
    private string _Url, _Title, _ToolTip;
    private bool _IsExternal;

    public MenuLink()
```

```
{
    _Url = "";
    _Title = "";
    _ToolTip = "";
    _IsExternal = false;
}

public MenuLink(string Url, string Title)
{
    _Url = Url;
    _Title = Title;
    _ToolTip = "";
    _IsExternal = false;
}

public MenuLink(string Url, string Title, bool IsExternal)
{
    _Url = Url;
    _Title = Title;
    IsExternal = IsExternal;
    _ToolTip = "";
}

public MenuLink(string Url, string Title, string ToolTip, bool
➥IsExternal)
{
    _Url = Url;
    _Title = Title;
    _ToolTip = ToolTip;
    _IsExternal = IsExternal;
}

public string Url
{
    get { return _Url; }
    set { _Url = value; }
}

public string Title
{
    get { return _Title; }
    set { _Title = value; }
}

public string ToolTip
{
    get { return _ToolTip; }
    set { _ToolTip = value; }
}

[XmlAttribute]
```

continues

Listing 10.5   **Continued**

```
public bool IsExternal
{
    get { return _IsExternal; }
    set { _IsExternal = value; }
}
}
```

Creating a *MenuManager*

We now have classes for the individual items in a menu, but we have no way of managing the individual menu items as an entity, so that becomes your next task. You'll create a class called MenuManager that's responsible for managing the menu as a whole. This class needs to keep track of all the individual menu items, handle adding and removing menu items, and returning the full list of menu items as an array of MenuItem objects. It needs to have built-in methods for loading the menu by deserializing it from an XML file, and for saving the menu back out to an XML file. You'll store the individual menu items in an ArrayList object, providing wrapper methods for most of the ArrayList methods. However, the wrapper methods only accepts objects of type MenuItem, or any class that inherits from MenuItem.

Add a new class file called MenuManager to the XMLMenu project. Listing 10.6 shows the portion of the MenuManager code that handles the ArrayList, which stores the MenuItems.

Listing 10.6   **A Partial Listing of the *MenuManager* Class**

```
public class MenuManager
{
    private ArrayList m_MenuItems;

    public MenuManager()
    {
        m_MenuItems = new ArrayList();
    }

    public int Add(MenuItem item)
    {
        return m_MenuItems.Add(item);
    }

    public void AddRange(MenuItem[] items)
    {
        m_MenuItems.AddRange(items);
```

```
        }

        public void Remove(MenuItem item)
        {
            m_MenuItems.Remove(item);
        }

        public void RemoveAt(int index)
        {
            m_MenuItems.RemoveAt(index);
        }

        public void Clear()
        {
            m_MenuItems.Clear();
        }

        public void Insert(int index, MenuItem item)
        {
            m_MenuItems.Insert(index, item);
        }

        public int IndexOf(MenuItem item)
        {
            return m_MenuItems.IndexOf(item);
        }

        public int Count
        {
            get { return m_MenuItems.Count; }
        }
    }
```

As you can see, a private `ArrayList` field called `m_MenuItems` is followed by a series of simple wrapper methods for the built-in `ArrayList` methods, which differ from the `ArrayList` methods in that they accept only `MenuItem` objects. This gives our `MenuManager` class all the flexibility and performance of an `ArrayList`, while ensuring that only classes that inherit from `MenuItem` can be used with it. Now you can add code to the class specifically for the menu, and for serialization and deserialization. Start with a read-only `Items` property that returns an array of `MenuItem` objects (which can, in reality, be either `MenuLinks` or `MenuSeparators`). The following code must be inserted into the `MenuManager` class after the `Count` property:

```
    public MenuItem[] Items
    {
        get
        {
```

```
        return (MenuItem[])_MenuItems.ToArray(typeof(MenuItem));
    }
}
```

Next, you need a method for saving the in-memory array of MenuItem objects to disk as XML. This is similar to the XML serialization already covered, except that this time, we're going to serialize an array. The following Save method must also be added to the existing MenuManager class:

```
public void Save(string path)
{
    // Lock to prevent multiple instances of
    // MenuManager from saving to the same file
    // at the same time.
    lock (path)
    {
        if (File.Exists(path))
            File.Delete(path);

        XmlSerializer serializer = new XmlSerializer(typeof(MenuItem[]));

        FileStream fs = new FileStream(path, FileMode.Create,
        ➥FileAccess.Write, FileShare.Read);
        XmlTextWriter writer = new XmlTextWriter(fs, Encoding.UTF8);
        writer.Formatting = Formatting.Indented;

        try
        {
            serializer.Serialize(writer, this.Items);
        }
        finally
        {
            writer.Close();
        }
    }
}
```

The first thing that you'll notice about this method is that the entire thing is enclosed in a lock statement. The lock statement, briefly, makes sure that a section of code cannot be executed by multiple threads at the same time. In this case, because you're locking on the path string passed into the method as the location to save the menu to, you can ensure that multiple instances of the MenuManager class do not try to save to the same file simultaneously, which can result in a collision and one of those nasty, hard-to-reproduce errors that nobody wants in their applications.

The next important difference from the XML serialization code you've examined previously is that you're passing the Type object for an array of MenuItem objects into the XmlSerializer constructor. Recall that the

XmlSerializer needs to know about the classes it will be expected to serialize, which, in this case, is an array rather than a single class. However, our array of MenuItem objects actually contains only objects that are inherited from MenuItem (either MenuLink or MenuSeparator). If you tried to run this code as it stands, it wouldn't work because the XmlSerializer doesn't know anything about those two classes. To correct this, you must go back to the definition of the MenuItem class and add the following code:

```
using System.Xml.Serialization;

[XmlInclude(typeof(MenuLink)), XmlInclude(typeof(MenuSeparator))]
public abstract class MenuItem
{
}
```

As you can see, two XmlInclude attributes have been added to the class definition, one for each of the derived classes that the XmlSerializer needs to know about. This is exactly what the XmlInclude attribute is for—it notifies the XmlSerializer which derived classes it should recognize when presented with the base class.

Now you can return to the MenuManager class and create a method to deserialize the menu from an XML file into live objects with which you can work:

```
public MenuItem[] Load(string path)
{
    XmlSerializer serializer = new XmlSerializer(typeof(MenuItem[]));
    FileStream fs = File.OpenRead(path);

    MenuItem[] loadedItems;
    try
    {
        loadedItems = (MenuItem[])serializer.Deserialize(fs);
    }
    finally
    {
        fs.Close();
    }

    this.AddRange(loadedItems);

    return loadedItems;
}
```

In this method, you deserialize the XML file into an array of MenuItem objects and then load the array into the internal ArrayList of the MenuManager by using the AddRange method, as well as returning it from the method. Add one more method to this class, purely for the sake of moving the example along. Add a `GenerateMenu` method that simply populates the menu with a series of default hard-coded menu items. In a real application, this method would most likely be replaced with an administrative tool for adding new menu items and editing or removing existing items:

```
public void GenerateMenu()
{
    this.Add(new MenuLink("~/Default.aspx", "Home", "Click here to return to
    ↪the home page.", false));
    this.Add(new MenuLink("~/ViewXML.aspx", "View XML Source", "Click here
    ↪to view the XML source behind the menu.", false));
    this.Add(new MenuLink("~/EditMenu.aspx", "Edit Menu", "Click here to
    ↪edit the menu.", false));
    this.Add(new MenuSeparator());
    this.Add(new MenuLink("http://www.newriders.com", "New Riders", true));
    this.Add(new MenuLink("http://www.microsoft.com/net", "Microsoft .NET",
    ↪true));
    this.Add(new MenuLink("http://www.gotdotnet.com", "GotDotNet", true));
    this.Add(new MenuSeparator());
    // the Url can be a client-side JavaScript call, as well as an actual
    ↪URL:
    this.Add(new MenuLink("javascript:window.close();", "Close Window",
    ↪"Click here to close this window.", false));
}
```

Listing 10.7 shows what the menu created by the `GenerateMenu` method looks like when it's serialized to XML.

Listing 10.7 **The Default Menu, Serialized to XML**

```
<?xml version="1.0" encoding="utf-8"?>
<ArrayOfMenuItem xmlns:xsd="http://www.w3.org/2001/XMLSchema"
xmlns:xsi="http://www.w3.org/2001/XMLSchema-instance">
  <MenuItem xsi:type="MenuLink" IsExternal="false">
    <Url>~/Default.aspx</Url>
    <Title>Home</Title>
    <ToolTip>Click here to return to the home page.</ToolTip>
  </MenuItem>
  <MenuItem xsi:type="MenuLink" IsExternal="false">
    <Url>~/ViewXML.aspx</Url>
    <Title>View Menu Source</Title>
    <ToolTip>Click here to view the XML source behind the menu.</ToolTip>
  </MenuItem>
  <MenuItem xsi:type="MenuLink" IsExternal="false">
    <Url>~/EditMenu.aspx</Url>
    <Title>Edit Menu</Title>
    <ToolTip>Click here to edit the menu.</ToolTip>
  </MenuItem>
  <MenuItem xsi:type="MenuSeparator" />
  <MenuItem xsi:type="MenuLink" IsExternal="true">
    <Url>http://www.newriders.com</Url>
```

```
    <Title>New Riders</Title>
    <ToolTip />
  </MenuItem>
  <MenuItem xsi:type="MenuLink" IsExternal="true">
    <Url>http://www.microsoft.com/net/</Url>
    <Title>Microsoft .NET</Title>
    <ToolTip />
  </MenuItem>
  <MenuItem xsi:type="MenuLink" IsExternal="true">
    <Url>http://www.gotdotnet.com</Url>
    <Title>GotDotNet</Title>
    <ToolTip />
  </MenuItem>
  <MenuItem xsi:type="MenuSeparator" />
  <MenuItem xsi:type="MenuLink" IsExternal="false">
    <Url>javascript:window.close();</Url>
    <Title>Close Window</Title>
    <ToolTip>Click here to close this window.</ToolTip>
  </MenuItem>
</ArrayOfMenuItem>
```

As you can see, serializing an array of derived objects is slightly different from serializing a single object. The root element of the XML document becomes ArrayOfMenuItem, while the individual menu items are not MenuLink and MenuSeparator elements; instead, they're all MenuItem elements with an xsi:type attribute that indicates what the true underlying object type should be.

If you reexamine the requirements for the XML-based menu, you have three main tasks left to complete: display, cache, and edit the menu.

Displaying, Caching, and Editing the Menu

Now that you're finished adding code to the XMLMenu class library project, the remainder of your work will be with the XMLSerialization web application project, which should have a project reference to the XMLMenu project.

You can take care of displaying and caching the menu by creating a UserControl, which has the additional advantage of making it easy to include the same menu in multiple pages on a site. You'll create a new UserControl in the XMLSerialization project, and call it Menu.ascx. Then, you'll place a panel control in the .ascx file and put all the code for loading the menu, caching it, and displaying it in the code-behind file for the control.

Here's the panel control into which the menu items will be inserted:

```
<asp:Panel runat="server"
    id="MenuPanel"
    BackColor="LightGray"
    BorderColor="Black"
    BorderStyle="Dotted"
```

```
        BorderWidth="1px"
        Width="150px"
        Style="padding:4px">
    </asp:Panel>
```

This defines the visual look for the menu and can be modified to fit the
design of most sites with minimal effort. The next step: Add the code that does
the actual work in the control to the code-behind file, Menu.ascx.cs. In the
event handler for the Page.Init event, you'll add the code to load the menu
data from the XML file. In the following example, you're storing the menu
data in a file called Menu.config because ASP.NET automatically denies access
to browsers that attempt to download any file with a config extension—you
want people to view the menu, not download its XML source code:

```
    private void Page_Init(object sender, EventArgs e)
    {
        //
        // CODEGEN: This call is required by the ASP.NET Web Form Designer.
        //
        InitializeComponent();

        // attempt to retrieve menu contents from cache
        MenuItem[] items = (MenuItem[])Page.Cache["MenuItems"];

        if (items == null)
        {
            // menu items were not in cache, so load from disk
            string filePath = Server.MapPath("~/Menu.config");

            MenuManager manager = new MenuManager();
            items = manager.Load(filePath);

            // place into cache with a dependency on the file we just loaded
            Page.Cache.Insert("MenuItems", items, new CacheDependency
            ↝(filePath));
        }

        this.DisplayMenuItems(items);
    }
```

This code is responsible for retrieving an array of MenuItem objects and passing
that array to the DisplayMenuItems method, which you'll write later in this
section. It also takes care of caching the loaded array of MenuItems in the
ASP.NET Cache object.

The first thing this method does (after the call to InitializeComponent
inserted by Visual Studio .NET) is attempt to load an array of menu items out
of the cache object. If the returned value is null, the array you're looking for
is not in the cache, so it must be loaded from disk. Instantiate the MenuManager

class and call its Load method, passing it the path to the Menu.config file. When you have the deserialized array of menu items, insert it into the cache with a dependency on the file from which you just loaded. The cache dependency ensures that the moment the underlying XML file is modified, the cached array is invalidated, forcing it to be reloaded from the file.

This technique gives a good combination of performance and responsiveness because the XML file needs be parsed only once each time it's modified, with the menu being served from the in-memory cache of MenuItem objects at all other times.

The last step in this method is to pass the MenuItem array (whether loaded from disk or retrieved from the cache) to the DisplayMenuItems method. This method, shown in Listing 10.8, needs to be included directly in the Menu.ascx.cs file with which you are currently working.

Listing 10.8   **The *DisplayMenuItems* Method**

```
private void DisplayMenuItems(MenuItem[] items)
{
    MenuLink thisLink;
    PlaceHolder holder = null;

    foreach (MenuItem item in items)
    {
        thisLink = item as MenuLink;

        if (thisLink == null)
        {
            // Current item is not a MenuLink,
            // so it must be a MenuSeparator.
            // Separators should only be displayed
            // if they are followed by a menu item,
            // so insert a placeholder for now and
            // keep a reference to it.
            holder = new PlaceHolder();
            MenuPanel.Controls.Add(holder);
        }
        else
        {
            // Current item is a MenuLink object - create
            // a HyperLink and add it to the output.
            HyperLink link = new HyperLink();
            link.NavigateUrl = thisLink.Url;
            link.Text = thisLink.Title;
            link.ToolTip = thisLink.ToolTip;

            // set external links to open in a new browser window
            if (thisLink.IsExternal)
                    link.Target = "_blank";
```

continues

Listing 10.8   **Continued**

```
MenuPanel.Controls.Add(link);
MenuPanel.Controls.Add(new LiteralControl("<br />\n"));

// if we have any current placeholders for a menu separator,
// insert an HR tag into the placeholder
if (holder != null)
{
        holder.Controls.Add(new LiteralControl("<hr noshade
        ➥color=\"#000000\" size=\"1\" />\n"));
        holder = null;
}
}
}
}
```

The `DisplayMenuItems` method is simple in concept, but its execution bears explanation. Conceptually, this method loops through the array of `MenuItem` objects passed to it, figures out if each object is actually a `MenuLink` or a `MenuSeparator`, and adds an ASP.NET `HyperLink` control to the menu for each `MenuLink` and a horizontal rule for each `MenuSeparator`. First off, these two code lines declare some variables that are reused multiple times as you loop through the menu items:

```
MenuLink thisLink;
PlaceHolder holder = null;
```

Next, you use the C# as operator to cast the current `MenuItem` to a `MenuLink`. The as operator works better for this operation than a normal cast because a normal cast would throw an exception if the underlying object were actually a `MenuSeparator` and you tried to cast it to a `MenuLink`. The as operator, however, simply returns `null` if the object that you're trying to cast to a `MenuLink` is actually a `MenuSeparator`. In this way, you can simply check to see if `thisLink` is `null` to determine what type of object you're working with. If it's `null`, you have a `MenuSeparator`; if it's not `null`, `thisLink` is ready to go with all the properties that you need to insert into the `HyperLink` control:

```
thisLink = item as MenuLink;
```

The rest of the code in this method is fairly straight forward, except for one detail. Rather than simply inserting a horizontal rule for each `MenuSeparator` that you encounter, you only want to display the separators that are followed by a `MenuLink`. This feature would be particularly useful if this example were extended in a real application so that `MenuLink` objects had additional properties that determined which users had permission to view certain links. In that case, a `MenuLink` between two separators might not be visible to some users. This code would prevent two consecutive separators from being displayed to those users. This is accomplished by inserting a `PlaceHolder` control into the output every time you encounter a `MenuSeparator`, holding onto a reference to that `PlaceHolder`, and inserting the horizontal rule into the `PlaceHolder` only when you next encounter a `MenuLink`.

You are now finished with everything that you need to display the menu. Using the completed `Menu` control requires only two lines of code on any page that needs a menu—one line to register the control with a particular tag prefix:

```
<%@ Register TagPrefix="nr" TagName="Menu" Src="~/Menu.ascx" %>
```

and one line of code to insert the menu into the page in the location you want it to appear:

```
<nr:Menu runat="server" />
```

Figure 10.1 shows what the output from the menu looks like, using the default

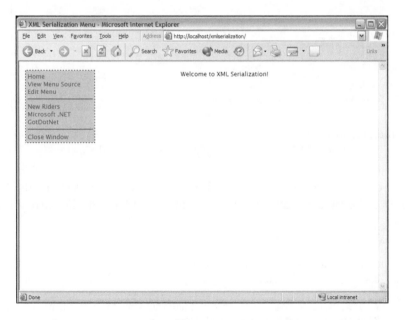

`Menu.config` that was generated earlier.

Figure 10.1   The completed menu control can be used on multiple pages.

The only remaining feature from the requirements is the ability to modify the menu. You'll create a simple web-based interface for editing the menu, but for the sake of brevity, we omit the HTML code and focus on the code that actually manipulates the menu. You can download the full source code from this book's website, located at www.xmlandasp.net.

The menu-editing page consists of a simple list box with all the menu items in it: a button to remove the currently selected menu item, a button to add a separator to the menu, and a form to add a new link to the menu. You can see

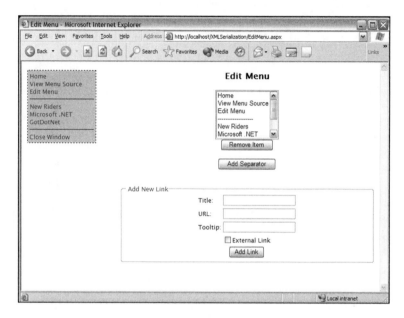

this interface in Figure 10.2.

Figure 10.2   A simple interface for modifying the menu.

The code to manipulate the menu consists of four methods. One method populates the list box (called CurrentMenu in this code) with the current menu items:

```
private void PopulateMenu()
{
    // clear any items currently in the list box
    CurrentMenu.Items.Clear();

    // instantiate a MenuManager and load the menu from the config file
    MenuManager manager = new MenuManager();
    string filePath = Server.MapPath("~/Menu.config");
    MenuItem[] items = manager.Load(filePath);

    // populate the ListBox
    MenuLink thisLink;
    for (int i=0; i < items.Length; i++)
    {
```

```
            thisLink = items[i] as MenuLink;

            if (thisLink == null)
            {
                // item is not a MenuLink, so it must be a MenuSeparator
                CurrentMenu.Items.Add(new ListItem("------------------",
    i.ToString()));
            }
            else
            {
                // add the title of the current link to the list box
                CurrentMenu.Items.Add(new ListItem(thisLink.Title,
    i.ToString()));
            }
        }
    }
```

The second method removes the currently selected item in the list box from the menu:

```
    private void Remove_Click(object sender, System.EventArgs e)
    {
        if (CurrentMenu.SelectedIndex != -1)
        {
            // instantiate a MenuManager and load the menu from the config file
            MenuManager manager = new MenuManager();
            string filePath = Server.MapPath("~/Menu.config");
            manager.Load(filePath);

            // The index number for the menu and for the List Box should be
            // identical, so we'll simply remove the corresponding item
            // from the menu.
            manager.RemoveAt(CurrentMenu.SelectedIndex);

            // save our changes
            manager.Save(filePath);

            // repopulate the list box with our changes
            PopulateMenu();
        }
    }
```

The third method adds a MenuSeparator to the end of the menu:

```
    private void AddSeparator_Click(object sender, System.EventArgs e)
    {
        // instantiate a MenuManager and load the menu from the config file
        MenuManager manager = new MenuManager();
        string filePath = Server.MapPath("~/Menu.config");
        manager.Load(filePath);

        // add a MenuSeparator
```

```
        manager.Add(new MenuSeparator());

        // save our changes
        manager.Save(filePath);

        // repopulate the list box with our changes
        PopulateMenu();
    }
```

The fourth and final method creates a new `MenuLink` object from the values entered into the form and adds it to the end of the menu:

```
    private void AddLink_Click(object sender, System.EventArgs e)
    {
        // instantiate a MenuManager and load the menu from the config file
        MenuManager manager = new MenuManager();
        string filePath = Server.MapPath("~/Menu.config");
        manager.Load(filePath);

        // create and populate a new MenuLink
        MenuLink link = new MenuLink();
        link.Title = Title.Text;
        link.Url = URL.Text;
        link.ToolTip = ToolTip.Text;
        link.IsExternal = IsExternal.Checked;

        // add the new link to the menu
        manager.Add(link);

        // save our changes
        manager.Save(filePath);

        // repopulate the list box with our changes
        PopulateMenu();
    }
```

My Changes Didn't Show Up!

If you downloaded the sample code to manipulate the menu and tried running it, you might have noticed that your changes are not immediately reflected in the live menu on the left (refer to Figure 10.2). The reason for this: The methods that modify the menu aren't executed until after the menu has been loaded in the sequence of events that make up the page execution life cycle. All subsequent page loads for yourself or any other user reflects the changes.

Completing the Menu Editor

In a real application, you would probably want to further enhance the editing tool by allowing new items to be inserted at specific locations in the menu (by using `MenuManager.Insert`) rather than always at the end, and also allowing the user to change the order of items in the menu (by using `MenuManager.RemoveAt` and `MenuManager.Insert`). Alternatively, if the menu isn't expected to change often, you might be happy with simply manually editing the `Menu.config` file when it needs to be modified.

Chapter Summary

In this chapter, you learned about XML serialization and some of the many and varied uses to which this extremely flexible tool can be put. You learned how to persist an object in XML format, and how to work with XML that conforms to a particular schema in an object-oriented fashion without touching the XML directly. You also learned how to control the formatting of the generated XML. This knowledge enables you to easily save and retrieve nearly any type of business-oriented data, and make interoperability with other XML-based systems almost trivial. As you saw with the menuing system you created, XML serialization can also be put to many uses that might not immediately spring to mind when you hear the words "XML serialization."

11

Creating and Using ASP.NET Web Services

WEB SERVICES ARE A MEANS TO EXPOSE your software as a service over the Internet so that it is accessible to a number of potentially disparate systems using ubiquitous Internet standards, such as XML and HTTP.

You can develop web services to expose some of the business data to the clients of a company or you can develop and expose web services that can be publicly available to any clients on the Internet.

As a client of a web service, you can build applications that integrate different web services found on the Internet. This enables you to provide a rich set of functionality into a single application. The application's functionality is not limited to what your application was basically intended to do, but by integrating other services, you can add value to the application. For example, if you have a scheduling application, you might integrate a web service that provides ticket reservations and enhances the users' experience while using your application. Again, you can expose your scheduling application as a web service so that other developers can integrate it into their applications. You can also develop a portal that assembles diverse web services, such as a news web service, a stock quote web service, a weather forecast web service, a travel reservation web service, an auction web service, and so on.

Web services depend heavily on the broad acceptance of XML and other Internet standards to create an infrastructure that supports application interoperability at a level that solves many of the problems that previously hindered such attempts. Web services use XML-based *Simple Object Access Protocol (SOAP)* as the wire format to achieve application interoperability. Web services are built on SOAP and other specifications, such as web services' description, discovery, and directories, which are covered in this chapter.

Benefits of SOAP over Other RPC Mechanisms

Some remote procedure call mechanisms have been in place, such as *Distributed Component Object Model (DCOM), Common Object Request Broker Architecture (CORBA), Java Remote Method Invocation (RMI)*, and so on. But the inherent problem with each mechanism is that it follows proprietary wire formats (CORBA is an exception).

In today's distributed systems application, integration is becoming an important requirement. Companies do not want to invest money and resources into rebuilding applications using a specific technology because a specific client that uses a different technology is unable to connect to an already existing application.

If a Java-based client needs to talk to a remote DCOM server, or a Visual Basic client needs to use the services of a CORBA server, they depend on *bridges*. These bridges are complex and require updates if the protocols change at all.

Wire protocols, such as Internet Inter-ORB Protocol (IIOP) used by CORBA, Object Remote Procedure Call (ORPC) used by DCOM, and Java Remote Method Protocol (JRMP) used by JAVA RMI, are binary protocols. SOAP, however, is a text-based protocol that uses XML. Using XML for data encoding makes it easier to debug applications because it's easier to read XML than a binary stream. Also, by using HTTP it's possible to transfer XML messages across firewall boundaries.

SOAP is built on vendor-agnostic technologies such as XML, HTTP, and Simple Mail Transfer Protocol (SMTP). Therefore, SOAP appeals to all vendors. Many leading software vendors have provided support for the evolution of this protocol.

SOAP alleviates the problem of application integration because it allows users to build loosely coupled distributed applications where the client and server communicate through a common XML-based wire protocol, irrespective of the underlying technologies used to build the client and the server.

Describing Web Services

The service description is an XML document called *Web Services Description Language (WSDL)*. WSDL defines the format of messages that the XML Web Service understands. The service description serves as an agreement that defines the behavior of a web service and instructs potential clients on how to interact with it. The WSDL document structure is covered in more detail in the section, "Consuming Web Services."

Locating Web Services Using the Discovery Process and the Web Services Directories

Web service discovery is the process of programmatically locating, or discovering, one or more related documents that describe a particular web service using the WSDL. Through this process, the web-service clients learn about the existence of a web service and the address of the web service's description document. The discovery process is enabled by a published .disco file, which is an XML document that contains links to other resources that describe the web service. The following code shows a sample structure of a .disco file that provides links to a news service and another stock-quote service on the same server:

```
<?xml version="1.0" encoding="utf-8" ?>
<disco:discovery xmlns:disco="http://schemas.xmlsoap.org/disco/"
➥xmlns:scl="http://schemas.xmlsoap.org/disco/scl/">
<scl:contractRef ref="http//MyWebServer/MyWebServices/NewsService.asmx?wsdl"
docRef="http://MyWebServer/MyWebServices/NewsService.asmx" />
<scl:contractRef ref="http://MyWebServer/MyWebServices/
➥StockQuoteService.asmx?wsdl"
➥docRef="http://MyWebServer/MyWebServices/StockQuoteService.asmx" />
</disco:discovery>
```

Web service directories provide central locations where web service providers can publish information about their available web services. So, a potential client application developer can easily locate an organization that provides web services for a particular purpose or determine what web services a particular organization provides.

Universal Description, Discovery, and Integration (UDDI) is an industry initiative to enable businesses to describe and publish their web services in a global registry. UDDI contains standards-based specifications for service description and discovery.

Understanding SOAP

You have already seen the benefits of using SOAP as a wire format for communication in a distributed system. The following paragraph is a formal definition of SOAP, as provided by the SOAP 1.1 Specification:

"SOAP provides a simple and lightweight mechanism for exchanging structured and typed information between peers in a decentralized, distributed environment using XML. SOAP does not itself define any application semantics such as a programming model or implementation specific semantics; rather it defines a simple mechanism for expressing application semantics by providing a modular packaging model and encoding mechanisms for encoding data within modules. This allows SOAP to be used in a large variety of systems ranging from messaging systems to RPC."

ASP.NET web services make the SOAP message transfers completely transparent to you. You are not required to learn the details of the SOAP message structure unless you want to customize the SOAP response that's sent to the client or intercept the SOAP request and response and alter them. Here, you look at the four main parts of the SOAP protocol specification:

- The first part defines a mandatory extensible envelope for encapsulating data. The SOAP envelope defines a SOAP message; it's the basic unit of exchange between SOAP message processors. This is the only mandatory part of the specification. (This part refers to Section 4 of the SOAP 1.1 Specification.)

- The second part defines optional data-encoding rules for representing application-defined data types and graphs of typed objects, and a uniform model for serializing data models that are independent of any language binding. (This part refers to Section 5 of the SOAP 1.1 Specification.)

- The third part defines an RPC-style (request/response) message-exchange pattern. Each SOAP message is a one-way transmission. RPC is not limited to being a request/response mechanism. Web services often combine SOAP messages to implement such patterns, but SOAP does not mandate a message-exchange pattern. This part of the specification is optional. (This part refers to Section 7 of the SOAP 1.1 Specification.)

- The fourth part defines a binding between SOAP and HTTP. However, this part is optional. You can use SOAP in combination with any transport protocol or mechanism that can transport the SOAP envelope, including SMTP or FTP. (This part refers to Section 6 of the SOAP 1.1 Specification.)

SOAP *Envelope*

The SOAP protocol follows the XML version 1.0 specification, which mandates the need for the single root XML element called `Envelope`. The following code shows a sample SOAP message with the root `Envelope` element containing the other elements, the optional `Header` and the mandatory `Body` elements:

```
<soap:Envelope xmlns:xsi="http://www.w3.org/2001/XMLSchema-instance"
xmlns:xsd="http://www.w3.org/2001/XMLSchema"
xmlns:soap="http://schemas.xmlsoap.org/soap/envelope/">
  <soap:Header>
     <!-- Optional SOAP Header. -->
  </soap: Header >
  <soap:Body>
     <!-- Mandatory SOAP Body. Serialized object information -->
  </soap:Body>
</soap:Envelope>
```

The `Envelope` element in the preceding code includes the `soap` namespace pointing to the URL `http://schemas.xmlsoap.org/soap/envelope/`. All the SOAP elements and attributes use this namespace qualifier. Not providing this exact URL causes your SOAP message to be treated as a version error by the SOAP application.

You can see the SOAP `Envelope` schema defined at `http://schemas.xmlsoap.org/soap/envelope/`.

The SOAP `encodingStyle` global attribute can indicate the serialization rules used in a SOAP message. This attribute has the default value of `http://schemas.xmlsoap.org/soap/encoding/`.

SOAP *Header*

The optional `Header` element, if present, must appear as the first child of the root `Envelope` element. The `Header` element provides special information, such as authentication, transaction management, payment, and so on, to be processed by the recipient application. The following code shows a sample `Header` element that contains transaction information for an application:

```
<soap:Header>
   <t:Transaction
       xmlns:t="some-URI" soap:mustUnderstand="1">
          10
   </t:Transaction>
</ soap:Header>
```

The SOAP `mustUnderstand` global attribute in the `Header` element is used to indicate that the `Header` entry is mandatory for the recipient to process the SOAP message.

SOAP *Body*

The mandatory SOAP `Body` element can represent a request message that contains information about the method names and the method parameters. The following code shows a sample SOAP request message with the `Body` element that contains the method name `GetQuote` and the parameter symbol with the value `MSFT`:

```
POST /mywebservices/StockQuoteService.asmx HTTP/1.1
Host: www.somedomain.com
Content-Type: text/xml; charset=utf-8
Content-Length: nnnn
SOAPAction: http://tempuri.org/GetQuote

<soap:Envelope xmlns:xsi="http://www.w3.org/2001/XMLSchema-instance"
xmlns:xsd="http://www.w3.org/2001/XMLSchema"
xmlns:soap="http://schemas.xmlsoap.org/soap/envelope/">
  <soap:Body>
    <GetQuote xmlns="http://tempuri.org/">
      <symbol>MSFT</symbol>
    </GetQuote>
  </soap:Body>
</soap:Envelope>
```

The SOAP `Body` can also represent a SOAP response message that's returned from the server. This contains the data returned from a method call on the remote server object. The following code shows a sample SOAP response:

```
HTTP/1.1 200 OK
Content-Type: text/xml; charset=utf-8
Content-Length: nnnn

<soap:Envelope xmlns:xsi="http://www.w3.org/2001/XMLSchema-instance"
xmlns:xsd="http://www.w3.org/2001/XMLSchema"
xmlns:soap="http://schemas.xmlsoap.org/soap/envelope/">
  <soap:Body>
    <GetQuoteResponse xmlns="http://tempuri.org/">
      <GetQuoteResult>69.5</GetQuoteResult>
    </GetQuoteResponse>
  </soap:Body>
</soap:Envelope>
```

The `Body` element can contain a SOAP `Fault` element to return error information to the calling client. This element must be the first child of the `Body` element. The following is a sample SOAP message with the `Fault` element showing an application-specific error:

```
<soap:Envelope
  xmlns:soap="http://schemas.xmlsoap.org/soap/envelope/">
  <soap:Body>
    <soap:Fault>
      <faultcode> soap:Server</faultcode>
```

```
              <faultstring>Server Error</faultstring>
              <detail>
<e:myfaultdetails
xmlns:e='http://newriders.com/webservices/addressbook/faults' >
              <message>Invalid User</message>
              <errorcode>1001</errorcode>
            </e:myfaultdetails>
            </detail>
          </soap:Fault>
      </soap:Body>
</soap:Envelope>
```

SOAP Encoding

The SOAP encoding rules define a serialization mechanism that can exchange instances of application–defined data types. Simple types and compound types are the main encoding data types found in a SOAP specification. SOAP's simple types include all the types found in the section "Built-In Datatypes" of the W3C XML Schema, Part 2: Datatypes Specification. Alternatively, a SOAP message can use the elements declared for every simple data type by the SOAP-ENC schema and namespace. The following shows you an example:

```
<SOAP-ENC:int  id="count">10</SOAP-ENC:int>
```

SOAP provides support for different compound types, such as structures, generic compound data types, and arrays. The following code gives you an example of how a string array can be encoded in a SOAP message:

```
<soap:Envelope
 xmlns:xsi="http://www.w3.org/2001/XMLSchema-instance"
 xmlns:xsd="http://www.w3.org/2001/XMLSchema"
 xmlns:soap="http://schemas.xmlsoap.org/soap/envelope/"
 soap:encodingStyle="http://schemas.xmlsoap.org/soap/encoding/"
 xmlns:SOAP-ENC="http://schemas.xmlsoap.org/soap/encoding/" >
 <soap:Body>
    <GetSOAPAuthorsListResponse xmlns="http://tempuri.org/"        >
          <AuthorListArray  href="#array"  />
    </GetSOAPAuthorsListResponse>
     <SOAP-ENC:Array  id="array"  SOAP-ENC:arrayType="xsd:string[8]">
        <SOAP-ENC:string>Don Box</SOAP-ENC:string>
        <SOAP-ENC:string>David Ehnebuske</SOAP-ENC:string>
     <SOAP-ENC:string>Gopal Kakivaya</SOAP-ENC:string>
        <SOAP-ENC:string>Andrew Layman</SOAP-ENC:string>
        <SOAP-ENC:string>Noah Mendelsohn</SOAP-ENC:string>
        <SOAP-ENC:string>Henrik Frystyk Nielsen</SOAP-ENC:string>
        <SOAP-ENC:string>Satish Thatte</SOAP-ENC:string>
        <SOAP-ENC:string>Dave Winer</SOAP-ENC:string>
      </SOAP-ENC:Array>
   </soap:Body>
</soap:Envelope>
```

Other array types, such as sparse arrays, partially transmitted arrays, and multi-dimensional arrays, are also supported by the SOAP 1.1 Specification.

> **Note**
>
> You can view the SOAP version 1.1 specification at www.w3.org/TR/SOAP/ and version 1.2, which is a working draft at the time of writing, at www.w3.org/TR/soap12/.

Exposing a Web Service

Exposing the methods of a C# or Visual Basic .NET class as an ASP.NET web service is fairly simple. The code is written in a file that ends with the .asmx extension and published into a web virtual directory, just what you normally do with a .aspx page. Listing 11.1 provides a simple Calculator web service that exposes two methods, Add and Subtract, that add and subtract two integers respectively.

Listing 11.1 **A Simple Inline Web Service** *(Calculator.asmx)*

```
<%@ WebService  Language="C#"   Class="Calculator" %>

using System.Web.Services;


public class Calculator : WebService
{
    [WebMethod]
    public int Add(int a , int b)
    {
        return a + b;
    }

    [WebMethod]
    public int Subtract(int a , int b)
    {
        return a - b;
    }
}
```

Adding the WebMethod attribute to a method within an XML Web Service makes the method callable from remote web clients. Methods within a class that have this attribute set are called *web service methods*. It's essential that the method and class are be defined as public.

A Visual Basic .NET web service uses the following syntax to add the WebMethod attribute:

```
<WebMethod> Public Function Add( a as Integer, b as Integer ) as Integer
```

> **Note**
> The WebMethod attribute is represented by the WebMethodAttribute class.

To expose your application logic, all that you need to do in the .asmx file is the following:

- Add an @ WebService directive at the top of the page, just as you provide a directive at the top of a .aspx page (for example, @ Page). The WebService directive supports two attributes, the Class that is required and an optional Language attribute. The Class attribute must be set to the name of the class, the methods and properties of which you want to expose as a web service. The .asmx file can have more than one class, but the class name assigned to the Class attribute in the directive at the top of the page alone can be used for the web service. By default, the Language attribute is set to VB (Visual Basic .NET). You can override that by setting it to any of the .NET languages (a language that provides a .NET compiler).

- Include a reference to the System.Web.Services class.

- Place the WebMethod attribute on any method or property you want to programmatically expose over the web.

- Inherit the class from the WebService base class. You need to inherit from this class in order to get access to the ASP.NET intrinsics, which are the class' properties. These ASP.NET intrinsics, such as the Application, Context, Session, Server, and User properties, can be accessed through HttpContext. Therefore, it is not mandatory to inherit from the WebService class. This fact allows you to have your class inherited from another base class instead of the WebService class.

Again, similar to the .aspx pages, the .asmx files are compiled upon first request. Navigating to the URL for the web service without any parameters in a web browser, you can view the Service help page. By default, the Service help page contains information from the clients about how to communicate with the XML Web Service and the XML Web Service methods it exposes. The Service help page is simply an ASP.NET web form, named DefaultWsdlHelpGenerator.aspx. It's located in the [system drive letter]: \WINNT\Microsoft.NET\Framework\vx.x.xxx\CONFIG directory. Figure 11.1 shows the web service (.asmx) file, as viewed in a browser.

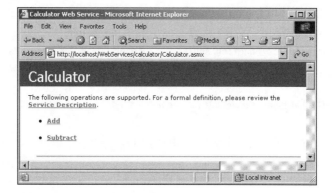

Figure 11.1   The .asmx file viewed in a browser.

You can modify or even replace the .asmx file to include other items, such as your company logo. If you want to change the filename, you must first change the default name specified in the <wsdlHelpGenerator> XML element of a configuration file (machine.config) in the same directory.

Testing the Web Service

You can test the web service in the browser using either HTTP-GET or HTTP-POST. Figure 11.2 shows the web service being tested by using the HTTP-GET method, which is the default.

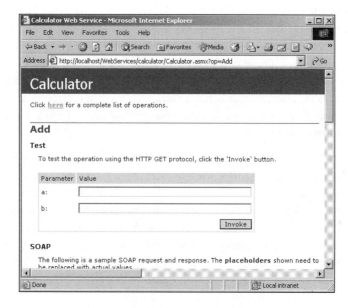

Figure 11.2   Testing the web service.

Entering the appropriate values (for example, 4 and 5), and clicking the Invoke button displays the window shown in Figure 11.3 with the XML returned by the web service.

Figure 11.3   Result of invoking the add web method.

To test the web service using the HTTP-POST method, you must send the parameter values within the body of the HTTP request rather than the querystring, which is the case for the GET method. For this test, you can create an HTML page. The following code shows the form element in the HTML page to test to the Calculator web service:

```
<form method=POST
action='http://localhost/WebServices/calculator/calculator.asmx/Add' >
      <input type="text" size="5" name='a'></td> -
      <input type="text" size="5" name='b'></td> =
      <input type=submit value="Add" NAME="Submit1"> </td>
   </form>
```

Pay attention to the format of the action URL and also note that the names of the input text controls match the parameter names in the web service method. Alternatively, you can modify the DefaultWsdlHelpGenerator.aspx page to set the flag showPost to true.

In the ASP.NET web services, the details of serializing .NET data types into SOAP data types and deserializing the SOAP data types into .NET data types are hidden from the developer, which allows him to concentrate on the business logic rather than the plumbing involved. The framework also takes care of interpreting the SOAP requests from a remote client, invoking the appropriate web service method and sending back a SOAP response to the clients. The ISAPI listener aspnet_isapi.dll instantiates the Http Handler class System.Web.Services.Protocols.WebServiceHandlerFactory to process the requests for any .asmx files published on your web server. You can view an *.asmx file's path mapped to the WebServiceHandlerFactory class in the httpHandlers element in the machine.config file.

Apart from creating a help document and serializing and deserializing a SOAP request response, the Http Handler class also generates the WSDL files. The WSDL file is discussed in the section, "Consuming Web Services."

Using Code Behind with ASP.NET Web Services

Listing 11.1 showed the .asmx file with inline code as all the application logic is contained within the file. Just as ASP.NET web forms provide an option for code behind, the ASP.NET web services also provide an option to add the application logic in an external assembly. This assembly should be placed in the application's bin directory.

We create the web service .asmx file that contains nothing more than the WebService directive, the Class assigned the name of the web service class, and the Codebehind attribute, which is assigned the name of the code behind file. The following is a line of code contained in the Calculator_Codebehind.asmx file:

```
<%@ WebService  Codebehind="Calulator.cs"  Class="Calculator" %>
```

Listing 11.2 shows the code for the code behind class Calculator.

Listing 11.2 **The Code Behind Calculator Class (*Calulator.cs*)**

```
using System;
using System.Web;
using System.Web.Services;


public class Calculator : WebService
{
    [WebMethod]
    public int Add(int a , int b)
    {
        return a + b;
    }

    [WebMethod]
    public int Subtract(int a , int b)
    {
        return a - b;
    }
}
```

You can compile this file into a .NET assembly by using the command-line compiler:

```
csc /t:library /r:System.Web.dll /r:System.Web.Services.dll Calculator.cs
```

You have to copy this assembly file into the `bin` directory before you can get your web service working. If you create your web service using Visual Studio .NET, by default, you will be using the code behind option. The advantage of using the code behind option is that the assembly can be used in other applications or ASP.NET pages.

The *WebMethod* Attribute

The `WebMethod` attribute supports some properties that you can set to make use of some features for a specific web service method, such as enabling session state management, buffering, and transactions.

You are probably familiar with some of these properties because they are similar to some of the `Response` object properties and the page directives in ASP.NET.

For example, the following `TransactionOption` property used with a web service method begins a new transaction when the method is called:

```
[WebMethod(TransactionOption= TransactionOption.RequiresNew)]
```

The following code line shows the syntax used for setting a description and enabling session state in a Visual Basic .NET web service method:

```
<WebMethod(Description := "Adds two integers", EnableSession := True)>
```

Table 11.1 lists all the public properties of the `WebMethodAttribute` class.

Table 11.1 **Public Properties of the *WebMethodAttribute* Class**

Property	Description
`BufferResponse`	Gets or sets whether the response for this request is buffered.
	Setting `BufferResponse` to true buffers the response of the XML Web Service before being sent to the web service client.
	When `BufferResponse` is false, the response to the XML Web Service method is sent back to the client as it is serialized. If the XML Web Service method returns large amounts of data to the client, it is recommended that you set `BufferResponse` to false because this consumes a large amount of the server memory. For smaller amounts of data, XML Web-Service performance is better with `BufferResponse` set to true. This property is set to true by default.

continues

Table 11.1   **Continued**

Property	Description
CacheDuration	Gets or sets the number of seconds the response should be held in the cache.
	The default is 0, which means the response is not cached. When caching is enabled, requests and responses are held in memory on the server for at least the duration of the cache. You must not set this property if you expect requests or responses to be large, or if you expect requests to vary widely.
Description	A descriptive message that describes the XML Web Service method.
	The descriptive message is displayed to prospective consumers of the XML Web Service when description documents for the XML Web Service are generated, such as the service description and the Service help page. The default value is String.Empty.
EnableSession	Indicates whether session state is enabled for an XML Web Service method.
	If this is set to true, you can use the ASP.NET HttpSessionState object to store session state. If session state is not needed for an XML Web Service method, disabling it can improve performance.
MessageName	The name used for the XML Web Service method in the data passed to and returned from an XML Web Service method. The default is the name of the XML Web Service method.
	If an XML Web Service contains two or more XML Web Service methods with the same name, you can uniquely identify the individual web service methods by setting the MessageName property to a name unique within the XML Web Service without changing the name of the actual method name in the code.
TransactionOption	Indicates the transaction support of an XML Web Service method. The default is TransactionOption.Disabled.
	When the XML Web Service method is executed with a transaction, the code is treated as an atomic unit of work that either fails or succeeds as a whole. Each XML Web Service method participates in its own transaction because an XML Web Service method can only act as the root

Property	Description
	object in a transaction. The following are the possible values for this property:
	TransactionOption.Disabled—The web service method is executed without a transaction.
	TransactionOption.NotSupported—No transaction support. The web service method is executed without a transaction.
	TransactionOption.Supported—Transactions are supported but the web service method is executed without a transaction.
	TransactionOption.Required—The web service method requires a transaction. Because web service methods can only participate as the root object in a transaction, a new transaction will be created for the web service method.
	TransactionOption.RequiresNew—The web service method requires a new transaction. When a request is processed, the XML Web Service is created within a new transaction.
TypeId	When implemented in a derived class, TypeId gets a unique identifier for this attribute. It is intended that the unique identifier be used to distinguish between two attributes of the same type.

The *WebService* Attribute

Just as the WebMethod attribute supports properties for the methods in a web service, the WebService attribute supports properties to configure the properties for the WebService class. This attribute is represented by the WebServiceAttribute class.

The following code changes the default http://tempuri.org namespace for an ASP.NET web service:

```
[WebService(Namespace="http://newriders.com/webservices/calculator")]
public class Calculator : WebService
```

The following code line changes the name of the web service:

```
<WebService(Name:="MyCalculatorService")> Public Class Calculator
```

These changes are reflected in the Web Service help page and the WSDL that's generated.

Table 11.2 lists all the public properties of the WebServiceAttribute class.

Table 11.2 **Public properties of the *WebServiceAttribute* class**

Property	Description
Description	A descriptive message for the XML Web Service. The message is displayed to prospective consumers of the XML Web Service when description documents for the XML Web Service are generated, such as the service description and the Service help page.
Name	Gets or sets the name for the XML Web Service. The default value is the name of the class implementing the XML Web Service.
Namespace	Gets or sets the default XML namespace to use for the XML Web Service.
TypeId	When implemented in a derived class, gets a unique identifier for this attribute. It's intended that the unique identifier be used to distinguish between two attributes of the same type.

Consuming Web Services

Now that you have seen how to create and expose a web service, this section looks at creating clients to consume these web services.

Web Service Description Language

At the time of writing, the WSDL specification (available at www.w3.org/TR/wsdl) is an acknowledged submission to W3C and is supported by industry leaders like Microsoft, IBM and Ariba. According to this specification, the official definition of Web Service Description Language (WSDL) states that, "WSDL is an XML format for describing network services as a set of endpoints operating on messages containing either document-oriented or procedure-oriented information." If you are familiar with the COM and CORBA component models, you can relate this to the Interface Description Language (IDL) file that describes the interfaces exposed by the components in a platform-neutral manner. Similar to IDL, a WSDL file defines a contract between a client and a server (a web service, in this case).

SOAP messages do carry type information; therefore, SOAP allows for dynamic determination of type. But without WSDL, it's impossible to call a function correctly unless the client application developer knows the name and the parameters in advance by reading the documentation or by examining wire messages. WSDL enables us to eliminate the human intervention required for acquiring the knowledge of the method names and the parameters, as it is possible to automate the generation of proxies for web services. Moreover, this happens in a truly language- and platform-independent way because WSDL uses XML syntax to describe the web service.

The SOAP Toolkit 2.0 provides a WSDL generation wizard that takes the COM component as the input and generates a WSDL file for you. A small drawback with this is that, if anything changes in the method signatures in the component, you must redo the process of the WSDL file generation. In an ASP.NET web service, you avoid the task of generating the WSDL file from the wizard. This is because when you simply append ?WSDL to the .asmx document URL, you get a WSDL file. Because this is generated dynamically by inspecting the methods marked with the WebMethod attribute in the .asmx file for every request, this is guaranteed to reflect the latest modifications in the .asmx file. Figure 11.4 shows the WSDL generated for the Calculator web service.

Figure 11.4   The WSDL for the Calculator web service.

The generated WSDL in Figure 11.4 describes the HTTP-GET, HTTP-POST, and SOAP protocols. You must look at the part of the WSDL document that describes the bindings for the SOAP protocol and try to understand the document structure. Listing 11.3 shows the WSDL using SOAP.

Listing 11.3   **The WSDL File for the Calculator Web Service**

```
<?xml version="1.0" encoding="utf-8" ?>
<definitions xmlns:s="http://www.w3.org/2001/XMLSchema"
             xmlns:http="http://schemas.xmlsoap.org/wsdl/http/"
             xmlns:mime="http://schemas.xmlsoap.org/wsdl/mime/"
             xmlns:tm="http://microsoft.com/wsdl/mime/textMatching/"
             xmlns:soap="http://schemas.xmlsoap.org/wsdl/soap/"
             xmlns:soapenc="http://schemas.xmlsoap.org/soap/encoding/"
             xmlns:s0="http://tempuri.org/"
             ↪targetNamespace="http://tempuri.org/"
             xmlns="http://schemas.xmlsoap.org/wsdl/">

    <types>
        <s:schema attributeFormDefault="qualified"
                  elementFormDefault="qualified"
                  targetNamespace="http://tempuri.org/">
            <s:element name="Add">
                <s:complexType>
                    <s:sequence>
                        <s:element minOccurs="1" maxOccurs="1"
                                   name="a" type="s:int" />
                        <s:element minOccurs="1" maxOccurs="1"
                                   name="b" type="s:int" />
                    </s:sequence>
                </s:complexType>
            </s:element>
            <s:element name="AddResponse">
                <s:complexType>
                    <s:sequence>
                        <s:element minOccurs="1" maxOccurs="1"
                                   name="AddResult" type="s:int" />
                    </s:sequence>
                </s:complexType>
            </s:element>
            <s:element name="Subtract">
                <s:complexType>
                    <s:sequence>
                        <s:element minOccurs="1" maxOccurs="1"
                                   name="a" type="s:int" />
                        <s:element minOccurs="1" maxOccurs="1"
                                   name="b" type="s:int" />
                    </s:sequence>
                </s:complexType>
            </s:element>
            <s:element name="SubtractResponse">
                <s:complexType>
                    <s:sequence>
                        <s:element minOccurs="1" maxOccurs="1"
                                   name="SubtractResult" type="s:int" />
```

```
                              </s:sequence>
                        </s:complexType>
                  </s:element>
                  <s:element name="int" type="s:int" />
            </s:schema>
      </types>

      <message name="AddSoapIn">
            <part name="parameters" element="s0:Add" />
      </message>
      <message name="AddSoapOut">
            <part name="parameters" element="s0:AddResponse" />
      </message>

      <message name="SubtractSoapIn">
            <part name="parameters" element="s0:Subtract" />
      </message>
      <message name="SubtractSoapOut">
            <part name="parameters" element="s0:SubtractResponse" />
      </message>

      <portType name="CalculatorSoap">
            <operation name="Add">
                  <input message="s0:AddSoapIn" />
                  <output message="s0:AddSoapOut" />
            </operation>
            <operation name="Subtract">
                  <input message="s0:SubtractSoapIn" />
                  <output message="s0:SubtractSoapOut" />
            </operation>
      </portType>

      <binding name="CalculatorSoap" type="s0:CalculatorSoap">
            <soap:binding transport="http://schemas.xmlsoap.org/soap/http"
            ➥style="document" />
            <operation name="Add">
                  <soap:operation soapAction="http://tempuri.org/Add"
                  ➥style="document" />
                  <input>
                        <soap:body use="literal" />
                  </input>
                  <output>
                        <soap:body use="literal" />
                  </output>
            </operation>
            <operation name="Subtract">
                  <soap:operation soapAction="http://tempuri.org/Subtract"
                  ➥style="document" />
                  <input>
                        <soap:body use="literal" />
                  </input>
```

continues

Listing 11.3 **Continued**

```
              <output>
                  <soap:body use="literal" />
              </output>
          </operation>
      </binding>

      <service name="Calculator">
          <port name="CalculatorSoap" binding="s0:CalculatorSoap">
              <soap:address
location="http://localhost/WebServices/Calculator/Calculator.asmx" />
          </port>
      </service>

  </definitions>
```

Five major sections are in the WSDL document, which can be categorized into two groups. The top group is comprised of abstract definitions, and the bottom group consists of concrete descriptions. The abstract sections define SOAP messages in a platform- and language-independent manner; they do not contain any machine- nor language-specific elements. This helps define a set of services that several diverse websites can implement. Site-specific matters, such as serialization, are then relegated to the bottom sections, which contain concrete descriptions.

Abstract Definitions

The following abstract definitions are found in the WSDL file:

- **Types**—The <types> element contains the parameters names and data type definitions for parameters and the return types of web service methods. This type definition is based on an XSD schema. This schema is referenced from the Messages section of the document.

- **Messages**—If you consider operations as functions, then a <message> element defines the parameters to that function. Each <part> child element in the <message> element corresponds to a parameter. Input parameters are defined in a single <message> element, separate from output parameters, which are in their own <message> element. Parameters that are both input and output have their corresponding <part> elements in both input and output <message> elements. The name of an output <message> element ends in Response, as in AddResponse, by convention. Each <part> element has name and type attributes, just as a function parameter has both a name and type.

- **PortTypes**—Refers to message definitions in a Messages section to describe function signatures (such as operation name, input parameters, and output pameters). Operation elements within a `PortType` define the syntax for calling all methods in the `PortType`. Each `<portType>` element groups together a number of related operations. In an `<operation>` element, there can be at most one `<input>` element, at most one `<output>` element, and at most one `<fault>` element. Each of these three elements has `name` and `message` attributes.

Concrete Descriptions

The following abstract definitions are found in the WSDL file:

- **Bindings**—The Binding section is where the protocol, serialization, and encoding on the wire corresponding to the operations defined in the `portType` element are fully specified. The `style` attribute in the `<binding>` element specifies the message serialization format as SOAP Section 5 RPC-style or document-style encoding. The `<soap:operation>` within the `<operation>` element specifies the value of the `SOAPAction` HTTP header. The `<input>` and `<output>` elements within the `<operation>` element specify how the input and output messages of the individual operation are encoded.

- **Services**—Specifies port address(es) of each binding. Therefore, a service is a set of `<port>` elements. Each `<port>` element associates a location with a `<binding>` in a one-to-one fashion. If more than one `<port>` element is associated with the same `<binding>`, the additional URL locations can be used as alternates. More than one `<service>` element can exist in a WSDL document.

> **Note**
> You can find the WSDL 1.1 Specification that has been submitted to the W3C as a Note at www.w3.org/TR/wsdl.

Creating a *proxy* Using Visual Studio .NET

For the development of the client of web services, Visual Studio .NET provides a new option to add a web reference to the web service. With this easy-to-use option, a `proxy` class is automatically generated. The Add Web Reference option is available from the Project menu or by right-clicking References in the Solution Explorer. Figure 11.5 shows a web reference being added in a Visual Studio .NET project.

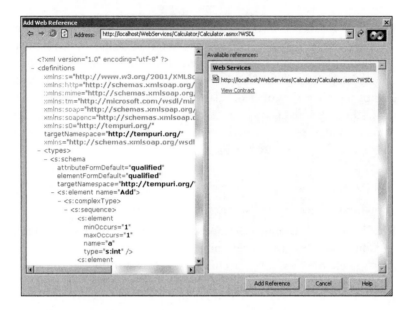

Figure 11.5 Adding a web reference in a Visual Studio .NET project.

Figure 11.6 shows the Solution Explorer with the added web reference.

Figure 11.6 The Solution Explorer showing the added web reference.

Now that you have a proxy automatically generated, use it to build a client. You can design a user interface for the client, as shown in Figure 11.7.

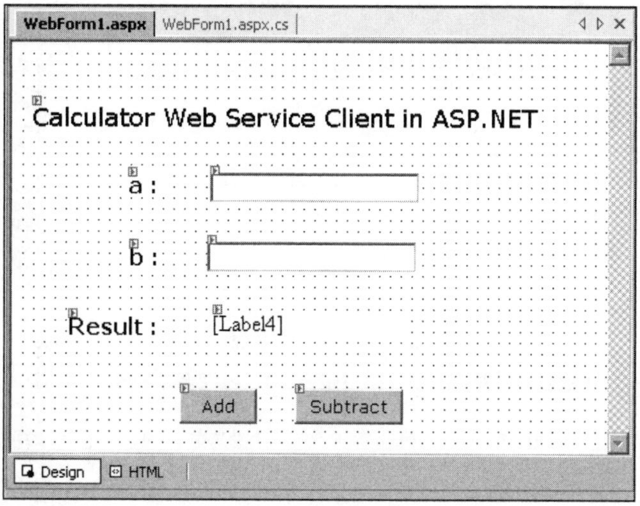

Figure 11.7 Designing the user interface with the designer in Visual Studio .NET.

The following code for the Add and Subtract button click events shows the use of the proxy to access the Calculator web service:

```
//Add
private void Button1_Click(object sender, System.EventArgs e)
{
CalculatorService.Calculator calc = new CalculatorService.Calculator();
Label4.Text =
calc.Add(Int32.Parse(TextBox1.Text),Int32.Parse(TextBox2.Text)).ToString();
}
//Subtract
private void Button2_Click(object sender, System.EventArgs e)
{
CalculatorService.Calculator calc = new CalculatorService.Calculator();
Label4.Text = calc.Subtract(Int32.Parse(TextBox1.Text),Int32.Parse
➥(TextBox2.Text)).ToString();
}
```

Figure 11.8 shows the result of clicking the Add button.

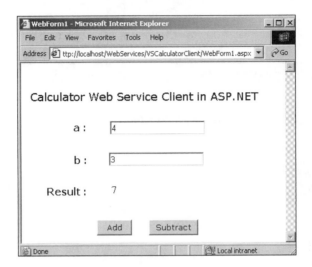

Figure 11.8 The web service client in action.

Creating a *proxy* Using the WSDL Tool

Running the WSDL tool with the following code creates a source file named `Calculator.cs` for the proxy object:

```
wsdl /o:Calculator.cs
http://localhost/WebServices/Calculator/Calculator.asmx?WSDL
```

Figure 11.9 shows the WSDL tool being used to create a proxy class.

```
C:\>wsdl /o:Calculator.cs http://localhost/WebServices/Calculator/Calculator.asm
x?WSDL
Microsoft (R) Web Services Description Language Utility
[Microsoft (R) .NET Framework, Version 1.0.3215.11]
Copyright (C) Microsoft Corporation 1998-2001. All rights reserved.

Writing file 'Calculator.cs'.

C:\>
```

Figure 11.9 Generating a source file using the WSDL tool.

For more information on all the options available for the WSDL tool refer to Chapter 4, "XML Tool Support in Visual Studio .NET."

Listing 11.4 shows the auto-generated proxy source created by the WSDL tool. Note that the proxy class generated by Visual Studio .NET has the same code as that's generated by the WSDL tool.

Listing 11.4 **Auto-Generated *proxy* Source for the Calculator Web Service *(Calculator.cs)***

```
using System.Diagnostics;
using System.Xml.Serialization;
using System;
using System.Web.Services.Protocols;
using System.ComponentModel;
using System.Web.Services;


/// <remarks/>
[System.Diagnostics.DebuggerStepThroughAttribute()]
[System.ComponentModel.DesignerCategoryAttribute("code")]
[System.Web.Services.WebServiceBindingAttribute(Name="CalculatorSoap",
➥Namespace="http://tempuri.org/")]
public class Calculator :
System.Web.Services.Protocols.SoapHttpClientProtocol {

    /// <remarks/>
    public Calculator() {
        this.Url = "http://localhost/WebServices/Calculator/Calculator.asmx";
    }

    /// <remarks/>

[System.Web.Services.Protocols.SoapDocumentMethodAttribute("http://tempuri.or
➥g/Add", RequestNamespace="http://tempuri.org/",
ResponseNamespace="http://tempuri.org/",
Use=System.Web.Services.Description.SoapBindingUse.Literal,
ParameterStyle=System.Web.Services.Protocols.SoapParameterStyle.Wrapped)]
    public int Add(int a, int b) {
        object[] results = this.Invoke("Add", new object[] {
                    a,
                    b});
        return ((int)(results[0]));
    }

    /// <remarks/>
    public System.IAsyncResult BeginAdd(int a, int b, System.AsyncCallback
    ➥callback, object asyncState) {
        return this.BeginInvoke("Add", new object[] {
                    a,
                    b}, callback, asyncState);
    }

    /// <remarks/>
    public int EndAdd(System.IAsyncResult asyncResult) {
        object[] results = this.EndInvoke(asyncResult);
        return ((int)(results[0]));
    }
```

continues

Listing 11.4 **Continued**

```
    /// <remarks/>

[System.Web.Services.Protocols.SoapDocumentMethodAttribute("http://tempuri.or
➥g/Subtract", RequestNamespace="http://tempuri.org/",
ResponseNamespace="http://tempuri.org/",
Use=System.Web.Services.Description.SoapBindingUse.Literal,
ParameterStyle=System.Web.Services.Protocols.SoapParameterStyle.Wrapped)]
    public int Subtract(int a, int b) {
        object[] results = this.Invoke("Subtract", new object[] {
                    a,
                    b});
        return ((int)(results[0]));
    }

    /// <remarks/>
    public System.IAsyncResult BeginSubtract(int a, int b,
➥System.AsyncCallback callback, object asyncState) {
        return this.BeginInvoke("Subtract", new object[] {
                    a,
                    b}, callback, asyncState);
    }

    /// <remarks/>
    public int EndSubtract(System.IAsyncResult asyncResult) {
        object[] results = this.EndInvoke(asyncResult);
        return ((int)(results[0]));
    }
}
```

The proxy class inherits from the System.Web.Services.Protocols.
SoapHttpClientProtocol base class. The generated proxy class and the
SoapHttpClientProtocol class wrap up the details of sending and receiving
SOAP requests and responses to the web service, thereby making the client
developer's job trivial. The client developer does not need to understand the
subtleties of the SOAP message structure unless he or she wants low-level
control over SOAP messages being serialized and deserialized.

Table 11.3 contains some useful public properties of the proxy object that it
inherits from the SoapHttpClientProtocol class. The clients can make use of
these properties to alter the default behavior of the generated proxy classes.

Table 11.3 **Public Properties of the *proxy* Object**

Property	Description
AllowAutoRedirect	Gets or sets whether the client automatically follows server redirections. If a client sends authentication information, such as a username and password, you do not want to enable the server to redirect because it might compromise security.

Property	Description
ClientCertificates	Gets the collection of client certificates. This property allows a client to pass one or more client certificates, also known as Authenticode X.509 v.3 certificates, when calling an XML Web Service method. If the XML Web Service method is configured to use client certificates, a client certificate can be used as one mechanism for authenticating a client.
CookieContainer	Gets or sets the collection of cookies. If an XML Web Service method uses session state, a cookie is passed back in the response headers to the XML Web Service client that uniquely identifies the session for that XML Web Service client. In order for the XML Web Service client to receive that cookie, a new instance of CookieContainer must be created and assigned to the CookieContainer property before the XML Web Service method is called. This ensures that the cookie is properly included in subsequent requests.
Credentials	Gets or sets security credentials for web service client authentication. When using the Credentials property, an XML Web Service client must instantiate a class implementing ICredentials, such as NetworkCredential, and set the client credentials specific to the authentication mechanism. The NetworkCredential class can set authentication credentials by using the basic, digest, NTLM, and Kerberos authentication mechanisms.
PreAuthenticate	When PreAuthenticate is true, the WWW-authenticate header is sent with the first request if the authentication mechanism supports doing so. When PreAuthenticate is false, a request is made to the XML Web Service method without initially attempting to authenticate the user. If the XML Web Service allows anonymous access, the XML Web Service method is executed. If anonymous access is disallowed, a 401 HTTP return code is sent back to the client. In response, the WebClientProtocol class returns authentication credentials to the web server. If the client is authenticated and subsequently authorized to access the XML Web Service, the XML Web Service method is executed; otherwise, the client is denied access.

continues

Table 11.3 **Continued**

Property	Description
Proxy	Gets or sets proxy information for making an XML Web Service request through a firewall. Use the proxy property if a client needs to use different proxy settings than those in the system settings. You can use the WebProxy class to set the proxy settings because it implements IWebProxy.
Timeout	Indicates the time an XML Web Service client waits for a synchronous XML Web Service request to complete (in milliseconds).
	Setting the Timeout property to Timeout.Infinite indicates that the request doesn't time out. Although an XML Web Service client can set the Timeout property to not time out, the web server can still cause the request to time out on the server side.
Url	Gets or sets the base URL of the XML Web Service that the client is requesting.
	The Url property can be changed to refer to any XML Web Service that implements the same service description from which the proxy class was generated.
UserAgent	Gets or sets the value for the user agent header that's sent with each request.

Consuming the ASP.NET Web Service from an ASP Client Using SOAP Toolkit 2.0

You can use SOAP Toolkit 2.0's high-level API to consume the Calculator web service from an ASP page. The example in this section demonstrates the interoperability of web services by showing you how a web service built in a managed environment can be consumed from an unmanaged environment. The same idea exists for a Visual Basic desktop client, a Java client, or potentially any client that can send valid SOAP requests to the service and read the SOAP requests sent by the service. Listing 11.5 shows the code for the Client.asp page. It's essential that you download and install the SOAP Toolkit before running this example.

Listing 11.5   **An ASP Client to Consume the ASP.NET Web Service**
            (Client.asp)

```
<%@ Language=VBScript %>
<%
Option Explicit
Dim  soapClient , c , a, b
a = 4
b = 3
Set soapClient = Server.CreateObject("MSSOAP.SoapClient")
call soapClient.mssoapinit(
"http://localhost/WebServices/Calculator/Calculator.asmx?WSDL" )

Response.Write     "<B> Add( a , b ) returned ::<B>" & _
                        soapClient.Add( a , b ) & "<BR>"
Response.Write     "<B> Subtract( a , b )   returned :: <B>" & _
                        soapClient.Subtract( a , b )
%>
```

Figure 11.10 shows the result in the browser.

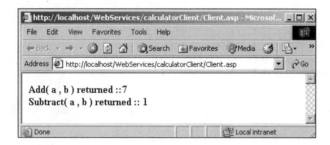

Figure 11.10   The result of running the ASP web service client.

Note

You can download the SOAP Toolkit 2.0 SP2 from Microsoft's download center at
http://msdn.microsoft.com/downloads/default.asp?URL=/code/sample.asp?url=/
MSDN-FILES/027/001/580/msdncompositedoc.xml.

Consuming the ASP.NET Web Service from IE 5.x Using XMLHTTP

In Chapter 5, "MSXML Parser," XMLHTTP was briefly introduced. In this
section, Listing 11.6 provides an example that consumes the web service
directly from a web browser by using XMLHTTP to send and receive the
SOAP request and response.

Listing 11.6 **An HTML Client to Consume the ASP.NET Web Service**
(Client.htm)

```
<HTML>
    <HEAD>
        <TITLE>XMLHTTP Browser Client for ASP.NET Web Service</TITLE>
    </HEAD>
    <BODY onload='makeSOAPCall(4,3)'>
    </BODY>
</HTML>

<SCRIPT LANGUAGE=javascript>
<!--
function makeSOAPCall( varA ,varB )
{
var    objXMLHTTP = new ActiveXObject("MSXML2.XMLHTTP")
//Specify the URL for the ASP.NET Web Service
objXMLHTTP.open("POST",
"http://localhost/WebServices/Calculator/Calculator.asmx" ,
                    false , "" , "" );
objXMLHTTP.setRequestHeader("SOAPAction","http://tempuri.org/Add" );
objXMLHTTP.setRequestHeader("Content-Type", "text/xml" );

//Create the SOAP Request
strSOAPRequest = '<?xml version="1.0" encoding="utf-8" ?>'
                    + '<soap:Envelope'
                    +      '
xmlns:soap="http://schemas.xmlsoap.org/soap/envelope/"'
                    +      ' xmlns:xsi="http://www.w3.org/2001/XMLSchema-
                          ⇒instance"'
                    +      ' xmlns:xsd="http://www.w3.org/2001/XMLSchema" >'
                    + '<soap:Body>'
                    + '<Add xmlns="http://tempuri.org/">'
                    + '<a>'+ varA +'</a>'
                    + '<b>'+ varB +'</b>'
                    + '</Add>'
                    + '</soap:Body>'
                    + '</soap:Envelope>'

alert("====================SOAP Request===================== \n"
        + strSOAPRequest)
//Send the Request to the .NET Web Service
objXMLHTTP.send(strSOAPRequest);
alert("====================SOAP Response==================== \n"
        + objXMLHTTP.responseXML.xml)

//Get the Envelope Node
var soapEnvelope =  objXMLHTTP.responseXML;
//Get the Body Node
var soapBody  = soapEnvelope.selectSingleNode("//soap:Body");
//Get the Result of the call.
```

```
alert( soapBody.selectSingleNode("AddResponse/AddResult").text )
}
//-->
</SCRIPT>
```

This code assumes that the request is successful. A production code should also expect that there might be exceptions within the code and handle the SOAP faults to show proper messages to the user. Figure 11.11 and Figure 11.12 show the request and response captured through JavaScript alerts.

Figure 11.11   The SOAP request created from an HTML page.

Figure 11.12   The SOAP response received by the HTML page.

When you use a SOAP implementation, a proxy generated on the client hides the details of the SOAP request and response formats. But when you deal with raw XML to create SOAP requests for an ASP.NET web service, you can get some help with the SOAP request and response formats by typing the URL for the web service with the ?op= + *WebMethod* name appended to the URL in a browser. Figure 11.13 shows a sample SOAP request and response.

As mentioned in the Chapter 5, you can also use the ServerXMLHTTP to consume the web service from an ASP page in the same manner as you did in the HTML page.

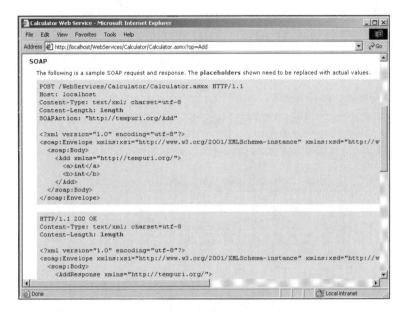

Figure 11.13   A sample SOAP request and response.

SOAP Extensions

Using ASP.NET SOAP extensions, you can inspect or alter a SOAP message in an XML Web Service at specific stages in message processing on either the client or the server. Altering messages gives you a chance to implement a layer for encryption or compression of messages on top of an existing XML Web Service. Inspecting the messages is useful to debug your web services.

ASP.NET SOAP extensions derive from the SoapExtension class. Overriding the ProcessMessage method in the SoapExtension base class gives you an opportunity to read or change the messages because this method can be called at each of the four stages defined in SoapMessageStage enum. (Note that the inline comments in Listing 11.7 explain these four stages.)

Using SOAP Extensions to Trace SOAP Messages

The .NET Framework does not provide a direct tool to trace SOAP messages, which is a useful aspect for a web service and the web service client developers. You can build a tracing mechanism to log the SOAP messages using the SOAP extensions. Listing 11.7 shows a sample web service that exposes a single method, GetAddressEntry(), and uses SOAP extension to log the SOAP request and response messages to a file.

Listing 11.7 **Tracing SOAP Messages Using SOAP Extensions** *(service1.asmx)*

```
<%@ WebService Language="c#" Class="TracingAddressEntries" %>
using System;
using System.IO;

using System.Web.Services;
using System.Web.Services.Protocols;

public class TracingAddressEntries : WebService
    {

        [WebMethod]
        //set a file name to log messages using the trace extension
        //attribute
        [TraceExtension(Filename="C:\\log.txt" )]
        public AddressEntry GetAddressEntry()
        {
            AddressEntry addrEntry = new AddressEntry();

            addrEntry.EntryId = 1000;
            addrEntry.FirstName = "Maria";
            addrEntry.LastName = "Anders";
            addrEntry.Email = "maria@alfreds-futterkiste.com" ;
            addrEntry.Phone = "030-0074321";

            return addrEntry;
        }
    }

public class AddressEntry
{
    public int EntryId;
    public string FirstName ;
    public string LastName ;
    public string Email ;
    public string Phone ;

}

//trace extension attribute class inheriting from the SoapExtensionAttribute
[AttributeUsage(AttributeTargets.Method)]
public class TraceExtensionAttribute : SoapExtensionAttribute {

    private string filename = "c:\\trace.txt";//default filename
    private int priority;

    public override Type ExtensionType {
        get { return typeof(TraceExtension); }
    }
```

continues

Listing 11.7 **Continued**

```
    public override int Priority {
        get { return priority; }
        set { priority = value; }
    }

    public string Filename {
        get {
            return filename;
        }
        set {
            filename = value;
        }
    }
}

public class TraceExtension : SoapExtension {

    Stream oldStream;
    Stream newStream;
    string filename;

// When the SOAP extension is accessed for the first time, the filename
//passed in using the corresponding SoapExtensionAttribute is stored.
    public override object GetInitializer(LogicalMethodInfo methodInfo,
    ⇒SoapExtensionAttribute attribute) {
        return ((TraceExtensionAttribute) attribute).Filename;
    }

    public override object GetInitializer(Type serviceType){
        return typeof(TraceExtension);
    }

// Receive the filename stored by GetInitializer and store it in a member
//variable for this specific instance.
    public override void Initialize(object initializer) {
        filename = (string) initializer;
    }

//overriding the ProcessMessage method. This method gives us a chance to
//alter the SOAP Messages before sending the SAOP messages to the network
//and soon after a SOAP message is available from a client.

    public override void ProcessMessage(SoapMessage message) {
        switch (message.Stage) {

        case SoapMessageStage.BeforeSerialize:
//The stage just prior to a SoapMessage being serialized. There is no XML
//Response yet so do nothing.
```

```
            break;

        case SoapMessageStage.AfterSerialize:
//The stage just after a SoapMessage is serialized, but before the SOAP
//message is sent over the wire. The XML SOAP Response is available. Capture
//it in a file.
            WriteOutput( message );
            break;

        case SoapMessageStage.BeforeDeserialize:
//The stage just before a SoapMessage is deserialized from the SOAP message
//sent across the network into a .NET object. The request from the client
//is available as XML. Capture it in a file.
            WriteInput( message );
            break;
        case SoapMessageStage.AfterDeserialize:
//The stage just after a SoapMessage is deserialized from a SOAP message into
//an object.
            break;

        default:
            throw new Exception("invalid stage");
        }
    }

// Save the Stream representing the SOAP request or SOAP response into a
//local memory buffer.
public override Stream ChainStream( Stream stream ){
        oldStream = stream;
        newStream = new MemoryStream();
        return newStream;
    }

//capturing the XML SOAP Response to the log file
    public void WriteOutput( SoapMessage message ){
        newStream.Position = 0;
            FileStream fs = new FileStream(filename, FileMode.Append,
            ➥FileAccess.Write);
        StreamWriter w = new StreamWriter(fs);
        w.WriteLine("-------------------------------- Response at " +
        ➥DateTime.Now);
        w.Flush();
        Copy(newStream, fs);
        fs.Close();
        newStream.Position = 0;
        Copy(newStream, oldStream);
    }

//capturing the XML SOAP Request to the log file
    public void WriteInput( SoapMessage message ){
        Copy(oldStream, newStream);
```

continues

Listing 11.7 **Continued**

```
              FileStream fs = new FileStream(filename, FileMode.Append,
              ➥<%FileAccess.Write);
        StreamWriter w = new StreamWriter(fs);
        w.WriteLine("================================== Request at " +
        ➥DateTime.Now);
        w.Flush();
        newStream.Position = 0;
        Copy(newStream, fs);
        fs.Close();
        newStream.Position = 0;
    }

    void Copy(Stream from, Stream to) {

        TextReader reader = new StreamReader(from);
        TextWriter writer = new StreamWriter(to);
        writer.WriteLine(reader.ReadToEnd());
        writer.Flush();
    }
}
```

Although in Listing 11.7 the two classes `TraceExtensionAttribute` and `TraceExtension` are placed in the same asmx file, you can place them in a different .cs file and convert the file into an assembly so that you can use it for all other web services on the web server.

The following is the SOAP request and response captured in the `log.txt` file:

```
================================== Request at 10/30/2001 6:05:07 AM
<?xml version="1.0" encoding="utf-8"?><soap:Envelope
xmlns:soap="http://schemas.xmlsoap.org/soap/envelope/"
xmlns:xsi="http://www.w3.org/2001/XMLSchema-instance"
xmlns:xsd="http://www.w3.org/2001/XMLSchema"><soap:Body><GetAddressEntry
xmlns="http://tempuri.org/" /></soap:Body></soap:Envelope>

------------------------------- Response at 10/30/2001 6:05:07 AM
<?xml version="1.0" encoding="utf-8"?><soap:Envelope
xmlns:soap="http://schemas.xmlsoap.org/soap/envelope/"
xmlns:xsi="http://www.w3.org/2001/XMLSchema-instance"
xmlns:xsd="http://www.w3.org/2001/XMLSchema"><soap:Body><GetAddressEntryResponse
xmlns="http://tempuri.org/"><GetAddressEntryResult><EntryId>1000</EntryId>
➥<FirstName>Maria</FirstName><LastName>Anders</LastName><Email>maria@alfreds
➥futterkiste.com</Email><Phone>030-0074321</Phone></GetAddressEntryResult>
➥</GetAddressEntryResponse></soap:Body></soap:Envelope>
```

To implement a custom encryption of messages, you must replace the WriteOutput() used in Listing 11.7 by a method (for example, Encrypt()) that encrypts the SOAP response before sending it over the wire and the WriteInput() method by a method (for example, Decrypt()) that decrypts an encrypted SOAP request that's sent by the client. These methods should not tamper with the entire SOAP messages, but only the contents inside the body of the SOAP messages. Tampering with the other structures makes them invalid SOAP messages for the underlying SOAP implementations.

Other Alternatives to Tracing

Apart from using the SOAP extension, you can use other tools, such as the SOAP Trace Utility (MsSoapT.exe) that is packaged along with the Microsoft SOAP Toolkit 2.0 and the tcpTrace available from www.pocketsoap.com/default.asp. MsSoapT.exe enables you to debug the SOAP request, and the tcpTrace.exe enables you to check out the entire HTTP conversation. Both tools make it possible for you to review SOAP requests by intercepting and forwarding the requests. To intercept a request, you must tell your client to talk to a port (for example, 8080) on which the chosen trace utility is listening. So it is required that you change the location attribute in the address element of the WSDL file, as shown in the following code.

The following code is the service section before changing:

```
<service name="TracingAddressEntries">
    <port name="TracingAddressEntriesSoap"
binding="s0:TracingAddressEntriesSoap">
        <soap:address
location="http://localhost/WebServices/SoapMessagesTracing/service1.asmx" />
    </port>
</service>
```

The following code is the service section after changing:

```
<service name="TracingAddressEntries">
    <port name="TracingAddressEntriesSoap"
binding="s0:TracingAddressEntriesSoap">
        <soap:address
location="http://localhost:8080/WebServices/SoapMessagesTracing/
➥service1.asmx" />
    </port>
</service>
```

But in the case of a .NET web service, where you have a dynamic WSDL file generated, you do not have the flexibility to make the previously mentioned changes. You can do this change in the client proxy code that's generated. This location is available to be changed through the Url property of the generated proxy. You can change it at run-time so you don't have to modify the generated proxy object's code. The following code shows how you can set the Url property in the client application:

```
localhost.TracingAddressEntries addrEntries = new
localhost.TracingAddressEntries();
addrEntries.Url =
"http://localhost:8080/WebServices/SoapMessagesTracing/service1.asmx";
localhost.AddressEntry addrEntry = addrEntries.GetAddressEntry();
```

Many other advantages of being able to dynamically change the Url property of the proxy object exist. If your call to a certain web service times out or fails due to some server error, you can use this feature to dynamically connect to another web service, provided that the other web service supports the same services.

Now you can view the SOAP messages using these tools, as shown in Figure 11.14 and Figure 11.15.

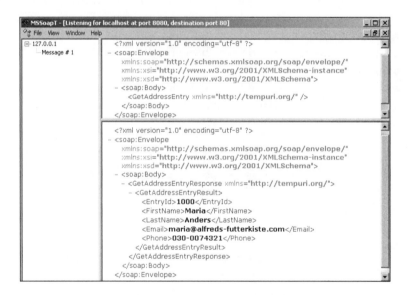

Figure 11.14   The SOAP messages viewed using the trace utility.

These tools will immensely help you as you discover the faults sent by the web service to the clients and convert them into a proper format or predefined error codes through the detail element:

```
<detail>
 <e:myfaultdetails
xmlns:e="http://newriders.com/webservices/addressbook/faults">
```

```
<message>Invalid User</message>
<errorcode>1001</errorcode>
</e:myfaultdetails>
</detail>
```

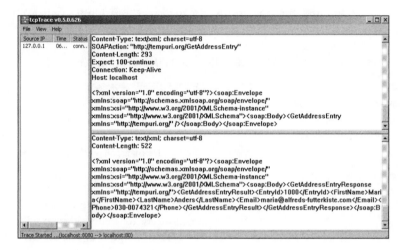

Figure 11.15   The HTTP conversation viewed using tcpTrace.

You can see an implementation of a web service returning error codes in the next section, "Building a Public Address Book Web Service." In cases where your server is not accepting the underlying TCP connection, or you are attempting to perform SOAP communications over a Secure Sockets Layer (SSL) channel, these two tools will not help much. So you might choose to use Microsoft Network Monitor, which is an administrative tool that enables you to monitor packets on your network, or you can write custom HTTP handler that views all the data that's received by and being sent to your web server.

Building a Public Address Book Web Service

This section shows you how to build a fictitious web service that provides RPC-oriented operations to store and manage users' Address Book Details. Developers can integrate this service into their applications and quickly provide an Address Book Management feature to attract the users of their application. These client application developers in turn can pay a licensing fee to use the Address Book service. (Note that the example provided in this section doesn't cover any of the details regarding licensing.)

The Address Book consists of address entries. Each address entry consists of an individual's name, nickname, email address, phone number, and address. The service defines the AddressEntry object that represents an individual address entry.

Table 11.4 contains the operations provided by the Address Book web service.

Table 11.4 **Operations Provided by the Address Book Web Service**

Operation	Description
AddUser(userName,password)	Adds an new user.
token= LogonUser (userName,password)	Authenticates the user's credentials and returns a token if the credentials supplied are valid. For a call with invalid credentials, this operation sends a SOAP fault to the client.
	The token is an encrypted string that the client needs to cache and send with all subsequent requests to the web service. This token expires after 20 minutes and the requests to an operation will fail. In such a situation, the client should call the LogonUser() operation to obtain a fresh token and retry the operation with the new token.
addrList = GetAddressList(token)	Returns all the address entries in the user's Address Book.
	This operation does not return all the fields in an address entry but only a summary that contains the name, email, and phone number. Other details can be obtained by using the AddAddressEntry() operation for a single address entry.
addrEntry = GetAddressEntry (token, addrEntryID)	Returns all the details of an address entry, including name, nickname, email, phone number, and address.
AddAddressEntry(token,addrEntry)	Adds a new address entry to the user's Address Book. It checks for a duplicate nickname and sends SOAP fault in the case of a duplicate nickname.

Operation	Description
`UpdateAddressEntry (token,addrEntry)`	Updates an existing address entry in the user's Address Book. It checks for a duplicate nickname and sends a SOAP fault in the case of a duplicate nickname.
`DeleteAddressEntry (token,addrEntryID)`	Deletes an existing address entry in the user's Address Book.

Table 11.5 contains the application specific errors returned by the web service.

Table 11.5 **Application-Specific Errors Returned by the Web Service**

Error Code	Messsage	Description
`1001`	`Invalid User`	This error is sent in the following cases: • The client sends an invalid username and password during logon. • The token is invalid and expired. • During registration, the client sends a username that's already in use.
`1002`	`Duplicate Nickname`	This error is sent when the client sends a nickname that already exists.

The Address Book web service stores the data on a SQL Server 7.0 (or later) database. Figure 11.16 shows the two tables, Users and AddressBook, used by this web service.

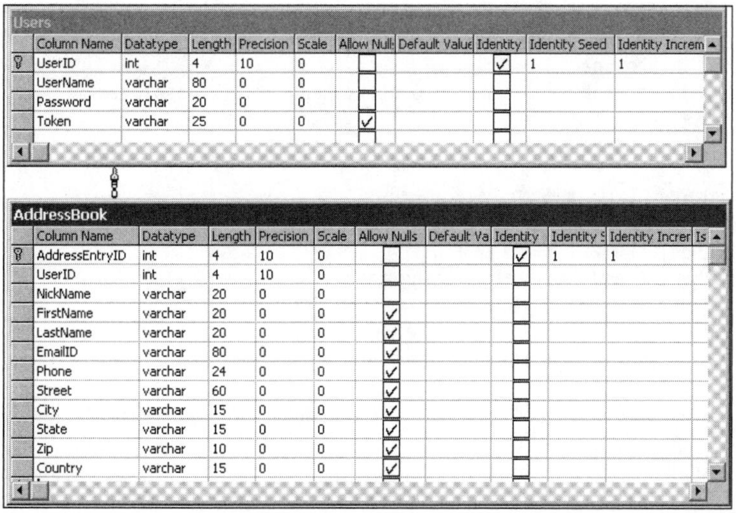

Users

Column Name	Datatype	Length	Precision	Scale	Allow Nulls	Default Value	Identity	Identity Seed	Identity Increm
UserID	int	4	10	0			✓	1	1
UserName	varchar	80	0	0					
Password	varchar	20	0	0					
Token	varchar	25	0	0	✓				

AddressBook

Column Name	Datatype	Length	Precision	Scale	Allow Nulls	Default Va	Identity	Identity S	Identity Incre	Is
AddressEntryID	int	4	10	0			✓	1	1	
UserID	int	4	10	0						
NickName	varchar	20	0	0						
FirstName	varchar	20	0	0	✓					
LastName	varchar	20	0	0	✓					
EmailID	varchar	80	0	0	✓					
Phone	varchar	24	0	0	✓					
Street	varchar	60	0	0	✓					
City	varchar	15	0	0	✓					
State	varchar	15	0	0	✓					
Zip	varchar	10	0	0	✓					
Country	varchar	15	0	0	✓					

Figure 11.16 The Users and AddressBook tables in SQL Server.

Listing 11.8 shows the Address Book web service. The code shows the web service class AddressBookService with the two custom SOAP Exception classes and a database configuration information class. The AddressBookService class is designed to handle the business processes and the two classes, AddressEntry and AddressBookUser, represent the business data.

Listing 11.8 **The Address Book Web Service** *(AddressBookService.asmx)*

```csharp
<%@ WebService Language="c#" Class="Service.AddressBookService" %>
using System;
using System.Web.Services;
using System.Web.Services.Protocols;
using System.Xml;

namespace Service
{
[WebService(Namespace="http://newriders.com/webservices/")]
public class AddressBookService : WebService
{

//Add a New Users of the Web service
[WebMethod]
public bool AddUser(string userName,string password)
{
    return AddressBookUser.CreateUser(userName, password );
}//AddUser


[WebMethod]
public string LogonUser(string userName,string password)
{
    int userID ;
    if( (userID = AddressBookUser.Authenticate(userName,password))== 0 )
        throw new
InvalidAddressBookUserException(Context.Request.Url.AbsoluteUri);

    return AddressBookUser.GetToken( userID );

}//AddUser

[WebMethod]
public bool AddAddressEntry(string token, AddressEntry addrEntry)
{
    int userID = 0;
    if( ( userID = AddressBookUser.Authenticate(token) )==0)
        throw new
InvalidAddressBookUserException(Context.Request.Url.AbsoluteUri);

    try
```

```
    {
        if (AddressEntry.Create( userID,  addrEntry ))
        return true;
        else
        return false;
    }
    catch(Exception ex )
    {
        if( ex.Message.Equals("Duplicate Nickname") )
            throw new
DuplicateNickNameException(Context.Request.Url.AbsoluteUri);
        else
            throw ex;
    }
}


[WebMethod]
public bool UpdateAddressEntry(string token, AddressEntry addrEntry)
{
    int userID = 0;
    if( ( userID = AddressBookUser.Authenticate(token) )==0)
        throw new
InvalidAddressBookUserException(Context.Request.Url.AbsoluteUri);

    try
    {
        if (AddressEntry.Update( userID,  addrEntry ))
            return true;
        else
            return false;
    }
    catch(Exception ex )
    {
        if( ex.Message.Equals("Duplicate Nickname") )
            throw new
DuplicateNickNameException(Context.Request.Url.AbsoluteUri);
        else
            throw ex;
    }
}


[WebMethod]
public bool DeleteAddressEntry(string token, int addrEntryID )
{
    int userID = 0;
    if( ( userID = AddressBookUser.Authenticate(token) )==0)
        throw new
InvalidAddressBookUserException(Context.Request.Url.AbsoluteUri);

    if (AddressEntry.Delete( userID, addrEntryID ))
```

Listing 11.8 **Continued**

```
            return true;
    else
            return false;

}

[WebMethod]
public AddressEntry GetAddressEntry(string token, int addrEntryID)
{

    if(  AddressBookUser.Authenticate(token) == 0 )
        throw new
InvalidAddressBookUserException(Context.Request.Url.AbsoluteUri);

    return new AddressEntry( addrEntryID ) ;
}

[WebMethod]
public AddressEntry[] GetAddressList(string token)
{
    int userID = 0;
    if( ( userID = AddressBookUser.Authenticate(token) )==0)
        throw new
InvalidAddressBookUserException(Context.Request.Url.AbsoluteUri);

    return  AddressEntry.GetAddressList(userID );
}


}


    //Database configuration details
    public class DBConfig
    {
        public static string CONNECT_STRING
        {
            get
            {
                return
"Server=NewRiders;uid=sa;pwd=;database=AddressBook";
            }
        }
    }

    //Exception thrown on Invalid Logon credentials or an Expired Token
    public class InvalidAddressBookUserException : SoapException
    {
        private static XmlNode node;
```

```
        static InvalidAddressBookUserException()
        {
        XmlDocument doc = new System.Xml.XmlDocument();
        node = doc.CreateNode(XmlNodeType.Element,
            SoapException.DetailElementName.Name,
            SoapException.DetailElementName.Namespace);
        //node.InnerText = "Invalid User";
        node.InnerXml =
        "<e:myfaultdetails xmlns:e='http://newriders.com/webservices/
        ➥addressbook/faults' >"
        +"    <message>Invalid User</message>"
        +"        <errorcode>1001</errorcode>"
        +"</e:myfaultdetails>";


        }
        public InvalidAddressBookUserException(string actor):
         base("Invalid User", SoapException.ClientFaultCode,actor,node )
        {
        }
    }

    //Exception thrown for a create request with an already existing
    //NickName
    public class DuplicateNickNameException : SoapException
    {
        private static XmlNode node;
        static DuplicateNickNameException()
        {
        XmlDocument doc = new System.Xml.XmlDocument();
        node = doc.CreateNode(XmlNodeType.Element,
            SoapException.DetailElementName.Name,
            SoapException.DetailElementName.Namespace);
        //node.InnerText = "Duplicate Nickname";
        node.InnerXml =
        "<e:myfaultdetails xmlns:e='http://newriders.com/webservices/
        ➥addressbook/faults' >"
        +"    <message>Duplicate Nickname</message>"
        +"        <errorcode>1002</errorcode>"
        +"</e:myfaultdetails>";


        }
        public DuplicateNickNameException(string actor):
         base("Duplicate Nickname", SoapException.ClientFaultCode,actor,
         ➥node )
        {
        }
    }

}
```

The preceding two custom SOAP Exception classes, InvalidAddressBookUser Exception and DuplicateNickNameException inherits from the System.Web. Services.Protocols.SoapException class and creates the application-specific error information in the detail element within the SOAP Fault element.

Listing 11.9 shows the AddressBookUser class used by the web service for user management and authentication.

Listing 11.9   **The *AddressBookUser* Class (*AddressBookUser.cs*)**

```csharp
using System;
using System.Data.SqlClient ;
using System.Web.Services.Protocols;
namespace Service
{
public class AddressBookUser
{
//Create new User with a unique userName
public static bool CreateUser(string userName,string password)
{
    bool created = false ;
    SqlConnection conn = new SqlConnection(DBConfig.CONNECT_STRING);
    SqlCommand command  = conn.CreateCommand();
    command.CommandText = "SELECT count(*) FROM Users WHERE
➥UserName='"+userName+"'";
    conn.Open();

    if (  (int) command.ExecuteScalar() == 0   )
    {
        //Add the User
        command.CommandText =  "INSERT INTO Users  (UserName,Password)
➥VALUES "
            + "('"+ userName +"','"+ password +"')";
        command.ExecuteNonQuery();
        created = true;
    }

    command.Dispose();
    conn.Close();
    return created;

}

//Authenticate user credentials
public static int Authenticate(string userName,string password)
{
    int userID = 0;
    SqlConnection conn = new SqlConnection(DBConfig.CONNECT_STRING);
    SqlCommand command  = conn.CreateCommand();
    command.CommandText = "SELECT UserID FROM Users WHERE
```

```
UserName='"+userName+"'"
        + "AND Password= '"+password+"'";

    conn.Open();

    SqlDataReader reader = command.ExecuteReader();
    if( reader.Read() )
    {
        userID = reader.GetInt32(0);
    }
    reader.Close();

    conn.Close();
    return  userID;

}

//Authenticate user credentials using the token and check for an expired
//token
public static int Authenticate(string token )
{
    int userID = 0;
    token = Decrypt(token);
    DateTime dtToken = Convert.ToDateTime(token);
    DateTime dtNow = DateTime.Now;

    if(    dtNow.Subtract(dtToken).TotalMinutes > 20  )//expire after 20
    ➥mins
    {
        return userID;
    }

    Object tempID ;
    SqlConnection conn = new SqlConnection(DBConfig.CONNECT_STRING);
    SqlCommand command  = conn.CreateCommand();
    command.CommandText = "SELECT UserID FROM Users WHERE
    ➥Token='"+token+"'";

    conn.Open();
    tempID =  command.ExecuteScalar();
    if (tempID!=null)
    {
        userID = (int) tempID;
    }

    conn.Close();
    return  userID;
}

//Fetch a fresh token
public static string GetToken( int  userID )
```

continues

Listing 11.9 **Continued**

```
{
    //For the token you can use the combination
    //"System.DateTime.Now.ToString()+userName+password"
    //to make it unique and secure. Here we only use the current time
    string token = Encrypt(System.DateTime.Now.ToString() );

    SqlConnection conn = new SqlConnection(DBConfig.CONNECT_STRING);
    SqlCommand command  = conn.CreateCommand();
    command.CommandText = "UPDATE Users SET Token = '"+ token +"'"
        + "WHERE  UserID= "+ userID  +" ";
    conn.Open();
    command.ExecuteNonQuery();
    conn.Close();
    return token;

}


private static string Encrypt(string str)
{     //Add   your Encryption logic here
    return str;
}
private static string Decrypt(string str)
{     //Add   your Decryption logic here
    return str;
}

}


}
```

Listing 11.10 shows the AddressEntry class that implements the operations related to the address entries in the Address Book.

Listing 11.10 **The *AddressEntry* Class *(AddressEntry.cs)***

```
using System;
using System.Data.SqlClient;

namespace Service
{
public class AddressEntry
{
  public int EntryID = 0;
  public string NickName;
  public string FirstName;
  public string LastName;
```

```
   public string EmailID;
   public string Phone;
   public Location AddrLocation;

//Default public constrcutor essential for searlization
public    AddressEntry()
{

}

public AddressEntry(int entryID)
{
SqlConnection conn = new SqlConnection(DBConfig.CONNECT_STRING);
SqlCommand command  = conn.CreateCommand();
command.CommandText = "SELECT * FROM AddressBook WHERE AddressEntryID='"+
➥entryID +"'";

conn.Open();
SqlDataReader reader = command.ExecuteReader();

if(reader.Read() )
{
    this.EntryID     = entryID;
    NickName = reader.GetString(2);

    FirstName        =  reader.IsDBNull(3)? null:reader.GetString(3);
    LastName =  reader.IsDBNull(4)? null:reader.GetString(4);
    EmailID     =  reader.IsDBNull(5)? null:reader.GetString(5);
    Phone            =  reader.IsDBNull(6)? null:reader.GetString(6);

    AddrLocation = new Location();

    AddrLocation.Street  =  reader.IsDBNull(7)? null:reader.GetString(7);
    AddrLocation.City    =  reader.IsDBNull(8)? null:reader.GetString(8);
    AddrLocation.State   =  reader.IsDBNull(9)? null:reader.GetString(9);
    AddrLocation.Zip     =  reader.IsDBNull(10)? null:reader.GetString(10);
    AddrLocation.Country =  reader.IsDBNull(11)? null:reader.GetString(11);
}

reader.Close();
conn.Close();

if( this.EntryID == 0 )
    throw new Exception("Invalid EntryID.");
}

//Create a new Address Entry
public static bool Create( int userID, AddressEntry addrEntry  )
{
Location loc = addrEntry.AddrLocation ;
String sql;
```

continues

Listing 11.10   **Continued**

```
SqlConnection conn = new SqlConnection(DBConfig.CONNECT_STRING);
SqlCommand command  = conn.CreateCommand();

command.CommandText = "SELECT Count(*) FROM AddressBook WHERE UserID='"+
➥userID +"'"
     +" AND  NickName= '"+ addrEntry.NickName +"'   ";

conn.Open();

if    ( (int) command.ExecuteScalar() > 0 )
{
    conn.Close();
    throw new Exception("Duplicate Nickname");
}


if (loc != null)
{
    sql = "INSERT INTO  AddressBook"
        +
"(UserID,NickName,FirstName,LastName,EmailID,Phone,Street,City,State,Zip,Coun
➥try )"
        + "VALUES ("+userID+","'"+addrEntry.NickName+"',
        ➥'"+addrEntry.FirstName+"',"
        + "'"+ addrEntry.LastName +"','"+addrEntry.EmailID +"',
        ➥'"+ addrEntry.Phone+ "',"
        + "'"+ loc.Street +"','"+ loc.City  +"','"+ loc.State +"','"+
        ➥loc.Zip +"','"
+ loc.Country +"'  )";
}
else
{
    sql = "INSERT INTO  AddressBook"
        + "(UserID,NickName,FirstName,LastName,EmailID,Phone )"
        + "VALUES ("+userID+","'"+addrEntry.NickName+"','"
        ➥+addrEntry.FirstName+"',"
        + "'"+ addrEntry.LastName +"','"+addrEntry.EmailID +"','"+
        ➥addrEntry.Phone +"' )" ;

}
command.CommandText = sql;

command.ExecuteNonQuery();
conn.Close();
return true;

}
```

```
//Update existing Address Entry
public static bool Update( int userID, AddressEntry addrEntry  )
{
Location loc = addrEntry.AddrLocation ;
String sql;
SqlConnection conn = new SqlConnection(DBConfig.CONNECT_STRING);
SqlCommand command  = conn.CreateCommand();

command.CommandText = "SELECT Count(*) FROM AddressBook WHERE UserID='"+
➥userID +"'"
     +" AND  AddressEntryID != '"+ addrEntry.EntryID +"' AND  NickName= '"+
     ➥addrEntry.NickName +"'";

conn.Open();

if    ( (int) command.ExecuteScalar() > 0 )
{
    conn.Close();
    throw new Exception("Duplicate NickName");
}


if (loc != null)
{
    sql = "UPDATE AddressBook "
        + " SET NickName = '"+addrEntry.NickName+"', FirstName =
        ➥'"+addrEntry.FirstName+"',"
        + " LastName    = '"+ addrEntry.LastName +"' ,EmailID = '"+
        ➥addrEntry.EmailID +"',"
        + " Phone ='"+ addrEntry.Phone+ "', Street= '"+ loc.Street +"',"
        + " City     = '"+ loc.City  +"' ,State = '"+ loc.State +"' ,Zip
        ➥= '"+ loc.Zip +"',"
        + " Country = '"+ loc.Country +"'"
        + " WHERE UserID = '"+ userID +"' AND AddressEntryID = '"+
        ➥addrEntry.EntryID +"'";
}
else
{
    sql = "UPDATE AddressBook"
        + " SET NickName = '"+addrEntry.NickName+"', FirstName =
        ➥'"+addrEntry.FirstName+"',"
        + " LastName    = '"+ addrEntry.LastName +"' ,EmailID = '"+
        ➥addrEntry.EmailID +"',"
        + " Phone ='"+ addrEntry.Phone+ "',"
        + " WHERE UserID = '"+ userID +"' AND AddressEntryID = '"+
        ➥addrEntry.EntryID +"'";
}
command.CommandText = sql;

command.ExecuteNonQuery();
conn.Close();
```

continues

Listing 11.10 **Continued**

```
return true;

}

//Delete existing Address Entry
public static bool Delete( int userID, int entryID  )
{
    SqlConnection conn = new SqlConnection(DBConfig.CONNECT_STRING);
    SqlCommand command  = conn.CreateCommand();

    command.CommandText = "DELETE FROM AddressBook WHERE UserID='"+ userID
    ⇒+"' "
        +" AND  AddressEntryID = '"+ entryID +"'    ";

    conn.Open();
    command.ExecuteNonQuery();
    conn.Close();
    return true;
}

//Get all existing Address entires for a specific user
public static AddressEntry[] GetAddressList(int userID)
{
    AddressEntry[] addressList = null ;
    int addrCount = 0;

    SqlConnection conn = new SqlConnection(DBConfig.CONNECT_STRING);
    SqlCommand command  = conn.CreateCommand();

    command.CommandText = "SELECT Count(*) FROM AddressBook WHERE UserID='"+
    ⇒userID +"'";

    conn.Open();
    addrCount =     (int) command.ExecuteScalar();

    if( addrCount != 0 )
    {
        addressList = new AddressEntry[addrCount];
        command.CommandText = "SELECT
        ⇒AddressEntryID,NickName,FirstName,LastName,EmailID,"
        + "Phone FROM AddressBook WHERE UserID='"+ userID +"' ORDER BY
        ⇒NickName"    ;

        SqlDataReader reader = command.ExecuteReader();
        int i=0;
        while( reader.Read() )
        {
            addressList[i] = new AddressEntry();
            addressList[i].EntryID  = reader.GetInt32(0);
```

```
                addressList[i].NickName  = reader.GetString(1);
                addressList[i].FirstName = reader.IsDBNull(2)?
null:reader.GetString(2);
                addressList[i].LastName  = reader.IsDBNull(3)?
null:reader.GetString(3);
                addressList[i].EmailID   = reader.IsDBNull(4)?
null:reader.GetString(4);
                addressList[i++].Phone   = reader.IsDBNull(5)?
null:reader.GetString(5);
            }
            reader.Close();
        }
        conn.Close();
        return addressList;
    }
}


public class Location
{
public string Street;
public string City;
public string State;
public string Zip;
public string Country;
}

}
```

Building an ASP.NET Client to Consume the Address Book Web Service

In this section, you examine the part of the code in a client of the Address Book web service that you saw in the previous section "Building a Public Address Book Web Service."

Listing 11.11 shows a part of the code for signing into the application. Here, you call the LogonUser() method exposed by the web service.

Listing 11.11   **Sign In** *(logon.aspx.cs)*

```
private void Button1_Click(object sender, System.EventArgs e)
{
localhost.AddressBookService service = new localhost.AddressBookService();

try
{
```

continues

Listing 11.11 **Continued**

```
        //call the LogonUser method
        Session["token"] = service.LogonUser(  TextBox1.Text.Trim()
    ➥,TextBox2.Text.Trim()   );
        Session["userName"]= TextBox1.Text.Trim();
        Session["password"]= TextBox2.Text.Trim();
    Response.Redirect( "AddressBook.aspx" , true ) ;
}
catch(SoapException soapEx )
{
    if( soapEx.Detail.SelectSingleNode("//message").InnerText.Equals(
    ➥AddressBookExceptions.INVALID_USER ) )
    {
        Label3.Text = AddressBookExceptions.INVALID_USER ;
    }
}
catch(Exception ex )
{
    Label3.Text = ex.Message;
}

}
```

Using the *GetAddressList()* and *DeleteAddressEntry()* Methods

Figure 11.17 shows an Address Book Manager in an ASP.NET client of the Address Book web service.

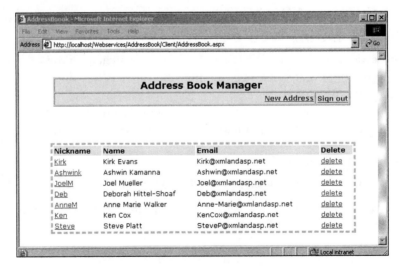

Figure 11.17 The Address Book Manager in an ASP.NET client of the Address Book web service.

Listing 11.12 shows the part of the code that's used to fetch the summary details of all the addresses in a user's Address Book and display them in a table.

Listing 11.12   Get All Addresses and Display in a Table
(*AddressBook.aspx.cs*)

```csharp
private void Page_Load(object sender, System.EventArgs e)
{
localhost.AddressBookService service = new localhost.AddressBookService();

//Delete Address Entry
if( Request.QueryString["delete"]=="true" )
{
int entryID =  Int32.Parse( Request.QueryString["entryid"]) ;
try
{
    service.DeleteAddressEntry( Session["token"].ToString(),entryID );
}
catch(SoapException soapEx )
{
//retry
if( soapEx.Detail.SelectSingleNode("//message").InnerText.Equals(
➥AddressBookExceptions.INVALID_USER) )
{

    Session["token"] =        service.LogonUser(
    ➥Session["userName"].ToString(), Session["password"].ToString() );
    try
    {
            service.DeleteAddressEntry( Session["token"].ToString()
            ➥,entryID );
    }
    catch( Exception innerEx  )
    {
            Label2.Text = innerEx.Message;
    }
}
}
catch(Exception ex )
{
    Label2.Text =  ex.Message;
}
}


//Get AddressList and display
try
{
    addrList = service.GetAddressList( Session["token"].ToString()  );
    DisplayAddressList();
```

continues

Listing 11.12 **Continued**

```
}
catch(SoapException soapEx )
{
//retry
if(soapEx.Detail.SelectSingleNode("//message").InnerText.Equals(
➥AddressBookExceptions.INVALID_USER ) )
{
    Session["token"] =    service.LogonUser(
    ➥Session["userName"].ToString(), Session["password"].ToString() );
    try
    {
        addrList = service.GetAddressList( Session["token"].ToString() );
        DisplayAddressList();
    }
    catch( Exception innerEx  )
    {
    Label2.Text = innerEx.Message;
    }
}
}
catch(Exception ex )
{
    Label2.Text =  ex.Message;
}


}

//Display addresses in a table
private void DisplayAddressList()
{
    HyperLink link ;
    for( int i=0 ;i <addrList.Length ;i++)
    {
        link = new HyperLink();
        link.Text = addrList[i].NickName;
        link.NavigateUrl = "AddressEntry.aspx?edit=true&entryid=" +
        ➥addrList[i].EntryID;

        TableRow row = new TableRow();
        row.Font.Name = "Verdana";
        row.Font.Size = 10;
        TableCell cell = new TableCell();

        cell.Controls.Add(link);
        row.Cells.Add(cell);
        cell = new TableCell();
        cell.Text = addrList[i].FirstName + " " + addrList[i].LastName;
        row.Cells.Add(cell);
```

```
        cell = new TableCell();
        cell.Text = addrList[i].EmailID;
        row.Cells.Add(cell);
        cell = new TableCell();

        link = new HyperLink();
        link.Text = "delete";
        link.NavigateUrl = "AddressBook.aspx?delete=true&entryid=" +
        ↩addrList[i].EntryID;

        cell.Controls.Add(link);
        row.Cells.Add(cell);
        Table1.Rows.Add(row);
    }
}
```

Using the *AddAddressEntry()* and *UpdateAddressEntry()* Methods

The AddAddressEntry()method adds new address entries to your Address Book, and the UpdateAddressEntry() method updates your existing address entries. In screen shown in Figure 11.17, if the user clicks on the "New Address" link, the Create/Edit screen appears in the create mode with all the fields empty. If the user clicks on an existing nickname, the Create/Edit screen appears in the edit mode.

Figure 11.18 shows an example of the Create/Edit screen of the Address Book in the Edit mode, when the user clicks on the nickname 'AshwinK' as seen in the Figure 11.17.

Listing 11.13 shows the code to display the Create/Edit screen and adding or updating address information.

In the edit mode, the address entry details for the specified nickname are retrieved into the addrEntry object using the GetAddressEntry() method. The InitAddressEntryForm() method, that is not shown here, initializes all the address fields in the form using the addrEntry object.

After updating the address information in the case of edit mode or entering new address information in the case of create mode, when the user clicks the Save button the Button1_Click event is fired. The event handler calls the UpdateAddressEntry() or the AddAddressEntry() method to update or add new address information respectively.

Figure 11.18 The Create/Edit Address screen in an Address Book.

Listing 11.13 **Displaying the Create/Edit screen and adding/updating address information.** *(AddressEntry.aspx.cs)*

```
private void Page_Load(object sender, System.EventArgs e)
{

Response.Cache.SetExpires( DateTime.Now );

if( Request.QueryString["edit"]== "true"  &&  !Page.IsPostBack )
{
    localhost.AddressBookService service = new
    ⇒localhost.AddressBookService();

    int entryID =  Int32.Parse( Request.QueryString["entryid"]) ;
    try
    {
        addrEntry = service.GetAddressEntry( Session["token"].ToString() ,
        ⇒entryID );
        InitAddressEntryForm();
    }
    catch(SoapException soapEx )
```

```
        {
        //retry
        if( soapEx.Detail.SelectSingleNode("//message").InnerText.Equals(
        ➥AddressBookExceptions.INVALID_USER  ) )
        {

            Session["token"] =    service.LogonUser(
            ➥Session["userName"].ToString(), Session["password"].ToString());
            try
            {
                addrEntry = service.GetAddressEntry(
                ➥Session["token"].ToString() , entryID );
                InitAddressEntryForm();
            }
            catch( Exception innerEx  )
            {
                Label_Message.Text = innerEx.Message;
            }
        }
        }
        catch(Exception ex )
        {
            Label_Message.Text =  ex.Message;
        }

}
}


//Save button click
private void Button1_Click(object sender, System.EventArgs e)
{
bool saved = false;
localhost.AddressBookService service = new localhost.AddressBookService();
InitAddressEntry();
try
{//Create
    if( addrEntry.EntryID == 0)
    {
        saved = service.AddAddressEntry( Session["token"].ToString()
        ➥,addrEntry );
    }
    else //update
    {
        saved = service.UpdateAddressEntry(
        ➥Session["token"].ToString(),addrEntry );
    }
}
catch(SoapException soapEx )
{
//retry
```

continues

Listing 11.13 **Continued**

```
if( soapEx.Detail.SelectSingleNode("//message").InnerText.Equals(
➥AddressBookExceptions.INVALID_USER  ) )
{
    Session["token"] =     service.LogonUser(
    ➥Session["userName"].ToString(), Session["password"].ToString() );
    try
    {
        Label_Message.Text += "-" + addrEntry.EntryID;
        if( addrEntry.EntryID == 0)//Create
            saved = service.AddAddressEntry(
            ➥Session["token"].ToString(),addrEntry );
        else //update
            saved = service.UpdateAddressEntry(
            ➥Session["token"].ToString(),addrEntry );
    }
    catch( Exception innerEx  )
    {
        Label_Message.Text = innerEx.Message;
    }
}
}
catch(Exception ex )
{
    Label_Message.Text =  ex.Message;
}

if( saved )
    Response.Redirect("AddressBook.aspx");

}

}
```

Exposing .NET Remoting Objects as Web Services

Now that you're more comfortable with exposing and consuming .NET web services, it's time to discuss the more advanced topic of the .NET Remoting Framework and how you can expose web services by using this Framework.

.NET Remoting Framework

Microsoft .NET Remoting provides a framework for objects that reside in different application domains, in different processes, and in different machines to seamlessly communicate with each other. .NET Remoting offers a powerful yet simple programming model and run-time support for making these interactions transparent. *.NET Channel Services* provides the underlying transport mechanism for this communication. The .NET Framework provides the HTTP and TCP channels. The HTTP channel uses SOAP by default to communicate, whereas the TCP channel uses binary payload by default. Different payload-protocol combinations are possible, but this section only discusses the SOAP/XML-HTTP payload-protocol combination.

Two main kinds of remotable objects exist:

- **Marshal-by-value (MBV) objects**—MBV objects are copied and passed out of the application domain. These objects declare their serialization rules (either by implementing `ISerializable` to implement their own serialization, or by being decorated with `SerializableAttribute`, which tells the system to serialize the object automatically), but do not extend `MarshalByRefObject`. The `AddressEntry` object that we shall be looking at in this section's example is a MBV object.

- **Marshal-by-reference (MBR) objects**—In MBR objects, a `proxy` is created and used by the client to access the object remotely. The `AddressEntries` object in the sample is a MBR object. MBR objects extend at least `System.MarshalByRefObject`.

Two types of activation for MBR objects exist:

- **Server-activated objects**—These objects are created by the server only when they are needed and not when the client `proxy` is created by calling new or `Activator.GetObject()`, but when the client invokes the first method on that `proxy`. These can be declared as `Singleton` or `SingleCall` objects. `Singleton` objects are objects for which there will always be only one instance, regardless of how many clients exist for that object, and which have a default lifetime. When an object is declared a `SingleCall` object, the system creates a new object for each client method invocation.

- **Client-activated objects**—These objects' lifetimes are controlled by the calling application domain, just as they would be if the objects were local to the client. These are created on the server when the client calls a new or `Activator.CreateInstance()`.

Creating a .NET Remoting Server Objects

Creating a Remoting Server Object is as simple as creating any other object. The only difference is that an MBR object extends System.MarshalByRefObject and the MBV object is serializable.

Listing 11.14 shows the AddressEntries Remotable Object.

Listing 11.14 **The Server Object** *(AddressEntries.cs)*

```
using System;

namespace RemotingAddressBookService
{
    //The AddressEntries class represents a Remote Object
    public class AddressEntries  : MarshalByRefObject
    {
        private int count = 10 ;

        public AddressEntry GetAddressEntry( int addrEntryID )
        {
            AddressEntry addrEntry  = new AddressEntry(addrEntryID);
            addrEntry.FirstName = "Maria";
            addrEntry.LastName  = "Anders";
                addrEntry.Email     = "maria@alfreds-futterkiste.com";
            addrEntry.Phone     = "030-0074321";

            return addrEntry;
        }

        public int GetCount( )
        {
            return count;
        }

    }
}
```

Listing 11.15 shows the AddressEntry Remotable Object, which is an MBV object.

Listing 11.15 **The Serializable Local Object** *(AddressEntry.cs)*

```
using System;

namespace RemotingAddressBookService
{
    //The AddressEntry class represents a local object
    //that can be serialized to the client
    [SerializableAttribute()]
```

```csharp
public class AddressEntry
{
    private int id;
    private string firstName ;
    private string lastName ;
    private string email ;
    private string phone ;

    public AddressEntry( int addrEntryId)
    {
        id = addrEntryId ;
    }

    public string FirstName
    {
        get
        {
            return firstName;
        }
        set
        {
            firstName = value;
        }
    }

    public string LastName
    {
        get
        {
            return lastName;
        }
        set
        {
            lastName = value;
        }
    }

    public string Email
    {
        get
        {
            return email;
        }
        set
        {
            email = value;
        }
    }
    public string Phone
    {
        get
```

continues

Listing 11.15 **Continued**

```
        {
            return phone;
        }
        set
        {
            phone = value;
        }
    }

  }
}
```

The Configuration File

The configuration file `Remoting.config` in Listing 11.15 specifies the Remoting-specific information for the `AddressEntries Remote` object.

Listing 11.16 **The *Remoting. config* File**

```
<configuration>
  <system.runtime.remoting>
    <application name="RemotingAddressBookService">
      <service>
      <wellknown mode="SingleCall"

type="RemotingAddressBookService.AddressEntries,RemoteObject"
                    objectUri="AddressEntries.soap" />
      </service>

      <channels>
        <channel port="8085" ref="http" />
      </channels>

    </application>
  </system.runtime.remoting>
</configuration>
```

Creating the Server

You can now create a managed executable to register the channels and start listening to the client requests at port 8085, as specified in the configuration file in Listing 11.16. Listing 11.17 shows the code for this listener.

Listing 11.17   **The Listener** *(Listener.cs)*

```csharp
using System;
using System.Runtime.Remoting;
using System.Runtime.Remoting.Channels;
using System.Runtime.Remoting.Channels.Http;

namespace RemotingAddressBookService
{
    public class Listener
    {

        public static int Main(string [] args)
        {
            try
            {
                RemotingConfiguration.Configure("Remoting.config");

//the Following commented code shows the programmatic approach which is
//an alternative to using a configuration file
                /*
                HttpChannel chan = new HttpChannel(8085);
                ChannelServices.RegisterChannel(chan);

                RemotingConfiguration.RegisterWellKnownServiceType
                ➥(Type.GetType("RemotingAddressBookService.AddressEntries,
                ➥RemoteObject"),
                    "AddressEntries.soap", WellKnownObjectMode.SingleCall);
                */

                System.Console.WriteLine("Address Book Remoting Service
                ➥is waiting "
                    + "for requests." );
            }
            catch(Exception e)
            {
                System.Console.WriteLine( e.Message );
            }NET;Remoting objects;exposing>

            System.Console.WriteLine("Press <Enter> to stop this
            ➥Service...");
            System.Console.ReadLine();
            return 0;
        }
    }
}
```

After you compile and run the executable, the service is running and listening to client requests, as shown in Figure 11.19.

Figure 11.19 The Remoting service is listening for requests.

Note

Instead of running an executable on the server machine, it is also possible to create a Windows Service. Creating a Windows Service is relatively simple in the .NET Framework. But because it is outside the scope of this book, it isn't discussed in this chapter. Another available option is to host the service in the Internet Information Server (IIS).

Consuming the Remote Service Through an ASP.NET Client Application

Now that you have the Remoting service running on the server, you must now look at creating an ASP.NET client to consume this service.

To compile a client that accesses the Remoting Server Object, we require the assembly reference for the Remote Object. This can be obtained if the client developer is provided with the Remote Object's assembly. The Remote Server Object developer can create an assembly, which defines the interface for the Remote object, and distribute this information to clients. Alternatively, the client can generate a proxy object by using the Soapsuds command-line utility and a WSDL file. This section looks at using the Soapsuds command-line utilityh and WSDL file. Note that a non-.NET consumer of the Remoting service can use a similar technique because this method doesn't depend on a .NET assembly.

The Soapsuds tool requires a WSDL file to generate the proxy object. The configuration file for the service specifies the HTTP channel running on port 8085 and the objectUri parameter as AddressEntries.soap. You can get a service description file by using the following URL:

```
http://localhost:8085/AddressEntries.soap?WSDL
```

You can check the generated WSDL by entering this URL in the address location of the browser. Figure 11.20 shows the generated WSDL file in a browser.

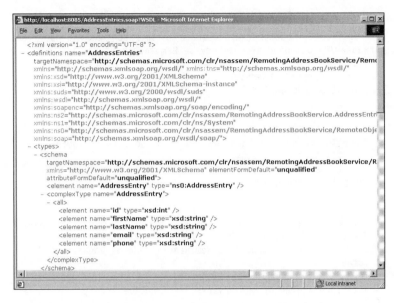

Figure 11.20 The generated WSDL file viewed in the browser.

Generating a *proxy* Using the *Soapsuds* Tool

After you have a WSDL file, you can create a `proxy` for the service by using the WSDL tool or by adding a web reference in a Visual Studio .NET project. Here, we use the `Soapsuds` tool to create the `proxy`. The following command creates the source file and the assembly for the `proxy`, which we can add to our client application:

```
Soapsuds -url:http://localhost:8085/AddressEntries.soap?WSDL -
oa:RemoteObject.dll
```

For more information on all the available options for the `Soapsuds` tool, refer to Chapter 4.

Listing 11.18 shows the source generated by the `Soapsuds` tool for the `proxy` object.

Listing 11.18 *Soapsuds* **Generated** *proxy* **Source Code** *(RemoteObject.cs)*

```
namespace RemotingAddressBookService {
using System;
using System.Runtime.Remoting.Messaging;
using System.Runtime.Remoting.Metadata;
using System.Runtime.Remoting.Metadata.W3cXsd2001;
```

continues

Listing 11.18 **Continued**

```
[Serializable, SoapType(XmlNamespace="http://schemas.microsoft.com/clr/
➡nsassem/RemotingAddressBookService/RemoteObject",
➡XmlTypeNamespace="http://schemas.microsoft.com/clr/nsassem/
➡RemotingAddressBookService/RemoteObject")]
public class AddressEntry
{
    // Class Fields
    public Int32 id;
    public String firstName; NET;Remoting objects;consuming>
    public String lastName;
    public String email;
    public String phone;
}

[SoapType(XmlNamespace="http://schemas.microsoft.com/clr/nsassem/Remoting
➡AddressBookService/RemoteObject",XmlTypeNamespace="http://
➡schemas.microsoft.com/clr/nsassem/RemotingAddressBookService/
➡RemoteObject")]
public class AddressEntries :
➡System.Runtime.Remoting.Services.RemotingClientProxy
{
    // Constructor
    public AddressEntries()
    {
        base.ConfigureProxy(this.GetType(),
"http://165.193.123.15:8085/AddressEntries.soap");

System.Runtime.Remoting.SoapServices.PreLoad(typeof(RemotingAddressBook
➡Service.AddressEntry));
    }
    // Class Methods

[SoapMethod(SoapAction="http://schemas.microsoft.com/clr/nsassem/Remoting
➡AddressBookService.AddressEntries/RemoteObject#GetAddressEntry")]
    public AddressEntry GetAddressEntry(Int32 addrEntryID)
    {
        return ((AddressEntries) _tp).GetAddressEntry(addrEntryID);
    }

[SoapMethod(SoapAction="http://schemas.microsoft.com/clr/nsassem/Remoting
➡AddressBookService.AddressEntries/RemoteObject#GetCount")]
    public Int32 GetCount()
    {
        return ((AddressEntries) _tp).GetCount();
    }

}
}
```

Listing 11.19 shows the part of the code from an ASP.NET page that uses the Remoting Server Object.

Listing 11.19 **An ASP.NET Client for the Remoting Server Object** *(Client.aspx)*

```
private void Page_Load(object sender, System.EventArgs e)
{
try
{
    HttpChannel channel = null;
    //Confirm that the channel is not alredy registered
    if ( ChannelServices.GetChannel("AddrHttpChannel")==null  )
    {
        IDictionary props = new Hashtable();
        props["name"] = "AddrHttpChannel";
        channel = new HttpChannel(
            props,
            null,
            new  BinaryServerFormatterSinkProvider()
            );
        //Register the channel
        ChannelServices.RegisterChannel(channel);
    }

    //Get the ObjRef for the  AddressEntries Remote Object
    AddressEntries addrEntires =
        (AddressEntries)Activator.GetObject(
        typeof(RemotingAddressBookService.AddressEntries)
        , "http://localhost:8085/AddressEntries.soap");
    if (addrEntires == null)
    {
        divAddrCount.InnerHtml = "<B>Could not locate server</B>";
    }
    else
    {
        //Call the method GetCount() on the AddressEntries Object
        divAddrCount.InnerHtml = "<B>Total number of Addresses in the"
            + " Address Book: </B>" + addrEntires.GetCount();

        //Call the method GetAddressEntry() on the AddressEntries Object
        AddressEntry addrEntry = addrEntires.GetAddressEntry(1);

        //Use the properties of the serialized AddressEntry Object
        divAddressEntry.InnerHtml = "<B>Details of Address Entry [id =
        ⇒1]:</B>"
            + "<BR><B>First Name :</B>" + addrEntry.firstName
            + "<BR><B>Last Name :</B>" + addrEntry.lastName ;
    }
}
```

continues

Listing 11.19 **Continued**

```
catch( RemotingException remEx )
{  //Handle Remoting Exception
     divAddrCount.InnerHtml = "<B>The following Remoting Exception occurred
     ➥:</B><BR>"
          + remEx.Message ;
}
catch(System.Net.WebException webEx )
{  //Handle Web Exception
     divAddrCount.InnerHtml = "<B>The following Web Exception occurred
     ➥:</B><BR>"
          + webEx.Message + " Confirm that the Remoting service is started
          ➥and try again.";

}
catch(Exception ex )
{  //Handle Web Exception
     divAddrCount.InnerHtml = "<B>The following Exception occurred :</B><BR>"
          + ex.Message ;

}
}
```

Figure 11.21 shows the result of invoking the `Client.aspx` page.

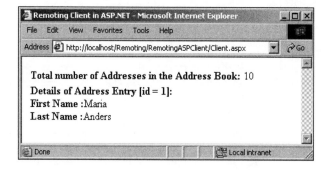

Figure 11.21 The result of invoking the `Client.aspx` page.

Chapter Summary

In this chapter, you saw the building of ASP.NET web services using the example of a simple Calculator web service.

The WSDL document structure was discussed. Then you saw how to build proxies using Visual Studio. NET and also the WSDL command-line tool. We walked through the creation of an ASP.NET client, an ASP client, and an HTML client to consume the ASP.NET Calculator web service.

You saw how to build an Address Book web service and consume it through an ASP.NET application. Then you learned how to expose .NET Remoting Objects as web services by using a sample application walk-through. You then built an ASP.NET client to use the Remote Object.

12

Sample Application: Developing an XML–Based Dynamic Web Page Builder Tool

DURING THE DEVELOPMENT CYCLE, WE all like to take advantage of shortcuts here and there. For example, you might have a code library that you reuse between projects, or several snippets of code that you routinely cut and paste into your projects. This chapter discusses another type of shortcut: a *code-blower* application.

A code-blower is essentially a wizard that you can use to ease development tasks. This wizard interface interrogates a database table and forms some type of user-interface and supporting database access code. This code-blower application enables you to dynamically generate ASP.NET web forms based on an existing database table.

The requirements for such an application are fairly simple: Develop some data about the underlying database table schema and create a user interface based on that schema. Most of the code is fairly static, so you can leverage the use of a template file to ease the amount of code generated.

Walk-Through of Code

This sample contains a bit of code that you might find useful in future projects. To set up the application, create a new C# web application called `pagebuilder`. We will explain the web forms that need to be added and the code they contain by focusing on each page that comprises the application individually. Table 12.1 shows the files that comprise the `pagebuilder` application.

Table 12.1 **Files in the *pagebuilder* Application**

Filename	Description
BuilderLib.cs	Contains a common set of methods used within the application.
CreateForm.aspx	Captures database connection information and the form name that is to be created.
ChooseTable.aspx	Provides the user with a drop-down list of tables within the database specified in `CreateForm.aspx`. The table chosen is used to create the generated code.
CreatePage.aspx	Creates the generated code and delivers the code to the user through email.
Template.txt	Contains the template code that is used to create the generated web form.
PageBuilder.css	Styles the output display.

The overall flow of the code is fairly simple. You collect data pertaining to the database connection and desired table to automate a user interface for. After the data is collected, connect to the database, retrieve the schema, and generate a user interface based on the table schema. To generate the `.aspx` page, use a template file, `Template.txt`, that holds placemarkers for the code that's unique to each usage of the application. You then simply build a string and replace the placemarkers in the template file to generate the `.aspx` page.

BuilderLib.cs

Throughout the code presented in this chapter, you might notice calls to a component called `BuilderLib`. This is a custom component developed for this application that provides several static helper methods. These methods are then reused in several pages in the application, reducing code redundancy.

BuilderLib. GetDataTable

The first method to note is the `GetDataTable` static function. This method retrieves an ADO.NET `DataTable` object using the SQL command and connection string passed to the component.

SQL Server allows the execution of multiple commands in a single command string. That is, you can execute multiple statements simply by separating them with a semicolon. For example, the following statement could be executed:

```
SELECT * FROM CUSTOMERS;DROP TABLE ORDERS
```

Because you build the command string directly from the UI elements, it is possible for the user to enter a semicolon into a UI element and enter malicious code. To avoid this possibility, simply remove the semicolon from the command string. The resulting command would be an invalid SQL call and would generate an error rather than allow potentially malicious code.

This function then uses a `SqlDataAdapter` to fill a `DataTable` object using the SQL command specified and returns the filled `DataTable`.

BuilderLib. GetNode

The `GetNode` method returns a node from an XML document if it exists, or creates a new node and appends it to the parent node if it doesn't exist. There are two overloaded versions of the `GetNode` method: one that specifies the node value and one that does not.

These functions are called by passing in a member of the `XmlNodeType` enumeration to specify what type of node is being retrieved. The method is only concerned with `Attribute` and `Element` nodes: Other node types, such as `ProcessingInstruction` and `CData` are not used in this sample application.

Listing 12.1 shows the code listing for the `BuilderLib` component.

CreateForm.aspx

The first `.aspx` page that we will walk through is `CreateForm.aspx`. This page should be set as the start page for the application by right-clicking the `.aspx` page in Visual Studio .NET and selecting Set as Start Page.

This page presents a UI that interrogates the user for database connectivity information. We do this through a very simple-looking UI. Figure 12.1 shows the first screen that captures connectivity information.

The information from this screen is stored in an `XmlDocument` object in memory in the `Session` object. Because this is not likely a high-volume application, this is a great use of the `Session` object to enable persistence of stateful data.

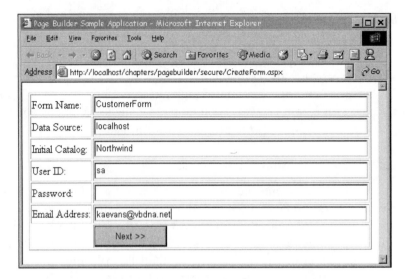

Figure 12.1   The first screen of the application
captures database connectivity information.

The form contains several text box controls and an `asp:Button` control. The button has its `OnClick` attribute set to the function that will fire when the button is clicked. You will use the `Button1_Click` custom method.

After the `Button1_Click` method is called, the connection string is formed by using elements from the UI. A `StringBuilder` object forms the string based on the values in the UI, and the connection string is tested against the database.

If the database connection cannot be made, the error is displayed in the HTML `div` server control. If the connection can be made, the form name and connection string are stored in an XML document. The XML document, in turn, is stored in Session state and the page is redirected.

Another point to note is the inclusion of the namespace `pagebuilder`. This namespace is necessary to access the methods in the `PageBuilder.cs` file, shown in Listing 12.1.

Listing 12.2 shows the code for the first page, `CreateForm.aspx`.

As you can see, the code so far is fairly simple: You are gathering the information needed to generate the code.

ChooseTable.aspx

The next screen of the application is even simpler. Use this screen to determine to which database table that the end user wants to connect. This code leverages the `BuilderLib` component again to retrieve the table names within the specified database. Figure 12.2 shows this simple drop-down listbox.

Figure 12.2 The second screen of the application captures the database table to use.

The code listing for the page shown in Figure 12.2 is fairly simple. When the page is loaded, the XML document created in `ChooseTable.aspx` is retrieved from Session state and the database connection string is retrieved from it. The `sp_tables` system stored procedure in SQL Server is called to retrieve the list of table names in the current catalog. This list of tables is contained in a `DataTable` that's returned from the `BuilderLib` component. The `DropDownList` control is bound to the `DataTable` object using the `TABLE_NAME` column as both the display and value of each item in the drop-down list.

After the button on the UI is clicked, the XML document is retrieved again from Session state and the chosen column is added to the document, after which the page is redirected to the final page, `CreatePage.aspx`.

Listing 12.3 shows the code for `ChooseTable.aspx`.

Template.txt

`Template.txt` is a simple text file that contains a template for an `.aspx` page. The code for `template.txt` is shown in Listing 12.4. Four placeholders are in the template file: `<##DATA_TABLE##>` will be replaced by the database table name, `<##CONNECTION_STRING##>` will be replaced by the database connection string, `<##BOUND_COLUMNS##>` will be replaced by the `asp:BoundColumn` elements that are to be bound to the `DataGrid`, and `<##UPDATE##>` will be replaced by the code that handles updating the database.

The UI it generates consists of a single editable `DataGrid`. The `DataGrid` allows editing of values in a single row by presenting an Edit link for each row. If the Edit link is clicked by the user, the links Update and Cancel are presented to the user. This is handled by using the `OnEditCommand`, `OnCancelCommand`, and `OnUpdateCommand` events of the `DataGrid`.

If Edit is clicked, the grid's `EditItemIndex` is set to the index of the clicked row. This causes the Update and Cancel links to appear. (This is a behavior of the `DataGrid`—no additional code is needed to display these.) Textboxes also appear in the editable columns for the `DataGrid`.

If Cancel is clicked for a row being edited, the `EditItemIndex` is set back to −1 and the grid is rebound. Because the `EditItemIndex` is −1, all rows show only the Edit link in the edit command column. The Update and Cancel links are hidden, as well as the `Textbox` controls that were shown when Edit was first clicked. Again, this is a behavior of the `DataGrid`; no additional code is necessary.

If Update is clicked, the code in the `resultGrid_Update` event handler is fired. The `DataGridCommandEventArgs` parameter of the Update event handler contains the objects that access the row information for the `DataGrid`. As previously stated, textboxes are displayed for inline editing. To retrieve the user's input from the grid, you must reference the cell and the first control in its `Controls` collection to retrieve the textbox.

Again, the code for `template.txt` is in Listing 12.4.

CreatePage.aspx

Now that you have determined which table will create your generated page, look at how you can achieve generating a dynamic page. So far, you have collected the form name, database connection string, and the database table name that will generate an `.aspx` page. The file `CreatePage.aspx` generates the file and delivers it to the end user.

The biggest point to make when looking at the code in Listing 12.5 is that you are writing code that is writing code. In other words, you are writing code that generates code, so the syntax might get confusing.

We will break up the code into manageable sections here with interspersed commentary, and the complete code is also found in Listing 12.5.

The driver function for the entire page is the `Page_Load` event because it controls the program flow:

```
private void Page_Load(object sender, System.EventArgs e)
    {
            FileStream file = new
FileStream(Server.MapPath("template.txt"),
            System.IO.FileMode.Open);
            StreamReader reader = new StreamReader(file);

            string contents = reader.ReadToEnd();
            reader.Close();
            file.Close();
```

In the Page_Load event, open the template file and read the template file's contents into a string. This string is used to build your generated page, and the template file is left untouched by your application.

```
XmlDocument doc = (XmlDocument)Session["doc"];
XmlElement root = doc.DocumentElement;
string tableName = root.Attributes["tableName"].Value;
string connectionString =
➥root.Attributes["connectionString"].Value;
string emailAddress = root.Attributes["emailAddress"].Value;
```

The next step in the Page_Load event: Retrieve the XML document from Session state and retrieve the settings from it:

```
//Replace the DATA_TABLE marker with the name of the database
//table
contents = contents.Replace("<##DATA_TABLE##>",
    ➥tableName);
//Replace the CONNECTION_STRING marker with the
//    database connection string
contents = contents.Replace("<##CONNECTION_STRING##>",
    ➥connectionString);
//Replace the UPDATE marker with the string returned
//    from the GetUpdate function.
contents = contents.Replace("<##UPDATE##>",
    ➥GetUpdate(root));
contents = contents.Replace("<##BOUND_COLUMNS##>",
    ➥GetBoundColumns(tableName,connectionString));
```

After you retrieve information from the XML document in Session state, generate the .aspx page based on the user's input. The template file's contents are replaced with the user's input and other generated code. The largest replacement occurs in the GetUpdate function, highlighted in this code snippet:

```
System.Web.Mail.MailMessage msg = new
➥System.Web.Mail.MailMessage();
msg.Subject="PageBuilder Generated Code";
msg.To = emailAddress;
msg.From = "pagebuilder@vbdna.net";
msg.Body = contents;
System.Web.Mail.SmtpMail.Send(msg);


}
```

After the .aspx web form is generated, the contents are mailed to the user at the specified email address. Figure 12.3 shows a sample email where the body of the email is the C# code for the web form.

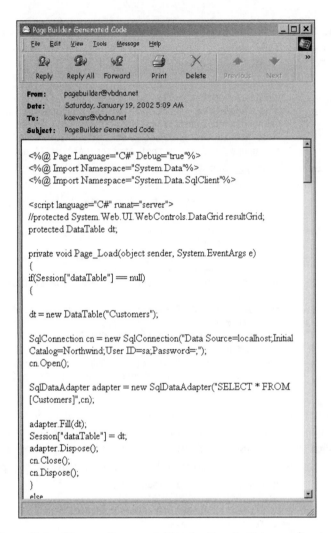

Figure 12.3   The email generated by the `PageBuilder` application.

Retrieving from Disconnected Workstations

If you are working on a workstation, you might have difficulty retrieving the generated code because your machine might not have SMTP services running. Start the default SMTP site in the Internet Services Manager MMC snap-in and start the default mail SMTP virtual server. Then go to your mailroot directory (mine is at `c:\inetpub\mailroot`) and look for your message in the `pickup` directory. If you see a message with a `.eml` extension, you can view it using Outlook Express to retrieve the generated code.

The GetUpdate function is the largest function: It contains the code that generates the UpdateCommand for the updated rows in the DataSet. Although the code is fairly lengthy, it is actually simple. The modified data is retrieved from the user interface as textboxes within the DataGrid. Code is then generated to create SqlParameter objects for use in the generated SQL statements.

It can be added to any C# web application. Just add a new web form to a C# web application and replace the code in the .cs file with the generated code received by email. Run the application, and the output will be similar to what's shown in Figure 12.4.

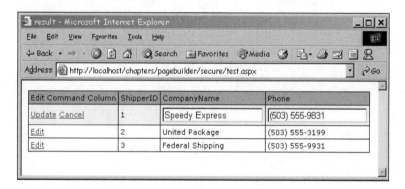

Figure 12.4 Running the generated code displays an editable DataGrid. An example is depicted of using the Shippers table in the Northwind database.

Code Listings

Listing 12.1 contains all code necessary for BuilderLib.cs.

Listing 12.1 *BuilderLib.cs*
```
using System;
using System.Data;
using System.Data.SqlClient;
using System.Configuration;
using System.Xml;

namespace pagebuilder
{

    public class BuilderLib
    {
```

continues

Listing 12.1 **Continued**

```
public static System.Data.DataTable GetDataTable(string
➥commandText, string connectionString)
{

    //Retrieve a DataTable object based on the command string
    ➥passed
    SqlConnection cn = new SqlConnection(connectionString);

    SqlDataAdapter adapter = new SqlDataAdapter();
    //Remove semicolons to avoid possibility of multiple commands
    commandText = commandText.Replace(";", "");

    adapter.SelectCommand = new SqlCommand(commandText, cn);
    adapter.SelectCommand.CommandType = CommandType.Text;

    DataTable dt = new DataTable();
    adapter.Fill(dt);

    adapter.Dispose();
    cn.Close();
    cn.Dispose();

    return (dt);
}


public static System.Xml.XmlNode GetNode(XmlNodeType nodeType,
        string nodeName, XmlNode parentNode)
{
    XmlNode node = null;
    switch(nodeType)
    {
        case XmlNodeType.Element:
            node = parentNode.SelectSingleNode(nodeName);
            if(node==null)
            {
                node = parentNode.OwnerDocument.CreateElement
                ➥(nodeName);
                parentNode.AppendChild(node);
            }
            break;
        case XmlNodeType.Attribute:
            node = parentNode.Attributes[nodeName];
            if(node==null)
            {
                node = parentNode.OwnerDocument.CreateAttribute
                ➥(nodeName);
                parentNode.Attributes.SetNamedItem(node);
```

```
                    }
                    break;
            }
            return(node);
    }


    public static System.Xml.XmlNode GetNode(XmlNodeType nodeType,
            string nodeName, XmlNode parentNode, string nodeValue)
    {
        XmlAttribute newAttrib = null;
        XmlElement newElem = null;
        XmlNode returnNode = null;
        XmlDocument parentDoc = parentNode.OwnerDocument;
        switch(nodeType)
        {
            case XmlNodeType.Element:
                //SelectSingleNode returns an XmlNode:  the XmlNode
                //must be cast as an XmlElement.
                newElem = (XmlElement)parentNode.SelectSingleNode
                ➥(nodeName);
                if(newElem==null)
                {
                    newElem = parentDoc.CreateElement(nodeName);
                }
                //remove any existing child nodes
                //of the current element
                newElem.RemoveAll();
                XmlText textNode = parentDoc.CreateTextNode
                ➥(nodeValue);
                textNode.Value = nodeValue;
                newElem.AppendChild(textNode);
                returnNode = newElem;
                break;
            case XmlNodeType.Attribute:
                //SelectSingleNode returns an XmlNode:  the XmlNode
                //must be cast as an XmlElement.
                newAttrib = parentDoc.CreateAttribute(nodeName);
                newAttrib.Value = nodeValue;
                returnNode = parentNode.Attributes.Set
                ➥NamedItem(newAttrib);
                break;
        }
        return(returnNode);
    }
    }
}
```

Listing 12.2 contains all the code necessary for the CreateForm.aspx web form. This page is set as the startup page in the web application.

Listing 12.2 *CreateForm.aspx*

```
<%@ Import Namespace="pagebuilder"%>
<%@ Import Namespace="System.Xml"%>
<%@ Import Namespace="System.Data.SqlClient"%>
<%@ Import Namespace="System.Data"%>
<HTML>
    <HEAD>
        <title>Page Builder Sample Application</title>
        <script language="C#" runat="server">
private void Button1_Click(object sender, System.EventArgs e)
{

    System.Text.StringBuilder sb = new System.Text.StringBuilder();
    sb.Append ("Data Source=" + dataSource.Text + ";");
    sb.Append ("Initial Catalog=" + dataBase.Text + ";");
    sb.Append ("User ID=" + userID.Text + ";");
    sb.Append ("Password=" + password.Text + ";");

    //Try to connect to the user's database
    SqlConnection cn = new SqlConnection(sb.ToString());

    Boolean hasError = false;
    try
    {
        cn.Open();
    }
    catch(System.Exception errOops)
    {
        messageUtility.InnerText = "Connection error:<br>" +
                ➥Server.HtmlEncode(errOops.ToString());
        hasError = true;
    }
    finally
    {
        if (!hasError) cn.Close();
        cn.Dispose();
    }
    if (!hasError)
    {
        //The database connection is valid.
        //Save the settings from the form.
        XmlDocument doc = new XmlDocument();
        XmlElement root = (XmlElement)doc.AppendChild(doc.CreateElement
        ➥("root"));

        BuilderLib.GetNode(System.Xml.XmlNodeType.Attribute,
            "formName",
            root,
            formName.Text);
```

```
        BuilderLib.GetNode(System.Xml.XmlNodeType.Attribute,
            "emailAddress",
            root,
            email.Text);
        BuilderLib.GetNode(System.Xml.XmlNodeType.Attribute,
            "connectionString",
            root,
            sb.ToString());

        Session["doc"] = doc;

        Response.Redirect("ChooseTable.aspx");
    }
}

    </script>
</HEAD>
<body>
    <form id="Form1" method="post" runat="server">
        <span id="messageUtility" runat="server" class="errorClass">
            <table border="1">
                <tr>
                    <td>Form Name:</td>
                    <td>
                        <asp:TextBox
                            id="formName"
                            runat="server"
                            Width="421px"
                            Height="25px">
                        </asp:TextBox>
                    </td>
                </tr>
                <tr>
                    <td>Data Source:</td>
                    <td>
                        <asp:TextBox
                            id="dataSource"
                            runat="server"
                            Width="421px"
                            Height="25px">localhost
                        </asp:TextBox>
                    </td>
                </tr>
                <tr>
                    <td>Initial Catalog:</td>
                    <td>
                        <asp:TextBox
                            id="dataBase"
                            runat="server"
                            Width="421px"
                            Height="25px">Northwind
                        </asp:TextBox>
```

continues

Listing 12.2 **Continued**

```
                        </td>
                    </tr>
                    <tr>
                        <td>User ID:</td>
                        <td>
                            <asp:TextBox
                                id="userID"
                                runat="server"
                                Width="421px"
                                Height="25px">sa
                            </asp:TextBox>
                        </td>
                    </tr>
                    <tr>
                        <td>Password:</td>
                        <td>
                            <asp:TextBox
                                id="password"
                                runat="server"
                                Width="421px"
                                Height="25px">
                            </asp:TextBox>
                        </td>
                    </tr>
                    <TR>
                        <TD>Email Address:</TD>
                        <TD>
                            <asp:TextBox
                                id="email"
                                runat="server"
                                Width="419px">
                            </asp:TextBox>
                        </TD>
                    </TR>
                    <tr>
                        <td></td>
                        <td>
                            <asp:Button
                                id="Button1"
                                runat="server"
                                Width="112px"
                                Height="31px"
                                Text="Next >>" OnClick="Button1_Click">
                            </asp:Button>
                        </td>
                    </tr>
                    </table>
            </form>
            </SPAN>
        </body>
    </HTML>
```

Listing 12.3 contains all code necessary for the ChooseTable.aspx web form.

Listing 12.3 *ChooseTable.aspx*

```
<%@ Import Namespace="System.Data"%>
<%@ Import Namespace="System.Data.SqlClient"%>
<%@ Import Namespace="System.Xml"%>
<%@ Import Namespace="pagebuilder"%>

<script language="C#" runat="server" >
    private void Page_Load(object sender, System.EventArgs e)
    {
        if(!IsPostBack)
        {

            XmlDocument doc = (XmlDocument)Session["doc"];
            XmlElement root = doc.DocumentElement;
            string connection = root.Attributes["connectionString"].Value;
            DataView dv = GetTableNames(connection);
            DropDownList1.DataSource = dv;
            DropDownList1.DataTextField = "TABLE_NAME";
            DropDownList1.DataValueField = "TABLE_NAME";
            DropDownList1.DataBind();
        }
    }

    private System.Data.DataView GetTableNames(string connectionString)
    {
        DataTable table = BuilderLib.GetDataTable("sp_tables",
                connectionString);
        DataView dv = new DataView(table);
        dv.RowFilter = "TABLE_TYPE IN ('TABLE','VIEW')";

        return(dv);
    }

    private void Button1_Click(object sender, System.EventArgs e)
    {
        //Get the values from the page
        XmlDocument doc = (XmlDocument)Session["doc"];
        XmlNode node = doc.DocumentElement;

        BuilderLib.GetNode(System.Xml.XmlNodeType.Attribute,
            "tableName",
            node,
            this.DropDownList1.SelectedItem.Value);

        Session["doc"] = doc;

        Response.Redirect("CreatePage.aspx");
    }
```

continues

Listing 12.3 **Continued**

```
</script>
<HTML>
    <HEAD>
        <title>Page Builder Sample Application - Choose Table</title>
        <LINK rel="stylesheet" type="text/css" href="PageBuilder.css">
    </HEAD>
    <body >
        <form id="Form1" method="post" runat="server">
            <table border="1">
                <tr>
                    <td>Table Source:</td>
                    <td>
                        <asp:DropDownList id="DropDownList1"
                            runat="server"
                            Width="198px"
                            Height="26px"/>
                    </td>
                </tr>
                <tr>
                    <td></td>
                    <td>
                        <asp:Button id="Button1"
                            runat="server"
                            Width="112px"
                            Height="31px"
                            Text="Next >>"
                            OnClick="Button1_Click"/>
                    </td>
                </tr>
            </table>
        </form>
    </body>
</HTML>
```

The file `Template.txt` as shown in Listing 12.4 contains the template code that's used to generate `.aspx` files. It contains the UI code to bind a `DataGrid` to a `DataTable`, as well as code to populate the `DataTable` object. It also contains placeholders that are replaced by code in `CreatePage.aspx`. This file is considered read-only: It's not generated or modified by the code.

Listing 12.4 *Template.txt*

```
<%@ Page Language="C#" Debug="true"%>
<%@ Import Namespace="System.Data"%>
<%@ Import Namespace="System.Data.SqlClient"%>

<script language="C#" runat="server">
        //protected System.Web.UI.WebControls.DataGrid resultGrid;
        protected DataTable dt;
```

```csharp
private void Page_Load(object sender, System.EventArgs e)
{
    if(Session["dataTable"] == null)
    {

        dt = new DataTable("<##DATA_TABLE##>");

        SqlConnection cn = new SqlConnection
        ("<##CONNECTION_STRING##>");
        cn.Open();

        SqlDataAdapter adapter = new SqlDataAdapter("SELECT *
        FROM [<##DATA_TABLE##>]",cn);

        adapter.Fill(dt);
        Session["dataTable"] = dt;
        adapter.Dispose();
        cn.Close();
        cn.Dispose();
    }
    else
    {
        dt = (DataTable)Session["dataTable"];
    }

    if(!IsPostBack)
    {
        BindResultGrid();
    }
}


protected void resultGrid_Edit(Object sender, DataGridCommand
EventArgs e)
{
    resultGrid.EditItemIndex = e.Item.ItemIndex;
    BindResultGrid();
}

protected void resultGrid_Cancel(Object sender, DataGridCommand
EventArgs e)
{
    resultGrid.EditItemIndex = -1;
    BindResultGrid();
}

protected void resultGrid_Update(Object sender, DataGridCommand
EventArgs e)
{
    // For bound columns, the edited value is stored in a TextBox.
    // The TextBox is the 0th element in the column's cell.
```

continues

Listing 12.4 **Continued**

```
                            //If read-only, then simply retrieve from position.
                            //Need to know the column name here
<##UPDATE##>

                            adapter.UpdateCommand = cm;
                            adapter.Update(dt);

                            resultGrid.EditItemIndex = -1;
                            BindResultGrid();
                        }

                        protected void BindResultGrid()
                        {
                            resultGrid.DataSource = dt;
                            resultGrid.DataBind();
                        }
        </script>

        <HTML>
            <HEAD>
                <title>result</title>
            </HEAD>
            <body>
                <form id="result" method="post" runat="server">
                    <asp:DataGrid id="resultGrid" runat="server"
                            BorderColor="black" BorderWidth="1" CellPadding="3"
                            Font-Name="Verdana" Font-Size="8pt"
                            OnEditCommand="resultGrid_Edit"
                            OnCancelCommand="resultGrid_Cancel"
                            OnUpdateCommand="resultGrid_Update"
                            AutoGenerateColumns="false">
                        <HeaderStyle BackColor="#aaaadd"></HeaderStyle>
                        <EditItemStyle BackColor="yellow"></EditItemStyle>
                        <Columns>
                            <asp:EditCommandColumn EditText="Edit"
                                    CancelText="Cancel" UpdateText="Update"
                                    HeaderText="Edit Command Column">
                                <ItemStyle Wrap="false"></ItemStyle>
                                <HeaderStyle Wrap="false"></HeaderStyle>
                            </asp:EditCommandColumn>

<##BOUND_COLUMNS##>
                        </Columns>
                    </asp:DataGrid>
                </form>
            </body>
        </HTML>
```

Listing 12.5 contains the code for `CreatePage.aspx.cs`.

Listing 12.5   *CreatePage.aspx.cs*

```
using System;
using System.Collections;
using System.ComponentModel;
using System.Data;
using System.Drawing;
using System.Web;
using System.Web.SessionState;
using System.Web.UI;
using System.Web.UI.WebControls;
using System.Web.UI.HtmlControls;
using System.Xml;
using System.Xml.Xsl;
using System.Xml.XPath;
using System.Text;
using System.IO;
namespace pagebuilder.secure
{
    /// <summary>
    /// Summary description for createpage.
    /// </summary>
    public class createpage : System.Web.UI.Page
    {

        private void Page_Load(object sender, System.EventArgs e)
        {
            FileStream file = new FileStream(Server.MapPath
            ➥("template.txt"),
                System.IO.FileMode.Open);
            StreamReader reader = new StreamReader(file);

            string contents = reader.ReadToEnd();
            reader.Close();
            file.Close();

            XmlDocument doc = (XmlDocument)Session["doc"];
            XmlElement root = doc.DocumentElement;
            string tableName = root.Attributes["tableName"].Value;
            string connectionString = root.Attributes["connectionString"]
            ➥.Value;
            string emailAddress = root.Attributes["emailAddress"].Value;
            //Replace the DATA_TABLE marker with the name
            //of the datbase table
            contents = contents.Replace("<##DATA_TABLE##>",
                tableName);
            //Replace the CONNECTION_STRING marker with the
            //     database connection string
            contents = contents.Replace("<##CONNECTION_STRING##>",
                connectionString);
            //Replace the UPDATE marker with the string returned
            //     from the GetUpdate function.
```

continues

Listing 12.5   **Continued**

```
        contents = contents.Replace("<##UPDATE##>",
            GetUpdate(root));
        contents = contents.Replace("<##BOUND_COLUMNS##>",
            GetBoundColumns(tableName,connectionString));

        System.Web.Mail.MailMessage msg = new System.Web.Mail.
        ➥MailMessage();
        msg.Subject="PageBuilder Generated Code";
        msg.To = emailAddress;
        msg.From = "pagebuilder@xmlandasp.net";
        msg.Body = contents;
        System.Web.Mail.SmtpMail.Send(msg);


        Response.Write("<html><head></head><body>");
        Response.Write("The file has been sent to the email address
        ➥specified.");
        Response.Write("</body></html>");
    }
    private string GetUpdate(XmlElement root)
    {
        string tableName = root.Attributes["tableName"].Value;
        string connectionString = root.Attributes["connectionString"].
        ➥Value;

        DataTable dt = BuilderLib.GetDataTableSchema(tableName,
        ➥connectionString);

        MemoryStream memstream = new MemoryStream();
        StreamWriter writer = new StreamWriter(memstream,System.Text.
        ➥Encoding.Unicode);

        writer.WriteLine("TextBox tempBox;");

        foreach(DataColumn col in dt.Columns)
        {
            int cellNum = col.Ordinal +1;
            if(col.ReadOnly )
            {
                //Read-only columns do not have a corresponding
                ➥textbox

                writer.WriteLine("String " + col.ColumnName + "Val =
                ➥e.Item.Cells[" + cellNum.ToString() + "].Text;");
            }
            else
            {
                //Retrieve the value from the user's input for the
                ➥textbox
                writer.WriteLine("tempBox = (TextBox)e.Item.Cells["
                ➥+ cellNum  +"].Controls[0];");
```

```
            writer.WriteLine("String " + col.ColumnName + "Val =
            ➥tempBox.Text;");
    }


    }

    //Create a view over the DataTable.
    writer.WriteLine("DataView dv = new DataView(dt);");
    writer.WriteLine("dv.RowStateFilter =
    ➥System.Data.DataViewRowState.CurrentRows;");

    //Write out the code to filter based on primary key(s)
    writer.Write("dv.RowFilter = \"");
    WritePKFilter(writer,dt.PrimaryKey);
    writer.WriteLine("\";");

    //Write out the code to update the column value
    foreach(DataColumn col in dt.Columns)
    {
        if(!col.ReadOnly)
        {
            writer.WriteLine("dv[0][\"" + col.ColumnName + "\"]
            ➥= " + col.ColumnName + "Val;");
        }
    }
    writer.WriteLine();
    writer.Write("SqlConnection cn = new SqlConnection(\"");
    writer.Write(root.Attributes["connectionString"].Value);
    writer.WriteLine("\");");
    writer.WriteLine("cn.Open();");
    writer.WriteLine();

    writer.WriteLine("SqlDataAdapter adapter = new
    ➥SqlDataAdapter();");
    writer.WriteLine();
    writer.WriteLine("SqlCommand cm;");
    writer.WriteLine();

    writer.Write("cm = new SqlCommand(\"SELECT ");

    int intLength = dt.Columns.Count -1;
    for (int i=0;i<=intLength;i++)
    {
        writer.Write(dt.Columns[i].ColumnName);
        //Separate column names with commas
        if(i<intLength)
        {
            writer.Write(", ");
        }
    }
    writer.WriteLine(" FROM " + tableName + "\",cn);");
    writer.WriteLine("adapter.SelectCommand =cm;");
```

continues

Listing 12.5 **Continued**

```
writer.WriteLine("SqlParameter parm;");
writer.WriteLine();
writer.Write("cm = new SqlCommand(\"UPDATE " + tableName + "
➥SET ");
intLength = dt.Columns.Count - 1;
foreach(DataColumn col in dt.Columns)
{
    writer.Write(col.ColumnName + "=@" + col.ColumnName );
    if ( col.Ordinal < intLength)
    {
        writer.Write(", ");
    }
}
writer.Write(" WHERE ");

intLength = dt.PrimaryKey.Length;
for(int i=0;i < intLength;i++)
{
    writer.Write(dt.PrimaryKey[i].ColumnName + "@" +
    ➥dt.PrimaryKey[i].ColumnName);
    if (i<intLength - 1)
        writer.Write(", ");

}
writer.WriteLine("\",cn);");
writer.WriteLine();

foreach(DataColumn col in dt.Columns)
{
    WriteParameter(writer,col.ColumnName);
}
writer.WriteLine();
writer.WriteLine("adapter.SelectCommand = cm;");
writer.WriteLine();

writer.Write("cm = new SqlCommand(\"UPDATE " + tableName + "
➥SET ");
intLength = dt.Columns.Count -1;
foreach(DataColumn col in dt.Columns)
{
    writer.Write(col.ColumnName + " = @" + col.ColumnName );
    if ( col.Ordinal < intLength)
    {
        writer.Write(", ");
    }
}
writer.Write(" WHERE ");

intLength = dt.PrimaryKey.Length;
for(int i=0;i < intLength;i++)
{
```

```
              writer.Write(dt.PrimaryKey[i].ColumnName + " = @" +
              ↪if (i < intLength - 1)
                 writer.Write(", ");

      }
      writer.WriteLine("\",cn);");
      writer.WriteLine();

      foreach(DataColumn col in dt.Columns)
      {
          WriteParameter(writer,col.ColumnName);
      }
      writer.WriteLine();
      writer.WriteLine("adapter.UpdateCommand = cm;");
      writer.WriteLine();


      writer.Flush();
      memstream.Position = 0;

      System.IO.StreamReader reader = new StreamReader
      ↪(memstream,System.Text.Encoding.Unicode);
      string results = reader.ReadToEnd();
      reader.Close();
      writer.Close();
      memstream.Close();

      return(results);
 }

 private string GetBoundColumns(string tableName,string
 ↪connectionString)
 {
     DataTable dt = BuilderLib.GetDataTableSchema
     ↪(tableName,connectionString);

     StringBuilder sb = new StringBuilder();

     foreach(DataColumn col in dt.Columns)
     {
         sb.Append ("<asp:BoundColumn HeaderText=\"");
         sb.Append(col.ColumnName + "\" ");
         sb.Append("DataField=\"" + col.ColumnName + "\" ");
         if(col.ReadOnly)
         {
             sb.Append("ReadOnly=\"true\"");
         }
         sb.Append(" />");
     }
     return(sb.ToString());
 }
```

continues

Listing 12.5   *Continued*

```
private void WritePKFilter(StreamWriter writer,DataColumn [] pk)
{
    //Write out the primary keys and their values,
    //used to filteron.    For instance
    //     CustomerID='ALFKI'
    //Because we are writing this as dynamic code,
    //the dynamic code will look like:
    //     dv.RowFilter="[CustomerID]='" + CustomerIDVal + "'"
    string [] filterConditions = new string[pk.Length] ;
    for(int i=0;i<= pk.Length -1;i++)
    {
        filterConditions[i] = "[" + pk[i].ColumnName + "] ='\" +
        ➥" + pk[i].ColumnName + "Val + \"'";
    }
    //Separate each filter condition with an AND clause
    writer.Write(string.Join(" AND ",filterConditions));
}

private void WriteParameter(StreamWriter writer,string columnName)
{
    System.Data.SqlClient.SqlParameter parm = new
    ➥System.Data.SqlClient.SqlParameter();

    writer.WriteLine("parm = new SqlParameter();");
    writer.WriteLine("parm.ParameterName=\"@" + columnName +
    ➥"\";");
    writer.WriteLine("parm.SourceColumn = \"" + columnName +
    ➥"\";");
    writer.WriteLine("cm.Parameters.Add(parm);");

}
#region Web Form Designer generated code
override protected void OnInit(EventArgs e)
{
    //
    InitializeComponent();
    base.OnInit(e);
}

/// <summary>
/// Required method for Designer support - do not modify
/// the contents of this method with the code editor.
/// </summary>
private void InitializeComponent()
{
    this.Load += new System.EventHandler(this.Page_Load);
}
#endregion
    }
}
```

Chapter Summary

This chapter looked at using the DOM as a storage mechanism behind the scenes. You saw how to retrieve information from the DOM, create nodes on the DOM, and how to update information.

This application made extensive use of ADO.NET, using various techniques to access columns within a `DataTable`. You saw how to determine the schema for a table quickly, and saw how you can build robust applications by using ADO.NET.

The generated code might not be what you are looking for in a production application. For example, it lacks the capability to add or delete rows. But, this sample gives you a great head start toward understanding code blowers and dynamic page generators. It also uses a bit of XML and ASP.NET behind the scenes, serving as a great tutorial application.

13

Sample Application: Mobile Device Programming with WAP, WML, and XHTML Basic

IN THIS CHAPTER, YOU ARE INTRODUCED TO mobile device development. You learn about the Wireless Application Protocol (WAP) and the Wireless Markup Language (WML), which is the most common development protocol and language used for mobile devices (at the time of writing). You are also introduced to a newer and more flexible way to develop mobile-device applications using XHTML Basic.

XHTML Basic is a cut-down version of XHTML. It's been specifically designed for use with mobile devices, such as mobile phones and PDAs.

After these two technologies are introduced and explained, you then look at a simple mobile-device application that uses some of the XML and XSL techniques that are shown throughout this book.

This sample application uses XML as a data source and multiple .xslt files for rendering either XHTML or WML content to mobile devices.

In this chapter, you learn the following:

- The history of WAP
- What WML is
- XHTML Basic

You also practice using these tools by doing work with a sample application.

The History of WAP

A little-known company called Unwired Planet created one of the first mass-market microbrowser and a markup language called *Handheld Device Markup Language (HDML)*. HDML met with limited success and was used by a few individual vendors in the U.S. Upon seeing that an interested market existed for this language, Unwired Planet established an open standard so that the company could make HDML the "next big thing" in mobile information access.

To do this, Unwired Planet talked to some of the major players in the mobile device world (at the time, mobile devices were essentially mobile phones—PDAs had not come onto the scene yet). Ericsson, Nokia, and Motorola were approached and introduced to the idea of an open and unified standard.

This standard was *Wireless Access Protocol (WAP)*. Almost immediately, a managing group for the standard was formed, called the *WAP Forum*. Because of WAP Forum's efforts, WAP has become the dominant medium for wireless application development.

You might be wondering what happened to HDML. It hasn't disappeared entirely; however, WAP has all but replaced it. WAP received more press coverage than HDML and it is the standard for handheld and mobile device development.

After the success of WAP and its predecessor HDML, Unwired Planet changed its name to Phone.com, the company behind the popular range of UP browsers and servers to most of the WAP vendors in the U.S.

What Exactly Is WAP?

WAP is simply a protocol that's used to access information and services through wireless devices, such as mobile phones and PDAs.

WAP is defined, coordinated, and developed by the WAP Forum. WAP Forum members have a vested interest in extending the kind of information and services that you have become used to accessing over the Internet to users of mobile devices. As previously mentioned, Phone.com, Ericsson, Nokia, and Motorola were the first members of the WAP Forum. Now the forum's members include most of the leading corporations in the industry, both in the IT and communications sectors. This includes all the major handset manufacturers, network operators, and software companies.

The objective of the WAP Forum was to define a standard application framework that is universal in nature. This allows for the interoperability of all the components required for a mobile device to access mobile network applications.

From the start, the WAP Forum aimed to define a standard that leverages existing Internet technologies wherever possible, and that also interoperates with third-party Internet technologies.

Do We Really Need Another Protocol?

The IT industry is plagued by protocols. It seems that almost every year, dozens of new technologies and protocols are defined. It can be a challenging task to keep up with all of them. So, why do we need another protocol?

The answer is not that technical. There's no big thesis on why we need WAP except for the fact that most Internet and network protocols are for PCs in general or larger capacity systems, not the lightweight processor and display area that challenge mobile devices.

Most of the protocols make many assumptions about the environment in which they operate. These assumptions include the type of network the protocol runs on, normally from the viewpoint of bandwidth and reliability, as well as the devices that will access the services offered by the protocols.

The following list outlines some of the requirements a PC needs when using the HTTP protocol:

- Constant bandwidth capability; speeds commonly in excess of 100kbps
- High reliability of data transfer
- A constant connection to work

Compare those requirements with the requirements of a mobile phone using WAP:

- Restricted bandwidth; in a many cases, no more 1.5k.
- High reliability when connected.
- Devices can rarely stay connected for long due to their method of data transfer. (For example, everyone's been cut off when using a mobile phone and everyone's had bad reception from time to time. You can imagine what that can do to sent data.)

As you can see, mobile devices have extra issues to deal with that a PC does not. This is a great segue into the key differences between PC applications and mobile-device applications. After all, it's what this chapter is about.

Mobile Device Development Issues

When developing mobile-device applications you must take the following into account:

- **Screen size**—A mobile device needs to be small enough to be easily transported and, ideally, it should fit in the palm of your hand or in your shirt pocket. For this reason, the available screen size is much smaller than a PC's screen size.

- **Physical display**—A mobile device's display is rarely in color and its size and ability are limited.

- **Data input**—Mobile devices typically do not have keyboards. If they do, the keyboards are limited in size and practicality. Therefore, data entry is more challenging for the user than it is for a PC-based system.

- **CPU**—In a mobile device, the CPU is not nearly as powerful as a PC's CPU, and it is almost certainly of a different architecture.

- **Memory**—Mobile devices tend to have a small storage capacity compared to PC-based systems. This is due to handset and PDA manufacturers being overly cost-sensitive because of the competition in the market place and their subsequent reluctance to add any additional components unless it's absolutely necessary. Note that some mobile devices do not have a persistent storage of their own (certain mobile phones fall under this category).

- **Battery**—Mobile devices are almost always battery powered. The need to have devices available for long periods of time between charges generally means that the CPU's processing cannot make significant demands on the battery.

- **Reliability**—A wireless network is different than a fixed-wire network. The bandwidth of the network is much smaller.

The reliability of a connection can vary considerably, especially when users move in and out of wireless network coverage areas, such as tunnels, certain buildings, and so on.

Other additional factors are latency and the large number of mobile network standards used around the world. These standards do not interoperate well. Some countries even have incompatible standards in different regions.

It is important to realize that, for wireless applications, the market is different. Applications that are suitable for use on mobile devices are different than those that are popular on fixed-wire environments.

For example, users of mobile applications are likely to be a broader selection of the population than PC users. Even the context in which applications are used is different. This highlights the most important part of mobile-device application development: making the application easy to use.

So What Does WAP Do to Help?

WAP was designed specifically to address all the issues mentioned in the previous section. The WAP standard defines a *Wireless Application Environment (WAE)*, which has been designed to maximize the developmental potential of mobile devices.

The WAE specification includes a microbrowser (a markup language browser). A microbrowser defines less control than most PC-based browsers in relation to specifying how a User Interface (UI) element is rendered. Instead, it concentrates on the functionality that's available.

Some directions can be given to the microbrowser, but it is the microbrowser itself that selects the onscreen representation of the UI element on the devices display area.

WAP defines a limited Virtual Machine (VM) for a simple scripting language to execute in, which is designed to operate in the limited environment of mobile devices.

The network issues are addressed through an optimized protocol stack, which was designed to take bandwidth limitations into account. It was decided to maintain compatibility with existing standards wherever possible. This is why WAP operates over standard Internet Protocol (IP) networks and uses the User Datagram Protocol (UDP) over IP whenever possible. (WAP is also capable of operating over non-IP networks.)

To help address the issue of restricted bandwidth, the content that's transmitted through WAP is encoded and compressed to reduce overall data volume. Most devices can only receive a small amount of data at a time; after compression, the actual amount of data varies depending on the device being used.

As previously mentioned, a microbrowser has its own scripting language; the standard language developed by the WAP Forum is *Wireless Markup Language (WML)*. WML is adapted to the constraints of mobile devices and wireless networks.

HTML is oriented towards the visual aspects of document rendering: what the specific UI elements should be and what they should look like.

This is good news for devices that are capable of complex rendering and have the ability to enable the user to interact with elements, such as push buttons and framesets. It's not appropriate for most mobile devices (mobile phones are a prime example).

Because of this, a smaller and more elegant markup language was required that's more appropriate for the wireless environment.

WML and its XML Origins

WML was derived from XML. It contains elements that are more useful to mobile devices than standard HTML elements.

For example, WML defines an <anchor> element, which a microbrowser renders in any way that's equivalent to the HTML <a> element.

Also, a scripting language called WMLScript is derived from the standard, ECMAScript. Again, compatibility has been maintained wherever possible.

How Does WAP Work?

The WAP protocols are similar to the World Wide Web's protocols (IP-based ones). WML is a dialect of XML and it uses the same tag-based format as *Hypertext Markup Language (HTML)*.

Most World Wide Web servers communicate with their clients by using an ASCII-based protocol called the *HyperText Transport Protocol (HTTP)*. HTTP is a simple protocol that consists of field names and field contents separated by carriage returns and line-feed characters.

HTML and HTTP are transported by using the *Transaction Control Protocol/Internet Protocol (TCP/IP)*. TCP/IP guarantees that data sent is either properly delivered or triggers an error condition back to the sender.

Although the WAP protocol is based on and uses Internet standards, it paradoxically is almost incompatible with them. This incompatibility means that WAP-enabled devices cannot directly communicate with WWW servers.

To do this, the WAP protocols must first be translated from their initial format to those of the protocols used by the WWW. This is why every WAP device needs access to a WAP gateway in order to request WML pages (or *decks* as they are referred to in WML) on a web server.

The WAP gateway's purpose is to translate the WAP binary-based protocol into one that's compatible with the HTTP text-based protocol.

The actual WAP protocol is a hierarchical set of layers, some of which are optional. The lowest layer is the WAP Datagram Protocol (WDP). It moves WAP data from the client to the server and back again.

WDP is based on the *User Datagram Protocol (UDP)*. Unlike TCP/IP, UDP makes no guarantees about the delivery of data. It is known as a best-effort delivery service. This means that some data can be lost or corrupted during its transportation. UDP is generally used on the Internet for data that's not affected too much if a few pieces are missing, such as audio and video streams.

UDP was chosen as the basis for the WAP transport (WDP) because of its compactness and simplicity. Like UDP, WDP is just as unreliable.

The next protocol layer is the *WAP Transaction Protocol (WTP)*. WTP was designed to replace the pieces UDP lacks compared to its bigger brother, TCP/IP. WTP is responsible for making sure that packets sent through WDP arrive at their destinations. This is done by waiting for an acknowledgement, or ACK, data back from the server. This means that any data that's sent between the client and server must be specifically acknowledged using WTP.

If an acknowledgement is not received for some data within a time window, WTP resends thee data. This happens a certain number of times. If all are unsuccessful, an error is generated. WTP is an optional protocol, however, and isn't present on all WAP gateway servers.

The next layer is the *WAP Session Protocol (WSP)*, which is responsible for two different modes of functionality. The first is the creation of a session between a WAP client and a WAP gateway server. Each session has a unique ID and must be explicitly started, stopped, resumed, or disconnected.

This mode, known as *connected mode WSP*, is always used in conjunction with WTP. A WAP client explicitly creates a session, and each part of data sent to a WAP gateway server is sent and acknowledged through WTP, which guarantees either delivery or an error condition. But, again, WTP is an optional protocol, as is using WSP connected mode.

The second mode of WSP is the same as HTTP session management. WSP's functionality, in this case, is not optional and is present in every WAP gateway server. If WAP is operating with just the WSP protocol, no sessions are created and communication becomes a simple request-response pairing.

What Is WML?

WML is a generalized markup language that's optimized for limited capability devices and networks. WML documents are based on the XML format. It borrowed some functionality and tags from HDML 2.0 and from HTML.

WML is the most popular mobile development technology used at the time of this writing; however, it might soon be exceeded by the XHTML standard in the future.

XHTML is outlined in this section on WML.

A Deck of Cards

WML follows the well-formed rules of XML, where each tag must have a closing tag, and only one root element is allowed.

WML is based on the metaphor of a deck of cards. A .wml document is referred to as a deck of cards, and a specific card is directly related to a specific area of functionality within the deck (normally UI elements, but sometimes this can be pure script).

The basic WML document structure is shown here:

```
<?xml version="1.0"?>
<!DOCTYPE wml PUBLIC "-//WAPFORUM//DTD WML 1.1//EN"
"http://www.wapforum.org/DTD/wml_1.1.xml">
<!--Deck Declaration-->
<wml>
<!--Card Declaration-->
    <card>
<!--Content of card goes here-->
    </card>
</wml>
```

WML focuses on the actual use of an element. By separating the rendering from the actual use allows the rendering and implementation on the device to be based on the abilities of the device being used.

In general, it is best to limit the number of cards to less than five per deck. An example of a .wml file is shown in Listing 13.1

Listing 13.1 **A Simple *.wml* File (*1501.wml*)**

```
<?xml version="1.0"?>
<!DOCTYPE wml PUBLIC "-//PHONE.COM//DTD WML 1.1//EN"
"http://www.phone.com/dtd/wml11.dtd" >
<wml>
    <card id="card1">
        <p>
        Card 1 - Displayed
          <anchor title="Card2">
              <go  href="#card2"/>
              Show Card 2
          </anchor>
          <br/>
        </p>
    </card>
    <card id="card2">
        <p>
        Card 2 - Displayed
        <anchor title="Card2">
              <go  href="#card1"/>
              Show Card 1
          </anchor>
          <br/>
        </p>
    </card>
</wml>
```

In the Listing 13.1, the XML version and namespace information is set up first:

```
<?xml version="1.0"?>
<!DOCTYPE wml PUBLIC "-//PHONE.COM//DTD WML 1.1//EN"
"http://www.phone.com/dtd/wml11.dtd" >
```

After this, Deck is defined, which holds two separate cards.

The next line contains the declaration of the first card. All information between the <card></card> tags apply to that specific card.

Note

The WML code looks similar to a standard XML document.

After declaring the card, you must assign it an ID of card1. To do this, simply display a text label that states the name of the card being displayed. All output on a WML card must be between the <p></p> tags; these tags are required for any output to a mobile device display:

```
<anchor title="Card2">
    <go  href="#card2"/>
    Show Card 2
</anchor>
```

Next, create a simple <anchor> element to act like an <a> tag from HTML. The only major difference between the WML <anchor> and that of HTML is that <anchor> has a title attribute that's used by the mobile device (normally, the text shown at the lower part of a mobile device display) and a sub element, <go>. The <go> element navigates to another URI. For now, note that the href value has a # in front of it, which tells the WML device to find another card with that name in the current deck and to display it.

The second card is the same as the first card, with one difference. It states that you are on the second card and enables you to navigate back to the first card.

WML Areas of Functionality

WML supports various elements that cover the following areas of functionality: presentation, navigation, and data entry.

Presentation

Presentation directions can be included with text and images; however, the microbrowser decides how to render the content.

The tags used for text and image presentation are outlined in Table 13.1.

Table 13.1   **WML Presentation Tags**

Basic WML Text Presentation Elements	Description
`<b></b>`	Adds a bold format
`<big></big>`	Increases font size
` `	Adds a line break
`<em></em>`	Adds emphasis; recommended over `<b>`
`<i></i>`	Adds italics
`<small></small>`	Decreases font size
`<strong></strong>`	Adds strong emphasis
`<u></u>`	Adds an underline
`<p></p>`	Paragraph text; required for text that's to be rendered onscreen
`<img></img>`	Renders an image to the mobile device display area
`<table />`	
`<tr />`	
`<td />`	Renders tables to a mobile device (not recommended)

The WML <p> Element

Of all the elements in Table 13.1, the most important presentation element is
`<p></p>`. This element is required to be around any free text rendering on a
mobile device.

The `<p></p>` element has two attributes:

- **Align**—Sets up the text alignment inside the control. Possible values are
  left, right, and center (left is the default).

- **Mode**—An important attribute for mobile phone development, mode tells
  the mobile device to either wrap text on the display or to disable line
  wrapping on a mobile display. Most mobile devices allow you to scroll
  horizontally when wrapping is disabled. The possible values for this
  attribute are wrap and nowrap (wrap is the default).

The WML Image Element

The `<img />` tag displays an image to the device screen.

Note that although most mobile devices can display images, it is not advised
because images can take up much space on the screen and slow the download
speed of a mobile device page. And you know that is not a good thing.

> **More on the <img /> Element**
>
> If the <img /> element is nested within a <p> element, the image is displayed on its own line; otherwise, the mobile device displays the image as it sees fit (on its own line also, most of the time).

Using Tables for Presentation

Although some mobile devices support the use of tables for presentation purposes, it is not recommended because most mobile devices decide how to render the table, if at all. Therefore, the table looks different on different devices.

If you are developing for only a single mobile device, however, tables can help organize your content. But be aware that if you create a table with more than two columns, you are asking for trouble. Most mobile devices have small screens that have no room for more than two columns.

Tables are also supported through the <table>, <tr>, and <td> elements. The number of columns in the table is specified as an attribute of the <table> element. The <tr> element contains a row of the table, and the <td> element contains a cell within the table; some browsers, however, do not support tables.

Navigation with WML

Generally, anchors link items to other cards in the form of menus or commands.

A URL references the first card in a deck, although other cards within the deck can be referenced by using *fragment anchors*.

For example, here's how to navigate to a new deck of cards by using <anchor>:

```
<anchor>
    <go href="card2.wml"/>
    Next
</anchor>
```

The <go> element navigates to a specified URI that is required and then pushes the current URI onto the history stack.

You can also specify the HTTP Post or Get method used to send variables that are to be transmitted to the server as part of the URI request.

Here's the same example, the <a> element is used instead:

```
<a href="card2.wml">Next</a>j
```

Here's how you can navigate to a card within the current deck by using the <anchor> element:

```
<anchor>
    <go href="#cardname"/>
    Next
</anchor>
```

The # symbol refers to the name of an existing card in the current deck. (The card name itself doesn't have a # symbol).

Here's the same example, but the <a> element is used instead:

```
<a href="#cardname">Next</a>
```

> **<a> Versus <anchor>**
>
> One of the main differences between <anchor> and <a> is that <anchor> must have an event or task assigned to it, but <a> can only have a URL for navigation.
>
> Generally, if you are using a link for navigation purposes only, you should use the more compact <a> element; if, however, you need to do some processing after the link is selected, <anchor> must be used.

Remember that one of the goals in WML is to minimize the amount of data being sent to the client device. Because of this, you need to keep card names as small as possible.

Instead of using the <anchor> and <go> element pair, whenever possible, use the <a> element. WML also supports the HTML anchor tag, <a>, as a shortcut.

Listing 13.2 creates a simple <anchor>-based menu system that displays a new card based on the selection made. The new card being displayed is navigated by the <go> task element that references another card in the deck.

Listing 13.2   **Creating a Simple *<anchor>*-Based Menu System**

```
<?xml version="1.0"?>
<!DOCTYPE wml PUBLIC "-//WAPFORUM//DTD WML 1.1//EN"
"http://www.wapforum.org/DTD/wml_1.1.xml"><wml>
<card id="SimpleMenu" title="Simple Menu">
    <p>
        <anchor>Option One
<go href="#OptionOne"/>
        </anchor><br/>
        <anchor>Option Two
<go href="#OptionTwo"/>
        </anchor><br/>
        <anchor>Option Three
<go href="#OptionThree"/>
        </anchor><br/>
    </p>
</card>
<card id="OptionOne">
        <p>
        Option One Selected!
    </p>
</card>
<card id="OptionTwo">
```

```
      <p>
      Option Two Selected!
</p>
</card>
<card id="OptionThree">
      <p>
      Option Three Selected!
</p>
</card>
</wml>
```

Data Entry in WML

Data entry is handled by using the <input> and <select> elements.

Input elements enable the user to enter data. Listing 13.3 creates two input fields: one field takes some text and the other requires a password. The password is obscured by asterisks onscreen. The card is also bound to a <go> task element that links it to a card that displays the card contents using a <do> element.

Listing 13.3   **Simple Example of a WML Data Entry Application**

```
<?xml version="1.0"?>
<!DOCTYPE wml PUBLIC "-//WAPFORUM//DTD WML 1.1//EN"
"http://www.wapforum.org/DTD/wml_1.1.xml"><wml>
<card id="Login" title="Login">
  <p>
  Email:<br/>
  <input type="text" name="email"/><br/>
  Password:<br/>
  <input type="password" name="password"/><br/>
  </p>
  <do type="accept" label="Login">
    <go href="#logmein"/>
  </do>
</card>
<card id="logmein">
  <p>
  Email is: $(email)<br/>
  Password is: $(password)<br/>
  </p>
</card>
</wml>
```

Other Features of WML and Further Reading

All the information on WML presented in this section is all that is required for the sample application at the end of this chapter.

The following list outlines some other areas of functionality that are available for more complex mobile device development with WML:

- Timers
- Variables
- Cookies and session management
- WMLScript (a script language for mobile devices)
- More data entry features, selection lists, and grouped option lists
- Stylesheet support
- 2-D graphics support
- Automatic phone dialing
- Development libraries for various tasks, extended math operations, vertical market solutions, and so on

For more information on WAP/WML application development, including WMLScript, variables, and user interaction, refer to the following web-based resources:

- www.wapforum.org
- www.WAP.net
- www.mobileWAP.com

Because you now have a basic overview of WAP and WML as a development medium, it's time to move on to XHTML Basic.

Enter XHTML Basic

XHTML Basic is a vastly cut-down version of XHTML. It's been designed with the more limited abilities of mobile devices in mind.

One of the biggest weaknesses with existing mobile device development technologies is that they are either propriety and tied to a specific device (Palm OS or Windows CE, for example), or they do not provide much control over the rendering of a UI to a client browser (such as WML).

To deal with the growing amount of mobile devices in use and the complexity of their UIs, not to mention the ever-increasing difficulty in developing for more than one device type, and taking into account screen and user input restrictions, W3C submitted and got approval for the XHTML Basic Standard, which, according to the W3C Specification, states that:

"XHTML Basic defines a document type that is rich enough to be used for content authoring and precise document layout yet can be shared across different classes of device—desktop, PDA, TV, and mobile handset. XHTML Basic is the mobile adaptation of XHTML 1.0, and includes everything in XHTML 1.0 except those capabilities that are not appropriate for devices with small screens, such as frames and the nesting of tables."

XHTML itself, according to the W3C, is the first big change to HTML since HTML 4.0 was released in 1997. Because the latest version of HTML (v.4.1) is the basis of XHTML, all common tag definitions and syntax are the same.

All XHTML does is simply add modularity and enforce strict XML-based language rules. XHTML brings a cleaner structure to web-page creation and content, which is important when you're developing for smaller screens and the limited power of mobile devices.

W3C is actively recommending XHTML for all future web development for desktop clients and all other devices, including mobile handsets.

W3C Activity on XHTML

According to the W3C's activity sheet on XHTML (www.w3.org/MarkUp/#xhtml-modularization):

The first step was to reformulate HTML 4 in XML, which resulted in XHTML 1.0. By following the HTML Compatibility Guidelines set forth in Appendix C of the XHTML 1.0 Specification, XHTML 1.0 documents could be compatible with existing HTML user agents.

The next step is to modularize the elements and attributes into convenient collections for use in documents that combine XHTML with other tag sets. The modules are defined in Modularization of XHTML. XHTML Basic is an example of fairly minimal build of these modules and is targeted at mobile applications.

XHTML 1.1 is an example of a larger build of the modules, and avoids many of the presentation features. Although XHTML 1.1 looks similar to XHTML 1.0 Strict, it is designed to serve as the basis for future extended XHTML Family document types, and its modular design makes it easier to add other modules as needed or integrate itself into other markup languages. XHTML 1.1 plus MathML 2.0 document type is an example of such XHTML Family document type.

Because XHTML is one of the major incentives of W3C's effort to create standards, web developers can provide richer content on more platforms than ever.

By using XHTML Basic, content is easier to provide on various platforms and with more success in creating uniform (expected) content rendering.

In contrast, WML never guarantees a consistent look and feel to its applications because the mobile devices decide how to render its content in almost all cases. This causes many issues for mobile device developers for content, layout, and manipulation (specifically those developing for mobile phones).

It's no surprise to discover that most mobile phone applications written in WML are no more than a collection of pages displaying raw text that use anchor links to navigate from page to page, and simple data entry based on either links or text-entry fields. Even then, the interface can differ substantially.

With XHTML Basic, there's a better solution. It's easier to get a more consistent UI with controls that are supported on most XHTML Basic-compliant devices (at the time of this writing, very few are on the market but plenty are planned).

What will happen to WML? Not much, probably, because XHTML Basic supports extensions that enable it to emulate WML. Also, newer versions of WML will have XHTML extensions. This is due to the fact that the W3C and the WAP Forum sanctioned XHTML Basic, which makes it a key part of the overall Internet standards. It also guarantees its widespread success in the market.

XHTML and Stylesheets

The key to XHTML Basics' ability to render UIs in a consistent manner lies in its support of Wireless Cascading Stylesheets (WCSS). XHTML Basic has no formatting ability; no <b>, <I>, <em>, or <u> elements exist, so you can only use simple-text rendering and layout options, such as tables. All other effects must be defined in a stylesheet that is linked to a main XHTML Basic file.

The W3C has actively promoted the use of CSS on the web for use with all desktop and mobile browsers. Through the usage of WCSS, XHTML Basic document developers can control the presentation of documents on a mobile device without loosing the ability to take advantage of each device's special characteristics.

WCSS is the mobile version of CSS, as defined by the WAP Forum. It is a subset of CSS that omits features inappropriate for small devices.

By using WCSS, a document developer can specify the presentation of an entire web application in one place: the stylesheet. If the developer needs to change the presentation at any time, the change is made once in the stylesheet and the modification is immediately applied throughout all the pages in the site that refer to that stylesheet. This enables web developers to easily create browser-specific versions of the same content by simply creating the appropriate stylesheet.

Using XHTML Basic

Now that you have an overview of XHTML Basic, it's time to see it in action.

Before going any further, look at Listing 13.4. It shows the basic structure of an XHTML Basic document.

Listing 13.4 **The Basic Structure of an XHTML Basic Document**

```
<?xml version="1.0"?>
<!DOCTYPE html PUBLIC "-//W3C//DTD XHTML Basic 1.0//EN"
"http://www.w3.org/TR/xhtml-basic/xhtml-basic10.dtd">
```

```
<html xmlns="http://www.w3.org/1999/xhtml">
    <head>
        <title>XHTML Basic Document</title>
      <!--
        <link rel="stylesheet" href="style.css" type="text/css"/>
        -->
        <!--
        <style> document-wide styles would go here </style>
        -->
    </head>
    <body>


        <p>
      Body Text
        </p>
    </body>
</html>
```

The top two lines of code in Listing 13.4 are the document declarations for the XML version that's used and the stylesheet for the XHTML Basic document.

```
<?xml version="1.0"?>
<!DOCTYPE html PUBLIC "-//W3C//DTD XHTML Basic 1.0//EN"
    "http://www.w3.org/TR/xhtml-basic/xhtml-basic10.dtd">
```

The next line in the code is also important in XHTML Basic documents—the <html> element:

```
<html xmlns="http://www.w3.org/1999/xhtml">
```

The <html> element has an xmlns attribute defining the XHTML namespace. Without this namespace, the XHTML document is not valid.

The rest of the document is exactly the same as a regular HTML document, with one main difference: It is XML-compliant. This means that every tag must have a closing tag.

Tag Closings

Closing certain tags on some browsers can cause errors. For example,

-
—Becomes
- <img>—Becomes <img/>

Both of these instances cause errors on Netscape browsers. This can be easily fixed by inserting a space before the / on the closing tag. Here's the result of doing this:

-
—Becomes
- <img>—Becomes <img />

To summarize, XHTML Basic is a subset of XHTML 1.0. XHTML Basic borrows syntax from HTML while following XML's well-formed rules. This creates a subset of HTML 4.0 that's targeted for mobile user agents. As such, the `<script>` tag and frames are not supported, as well as other features of HTML 4.0 that a desktop-based browser can support.

> **Note**
>
> For further information on the XHTML Basic Specification, and XHTML in general, visit the W3C website, located at www.wc3.org.

I Thought This Was an XML Book

The advent of WAP is a dream come true for consumers wanting information at their fingertips. However, it's a nightmare for website developers. Not only must they maintain multiple sets of web pages for different web browsers, they now have to add a new set of documents to serve information to WAP users. To make matters worse, different WAP devices support different subsets of the WAP standards.

One of the ways for website developers to approach the problem is to maintain two main sets of pages: XHTML Basic and WML for WAP-based users.

However, this increases source code, maintenance, and means maintaining multiple UIs for essentially the same content.

What can be done about this? You can make use of XML and XSLT. The last half of this chapter shows you how to do just that.

The source code shown in this chapter is for both XHTML and WML; however, only the XHTML code is walked through with the differences between the codes highlighted.

A Simple Online Voting System

Online polls have become popular and are fun, so in this section, you're going to create an online voting system.

Design Objectives

Because of the need to support both an XHTML and a WML front-end to the system, and because the system's clients will be a mix of desktop- and mobile phone-based browsers, you'll use XML and XSLT to provide a common UI and a common experience.

The actual vote questions need to be stored in an easy-to-maintain file format that non-technical people can use. For this reason, XML will serve as the storage mechanism.

The voting system UI must support the following functionalities:

- Easy update of questions used for polls.
- The user must be able to select any vote question that he or she wants to answer.
- The system must record and display the total number of votes per question and per vote item.
- Votes are in the following format:
    - Question text
        - Response text 1
        - Response text 2
        - …

For example:

Which is your favorite Swiss Army product?

Pocket knife

Watch

Perfume

Apparel

Pens

Now that you have a set of system requirements and made a few choices about the implementation, look at the diagram of the application's UI flow-chart (see Figure 13.1).

In Figure 13.1, you can see that the UI starts by showing a list of available vote polls and allows the user to select one. After a selection is made, the user is presented with the actual poll question and the items on which to vote. The user can also return to the vote list if they desire.

If the user decides to vote by selecting a vote option, the system records the vote data and displays a brief message that thanks the user for his vote. It then allows the user to view the current statistics for the vote question on which they just voted.

The Vote Statistics screen simply shows the vote question, the total number of votes made for all options, and a breakdown of each vote item. The user also has the opportunity to return to the list of votes from this card.

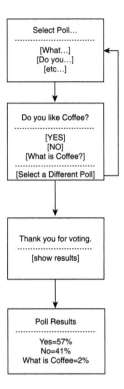

Figure 13.1 The application flowchart.

How can you do this by using XML? First, you must define the XML data file and how you're going to use it.

The XML File

What do you know about the data? It's a poll (or there can be a list of polls), each poll has a question, and each question has a list of items on which to vote.

The following list shows the general data hierarchy:

- Polls
  - Question
    - Item 1
    - Item 2
  - Question

From here, it is simple to see a basic XML structure, as follows:

```
<polls>
    <question>
        <item> </item>
    </question>
</polls>
```

For your needs, however, you must add some data. Listing 13.5 shows the appropriate XML structure. For clarity, a sample poll question's data is shown in the code.

Listing 13.5   *polls.xml*

```
<polls>
  <poll text="What is your favourite Swiss Army product">
    <item text="Pocket knife" votes="4" />
    <item text="Watch" votes="0" />
    <item text="Perfume" votes="2" />
    <item text="Apparel" votes="0" />
    <item text="Pens" votes="1" />
  </poll>
  <poll text="What size computer monitor are you using">
    <item text="15 inch" votes="1" />
    <item text="17 inch" votes="0" />
    <item text="20+ inch" votes="0" />
    <item text="Less than 15 inch." votes="0" />
  </poll>
  <poll text="Where do you get most of your world news">
    <item text="Television" votes="1" />
    <item text="Radio" votes="0" />
    <item text="Daily newspaper" votes="0" />
    <item text="Internet sites" votes="0" />
    <item text="Word of mouth" votes="0" />
    <item text="None of the above" votes="1" />
  </poll>
  <poll text="Do you think computer hacking should be considered terrorism">
    <item text="Yes, hacking is a form of terrorism." votes="0" />
    <item text="No, hacking is a crime but not terrorism." votes="0" />
    <item text="No, hacking is just a prank that tests vulnerabilities."
    ➥votes="1" />
  </poll>
  <poll text="When shopping for blue jeans are you more likely to">
    <item text="Buy the name brand even though it is more expensive."
    ➥votes="0" />
    <item text="Buy a generic/unknown brand that is cheaper." votes="0" />
    <item text="Wait for the name brand to go on sale." votes="0" />
  </poll>
  <poll text="How do you get to work">
    <item text="Personal automobile" votes="0" />
    <item text="Public transit" votes="0" />
```

continues

Listing 13.5 **Continued**

```
      <item text="Bicycle" votes="0" />
      <item text="Motorcycle" votes="0" />
      <item text="Walk" votes="0" />
      <item text="Don't work/work at home." votes="0" />
    </poll>
    <poll text="What do you read first in a newspaper">
      <item text="Front page stories" votes="0" />
      <item text="Entertainment" votes="0" />
      <item text="Comics" votes="0" />
      <item text="Sports" votes="0" />
      <item text="Business" votes="0" />
      <item text="Classified" votes="0" />
      <item text="Births/Deaths" votes="0" />
    </poll>
    <poll text="Do you own or use a Global Positioning System (GPS) receiver">
      <item text="Yes, I have a GPS receiver." votes="0" />
      <item text="No, I don't have one." votes="0" />
      <item text="I don't have one and don't know what it is." votes="0" />
    </poll>
    <poll text="When was the last time you played a 33 RPM record">
      <item text="Have never played one." votes="1" />
      <item text="Played one this week." votes="0" />
      <item text="It has been months." votes="0" />
      <item text="Last played a vinyl record years ago." votes="0" />
      <item text="Don't have one to play." votes="0" />
    </poll>
    <poll text="How many TV do you own">
      <item text="None. I don't watch TV." votes="0" />
      <item text="One." votes="1" />
      <item text="Two." votes="1" />
      <item text="Three." votes="1" />
      <item text="Too many." votes="0" />
    </poll>
    <poll text="Which PDA is most appealing to you">
      <item text="Palm" votes="0" />
      <item text="Pocket PC" votes="1" />
    </poll>
  </polls>
```

If you look at the code in Listing 13.5, you can see that there's a root element of <polls>, which contains a collection of <poll> elements. A <poll> element has a text attribute that holds the question text to be displayed. Inside the <poll> attribute are a collection of <item> elements, each with two attributes (text and votes). The text attribute holds the text label of a reply to a vote question, while the votes attribute holds a value that represents the total amount of votes for a vote reply.

This XML is used as both the basis of the voting system's UI and as its storage mechanism.

Transforming XML Using XSLT and ASP.NET

When designing this application, I was faced with how I would automatically render the correct UI for each client that I aimed to support (either XHTML Basic or WML).

To facilitate this, I came up with some logic that allowed me to detect the browser type being used and to select the correct .xsl translation file and render it to the client device.

ASP.NET provides various classes that enable you to load existing XML documents into memory for transformation by an XSL file.

Listing 13.6 demonstrates a simple XML translation process by using ASP.NET.

Listing 13.6 *xmlwmltext.aspx*

```
<%@ Import Namespace="System.Text" %>
<%@ Import Namespace="System.Xml" %>
<%@ Import Namespace="System.Xml.Xsl" %>

<script language="c#" runat="server">


private void Page_Load(object sender, System.EventArgs e)
{

XmlDocument xmlDoc = new XmlDocument();
XslTransform xslDoc = new XslTransform();
XmlDocument worker = new XmlDocument();

// Load the source xml
xmlDoc.Load(Server.MapPath("polls.xml"));

// load the source xsl
xslDoc.Load(Server.MapPath("pollsWML.xsl"));

// Transform the xmlDoc, using xslDoc and load results into the worker object
worker.Load(xslDoc.Transform(xmlDoc.DocumentElement.CreateNavigator(),
null));

// Print the result to the output stream
Response.ContentType = "text/vnd.wap.wml";
Response.Write(worker.InnerXml);


}

</script>
```

Listing 13.6 shows an .aspx file used to load the polls.xml file, and applies an .xsl translation to it (stored in the pollsWML.xsl file). Finally, the results are rendered onscreen.

The first three lines of code declare the namespaces required for this example:

```
<%@ Import Namespace="System.Text" %>
<%@ Import Namespace="System.Xml" %>
<%@ Import Namespace="System.Xml.Xsl" %>
```

Next, a script block is declared to run server-side and to use the language of C#:

```
<script language="c#" runat="server">
```

The page load event is then defined and three objects are defined for use:

- xmlDoc—Holds the XML document to process
- xslDoc—Holds the XSL transformation file to use
- worker—An XML document object that's used to hold the transformed XML document

```
private void Page_Load(object sender, System.EventArgs e)
{

XmlDocument xmlDoc = new XmlDocument();
XslTransform xslDoc = new XslTransform();

XmlDocument worker = new XmlDocument();
```

Next, the polls.xml file is loaded and stored by the xmlDoc object, as shown here:

```
// Load the source xml
xmlDoc.Load(Server.MapPath("polls.xml"));
```

Then we load and store the pollsWML.xsl XSL file we going to use for the transform in the xslDoc object

```
// load the source xsl

xslDoc.Load(Server.MapPath("pollsWML.xsl"));
```

Next, the actual transformation of the xmlDoc is performed by using the xslDoc object. The result is stored in the worker object:

```
// Transform the xmlDoc, using xslDoc and load results into the worker object
worker.Load(xslDoc.Transform(xmlDoc.DocumentElement.CreateNavigator(),
→null));
```

Finally we set the return content type to text/vnd.wap.wml to make sure content is delivered in a WAP/WML friendly format, and then we finally write the results back to the client device. Before closing the function and a script block.

```
// Print the result to the output stream
Response.ContentType = "text/vnd.wap.wml";
Response.Write(worker.InnerXml);


}

</script>
```

The Poll's System Code and Walk-Throughs

This section walks you through all the source code that makes up this application.

The *Default.aspx* File

The default.aspx is the heart and soul of the polling application; from here, the web server decides what .xsl transformation will take place to produce a UI for the client.

There are three possible pages in the poll's system:

- A list of polls
- Voting form
- Poll results

The default.aspx file also decides what version of the UI to render to the client, either WML for WML-compliant devices or XHTML for all other devices.

To see how this is done, look at Listing 13.7 and the code walk-through, which follows it.

Listing 13.7 *default.aspx*

```
<%@ Import Namespace="System.Text" %>
<%@ Import Namespace="System.Xml" %>
<%@ Import Namespace="System.Xml.Xsl" %>

<script language="c#" runat="server">
private void Page_Load(object sender, System.EventArgs e)
{
    string sPage = "";
    string sVoteOn = "";
    string sVoteItem ="";
    XmlDocument xmlDoc = new XmlDocument();
    XslTransform xslDoc = new XslTransform();
    XmlDocument worker = new XmlDocument();
    XsltArgumentList args = new XsltArgumentList();
```

continues

Listing 13.7 **Continued**

```
int iQueryParams = Context.Request.QueryString.Count;

//if less than two params show list of polls
if(iQueryParams < 2)
{
if (isWML()) { sPage="pollsWML.xsl";}
else {sPage="pollsXHTML.xsl";}

// Load the source xml
xmlDoc.Load(Server.MapPath("polls.xml"));

//' load the source xsl
xslDoc.Load(Server.MapPath(sPage));

// Get the resulting output and load it into a new document
worker.Load(xslDoc.Transform(xmlDoc.DocumentElement.CreateNavigator(),
➥null));

// Print the result to the output stream
if (isWML()) { Response.ContentType = "text/vnd.wap.wml";  }
Response.Write(worker.InnerXml);
}

//2 params so display vote page or Results page
if(iQueryParams == 2)
{
    sPage = Context.Request.QueryString["displayPage"];
sVoteOn = Context.Request.QueryString["voteon"];

// Load the source xml
xmlDoc.Load(Server.MapPath("polls.xml"));

// load the source xsl
xslDoc.Load(Server.MapPath(sPage));

//setup parameter value
args.AddParam("voteon", string.Empty, sVoteOn);

// Get the resulting output and load it into a new document
worker.Load(xslDoc.Transform(xmlDoc.DocumentElement.CreateNavigator(),
➥args));

// Print the result to the output stream
if (sPage.IndexOf("WML") >=0) { Response.ContentType =
➥"text/vnd.wap.wml"; }
Response.Write(worker.InnerXml);
}

//3 params so update xml file., then redirect and show vote results
if(iQueryParams == 3)
```

```
    {
    sPage = Context.Request.QueryString["displayPage"];
    sVoteOn = Context.Request.QueryString["voteon"];
    sVoteItem = Context.Request.QueryString["voteitem"];

            XmlDocument xDoc = new XmlDocument();
    xDoc.Load(Server.MapPath("polls.xml"));
    XmlElement xPoll = (XmlElement)xDoc.SelectSingleNode("polls/poll
    ➥[@text='"+sVoteOn+"']");
    XmlElement xItem = (XmlElement)xPoll.SelectSingleNode("item[@text='" +
    ➥sVoteItem + "']");
    XmlAttribute xVotes = (XmlAttribute)xItem.Attributes["votes"];
    xVotes.Value = Convert.ToString(Convert.ToInt32(xVotes.Value)+1);
    xDoc.Save(Server.MapPath("polls.xml"));

    if(sPage.IndexOf("WML")>=0){
Response.Redirect("default.aspx?displayPage=ResultWML.xsl&voteon="+
➥HttpUtility.HtmlEncode(sVoteOn)); }
    else {Response.Redirect("default.aspx?displayPage=ResultXHTML
    ➥.xsl&voteon="+sVoteOn);}
    }


}


///
/// Function used to tell whether the client device is WML
///

bool isWML()
{
    //Get required server variables used by function
    string userBrowser =
Context.Request.ServerVariables["HTTP_USER_AGENT"];

    //  if MOZ in the string its a XHTML Compliant browser
    //  else it is a WML compliant browser

    userBrowser = userBrowser.ToUpper();

    if(userBrowser.IndexOf("MOZ") >= 0) {
        return(false);
    }
    else {
        return(true);
    }
}

</script>
```

Listing 13.7 is complex, so let's walk-through it a section at a time.

One of the main purposes of the page load event code is to decide what transform file to use with the XML poll data. This is done by checking the query string parameter count, based on the following logic.

The parameters that are passed by query string are as follows:

- `displayPage`—The page to display (poll, vote, result, or update)
- `Voteon`—The question to vote on, see statistics for, or to update in the XML file
- `VoteItem`—Holds the text label of the vote item on which to vote

The following logic is used to select a page for processing:

1. If no parameters passed, display a list of votes.
2. If two parameters passed, use the passed `displaypage` as the XSL file.
3. If three parameters passed update the XML file with new data from inside default `aspx` file and then redirect the user to the results page for their browser type.

Now you know what the `default.aspx` is meant to do logicwise. Take a closer look at the code.

The *isWML()* Function

The `default.aspx` also detects what client browser is being used and selects the initial `.xsl` file based on the client browser type. This is done in the `isWML()` support function in the `default.aspx` file. It's also shown in the following code:

```
bool isWML()
{
    //Get required server variables used by function
    string userBrowser =
Context.Request.ServerVariables["HTTP_USER_AGENT"];
    userBrowser = userBrowser.ToUpper();

    //  if MOZ in the string its a XHTML Compliant browser
    //  else it is a WML compliant browser
    if(userBrowser.IndexOf("MOZ") >= 0) {
        return(false);
    }
    else {
        return(true);
    }
}
```

The `isWML()` function returns a boolean value that indicates whether the client browser can support WML or not. This is done by checking the `HTTP_USER_AGENT` server variable for the value of `MOZ`. This value is in the user agent string for all desktop-based browsers (Internet Explorer and Netscape, for example).

If the value of `MOZ` does not exist, the client browser is assumed to be a WML-compliant one.

The *Page_Load()* Event

The `Page_Load` event carries out all the processing in the `default.aspx` file. Its sole purpose is to generate the UI of the poll's system and to update the `polls.xml` file with new vote information.

To start, declare all the objects that you are going to use in this routine:

- **sPage**—The current display page (page to render)
- **sVoteOn**—The current poll on which to vote
- **sVoteItem**—The item to vote on in a poll
- **xmlDoc**—The object used to hold the `polls.xml` file
- **xslTransform**—The object used to hold the `.xsl` transformation file
- **worker**—The object used to hold the transformed XML file results
- **args**—An `Xsl Arg.` list for `.xsl` files that use parameters
- **iQueryParams**—The total number of `QueryString` variables in page request

```
private void Page_Load(object sender, System.EventArgs e)

    string sPage = "";
    string sVoteOn = "";
    string sVoteItem ="";
    XmlDocument xmlDoc = new XmlDocument();
    XslTransform xslDoc = new XslTransform();
    XmlDocument worker = new XmlDocument();
    XsltArgumentList args = new XsltArgumentList();
```

Store the total `QueryString` parameters in a variable for easy access:

```
int iQueryParams = Context.Request.QueryString.Count;
```

Next, check the `iQueryParams` variable to see if less than two `QueryString` variables have been passed. If so, you know that this is the first access to the page and that you should display a list of polls from which the user can select.

After this check is made, define which page you are going to use by checking to see if the requesting device is WML-compliant by using the `isWML()` function. If the device can support WML, set the `sPage` variable to hold the name of the WML `.xsl` file for the poll's list; otherwise, store the filename of the XHTML version.

There are better ways of doing this, but because the main purpose of this example is to show how to use various `.xsl` transformations for mobile device development, some values have been hard-coded for simplicity. In a real application, you would create more sophisticated logic for selecting and rendering each device type, probably by using a XML file as a data store of what devices are supported and the names of the pages that they should use.

After these filenames are stored, load the `polls.xml` file into the `xmlDoc` object, then load the defined XSL file into the `xslDoc` object.

Now that the `xmlDoc` and `xslDoc` objects are defined, apply a transformation and store the results in the worker object.

The next line checks again whether the rendering device is WML based. If it is, you must change the response content type to `text/vnd.wap.wml` so that it renders correctly on a mobile device that supports WML.

Finally, render the contents of the worker object (the translated XML document results) to the client browser, as shown here:

```
//if less than two params show list of polls
if(iQueryParams < 2)
{
if (isWML()) { sPage="pollsWML.xsl";}
else {sPage="pollsXHTML.xsl";}

// Load the source xml
xmlDoc.Load(Server.MapPath("polls.xml"));

//' load the source xsl
xslDoc.Load(Server.MapPath(sPage));

// Get the resulting output and load it into a new document
worker.Load(xslDoc.Transform(xmlDoc.DocumentElement.CreateNavigator(),
➥null));

// Print the result to the output stream
if (isWML()) { Response.ContentType = "text/vnd.wap.wml";  }
Response.Write(worker.InnerXml);
}
```

You have now just seen what happens if it is the first access to the page. Now look at the other page requests:

- Displaying the poll and letting the user vote

- Displaying the poll results
- Updating the `polls.xml` file with updated poll information

The first two of these page requests are dealt with in the next code walk-through and the final one.

If two `QueryString` variables have been passed, you must be either allowing the user to vote on a poll or displaying a poll's voting results.

The decision on which page to display is driven purely by the `displayPage` `QueryString` parameter. This actually holds the name of the `.xsl` transform file to use for rendering. (This is defined in the `.xsl` file that displays the polls list; all the `.xsl` files are explained in the next section.)

The `displayPage` value is stored in `sPage` variable for easy reference.

After you know what `.xsl` page to use for transformation of the XML file, you can store both the `polls.xml` and the file referenced in the `sPage` variable in their relevant objects (`xmlDoc` and `xslDoc`).

Next, create an `xslt` argument (based on the `sVoteOn` value) and add it to the `args` object. This value is used by the `.xsl` files to select the correct poll from the poll's XMLS file. (This is covered in more detail in the next section where I detail the workings of the `.xsl` files used by the polls system).

After defining the parameter value for the XSL transformation, you can actually perform the transformation and save it in the worker object prior to rendering its contents to the client devices display.

After this is done, check to see if the `.xsl` file you're using is for WML. This is done by looking for the value of `WML` in the `sPage` variable. If it's found, you are doing an WML-based client and need to set the response type of the client browser to the relevant type.

Now render the results to the browser, as shown here:

```
if(iQueryParams == 2)
{
    sPage = Context.Request.QueryString["displayPage"];
sVoteOn = Context.Request.QueryString["voteon"];

// Load the source xml
xmlDoc.Load(Server.MapPath("polls.xml"));

// load the source xsl
xslDoc.Load(Server.MapPath(sPage));

//setup parameter value
args.AddParam("voteon", string.Empty, sVoteOn);

// Get the resulting output and load it into a new document
worker.Load(xslDoc.Transform(xmlDoc.DocumentElement.CreateNavigator(),
➥args));
```

```
// Print the result to the output stream
if (sPage.IndexOf("WML") >=0) { Response.ContentType =
↝"text/vnd.wap.wml"; }
Response.Write(worker.InnerXml);
}
```

The final bit of processing that the `default.aspx` file does is actually update the `polls.xml` file with updated information on a poll after voting.

If the `QueryString` variable has three variables in it, you are updating the poll's XML file, so first you must store the page's `sPage`, `sVoteOn`, and `sVoteItem` variables.

Then, you load the `polls.xml` file into the `xmlDoc` object so that it is ready for processing. After this, declare an `XmlElement` to reference the poll with which you are working. Next, create another `XmlElement` to reference the item of the poll on which the client has voted.

Now that you have the poll and vote item that you require, you must access the correct attribute of the vote item so that you can increase its vote count by one. This is done by declaring an `xmlAttribute` object to get the `votes` attribute of the `<item>` tag in the `polls.xml` file.

After you have this value, increment it by one, and save the changed XML file to disk.

Now that the XML file is updated, simply redirect the user to the results page for the specified client browser. This is done by checking the `sPage` variable for the value of WML, just as you did earlier.

That's the processing of the `default.aspx`. It is not complex after you get familiar with it, but until then, it can be a bit tough.

XSL Translations

This section lists each of the `.xsl` translation files that the poll's system uses. Most of these files are identical in operation except for the differences in client rendering. These differences are summarized in the following section.

XSL Files Used for Rendering to a Client Device

The three `.xsl` files used by the XHTML Basic version of the poll's system are the following:

- **pollsXHTML.xsl**—Displays a list of polls to the user
- **voteXHTML.xsl**—Displays a poll and allows the user to vote
- **resultXHTML.xsl**—Displays the results of a poll just voted on

The three `.xsl` files used by the WML version of the poll's system are the following:

- `pollsWML.xsl`—Displays a list of polls to the user
- `voteWML.xsl`—Displays a poll and allows the user to vote
- `resultWML.xsl`—Displays the results of a poll just voted on

Note that the rendering in the XSL files has been kept simplistic. For XHTML Basic, I am not using WCSS or any other rendering features other than the following elements:

- `<br />`—Breaks a row to start a new line on the browser display
- `<a />`—Displays a hyperlink to a new page, used for all navigation and data entry in poll's system
- `text`—Frees text for all text labels in the system

For WML, stylesheets are not being used; only the following elements are used:

- `<p />`—Used to separate text and set wrapping on or off for a line of text
- `<a />`—To display a hyperlink to a new page, used for all navigation and data entry in polls system
- `text`—Free text for all text labels in the system

The reason for making the interface so simple is twofold: The first reason is so that it is simple for you to convert the `.xsl` for the XHTML version of the application into a WML version. The second reason is to demonstrate that, with mobile devices, you can create effective UIs without all the bells and whistles of a full-blown hypertext language.

The other main difference in the code is that the XML stylesheet declaration generated by the XHTML .xsl files is different to that of the WML version; also, the XHTML version has `<html><title>` and `<body>` tags whereas the WML version uses `<wml>` and `<card>` tags in their place.

So now that you know the key rendering differences, it's time to look at the code for all the translations and walk-through the WML translation of each one.

The *pollsWML.xsl* File

As previously stated, the polls WML Basic file displays a list of questions in the `polls.xml` file. The `.xsl` file is shown in Listing 13.8, and a walk-through is provided thereafter.

Listing 13.8   *pollsWML.xsl*

```
<?xml version="1.0"?>
<xsl:stylesheet xmlns:xsl="http://www.w3.org/1999/XSL/Transform"
version="1.0">
<xsl:output method="xml" omit-xml-declaration="no" doctype-
system="http://www.phone.com/dtd/wml11.dtd" standalone="yes" indent="yes"
doctype-public="-//PHONE.COM//DTD WML 1.1//EN" />
<xsl:template match="polls">
      <xsl:variable name="polls" select="//poll" />
      <wml>

          <card>
          <p> Please Select Poll</p>
          <p mode="nowrap">
          <!-- show all polls -->
          <xsl:for-each select="$polls">
               <a><xsl:attribute
name="href">default.aspx?displayPage=VoteWML.xsl&amp;voteOn=<xsl:value-of
select="current()/@text"/></xsl:attribute><xsl:value-of
select="current()/@text"/></a><br />
          </xsl:for-each>
          </p>
      </card>
</wml>
</xsl:template>
</xsl:stylesheet>
```

Starting from the top of the file, you have the normal XML and XSL declarations, plus one new addition for the XML file. This is an `xsl:output` directive,
which creates the WML stylesheet declaration that's needed for the generated
XHTML file.

```
<?xml version="1.0"?>
<xsl:stylesheet xmlns:xsl="http://www.w3.org/1999/XSL/Transform"
version="1.0">
<xsl:output method="xml" omit-xml-declaration="no" doctype-
system="http://www.phone.com/dtd/wml11.dtd" standalone="yes" indent="yes"
doctype-public="-//PHONE.COM//DTD WML 1.1//EN" />
```

Next, you define a global template for the transformation that sets its root to
the <polls> tag, which as you might remember, is the outermost tag in the
XML file `polls.xml`.

```
<xsl:template match="polls">
```

Next, an `xsl:variable` ($polls) is declared to hold all the poll elements. Then
the top area of the WML card is rendered.

```
      <xsl:variable name="polls" select="//poll" />
      <wml>
```

```
<card>
<p> Please Select Poll</p>
<p mode="nowrap">
```

An xsl:for-each directive is used to loop through each poll element in the $polls variable that was declared earlier.

In each iteration of the loop, I transform and output simple <a></a> hyperlinks for each item in the loop. Take note of the usage of the current()/@text tag, which creates the text label used by the link and as part of the URL to which the link will redirect.

```
    <!-- show all polls -->
    <xsl:for-each select="$polls">
        <a><xsl:attribute
name="href">default.aspx?displayPage=VoteWML.xsl&amp;voteOn=<xsl:value-of
select="current()/@text"/></xsl:attribute><xsl:value-of
select="current()/@text"/></a><br />
    </xsl:for-each>
```

After the loop is complete, render the last section of the WML card:

```
        </p>
    </card>
</wml>
</xsl:template>
</xsl:stylesheet>
```

The XHTML version does the same XSL processing except that it renders XHTML content. The full code for this is shown in Listing 13.9.

Listing 13.9 **An XHTML Translation File for the Vote Page**

```
<?xml version="1.0" encoding="utf-8"?>

<xsl:stylesheet version="1.0"
xmlns:xsl="http://www.w3.org/1999/XSL/Transform">

<xsl:output method="xml" omit-xml-declaration="no" doctype-
➥system="http://www.w3.org/TR/xhtml-basic/xhtml-basic10.dtd"
➥standalone="yes" indent="yes" doctype-public="-//W3C//DTD XHTML Basic
➥1.0//EN" />

<xsl:template match="polls">

    <xsl:variable name="polls" select="//poll" />

    <html xmlns="http://www.w3.org/1999/xhtml">
    <head>
        <title>vote page</title>
    </head>
    <body>
```

continues

Listing 13.9 **Continued**

```
    <h1>Please Select an Item to vote on.</h1>

    <!-- show all polls -->
    <xsl:for-each select="$polls">
        <a><xsl:attribute
name="href">default.aspx?displayPage=VoteXHTML.xsl&amp;voteOn=<xsl:value-of
select="current()/@text"/></xsl:attribute><xsl:value-of
select="current()/@text"/></a><br />
    </xsl:for-each>

    </body>
    </html>

</xsl:template>

</xsl:stylesheet>
```

This transformation page produces what's shown in Figure 13.2 (XHTML version in Internet Explorer).

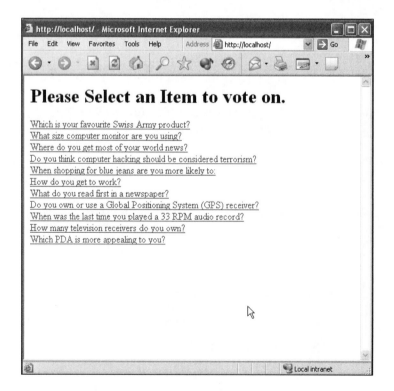

Figure 13.2 The list of polls available.

The *voteWML.xsl* File

The VoteWML file displays a specific question that has been selected through the output of the previous transformation that produced a list of questions from the polls.xml file. The question is displayed on the screen as text and then a list of hyperlinks are displayed for each of the possible options on which a user can vote (again, links are used for UI consistency). The XSL file is shown in Listing 13.10 and a walk-through is provided thereafter.

Listing 13.10   *voteWML.xsl*

```
<?xml version="1.0"?>
<xsl:stylesheet version="1.0"
xmlns:xsl="http://www.w3.org/1999/XSL/Transform">
<xsl:output method="xml" omit-xml-declaration="no" doctype-
system="http://www.phone.com/dtd/wml11.dtd" standalone="yes" indent="yes"
doctype-public="-//PHONE.COM//DTD WML 1.1//EN" />
<xsl:param name="voteon" />
<xsl:template match="polls">
    <wml>
    <card>
    <p mode="nowrap">Please vote<br />
    <xsl:for-each select="//poll[@text=$voteon]">
        <xsl:value-of select="current()/@text" /><br />
            <xsl:for-each select="current()/item">
                    <a><xsl:attribute
name="href">default.aspx?displayPage=UpdateWML&amp;voteOn=<xsl:value-of
select="$voteon" />&amp;voteitem=<xsl:value-of
select="current()/@text"/></xsl:attribute><xsl:value-of
select="current()/@text"/></a>
                </xsl:for-each>
    </xsl:for-each>
    </p>
    </card>
    </wml>
</xsl:template>
</xsl:stylesheet>
```

At the top of the file is the normal XML and XSL declarations:

```
<?xml version="1.0"?>
<xsl:stylesheet version="1.0"
xmlns:xsl="http://www.w3.org/1999/XSL/Transform">
<xsl:output method="xml" omit-xml-declaration="no" doctype-
system="http://www.phone.com/dtd/wml11.dtd" standalone="yes" indent="yes"
doctype-public="-//PHONE.COM//DTD WML 1.1//EN" />
```

Next, an xsl:parameter is declared. (The exact usage of this was covered earlier in this chapter.) This parameter performs an XPath select for the poll question that you want to render to the display. This parameter is the `voteon` parameter.

```
<xsl:param name="voteon" />
```

Set the root of the document that you want to transform to the `<polls>` outermost element:

```
<xsl:template match="polls">
    <wml>
    <card>
    <p mode="nowrap">Please vote<br />
```

Create a `for-each` loop as you did earlier, except that the actual select XPath statement now looks for a specific vote poll based on the text attribute of the `<poll>` tag. Then display the poll question text.

Followed by another `xsl:for-each` loop, this time for all the `<item>` elements in the `<poll>` tag. After that's done, create a hyperlink for each vote item, as you did earlier. Again, note the use of `current()/@text` and its use for the URL and rendering text:

```
        <xsl:for-each select="//poll[@text=$voteon]">
            <xsl:value-of select="current()/@text" /><br />
                <xsl:for-each select="current()/item">
                    <a><xsl:attribute
name="href">default.aspx?displayPage=UpdateWML&amp;voteOn=<xsl:value-of
select="$voteon"/>&amp;voteitem=<xsl:value-of
select="current()/@text"/></xsl:attribute><xsl:value-of
select="current()/@text"/></a>
                </xsl:for-each>
        </xsl:for-each>
```

After both loops are complete, generate the footer information for the output WML file:

```
        </p>
        </card>
        </wml>
    </xsl:template>
    </xsl:stylesheet>
```

The XHTML version does the same XSL processing except it renders for the XHTML browser. The full code is shown in Listing 13.11.

Listing 13.11   *voteXHTML.xsl*

```
<?xml version="1.0" encoding="utf-8"?>
<xsl:stylesheet version="1.0"
xmlns:xsl="http://www.w3.org/1999/XSL/Transform">
<xsl:param name="voteon" />
<xsl:output method="xml" omit-xml-declaration="no" doctype-
system="http://www.w3.org/TR/xhtml-basic/xhtml-basic10.dtd" standalone="yes"
indent="yes" doctype-public="-//W3C//DTD XHTML Basic 1.0//EN" />
<xsl:template match="polls">
     <html xmlns="http://www.w3.org/1999/xhtml">
     <head>
     <title>Mobile Polls</title>
     </head>
     <body>
     Please select link below to place vote

     <xsl:for-each select="//poll[@text=$voteon]">
          <xsl:value-of select="current()/@text" />
          <br />
          <xsl:for-each select="current()/item">
               <a><xsl:attribute name="href">

default.aspx?displayPage=UpdateXHTML&amp;voteOn=<xsl:value-of
select="$voteon"/>&amp;voteitem=<xsl:value-of select="current()/@text" />
               </xsl:attribute><xsl:value-of select="current()/@text"/></a>
               <br />
          </xsl:for-each>
          <br />
     </xsl:for-each>
     </body>
     </html>
</xsl:template>
</xsl:stylesheet>
```

When the file is combined with the polls.xml file, you get the output that's shown in Figure 13.3 (XHTML version rendered to Internet Explorer).

The *resultWML.xsl* File

The resultWML.xsl file displays the statistics for a specific question that has been selected by the output from the previous XSL transformation that allowed people to vote on a question. The question is displayed onscreen as text, but a total vote count displayed is displayed, and a list of the possible options that a user could have voted on with a percentage value next to it showing what percentage of votes that item received. The XSL file is shown in Listing 13.12, and a walk-through is provided thereafter.

Figure 13.3 Placing a vote.

Listing 13.12 **Vote Results XHTML Translation File**

```
<?xml version="1.0" encoding="utf-8"?>
<xsl:stylesheet version="1.0"
xmlns:xsl="http://www.w3.org/1999/XSL/Transform">
<xsl:output method="xml" omit-xml-declaration="no" doctype-
system="http://www.phone.com/dtd/wml11.dtd" standalone="yes" indent="yes"
doctype-public="-//PHONE.COM//DTD WML 1.1//EN" />
<xsl:param name="voteon" />
<xsl:template match="polls">
    <wml>
    <card>
    <xsl:for-each select="//poll[@text=$voteon]">
        <p>
        <xsl:value-of select="current()/@text" />
        <xsl:variable name="totalvotes" select="sum(//poll[@text=current()
        ➥/@text]/item/@votes)" />
        Total Votes: <xsl:value-of select="$totalvotes" />
```

```
        </p>
        <p mode="nowrap">
        <xsl:for-each select="current()/item">
            <xsl:choose >
                <xsl:when test="current()/@votes &gt; 0" >
                    <xsl:variable name="votepercentage"
                    ⇥select="round(current()/@votes div $totalvotes *
                    ⇥100)" />
                    <xsl:value-of select="current()/@text" />
                    ⇥[<xsl:value-of select="$votepercentage" />%]
                </xsl:when>
                <xsl:otherwise>
                    <xsl:value-of select="current()/@text" /> [0%]
                </xsl:otherwise>
            </xsl:choose>
        </xsl:for-each>
        </p>
        </xsl:for-each>
    </card>
    </wml>
</xsl:template>
</xsl:stylesheet>
```

As always, at the top of the file you have the normal XML and XSL declarations:

```
<?xml version="1.0" encoding="utf-8"?>
<xsl:stylesheet version="1.0"
xmlns:xsl="http://www.w3.org/1999/XSL/Transform">
<xsl:output method="xml" omit-xml-declaration="no" doctype-
system="http://www.phone.com/dtd/wml11.dtd" standalone="yes" indent="yes"
doctype-public="-//PHONE.COM//DTD WML 1.1//EN" />
```

Next, declare an `xsl:parameter`. To put it briefly, however, the parameter performs an XPath select for the poll question that you want to render to the display. This parameter is the `voteon` parameter.

```
<xsl:param name="voteon" />
```

By now, you should be familiar with this first step of isolating all the polls and then selecting the poll for which you want to see results:

```
<xsl:template match="polls">
    <wml>
    <card>
    <xsl:for-each select="//poll[@text=$voteon]">
```

Next, display the poll name that's statistics you will display.

After this is done, you can get to an interesting bit of transformation magic. First, have create a new xsl:variable ($totalvotes). This variable holds the total votes for each <item> in the selected <poll> element. The select calculates the sum of the <item/@votes> in the selected text item:

```
<p>
     <xsl:value-of select="current()/@text" />
     <xsl:variable name="totalvotes"
select="sum(//poll[@text=current()/@text]/item/@votes)" />
     Total Votes: <xsl:value-of select="$totalvotes" />
</p>
```

Now that you have the totalvotes value for the question, loop through each of the <items> and display their text, followed by the total percentage of the overall votes that the current item has.

For each <item> element in the loop, check whether their <votes> attribute is 0 or not. Doing this avoids annoying issues such as "divide by 0" errors. I have done this check by using the xsl:choose statement and testing if the current() element's <votes> attribute is > 0; if it is, I render the text and calculate the percentage and render that as well. Otherwise, I simply render the text of the <item> and some text as [0%].

```
              <p mode="nowrap">
              <xsl:for-each select="current()/item">
                    <xsl:choose >
                          <xsl:when test="current()/@votes &gt; 0" >
                               <xsl:variable name="votepercentage"
select="round(current()/@votes div $totalvotes * 100)" />
                               <xsl:value-of select="current()/@text" />
[<xsl:value-of select="$votepercentage" />%]
                          </xsl:when>
                          <xsl:otherwise>
                               <xsl:value-of select="current()/@text" /> [0%]
                          </xsl:otherwise>
                    </xsl:choose>
              </xsl:for-each>
              </p>
              </xsl:for-each>
```

Finally, after the loops are finished, simply render the rest of the WML card:

```
              </card>
              </wml>
       </xsl:template>
       </xsl:stylesheet>
```

The XHTML version does the same XSL processing except that it renders for the XHTML browser. The full code for this is shown in Listing 13.13.

Listing 13.13 **XHTML Translation File for the Vote Results Page**

```
<?xml version="1.0" encoding="utf-8"?>
<c:stylesheet version="1.0" xmlns:xsl="http://www.w3.org/1999/XSL/Transform">
<xsl:param name="voteon" />
<xsl:output method="xml" omit-xml-declaration="no" doctype-
system="http://www.w3.org/TR/xhtml-basic/xhtml-basic10.dtd" standalone="yes"
indent="yes" doctype-public="-//W3C//DTD XHTML Basic 1.0//EN" />
<xsl:template match="polls">
    <html xmlns="http://www.w3.org/1999/xhtml">
    <head>
    <title>Mobile Polls</title>
    </head>
    <body>
    <xsl:for-each select="//poll[@text=$voteon]">
        <xsl:value-of select="current()/@text" />
        <br />
        <xsl:variable name="totalvotes"
select="sum(//poll[@text=current()/@text]/item/@votes)" />
        Total Votes: <xsl:value-of select="$totalvotes" /><br />
        <xsl:for-each select="current()/item">
            <xsl:choose >
                <xsl:when test="current()/@votes &gt; 0" >
                    <xsl:variable name="votepercentage"
select="round(current()/@votes div $totalvotes * 100)" />
                    <xsl:value-of select="current()/@text" />
[<xsl:value-of select="$votepercentage" />%]
                </xsl:when>
                <xsl:otherwise>
                    <xsl:value-of select="current()/@text" /> [0%]
                </xsl:otherwise>
            </xsl:choose>
            <br />
        </xsl:for-each>
        <br />
    </xsl:for-each>
    </body>
    </html>
</xsl:template>
</c:stylesheet>
```

When this XSL transformation is rendered, you get the output that is shown in Figure 13.4. (The XHTML output was rendered by Internet Explorer.)

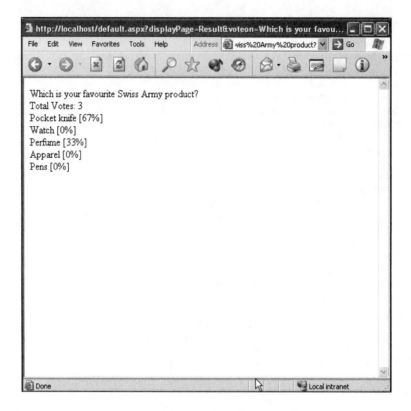

Figure 13.4 The Vote Results screen shot.

Chapter Summary

In this chapter, you were introduced to WAP/WML. You also learned how to use XHTML and WML with XML to produce a simple, yet functional, polling application.

III
Appendixes

ASP.NET Objects Reference

THIS APPENDIX LISTS THE PROPERTIES, METHODS, and events for the most commonly used classes within ASP.NET applications. The classes included are the following:

- `System.UI.Web.Page`
- `System.Web.HttpApplication`
- `System.Web.HttpApplicationState`
- `System.Web.HttpRequest`
- `System.Web.HttpResponse`
- `System.Web.HttpServerUtility`
- `System.Web.SessionState.HttpSessionState`

Some class members are omitted for brevity. Any methods or properties intended purely for .NET infrastructure support are not included in this appendix.

System.Web.UI.Page

The `System.Web.UI.Page` class provides server-side events and capabilities for a `.aspx` file. It includes properties (specifically, `Application`, `Context`, `Request`, `Response`, `Session`, and `Server`) to quickly access contextual information. Table A.1 lists the methods of the `Page` class, Table A.2 lists the available properties of the `Page` class, and Table A.3 lists the available events of the `Page` class.

Table A.1   **Methods of the *System.Web.UI.Page* Class**

Method Name	Description
DataBind	Binds a data source to the page and all its child controls.
DeterminePostBackMode	Determines if the page was the result of an `HTTP POST` or `GET` postback operation. If it was not a postback request, `null` is returned in C# (`Nothing` in Visual Basic). If it was an `HTTP POST` postback, the `Form` collection information is returned. If it was an `HTTP GET` postback, the `QueryString` collection information is returned.
FindControl	Finds a specified server control.
GetPostBackClientEvent	Obtains a reference to a client-side script function that causes a server postback when invoked.
GetPostBackClientHyperlink	Appends JavaScript to the beginning of the return from a `GetPostBackEventReference` call to allow hyperlink postback processing on the server. Returns the name of the client-side function and the `ID` property of the server control that processed the function and argument passed to the control.
HasControls	Determines if the server control contains any child controls.
GetPostBackEventReference	Obtains a reference to a client-side script function that causes a server postback when invoked.
IsClientScriptBlockRegistered	Determines if a named client script block is already registered within the page.
IsStartupScriptRegistered	Determines if a named startup script block is already registered within the page.

Method Name	Description
LoadPageStateFromPersistenceMedium	Loads the view state information from the specified persistence medium. Stores view state in a medium other than hidden form variables.
MapPath	Retrieves the physical path for a virtual path.
ParseControl	Parses a string argument to create a `System.Web.UI.Control` object reference.
RaisePostBackEvent	Notifies the server control that caused the postback that it must handle an incoming postback event.
RegisterArrayDeclaration	Creates a client-side array declaration and populates it with the specified contents.
RegisterClientScriptBlock	Creates a client-side script block from server controls.
RegisterHiddenField	Registers a hidden form field from a server control.
RegisterOnSubmitStatement	Registers a client-side script (registered with `RegisterClientScriptBlock`) to respond to a client `OnSubmit` event.
RegisterRequiresPostBack	Registers a control as requiring postback handling.
RegisterRequiresRaiseEvent	Registers a server control as requiring a page process event.
RegisterStartupScript	Registers a client-side script (previously registered with `RegisterClientScriptBlock`) as a startup script.
RegisterViewStateHandler	Persists the page view state.
SavePageStateToPersistenceMedium	Saves the page view state to the specified object.
Validate	Instructs validation controls in the page to perform validation.
VerifyRenderingInServerForm	Confirms that a `System.Web.UI.HtmlControls.HtmlForm` control is rendered for the specified ASP.NET server control at run-time.

Table A.2   **Properties of the *System. Web. UI. Page* Class**

Property Name	Description
Application	Gets a reference to the HttpApplicationState (application intrinsic object) instance object for the current application.
Cache	Gets the System.Web.Caching.Cache object associated with the application to which the page belongs.
ClientTarget	Disables browser capabilities detection and uses the capabilities defined in web.config.
Context	Gets an HttpContext (context intrinsic control) instance object, allowing access to the context under which the web server processes requests.
EnableViewState	Gets or sets a Boolean indicating if the page (and any server controls it contains) maintains its view state when the current request ends.
ErrorPage	Gets or sets the page that is redirected to in case of an unhandled exception within the page.
ID	Gets or sets an identifier for the page.
IsPostBack	Gets a value indicating if the page is being loaded as the result of a postback operation.
IsValid	Gets a value indicating if page validation succeeded.
Request	Gets the HttpRequest (request intrinsic object) instance object for the current request, allowing access to HTTP information, such as POST and GET data.
Response	Gets the HttpResponse (response intrinsic object) instance object for the current request.
Server	Gets the HttpServerUtility (server intrinsic object) instance object for the current web request, providing utility functions for use in the current application.
Session	Gets the HttpSessionState (session intrinsic object) instance object for the current web request, enabling access to state persistence between stateless requests.
SmartNavigation	Gets or sets a value indicating if smart navigation is enabled.
Trace	Gets the System.Web.TraceContext instance object for the current web request, enabling access to performance information.
User	Gets a System.Security.IPrincipal interface object representing the current user's identity and roles.
Validators	Gets a ValidatorCollection collection of the validation controls for the page.
Visible	Gets or sets a Boolean indicating if the page is to be rendered.

Table A.3   **Events of the** *System. Web. UI. Page* **Class**

Event Name	Occurs When
AbortTransaction	A transaction is aborted.
CommitTransaction	A transaction is completed.
DataBinding	The server control binds to a data source.
Disposed	A server control is released from memory.
Error	An unhandled exception occurs.
Init	The server control is initialized.
Load	The server control is loaded into the Page object.
PreRender	A server control is about to render to its containing Page object.
Unload	The server control is unloaded from memory.

System. Web. HttpApplication

The System.Web.HttpApplication class accesses information for the current application. Table A.4 shows the properties of the HttpApplication class, Table A.5 shows its methods, and Table A.6 lists its events.

Table A.4   **Properties of the** *System. Web. HttpApplication* **Class**

Property Name	Description
Application	Gets the HttpApplicationState (application intrinsic object) for the current request.
Context	Gets an HttpContext (context intrinsic control) instance object, allowing access to the context under which the web server processes requests.
Modules	Provides access to a collection of all HttpModules registered for the application.
Request	Gets the HttpRequest (request intrinsic object) instance object for the current request, allowing access to HTTP information such as POST and GET data.
Response	Gets the HttpResponse (response intrinsic object) instance object for the current request.
Server	Gets the HttpServerUtility (server intrinsic object) instance object for the current web request, providing utility functions for use in the current application.
Session	Gets the HttpSessionState (session intrinsic object) instance object for the current web request, which enables access to state persistence between stateless requests.

Table A.5 **Methods of the *System.Web.Application* Class**

Method Name	Description
CompleteRequest	Bypasses all other events in the pipeline and forces the request to terminate prematurely.
Dispose	Cleans up HttpModule object instances.
Init	Initializes IHttpModule object instances and executes custom initialization code.

Table A.6 **Events of the *System.Web.Application* Class**

Event Name	Occurs When
AuthenticateRequest	The user's identity (System.Security.IPrincipal) is established.
AuthorizeRequest	The user is verified as authorized for the request.
BeginRequest	A new request is made.
EndRequest	A new request is completed.
Error	The application encounters an unhandled exception.

System.Web.HttpApplicationState

The System.Web.HttpApplicationState class (or application intrinsic object) enables access to persisted state information across user context boundaries but within a single application context boundary. Each application on the web server creates an instance of the HttpApplicationState class. Table A.7 shows the properties of the HttpApplicationState class, and Table A.8 shows its methods.

Table A.7 **Properties of the *System.Web.HttpApplicationState* Class**

Property Name	Description
AllKeys	Exposes the keys in the HttpApplicationState collection.
Contents	Provides reference to the HttpApplicationState collection object.
Count	Gets the number of objects in the HttpApplicationState collection.
Item	Provides access to an item in the HttpApplicationState collection object by name or index.
Keys	Returns a collection of keys for the HttpApplicationState collection.
StaticObjects	Returns objects declared in the global.asax file by the following tag: `<object runat="server" scope="application">`

Table A.8   **Methods of the *System.Web.HttpApplicationState* Class**

Method Name	Description
Add	Adds an object to the `HttpApplicationState` collection.
Clear	Removes all objects from the `HttpApplicationState` collection.
Get	Gets an object from the `HttpApplicationState` collection by index or name.
Lock	Locks access to the `HttpApplicationState` variable to enable synchronization.
Remove	Removes a specific item from the `HttpApplicationState` collection.
RemoveAll	Removes all objects from the `HttpApplicationState` collection.
RemoveAt	Removes an object from the `HttpApplicationState` collection by index.
Set	Updates the value of an object in the `HttpApplicationState` collection.
UnLock	Unlocks access to the `HttpApplicationState` variable to enable synchronization.

System.Web.HttpRequest

The `System.Web.HttpRequest` class (or request intrinsic object) enables access to the HTTP request made by the user. A new request is created each time a user loads a page in his or her browser. Table A.9 shows the properties of the `HttpRequest` class, and Table A.10 shows its methods.

Table A.9   **Properties of the *System.Web.HttpRequest* Class**

Property Name	Description
AcceptTypes	Gets an array of client-supported Multipurpose Internet Mail Extensions (MIME) accept types.
ApplicationPath	Gets the path for the current application's virtual directory.
Browser	Gets a `System.Web.HttpBrowserCapabilities` object that represents the client browser's capabilities.
ClientCertificate	Gets the current request's client security certificate. Corresponds to server variables prefixed with `CERT_`.

continues

Table A.9 **Continued**

Property Name	Description
ContentEncoding	Gets a System.Text.Encoding object for the client browser's character set.
ContentLength	The length, in bytes, of data sent by the client. Corresponds to the CONTENT_LENGTH server variable.
ContentType	Gets the MIME type of the incoming request.
Cookies	Gets the collection of the client's cookies for the current server.
CurrentExecutionFilePath	Gets the virtual path of the current request.
FilePath	Gets the virtual path of the current request.
Files	Gets the collection of files uploaded by the client.
Filter	Gets or sets the filter to use when reading the current input stream.
Form	Gets a collection of form variables.
Headers	Gets a collection of header variables.
HttpMethod	Gets the HTTP data transfer method (GET, POST, or HEAD) used by the client.
InputStream	Provides access to the raw HTTP stream.
IsAuthenticated	Gets a value that indicates if the user has been authenticated for the HTTP request.
IsSecureConnection	Gets a value that indicates if the HTTP request is secure (over HTTPS). Corresponds to the HTTPS server variable.
Params	Gets a combined collection of QueryString, Form, ServerVariables, and Cookies items.
Path	Gets the virtual path of the current request. Corresponds to PATH_INFO server variable.
PathInfo	Gets additional path information for a resource.
PhysicalApplicationPath	The physical file system path of the current application's root directory. Corresponds to the APPL_PHYSICAL_PATH server variable.
PhysicalPath	Gets the physical file path associated with the requested URL.
QueryString	Gets the collection of querystring variables.
RawUrl	Gets the raw URL of the current request.

Property Name	Description
RequestType	Gets the HTTP data transfer method (GET, POST, or HEAD) used by the client. Corresponds to the REQUEST_METHOD server variable.
ServerVariables	Returns a collection of web server variables.
TotalBytes	Gets the number of bytes in the current input stream.
Url	Returns a System.Uri object that contains information about the URL of the current request.
UrlReferrer	Returns the URL from which this page was redirected. Corresponds to the HTTP_REFERRER server variable.
UserAgent	Gets the raw user agent string of the client browser. Corresponds to the HTTP_USER_AGENT server variable.
UserHostAddress	Gets the IP host address of the remote client. Corresponds to the REMOTE_ADDR server variable.
UserHostName	Gets the DNS name of the remote client. Corresponds to HTTP_HOST server variable.
UserLanguages	Retrieves a string array of client language preferences.

Table A.10 **Methods of the** *System.Web.HttpRequest* **Class**

Method Name	Description
BinaryRead	Reads a specified number of bytes from the input stream.
MapImageCoordinates	Maps an incoming image-field form parameter to appropriate X-Y coordinate values.
MapPath	Maps the specified virtual path to a physical path.
SaveAs	Saves an HTTP request to disk.

System.Web.HttpResponse

The System.Web.HttpResponse class (or response intrinsic object) enables access to the HTTP response stream as it is being formed. This class writes information to the client browser. Table A.11 shows the properties of the HttpResponse class, and Table A.12 shows its methods.

Table A.11 **Properties of the *System.Web.HttpResponse* Class**

Property Name	Description
Buffer	Gets or sets a value that indicates if the output stream should be buffered before sending or not.
BufferOutput	Gets or sets a value that indicates whether the output stream should be buffered before sending after the page completes processing.
Cache	Gets the caching properties of the page (expiration time, privacy, and vary clauses).
CacheControl	Sets the CacheControl HTTP header to Public or Private.
Charset	Gets or sets the HTTP character set of the output stream.
ContentEncoding	Gets or sets the character (or maybe content) encoding of the output stream.
ContentType	Gets or sets the MIME type for the output stream.
Cookies	Gets the HttpCookie collection sent by the response.
Expires	Gets or sets the number of minutes before a page cached on a client browser expires.
ExpiresAbsolute	Gets or sets the date and time when cached content on the client browser expires.
IsClientConnected	Gets a value indicating if the client is still connected to the server.
Output	Enables output of text to the outgoing response stream.
OutputStream	Enables binary output to the outgoing response stream. Used for methods that require a System.IO.Stream object reference to be written to.
StatusCode	Gets or sets the HTTP status code of the output returned to the client. The default is 200.
StatusDescription	Gets or sets the HTTP status string of the output returned to the client.
SuppressContent	Gets or sets a value indicating whether to send HTTP content to the client.

Table A.12 **Methods of the** *System.Web.HttpResponse* **Class**

Method Name	Description
AddCacheItemDependencies	Accepts an array of keys to other cache items, making the validity of a cached item dependent on various other items in the cache.
AddCacheItemDependency	Makes the validity of a cached item dependent on another item in the cache.
AddFileDependencies	Adds a group of filenames to the collection of filenames on which the current response is dependent.
AppendHeader	Adds an HTTP header to the output stream.
AppendToLog	Adds custom information to the IIS log file.
ApplyAppPathModifier	Appends the session ID to the virtual path.
BinaryWrite	Writes binary information to the output stream.
Clear	Clears buffered information from the output stream.
ClearContent	Clears all buffered content output from the output stream.
ClearHeaders	Clears all buffered headers from the output stream.
Close	Closes the socket connection to a client.
End	Sends all buffered output to the client and stops execution of the page.
Flush	Flushes buffered content.
Pics	Appends a Platform for Internet Content Selection (PICS)-Label HTTP header to the output stream.
Redirect	Directs the client to a new URL.
RemoveOutputCacheItem	Removes all cached items related to the specified path from the cache.
Write	Writes the specified values to the output stream.
WriteFile	Writes a file directly to the output stream.

System. Web. HttpServerUtility

The System.Web.HttpServerUtility class (or server intrinsic object) provides access to utility functions for processing web requests. Table A.13 shows the properties of the HttpServerUtility class, and Table A.14 shows its methods.

Table A.13 **Properties of the *System. Web. HttpServerUtility* Class**

Property Name	Description
MachineName	Gets the web server's name.
ScriptTimeout	Gets or sets the request timeout in seconds.

Table A.14 **Methods of the *System. Web. HttpServerUtility* Class**

Method Name	Description
ClearError	Clears the previous exception.
CreateObject	Creates a COM object from the specified progid.
CreateObjectFromClsId	Creates a COM object from the specified clsid.
Execute	Executes a request to another page.
GetLastError	Returns the previous exception.
HtmlDecode	HTML decodes a string.
HtmlEncode	HTML encodes a string.
MapPath	Gets the physical path for the specified virtual path.
Transfer	Terminates execution of the current page and begins execution of a new request by using the supplied URL path.
UrlDecode	URL decodes a string.
UrlEncode	URL encodes a string.
UrlPathEncode	URL encodes the path portion of a string.

System. Web. SessionState. HttpSessionState

The System.Web.SessionState.HttpSessionState class (or session intrinsic object) provides a means to persist stateful information between requests for a single user. Table A.15 shows the properties of the HttpSessionState class, and Table A.16 shows its methods.

Table A.15   **Properties of the** *System. Web. SessionState. HttpSessionState* **Class**

Property Name	Description
CodePage	Gets or sets the code page identifier for the current session.
Contents	Gets a reference to the current session state collection.
Count	Gets a count of items in the session state collection.
IsCookieless	Gets a value indicating if the session is cookieless, meaning the session ID is embedded in the URL.
IsNewSession	Gets a value indicating if the current request created the session.
IsReadOnly	Gets a value indicating if the session is read only.
Item	Gets a session variable value.
IsSynchronized	Gets a value indicating if the current session is thread safe.
Keys	Gets the collection of keys for the current session.
LCID	Gets the locale identifier (LCID) for the current session.
Mode	Gets one of the SessionStateMode enumeration members representing the current session state mode (InProc, Off, SQLServer, or StateServer).
SessionID	Gets the session ID for the current session.
StaticObjects	Gets the collection of objects defined in global.asax with the following tag: `<object runat="server" scope="session">`
Timeout	Gets or sets the number of minutes between requests until the current session times out.

Table A.16   **Methods of the** *System. Web. HttpSessionState* **Class**

Method Name	Description
Abandon	Tears down the current session.
Add	Adds an item to the session state collection.
Clear	Clears all values from the session state.
CopyTo	Copies the collection of session state values to an array.
GetEnumerator	Gets an enumerator to iterate through the collection of session state items.
Remove	Removes an item from the session state collection.
RemoveAll	Removes all items from the session state collection.
RemoveAt	Removes an item from the session state collection by index.

B

Side-By-Side MSXML Reference

Chapter 6 "Exploring the System.Xml Namespace," discusses the System.Xml namespace in depth, and Chapter 5, "MSXML Parser," discusses the MSXML Parser. Here, you can see a comprehensive reference to the important classes in the System.Xml namespace and their corresponding MSXML implementations side by side.

System.Xml.XmlNode and IXMLDOMNode

XmlNode class in the System.Xml namespace is the implementation of the W3C Node interface. It's an abstract class and is implemented and extended by the other classes in the System.Xml namespace, such as XmlAttribute, XmlDocument, XmlDocumentFragment, XmlEntity, XmlLinkedNode and XmlNotation. Because these classes represent the items in the XML document, these items can be treated as nodes and can be accessed through DOM. XmlNode class provides different properties and methods to work with different types of nodes in an XML document. Table B.1 and Table B.2 list these properties and methods, respectively. The corresponding MSXML interface IXMLDOMNode provides methods for XSLT transformation, like transformNode. In the System.Xml namespace, this is achieved by using the Transform method in the System.Xml.Xsl.xslTransform class.

Table B.1   *System.Xml.XmlNode* and *IXMLDOMNode* Properties

XmlNode	Description	MSXML *IXMLDOMNode*
Attributes	Gets an XmlAttributeCollection containing the attributes of this node. XmlAttributeCollection inherits from System.Xml.XmlNamedNodeMap.	Gets IXMLDOMNamedNodeMap.
BaseURI	Gets the base URI of the current node. Indicates where the node was loaded from.	
ChildNodes	Gets all the children of the current node.	childNodes
FirstChild	Gets the first child of the current node.	firstChild
HasChildNodes	Returns Boolean indicating if the current node has child nodes.	Implements this functionality as a method named hasChildNodes.
InnerText	Gets or sets the concatenated values of the node and all its children.	text*
InnerXml	Gets or sets the markup representing the children of the current node.	
IsReadOnly	Returns a Boolean indicating whether the current node is read-only.	
Item	Returns the specified child element (XmlElement). This is the indexer in C# for the XmlDocument class.	
LastChild	The last child of the node.	lastChild
LocalName	Gets the name of the node without the namespace prefix.	baseName
Name	Should get the qualified name of the current node when overridden in the derived classes.	nodeName
NamespaceURI Gets the namespace URI of this node.	Returns the namespace URI of the current node.	namespaceURI
NextSibling	Returns the node following this node at the same level in the document hierarchy.	nextSibling

XmlNode	Description	**MSXML** *IXMLDOMNode*
`NodeType`	Should get the type of the current node when overridden in the derived classes. (Type is an `XmlNodeType` Enumeration member.)	`nodeType` (Type is an `IXMLDOMNodeType` Enumeration member.)
`OuterXml`	Gets the XML markup representing the current node and its children. Similar to `InnerXml`, except the current node is also returned.	`xml`
`OwnerDocument`	Gets the `XmlDocument` to which the current node belongs.	`ownerDocument`
`ParentNode`	Gets the parent of the current node. If the node has been created but not added to the tree, this returns a null reference in C#, or Nothing in Visual Basic .NET.	`parentNode`
`Prefix`	Gets or sets the namespace prefix for the current node.	`Prefix`
`PreviousSibling`	Gets the node previous to this node at the same level in the document hierarchy.	`previousSibling`
`Value`	Gets or sets the value (text) of the current node.	`nodeValue`

Table B.2 *System.Xml.XmlNode* **and** *IXMLDOMNode* **Methods**

XmlNode	Description	**MSXML** *IXMLDOMNode* **Implementation**
`AppendChild`	Adds the specified node to the end of the list of children of the current node.	`appendChild` Appends new `Child` as the last child of this node.
`Clone`	Creates a duplicate of the current node.	`CloneNode`
`CloneNode`	. . . . Similar to `Clone`, but accepts a deep Boolean parameter indicating if the subtree should be duplicated.	

continues

Table B.2 **Continued**

XmlNode	**Description**	**MSXML** *IXMLDOMNode* **Implementation**
CreateNavigator	Creates an XpathNavigator for navigating this object as a DOM structure.	
GetEnumerator	Enables For Each enumerations on the object.	
GetNamespace OfPrefix	Retrieves the namespace URI in the closest xmlns declaration for the given prefix.	
GetPrefix OfNamespace	Retrieves the prefix in the closest xmlns declaration for the given URI.	
InsertAfter	Inserts the node immediately after the specified reference node.	
InsertBefore	Inserts the node immediately before the specified reference node or at the end of the list.	insertBefore
Normalize	Puts all XmlText nodes in the full depth of the sub-tree underneath this XmlNode into a normal form where only markup (that is, tags, comments, processing instructions, CDATA sections, and entity references) separates XmlText nodes; that is, there are no adjacent XmlText nodes.	
PrependChild	Adds the specified node as the first child of the current node.	
RemoveAll	Removes all children and/or attributes of the current node.	
RemoveChild	Removes the specified child node associated with the current node.	removeChild
ReplaceChild	Removes the old child node and replaces it with the new child node.	replaceChild
SelectNodes	Selects an XmlNodeList of nodes matching the specified XPath expression.	selectNodes* Selects IXMLDOMNodeList.
SelectSingle Node	Selects an XmlNode matching the specified XPath expression. If more than one match is found, only the first match is returned.	selectSingleNode* Selects an IXMLDOMNode.

XmlNode	Description	**MSXML** *IXMLDOMNode* **Implementation**
Supports	Tests if the DOM implementation supports a specific feature.	
WriteContentTo	Should save the contents of the XmlDocument node to the specified XmlWriter when overridden in the derived classes.	
WriteTo When over ridden in a derived class, saves the current node to the specified XmlWriter.	Should save the XmlDocument node to the specified XmlWriter when overridden in the derived classes.	

System. Xml. XmlDocument and *DOMDocument*

XmlDocument class in the System.Xml namespace is the implementation of the W3C Document interface. This class inherits from the XmlNode class and provides functionality such as loading XML documents into the DOM structure and creating XML documents. Table B.3 and Table B.4 list the properties and methods respectively found in the XmlDocument class.

Table B.3   *System. Xml. XmlDocument* **and** *DOMDocument Properties*

XmlDocument (Inherits *XmlNode*)	Description	**MSXML** *DOMDocument*
BaseURI (Overrides XMLNode::BaseURI)	Gets the base URI of the current node. Indicates from where the node was loaded from.	
DocumentElement	Retrieves the root element of the XML document as an XmlElement object.	documentElement
DocumentType	Gets the <!DOCTYPE..> declaration if one exists as an XmlDocumentType object.	doctype Get it as an IXMLDOMDocumentType object.

continues

Table B.3 **Continued**

XmlDocument (Inherits *XmlNode*)	Description	MSXML *DOMDocument*
Implementation	Returns the Xml Implementation object for the XML document.	implementation Returns the IXMLDOMImplementation object for the XML document.
InnerXml (Overrides XMLNode::InnerXml)	Gets or sets the markup representing the children of the current node.	
IsReadOnly (Overrides XMLNode::IsReadOnly)	Returns a Boolean indicating whether the current node is read only.	
LocalName (Overrides XMLNode::LocalName)	Gets the name of the node without the namespace prefix.	baseName
Name (Overrides XMLNode::Name)	Gets the qualified name of the node.	nodeName
NameTable	Returns the XmlNameTable associated with this implementation.	
NodeType (Overrides XMLNode::NodeType)	Returns an XmlNodeType enumeration member representing this node's type.	nodeType (Gets an IXMLDOMNodeType Enumeration member.)
OwnerDocument (Overrides XMLNode::OwnerDocument)	Gets the XmlDocument to which the current node belongs.	ownerDocument Gets the IXMLDOMDocument root note to which the current node belongs.
PreserveWhitespace	Gets or sets a Boolean indicating if white space would be preserved or stripped.	preserveWhiteSpace
XmlResolver	Sets the XmlResolver to use for resolving external resources.	

Table B.4 *DOMDocument* and *System.Xml.XmlDocument* Methods

XmlDocument (Inherits *XmlNode*)	Description	MSXML *DOMDocument*
CloneNode (Overrides XMLNode::CloneNode)	Similar to XMLNode::Clone, but accepts a deep Boolean parameter indicating if the subtree should be duplicated.	cloneNode
CreateAttribute Overloaded. Creates an XmlAttribute with the specified name.	Creates an XmlAttribute node with the specified name.	createAttribute Creates a new object of type IXMLDOMAttributeat-tribute with the specified name.
CreateCDataSection	Creates an XmlCDATASection containing the specified data.	createCDATASection Creates a IXMLDOMCDATASection node.
CreateComment	Creates an XmlComment containing the data specified.	createComment Creates an IXMLDOMComment.
CreateDocumentFragment	Creates an empty XmlDocumentFragment used for tree inserts.	createDocument Fragment Creates an empty DocumentFragment object.
CreateDocumentType	Creates an XmlDocumentType object.	
CreateElement	Creates an empty XmlElement. Use the Value property to specify text data for the element, or append an XmlTextNode as the element's child.	createElement Creates an empty IXMLDOMElement object.
CreateEntityReference	Creates an XmlEntityReference with the specified name.	createEntity Reference Creates an IXMLDOMEntity Reference object.
CreateNode	Creates an XmlNode object with the specified XmlNodeType.	createNode Creates an IXMLDOMNode object.

continues

Table B.4 **Continued**

XmlDocument (Inherits *XmlNode*)	Description	MSXML *DOMDocument*
CreateProcessing Instruction	Creates an XmlProcessingInstruction that contains the specified target and data. For working with the `<?xml version="1.0"?>` XML declaration, use the CreateXmlDeclaration method.	createProcessing Instruction Creates an IXMLDOMProcessing Instruction object.
CreateSignificant Whitespace	Creates an XmlSignificantWhitespace node containing only the characters &#20;,
, , and 	.	
CreateTextNode	Creates an XmlTextNode with the passed in text.	createTextNode Creates an IMLDOMText object.
CreateWhitespace	Creates an XmlWhitespace node containing only the characters &#20;,
, , and 	.	
CreateXmlDeclaration	Creates an XmlDeclaration object with the specified values. Accepts parameters for version, encoding, and standalone.	
GetElementById	Gets the XmlElement with the specified ID attribute. If multiple matches are found, returns only the first match.	
GetElementsByTagName	Returns an XmlNodeList containing all the descendant elements with the specified name.	getElementsByTagName Returns IXMLDOMNodeList
ImportNode	Imports a node from an external document to the current document.	

XmlDocument (Inherits *XmlNode*)	Description	**MSXML** *DOMDocument*
Load	Loads the XML data. Sources for the XML data include from a URL, a Stream, a TextReader, and an XmlReader.	load Sources include URL, IStream, Internet Information Services (IIS) Request object.
LoadXml	Loads the XML document from the string parameter.	loadXML
ReadNode	Creates an XmlNode object based on the information in the XmlReader. The reader must be positioned on a node or attribute. If positioned on an element node, it advances the reader to the next position. If positioned on an attribute, it does not advance the reader.	
Save	Saves the XML document to the specified location.	save
WriteContentTo (Overrides XMLNode:: WriteContentTo)	Saves the contents of the XmlDocument node to the specified XmlWriter.	
WriteTo (Overrides XMLNode:: WriteTo)	Saves the XmlDocument node to the specified XmlWriter.	

System.Xml.XmlImplementation and *IXMLDOMImplementation*

XmlImplementation class in the System.Xml namespace is the implementation of the W3C DOMImplementation interface. You can get the XmlImplementation object for a document using the XmlDocument object's Implementation property. XmlImplementation class provides methods that are independent of any particular instance of the DOM. Table B.5 list these methods.

Table B.5 *System. Xml. XmlImplementation* and *IXMLDOMImplementation*
Methods

XmlImplementation	Description	MSXML *IXMLDOM* Implementation
CreateDocument	Creates a new XmlDocument object.	
HasFeature	Returns a Boolean indicating whether the DOM implementation implements a specific feature passed in as a parameter.	hasFeature

System. Xml. XmlDocumentFragment and IXMLDOMDocumentFragment

XmlDocumentFragment class in the System.Xml namespace is an implementation of the W3C DocumentFragment interface. This class represents a lightweight object that inherits the XmlNode class and is useful for tree insert operations. This can be used as an alternative to XmlDocument class, which might prove to be comparatively heavyweight for some operations on the document. Table B.6 and Table B.7 list the properties and methods respectively found in the XmlDocumentFragment class.

Table B.6 *IXMLDOMDocumentFragment* and
System. Xml. XmlDocumentFragment Properties

XmlDocumentFragment (Inherits *XmlNode*)	Description	IXMLDOMDocument Fragment
InnerXml (Overrides XMLNode::InnerXml)	Gets or sets the markup representing the children of the current node.	
LocalName (Overrides XMLNode::LocalName)	Gets the name of the node without the namespace prefix.	baseName
Name (Overrides XMLNode::Name)	Gets the qualified name of the node.	nodeName
NodeType (Overrides XMLNode::NodeType)	Returns an XmlNodeType enumeration member representing this node's type.	nodeType (Gets an IXMLDOMNodeType enumeration member)

XmlDocumentFragment (Inherits *XmlNode*)	Description	*IXMLDOMDocument Fragment*
`OwnerDocument` (Overrides `XMLNode::OwnerDocument`)	Gets the `XmlDocument` to which the current node belongs.	`ownerDocument` Gets the `IXMLDOMDocument` root note to which the current node belongs.
`ParentNode` (Overrides `XMLNode::ParentNode`)	Gets the parent of the current node. If the node has been created but not added to the tree, this returns a null reference in C#, or Nothing in Visual Basic .NET.	`parentNode`

Table B.7   *System.Xml.XmlDocumentFragment* and *IXMLDOMDocumentFragment* Methods

XmlDocumentFragment	Description	*IXMLDOMDocument Fragment*
`CloneNode` (Overrides `XMLNode::CloneNode`)	Similar to `XMLNode::Clone`, but accepts a deep Boolean parameter indicating if the subtree should be duplicated.	`cloneNode`
`WriteContentTo` (Overrides `XMLNode::WriteContentTo`)	Saves the contents of the `XmlDocument` node to the specified `XmlWriter`.	
`WriteTo` (Overrides `XMLNode::WriteTo`)	Saves the `XmlDocument` node to the specified `XmlWriter`.	

System.Xml.XmlNodeList and *IXMLDOMNodeList*

`XmlNodeList` class in the `System.Xml` namespace is an implementation of the W3C `NodeList` interface. This class represents an ordered collection of nodes that can be iterated through. The `XmlDocument`'s `ChildNodes` property and the `GetElementsByTagName` method return an `XmlNodeList` object. Table B.8 and Table B.9 list the properties and methods respectively found in the `XmlNodeList` class.

Table B.8 *System.Xml.XmlNodeList* and *IXMLDOMNodeList* **Properties**

XmlNodeList (Inherits *IEnumerable*)	Description	IXMLDOMNodeList
Count	Gets the number of nodes in the XmlNodeList.	length Gets the number of nodes in the IXMLDOMNodeList collection.
ItemOf	Gets a node corresponding to the index specified. In C#, this property is the indexer for the XmlNodeList class.	

Table B.9 *System.Xml.XmlNodeList* and *IXMLDOMNodeList* **Methods**

XmlNodeList	Description	IXMLDOMNodeList
Item	Gets a node in the collection corresponding to the index specified.	item
GetEnumerator	Enables For Each enumerations on the object.	

System.Xml.XmlElement and *IXMLDOMElement*

XmlElement class in the System.Xml namespace is an implementation of the W3C Element interface. This class represents an element in an XML document. Table B.10 and Table B.11 list the properties and methods respectively found in the XmlElement class.

Table B.10 *System.Xml.XmlElement* and *IXMLDOMElement* **Properties**

XmlElement (Inherits *XmlLinkedNode*)	Description	IXMLDOMElement
Attributes (Overrides XMLNode::Attributes)	Gets an XmlAttributeCollection containing the attributes of this node.	attributes Gets IXMLDOMNamedNodeMap.
HasAttributes	Returns a Boolean value indicating whether the current node has any attributes.	

XmlElement (**Inherits** *XmlLinkedNode*)	**Description**	*IXMLDOMElement*
IsEmpty	Returns true if the tag form at is in the form "`<book/>`"; false for the form "`<book></book>`".	
LocalName (Overrides XMLNode::LocalName)	Gets the name of the node without the namespace prefix.	baseName
NamespaceURI (Overrides XMLNode::NamespaceURI)	Returns the namespace URI of the current node.	namespaceURI
NextSibling (Overrides XMLNode::NextSibling)	Returns the node following this node at the same level in the document hierarchy.	nextSibling
Name (Overrides XMLNode::Name)	Gets the qualified name of the node.	nodeName
NodeType (Overrides XMLNode::NodeType)	Returns an XmlNodeType enumeration member representing this node's type.	nodeType (Gets an IXMLDOMNodeType enumeration member)
OwnerDocument (Overrides XMLNode::OwnerDocument)	Gets the XmlDocument to which the current node belongs.	ownerDocument Gets the IXMLDOMDocument root note to which the current node belongs.
Prefix (Overrides XMLNode::Prefix)	Gets the namespace prefix associated with the current node.	prefix
PreviousSibling (Inherited from XmlLinkedNode)	Gets the node previous to this node at the same level in the document hierarchy.	previousSibling
InnerText (Overrides XMLNode::InnerText)	Gets or sets the concatenated values of the node and all its children.	text
InnerXml (Overrides XMLNode::InnerXml)	Gets or sets the markup representing the children of the current node.	

Table B.11 *System.Xml.XmlElement* **and** *IXMLDOMElement* **Methods**

XmlElement	Description	IXMLDOMElement
CloneNode (Overrides XMLNode::CloneNode)		Similar to XMLNode::Clone, but accepts a deep Boolean parameter indicating if the subtree should be duplicated.
GetAttribute	Gets the attribute value of the attribute passed as a string parameter.	getAttribute
GetAttributeNode	Return the XmlAttribute for the attribute passed as a string parameter.	getAttributeNode Returns an IXMLDOMAttribute.
GetElementsByTagName	Returns an XmlNodeList containing all the descendant elements with the specified name.	getElementsByTagName Returns IXMLDOMNodeList.
HasAttribute	Returns a Boolean indicating whether the current node has a specified attribute.	
RemoveAll (Overrides XMLNode::RemoveAll)	Removes all specified attributes and child nodes of the current node with the exception of default attributes.	
RemoveAllAttributes	Removes all specified attributes and child nodes of the current element with the exception of default attributes.	
RemoveAttribute	Removes the specified attribute.	removeAttribute
RemoveAttributeAt	Removes the attribute node with the index specified.	
RemoveAttributeNode	Removes an XmlAttribute object.	removeAttributeNode Removes an IXMLDOMAttribute.
SetAttribute	Sets the value of the specified named attribute.	setAttribute
SetAttributeNode	Adds or changes the supplied XmlAttribute.	setAttributeNode Adds or changes the supplied IXMLDOMAttribute.

XmlElement	Description	*IXMLDOMElement*
WriteContentTo (Overrides XMLNode::WriteContentTo)	Saves the contents of the XmlDocument node to the specified XmlWriter.	
WriteTo (Overrides XMLNode::WriteTo)	Saves the XmlDocument node to the specified XmlWriter.	

System.Xml.XmlNamedNodeMap and *IXMLDOMNamedNodeMap*

XmlNamedNodeMap class in the System.Xml namespace is an implementation of the W3C NamedNodeMap interface. This class represents a collection of nodes that can be accessed by name or index. Table B.12 and Table B.13 list the properties and methods respectively found in the XmlNamedNodeMap class.

Table B.12 *System.Xml.XmlNamedNodeMap* and *IXMLDOMNamedNodeMap* **Properties**

XmlNamedNodeMap (**Implements** *IEnumerable*)	Description	**MSXML** *IXMLDOMNamed NodeMap*
Count	Gets the number of nodes in the XmlNamedNodeMap.	length Gets the number of items in the IXMLDOMNamedNodeMap.

Table B.13 *System.Xml.XmlNamedNodeMap* and *IXMLDOMNamedNodeMap* **Methods**

XmlNamedNodeMap (**Implements** *IEnumerable*)	Description	**MSXML** *IXMLDOMNamed NodeMap*
GetEnumerator	Enables For Each enumerations on the object.	
GetNamedItem Retrieves the specified XmlNode from the collection of nodes in the XmlNamedNodeMap.	Gets the specified XmlNode from the XmlNamedNodeMap.	getNamedItem Gets the specified attribute from the IXMLDOMNamedNodeMap.

continues

Table B.13 **Continued**

XmlNamedNodeMap (Implements IEnumerable)	Description	MSXML IXMLDOMNamed NodeMap
Item	Gets the node at the specified index in the XmlNamedNodeMap.	item Gets the node at the specified index in the IXMLDOMNamedNodeMap.
RemoveNamedItem	Removes the specified node from the XmlNamedNodeMap.	removeNamedItem Removes the specified node from the IXMLDOMNamedNodeMap.
SetNamedItem	Adds the specified XmlNode to the XmlNamedNodeMap.	setNamedItem Adds the specified IXMLDOMNode to the IXMLDOMNamedNodeMap.

System.Xml.XmlAttribute and IXMLDOMAttribute

XmlAttribute class in the System.Xml namespace is an implementation of the W3C Attr interface. This class represents an attribute in an XmlElement object. Valid and default values for the attribute are defined in a DTD or schema. XmlAttribute inherits from the XmlNode class, but it is important to remember that the DOM does not consider them part of the document tree. Table B.14 and Table B.15 list the properties and methods respectively found in the XmlAttribute class.

Table B.14 *System.Xml.XmlAttribute* and *IXMLDOMAttribute* **Properties**

XmlAttribute (Inherits XmlNode)	Description	MSXML IXMLDOMAttribute
BaseURI Overridden. Gets the base URI of the node.		
LocalName (Overrides XMLNode::LocalName)	Gets the name of the node without the namespace prefix.	baseName

XmlAttribute (Inherits *XmlNode*)	Description	MSXML *IXMLDOMAttribute*
Name (Overrides `XMLNode::Name`)	Gets the qualified name of the node.	`nodeName`
NamespaceURI (Overrides `XMLNode::NamespaceURI`)	Returns the namespace URI of the current node.	`namespaceURI`
NodeType (Overrides `XMLNode::NodeType`)	Returns an `XmlNodeType` enumeration member representing this node's type.	`nodeType` (Gets an `IXMLDOMNodeType` enumeration member)
Value (Overrides `XMLNode::Value`)	Gets or sets the value (text) of the current node.	`nodeValue`
OwnerDocument (Overrides `XMLNode::OwnerDocument`)	Gets the `XmlDocument` to which the current node belongs.	`ownerDocument` Gets the `IXMLDOMDocument` root note that the current node belongs to.
OwnerElement	Gets the `XmlElement` to which the current attribute belongs.	
ParentNode (Overrides `XMLNode::ParentNode`)	Gets the parent of the current node. For `XmlAttribute` nodes, this returns a null reference in C#, or `Nothing` in Visual Basic .NET.	`parentNode`
Prefix (Overrides `XMLNode::Prefix`)	Gets the namespace prefix associated with the current node.	`prefix`
Specified	Gets a Boolean value indicating whether the attribute value was explicitly set.	`specified`
InnerText (Overrides `XMLNode::InnerText`)	Gets or sets the concatenated values of the node and all its children.	`text`

continues

Table B.14   **Continued**

XmlAttribute (Inherits XmlNode)	Description	MSXML IXMLDOMAttribute
InnerXml (Overrides XMLNode::InnerXml)	Gets or sets the markup representing the children of the current node.	
Value (Overrides XMLNode::Value)	Gets or sets the value (text) of the current node.	nodeValue

Table B.15   *System.Xml.XmlAttribute* and *IXMLDOMAttribute* **Methods**

XmlAttribute (Inherits XmlNode)	Description	MSXML IXMLDOMAttribute
CloneNode (Overrides XMLNode::CloneNode)	Similar to XMLNode::Clone, but accepts a deep Boolean parameter indicating if the subtree should be duplicated.	cloneNode
WriteContentTo (Overrides XMLNode::WriteContentTo)	Saves the contents of the XmlDocument node to the specified XmlWriter.	
WriteTo (Overrides XMLNode::WriteTo)	Saves the XmlDocument node to the specified XmlWriter.	

System.Xml.XmlCharacterData and *IXMLDOMCharacterData*

XmlCharacterData class in the System.Xml namespace is an implementation of the W3C CharacterData interface. This class provides text manipulation methods that are used by several classes. Table B.16 and Table B.17 list the properties and methods respectively found in the XmlCharacterData class.

Table B.16 *System.Xml.XmlCharacterData* **and** *IXMLDOMCharacterData*
            Properties

XmlCharacterData (**Inherits** *XmlLinkedNode*)	**Description**	**MSXML** *IXMLDOMCharacterData*
Data	Contains the node's data.	data
Length	Gets the length, in characters, of the data.	length
NextSibling (Inherited from XmlLinkedNode)	Returns the node following this node at the same level in the document hierarchy.	nextSibling
Value (Overrides XMLNode:: Value)	Gets or sets the value (text) of the current node.	nodeValue
PreviousSibling (Inherited from XmlLinkedNode)	Gets the node previous to this node at the same level in the document hierarchy.	previousSibling
InnerText (Overrides XMLNode:: InnerText)	Gets or sets the concatenated values of the node and all its children.	text

Table B.17 *System.Xml.XmlCharacterData* **and** *IXMLDOMCharacterData*
            Methods

XmlCharacterData	**Description**	**MSXML** *IXMLDOMCharacterData*
AppendData	Appends the supplied string to the character data of the node.	appendData Appends the supplied string to the existing string data.
DeleteData	Deletes a range of characters from the node.	deleteData
InsertData	Inserts the supplied string at the specified character offset.	insertData

continues

Table B.17 *System.Xml.XmlCharacterData* and *IXMLDOMCharacterData* **Methods**

XmlCharacterData	Description	**MSXML** *IXMLDOMCharacterData*
ReplaceData	Replaces the specified number of characters with the supplied string.	replaceData
Substring	Gets a substring of the full string from the range specified.	substringData

System.Xml.XmlText and *IXMLDOMText*

XmlText class in the System.Xml namespace is an implementation of the W3C Text interface. This class represents the text content of an element or attribute. Table B.18 and Table B.19 list the properties and methods respectively found in the XmlText class.

Table B.18 *System.Xml.XmlText* and *IXMLDOMText* **Methods**

XmlText (**Inherits** *XmlCharacterData*)	Description	**MSXML** *IXMLDOMText*
LocalName (Overrides XMLNode::LocalName)	Gets the name of the node without the namespace prefix.	baseName
NextSibling (Inherited from XmlLinkedNode)	Returns the node following this node at the same level in the document hierarchy.	nextSibling
Name (Overrides XMLNode:: Name)	Gets the qualified name of the node.	nodeName
NodeType (Overrides XMLNode::NodeType)	Returns an XmlNodeType enumeration member representing this node's type.	nodeType (Gets an IXMLDOMNode Type enumeration member)
Value (Overrides XMLNode:: Value)	Gets or sets the value (text) of the current node.	nodeValue

XmlText (Inherits *XmlCharacterData*)	Description	MSXML *IXMLDOMText*
PreviousSibling (Inherited from `XmlLinkedNode`)	Gets the node previous to this node at the same level in the document hierarchy.	`previousSibling`
InnerText (Overrides `XmlCharacterData:: InnerText`)	Gets or sets the concatenated values of the node and all its children.	`text`

Table B.19 *System.Xml.XmlText and IXMLDOMText Methods*

XmlText (Inherits *XmlCharacterData*)	Description	MSXML *IXMLDOMText*
CloneNode (Overrides `XMLNode::CloneNode`)	Similar to `XMLNode::Clone`, but accepts a deep Boolean parameter indicating if the subtree should be duplicated.	`cloneNode`
SplitText	Splits the text node into two text nodes at the specified offset, keeping both in the tree as siblings.	`splitText` Breaks this text node into two text nodes at the specified offset and inserts the new text node into the tree as a sibling that immediately follows this node.
WriteContentTo (Overrides `XMLNode::WriteContentTo`)	Saves the contents of the `XmlDocument` node to the specified `XmlWriter`.	
WriteTo (Overrides `XMLNode::WriteTo`)	Saves the `XmlDocument` node to the specified `XmlWriter`.	

System.Xml.XmlComment and IXMLDOMComment

`XmlComment` class in the `System.Xml` namespace is an implementation of the W3C `Comment` interface. This class represents the content of an XML comment. Table B.20 and Table B.21 list the properties and methods respectively found in the `XmlComment` class.

Table B.20   *System.Xml.XmlComment* and *IXMLDOMComment* **Properties**

XmlComment (Inherits *XmlCharacterData*)	Description	MSXML IXMLDOMComment
LocalName (Overrides XMLNode::LocalName)	Gets the name of the node without the namespace prefix.	baseName
NextSibling (Inherited from XmlLinkedNode)	Returns the node following this node at the same level in the document hierarchy	nextSibling
Name (Overrides XMLNode:: Name)	Gets the qualified name of the node.	nodeName
NodeType (Overrides XMLNode:: NodeType)	Returns an XmlNodeType enumeration member representing this node's type.	nodeType (Gets an IXMLDOMNodeType enumeration member)
Value (Inherited from XmlCharacterData)	Gets or sets the value (text) of the current node.	nodeValue
PreviousSibling (Inherited from XmlLinkedNode)	Gets the node previous to this node at the same level in the document hierarchy.	previousSibling
InnerText (Inherited from XmlCharacterData)	Gets or sets the concatenated values of the node and all its children.	text

Table B.21   *System.Xml.XmlComment* and *IXMLDOMComment* **Methods**

System.Xml.XmlComment	Description	MSXML IXMLDOMComment
CloneNode (Overrides XMLNode::CloneNode)	Similar to XMLNode::Clone, but accepts a deep Boolean parameter indicating if the subtree should be duplicated.	cloneNode
WriteContentTo (Overrides XMLNode:: WriteContentTo)	Saves the contents of the XmlDocument node to the specified XmlWriter.	
WriteTo (Overrides XMLNode::WriteTo)	Saves the XmlDocument node to the specified XmlWriter.	

System.Xml.XmlCDataSection and IXMLDOMCDATASection

XmlCDataSection class in the System.Xml namespace is an implementation of the W3C CDATASection interface. This class represents a CDATA section. Table B.22 and Table B.23 list the properties and methods respectively found in the XmlCDataSection class.

Table B.22   *System.Xml.XmlCDataSection* **and** *IXMLDOMCDATASection*
             Properties

System.Xml.XmlCDataSection (Inherits XmlCharacterData)	Description	MSXML IXMLDOMC DATASection
LocalName (Overrides XMLNode:: LocalName)	Gets the name of the node without the namespace prefix.	baseName
NextSibling (Inherited from XmlLinkedNode)	Returns the node following this node at the same level in the document hierarchy.	nextSibling
Name (Overrides XMLNode:: Name)	Gets the qualified name of the node.	nodeName
NodeType (Overrides XMLNode:: NodeType)	Returns an XmlNodeType enumeration member representing this node's type.	nodeType (Gets an IXMLDOMNodeType Enumeration member)

Table B.23   *System.Xml.XmlCDataSection* **and** *IXMLDOMCDATASection*
             Methods

XmlCDataSection (Inherits XmlCharacterData)	Description	MSXML IXMLDOMC DATASection
CloneNode (Overrides XMLNode::CloneNode)	Similar to XMLNode:: Clone, but accepts a deep Boolean parameter indicating if the subtree should be duplicated.	cloneNode
WriteContentTo (Overrides XMLNode:: WriteContentTo)	Saves the contents of the XmlDocument node to the specified XmlWriter.	

Table B.23 **Continued**

XmlCDataSection (Inherits *XmlCharacterData*)	Description	*MSXML IXMLDOMC DATASection*
WriteTo (Overrides XMLNode::WriteTo)	Saves the XmlDocument node to the specified XmlWriter.	

System. Xml. XmlDocumentType and *IXMLDOMDocumentType*

XmlDocumentType class in the System.Xml namespace is an implementation of the W3C DocumentType interface. This class represents the document type declaration. Table B.24 and Table B.25 list the properties and methods respectively found in the XmlDocumentType class.

Table B.24 *System. Xml. XmlDocumentType* and *IXMLDOMDocumentType*
Properties

XmlDocumentType (Inherits *XmlLinkedNode*)	Description	*MSXML IXMLDOM DocumentType*
Entities	Gets an XmlNamedNodeMap containing XmlEntity nodes declared in the document type declaration.	entities Gets an IXMLDOMNamedNodeMap.
InternalSubset	Returns the value of the DTD internal subset on the DOCTYPE declaration.	
IsReadOnly (Overrides XMLNode::IsReadOnly)	Returns a Boolean indicating whether the current node is read only.	
LocalName (Overrides XMLNode::LocalName)	Gets the name of the node without the namespace prefix.	baseName
Name (Overrides XMLNode:: Name)	Gets the qualified name of the node.	nodeName
Notations Gets the collection of XmlNotation nodes present in the document type declaration.	Gets an XmlNamedNodeMap containing XmlNotation nodes present in the document type declaration.	notations Gets an IXMLDOMNamedNodeMap.

XmlDocumentType (Inherits XmlLinkedNode)	Description	MSXML IXMLDOM DocumentType
PreviousSibling (Inherited from XmlLinkedNode)	Gets the node previous to this node at the same level in the document hierarchy.	previousSibling
PublicId	Returns the value of the public identifier on the DOCTYPE declaration.	
SystemId	Returns the value of the system identifier on the DOCTYPE declaration.	

Table B.25 *System.Xml.XmlDocumentType* and *IXMLDOMDocumentType* Methods

XmlDocumentType	Description	MSXML IXMLDOM DocumentType
CloneNode (Overrides XMLNode::CloneNode)	Similar to XMLNode::Clone but accepts a deep Boolean parameter indicating if the subtree should be duplicated.	cloneNode
WriteContentTo (Overrides XMLNode::WriteContentTo)	Saves the contents of the XmlDocument node to the specified XmlWriter.	
WriteTo (Overrides XMLNode::WriteTo)	Saves the XmlDocument node to the specified XmlWriter.	

System.Xml.XmlNotation and *IXMLDOMNotation*

XmlNotation class in the System.Xml namespace is an implementation of the W3C Notation interface. This class represents a notation declaration <!NOTATION ... >. Table B.26 and Table B.27 list the properties and methods respectively found in the XmlNotation class.

Table B.26 *System.Xml.XmlNotation* and *IXMLDOMNotation* Properties

System.Xml.XmlNotation (Inherits *XmlNode*)	Description	MSXML *IXMLDOMNotation*
CloneNode (Overrides XMLNode::CloneNode)	Similar to XMLNode::Clone, but accepts a deep Boolean parameter indicating if the subtree should be duplicated.	cloneNode
InnerXml (Overrides XMLNode::InnerXml)	Gets or sets the markup representing the children of the current node.	InnerXml (Overrides XMLNode::InnerXml)
IsReadOnly (Overrides XMLNode::IsReadOnly)	Returns a Boolean indicating whether the current node is read only.	
Name (Overrides XMLNode:: Name)	Gets the qualified name of the node.	nodeName
NodeType (Overrides XMLNode::NodeType)	Returns an XmlNodeType enumeration member representing this node's type.	nodeType (Gets an IXMLDOMNodeType enumeration member)
PublicId	Returns the value of the public identifier on the notation declaration.	publicId
SystemId	Returns the value of the system identifier on the notation declaration.	systemId
OuterXml (Overrides XmlNode::OuterXml)	Gets the XML markup representing the current node and its children. Similar to InnerXml, except the current node is also returned.	xml

Table B.27 *System.Xml.XmlNotation* and *IXMLDOMNotation* Methods

XmlNotation	Description	MSXML *IXMLDOMNotation*
CloneNode (Overrides XMLNode::CloneNode)	Similar to XMLNode::Clone, but accepts a deep Boolean parameter indicating if the subtree should be duplicated.	cloneNode

XmlNotation	Description	**MSXML** *IXMLDOMNotation*
WriteContentTo (Overrides XMLNode::WriteContentTo)	Saves the contents of the XmlDocument node to the specified XmlWriter. No effect for XmlNotation nodes.	
WriteTo (Overrides XMLNode::WriteTo)	Saves the XmlDocument node to the specified XmlWriter. No effect for XmlNotation nodes.	

System.Xml.XmlEntity and *IXMLDOMEntity*

XmlEntity class in the System.Xml namespace is an implementation of the W3C Entity interface. This class represents an entity declaration <!ENTITY ... >. Table B.28 and Table B.29 list the properties and methods respectively found in the XmlEntity class.

Table B.28   *System.Xml.XmlEntity* and *IXMLDOMEntity* Properties

XmlEntity (Inherits *XmlNode*)	Description	**MSXML** *IXMLDOMEntity*
BaseURI (Overrides XMLNode::BaseURI)	Gets the base URI of the current node. Indicates from where the node was loaded.	
LocalName (Overrides XMLNode::LocalName)	Gets the name of the node without the namespace prefix.	baseName
InnerXml (Overrides XMLNode::InnerXml)	Gets or sets the markup representing the children of the current node.	
IsReadOnly (Overrides XMLNode::IsReadOnly)	Returns a Boolean indicating whether the current node is read only.	
Name (Overrides XMLNode:: Name)	Gets the qualified name of the node.	nodeName
NodeType (Overrides XMLNode:: NodeType)	Returns an XmlNodeType enumeration member representing this node's type.	nodeType (Gets an IXMLDOMNodeType enumeration member)

continues

Table B.28 **Continued**

XmlEntity (Inherits XmlNode)	Description	MSXML IXMLDOMEntity
NotationName	Returns the name of the optional NDATA attribute on the entity declaration.	notationName
OuterXml (Overrides XmlNode:: OuterXml)	Gets the XML markup representing the current node and its children. Similar to InnerXml, except the current node is also returned.	OuterXml (Overrides XmlNode:: OuterXml)
PublicId	Returns the value of the public identifier on the entity declaration.	publicId
SystemId	Returns the value of the system identifier on the entity declaration.	systemId

Table B.29 *System.Xml.XmlEntity* and *IXMLDOMEntity* **Methods**

XmlEntity (Inherits XmlNode)	Description	MSXML IXMLDOMEntity
CloneNode (Overrides XMLNode::CloneNode)	Similar to XMLNode::Clone, but accepts a deep Boolean parameter indicating if the subtree should be duplicated.	cloneNode
WriteContentTo (Overrides XMLNode:: WriteContentTo)	Saves the contents of the XmlDocument node to the specified XmlWriter. No effect for XmlEntity nodes.	
WriteTo (Overrides XMLNode::WriteTo)	Saves the XmlDocument node to the specified XmlWriter. No effect for XmlEntity nodes.	

System.Xml.XmlEntityReference and *IXMLDOMEntityReference*

XmlEntityReference class in the System.Xml namespace is an implementation of the W3C EntityReference interface. This class represents an entity reference node. Table B.30 and Table B.31 list the properties and methods respectively found in the XmlEntityReference class.

Table B.30   *System.Xml.XmlEntityReference* and *IXMLDOMEntityReference* Properties

XmlEntityReference (Inherits *XmlLinkedNode*)	Description	MSXML *IXMLDOM EntityReference*
BaseURI (Overrides XMLNode::BaseURI)	Gets the base URI of the current node. Indicates from where the node was loaded.	
LocalName (Overrides XMLNode:: LocalName)	Gets the name of the node without the namespace prefix.	baseName
IsReadOnly (Overrides XMLNode::IsReadOnly)	Returns a Boolean indicating whether the current node is read only.	
NextSibling (Inherited from XmlLinkedNode)	Returns the node following this node at the same level in the document hierarchy.	nextSibling
Name (Overrides XMLNode:: Name)	Gets the qualified name of the node.	nodeName
NodeType (Overrides XMLNode:: NodeType)	Returns an XmlNodeType enumeration member representing this node's type.	nodeType (Gets an IXMLDOMNodeType enumeration member)
Value (Overrides XMLNode:: Value)	Gets or sets the value (text) of the current node.	nodeValue
PreviousSibling (Inherited from XmlLinkedNode)	Gets the node previous to this node at the same level in the document hierarchy.	previousSibling

Table B.31   *System.Xml.XmlEntityReference* and *IXMLDOMEntityReference*
             Methods

XmlEntityReference (Inherits *XmlLinkedNode*)	Description	MSXML *IXMLDOM* *EntityReference*
CloneNode (Overrides XMLNode::CloneNode)	Similar to XMLNode::Clone but accepts a deep Boolean parameter indicating if the subtree should be duplicated.	cloneNode
WriteContentTo (Overrides XMLNode:: WriteContentTo)	Saves the contents of the XmlDocument node to the specified XmlWriter.	
WriteTo (Overrides XMLNode::WriteTo)	Saves the XmlDocument node to the specified XmlWriter.	

System.Xml.XmlProcessingInstruction and IXMLDOMProcessingInstruction

XmlProcessingInstruction class in the System.Xml namespace is an implementation of the W3C ProcessingInstruction interface. This class represents a processing instruction, which XML defines to keep processor-specific information in the text of the document. Table B.32 and Table B.33 list the properties and methods respectively found in the XmlProcessingInstruction class.

Table B.32   *System.Xml.XmlProcessingInstruction* and
             IXMLDOMProcessingInstruction **Properties**

XmlProcessingInstruction (Inherits *XmlLinkedNode*)	Description	MSXML *IXMLDOM* *ProcessingInstruction*
LocalName (Overrides XMLNode:: LocalName)	Gets the name of the node without the namespace prefix.	baseName
Data	Gets or sets the content of the processing instruction, excluding the target.	data

XmlProcessingInstruction (Inherits *XmlLinkedNode*)	Description	MSXML *IXMLDOM ProcessingInstruction*
`NextSibling` (Inherited from `XmlLinkedNode`)	Returns the node following this node at the same level in the document hierarchy.	`nextSibling`
`Name` (Overrides `XMLNode:: Name`)	Gets the qualified name of the node.	`nodeName`
`NodeType` (Overrides `XMLNode:: NodeType`)	Returns an `XmlNodeType` enumeration member representing this node's type.	`nodeType` (Gets an `IXMLDOMNodeType` enumeration member)
`Value` (Overrides `XMLNode:: Value`)	Gets or sets the value (text) of the current node.	`nodeValue`
`PreviousSibling` (Inherited from `XmlLinkedNode`)	Gets the node previous to this node at the same level in the document hierarchy.	`previousSibling`
`Target`	Returns the target of the processing instruction.	`target`
`InnerText` (Overrides `XMLNode:: InnerText`)	Gets or sets the concatenated values of the node and all its children.	`text`

Table B.33 *System.Xml.XmlProcessingInstruction* and *IXMLDOMProcessingInstruction Methods*

XmlProcessingInstruction (Inherits *XmlLinkedNode*)	Description	MSXML *IXMLDOM ProcessingInstruction*
`CloneNode` (Overrides `XMLNode::CloneNode`)	Similar to `XMLNode::Clone` but accepts a deep Boolean parameter indicating if the subtree should be duplicated.	`cloneNode`

continues

Table B.33 **Continued**

XmlProcessingInstruction (Inherits *XmlLinkedNode*)	Description	**MSXML** *IXMLDOM ProcessingInstruction*
`WriteContentTo` (Overrides `XMLNode:: WriteContentTo`)	Saves the contents of the `XmlDocument` node to the specified `XmlWriter`. No effect for `ProcessingInstruction` nodes because they do not have children.	
`WriteTo` (Overrides `XMLNode::WriteTo`)	Saves the `XmlDocument` node to the specified `XmlWriter`. No effect for `XmlEntity` nodes.	

C

XSLT Reference

THE CONTENT IN THIS APPENDIX IS A MIXTURE between the XSLT reference at
`www.w3.org/TR/1999/REC-xslt-19991116`[1] and the MSDN documentation for
the MSXML SDK.

xsl:apply-imports

`xsl:apply-imports` invokes an overridden template rule in an imported
stylesheet.

A template rule that's being used to override a template rule in an imported
stylesheet can use the `xsl:apply-imports` element to invoke the overridden
template rule.

At any point in the processing of a stylesheet, a current template rule exists.
Whenever a template rule is chosen by matching a pattern, the template rule
becomes the current template rule for the instantiation of the rule's template.
When an `xsl:for-each` element is instantiated, the current template rule
becomes null for the instantiation of the content of the `xsl:for-each` element.

`xsl:apply-imports` processes the current node using only template rules that were imported into the stylesheet element containing the current template rule; the node is processed in the current template rule's mode. It is an error if `xsl:apply-imports` is instantiated when the current template rule is null.

Attributes

None.

Example

Suppose the stylesheet `doc.xsl` contains a template rule for example elements:

```
<xsl:template match="example">
  <pre><xsl:apply-templates/></pre>
</xsl:template>
```

Another stylesheet could import `doc.xsl` and modify the treatment of example elements, as shown here:

```
<xsl:import href="doc.xsl"/>

<xsl:template match="example">
  <div style="border: solid red">
    <xsl:apply-imports/>
  </div>
</xsl:template>
```

Parent Elements

xsl:attribute, xsl:comment, xsl:copy, xsl:element, xsl:for-each, xsl:if, xsl:otherwise, xsl:param, xsl:processing-instruction, xsl:template, xsl:variable, xsl:when, xsl:with-param, output elements

Child Elements

None.

xsl:apply-templates

`xsl:apply-templates` recursively processes the children of the source element.

Template rules are defined using `xsl:template`, imported using `xsl:import`, or included using `xsl:include`. If the `select` attribute is specified, a node list is generated that is applied to the rest of the stylesheet. If the `select` attribute is missing, all children of the current element are used in the resulting node list.

Each node is then tested against the templates to see if it applies to the definition of the template rule, following the recommendation for conflict resolution for template rules (defined in the W3C recommendation, Section 5.5, at www.w3.org/TR/xslt).

Both `xsl:template` and `xsl:apply-templates` have an optional `mode` attribute. The value of the `mode` attribute is a `QName`. If `xsl:template` does not have a `match` attribute, it must not have a `mode` attribute. If an `xsl:apply-templates` element has a `mode` attribute, it applies only to those template rules from `xsl:template` elements that have a `mode` attribute with the same value; if an `xsl:apply-templates` element does not have a `mode` attribute, it applies only to those template rules from `xsl:template` elements that do not have a `mode` attribute.

Attributes

Attribute Name	Enforced	Description	Values
select	Optional	Specifies the node list to return	An expression returning a node set
mode	Optional	Allows an element to be processed multiple times, each time returning a different result	QName

Example

Suppose that you have a series of links that you want to display on a page. Each link is represented here by a link element with properties for its unique identifier, its location on the web, a memorable name for the link, and a brief description of the site:

```xml
<?xml version="1.0" encoding="utf-8" ?>
<links>
    <link id="newriders" URL="http://www.newriders.com" name="NewRiders.com"
    ➥description="Available books by New Riders" />
    <link id="/xmlandasp" URL="http://www.xmlandasp.net" name="Xmlandasp.net"
    ➥description="Articles and samples available for VB, DNA, and .NET" />
    <link id="gotdotnet" URL="http://www.gotdotnet.com" name="GotDotNet.com"
    ➥description="Samples, walkthroughs, and more" />
    <link id="msdn" URL="http://msdn.microsoft.com/library" name="MSDN
    ➥Online Library" description="MSDN Online" />
    <link id="devx" URL="http://www.devx.com" name="DevX.com"
    ➥description="Fawcette Technical Publications" />
</links>
```

The stylesheet doc.xsl contains template rules to process each link element twice—once to generate an index of links, and the second to generate the named anchor tag, its URL, name, and description. Notice that the character entity reference # for the hash (#) symbol is used because the pound symbol has meaning in XSLT.

```xml
<?xml version="1.0" encoding="UTF-8" ?>
<xsl:stylesheet version="1.0"
xmlns:xsl="http://www.w3.org/1999/XSL/Transform">
    <xsl:template match="/">
        <html>
            <body>
                <xsl:apply-templates select="links/link" />
                <hr />
                <xsl:apply-templates select="links/link"
                ↪mode="description" />
            </body>
        </html>
    </xsl:template>
    <xsl:template match="link">
        <a>
            <xsl:attribute name="href">
                &#035;<xsl:value-of select="@id" />
            </xsl:attribute>
            <xsl:value-of select="@name" />
        </a>
        <br />
    </xsl:template>
    <xsl:template match="link" mode="description">
        <a>
            <xsl:attribute name="name">
                <xsl:value-of select="@id" />
            </xsl:attribute>
            <h1>
                <xsl:value-of select="@name" />
            </h1>
        </a>
        <a>
            <xsl:attribute name="href">
                <xsl:value-of select="@URL" />
            </xsl:attribute>
            <xsl:value-of select="@URL" />
        </a>
        <br />
        <xsl:value-of select="@description" />
        <br />
    </xsl:template>
</xsl:stylesheet>
```

Parent Elements

```
xsl:attribute, xsl:comment, xsl:copy, xsl:element, xsl:for-each, xsl:if,
xsl:otherwise, xsl:param, xsl:processing-instruction, xsl:template,
xsl:variable, xsl:when, xsl:with-param, output elements
```

Child Elements

```
xsl:sort, xsl:with-param
```

xsl:attribute

`xsl:attribute` creates an attribute of an output element.

Attributes

Attribute Name	Enforced	Description	Values
name	Required	The name of the attribute to add to the output element	QName
namespace	Optional	The namespace to be used for the attribute	URI reference

Example

Given the XML instance document, `links.xml`:

```
<?xml version="1.0" encoding="utf-8" ?>
<links>
    <link id="newriders" URL="http://www.newriders.com" name="NewRiders.com"
description="Available books by New Riders" />
</links>
```

The following template rule generates an anchor tag:

```
<xsl:template match="link">
    <a>
        <xsl:attribute name="href">
            <xsl:value-of select="@URL"/>
        </xsl:attribute>
        <xsl:value-of select="@name" />
    </a>
</xsl:template>
```

This results in the following markup:

```
<a href=http://www.newriders.com>Available books by New Riders</a>
```

Parent Elements

```
xsl:copy, xsl:element, xsl:for-each, xsl:if, xsl:otherwise, xsl:param,
xsl:template, xsl:variable, xsl:when, xsl:with-param
```

Child Elements

```
xsl:apply-templates, xsl:call-template, xsl:choose, xsl:copy, xsl:copy-of,
xsl:for-each, xsl:if, xsl:text, xsl:variable
```

xsl:attribute-set

Defines a named set of attributes.

Attribute sets are used by specifying a `use-attribute-sets` attribute on `xsl:element`, `xsl:copy`, or `xsl:attribute-set` elements.

Attributes

Attribute Name	Enforced	Description	Values
name	Required	The name of the attribute set definition	QName
use-attribute-sets	Optional	A list of attribute set names to use for the definition	White space delimited list of attribute set QNames

Example

Given the XML instance document, `links.xml`:

```
<?xml version="1.0" encoding="utf-8" ?>
<links>
    <link id="newriders" URL="http://www.newriders.com" name="NewRiders.com"
    ↪description="Available books by New Riders" />
    <link id="vbdna" URL="http://www.xmlandasp.net" name="Xmlandasp.net"
    ↪description="Articles and samples available for VB, DNA, and .NET" />
</links>
```

The following template rule generates a table with cells left-aligned and backcolor silver:

```
<html>
      <body>
            <table>
<xsl:template match="link">
            <tr>
                  <td xsl:use-attribute-sets="leftsilver">
                        <xsl:value-of select="@name" />
                  </td>
            </tr>
      </xsl:template>
      <xsl:attribute-set name="leftsilver">
            <xsl:attribute name="align">left</xsl:attribute>
            <xsl:attribute name="bgcolor">silver</xsl:attribute>
      </xsl:attribute-set>
            </table>
      </body>
</html>
```

This results in the following markup:

```
<html>
      <body>
            <table>
                  <tr>
                        <td align="left" bgcolor="silver">
                        NewRiders.com
                         </td>
                  </tr>
                  <tr>
                        <td align="left" bgcolor="silver">
                        Xmlandasp.net
                         </td>
                  </tr>
            </table>
      </body>
</html>
```

Parent Elements

```
xsl:stylesheet, xsl:transform
```

Child Elements

```
xsl:attribute
```

xsl:call-template

xsl:call-template calls a named template.

The xsl:call-template element defines template rules that perform as functions in C# or Visual Basic .NET. It can also contain xsl:with-param child elements to be used as parameters to the template rule.

Attributes

Attribute Name	Enforced	Description	Values
name	Required	The name of the template rule to call	QName

Example

Given the XML instance document, links.xml:

```
<?xml version="1.0" encoding="utf-8" ?>
<links>
    <link name="NewRiders.com" lastevaluated="2001-09-08T19:01:55"/>
</links>
```

The following stylesheet would parse the last evaluated attribute to display in mm/dd/yyyy format:

```
<?xml version="1.0" encoding="UTF-8" ?>
<xsl:stylesheet version="1.0"
xmlns:xsl="http://www.w3.org/1999/XSL/Transform">
    <xsl:template name="sqlserver_date">
        <xsl:param name="date" />
        <xsl:value-of select="substring($date, 6, 2)" />
        <xsl:text>/</xsl:text>
        <xsl:value-of select="substring($date, 9, 2)" />
        <xsl:text>/</xsl:text>
        <xsl:value-of select="substring($date, 1, 4)" />
    </xsl:template>
    <xsl:template match="/">
        <xsl:apply-templates select="links/link" />
    </xsl:template>
    <xsl:template match="link">
        <tr>
            <td>
                <xsl:call-template name="sqlserver_date">
                    <xsl:with-param name="date">
                        <xsl:value-of select="@lastevaluated" />
                    </xsl:with-param>
                </xsl:call-template>
            </td>
        </tr>
    </xsl:template>
</xsl:stylesheet>
```

This results in the following output:

```
<?xml version="1.0" encoding="UTF-16"?><tr><td>09/08/2001</td></tr>
```

Parent Elements

```
xsl:attribute, xsl:comment, xsl:copy, xsl:element, xsl:for-each, xsl:if,
xsl:otherwise, xsl:param, xsl:processing-instruction, xsl:template,
xsl:variable, xsl:when, xsl:with-param, output elements
```

Child Elements

```
xsl:with-param, output elements
```

xsl:choose

xsl:choose provides conditional processing, supporting the selection of one choice of several possibilities.

The xsl:choose element can be thought of as analgous to the C# switch statement or the Visual Basic Select Case statement. The xsl:when element is used in conjunction with the xsl:choose element to provide the functionality for each condition.

Attributes

None.

Example

You can use the xsl:choose element to test if an attribute exists or not. Using the following XML instance document, the image attribute is not specified for NewRiders.com but is available for xmlandasp.net:

```
<?xml version="1.0" encoding="utf-8" ?>
<links>
    <link name="NewRiders.com" />
    <link name="xmlandasp.net" image="images/xmlandasp.gif"/>
</links>
```

The following stylesheet displays images when the image attribute is specified; otherwise, it displays the value of the name attribute:

```
<?xml version="1.0" encoding="UTF-8" ?>
<xsl:stylesheet version="1.0"
xmlns:xsl="http://www.w3.org/1999/XSL/Transform">
    <xsl:template match="/">
        <xsl:apply-templates select="links/link" />
```

```
        </xsl:template>
        <xsl:template match="link">
            <xsl:choose>
                <xsl:when test="@image">
                    <img>
                        <xsl:attribute name="src">
                            <xsl:value-of select="@image" />
                        </xsl:attribute>
                    </img>
                </xsl:when>
                <xsl:otherwise>
                    <xsl:value-of select="@name"/>
                </xsl:otherwise>
            </xsl:choose>
        </xsl:template>
    </xsl:stylesheet>
```

Parent Elements

```
xsl:attribute, xsl:comment, xsl:copy, xsl:element, xsl:for-each, xsl:if,
xsl:otherwise, xsl:param, xsl:processing-instruction, xsl:template,
xsl:variable, xsl:when, xsl:with-param, output elements
```

Child Elements

```
xsl:otherwise, xsl:when
```

xsl:comment

xsl:comment generates a comment in the output.

Attributes

None.

Example

Consider this XML instance document, sample.xml:

```
<?xml version="1.0" encoding="utf-8" ?>
<foo>
    <bar>Testing</bar>
</foo>
```

The following stylesheet, sample.xslt, is applied to the sample XML document.

```
<xsl:stylesheet version="1.0"
xmlns:xsl="http://www.w3.org/1999/XSL/Transform">
    <xsl:template match="/">
```

```
        <xsl:comment>
            <xsl:value-of select="foo/bar"/>
        </xsl:comment>
    </xsl:template>
</xsl:stylesheet>
```

This produces the following result:

```
<?xml version="1.0" encoding="UTF-16"?><!--Testing-->
```

xsl:copy

xsl:copy copies the current node to the result.

Attributes

Attribute Name	Enforced	Description	Values
use-attribute-sets	Optional	A white space-separated list of attribute sets	QName

Example

Consider the XML instance document, links.xml:

```
<?xml version="1.0" encoding="utf-8" ?>
<links>
    <link name="NewRiders.com" URL="http://www.newriders.com" />
    <link name="Xmlandasp.net" URL="http://www.xmlandasp.net" />
    <link name="MSDN Online Library" URL="http://msdn.microsoft.com/library"
/>
</links>
```

The following stylesheet uses the xsl:copy element to copy all elements and attributes by matching each attribute (@*) or element (node()) in the second template rule, which creates an XML data island that's bound to a table and is usable in Internet Explorer:

```
<?xml version="1.0" encoding="UTF-8" ?>
<xsl:stylesheet version="1.0"
xmlns:xsl="http://www.w3.org/1999/XSL/Transform">
    <xsl:template match="/">
        <xml>
            <xsl:attribute name="id">dataisland</xsl:attribute>
            <xsl:apply-templates />
        </xml>
        <table>
            <xsl:attribute name="datasrc">&#035;dataisland</xsl:attribute>
            <tr>
                <td>
                    <div>
```

```
                    <xsl:attribute name="datafld">name</xsl:attribute>
                </div>
            </td>
            <td>
                <div>
                    <xsl:attribute name="datafld">URL</xsl:attribute>
                </div>
            </td>
        </tr>
    </table>
</xsl:template>
<xsl:template match="@* | node()">
    <xsl:copy>
        <xsl:apply-templates select="@* | node()" />
    </xsl:copy>
</xsl:template>
</xsl:stylesheet>
```

This results in the following output:

```
<?xml version="1.0" encoding="UTF-16"?>
    <xml id="dataisland">
        <links>
        <link name="NewRiders.com" URL="http://www.newriders.com" />
        <link name="Xmlandasp.net" URL="http://www.xmlandasp.net" />
        <link name="MSDN Online Library"
        ⇒URL="http://msdn.microsoft.com/library" />
        </links>
    </xml>
    <table datasrc="#dataisland">
        <tr>
            <td>
                <div datafld="name" />
            </td>
            <td>
                <div datafld="URL" />
            </td>
        </tr>
    </table>
```

When this code is displayed in Internet Explorer, version 5.0 or 5.5, the following HTML table is visible to the user.

NewRiders.com	www.newriders.com
Xmlandasp.net	www.xmlandasp.net
MSDN Online Library	http://msdn.microsoft.com/library

Parent Elements

```
xsl:attribute, xsl:comment, xsl:copy, xsl:element, xsl:for-each, xsl:if,
xsl:otherwise, xsl:param, xsl:processing-instruction, xsl:template,
xsl:variable, xsl:when, xsl:with-param, output elements
```

Child Elements

```
xsl:apply-templates, xsl:attribute, xsl:call-template, xsl:choose,
xsl:comment, xsl:copy, xsl:copy-of, xsl:element, xsl:for-each, xsl:if,
xsl:processing-instruction, xsl:text, xsl:value-of, xsl:variable, output
elements
```

xsl:copy-of

xsl:copy-of inserts subtrees into the result document without converting the
result into a string.

It's similar to xsl:copy, but provides an explicit select attribute to specify
the fragment to be included.

Attributes

Attribute Name	Enforced	Description	Values
Select	Required	The name of the template rule to call	QName

Example

Given the XML instance document, links.xml.

```
<?xml version="1.0" encoding="utf-8" ?>
<links>
    <link>
        <name>NewRiders.com</name>
        <URL>http://www.newriders.com</URL>
    </link>
    <link>
        <name>Xmlandasp.net</name>
        <URL>http://www.xmlandasp.net</URL>
    </link>
</links>
```

The preceding stylesheet used for the xsl:copy example is modified so that
only a single template rule is needed to match the root node. The character
entity reference # is used to display the pound (#) symbol because the #
symbol has meaning in XSLT.

```
<?xml version="1.0" encoding="UTF-8" ?>
<xsl:stylesheet version="1.0"
xmlns:xsl="http://www.w3.org/1999/XSL/Transform">
    <xsl:template match="/">
        <xml>
            <xsl:attribute name="id">dataisland</xsl:attribute>
            <xsl:copy-of select="@* | node()" />
        </xml>
```

```
                    <table border="1" datasrc="&#035;dataisland">
                        <tr>
                            <td>
                                <div>
                                    <xsl:attribute name="datafld">name<
                                    ➥/xsl:attribute>
                                </div>
                            </td>
                            <td>
                                <div>
                                    <xsl:attribute name="datafld">URL<
                                    ➥/xsl:attribute>
                                </div>
                            </td>
                        </tr>
                    </table>
                </xsl:template>
            </xsl:stylesheet>
```

This results in the following output, which is the same output yielded in the
xsl:copy example.

```
<?xml version="1.0" encoding="UTF-16" ?>
<xml id="dataisland">
    <links>
        <link>
            <name>NewRiders.com</name>
            <URL>http://www.newriders.com</URL>
        </link>
        <link>
            <name>Xmlandasp.net</name>
            <URL>http://www.xmlandasp.net</URL>
        </link>
    </links>
</xml>
<table border="1" datasrc="#dataisland">
    <tr>
        <td><div datafld="name" /></td>
        <td><div datafld="URL" /></td>
    </tr>
</table>
```

When this document is viewed in Internet Explorer 5.0 or higher as an
HTML document, the following HTML table is visible in the browser.

NewRiders.com	www.newriders.com
Xmlandasp.net	www.xmlandasp.net

Parent Elements

```
xsl:attribute, xsl:comment, xsl:copy, xsl:element, xsl:for-each, xsl:if,
xsl:otherwise, xsl:param, xsl:processing-instruction, xsl:template,
xsl:variable, xsl:when, xsl:with-param, output elements
```

Child Elements

None.

xsl:decimal-format

The `xsl:decimal-format` element declares a decimal-format, which controls the interpretation of a format pattern used by the format-number function. If there is a `name` attribute, then the element declares a named decimal-format; otherwise, it declares the default decimal-format.

Attributes

Attribute Name	Enforced	Description	Values
Name	Optional	The name of the decimal format.	QName
decimal-separator	Optional	The character used for a decimal sign. The default is a period (.).	Character
grouping-separator	Optional	The character used as a grouping (for example, thousands) separator. The default is a comma (,).	Character
infinity	Optional	The string used to represent infinity. The default is the string Infinity.	String
minus-sign	Optional	The character used as the default minus sign. The default is the hyphen-minus character (-, #x2D).	Character

continues

Attribute Name	Enforced	Description	Values
NaN	Optional	The string used to represent the NaN value. The default is the string NaN.	String
percent	Optional	The character used as a percent sign. The default is the percent character (%).	Character
per-mile	Optional	The character used as a per mille sign. The default is the Unicode per-mille character (#x2030).	Character
zero-digit	Optional	The character used as a digit zero. The default is the digit zero (0).	Character
digit	Optional	The character used for a digit in the format pattern. The default is the pound sign (#).	Character
pattern-separator	Optional	The character used to separate positive and negative subpatterns in a pattern. The default value is the semicolon character (;).	Character

Example

The following example relies on the fact that division by 0 for a non-zero number yields Infinity, while division of 0 by 0 yields NaN (Not a Number). We change the output of the value displayed for both NaN and Infinity values by declaring a default decimal format.

```
<?xml version="1.0" encoding="UTF-8" ?>
<xsl:stylesheet version="1.0"
    xmlns:xsl="http://www.w3.org/1999/XSL/Transform">
    <xsl:decimal-format infinity="An infinite number" NaN="Not a number"
    ➥digit="9" />
    <xsl:template match="/">
        <!--Infinity-->
        <xsl:value-of select="format-number(1 div 0,'999,9999.99')" />
        <br />
        <!--NaN-->
```

```
            <xsl:value-of select="format-number(0 div 0,'999,9999.99')" />
        </xsl:template>
    </xsl:stylesheet>
```

This results in the following output:

```
<?xml version="1.0" encoding="UTF-16"?>An infinite number<br />Not a number
```

Parent Elements

xsl:stylesheet or xsl:tranform.

Child Elements

None.

xsl:element

xsl:element creates an output element.

Attributes

Attribute Name	Enforced	Description	Values
Name	Required	The name of the element to output.	QName
namespace	Optional	The character used for a decimal sign. The default is a period (.).	URI Reference
use-attribute-sets	Optional	The character used as a grouping (for example, thousands) separator. The default is a comma (,).	QNames

Example

Given the following XML instance document, links.xml:

```
<?xml version="1.0" encoding="utf-8" ?>
<links>
    <link id="newriders" URL="http://www.newriders.com" name="NewRiders.com"
description="Available books by New Riders" />
</links>
```

continues

The following template rule generates an anchor tag:

```
<xsl:template match="link">
    <xsl:element name="a">
        <xsl:attribute name="href">
            <xsl:value-of select="@URL"/>
        </xsl:attribute>
        <xsl:value-of select="@name" />
    </xsl:element>
</xsl:template>
```

This results in the following markup:

```
<a href="http://www.newriders.com">NewRiders.com</a>
```

Parent Elements

```
xsl:copy, xsl:element, xsl:for-each, xsl:if, xsl:otherwise, xsl:param,
xsl:template, xsl:variable, xsl:when, xsl:with-param, output elements
```

Child Elements

```
xsl:apply-templates, xsl:attribute, xsl:call-template, xsl:choose,
xsl:comment, xsl:copy, xsl:copy-of, xsl:element, xsl:for-each, xsl:if,
xsl:processing-instruction, xsl:text, xsl:value-of, xsl:variable, output
elements
```

xsl:fallback

`xsl:fallback` attempts to use future implementations or extensions that the processor might not be able to currently implement.

Attributes

None.

Example

Given the following XML instance document, `links.xml`:

```
<?xml version="1.0" encoding="utf-8" ?>
<links>
    <link id="newriders" URL="http://www.newriders.com" name="NewRiders.com"
description="Available books by New Riders" />
</links>
```

The following stylesheet uses a newer version than the current processor has implemented, 1.1 (recall that the current version is 1.0). A new element is also added, bogus, to show what happens if the processor cannot process an extension:

```
<?xml version="1.0" encoding="UTF-8" ?>
<xsl:stylesheet version="1.1"
xmlns:xsl="http://www.w3.org/1999/XSL/Transform">
    <xsl:template match="/">
        <head>
            <body>
                <xsl:bogus>
                    <xsl:fallback>
                        Oops, the parser does not recognize the bogus
                        ➥element.
            </xsl:fallback>
                </xsl:bogus>
            </body>
        </head>
    </xsl:template>
</xsl:stylesheet>
```

This results in the following markup:

```
<?xml version="1.0" encoding="UTF-16"?>
<head><body>
    Oops, the parser doesn't recognize the "bogus" element.
</body></head>
```

Parent Elements

Any element where the content is a template.

Child Elements

Any element that can occur in a template.

xsl:for-each

xsl:for-each provides iterative looping over a node set to apply a template to each node in the node set. The xsl:for-each element contains a template that's applied to each node in the node set selected by the expression in the select attribute.

Attributes

Attribute Name	Enforced	Description	Values
select	Required	An expression that evaluates to a node set	Expression

Example

Given the following XML instance document, `links.xml`:

```
<links>
    <link name="NewRiders.com" URL="http://www.newriders.com" />
    <link name="Xmlandasp.net" URL="http://www.xmlandasp.net" />
    <link name="MSDN Online Library" URL="http://msdn.microsoft.com/library"
/>
</links>
```

The following stylesheet selects the node list containing all `link` nodes. Each iteration applies the local template that outputs the `name` attribute and the `<br/>` tag:

```
<?xml version="1.0" encoding="UTF-8" ?>
<xsl:stylesheet version="1.1"
➥xmlns:xsl="http://www.w3.org/1999/XSL/Transform">
    <xsl:template match="/">
        <xsl:for-each select="links/link">
            <xsl:value-of select="@name" />
            <br />
        </xsl:for-each>
    </xsl:template>
</xsl:stylesheet>
```

This results in the following markup:

```
<?xml version="1.0" encoding="UTF-16"?>
NewRiders.com<br />Xmlandasp.net<br />GotDotNet.com<br
➥/>MSDN Online Library<br />
```

Parent Elements

```
xsl:attribute, xsl:comment, xsl:copy, xsl:element, xsl:for-each, xsl:if,
xsl:otherwise, xsl:param, xsl:processing-instruction, xsl:template,
xsl:variable, xsl:when, xsl:with-param, output elements
```

Child Elements

```
xsl:apply-templates, xsl:attribute, xsl:call-template, xsl:choose,
xsl:comment, xsl:copy, xsl:copy-of, xsl:element, xsl:for-each, xsl:if,
xsl:processing-instruction, xsl:sort, xsl:text, xsl:value-of, xsl:variable,
output elements
```

xsl:if

`xsl:if` provides simple conditional evaluation.

Attributes

Attribute Name	Enforced	Description	Values
test	Required	An expression that evaluates to a Boolean	Boolean expression

Example

Given the following XML instance document, links.xml:

```
<links>
    <link name="NewRiders.com" URL="http://www.newriders.com" />
    <link name="Xmlandasp.net" URL="http://www.xmlandasp.net" />
    <link name="MSDN Online Library" URL="http://msdn.microsoft.com/library" />
</links>
```

The following stylesheet displays all the elements in a table with every other row colored medium gray:

```
<?xml version="1.0" encoding="UTF-8" ?>
<xsl:stylesheet version="1.1"
xmlns:xsl="http://www.w3.org/1999/XSL/Transform">
    <xsl:template match="/">
        <table>
            <xsl:for-each select="links/link">
                <tr>
                    <td>
                        <xsl:if test="position() mod 2 = 0">
                        <xsl:attribute name="bgcolor">silver<
                        ⇒/xsl:attribute>
                        </xsl:if>
                        <xsl:value-of select="@name" />
                    </td>
                </tr>
            </xsl:for-each>
        </table>
    </xsl:template>
</xsl:stylesheet>
```

This results in the following markup:

```
<?xml version="1.0" encoding="UTF-16"?>
<table>
    <tr>
      <td>NewRiders.com</td>
    </tr>
    <tr>
      <td bgcolor="silver">Xmlandasp.net</td>
    </tr>
    <tr>
      <td>MSDN Online Library</td>
    </tr>
</table>
```

Parent Elements

```
xsl:attribute, xsl:comment, xsl:copy, xsl:element, xsl:for-each, xsl:if,
xsl:otherwise, xsl:param, xsl:processing-instruction, xsl:template,
xsl:variable, xsl:when, xsl:with-param, output elements
```

Child Elements

```
xsl:apply-templates, xsl:attribute, xsl:call-template, xsl:choose,
xsl:comment, xsl:copy, xsl:copy-of, xsl:element, xsl:for-each, xsl:if,
xsl:processing-instruction, xsl:text, xsl:value-of, xsl:variable, output
elements
```

xsl:import

xsl:import imports the referenced XSLT stylesheet. Any template rules in the stylesheet take precedence over the included template rules.

Attributes

Attribute Name	Enforced	Description	Values
href	Required	The location of the XSLT stylesheet to import	URI Reference

Example

Given the following XML instance document, links.xml:

```
<links>
    <link name="NewRiders.com" URL="http://www.newriders.com" />
    <link name="Xmlandasp.net" URL="http://www.xmlandasp.net" />
    <link name="MSDN Online Library" URL="http://msdn.microsoft.com/library" />
</links>
```

The following stylesheet selects the node list containing all link nodes. Each iteration applies the local template that outputs the name attribute and the <br/> tag:

```
<?xml version="1.0" encoding="UTF-8" ?>
<xsl:stylesheet version="1.1" xmlns:xsl=
▪"http://www.w3.org/1999/XSL/Transform">
    <xsl:import href="styles.xsl"/>
        <xsl:template match="/">
          <xsl:apply-templates/>
        </xsl:template>
</xsl:stylesheet>
```

This stylesheet imports template rules from `style.xsl`, as shown here:

```
<?xml version="1.0" encoding="UTF-8" ?>
<xsl:stylesheet version="1.0" xmlns:xsl=
➥"http://www.w3.org/1999/XSL/Transform">
    <xsl:template match="links/link">
        <tr>
            <td>
                <xsl:value-of select="@name" />
            </td>
        </tr>
    </xsl:template>
</xsl:stylesheet>
```

This imports all the template rules and definitions from `styles.xsl`. Furthermore, if a template rule for the root context is provided, the current template rule overrides it.

Parent Elements

`xsl:stylesheet` or `xsl:transform`

Child Elements

None.

xsl:include

`xsl:include` includes the referenced XSLT stylesheet. It allows stylesheets to be combined without changing the semantics of the stylesheets being combined. Including a stylesheet is the same as importing a stylesheet using `xsl:include`, except that `xsl:import` causes the including stylesheet to override the included stylesheet.

Attributes

Attribute Name	Enforced	Description	Values
href	Required	The location of the XSLT stylesheet to include	URI Reference

Example

Given the following XML instance document, `links.xml`,

```
<links>
    <link name="NewRiders.com" URL="http://www.newriders.com" />
    <link name="Xmlandasp.net" URL="http://www.xmlandasp.net" />
```

```
        <link name="MSDN Online Library" URL="http://msdn.microsoft.com/library" />
    </links>
```

The following stylesheet, links.xsl, includes the referenced stylesheet, styles.xsl.

links.xsl

```
    <?xml version="1.0" encoding="UTF-8" ?>
    <xsl:stylesheet version="1.1"
    xmlns:xsl="http://www.w3.org/1999/XSL/Transform">
        <xsl:import href="styles.xsl" />
        <xsl:template match="/">
            <table>
                <xsl:apply-templates />
            </table>
        </xsl:template>
    </xsl:stylesheet>
```

styles.xsl

```
    <?xml version="1.0" encoding="UTF-8" ?>
    <xsl:stylesheet version="1.0"
    xmlns:xsl="http://www.w3.org/1999/XSL/Transform">
        <xsl:template match="links/link">
            <tr>
                <td>
                    <xsl:value-of select="@name" />
                </td>
            </tr>
        </xsl:template>
    </xsl:stylesheet>
```

This imports all the template rules and definitions from styles.xsl. The following markup is generated. Notice that the table element was generated from links.xsl and the table rows and cells were generated from styles.xsl:

```
    <?xml version="1.0" encoding="UTF-16"?>
    <table>
        <tr><td>NewRiders.com</td></tr>
        <tr><td>Xmlandasp.net</td></tr>

        <tr><td>DevX.com</td></tr>
    </table>
```

Parent Elements

```
    xsl:stylesheet or xsl:transform
```

Child Elements

None.

xsl:key

xsl:key defines a named key for a node or set of nodes that are accessed through the XSLT key() function. Keys are comprised of three components: the node(s) referenced by the key, the name of the key, and the value of the key. Keys can be useful for lookup information or temporarily caching values for later use. Keys can also help avoid complex queries for decendants of ancestors.

The key function does for keys what the id function does for IDs. The first argument specifies the name of the key. The value of the argument must be a QName, which is expanded. When the second argument to the key function is of type node-set, the result is the union of the result of applying the key function to the string value of each of the nodes in the argument node-set. When the second argument to key is of any other type, the argument is converted to a string as if by a call to the string function; it returns a node-set that contains the nodes in the same document as the context node that has a value for the named key equal to this string.

Attributes

Attribute Name	Enforced	Description	Values
Name	Required	The name of the key	QName
Match	Required	The pattern that matches the key	Pattern
Use	Required	Indicates the value of the key	Expression

Example

Suppose that you have a list of keywords that you'd like to provide a hyperlink to each time the keyword is referenced. Instead of including the definition as a child element for each instance of the keyword, you can separate the references to the keywords and the definitions themselves. Consider the following XML instance document, definitions.xml:

```
<?xml version="1.0" encoding="utf-8" ?>
<root>
    <p>
    This document explains some of the relationships between
    ➥<keyword>XML</keyword>,
    and <keyword>XSLT</keyword>.  <keyword>HTML</keyword>
    is familiar to most people.  <keyword>XSLT</keyword> is a growing
    ➥technology that
    is rapidly gaining interest.
     </p>
```

```
    <defs>
        <def name="XML">Extensible Markup Language</def>
        <def name="XSLT">Extensible Stylesheet Language
        ➥Transformations</def>
        <def name="HTML">Hypertext Markup Language</def>
    </defs>
</root>
```

The following stylesheet, defs.xsl, generates hyperlinks between instances of keywords in text and the definitions of the keywords:

```
<?xml version="1.0" encoding="UTF-8" ?>
<xsl:stylesheet version="1.0"
xmlns:xsl="http://www.w3.org/1999/XSL/Transform">
<xsl:output method="html"/>
    <xsl:key name="definition" match="def" use="@name" />
    <xsl:template match="/">
        <html>
            <body>
                <xsl:apply-templates />
            </body>
        </html>
    </xsl:template>
    <xsl:template match="p">
        <xsl:apply-templates />
    </xsl:template>
    <xsl:template match="keyword">
        <b>
            <a href="#{generate-id(key('definition',.))}">
                <xsl:apply-templates />
            </a>
        </b>
    </xsl:template>
    <xsl:template match="def">
        <p>
            <a name="{generate-id()}">
                <b>
                    <xsl:value-of select="@name" />
                </b>
                <xsl:text> - </xsl:text>
                <xsl:value-of select="." />
            </a>
        </p>
    </xsl:template>
</xsl:stylesheet>
```

The result of this transformation is as follows:

```
<html>
<body>
    This document explains some of the relationships between <b>
    ➥<a href="#IDA3TZCB">XML</a></b>,
    and <b><a href="#IDAAUZCB">XSLT</a></b>.  <b>
    ➥<a href="#IDADUZCB">HTML</a></b>
```

```
       is familiar to most people.   <b><a href="#IDAAUZCB">XSLT</a>
       ↵</b> is a growing technology that
       is rapidly gaining interest.
        <p><a name="IDA3TZCB"><b>XML</b> - Extensible Markup Language</a></p>
   <p><a name="IDAAUZCB"><b>XSLT</b> - Extensible Stylesheet Language
   ↵Transformations</a></p>
   <p><a name="IDADUZCB"><b>HTML</b> - Hypertext Markup Language</a></p>
   </body>
   </html>
```

Parent Elements

xsl:stylesheet or xsl:transform

Child Elements

None.

xsl:message

xsl:message raises a message in a way that's dependent on the XSLT processor. For MSXML 3.0 and higher, this causes a message to either be sent to the message buffer or a message dialog box, depending on the environment in which the element call is made.

For MSXML 3.0 and the preview release of MSXML 4.0, if the value of the terminate attribute is no, the call is ignored. If the value of the terminate attribute is yes, the message results in a trappable error.

For the .NET base classes, the xsl:message element does not cause a trappable error. Instead, the message is output to the default message handler. For a Windows application project, the default handler is the output window. For a Console application, the default handler is the console window. For web forms applications, the message is suppressed.

The default handler can be overridden in .NET. See the .NET SDK documentation for information on the DefaultTraceListener class.

Attributes

Attribute Name	Enforced	Description	Values
terminate	Required	Specifies if the XSLT processor should halt processing	Either yes or no

Example

Consider the following XML document, `links.xml`:

```
<?xml version="1.0" encoding="UTF-8" ?>
<links>
    <link name="NewRiders.com" URL="http://www.newriders.com/">
    ↩"http://www.newriders.com" />

    <link name="Xmlandasp.net" URL="http://www.xmlandasp.net" />
    <link name="MSDN Online Library" URL="http://msdn.microsoft.com/library" />
</links>
```

The following stylesheet fragment would act differently when parsed with
MSXML 4.0 versus being parsed with the .NET base classes. The MSXML
parser would generate an error, with the error text being, "The Xmlandasp.net
node was reached," while the .NET classes would send the same message to
the default trace listener.

```
<?xml version="1.0" encoding="UTF-8" ?>
<xsl:stylesheet version="1.0"
xmlns:xsl="http://www.w3.org/1999/XSL/Transform">
    <xsl:template match="/">
        <table>
            <xsl:apply-templates />
        </table>
    </xsl:template>
    <xsl:template match="links/link">
        <tr>
            <td>
                <xsl:choose>
                    <xsl:when test="@name='Xmlandasp.net'">
                        <xsl:message terminate="yes">The Xmlandasp.net
                        ↩node was reached</xsl:message>
                    </xsl:when>
                    <xsl:otherwise>
                        <xsl:value-of select="@name" />
                    </xsl:otherwise>
                </xsl:choose>
            </td>
        </tr>
    </xsl:template>
</xsl:stylesheet>
```

The MSXML Parser would not return any text as the result of the transformation. The .NET parser would return text up until the message was generated.
If the `terminate` attribute is changed to have a value of no, the MSXML Parser
would ignore the element. The .NET classes would emit the message to the
default trace listener and continue processing past the message.

Parent Elements

Any element where the content is a template.

Child Elements

Any element that can occur in a template.

xsl:namespace-alias

xsl:namespace-alias aliases a prefix name in the stylesheet. This is useful for creating stylesheets as the result of a transformation.

Attributes

Attribute Name	Enforced	Description	Values
terminate	Required	Specifies if the XSLT processor should halt processing	Either yes or no

Example

Suppose that you want to generate a stylesheet to transform data from HTML to PDF format. Consider the following XML document, elements.xml:

```
<?xml version="1.0" encoding="utf-8" ?>
<elements>
     <block>p</block>
     <block>h1</block>
     <block>h2</block>
     <block>h3</block>
     <block>h4</block>
</elements>
```

You can use this set of elements to generate a stylesheet by aliasing the axsl prefix so that it appears in the result tree with the xsl prefix:

```
<xsl:stylesheet
  version="1.0"
  xmlns:xsl="http://www.w3.org/1999/XSL/Transform"
  xmlns:fo="http://www.w3.org/1999/XSL/Format"
  xmlns:axsl="http://www.w3.org/1999/XSL/TransformAlias">

<xsl:namespace-alias stylesheet-prefix="axsl" result-prefix="xsl"/>

<xsl:template match="/">
  <axsl:stylesheet>
    <xsl:apply-templates/>
```

```
    </axsl:stylesheet>
  </xsl:template>

  <xsl:template match="block">
    <axsl:template match="{.}">
      <fo:block><axsl:apply-templates/></fo:block>
    </axsl:template>
  </xsl:template>

</xsl:stylesheet>
```

The result of this transformation is another stylesheet. Notice that elements prefixed with axsl in the source stylesheet are output in the result with the xsl prefix.

```
<?xml version="1.0" encoding="UTF-16"?>
<xsl:stylesheet xmlns:fo="http://www.w3.org/1999/XSL/Format"
xmlns:xsl="http://www.w3.org/1999/XSL/Transform">
    <xsl:template match="p"><fo:block><xsl:apply-templates />
    ➥</fo:block></xsl:template>
    <xsl:template match="h1"><fo:block><xsl:apply-templates />
    ➥</fo:block></xsl:template>
    <xsl:template match="h2"><fo:block><xsl:apply-templates />
    ➥</fo:block></xsl:template>
    <xsl:template match="h3"><fo:block><xsl:apply-templates />
    ➥</fo:block></xsl:template>
    <xsl:template match="h4"><fo:block><xsl:apply-templates />
    ➥</fo:block></xsl:template>
</xsl:stylesheet>
```

Parent Elements

xsl:stylesheet

Child Elements

None.

xsl:number

xsl:number inserts a formatted number into the result tree.

Attributes

Attribute Name	Enforced	Description	Values
level	Optional	Specifies what level of the source tree should be considered. The default is single.	single, multiple, or any

count	Optional	A pattern that specifies what nodes should be counted at those levels. If `count` attribute is not specified, it defaults to the pattern that matches any node with the same node type as the current node and, if the current node has an expanded-name, with the same expanded-name as the current node.	A pattern
from	Optional	Specifies where counting starts.	A pattern
value	Optional	Allows specifying the numeric value rather than maintaining a running list. If no `value` attribute is specified, `xsl:number` inserts one based on the current node in the source tree.	A number-expression, such as `count()` or `position()`.
format	Optional	Specifies the format that can be used.	A string. A formats as a capital letter. 1 formats as a decimal. I formats as a capital roman numeral, and i formats as a lower-case roman numeral.
lang	Optional	Specifies the language's alphabet to use. If no language is specified, the language is determined from the system's environment.	`NMToken`

continues

Attribute Name	Enforced	Description	Values
letter-value	Optional	Specifies how sorting should occur for characters. For example, an alphabetic sort of the sequence (1,2,11,12) might yield (1,11,12,2) while traditional would yield (1,2,11,12).	alphabetic or traditional. The default is traditional.
grouping-separator	Optional	Specifies the grouping separator in decimal numbering sequences. An example is a thousands separator.	A character. If grouping-size is x, attribute is ignored.
grouping-size	Optional	Specifies the size of the decimal to group on. Separating thousands would mean a grouping-size of three.	A number. If grouping-separator is not specified, this attribute is ignored.

Example

Suppose that you want to create a numbered outline from the data in an XML file. Consider the following XML file, links.xml:

```xml
<?xml version="1.0" encoding="utf-8" ?>
<links>
    <link URL="http://www.newriders.com">
        <section name="New Books">
            <feature>XML and ASP.NET</feature>
            <feature>Inside XML</feature>
            <feature>Inside XSLT</feature>
        </section>
        <section name="Contact Us">
            <feature>Contact by email</feature>
            <feature>Contact by Phone</feature>
        </section>
    </link>
    <link URL="http://msdn.microsoft.com">
        <section name="MSDN Library" />
        <section name="Downloads" />
    </link>
    <link URL="http://www.xmlandasp.net">
        <section name="Articles">
```

```
                <feature>Obtaining ObjectContext</feature>
                <feature>Calling Java from ASP</feature>
                <feature>Introduction to XSLT</feature>
            </section>
        </link>
    </links>
```

Using the xsl:number element, you can use the level attribute with a value of multiple to generate the outline. The URL is displayed with a roman numeral, the section is displayed with a capital letter, and the feature is displayed with a decimal. This stylesheet is called outline.xslt.

```
<?xml version="1.0" encoding="UTF-8" ?>
<xsl:stylesheet version="1.0"
xmlns:xsl="http://www.w3.org/1999/XSL/Transform">
        <xsl:output omit-xml-declaration="yes" />
    <xsl:template match="/">
            <xsl:apply-templates />
    </xsl:template>
    <xsl:template match="link">
            <xsl:number level="multiple" format="I. " />
            <xsl:value-of select="@URL" />
            <xsl:apply-templates />
    </xsl:template>
    <xsl:template match="section">
            <xsl:number level="multiple" format="A. " />
            <xsl:value-of select="@name" />
            <xsl:apply-templates />
    </xsl:template>
    <xsl:template match="feature">
            <xsl:number level="multiple" format="1. " />
            <xsl:value-of select="." />
    </xsl:template>
</xsl:stylesheet>
```

Applying the stylesheet outline.xslt to the XML document links.xml produces the following output. This result is not XML, and you have omitted the XML decaration. The document is formatted with carriage returns for clarity:

```
    I. http://www.newriders.com
        A. New Books
            1. XML and ASP.NET
            2. Inside XML
            3. Inside XSLT

        B. Contact Us
            1. Contact by email
            2. Contact by Phone
```

```
    II. http://msdn.microsoft.com
        A. MSDN Library
        B. Downloads

    III. http://www.xmlandasp.net
        A. Articles
            1. Obtaining ObjectContext
            2. Calling Java from ASP
            3. Introduction to XSLT
```

Parent Elements

xsl:copy, xsl:element, xsl:for-each, xsl:if, xsl:otherwise, xsl:param, xsl:template, xsl:variable, xsl:when, xsl:with-param, output elements

Child Elements

None.

xsl:otherwise

xsl:otherwise provides a default for multiple condition testing, used with the xsl:choose and xsl:when elements. A similar construct is the else keyword in most programming languages that is used with an if statement.

Attributes

None.

Example

Suppose that you want to create a numbered outline from the data in an XML file. Consider the following XML file, links.xml:

```
<links>
    <link name="NewRiders.com" URL="http://www.newriders.com"> />

    <link name="Xmlandasp.net" URL="http://www.xmlandasp.net" />
    <link name="MSDN Online Library" URL="http://msdn.microsoft.com/library"
/>
</links>
```

Specify that you are outputting version 4.0 HTML and do not want an XML declaration at the beginning of the output:

```
<?xml version="1.0" encoding="UTF-8" ?>
<xsl:stylesheet version="1.0"
xmlns:xsl="http://www.w3.org/1999/XSL/Transform">
```

```
<xsl:output method="html" version="4.0" omit-xml-declaration="yes" />
<xsl:template match="/">
    <html>
        <head></head>
        <body></body>
        <table>
            <xsl:apply-templates />
        </table>
    </html>
</xsl:template>
<xsl:template match="link">
    <tr>
        <td>
            <xsl:value-of select="@name" />
        </td>
    </tr>
</xsl:template>
</xsl:stylesheet>
```

Applying the stylesheet to links.xml would produce version 4.0-compliant HTML. Notice the meta tag generated that specifies the content type, and the lack of an XML declaration at the beginning of the HTML output:

```
<html>
    <head>
        <META http-equiv="Content-Type" content="text/html; charset=UTF-16">
    </head>
    <body>
    </body>
    <table>
        <tr>
            <td>
                NewRiders.com
            </td>
        </tr>
        <tr>
            <td>
                Xmlandasp.net
            </td>
        </tr>
        <tr>
            <td>
                MSDN Online Library
            </td>
        </tr>
    </table>
</html>
```

Parent Elements

xsl:choose

Child Elements

xsl:apply-templates, xsl:attribute, xsl:call-template, xsl:choose, xsl:comment, xsl:copy, xsl:copy-of, xsl:element, xsl:for-each, xsl:if, xsl:processing-instruction, xsl:text, xsl:value-of, xsl:variable, output elements

xsl:param

xsl:param provides a variable parameter for an xsl:stylesheet or an xsl:template element.

The xsl:param element is identical to the xsl:variable element, except that the xsl:param element can specify a default value.

Attributes

Attribute Name	Enforced	Description	Values
method	Optional	Specifies the overall method that should be used for outputting the result tree.	xml, html, text, or any QName that is not an NCName.
version	Optional	Specifies the version of the output method	NMToken
encoding	Optional	Specifies the preferred character encoding that the XSLT processor should use to encode sequences of characters as sequences of bytes; the value of the attribute should be treated case insensitively.	The value must contain only characters in the range #x21 to #x7E (for example, printable ASCII characters); the value should either be a charset registered with the Internet Assigned Numbers Authority, RFC2278, or start with X-.

omit-xml-declaration	Optional	Specifies whether the XSLT processor should emit an XML declaration.	yes or no.
standalone	Optional	Indicates if the XSLT processor should output a standalone document declaration. The default is no.	yes or no.
doctype-public	Optional	Specifies the public identifier to be used in the document type declaration.	String
doctype-system	Optional	Specifies the system identifier to be used in the document type declaration.	String
cdata-section-elements	Optional	Specifies a list of element names whose text node children should be output as CDATA sections.	QNames
indent	Optional	Indicates if the XSLT processor might add additional white space when outputting the result tree.	yes or no.
media-type	Optional	Specifies the MIME content type of the data that results from outputting the result tree.	String

Example

Suppose that you want to display an HTML table with alternating rows colored differently. One way to do this is to set up a template rule that accepts the color to use. Here, you can see that even-numbered rows use the default value of the template rule named output-row, while odd-numbered rows specify the color parameter as silver:

```
<?xml version="1.0" encoding="UTF-8" ?>
<xsl:stylesheet version="1.0"
xmlns:xsl="http://www.w3.org/1999/XSL/Transform">
    <xsl:output method="html" version="4.0" omit-xml-declaration="yes" />
    <xsl:template match="/">
        <html>
            <head></head>
            <body></body>
            <table>
                <xsl:for-each select="links/link">
                    <xsl:choose>
                        <xsl:when test="position() mod 2 = 0">
                            <xsl:call-template name="output-row" />
                        </xsl:when>
                        <xsl:otherwise>
                            <xsl:call-template name="output-row">
                                <xsl:with-param name="bgcolor"
                                ↪select="'silver'" />
                            </xsl:call-template>
                        </xsl:otherwise>
                    </xsl:choose>
                </xsl:for-each>
            </table>
        </html>
    </xsl:template>
    <xsl:template name="output-row">
        <xsl:param name="bgcolor" select="'blue'" />
        <tr>
            <xsl:attribute name="bgcolor">
                <xsl:value-of select="$bgcolor" />
            </xsl:attribute>
            <td>
                <xsl:value-of select="@name" />
            </td>
        </tr>
    </xsl:template>
</xsl:stylesheet>
```

This stylesheet emits the following results. Notice that the odd-numbered rows have the specified color of silver, while the even-numbered rows have the default color of blue.

```
<html>
<head>
<META http-equiv="Content-Type" content="text/html; charset=UTF-16">
</head>
<body></body>
<table>
<tr bgcolor="silver">
```

```
<td>NewRiders.com</td>
</tr>
<tr bgcolor="blue">
<td>Xmlandasp.net</td>
</tr>
<tr bgcolor="silver">
<td>MSDN Online Library</td>
</tr>
</table>
</html>
```

Parent Elements

xsl:stylesheet, xsl:template, xsl:transform

Child Elements

xsl:apply-templates, xsl:attribute, xsl:call-template, xsl:choose,
xsl:comment, xsl:copy, xsl:copy-of, xsl:element, xsl:for-each, xsl:if,
xsl:processing-instruction, xsl:text, xsl:value-of, xsl:variable, output
elements

xsl:preserve-space

xsl:preserve-space specifies the elements whose text node children are not to
be removed from the result tree if they contain only spaces.

XSLT parsers will remove text nodes from the constructed source tree if
their content contains only spaces. It does not strip text nodes unless their
content contains only spaces. The xsl:preserve-space element allows for the
preservation of those child text nodes so they are still contained in the source
tree upon parsing.

The MSXML Parser requires loading the source document into a DOM
tree before parsing. The act of loading the source into the DOM may
strip significant white space before the stylesheet is rendered, so the
xsl:preserve-space might seem to have no effect. To preserve significant
white space when initially loading the source tree into the DOM, set the
preserveWhiteSpace property of the DomDocument object to True before loading
the XML.

The .NET parser handles white space differently. A property of the
XmlReader is WhiteSpaceHandling, which is one of the WhiteSpaceHandling
enumeration members. This is covered in detail in Chapter 3, "XML
Presentation."

Attributes

Attribute Name	Enforced	Description	Values
Elements	Required	The list of elements that are to have text node children preserved if they contain only spaces.	NMTokens

Example

Consider the following document, `source.xml`:

```
<?xml version="1.0" encoding="UTF-8" ?>
<links>
     <link>      </link>
     <link>            </link>
     <link>                  </link>
</links>
```

We experiment with different combinations of `xsl:preserve-space` to show the effects of each setting. We begin with a simple stylesheet that does not preserve any white space. This stylesheet is `trans.xslt`. The stylesheet simply displays the number of spaces for each node in the selected nodes:

```
<?xml version="1.0" encoding="UTF-8" ?>
<xsl:stylesheet version="1.0"
xmlns:xsl="http://www.w3.org/1999/XSL/Transform">
     <xsl:output method="xml" version="1.0" />
     <xsl:template match="/">
          <xsl:for-each select="links/link">
               <xsl:text>[</xsl:text>
               <xsl:value-of select="string-length(.)" />
               <xsl:text>]</xsl:text>
          </xsl:for-each>
     </xsl:template>
</xsl:stylesheet>
```

The MSXML Parser handles white space somewhat differently than other parsers. To demonstrate this, parse the document using MSXML 4.0 with Visual Basic 6. You are only using VB6 here as a control to avoid issues where the browser might not have the correct version installed:

```
Option Explicit

Private Sub Command1_Click()
    Dim xml As New MSXML2.DOMDocument40
    Dim trans As New MSXML2.DOMDocument40
    Dim fso As New Scripting.FileSystemObject
    Dim strm As Scripting.TextStream
```

```
    On Error GoTo eh
    xml.Load "c:\temp\source.xml"

    trans.Load "c:\temp\trans.xslt"

    Set strm = fso.OpenTextFile("c:\outfile.txt", ForWriting, True)
    strm.Write xml.transformNode(trans)
    strm.Close
    Set xml = Nothing
    Set trans = Nothing
    Exit Sub
eh:
    Debug.Assert False
    strm.Close
    Set strm = Nothing
    Set fso = Nothing
    Set trans = Nothing
    Set xml = Nothing
End Sub
```

This results in the following output in the file `outfile.txt`:

```
<?xml version="1.0"?>[1][1][1]
```

To preserve white space, you need to preserve white space in the source XML DOM and within the stylsheet. To do this, alter the stylesheet to include the `xsl:preserve-space` element:

```
<?xml version="1.0" encoding="UTF-8" ?>
<xsl:stylesheet version="1.0"
xmlns:xsl="http://www.w3.org/1999/XSL/Transform">
    <xsl:preserve-space elements="link"/>
    <xsl:output method="xml" version="1.0" />
    <xsl:template match="/">
        <xsl:for-each select="links/link">
            <xsl:text>[</xsl:text>
            <xsl:value-of select="string-length(.)" />
            <xsl:text>]</xsl:text>
        </xsl:for-each>
    </xsl:template>
</xsl:stylesheet>
```

Also alter the code for MSXML by setting the `preserveWhiteSpace` property to True prior to loading the XML source:

```
    On Error GoTo eh
    xml.preserveWhitespace = True
    xml.Load "c:\temp\source.xml"
```

This combination of steps yields the expected result.

[5][13][21]

To achieve the same result in .NET, you again need to preserve white space in the parser prior to loading the document. You can achieve this by using an XmlDocument object to load the source XML and set the PreserveWhitespace property of the XmlDocument object to True:

```
Sub Main()
    Dim xsltReader As System.Xml.XmlTextReader = New
    ⇒System.Xml.XmlTextReader("c:\temp\trans.xslt")
    Dim xsltdoc As System.Xml.XPath.XPathDocument = New
    ⇒System.Xml.XPath.XPathDocument(xsltReader, XmlSpace.Preserve)
    Dim xmldoc As System.Xml.XmlDocument = New System.Xml.XmlDocument()

    'Preserve whitespace and then load the xml source
    xmldoc.PreserveWhitespace = True
    xmldoc.Load("c:\temp\source.xml")

    'Create the XslTransform object and load the stylesheet.
    Dim xslt As XslTransform = New XslTransform()
    xslt.Load(xsltdoc)

    'Create an XmlTextWriter which outputs to the console.
    Dim writer As XmlTextWriter = New XmlTextWriter(Console.Out)

    'Transform the file and send the output to the console.
    xslt.Transform(xmldoc, Nothing, writer)
    writer.Close()
End Sub
```

The output in the console window is the same as this result:

```
[5][13][21]
```

Parent Elements

```
Xsl:stylesheet, xsl:transform
```

Child Elements

None.

xsl:processing-instruction

xsl:processing-instruction creates a processing instruction in the result tree.

Attributes

Attribute Name	Enforced	Description	Values
Name	Required	The name of the processing instruction	String (pi-name)

Example

The following stylesheet suppresses the xml declaration and creates a processing instruction named my-ml with a version of 1.0. Note that the
xsl:attribute element is not a valid child of the xsl:processing-instruction
element. It is also not legal to name a processing instruction "xml" or "XML":
manually creating the xml declaration requires output escaping a string or
using the xsl:output element with a value of "no" for the omit-xml-declara-
tion attribute:

```
<?xml version="1.0" encoding="UTF-8" ?>
<xsl:stylesheet version="1.0"
xmlns:xsl="http://www.w3.org/1999/XSL/Transform">
    <xsl:output omit-xml-declaration="yes" />
    <xsl:template match="/">
        <xsl:processing-instruction name=
    ⇥"my-ml">version="1.0"</xsl:processing-instruction>
    </xsl:template>
</xsl:stylesheet>
```

Parent Elements

```
xsl:attribute, xsl:comment, xsl:copy, xsl:element, xsl:for-each,
xsl:if, xsl:otherwise, xsl:param, xsl:processing-instruction,
xsl:template, xsl:variable, xsl:when, xsl:with-param, output elements
```

Child Elements

```
xsl:apply-templates, xsl:call-template, xsl:choose, xsl:copy, xsl:copy-of,
xsl:for-each, xsl:if, xsl:text, xsl:value-of, xsl:variable, output elements
```

xsl:sort

xsl:sort specifies sort criteria for a node list selected by xsl:value-of or
xsl:apply-templates.

Attributes

Attribute Name	Enforced	Description	Values
select	Optional	The sort key for the node. If not specified, uses the value of the current node (.) as the sort key.	A string value, usually an XPath expression.

Attribute Name	Enforced	Description	Values
data-type	Optional	Specifies the data type for the strings.	text, number, or a QName that's expanded into a dt-expanded-name. The expanded-name identifies the data type.
order	Optional	Specifies the sort order.	ascending or descending
lang	Optional	Specifies which language's alphabet is used to determine sort order.	NMToken. If unspecified, the language is determined from the system's environment.
case-order	Optional	Determines if strings will be sorted with uppercase first or lowercase first.	upper-first or lower-first. The default is lower-first (despite the documentation in MSDN to the contrary).

Example

Consider the following XML document, test.xml:

```
<?xml version="1.0" encoding="utf-8" ?>
<links>
    <link name="C" id="1" />
    <link name="B" id="2" />
    <link name="A" id="11" />
    <link name="b" id="22" />
    <link name="a" id="12" />
    <link name="c" id="23" />
</links>
```

The following stylesheet examples have a single template rule that matches the root node. They iterate through the link elements, which are sorted. The only difference is their xsl:sort element's parameters and the output generated:

```
<?xml version="1.0" encoding="UTF-8" ?>
<xsl:stylesheet version="1.0"
xmlns:xsl="http://www.w3.org/1999/XSL/Transform">
    <xsl:output method="text" omit-xml-declaration="yes" />
    <xsl:template match="/">
```

```
    <xsl:for-each select="links/link">
        <xsl:sort select="attribute::name" order="descending" case-
        ↦order="lower-first" />
        <xsl:value-of select="@name" />
        <xsl:if test="position() != last()">
            <xsl:text>,</xsl:text>
        </xsl:if>
    </xsl:for-each>
    </xsl:template>
</xsl:stylesheet>
```

The preceding stylesheet yields the following:

```
C,c,B,b,A,a
```

Notice that we specified the case-order attribute as lower-first. The upper-case letters are rendered first in the example. This is because the document is first sorted using the case-order and then the sort order is applied. To see this more clearly, sort in ascending order and change the previous stylesheet rule's xsl:sort element to the following declaration:

```
<xsl:sort select="attribute::name" case-order="upper-first" />
```

This yields the following:

```
A,a,B,b,C,c
```

Changing the line of text to use all the defaults looks like this:

```
<xsl:sort select="attribute::name" />
```

The default behavior yields the following.

```
a,A,b,B,c,C
```

The preceding examples are sorted based on text. The following examples show sorting with numeric data. We are now sorting based on the id attribute:

```
<?xml version="1.0" encoding="UTF-8" ?>
<xsl:stylesheet version="1.0"
xmlns:xsl="http://www.w3.org/1999/XSL/Transform">
    <xsl:output method="text" omit-xml-declaration="yes" />
    <xsl:template match="/">
        <xsl:for-each select="links/link">
            <xsl:sort select="attribute::id" />
            <xsl:value-of select="@id" />
            <xsl:if test="position() != last()">
             <xsl:text>,</xsl:text>
            </xsl:if>
        </xsl:for-each>
    </xsl:template>
</xsl:stylesheet>
```

This stylesheet yields the following:

```
1,11,12,2,22,23
```

Instead of using the default data type, text, you can specify the `data-type` attribute as `number`:

```
<xsl:sort select="attribute::id" data-type="number"/>
```

This yields a numeric sorting instead of character sorting:

```
1,2,11,12,22,23
```

Parent Elements

```
xsl:apply-templates, xsl:for-each
```

Child Elements

None.

xsl:strip-space

`xsl:strip-space` adds the text nodes to the list of nodes to be stripped if their content contains only spaces.

XSLT parsers remove text nodes from the constructed source tree if their content contains only spaces. They do not strip text nodes unless their content contains only spaces. The `xsl:preserve-space` element allows preserving those child text nodes so they are still contained in the source tree upon parsing.

The MSXML Parser requires loading the source document into a DOM tree before parsing. The act of loading the source into the DOM might strip significant white space before the stylesheet is rendered, so the `xsl:preserve-space` or `xsl:strip-space` elements might seem to have no effect. To preserve significant white space when initially loading the source tree into the DOM, set the `preserveWhiteSpace` property of the `DomDocument` object to True before loading the XML.

The .NET parser handles white space differently. A property of the `XmlReader` is `WhiteSpaceHandling`, which is one of the `WhiteSpaceHandling` enumeration members. You can also handle white space stripping/preservation at the node level by using `XsltContext`. Finally, you can control white space using the `XmlDocument` object's `preserveWhitespace` property. These techniques and objects are covered in more detail in Chapter 3.

Attributes

Attribute Name	Enforced	Description	Values
elements	Required	The list of elements that are to have text node children preserved if they contain only spaces.	NMTokens

Example

Consider the following document, source.xml:

```
<?xml version="1.0" encoding="UTF-8" ?>
<links>
    <link>        </link>
    <link>            </link>
    <link>                    </link>
</links>
```

We experiment with different combinations of xsl:preserve-space to show the effects of each setting. We begin with a simple stylesheet that does not preserve any white space. This stylesheet is trans.xslt. The stylesheet simply displays the number of spaces for each node in the selected nodes:

```
<?xml version="1.0" encoding="UTF-8" ?>
<xsl:stylesheet version="1.0"
xmlns:xsl="http://www.w3.org/1999/XSL/Transform">
    <xsl:output method="xml" version="1.0" />
    <xsl:template match="/">
        <xsl:for-each select="links/link">
            <xsl:text>[</xsl:text>
            <xsl:value-of select="string-length(.)" />
            <xsl:text>]</xsl:text>
        </xsl:for-each>
    </xsl:template>
</xsl:stylesheet>
```

To parse the result tree, you must first examine using the MSXML 4.0 Parser with Visual Basic 6:

```
Option Explicit

Private Sub Command1_Click()
    Dim xml As New MSXML2.DOMDocument40
    Dim trans As New MSXML2.DOMDocument40
    Dim fso As New Scripting.FileSystemObject
    Dim strm As Scripting.TextStream
```

```
    On Error GoTo eh
    xml.Load "c:\temp\source.xml"

    trans.Load "c:\temp\trans.xslt"

    Set strm = fso.OpenTextFile("c:\outfile.txt", ForWriting, True)
    strm.Write xml.transformNode(trans)
    strm.Close
    Set xml = Nothing
    Set trans = Nothing
    Exit Sub
eh:
    Debug.Assert False
    strm.Close
    Set strm = Nothing
    Set fso = Nothing
    Set trans = Nothing
    Set xml = Nothing
End Sub
```

This results in the following output in the file `outfile.txt`:

```
[1][1][1]
```

To preserve white space, you need to preserve white space in the source XML DOM and within the stylsheet. To do this, alter the stylesheet to include the `xsl:preserve-space` element:

```
<?xml version="1.0" encoding="UTF-8" ?>
<xsl:stylesheet version="1.0"
xmlns:xsl="http://www.w3.org/1999/XSL/Transform">
    <xsl:preserve-space elements="link"/>
    <xsl:output method="xml" version="1.0" />
    <xsl:template match="/">
        <xsl:for-each select="links/link">
            <xsl:text>[</xsl:text>
            <xsl:value-of select="string-length(.)" />
            <xsl:text>]</xsl:text>
        </xsl:for-each>
    </xsl:template>
</xsl:stylesheet>
```

Also alter the code for MSXML by setting the `preserveWhiteSpace` property to True prior to loading the XML source:

```
On Error GoTo eh
xml.preserveWhitespace = True
xml.Load "c:\temp\source.xml"
```

This combination yields the expected result:

```
[5][13][21]
```

To achieve the same result in .NET, you again need to preserve white space in the parser prior to loading the document. You can achieve this by using an XmlDocument object to load the source XML and set the PreserveWhitespace property of the XmlDocument object to True:

```
Sub Main()
    Dim xsltReader As System.Xml.XmlTextReader = New
    ▬System.Xml.XmlTextReader("c:\temp\trans.xslt")
    Dim xsltdoc As System.Xml.XPath.XPathDocument = New
    ▬System.Xml.XPath.XPathDocument(xsltReader, XmlSpace.Preserve)
    Dim xmldoc As System.Xml.XmlDocument = New System.Xml.XmlDocument()

    'Preserve whitespace and then load the xml source
    xmldoc.PreserveWhitespace = True
    xmldoc.Load("c:\temp\source.xml")

    'Create the XslTransform object and load the stylesheet.
    Dim xslt As XslTransform = New XslTransform()
    xslt.Load(xsltdoc)

    'Create an XmlTextWriter which outputs to the console.
    Dim writer As XmlTextWriter = New XmlTextWriter(Console.Out)

    'Transform the file and send the output to the console.
    xslt.Transform(xmldoc, Nothing, writer)
    writer.Close()
End Sub
```

The output in the console window is the same as the previous result:

```
[5][13][21]
```

Parent Elements

```
Xsl:stylesheet, xsl:transform
```

Child Elements

None.

xsl:stylesheet or xsl:transform

The document element of a stylesheet, containing all other stylesheet elements.

Attributes

Attribute Name	Enforced	Description	Values
version	Required	The version of XSLT transformations the stylesheet uses. The current value is 1.0.	Number
id	Optional	A unique identifier to facilitate embedding stylesheets.	ID
extension-element-prefixes	Optional	Specifies a namespace as an extension namespace.	White space separated list of NMTokens
exclude-element-prefixes	Optional	Specifies the namespace URIs that are excluded from the result tree.	White space separated list of NMTokens.
case-order	Optional	Determines if strings will be sorted with uppercase first or lowercase first.	upper-first or lower-first. The default is lower-first (despite the documentation in MSDN to the contrary).

Example

The following is a complete stylesheet:

```
<?xml version="1.0" encoding="UTF-8" ?>
<xsl:stylesheet version="1.0"
xmlns:xsl="http://www.w3.org/1999/XSL/Transform">
    <xsl:output method="text" omit-xml-declaration="yes" />
    <xsl:template match="/">
        <xsl:for-each select="links/link">
            <xsl:sort select="attribute::name" order="descending" case-
            ➥order="lower-first" />
            <xsl:value-of select="@name" />
            <xsl:if test="position() != last()">
                <xsl:text>,</xsl:text>
            </xsl:if>
        </xsl:for-each>
    </xsl:template>
</xsl:stylesheet>
```

Parent Elements

None.

Child Elements

```
xsl:attribute-set, xsl:import, xsl:include, xsl:output, xsl:param,
xsl:template, xsl:variable
```

xsl:template

xsl:template defines a template rule that can generate result output. Template rules can be thought of several different ways. They can be thought of as functions with parameters (pull model programming). They can also be thought of as events, where a message is tested against all event declarations for an applicable event prototype (push model programming). They generally define a rule that is tested against a node.

Attributes

Attribute Name	Enforced	Description	Values
name	Optional	Defines a named template that can be called as a function using the xsl:call-template element.	QName
match	Optional	Identifies the source node or nodes to which the rule applies.	Pattern
priority	Optional	Specifies the priority for the template rule, to be used for conflict resolution. If two templates with matching criteria are in the same scope, the priority attribute can determine which rule applies.	Number
mode	Optional	Allows a template to be processed multiple times, each time producing a different result.	QName

Example

Suppose that you have a series of links that you want to display on a page.
Each link is represented here by a link element with properties for its unique
identifier, its location on the web, a memorable name for the link, and a brief
description of the site:

```
<?xml version="1.0" encoding="utf-8" ?>
<links>
    <link id="newriders" URL="http://www.newriders.com" name="NewRiders.com"
    ▬description="Available books by New Riders" />
    <link id="vbdna" URL="http://www.xmlandasp.net" name="Xmlandasp.net"
    ▬description="Articles and samples available for VB, DNA, and .NET" />
    <link id="gotdotnet" URL="http://www.gotdotnet.com" name="GotDotNet.com"
    ▬description="Samples, walkthroughs, and more" />
    <link id="msdn" URL="http://msdn.microsoft.com/library" name="MSDN
    ▬Online Library" description="MSDN Online" />
    <link id="devx" URL="http://www.devx.com" name="DevX.com"
    ▬description="Fawcette Technical Publications" />
</links>
```

The stylesheet doc.xsl contains template rules to process each link element
twice: once to generate an index of links, and the second to generate the
named anchor tag, its URL, name, and description:

```
<?xml version="1.0" encoding="UTF-8" ?>
<xsl:stylesheet version="1.0"
xmlns:xsl="http://www.w3.org/1999/XSL/Transform">
    <xsl:template match="/">
        <html>
            <body>
                <xsl:apply-templates select="links/link" />
                <hr />
                <xsl:apply-templates select="links/link"
                ▬mode="description" />
            </body>
        </html>
    </xsl:template>
    <xsl:template match="link">
        <a>
            <xsl:attribute name="href">
                &#035;<xsl:value-of select="@id" />
            </xsl:attribute>
            <xsl:value-of select="@name" />
        </a>
        <br />
    </xsl:template>
    <xsl:template match="link" mode="description">
        <a>
            <xsl:attribute name="name">
                <xsl:value-of select="@id" />
            </xsl:attribute>
```

```
        <h1>
              <xsl:value-of select="@name" />
        </h1>
     </a>
     <a>
        <xsl:attribute name="href">
              <xsl:value-of select="@URL" />
        </xsl:attribute>
        <xsl:value-of select="@URL" />
     </a>
     <br />
     <xsl:value-of select="@description" />
      <br />
   </xsl:template>
</xsl:stylesheet>
```

Parent Elements

```
xsl:stylesheet, xsl:transform
```

Child Elements

```
xsl:apply-templates, xsl:attribute, xsl:call-template, xsl:choose,
xsl:comment, xsl:copy, xsl:copy-of, xsl:element, xsl:for-each, xsl:if,
xsl:param, xsl:processing-instruction, xsl:text, xsl:value-of, xsl:variable,
output elements
```

xsl:text

`xsl:text` outputs literal text that can be escaped depending on the value of the `disable-output-escaping` attribute.

Generally, it is considered bad form to disable output escaping to generate HTML tags such as `<p>` or `<br>` that do not require closing tags and should be avoided.

Attributes

Attribute Name	Enforced	Description	Values
`disable-output-escaping`	Optional	Determines if the element will be output without escaping. The default is `no`.	`yes` or `no`

Example

Consider the following XML file, `links.xml`:

```
<?xml version="1.0" encoding="UTF-8" ?>
<links>
    <link name="NewRiders.com" URL="http://www.newriders.com" />
    <link name="Xmlandasp.net" URL="http://www.xmlandasp.net" />
    <link name="MSDN Online Library" URL="http://msdn.microsoft.com/library" />
</links>
```

The following stylesheet can be applied to the XML file to generate brackets around each of the values specified:

```
<?xml version="1.0" encoding="UTF-8" ?>
<xsl:stylesheet version="1.0"
xmlns:xsl="http://www.w3.org/1999/XSL/Transform">
    <xsl:template match="/">
        <xsl:for-each select="links/link">
            <xsl:text>[</xsl:text>
            <xsl:value-of select="@name" />
            <xsl:text>]</xsl:text>
        </xsl:for-each>
    </xsl:template>
</xsl:stylesheet>
```

This yields the following result:

```
<?xml version="1.0" encoding="UTF-16"?>[NewRiders.com][Xmlandasp.net][MSDN
Online Library]
```

Parent Elements

```
xsl:attribute, xsl:comment, xsl:copy, xsl:element, xsl:for-each, xsl:if,
xsl:otherwise, xsl:param, xsl:processing-instruction, xsl:template,
xsl:variable, xsl:when, xsl:with-param, output elements
```

Child Elements

None.

xsl:value-of

`xsl:value-of` inserts the value of the selected node as text.

Attributes

Attribute Name	Enforced	Description	Values
select	Required	Expression to be evaluated against the current context. The results are converted to a string.	Expression
disable-output-escaping	Optional	Determines if the result element should no longer be escaped. The default is no.	yes or no

Example

Consider the following XML file, `links.xml`:

```
<?xml version="1.0" encoding="UTF-8" ?>
<links>
    <link name="NewRiders.com" URL="http://www.newriders.com" />
    <link name="Xmlandasp.net" URL="http://www.xmlandasp.net" />
    <link name="MSDN Online Library" URL="http://msdn.microsoft.com/library"
/>
</links>
```

The following stylesheet can be applied to the XML file to generate brackets around each of the values specified:

```
<?xml version="1.0" encoding="UTF-8" ?>
<xsl:stylesheet version="1.0"
xmlns:xsl="http://www.w3.org/1999/XSL/Transform">
    <xsl:template match="/">
        <table>
            <xsl:for-each select="links/link">
                <tr>
                    <td>
                        <xsl:value-of select="@name" />
                    </td>
                </tr>
            </xsl:for-each>
        </table>
    </xsl:template>
</xsl:stylesheet>
```

This yields the following result:

```
<?xml version="1.0" encoding="UTF-16"?>
<table><tr><td>NewRiders.com</td></tr><tr><td>Xmlandasp.net</td></tr><tr><td>
➥MSDN Online Library</td></tr></table>
```

If the `select` attribute's value yields more than one node in the result tree, only the first result node is returned. If the node has substructure, the child structure is concatenated to the result with markup removed. For example, consider the following XML document:

```
<?xml version="1.0" encoding="utf-8" ?>
<paragraph>
    <sentence>Click <href URL="http://msdn.microsoft.com">here</href> for
    ➥the MSDN library.</sentence>
    <sentence>This is another sentence.</sentence>
    <sentence>This is yet another sentence.</sentence>
</paragraph>
```

A stylesheet can be applied to this document that selects all `sentence` nodes:

```
<?xml version="1.0" encoding="utf-8" ?>
<xsl:stylesheet version="1.0"
xmlns:xsl="http://www.w3.org/1999/XSL/Transform">
    <xsl:template match="/">
        <xsl:value-of select="paragraph/sentence" />
    </xsl:template>
</xsl:stylesheet>
```

Because more than one `sentence` node is returned by the `select` attribute, only the first is included in the result tree. Because the selected node has substructure, its child structure is also included in the result tree with markup removed:

```
<?xml version="1.0" encoding="UTF-16"?>Click here for the MSDN library.
```

Parent Elements

```
xsl:attribute, xsl:comment, xsl:copy, xsl:element, xsl:for-each, xsl:if,
xsl:otherwise, xsl:param, xsl:processing-instruction, xsl:template,
xsl:variable, xsl:when, xsl:with-param, output elements
```

Child Elements

None.

xsl:variable

`xsl:variable` specifies a variable bound in an expression. A variable has scope, which means that a variable is only visible as a child of the parent element in which it was declared.

A variable's contents can be specified through either the `select` attribute or as a child element. For example, consider the declaration:

```
<xsl:variable name="foo">
<xsl:value-of select="bar"/>
</xsl:variable>
```

This declaration is equivalent to the following:

```
<xsl:variable name="foo" select="bar"/>
```

The difference is that the first method always binds the variable to a result-tree fragment, whereas the second method can bind the variable to a string or number.

Attributes

Attribute Name	Enforced	Description	Values
name	Required	The name of the variable.	QName
select	Optional	The value of the variable. If specified, the content of the `xsl:variable` element must be empty.	Expression

Example

Given the XML instance document, `links.xml`:

```
<?xml version="1.0" encoding="utf-8" ?>
<links>
    <link name="NewRiders.com" lastevaluated="2001-09-08T19:01:55"/>
</links>
```

The following stylesheet would parse the last evaluated attribute to display the month number:

```
<?xml version="1.0" encoding="UTF-8" ?>
<xsl:stylesheet version="1.0"
xmlns:xsl="http://www.w3.org/1999/XSL/Transform">
    <xsl:template name="showmonth">
        <xsl:param name="date" />
        <xsl:text>Month:</xsl:text><xsl:value-of select="substring
        ↪($date, 6, 2)" />
        </xsl:template>
    <xsl:template match="/">
        <xsl:apply-templates select="links/link" />
    </xsl:template>
    <xsl:template match="link">
        <tr>
```

```
        <td>
            <xsl:call-template name="showmonth">
              <xsl:with-param name="date">
               <xsl:value-of select="@lastevaluated" />
              </xsl:with-param>
            </xsl:call-template>
        </td>
      </tr>
    </xsl:template>
</xsl:stylesheet>
```

This results in the following output:

```
<?xml version="1.0" encoding="UTF-16"?><tr><td>Month:09</td></tr>
```

Parent Elements

xsl:attribute, xsl:comment, xsl:copy, xsl:element, xsl:for-each, xsl:if,
xsl:otherwise, xsl:param, xsl:processing-instruction, xsl:stylesheet
xsl:template, xsl:variable, xsl:when, xsl:with-param, output elements

Child Elements

xsl:apply-templates, xsl:attribute, xsl:call-template, xsl:choose,
xsl:comment, xsl:copy, xsl:copy-of, xsl:element, xsl:for-each, xsl:if,
xsl:processing-instruction, xsl:text, xsl:value-of, xsl:variable, output
elements

xsl:when

xsl:when provides for multiple condition evaluation.

The xsl:when element is analgous to a case statement in formal programming languages.

Attributes

Attribute Name	Enforced	Description	Values
test	Required	The condition to test. If the expression evaluates to Boolean True, the results are included in the output.	A Boolean expression
select	Optional	The value of the variable. If specified, the content of the xsl:variable element must be empty.	Expression

Example

You can use the xsl:choose element to test if an attribute exists or not. Using the following XML instance document, the image attribute is not specified for NewRiders.com but is available for xmlandasp.net:

```
<?xml version="1.0" encoding="utf-8" ?>
<links>
    <link name="NewRiders.com" />
    <link name="xmlandasp.net" image="images/xmlandasp.gif"/>
</links>
```

The following stylesheet displays images when the image attribute is specified; otherwise, it displays the value of the name attribute:

```
<?xml version="1.0" encoding="UTF-8" ?>
<xsl:stylesheet version="1.0"
xmlns:xsl="http://www.w3.org/1999/XSL/Transform">
    <xsl:template match="/">
        <xsl:apply-templates select="links/link" />
    </xsl:template>
    <xsl:template match="link">
        <xsl:choose>
            <xsl:when test="@image">
                <img>
                  <xsl:attribute name="src">
                   <xsl:value-of select="@image" />
                  </xsl:attribute>
                </img>
            </xsl:when>
            <xsl:otherwise>
                <xsl:value-of select="@name"/>
            </xsl:otherwise>
        </xsl:choose>
    </xsl:template>
</xsl:stylesheet>
```

Parent Elements

```
xsl:choose
```

Child Elements

```
xsl:apply-templates, xsl:attribute, xsl:call-template, xsl:choose,
xsl:comment, xsl:copy, xsl:copy-of, xsl:element, xsl:for-each, xsl:if,
xsl:processing-instruction, xsl:value-of, xsl:variable, output elements
```

xsl:with-param

xsl:with-param passes a variable to a template.

Attributes

Attribute Name	Enforced	Description	Values
Name	Required	The condition to test. If the expression evaluates to Boolean True, the results are included in the output.	QName
Select	Optional	An expression to be matched against the current context.	Expression

Example

Given the XML instance document, links.xml:

```
<?xml version="1.0" encoding="utf-8" ?>
<links>
    <link name="NewRiders.com" lastevaluated="2001-09-08T19:01:55"/>
</links>
```

The following stylesheet would parse the last evaluated attribute to display in mm/dd/yyyy format:

```
<?xml version="1.0" encoding="UTF-8" ?>
<xsl:stylesheet version="1.0"
xmlns:xsl="http://www.w3.org/1999/XSL/Transform">
    <xsl:template name="sqlserver_date">
        <xsl:param name="date" />
        <xsl:value-of select="substring($date, 6, 2)" />
        <xsl:text>/</xsl:text>
        <xsl:value-of select="substring($date, 9, 2)" />
        <xsl:text>/</xsl:text>
        <xsl:value-of select="substring($date, 1, 4)" />
    </xsl:template>
    <xsl:template match="/">
        <xsl:apply-templates select="links/link" />
    </xsl:template>
    <xsl:template match="link">
        <tr>
            <td>
                <xsl:call-template name="sqlserver_date">
                    <xsl:with-param name="date">
```

```
                    <xsl:value-of select="@lastevaluated" />
                </xsl:with-param>
            </xsl:call-template>
          </td>
      </tr>
    </xsl:template>
</xsl:stylesheet>
```

This results in the following output:

```
<?xml version="1.0" encoding="UTF-16"?>
<tr><td>09/08/2001</td></tr>
```

Parent Elements

```
xsl:call-template, xsl:apply-templates
```

Child Elements

```
xsl:apply-templates, xsl:attribute, xsl:call-template, xsl:choose,
xsl:comment, xsl:copy, xsl:copy-of, xsl:element, xsl:for-each, xsl:if,
xsl:processing-instruction, xsl:text, xsl:value-of, xsl:variable
```

Resources

Index

E

S

T

X-Z

VOICES THAT MATTER

HOW TO CONTACT US

VISIT OUR WEB SITE

WWW.NEWRIDERS.COM

On our web site, you'll find information about our other books, authors, tables of contents, and book errata. You will also find information about book registration and how to purchase our books, both domestically and internationally.

EMAIL US

Contact us at: **nrfeedback@newriders.com**

- If you have comments or questions about this book
- To report errors that you have found in this book
- If you have a book proposal to submit or are interested in writing for New Riders
- If you are an expert in a computer topic or technology and are interested in being a technical editor who reviews manuscripts for technical accuracy

Contact us at: **nreducation@newriders.com**

- If you are an instructor from an educational institution who wants to preview New Riders books for classroom use. Email should include your name, title, school, department, address, phone number, office days/hours, text in use, and enrollment, along with your request for desk/examination copies and/or additional information.

Contact us at: **nrmedia@newriders.com**

- If you are a member of the media who is interested in reviewing copies of New Riders books. Send your name, mailing address, and email address, along with the name of the publication or web site you work for.

BULK PURCHASES/CORPORATE SALES

If you are interested in buying 10 or more copies of a title or want to set up an account for your company to purchase directly from the publisher at a substantial discount, contact us at 800-382-3419 or email your contact information to corpsales@pearsontechgroup.com. A sales representative will contact you with more information.

WRITE TO US

New Riders Publishing
201 W. 103rd St.
Indianapolis, IN 46290-1097

CALL/FAX US

Toll-free (800) 571-5840
If outside U.S. (317) 581-3500
Ask for New Riders
FAX: (317) 581-4663

New Riders

WWW.NEWRIDERS.COM

RELATED NEW RIDERS TITLES

Inside ASP.NET

Scott Worley

Discover the sheer power and flexibility of the ASP.NET development environment and prepare yourself for the future of web development.

ISBN: 0735711356
736 pages
US$49.99

ISBN: 0735710201
1152 pages
US$49.99

Inside XML

Steven Holzner

Inside XML is a foundation book that covers both the Microsoft and non-Microsoft approach to XML programming. It covers in detail the hot aspects of XML, such as, DTD's vs. XML schemas, CSS, XSL, XSLT, Xlinks, Xpointers, XHTML, RDF, CDF, parsing XML in Perl and Java, and much more.

Debugging ASP.NET

Jonathan Goodyear, Brian Peek, Brad Fox

This first book to cover debugging for ASP.NET will save you hundreds of hours, dollars, and headaches by providing real-world problems and their real-world coding solutions.

ISBN: 0735711410
376 pages
US$34.99

ISBN: 073570970X
768 pages
US$49.99

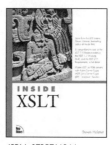

ISBN: 0735711364
640 pages
US$49.99

ISBN: 0735711127
384 pages
US$44.99

ISBN: 073571052X
336 pages with CD-ROM
US$39.99

PHP Functions Essential Reference

Torben Wilson, Zak Greant, Graeme Merrall, Brett Michlitsch

Co-authored by some of the leading developers in the PHP community, *PHP Functions Essential Reference* is guaranteed to help you write effective code that makes full use of the rich variety of functions available in PHP 4.

Inside XSLT

Steven Holzner

To work with XML fully, you need to be up to speed with XSLT and this is the book to get you there. Covering everything from creating XPath expressions to transforming XML to HTML, *Inside XSLT* will have you heading straight down the road to programming efficiency.

XML and SQL Server 2000

John Griffin

SQL Server 2000 has added several new features that make working with XML easier for the developer. *XML and SQL Server 2000* helps SQL developers to understand and utilize these new XML capabilities.

C++ XML

Fabio Arciniegas

The demand for robust solutions is at an all-time high. Developers and programmers are asking the question, "How do I get the power performance found with C++ integrated into my web applications?" Fabio Arciniegas knows how. He has created the best way to bring C++ to the web through development with XML. In this book, he shares the secrets developers and programmers worldwide are searching for.

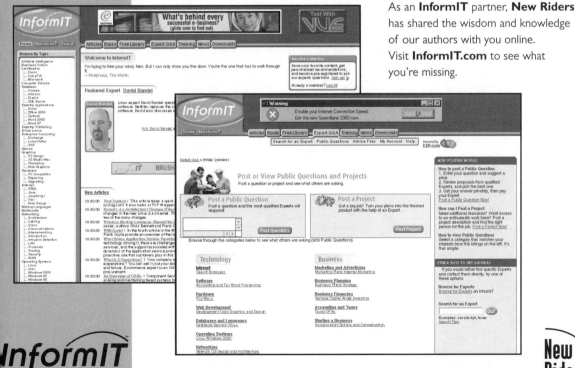

Colophon

Pictured on the cover is a photograph by Phillippe Colombi of the ruins of Pelenque, Mexico. Pelenque is considered to be one of the most beautiful Mayan city-states in Mexico dating back to Mayan rule between 300 B.C. and 600 A.D. It is surrounded by a vast jungle, which had kept Pelenque hidden even after its initial discovery in 1773. It wasn't until 1841 that this region was rediscovered by explorers. The Palace, believed to be the subject of this picture, was quite structurally advanced. It contained aquaducts designed to flush out the sewage. The Palace was also the center of Pelenque kingdom rule, in which the power belonged to women.

This book was written and edited in Microsoft Word, and laid out in QuarkXPress. The fonts used for the body text are Bembo and MCPdigital. It was printed on 50# Husky Offset Smooth paper at R.R. Donnelley & Sons in Crawfordsville, Indiana. Prepress consisted of PostScript computer-to-plate technology (filmless process). The cover was printed at Moore Langen Printing in Terre Haute, Indiana, on 12 pt, coated on one side.